# Windows PowerShell™ v1.0: TFM™

## SECOND ᴵᴵ EDITION

D0860784

Don Jones and Jeffery Hicks

SAPIEN
PRESS

3212 Jefferson St #288
Napa, CA 94558
www.SAPIENPress.com

# Windows PowerShell v1.0: TFM
## 2nd Edition
### by Don Jones and Jeffery Hicks

ISBN: 0-9776597-6-3
Printed in the United States of America
First printing: November 2007
10 9 8 7 6 5 4 3 2 1

**Publisher**
Ferdinand Rios

**Associate Publisher**
Don Jones

**Copy Editor**
Amy Tipton

**Indexer**
Julie Bess

## Trademarks
All terms mentioned in this book that are known to be trademarks or service marks have been appropriately capitalized. SAPIEN Press cannot attest to the accuracy of this information. Use of a term in this book should not be regarded as affecting the validity of any trademark or service mark. All marks remain the property of their respective owner(s) and are used herein only for reference.

## Warning and Disclaimer
Every effort has been made to make this book as complete and as accurate as possible, but no warranty or fitness is implied. The information provided is on an "as is" basis. The author(s) and the publisher shall have neither liability nor responsibility to any person or entity with respect to any loss or damages arising from the information contained in thi book.

## Get More... Online!
Access downloads, technical support, and other resources for this book at www.SAPIENPress.com. Discussion forums related to this book's content may be maintained at www.ScriptingAnswers.com, or on the author(s)' private Web sites.

## If You're Legal... We Thank You
If you legally purchased this book, in either electronic or print format, both the publisher and the author(s) would like to extend their sincere gratitude. Publishers and authors earn their income from the sale of their books; that income enables them to pay for their homes, feed and support their families, and remain financially solvent. By legally purchasing this book, you are encourging technical authors everywhere to continue writing books that deliver the information you need. Thank you.

## Available in Print and Electronic Editions
This book is available in electronic format exclusively from www.ScriptingOutpost.com. Print editions are available from all major booksellers and from www.ScriptingOutpost.com.

*For Christopher… now, as always.*
*—Don*

*For Beth, who makes all my dreams come true.*

*—Jeffery*

# Foreword

My co-author and I are incredibly proud of this second edition of our PowerShell book. It's more than one-quarter larger than the original edition (in content, not just physical size), and contains probably more than 60% new material—and even the remaining 40% has been thoroughly re-visited and revised where necessary. It's a testament to the power of a "small" publishing firm like SAPIEN Press than we could release this second edition less than a year after the first edition launched. It's also a testament to the popularity of Windows PowerShell itself, since it's that popularity that has led so many administrators into the intermediate and advanced topics that we're covering in this edition for the first time.

We've been fortunate to receive a lot of feedback—both constructive and sometimes not-so-constructive—from the first edition, and we've taken it *all* to heart. In addition to the new material we've created for this edition, we've also rewritten major sections of this book to provide clearer explanations of core concepts, and we've vastly expanded our explanations of other areas of Windows PowerShell that we didn't originally realize would be so interesting to Windows administrators. We've made a tremendous effort to make sure this book includes *everything* you might need, now and well into your PowerShell future.

Writing any book of this size is a labor of love. In the case of Windows PowerShell, it *has* to be, because so little in the way of formal documentation is available anywhere. Many things—such as PowerShell's custom formatting and type extensions—are either poorly documented, or completely undocumented by Microsoft (at least at the time we wrote this). So, we had to reverse-engineer a lot of these things in order to explain how they work and provide some practical examples for you. But we were happy to do it, because we know there are folks out there who will *really* utilize those features, using our examples as a jumping-off point for their own experimentation.

We're delighted that you've chosen our book for your Windows PowerShell learning needs. We hope you'll take advantage of our blog, at http://blog.sapien.com, and our discussion forums, at http://www. ScriptingAnswers.com, for any follow-up questions, comments, or suggestions you may have. We also invite you to one of the many conferences we speak at, most of which we mention in our blog from time to time. Most important, we don't want to be faceless entities, floating out in space somewhere writing books and magazine articles; we want to work *with* you to find answers to questions, and to find ways to put Windows PowerShell to practical uses in every Windows-based environment. Let this book be the *beginning* of your PowerShell career, but don't let it be the end. Drop by and say "hi."

Don Jones,
Series Editor, SAPIEN Press
June, 2007

# About the Authors

**Don Jones** has been in the Information Technology industry for more than a decade, and has written more than thirty published books on IT topics. Today, he's a Windows PowerShell MVP Award recipient, an in-demand speaker at international conferences, and the Director of Projects and Services for SAPIEN Technologies. Don is a columnist for *Microsoft TechNet Magazine* and in the past has written for *Windows IT Pro* and *REDMOND* magazines, among other publications. He founded ScriptingAnswers.com and continues to be one of the industry's leading advocates and experts for Windows administrative scripting and automation.

**Jeffery Hicks** is a Scripting Guru for SAPIEN Technologies and a Windows PowerShell MVP Award recipient. He is the author of *WSH and VBSCript Core:TFM* (SAPIEN Press 2007) and the co-author of *Advanced VBScript for Microsoft Windows Administrators* (Microsoft Press 2006) and *Windows PowerShell:TFM* (SAPIEN Press 2007). He is also the author of several training videos on administrative scripting. He is currently a columnist and contributing editor for *REDMOND* Magazine, where he writes the popular "Mr. Roboto" column and Powershell-oriented column for MCPMag.com. Jeff is a frequent contributor to several online IT community web sites as well as an invited speaker at computer conferences and seminars. Jeff has been an IT professional for 16 years, much of it spent as a professional consultant. Throughout his entire career, Jeff has leveraged the available tools and techniques for automating Windows administration. His experience with a wide range of organizations and technologies provides a wealth of knowledge he is eager to share through speaking, teaching, writing, community participation, and mentoring.

# Acknowledgements

We'd like to express our sincere gratitude to everyone who purchased the first edition of this book and took the time to send us their questions, comments, suggestions, and even the odd correction. Whether you contacted us via e-mail at errata@sapien.com (an address you're still welcome to use) or in the forums on ScriptingAnswers.com, we appreciate it, and we want you to know that everything you brought to our attention has in some way been incorporated into this new edition.

We'd also like to specifically thank the team at SAPIEN Technologies who have supported the SAPIEN Press brand and this revised edition of the brand's first book: CEO Ferdinand Rios and CTO Alex Riedel, along with Christopher Gannon, Margaret Pratt, Stephen Poon, and Maricela Soria.

We'd also like to thank the folks who provided such useful feedback during our Table of Contents review, including Marco Shaw, Michel Klomp, Bruno Guerpillon, Adam Ball, Hector Hernandez, Mark Ingalls, and especially Matthew Grogan, Greg Milner, and Jamie Bradford, who all provided very detailed feedback that directly resulted in many of the things you'll find in this book.

The following folks also deserve thanks for their help in reviewing the draft chapters (but they deserve no blame for any mistakes you may find—those belong to use): Fellow MVP Marco Shaw, Andy Bidlen, Michel Klomp, Colin Halford, Jamie Bradford, Shane Dovers, Alan Finn, and Adam Ball.

Finally, we'd like to thank our families and co-workers for their patience and understanding as we worked long hours on this project.

# Contents

Ground Zero
# Windows PowerShell Seven-Step Speed Start

You've picked up a new book on Windows PowerShell and you're ready to get started! You want to see PowerShell in action! You want to see what it can do! You want to see if the authors will end every sentence with an exclamation point! That's what this chapter is all about: Putting PowerShell through its paces. We won't be explaining a lot as we go, since the goal here is just to show off some of PowerShell's capabilities. In fact, if you've already been tinkering with PowerShell, you might want to just skim this chapter and move right on to the next one, which is where the meaty stuff starts. Oh, and no, we won't use very many exclamation points from here on out.

## 1. Installing Windows PowerShell

The first thing you need to do is install Windows PowerShell. Exactly how you do that depends a bit on the operating system you're running, and we have to caution you: While this information was accurate at the time we wrote the book, it may change a bit, since Microsoft may add PowerShell to the base Windows operating system in more versions of Windows.

You need to be running Windows XP, Windows Server 2003, Windows Vista, Windows Server 2008, or a later version of Windows in order to install PowerShell. It *will not* install on Windows 2000 or anything older.

### Framework First

First, you need to make sure you have v2.0 (or v3.0) of the .NET Framework installed. Some versions of Windows, like Windows Vista and Windows Server 2008, may already have it installed. Look in your Windows folder (usually C:\Windows), and then under the Microsoft.NET folder. Under there, you'll either see a folder named Framework, or something similar—it has a different name on 32- and 64-bit systems. Under *there*, you're looking for the v2.0.xxxx folder. If it exists, you're good to go. If not, go to http://www.Microsoft.com/download and download the .NET Framework runtime for v2.0 or v3.0 (v3.0 will actually install v2.0 as well). You'll probably need to be a local administrator on your computer in order to do this. You might also be able to use the Windows Update or Microsoft Update feature of Windows to install the Framework; it'll be listed under Optional Components.

## Download and Install the Shell

With the Framework installed, see if Windows PowerShell is already installed—usually, you'll find it right on your Start menu if it is. If not, you can also look for its installation folder: On 32-bit systems, it's in Windows\System32\
WindowsPowerShell\v1.0. On 64-bit systems, it's more or less than same path, just usually under System64 instead of System32.

If you don't have PowerShell installed, go to http://www.Microsoft.com/PowerShell. From there, you'll find links to download it. *Be sure to download the right build!* A different build is available for *each* different version of Windows, and there's a different build for 32- or 64-bit editions, also.

----

**Don't See a Download for Your Version of Windows?**
If you go to the download page and don't see a build for your operating system, then either (a) your operating system isn't supported (that's the case for Windows 2000 and earlier), or (b) your operating system comes with Windows PowerShell as an optional installation component (as is the case for Windows Server 2008, which was code-named "Longhorn"). In the latter situation, you'll need to install Windows PowerShell by using Windows Setup, Add/Remove Windows Components, or whatever other functionality is provided by the operating system itself to add components that are included on the Windows Setup disc.

----

Once you've downloaded the installer, just double-click it. As with the Framework, you'll probably need to be an administrator in order to complete the installation properly. The installer will install not only PowerShell itself, but also the documentation provided by Microsoft. It'll create Start Menu items for the shell and for the documentation. We like to pin the PowerShell icon to the Start Menu so it's easier to find.

----

**Updates!**
If you *downloaded* PowerShell, then you'll probably also have to download any new versions which are released. As of this writing, at least, Microsoft hadn't decided if PowerShell updates would be pushed down through the Windows/Microsoft Update Service. If PowerShell *came with* your version of Windows (as an optional installation component), then updated will be pushed down through the Windows/Microsoft Update Service, either as "hotfixes" or in service packs.

----

## 2. Customizing the Shell

By default, the shell uses a blue background and white text. By clicking the control box (in the upper-left corner of the window), you can select Properties to modify the font, the colors, and even the window size. For the window size, you can control the physical size—that is, how many lines tall and how many columns wide the window is. You can also control the *buffer*, which is how many lines and columns actually exist. For example, if you configure the shell to use a 100-column window with a 200-column buffer, you'll see a horizontal scroll bar. Take a moment to tweak the shell to meet your liking—the wider the window, the better!

## 3. Performing Some Familiar Tasks in the New Shell

PowerShell works a lot like the shell you may have used before: Windows' Cmd.exe shell. For example, try these quick tasks:

- Enter **Cd \** to change to the root folder of your drive.

- Enter **Cd /Windows** to change into the Windows folder. Notice that you can use forward or backward slashes in paths!

- Enter **Cd ..** to go back up one folder level. Notice that you do need a space between "Cd" and ".."—that's a difference in PowerShell. PowerShell isn't case-sensitive, though: "CD," "Cd," and "cd" work equally well.

- Enter **Dir** to see a directory listing.

- Press Up Arrow or Down Arrow to cycle through previously-entered commands, known as the *command history*.

Many of the other commands you're familiar with will work, too: **Ren, Copy, Del, MkDir, RmDir**, and so forth. Commands like **Type** and **More** also work fine.

You can also run the external command-line utilities you're accustomed to. For example, **Ping** and **TraceRt** work perfectly, as does **Net, Nbtstat, Netsh**, and many others. Try a few now to convince yourself. You'll even have access to some advanced commands, like **Ps** for a process list or **Kill** to terminate a process.

If you've used UNIX before, and prefer to use commands like **Ls** or **Man**, you'll find that those work, too.

## 4. Working with More Drives than C:

Now try this:

```
PS C:\> cd hkcu:
```

Then type:

```
PS C:\> cd software
PS C:\> dir
```

Cool, huh? PowerShell exposes your registry, your certificate store, and other forms of storage as if they were disks. You can use all the familiar disk commands to change keys, delete keys, and so forth. You can see a list of all available "drives" by entering **Get-PSDrive**. And yes, you can map a network drive in PowerShell, too: Use **New-PSDrive**.

# 5. Finding Help at Your Fingertips

PowerShell has a built-in help facility. Just run **Help** *command* (or, as we mentioned, **Man** *command*) to get help on any command. For example:

```
PS C:\> Help dir
```

Displays help on using the **Dir** command. You'll notice that it's a bit different from the old Cmd.exe version of Dir. For example, you can't use **/s** to include subdirectories. Instead, you'd run **Dir -recurse**. When asking for help, the default screen is pretty concise. You can get more extensive help by running something like this:

```
PS C:\> Help dir -detailed
```

Or, for even more help:

```
PS C:\> Help dir -full
```

You can even ask for some examples of the command in use:

```
PS C:\> Help dir -example
```

The cool part about the **Help** command is that it'll show you what help is available. For example, to see a list of everything it knows about:

```
PS C:\> Help *
```

Or, if you'd like to see what help is available for working with Windows services, run this:

```
PS C:\> Help *service*
```

Wildcards like **\*** can be used with many PowerShell commands, and in this case they're a great way to discover what PowerShell has to offer.

# 6. Performing Real Administrative Tasks Without Scripting

Try these quick tasks, which go far beyond what Cmd.exe could do:

- **Get-Service** will show a list of running services. **Stop-Service** and **Start-Service** provide control over those services.

- **Get-Process** and **Stop-Process** provide functionality similar to the Resource Kit tools Plist.exe and Kill.exe.

- **Get-ACL C:\Windows** will show you who has permissions to the Windows folder (note that if you're running on Windows Vista with User Account Control enabled, this may not work—try right-clicking the PowerShell shortcut to run it as Administrator, and then try again, or try a different folder).

- **Get-EventLog System** will get your System event log. Yes, it will probably take a few minutes to finish running! Try **Get-EventLog System | Select -first 10** to just see the first ten entries. Or, press Ctrl+C if you're tired of waiting for it to finish.

- Run just **Notepad** to open a new instance of Notepad. Then run **Kill -name Notepad** to kill the process.

......................................................................................................................................................................

**Leverage What You've Learned**
Don't be afraid to try something new. Not sure what **Get-EventLog** does? Use **Help** to find out. Wondering what other things you can do with event logs? Try **Help *event*** and see if anything comes up. Running a script and want to stop? We just showed you Ctrl+C, which will stop a script as well as a command like **Get-EventLog**. Many of the things we'll show you in this book can be used elsewhere in PowerShell, too—don't be afraid to try using things that we've shown you in different combinations.

PowerShell has a lot of built-in commands that perform useful tasks. For example, try running **Help *service*** to see what commands are available for working with services—you may be pleasantly surprised! Always remember to use **Help** to discover more about what PowerShell can do, and to learn how a particular command works.

# 7. Taking a Peek at the Pipeline

PowerShell's commands—they're technically called *cmdlets* (pronounced, "command-lets")—don't actually produce text lists, although so far it seems like they do. Instead, they work with rich, fully-functional *objects*. PowerShell's *pipeline* lets you pass (or "pipe") objects from one cmdlet to another. For example, try this to get a list of all running services:

```
PS C:\> Get-Service | Where { $_.Status -eq "Running" } | Format-Wide
```
*local*

......................................................................................................................................................................

**Hey, I Still Got a List!**
At the end of every pipeline, PowerShell automatically takes whatever's left and makes a text list or table out of it. In this case, we specifically told it to make a *wide* list, so that's what it did.

We got a collection of all the services by using **Get-Service**, and then piped those to **Where.** The **Where** command passed along all those with a Status of Running, and dropped everything else. Finally, **Format-Wide** reformatted the results into a wide list of just the service names.

Want to see which processes on your computer have the largest memory working set?

```
PS C:\> ps | sort workingset -desc | select name,workingset | format-table -auto
```

**Ps** got a bunch of processes, and **Sort** ordered them by their working set in descending order (so the biggest users would be at the top of the list). We then asked **Select** to just grab the name and working set information, and then used **Format-Table** to format the information into an automatically-sized set of columns—a table, in other words.

We'll spend lots of time on the pipeline, later—but for right now you can see that it enables some pretty powerful tasks, and it doesn't require you to use a bit of scripting.

## Ready for More?

There's so much to learn in Windows PowerShell! Hopefully, these few pages have given you a peek at what you can do with this new shell, and the entire rest of this book will be devoted to expanding upon and explaining those capabilities.

In Part I of this book, we'll be focused on using PowerShell interactively—that is, just running commands, not writing scripts. You'll be amazed at how much you can accomplish that way! We'll look at a lot of PowerShell's major cmdlets so that you can understand what the shell can do (and don't forget that products like Exchange Server 2007 and System Center all add more capabilities to the shell).

Part II is all about scripting, although most of these topics can also be used directly from the command line. We'll look at PowerShell's scripting language, dive more deeply into variables, and so forth. We'll even provide some information on debugging!

Part III is a collection of real-world administrative examples for various tasks. In this Part, we'll look at how PowerShell can be used to accomplish some straightforward tasks, along with a few more complex tasks.

Finally, Part IV dives into more advanced topics, like working directly with the .NET Framework, working with databases, building a graphical user interface, and more. You don't *need* any of these things to use PowerShell effectively, but as you become more experienced and proficient in the new shell, you may want to explore some of these additional options.

Let's get started!

# Part I

# Using Windows PowerShell Interactively

# Chapter 1
# Windows PowerShell Architecture and Overview

Windows PowerShell occupies a fairly unique place in the Microsoft world. Never before has Microsoft really created a command-line shell: The original MS-DOS of the 1980s wasn't a *shell*; it was the entire *operating system*. The original Windows was a *graphical* shell on top of MS-DOS, but when Windows NT came out the *operating system* was a graphical environment; the Cmd.exe "shell" that we're accustomed to is really just a Windows console application; it doesn't actually "wrap around" the operating system in the way that a UNIX shell, like Bash, does. PowerShell, however, is a *true* shell that is uniquely designed for the complex Windows operating system and the various server products—such as Exchange Server and the System Center family—that we all use every day.

## What Is PowerShell, and Why Should I Care?

Administrators of UNIX and Linux systems (collectively referred to as "*nix" throughout this book) have always had the luxury of administrative scripting. In fact, most *nix operating systems are built on a command-line interface (CLI). The graphical operating environment of *nix systems—often the "X Windows" environment—is itself a type of shell; the operating system is fully-functional without this graphical interface. This presents a powerful combination: Because the operating system is typically built from the command line, there's nothing you can't do, from an administrative sense, *from the command line.* That's why *nix administrators are so fond of scripting languages like Python and Perl: They can accomplish real administration tasks with them.

Windows, however, has always been different. When a Microsoft product group sat down to develop a new feature—say, the Windows DNS Server software—they had certain tasks that were simply required. First and foremost, of course, was the actual product functionality—such as the DNS Server service, the bit of the software that actually performs as a DNS server. Some form of management interface was also required, and the Windows Common Engineering Criteria specified that the minimum management interface was a Microsoft Management Console (MMC) snap-in—that is, a *graphical* administrative interface. If they had extra time, the product team might create a Windows Management Instrumentation (WMI) provider, "connecting" their product to WMI, or they might develop a few command-line utilities or Component Object Model (COM) objects, allowing for some scriptable administrative capability. Rarely did the WMI or COM interfaces fully duplicate all the functionality available in the graphical console; this often meant that *some* administrative tasks could be accomplished via the command line or a language like VBScript, but you couldn't do *everything* that way. You'd always be back in the graphical console for something, at some point.

Not that graphical interfaces are *bad,* mind you. After all, they're how Microsoft has made billions from the Windows operating system. But clicking buttons and checkboxes can only go so fast, and with commonly performed tasks like creating new users, manual button-clicking is not only tedious, it's prone to mistakes and inconsistencies. Administrators of *nix systems have spent the better part of a decade laughing at Windows' pitiable administrative automation, and third parties have done very well creating tools like AutoIt or KiXtart to help fill in the gaps for Windows' automation capabilities.

That's no longer the case, though. Windows PowerShell is now a part of the Windows Common Engineering Criteria, and it occupies a similar position of importance with product groups outside the Windows operating system. Now, *administrative functionality is built in Windows PowerShell first.* Any other form of administration, including graphical consoles, utilizes the Windows PowerShell-based functionality. Essentially, graphical consoles are merely "script wizards" that run PowerShell commands in the background to accomplish whatever they're doing. Exchange Server 2007 is the first example of this: The graphical console simply runs PowerShell commands to do whatever corresponds to the buttons you click (the console even helpfully displays the commands it's running, so you can use those as examples to learn from). In fact, that graphical console only exposes roughly 80% of the product's total functionality: For everything else, you have to use the PowerShell command line. PowerShell is now the single source for administrative functionality; as it is a command-line interface, that means *every piece of functionality* can potentially be scripted or automated!

Of course, only *new* Microsoft products conform to this vision. Even Windows Server 2008 doesn't, since its development—under the code-name "Longhorn"—began prior to PowerShell's availability. But the next version of Windows will have to be built on PowerShell. It's a huge step, and it's a major change for the way administrators work with Windows. A change, we might add, that we feel is definitely for the better.

## How Do I Use PowerShell?

When you open a new PowerShell window, you're actually running a program called PowerShell.exe. It's a small application—just about 300 kilobytes, in fact. Its job is to fire up the *real* PowerShell, what we call the "PowerShell engine," an application written in C# and housed in a DLL file. PowerShell.exe—called a *hosting application*—is what provides you with the command-line interface to issue instructions to the PowerShell engine, and provides you with a means of reviewing the results that the engine generates.

You operate PowerShell primarily by running *cmdlets* (pronounced, "command-lets"). These are special mini-applications written in a .NET language, such as C# or Visual Basic. They're designed to run exclusively within PowerShell, and they form the basis of PowerShell's functionality. Cmdlets are named according to a consistent, documented standard created by Microsoft. All cmdlet names are constructed of a verb, such as *get* or *set,* and a noun, such as *service* or *process.* Nouns are always singular; even though **Get-Process** returns all running processes, the noun is still the singular *process.*

PowerShell comes with about 130 cmdlets built-in, including ones that work with services, permissions, processes, WMI, and more. More cmdlets can be "snapped in" to PowerShell. Exchange Server 2007, for example, snaps in about 300 or so additional cmdlets, which handle Exchange administration tasks. Most cmdlets provide instant gratification: Open PowerShell, type **Get-Service**, and press Enter, and you'll see a list of services installed on your computer. But that's really just scratching the surface: These cmdlets can, as you'll learn, do much more.

## Parameters

Like the command-line utilities you may have used in the past, PowerShell cmdlets often support a number of parameters. Unlike the old command-line utilities, however, PowerShell's cmdlet parameters use a consistent naming pattern, which makes the parameters easier to learn. For example, both the **Get-Content** and **Set-Content** cmdlets allow you to specify a path—such as a file path—and so both use the same parameter name, -**path**, for that parameter.

PowerShell uses spaces as parameter delimiters. For example:

```
PS C:\> Get-Content -path C:\Content.txt
```

If a parameter value contains spaces, then the value must be enclosed in either single or double quotation marks:

```
PS C:\> Get-Content -path "C:\Test Files\content.txt"
```

Typically, the most commonly-used parameter for any given cmdlet is *positional*, meaning you don't even have to specify the parameter name. Therefore, the following is also valid:

```
PS C:\> Get-Content C:\Content.txt
```

What's more, when you *do* need to type a parameter name, you need to type only as much of the name as necessary to distinguish the parameter from others. For example, here's a command that will retrieve operating system information from a remote computer, passing along a previously created set of alternate credentials:

```
PS C:\> Get-Wmiobject win32_operatingsystem -computer Server02 -credential $cred
```

The following, however, would also be valid, because the parameter -**credential** can be abbreviated to just a couple of letters and no other parameter begins with *cr*. The computer parameter can also be abbreviated:

```
PS C:\> Get-Wmiobject win32_operatingsystem -co Server02 -cr $cred
```

Parameters allow you to customize the way cmdlets behave. For example, when retrieving a list of files from a folder, you can specify a parameter that causes the cmdlet to recurse subfolders.

## Aliases

We've already described how aliases are a sort of nickname for cmdlets. After all, it's certainly easier to type **Dir** than to type **Get-ChildItem** all the time! PowerShell comes with a number of predefined aliases that can make typing faster. For a complete list, simply run **Get-Alias**, and you'll see a list of all aliases, as well as the cmdlets they point to.

You can make your own aliases, too. For example, we like to occasionally pop up Windows Notepad to jot down a few notes as we're working in the shell, and simply typing **Notepad** over and over takes too long. Instead, we prefer the shorter alias, **Np**, which we created by running this:

```
PS C:\>new-alias np notepad
```

Notice that we didn't even have to type the parameter names, since with this cmdlet both of the required parameters—alias name and command name—are positional, and don't need to be specifically named. Also notice that *we aliased an external command!* **Notepad** isn't a PowerShell cmdlet, but it is something you can run in PowerShell. Therefore, you can create an alias for it. Of course, our alias will "go away" the minute we close the shell session, and so we added it to our profile script and now the alias is added each time we run PowerShell. We'll cover profile scripting in "Scripting Overview."

Aliases have some downsides. For one, while they're certainly easier to type, they can be harder to read. Consider this:

```
ps | ? { $_.CPU -gt 50 } | % { $_.Name }
```

Yikes. Even punctuation marks like **?** and **%** get into the act with aliases! This is a lot easier to figure out when full cmdlet names are used:

```
Get-Process | '
  Where-Object { $_.CPU -gt 50 } | '
  ForEach-Object { $_.Name }
```

This command retrieves all currently running processes, selects those instances that have CPU utilization greater than 50, and then for each of those instances, just displays the process name. We're getting ahead of ourselves with the functionality, but you can probably see how the full cmdlet names make this easier to follow than the aliases.

In the first version of PowerShell, aliases are limited to providing a shorter, alternate name. You cannot create an alias for an expression that includes a parameter:

```
PS C:\ > new-alias -name os -value get-wmiobject win32_operatingsystem
New-Alias : A parameter cannot be found that matches parameter name 'win32_operatingsystem'.
At line:1 char:10
+ new-alias <<<< -name os -value get-wmiobject win32_operatingsystem
```

This is not to say you can't create a shortcut for something like the above expression. You'll have to create a function or use a script block, which we cover later in the book, not an alias. You can only create an alias for a cmdlet name:

```
PS C:\ > new-alias -name wmi -value get-wmiobject
```

Another downside to aliases is that, unless you stick to the aliases predefined in PowerShell itself, any scripts you write won't run on another computer unless you first take the time to define your custom aliases on that computer.

When it comes to writing scripts, you can work around both of these downsides by using a script editor like SAPIEN PrimalScript (www.primalscript.com). Type all the aliases you want—after all, they *are* faster—and then go to PrimalScript's Edit menu. Open the Convert submenu, and select Alias to Cmdlet to have PrimalScript expand all of your aliases into their full cmdlet names. You'll get instant readability and portability!

There are a couple of other cmdlets that you can use to work with aliases. **Remove-Alias**, for example, does exactly what its name suggests: It deletes an alias from your system. **Export-Alias** exports your aliases into a special export file, allowing you to import those aliases on another system using **Import-Alias**. The **Set-Alias** cmdlet lets you change an existing alias. Remember, you can read more about using these cmdlets by asking PowerShell for help—read on, and we'll tell you how.

## Backward-Compatible

PowerShell doesn't require you to give up all the external command-line utilities you've become accustomed to over the years. With few exceptions, utilities like Nslookup.exe, Ping.exe, Tracert.exe, Pathping.exe, and nearly any other will still run from within PowerShell—meaning you don't need to maintain two separate shells. These older command-line utilities are used in more or less the same way that they always have been; sometimes, you'll run into situations where you need to enclose command-line parameters in quotes from within PowerShell, but that's about the only major difference. You'll also notice that most of your batch files and VBScript files should also run from within PowerShell. If you run into something that just won't run under PowerShell, you can always resort to calling CMD:

```
PS C:\ > cmd /c c:\scripts\myoldscript.bat
```

When we speak at conferences we're often asked, "Can PowerShell also run graphical applications?" We're glad you asked, although, really, you should just try it and see! After all, what's the worst that could happen? In fact, if you open PowerShell and run **Calc** or **Notepad** or even **MSPaint**, you'll find that the graphical application pops right up, exactly as it would if you ran those applications from Cmd.exe or even Windows' "Run" dialog box. So, there aren't many reasons to keep Cmd.exe around, Consider deleting its shortcuts from your Start menu or wherever else and replacing those with shortcuts to PowerShell!

## Navigation

Much like the Cmd.exe interface, PowerShell allows you to quickly and easily navigate the file system on your computer. Commands like **Dir**, **Cd**, **Del**, **Mkdir**, and others work almost flawlessly. We say *almost* because these are in fact *not* PowerShell commands or cmdlets. Instead, they're *aliases*, or nicknames, to built-in PowerShell cmdlets. For example, **Dir** is an alias to the **Get-ChildItem** cmdlet, which retrieves a list of child items for a given object. Since a folder's "children" are its files and subfolders, **Get-ChildItem** has the same practical use as the old **Dir** command. However, when using **Dir** in Cmd.exe, you'd type something like **Dir /s** to see a list of files and folders and to recurse through subfolders. In PowerShell the same command line would be **Dir -recurse**, because **-recurse** is the equivalent parameter of **Get-ChildItem**.

Interestingly, cmdlets can have more than one alias. For example, **Get-ChildItem** is aliased to **Dir**, but also to **Ls**, the *nix equivalent to **Dir**. This lets folks with some *nix experience quickly jump in and start navigating. For the same reason, PowerShell will accept both backslashes and slashes in file paths, helping to bridge the gap between the MS-DOS world and the *nix world.

## Scripting

PowerShell scripts are simple text files with a .PS1 filename extension. Inside each file is a list of PowerShell command lines *exactly as you might type them interactively in the command-line window*. There is *no difference* in functionality between using the shell interactively and running a script. Essentially, you can type commands interactively until they do what you want and then paste them into a script for long-term use. PowerShell does have some scripting-specific language elements, which we explore in Part II of this book, but these elements can also be used interactively at the shell's command line—you don't have to "save" them for a PS1 file.

As we'll cover in "Security Features," PowerShell scripts are also capable of being fully secured, much more so than prior Microsoft scripting languages like KiXtart, VBScript, or JScript.

## Variables

Like any good scripting environment, PowerShell supports the use of variables (which we'll discuss in full detail in "Variables, Arrays, and Escape Characters"). However, as we already mentioned, there's no strict difference in functionality between using the shell interactively and writing a script. Therefore, you can use variables interactively! For example, the following will retrieve a list of services that are installed on the remote computer Server2:

```
PS C:\> Get-WmiObject Win32_Service -computerName Server2
```

The results will simply be listed on your screen. However, you *could* save those results into a variable:

```
PS C:\> $wmi = Get-WmiObject Win32_Service -computerName Server2
```

The variable $wmi is easy to spot: Variable names always begin with a dollar sign. Once the variable contains the results of the **Get-WmiObject** cmdlet, you can display those results simply by typing the variable name and pressing Enter:

```
PS C:\> $wmi
```

You can, of course, expect more than one service to be installed on that remote computer, and $wmi would contain them all. To view just the *first* service—something it's tougher to do by just using **Get-WmiObject** alone—you could do something like this:

```
PS C:\> $wmi[0]
```

Of course, we're getting a bit ahead of ourselves, but this does illustrate how powerful and flexible the shell is without ever needing to use a script.

## Built-in Help

Microsoft ships PowerShell with extensive help for all of the built-in cmdlets. To ask for help, simply type the keyword **Help** (which is actually a special, built-in function that utilizes the **Get-Help** cmdlet), followed by whatever you want help on:

```
PS C:\> Help Get-WmiObject
```

If all you know is an alias name, you can use that, too:

```
PS C:\> Help Dir
```

If you're not even sure what you need help on, try using wildcards. For example, to see everything PowerShell can do with services, try this:

```
PS C:\> Help *service*
```

The default help display is fairly concise, designed to fit on a single screen. Use parameters like -**full**, -**detailed**, or -**example** to get full help, moderately detailed help, or command examples, when available. To see **Get-ACL** in action, for example:

```
PS C:\> Help Get-ACL -example
```

This help functionality makes PowerShell's capabilities easier to discover.

In addition to cmdlet help, PowerShell includes a number of topic-oriented help files. Want to know more about associative arrays? Run this:

```
PS C:\ > help about_associative_array
```

You'll get a useful summary with examples. If you want to see a listing of all the available topics, run:

```
PS C:\ > help about*
```

Of course, sometimes it can be a distraction to have to refer to help while you're trying to work out a command line, and sometimes you don't want to have to page through the information the way the **Help** function does. If you'd prefer an on-screen, electronic cmdlet reference, there are several options available. We suggest that you go to www.PrimalScript.com/freetools and download the free PowerShell Help tool. It provides a nicely formatted version of help in a graphical window that you can have up and running alongside your PowerShell console, giving you access to the built-in help without distracting you from the command you're trying to construct.

## Object Oriented

Perhaps the most important part of Windows PowerShell—and for us, the toughest concept to grasp when we first started—is that PowerShell is completely object oriented. If you're an old hand at *nix, this object orientation is a big conceptual leap; PowerShell looks and feels so much like a *nix shell (such as Bash, which provided a lot of PowerShell's inspiration), that it's easy to think of PowerShell as a text-based shell. But it isn't.

Almost all PowerShell cmdlets deal with *objects*. This is perhaps easiest to see with a cmdlet like **Get-Service**.

```
PS C:\> $services = Get-Service
PS C:\> $services[0]
PS C:\> $services[0].Name
PS C:\> $services[0].Pause()
```

The first line retrieves all installed services and stores the result in the variable $services. The "result," in this case, is a *collection* of service *objects*. That is, for each service installed on your computer, Windows produces a unique software component to represent the service. That component can do all the things a service can do, such as starting or stopping. The component also contains all the properties, or attributes, that service has, such as a name and description and start mode.

The second line displays the first service in the collection. Collections are zero-based, so the first item has an index of zero, the second and index of one, and so forth. Placing the index in square brackets just retrieves that particular item. The third line is still working with the first service, but now PowerShell will *just* display the contents of that service's Name property.

Finally, the last line grabs the first service and executes its **Pause()** *method*. A method is essentially a command, telling the object—in this case, a service—to do something, such as pause itself.

The thing to remember is that even when you're looking at a text list in PowerShell—such as the list you see when you run **Get-Service**—what really happened under the hood is that a cmdlet produced one or more objects. Having nothing else to do with those objects, PowerShell selected certain properties of those objects and used those properties to construct a text list. That doesn't mean the **Get-Process** cmdlet creates a list of processes. The cmdlet assembles a *collection* of process *objects*. It's PowerShell that selected key properties of those objects to create that text list. PowerShell will only create a text list when you haven't given it something else to do with those objects. "The PowerShell Pipeline" will show you what else you can have it do.

Objects are a software way of representing complex computer functionality. For example, the objects returned by **Get-Service** represent services and all the things a service can do; the objects returned by **Get-Process** are quite different, since processes have different attributes and capabilities than a service. Even strings of text are, to PowerShell's way of thinking, a kind of object:

```
PS C:\> "this is a string".ToUpper()
THIS IS A STRING
```

The string of characters, "this is a string" is enclosed in double quotation marks, identifying them to PowerShell as a single unit. That single unit is an *object* of the String type; that is, the object is a string of characters. PowerShell knows how to do certain things with strings, including displaying an all-uppercase version of them. That particular capability is accessed via the **ToUpper()** method of the String object, as shown in the example. The object itself is followed by a period, which indicates that you're ready to type a property or method name, then the method name, **ToUpper()** (methods always have parentheses after their name).

This example illustrates that anything, even a literal string, can be treated as an object. If the string were in a variable, as we did with our earlier example on pausing a service, things would work exactly the same:

```
PS C:\> $var = "this is a string"
PS C:\> $var.ToUpper()
THIS IS A STRING
```

In this case, we put the string of characters into a variable, $var. At that point, $var represents that string of characters and has the same capabilities. In programmer-speak, then, $var is a String variable, with all the capabilities of any String, including the **ToUpper()** method.

Curious about the capabilities a particular object might have? PowerShell has a cmdlet, **Get-Member**, which displays the properties and methods of any object. To use **Get-Member**, simply *pipe* the object you're curious about to **Get-Member**:

```
PS C:\> $var = 5
PS C:\> $var | get-member


   TypeName: System.Int32
```

```
Name         MemberType  Definition
----         ----------  ----------
CompareTo    Method      System.Int3...
Equals       Method      System.Bool...
GetHashCode  Method       System.Int3...
GetType      Method      System.Type...
GetTypeCode  Method       System.Type...
ToString     Method      System.Stri...


PS C:\>
```

In this example, we put the number 5 into $var and piped it to **Get-Member**. The results, as you can see, indicate that $var represents an Int32 type of variable—that is, an integer—and that the Int32 type as six methods we could use. Try putting the results of **Get-Process** into a variable, and then piping that variable to **Get-Member**. What can you do with a process object, once you have one?

We'll spend a lot more time on objects, variables, and piping in upcoming chapters, so if this didn't make a lot of sense right now, don't worry. We'll have more elaborate examples later to help make things clearer.

## Danger! Danger! Danger!

We're often asked, "Is PowerShell dangerous?" To which we always answer, "Of course it is!" After all, PowerShell is an administrative tool, capable of doing the same amount of damage as any such tool. Imagine, for example, what you could do in Active Directory Users & Computers with an injudicious mouse click and the Delete key on your keyboard!

But PowerShell does try and offer you some protection through two common parameters, **-whatIf** and **-confirm**. Supported by almost any cmdlet that has the potential to do something damaging or irreversible, these parameters give you an opportunity to see what the cmdlet *would do*, without actually doing it, and a chance for you to change your mind. To see how they work, consider this:

> **Caution:** Please don't actually run this in PowerShell until you've read this entire section. Seriously.

```
PS C:\> Get-Process | Stop-Process
```

The first cmdlet there retrieves all running process, and then *pipes,* or sends, them to the second cmdlet, which will stop them all one at a time. The result is that your computer crashes. Whoops. Now consider this safer alternative:

```
PS C:\> Get-Process | Stop-Process -whatif
```

You can run the above safely because it won't *do* anything. Instead, **Stop-Process** simply shows you *what it would have done,* if you'd let it. This is an excellent way of testing a command line to see what would happen, without actually letting anything happen that might get you into trouble with the boss. As a next step, you might try this:

```
PS C:\> Get-Process | Stop-Process -confirm
```

Now, **Stop-Process** will stop before every process and ask you what you want to do. You'll have the option to stop each process, one at a time, or skip ones that you've changed your mind about. This is essentially the same as the "Are you sure?" dialog boxes you'd find in a graphical user interface, and it's a good way to help avoid potentially damaging situations. Remember, shells don't' damage systems, *people* damage systems: By using -**whatif** and -**confirm** appropriately, you'll help yourself avoid any unintended damage to your computers.

## Bottom Line: Do I Need to Know All This?

Yes. Look, we acknowledge that graphical user interfaces are easier to use than esoteric command-line utilities. Hopefully, though, PowerShell's consistent naming and architecture make its utilities less esoteric and easier to use. But, in the end, it's all about the command line. A Windows administrator who operates from the command line can create a hundred new users in the time it takes to create just *one* in the graphical user interface. That's an efficiency savings managers just can't ignore. PowerShell lets you perform tasks *en masse* that can't be done at all with the GUI, like updating the password a particular service uses to log on across dozens of computers.

If you've been with Windows since the NT 4.0 days, you may remember a time when earning your Microsoft Certified Systems Engineer (MCSE) certification was not only a way to differentiate yourself from the rest of the administrators out there, it was also a ticket to a $20,000 or more pay raise. Those days, of course, are gone; today, management is looking at production-applicable skills to differentiate the highly-paid administrators from the entry-level ones. And before long, PowerShell is going to be *the* skill management is after. As an industry, we know it, because we've seen it: Try finding an IT manager who'll pay top dollar for a *nix administrator who can't script in Perl, or Python, or some similar language. Before long, Windows managers will have figured it out, too: A PowerShell-savvy administrator can do more work, in less time and with fewer mistakes, than an administrator who doesn't know PowerShell. That's the type of bottom-line, dollars-and-cents criteria that any smart manager can understand. So, *yes,* you will need to know this stuff. Better to learn it now, when PowerShell is version 1.0. Wait a few years and there will be *even more* to learn, and it'll become increasingly difficult for someone starting from scratch.

## Is PowerShell a Good Investment of My Time?

Absolutely. That can be tough to believe, given all the scripting technologies Microsoft has inflicted on the world in the past and then quickly abandoned: KiXtart, VBScript, batch files, JScript, and more—the list goes on. But PowerShell's different. First of all, PowerShell is currently in version 1.0 (and that's the version this book covers). But there *will be* a v2.0, and a v3.0… so while today's PowerShell is far from perfect, it's pretty darn good, and in almost all ways it's already better than any similar technology we've had in the past.

But, as we already described, PowerShell is here to *stay.* Microsoft's not going to be able to walk away from PowerShell as easily as they did VBScript, primarily because so many products are being built *on top of* PowerShell. With PowerShell embedded in Exchange Server 2007, the System Center family, and future versions of Windows, well, it's a safe bet that we're going to be working with PowerShell for a decade or more, at least. In computer time that's about a century, so it's definitely a good investment.

## Where Do I Go from Here?

PowerShell is ready to use right out of the box; you don't need to start writing scripts. The remainder of Part I of this book, in fact, focuses on using the shell interactively to perform real administrative tasks. What's more, Part I introduces you to the core functionality of PowerShell that you'll use if you ever do venture into scripting. Part II gets into script, including all of the advanced things you can do with

PowerShell's simple, yet powerful scripting keywords and concepts. Part III of this book is more of a "cookbook," providing some simple, real-life examples of PowerShell scripts that perform real administrative tasks. We work from simpler to more complex, and show you how to work with various aspects of Windows, such as files and folders, services, permissions, and more. Finally, Part IV of this book focuses on intermediate and advanced topics, like working with databases, creating a graphical user interface by using Windows Forms, and ways to extend PowerShell's functionality.

## Help and Additional Resources

If you ever get stuck, please know that www.ScriptingAnswers.com is available to help. It's a free online community for Windows scripting, which we're on almost daily. We have a dedicated forum for PowerShell questions, and we encourage you to post any questions you run across.

If you're looking for additional training resources, visit www.ScriptingTraining.com, which offers a variety of instructor-led and self-paced training products related to Windows PowerShell.

Finally, we encourage you to download a trial version of PrimalScript from www.PrimalScript.com. This all-in-one visual development environment supports Windows PowerShell scripting, as well as cmdlet development, should you ever venture in that direction. It makes PowerShell scripting vastly easier and more intuitive, and provides a lot of little tricks to help you construct scripts more quickly and efficiently.

If you're interested in participating in the larger Windows PowerShell community, start at http://blogs.msdn.com/powershell, which is the home of the Windows PowerShell Team Blog. There, you'll find many members of the Windows PowerShell product team—that's right, real Microsoft employees—sharing tips and tricks about their product. Our own blog, at http://blog.sapien.com, is also chock-full of scripts, tips, techniques, news, and more, and we hope you'll take a moment to check it out.

So, that's our introduction! Now, let's dive in and see how this PowerShell thing ticks.

# Chapter 2
# PowerShell Drives

PowerShell introduces a unique concept called *PSDrives*, or PowerShell Drives. There's an interesting philosophy behind these: The team that created PowerShell knew that they'd have an uphill battle convincing administrators to drop their graphical tools and turn to the command line. They figured the switch would be easier if they could leverage the relatively small set of command-line skills that most Windows administrators already had. PowerShell's cmdlets, with their command-line parameters, are one example of that. Most admins are already familiar with command-line utilities and switches, and PowerShell simply expands on that familiarity, adding in better consistency for a shorter learning curve. The other main skill that the team wanted to leverage was the ability to navigate a complex hierarchical object store. Bet you didn't know you had that skill, but you do!

## Navigating a Hierarchical Object Store

Suppose you were using an operating system, like Windows that had the ability to store long strings of text in some sort of container. That container would have various properties, such as a name, its size, and information about when it was created and last accessed. You'd be able to view those properties at any time, modify some of them, like the name, and access the contents of the container. Now suppose that "container" was called a "text file" and you'll realize that you already know all about them! You probably even know how to manipulate them, to a degree, from the command line. You probably know how to use **Ren** to rename a file, **Type** to see its contents, and **Del** to remove it from the storage device. In fact, PowerShell supports all three of those commands by aliasing them to actual PowerShell cmdlets.

Now suppose your operating system had *tens of thousands* of files like these. You'd need some way to organize them, right? Something like the hierarchy of folders and subfolders that you've doubtless seen in Windows Explorer. And you probably know how to work with that hierarchy from the command line, too, using commands like **Cd** to change into a different folder, **Cd ..** to move up one level in the hierarchy, **Rmdir** to remove a folder, **Mkdir** to create a new folder, and **Dir** to see a list of the objects (files and subfolders) within a folder. And again, PowerShell supports these commands by aliasing them to the appropriate PowerShell cmdlets.

In other words, you can jump right into PowerShell and navigate a complex, hierarchical, object-based store, using the same commands and techniques that you've probably been using for years in something like Cmd.exe.

So, why can't *all* of Windows' hierarchical stores be navigated in the same fashion?

## More Stores than Just the File System

Windows has several different hierarchical stores aside from the file system. The registry, for example, looks a lot like the file system, don't you think? It has folders (registry keys) and files (registry settings), and the files have contents (the values within settings). The Certificate Store in Windows is similar, too. So is Active Directory, for that matter.

PowerShell lets you leverage all of these hierarchical stores using the same techniques you use to work with the file system (well, not *all*—PowerShell v1.0 doesn't ship with a way to make Active Directory look like a file system). Open a PowerShell console and run **Get-PSDrive**. You'll see a list of all the "drives" attached to your PowerShell console, and you'll see the *provider* that connects each drive. For example, you'll doubtless see drives C: and D:, and perhaps others, using the FileSystem provider—and these drives are the ones you're probably already familiar with. But you'll also see drives HKCU: and HKLM:, which use the registry provider. You'll see a CERT: drive for the Certificate Store, and an ENV: drive for environment variables. Other drives like Function: and Variable: connect to PowerShell's own internal storage mechanisms.

Try accessing the HKEY_LOCAL_MACHINE hive of the registry. How? The same way you'd access your D: drive:

```
PS C:\> cd hklm:
```

Simply change to the HKLM: drive and you're there. Need to see the keys that are available at list level? Ask for a list:

```
PS HKLM:\> dir
```

Want to change into the SOFTWARE key? You can probably guess how that's done:

```
PS HKLM:\> cd software
PS HKLM:\Software >
```

Note that PowerShell isn't even case sensitive! Want to delete a registry key (be careful)? The **Del** command will do it. There is much more that you can do, and we'll cover working with the registry in more detail in "Managing the Registry." But we wanted to demonstrate the flexibility of PSDrives.

## Mapping Drives

You can create your own drives using whatever providers you have installed. For example, to map your Z: drive to \\Server\Share, you'd run something like this:

```
PS C:\> new-psdrive Z -psprovider FileSystem -root \\server1\share
```

The **-Psprovider** parameter tells PowerShell exactly which provider you're using. You can even map to local folders:

```
PS C:\> new-psdrive Z -psprovider FileSystem -root C:\test
```

This maps the Z: drive to the local C:\Test folder. Unfortunately, PowerShell v1.0 doesn't provide any means for using the other providers remotely. Mapping to a remote UNC is about your only option, and that only works with the FileSystem provider. You can't map to remote registries or certificate stores. That'd be a useful capability, but it doesn't exist in v1.0.

Any mappings you create in PowerShell are preserved only for the current session. Once you close PowerShell, they're gone. Also, your drive mappings don't show up in Windows Explorer; they only exist in PowerShell. If you need to re-create a particular mapping each time you open a PowerShell console, then add the appropriate **New-PSDrive** command to a PowerShell profile (more on that in "Scripting Overview").

We should call special attention to the fact that PowerShell's drives *exist only within PowerShell itself.* For example, if you map the Z: drive to a UNC, and then try to launch Windows Notepad to open a file on the Z: drive, *it won't work.* That's because the path is passed to Notepad, which has to ask *Windows*, not PowerShell, to get the file. Since *Windows* doesn't "have" the Z: drive, the operation will fail.

## More Providers!

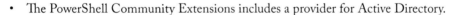

You're not limited to the providers supplied by Microsoft. Go to www.codeplex.com and, in the search box near the top of the page, type **powershell** and hit Enter. You'll find a variety of projects that extend PowerShell's functionality. Some of these include providers for other hierarchical storage systems, allowing you to "attach" them as PSDrives:

- The PowerShell Community Extensions includes a provider for Active Directory.

- A SharePoint Provider connects SharePoint 2003 and 2007 as a PSDrive.

- A BizTalk provider connects BizTalk Server as a file system, including applications, orchestrations, and schemas.

The possibilities are endless. Microsoft also releases new providers, as appropriate, with server products, and it's currently expected that PowerShell v2.0 will include an officially-supported PSDrive provider for Active Directory. Imagine being able to delete users using the **Del** command, or being able to navigate organizational units (OUs) using **Cd**!

## PSDrives = Ease of Use

The beauty of the PSDrive model is that *any* hierarchical store supported by a PSDrive provider looks like a file system. If Microsoft releases yet another hierarchical storage product in the future, it can be "snapped" into PowerShell to look like a file system, meaning your investment in file system-management commands will last you for a good, long time. You also have to be creative in using PSDrives. For example, if you know how to write a batch file that copies a bunch of files from one place to another, then you also know how to write a PowerShell script that copies *registry keys* from one place to another! Every skill you already possess for managing files from the command line can now be re-purposed for many different types of storage—and that's a *real* benefit of using PowerShell.

## Chapter 3
# Key Cmdlets for Windows Administration

Now that you've had a quick overview of PowerShell and you know how to navigate your computer's various storage systems, it's time to put PowerShell to use. Understand that the rest of this book will build on these concepts, and in fact go into more depth on a lot of what we'll show you right now, but we want you to be able to do something *useful* with PowerShell as quickly as possible. Also, don't think that this chapter represents the sum total of PowerShell's capabilities—nothing could be further from the truth! Our plan right now is to just scratch the surface a little bit and introduce you to some key cmdlets that you'll use almost every day in Windows PowerShell. We want to show you how these cmdlets relate directly to production administration tasks. Ready to get started?

## Cmdlets for Navigating Your System

We reviewed a bunch of these in "Windows PowerShell Architecture and Overview" and "PowerShell Drives," but we primarily focused on their aliases—such as **Dir**, **Cd**, **Ls**, **MkDir**, and so forth. Now, we'd like to focus on the actual underlying cmdlets. Hey, you're still welcome to type the aliases, if you prefer them, but knowing the names for these particular cmdlets gives you some valuable insight into how PowerShell thinks.

## Listing Child Items

First up, remember that PowerShell thinks of *everything* as an object. A folder on your hard drive, for example, is an object. Of course, folders have subfolders and files, too, which PowerShell thinks of as *children* of the folder. That's not an uncommon term: Many of us are accustomed to thinking of "parent folders" and so forth, for example. So, if you're working with a particular folder, meaning that PowerShell is "inside" that folder, then the way you'd get a list of child items is simple: **Get-ChildItem**. Remember,

PowerShell cmdlets always use a singular noun, so it's not "Get-Children" or "Get-ChildItems," it's **Get-ChildItem**. Typed alone, the cmdlet—or one of its aliases, such as **Dir**, **Ls**, or **GCI**—will return a list of child items for the current object; that is, the folder the shell is currently "in." Like this:

```
PS C:\test> Get-ChildItem

    Directory: Microsoft.PowerShell.Core\FileSystem::C:\test

Mode                LastWriteTime     Length Name
----                -------------     ------ ----
d----         4/9/2007  11:10 AM             subfolder
-a---        3/20/2007  11:37 AM        435 demo1.ps1
-a---        3/20/2007  11:46 AM        481 demo2.ps1
-a---        3/20/2007   9:44 AM        354 demo3.ps1
-a---        3/20/2007   9:44 AM        349 demo4.ps1
-a---        3/20/2007  11:55 AM        676 scope.ps1
-a---        3/19/2007  11:15 AM       1825 webcast.zip
```

By default, this information is displayed in a table format. If you ask for help on **Get-ChildItem**, however, you'll see that it has a lot of additional options, which are exposed via parameters. For example, one useful parameter is --**recurse**, which forces the cmdlet to retrieve *all* child items, even those deeply nested within subfolders.

You can get the child items for a specific path, too:

```
PS C:\> gci -path c:\test
```

Notice that we've used the **GCI** alias, and specified the name of the --**path** parameter. The online help indicates that the actual parameter name is optional, in this case, because the first parameter is positional. Therefore, the following would achieve the same thing:

```
PS C:\> dir c:\test
```

Of course, we used a different alias, but it doesn't matter. The command works the same either way. Other parameters let you filter the results. For example, consider this:

```
PS C:\test> dir -exclude *.ps1


    Directory: Microsoft.PowerShell.Core\FileSystem::C:\test


Mode                LastWriteTime     Length Name
----                -------------     ------ ----
d----         4/9/2007  11:10 AM             subfolder
-a---        3/19/2007  11:15 AM       1825 webcast.zip
```

The -**exclude** parameter accepts wildcards, such as * and **?**, and removes matching items from the result set. Similarly, the -**include** parameter filters out everything *except* those items which match your criteria. One important thing to remember about -**include** and -**exclude** is that they force the cmdlet to retrieve all of the child items *first,* and *then* filter out the items you didn't want. That can be slow, sometimes, when a lot of items are involved. An alternate technique is to use the -**filter** parameter. Its use differs depending on the PSDrive provider you're working with, although with the file system it uses the familiar * and **?** wildcards, like this:

```
PS C:\test> dir -filter *.ps1


    Directory: Microsoft.PowerShell.Core\FileSystem::C:\test


Mode                LastWriteTime     Length Name
----                -------------     ------ ----
-a---         3/20/2007 11:37 AM        435 demo1.ps1
-a---         3/20/2007 11:46 AM        481 demo2.ps1
-a---         3/20/2007  9:44 AM        354 demo3.ps1
-a---         3/20/2007  9:44 AM        349 demo4.ps1
-a---         3/20/2007 11:55 AM        676 scope.ps1
```

Only items matching your criteria are included in the output. If that output contains too much information, you can just have the cmdlet return the names of the child items:

```
PS C:\test> dir -filter *.ps1 -name
demo1.ps1
demo2.ps1
demo3.ps1
demo4.ps1
scope.ps1
```

Here, by combining the -**filter** and -**name** parameters, we've generated a very customized list: just the names of the PowerShell scripts in this folder.

Occasionally, PowerShell can annoy you by attempting to interpret characters in a path as a wildcard. For example, in the file system, it is used as a single character wild card:

```
PS C:\temp > dir t?st.txt


    Directory: Microsoft.PowerShell.Core\FileSystem::C:\temp


Mode                LastWriteTime     Length Name
----                -------------     ------ ----
-a---         8/23/2007  4:40 PM      44194 tast.txt
-a---         8/23/2007  4:40 PM      44194 test.txt
-a---         8/23/2007  4:40 PM      44194 tzst.txt
PS C:\temp >
```

However, within the Windows registry, the question mark character is a legitimate character. To see how this works temporarily, create some new keys in the registry:

```
PS HKCU:\software > mkdir Micr?soft
PS HKCU:\software > mkdir Micr?soft\test1\
```

Now try the following:

```
PS HKCU:\> dir Micr?soft -recurse
```

You might be expecting a listing of registry keys underneath the key "Micr?Soft," but PowerShell interprets the question mark as a wildcard, and will instead search for any key like "MicrzSoft," "Micr0soft," and so forth. If you run into this situation, just use a slightly different technique:

```
PS HKCU:\> dir -literalPath Micr?soft -recurse
```

Here, the **-literalPath** parameter tells PowerShell to take the path literally—that is, to not try and inter-pret any characters as wildcards. Now you should see only the specified key and its children.

Finally, remember that PowerShell is designed to work with a variety of different storage systems. When you're working with the CERT: drive—the "disk drive" that's connected to your local certificate store—**Get-ChildItem** supports a parameter named **-codeSigningCert**. It filters the display of child items to those which are code-signing certificates rather than other types; this makes it easier to retrieve a code-signing certificate when you want to digitally sign a PowerShell script file. For example:

```
PS CERT:\> get-childitem -codesign
```

Notice that we didn't specify the full name of **-codeSigningCert**; we didn't need to, because only a few characters are needed to differentiate the parameter name from the other ones available (actually, we could have used fewer characters, but this way it's still relatively obvious what's going on when you read the command line).

## Changing Location

Now that you know how to get a list of child items from a single location, you'll also need to know how to change locations. In MS-DOS and *nix, that's done with the **Cd** command, short for "Change Directory," and in many operating systems the longer **ChDir** command will also work. PowerShell aliases **Cd** to **Set-Location**.

Generally speaking, you just tell **Set-Location** where you want to go:

```
PS C:\> Set-Location -path CERT:
```

Or, using an alias and omitting the parameter name:

```
PS C:\> cd C:\Test\Subfolder
```

As with the **Get-ChildItem** cmdlet, you can also specify a literal path, if you don't want PowerShell interpreting wildcard characters:

```
PS C:\> cd -literal HKCU:\SOFTWARE\Manu?\Key
```

If you're curious, you *can* provide wildcards if you don't use the **-literalPath** parameter:

```
PS C:\> cd tes*
```

On our test system, the above changes into the C:\Test folder. You'll get an error if the path you specify resolves to more than one path; this is different than the Cmd.exe behavior of simply changing into the first matching path in the event of multiple matches.

By the way, you *will* notice some quirks in how **Set-Location** behaves compared to Cmd.exe. For exam-ple, the following will produce an error:

```
PS C:\test> cd..
```

In Cmd.exe, that would move up one directory level to C:\; in PowerShell it generates an error because PowerShell needs a space between the command and any parameters:

```
PS C:\test> cd ..
```

That's just a little thing you'll have to get used to as you work with PowerShell. Before long, you'll be dropping your old Cmd.exe habits and picking up new PowerShell habits!

## Cmdlets for Working with Items

Remember, PowerShell uses the word *item* to generically refer to the "stuff located in a PSDrive." That means an *item* could be a file, a folder, a registry value, a registry key, a certificate, an environment variable, and so forth. For example, try this:

```
PS C:\> cd env:
PS Env:\> type systemroot
C:\Windows
PS Env:\>
```

This uses **Set-Location** (or its alias, **Cd**) to change to the ENV: drive—the "disk drive" that contains all the environment variables on your computer. It then uses the **Type** alias—that's the **Get-Content** cmdlet, by the way—to retrieve the contents of the item named "systemroot." In this case, that "item" is an environment variable and **Get-Content** displays its contents: "C:\Windows." So, you've just learned a new cmdlet: **Get-Content**! That cmdlet has a *lot* of parameters that customize its behavior, allowing you to filter the content as it's being displayed, read only a specified number of characters, and so forth; we won't be covering the cmdlet in any more depth right now, but feel free to look it up in PowerShell's help if you like.

PowerShell has a variety of cmdlets for manipulating items:

- Copy-Item
- Clear-Item
- Get-Item
- Invoke-Item
- New-Item
- Move-Item
- Remove-Item
- Rename-Item
- Set-Item

Some of these will look familiar to you. For example, **Remove-Item** is an alias for s **Del**, and is used to delete items, whether they are files, folders, registry keys, or whatever. The old **Move**, **Ren**, and **Copy** commands are now aliases to **Move-Item**, **Rename-Item**, and **Copy-Item**. For example, here you can see a directory listing that includes a folder named Subfolder; the **Copy-Item** cmdlet is then used to create a copy of it named Newfolder:

```
PS C:\test> dir
```

```
    Directory: Microsoft.PowerShell.Core\FileSystem::C:\test


Mode            LastWriteTime     Length Name
----            -------------     ------ ----
d----       4/9/2007 11:10 AM            subfolder
-a---       3/20/2007 11:37 AM       435 demo1.ps1
-a---       3/20/2007 11:46 AM       481 demo2.ps1
-a---       3/20/2007  9:44 AM       354 demo3.ps1
-a---       3/20/2007  9:44 AM       349 demo4.ps1
-a---       3/20/2007 11:55 AM       676 scope.ps1
-a---       3/19/2007 11:15 AM      1825 webcast.zip


PS C:\test> copy subfolder newfolder
PS C:\test> dir


    Directory: Microsoft.PowerShell.Core\FileSystem::C:\test


Mode            LastWriteTime     Length Name
----            -------------     ------ ----
d----       4/9/2007 11:37 AM            newfolder
d----       4/9/2007 11:10 AM            subfolder
-a---       3/20/2007 11:37 AM       435 demo1.ps1
-a---       3/20/2007 11:46 AM       481 demo2.ps1
-a---       3/20/2007  9:44 AM       354 demo3.ps1
-a---       3/20/2007  9:44 AM       349 demo4.ps1
-a---       3/20/2007 11:55 AM       676 scope.ps1
-a---       3/19/2007 11:15 AM      1825 webcast.zip
```

The **Copy-Item** cmdlet is incredibly powerful, though. It supports a -**recurse** parameter which lets it work with entire trees of objects, and supports the -**include** and -**exclude** filtering parameters, as well as -**filter.** For example, the following will copy all files with a .PS1 filename extension to a folder named Newfolder. It will not, however, copy files matching the wildcard pattern Demo?.ps1:

```
PS C:\test> copy *.ps1 newfolder -exclude demo?.ps1
```

The cmdlet also supports the -**whatif** and -**confirm** parameters we introduced in "Windows PowerShell Architecture and Overview." The **Move-Item** cmdlet supports a similar set of functionality. Even **Rename-Item** supports the -**whatif** and -**confirm** parameters, so that you can test what it's doing before actually committing yourself.

**Clear-Item** works similarly to **Remove-Item**. However, it leaves the original item in place, and clears out its contents, making it a zero-length file. That might not seem useful with files and folders, but it's definitely useful with other PSDrive providers, such as the registry, where **Clear-Item** can eliminate the value from a setting but leave the setting itself intact. Similarly, **Set-Item** might not seem to have any use in the file system, but it's useful for changing the value of registry settings.

Last up is **New-Item**, which, as you might guess, creates an all-new item. Of course, you will need to tell PowerShell what *kind* of item you'd like created, and that type of item must match the drive where the item is being created. You can't, for example, create a new file within one of the registry "drives," because the registry can't store a file. For example, this will create a new file and place some text in it:

```
PS C:\> New-Item -path . -name example.txt -type "file" -value "hello!"
```

The **-path** parameter indicates where the item should be created, and the remaining parameters specify its name, its type, and its initial contents. You might also specify "directory" to create a new directory—and, by the way, you've just found the cmdlet that's used instead of the old **MkDir** command! Unfortunately, PowerShell doesn't contain an alias for **MkDir**, because an alias can't specify parameters—and in order to create a new folder, you must specify the **-type directory** parameter.

> You don't *have* to include parameter values like "file" in quotation marks, unless the value contains a space. It doesn't hurt to enclose them in quotation marks, though, and it's not a bad habit to get into, because quotes will *always* work, even if the value contains spaces.

Use PowerShell's built-in help to explore some of the other options available to these cmdlets, and you'll soon be working with all types of items from the various PSDrives available to you.

# Cmdlets for Working with Text Data

Although PowerShell itself always works with objects, as an administrator you're often forced to work with text, or strings of characters. For example, some administrators need to scan through Internet Information Server (IIS) log files, searching for HTTP application errors, so that the errors can be reported to the appropriate Web developers for resolution. This is a bit tricky: The HTTP error code you're after is 500, but you can't just search for the string "500," since it'll also occur in page names, port numbers, byte counts, and so forth. Here's an example log file line with HTTP status code 500 logged:

```
2007-03-05 09:08:45 W3SVC122167217 DATAPIPE-OG0E5E 65.17.251.151 GET /forum/member_profile.asp
PF=|110|800a000d|Type_mismatch:_'CLng' 80 - 66.249.65.243 HTTP/1.1 Mozilla/5.0+(compatible;+Google
bot/2.1;++http://www.google.com/bot.html) - - www.sapien.com 500 0 0 641 248 93
```

The status code immediately follows the domain—in this case, "www.sapien.com 500" is the string we're after. The **Select-String** cmdlet can help quickly scan an entire log file looking for lines with this pattern of characters:

```
PS C:\> get-content c:\sample.log | select-string "www.sapien.com 500" -simple
```

The **-simple** parameter tells **Select-String** that we're not matching on a regular expression, but rather a simple string of characters. The output is every line of the input that has a match for our pattern. We could have stored those matches in a variable, if desired:

```
PS C:\> $matches = get-content c:\sample.log | select-string "www.sapien.com 500" -simple
```

We didn't even have to use **Get-Content** to retrieve our text file, as **Select-String** provides a **-path** argument, which loads the file automatically:

```
PS C:\> $matches = select-string "www.sapien.com 500" -simple -path c:\sample.log
```

Now, our $matches variable actually includes a collection of MatchInfo object, not just pure text. For example, by treating it as a collection, we can refer to specific matches:

```
PS C:\> $matches.filename
sample.log
PS C:\> $matches.line
2007-03-05 09:08:45 W3SVC122167217 DATAPIPE-OG0E5E 65.17.251.151 GET /forum/member_profil
```

```
e.asp PF=|110|800a000d|Type_mismatch:_'CLng' 80 - 66.249.65.243 HTTP/1.1 Mozilla/5.0+(com
patible;+Googlebot/2.1;++http://www.google.com/bot.html) - - www.sapien.com 500 0 0 641 2
48 93
PS C:\> $matches.linenumber
5416
PS C:\> $matches.path
C:\sample.log
PS C:\> $matches.pattern
www.sapien.com 500
PS C:\>
```

You can see that the Filename, Line, LineNumber, Path, and Pattern properties all return useful information. Now, in this example our $matches variable only contained one match (the $matches.Count property would verify this). But we can modify our search slightly:

```
PS C:\> $matches = select-string "500" -simple -path c:\sample.log
```

Now we're not just getting HTTP 500 errors, but also anything with "500," including byte counts and other data. This time our log generated 503 matches:

```
PS C:\> $matches.count
503
```

And we can reference individual matches by using their index number:

```
PS C:\> $matches[0].linenumber
93
```

This tells us that our first match was on line 93. The **Select-String** cmdlet also works with regular expressions; in fact, it's *primarily* designed to work with regular expressions, although we've been using it in a simpler fashion in our examples.

# Cmdlets for Working with Windows

Even though current versions of Windows—Vista, XP, Server 2003, and Server 2008—aren't specifically built on PowerShell, you can still perform a lot of administrative automation in PowerShell. That's because PowerShell comes pre-packed with cmdlets designed for administering specific portions of Windows, and because PowerShell makes it easy to utilize Windows Management Instrumentation (WMI), a key management technology that's present in all modern versions of Windows.

---

**Note**

Keep in mind that files, folders, registries, and other aspects of Windows are also manageable through Windows PowerShell, using the various cmdlets and techniques we discussed earlier in this chapter. There aren't specific cmdlets used to deal with files or folders, for example; you use the "generic" Item cmdlets to move, copy, rename, delete, and create these items.

---

Our goal here is *not* an exhaustive exploration of these cmdlets. In fact, Part III of this book focuses on using these and other cmdlets to perform administrative tasks. The goal right now is just to make you aware of these cmdlets, since we'll be using them in a lot of examples and samples in upcoming chapters.

Perhaps the easiest cmdlet to start working with is **Get-Process**. By itself, it returns a collection of all the currently running processes on your computer. You can also give it a specific process name, or a numeric process ID, and it'll retrieve just the specified process. The following example retrieves a specific process and stores it in the variable $psh. Then, it displays the path of the executable that the process is running by using the Path property of the process object.

```
PS C:\test> $psh = get-process PowerShell
PS C:\test> $psh.path
C:\WINDOWS\system32\WindowsPowerShell\v1.0\powershell.exe
```

The other cmdlet used to work with processes is **Stop-Process**. It can also accept a process name or ID, or you can simply give it a process object. It supports the -**whatif** and -**confirm** parameters we described in "Windows PowerShell Architecture and Overview." In the following example, we're continuing to use the $psh variable we created in the previous example. As you can see, we choose *not* to stop the process after all. But by using the -**confirm** parameter, we can see what the **Stop-Process** cmdlet was doing:

```
PS C:\test> stop-process -inputobject $psh -confirm

Confirm
Are you sure you want to perform this action?
Performing operation "Stop-Process" on Target "powershell (2008)".
[Y] Yes [A] Yes to All [N] No [L] No to All
[S] Suspend[?] Help (default is "Y"): n
PS C:\test>
```

> We'll give you more examples of process management in "Managing Processes."

Another straightforward cmdlet is **Get-Service**, which retrieves one or more Windows services. It supports the same -**include** and -**exclude** parameters that the various Item cmdlets did, allowing you to filter the results that the cmdlet provides. You can specify either the name of the service you want, or its display name. If you don't specify any name, you get a collection of all installed services. For example, we'll retrieve the LanManServer service and display its status:

```
PS C:\> $svc = get-service lanmanserver
PS C:\> $svc.status
Running
PS C:\>
```

Other cmdlets used to work with services include **Stop-Service**, **Start-Service**, **Suspend-Service**, **Resume-Service**, and **Set-Service**, which allows you to reconfigure a service. **New-Service** permits you to create new services. For example, the following would stop our LanManServer service (stored in the variable $svc)—would stop it, that is, if we hadn't specified the -**whatif** parameter:

```
PS C:\> stop-service -inputobject $svc -whatif
What if: Performing operation "Stop-Service" on Target "Serv
er (LanmanServer)".
```

> "Managing Services" provides examples of performing various service management tasks using these cmdlets.

The last set basic cmdlet we'll explore for now is for event log management. **Get-EventLog** retrieves an event log, such as the Application, System, or Security log. Not sure what logs are installed? Try this:

```
PS C:\> get-eventlog -list

Max(K) Retain OverflowAction     Entries Name
------ ------ --------------     ------- ----
   512      7 OverwriteOlder         109 ACEEventLog
20,480      7 OverwriteOlder       1,296 Application
15,168      0 OverwriteAsNeeded        6 DFS Replic...
20,480      0 OverwriteAsNeeded        0 Hardware E...
   512      7 OverwriteOlder           0 Internet E...
   512      7 OverwriteOlder           0 Key Manage...
 8,192      0 OverwriteAsNeeded        0 Media Center
16,384      0 OverwriteAsNeeded        0 Microsoft ...
16,384      0 OverwriteAsNeeded      117 Microsoft ...
20,480      7 OverwriteOlder          25 Security
20,480      7 OverwriteOlder       4,677 System
15,360      0 OverwriteAsNeeded      345 Windows Po...
```

Yes, that last one *is* "Windows PowerShell." Bet you didn't realize Windows PowerShell had a log all its own! When you retrieve a log, what you're really retrieving is a collection of the log's entries. For example, here's part of a Security log:

```
PS C:\> get-eventlog security

Index Time          Type Source              EventID Mess
                                                     age
----- ----          ---- ------              ------- ----
   25 Apr 04 03:05  Succ Microsoft-Windows...    1108 T...
   24 Apr 04 03:05  Succ Microsoft-Windows...    1100 T...
   23 Mar 30 14:46  Succ Microsoft-Windows...    4616 T...
   22 Mar 30 14:46  Succ Microsoft-Windows...    4616 T...
   21 Mar 23 14:48  Succ Microsoft-Windows...    4616 T...
   20 Mar 23 14:48  Succ Microsoft-Windows...    4616 T...
   19 Mar 23 08:09  Succ Microsoft-Windows...    4616 T...
   18 Mar 23 08:09  Succ Microsoft-Windows...    1100 T...
   17 Mar 19 17:45  Succ Microsoft-Windows...    1108 T...
   16 Mar 19 17:45  Succ Microsoft-Windows...    1100 T...
```

> We're truncating our output throughout this book to save space and to prevent unnecessary line-wrapping. When you run this on a full-sized monitor, you'll see more comprehensive results.

Don't want the full list of events? No problem!

```
PS C:\> get-eventlog security -newest 10

Index Time          Type Source              EventID Message
----- ----          ---- ------              ------- -------
   25 Apr 04 03:05  Succ Microsoft-Windows...    1108 The description for E...
   24 Apr 04 03:05  Succ Microsoft-Windows...    1100 The description for E...
   23 Mar 30 14:46  Succ Microsoft-Windows...    4616 The description for E...
   22 Mar 30 14:46  Succ Microsoft-Windows...    4616 The description for E...
   21 Mar 23 14:48  Succ Microsoft-Windows...    4616 The description for E...
   20 Mar 23 14:48  Succ Microsoft-Windows...    4616 The description for E...
   19 Mar 23 08:09  Succ Microsoft-Windows...    4616 The description for E...
   18 Mar 23 08:09  Succ Microsoft-Windows...    1100 The description for E...
   17 Mar 19 17:45  Succ Microsoft-Windows...    1108 The description for E...
```

```
16 Mar 19 17:45 Succ Microsoft-Windows...    1100 The description for E...
```

"Managing Event Logs" provides samples for production event log management in PowerShell.

Just this handful of cmdlets provides a lot of administrative functionality. Of course, we haven't even talked about WMI, yet, or about ways of managing Directory Services from PowerShell—those topics will come later in this Part. But right now you know enough cmdlets to start working with PowerShell in more depth.

# Cmdlets for Working with PowerShell

Another category of cmdlets is used to manipulate PowerShell itself, working with the shell's variables, commands, and so forth (and, remember, we covered commands to work with aliases in "Part I: Using Windows PowerShell").

## Creating Output

PowerShell supports a number of different *output streams*. These can be kind of tough to visualize in the console, because in the end, everything appears as text within the console window. But, if you can imagine PowerShell being embedded inside another application—such as the Exchange Server 2007 graphical management console, where the PowerShell command line itself isn't visible—you can start to imagine how these different "streams" can be used. PowerShell provides a cmdlet for writing to each of these streams:

- **Write-Debug** writes debugging information—primarily from a script. Whether or not the information written to the debugging stream is displayed depends upon the contents of a special PowerShell variable named $DebugPreference. Its default value, "SilentlyContinue", suppresses anything written to the debugging stream. Any other valid value—"Stop", "Continue", and "Inquire"—will display the information written to the debugging stream. This cmdlet is useful within scripts, where you can use it to output status information as the script runs. By setting $DebugPreference to "SilentlyContinue", you can then suppress the debug output without having to remove the **Write-Debug** commands from the script.

- **Write-Error** writes information to the error stream. This cmdlet has a large number of parameters that permit you to customize its output. Generally speaking, this should be used only when a script needs to output an error message. By default, the console displays errors in red text, helping them stand out from other output.

- **Write-Host** writes information to the application that is hosting PowerShell. Remember, when you're using PowerShell.exe, *this* is the hosting application, and it's what provides you with the command-line interface you're accustomed to seeing. Other applications can host the PowerShell engine, though, and what *those* applications do with **Write-Host** output may differ. We typically use **Write-Host** only when we *know* our scripts will only be run in the PowerShell.exe host and when we want to take advantage of the formatting options **Write-Host** offers, like alternate text colors.

- **Write-Output** sends output to the "success" output stream. This has a number of uses. Within the PowerShell.exe console host, the "success" output stream is usually just whatever output you want the user to see. Within a PowerShell function, the "success" output stream is where you send the information you want to return from the function when the function completes. From the command line, **Write-Output** may seem indistinguishable from **Write-Host** (except that **Write-Host** offers some formatting options for text), but under the hood these two cmdlets do serve different purposes. **Write-Host** always creates output to be displayed in a host window. **Write-Output** sends output to a specific output stream, which doesn't, in all cases, display as text to the user.

- **Write-Progress** creates a progress bar within the PowerShell window. Whether or not the bar is displayed depends upon the special $ProgressPreference variable. When set to "SilentlyContinue", then no progress bar is displayed; other values—"Continue", "Stop", and "Inquire"—will display the progress bar. Note that you can generally display a progress bar only within a script or some other construct; if you issue a single call to **Write-Progress** from the command line, the bar will appear and disappear too quickly to even see.

- **Write-Verbose** writes a string to the hosting application's "verbose" stream. The contents of the special $VerbosePreference variable determines whether or not verbose output is actually displayed. A value of "SilentlyContinue" suppresses output, while other values—"Continue", "Stop", and "Inquire"—will display the output.

- **Write-Warning** writes a string to the hosting application's "warning" stream. The contents of the special $WarningPreference variable determines whether or not verbose output is actually displayed. A value of "SilentlyContinue" suppresses output, while other values—"Continue", "Stop", and "Inquire"—will display the output. By default, warnings are displayed in reversed colors to help make them stand out from other output.

Now, here's where things may get confusing. In reality, none of the Write cmdlets *actually produce output*. As we describe above, these cmdlets simply write to various different streams (or pipelines—same thing). *Rendering* those streams—that is, turning the objects in the streams (which are technically called *pipelines*) into text output—is the job of the various Out cmdlets:

- **Out-Default** is a placeholder; that is, it doesn't really do anything except pass objects right along to the shell's default output cmdlet, **Out-Host**. The only reason **Out-Default** exists is in case a developer wanted to create a different default behavior.

- **Out-Host** turns objects into strings and displays them in the console host; that is, it creates command-line output. The cmdlet does not pass any objects down the pipeline.

- **Out-Printer** turns objects into strings and sends them to the specified Windows printer. The cmdlet does not pass any objects down the pipeline.

- **Out-File** turns objects into strings, and writes them to the specified file. Cmdlet parameters can be used to append to an existing file rather than overwriting it, and so forth. The cmdlet does not pass any objects down the pipeline.

- **Out-Null** doesn't do anything with whatever it's given; it just discards it. The cmdlet does not pass any objects down the pipeline.

- **Out-String** turns objects into strings, and then passes them down the pipeline. This is the only Out cmdlet that passes things down the pipeline. **Out-String** is designed to render objects into strings so that they can be passed to older, external utilities that can work only with strings and not with objects.

For example, when you run this:

```
Write-Output "Hello"
```

You're really running a lot more than that: The cmdlet is writing the text "Hello" to the success pipeline; since there are no other cmdlets in the pipeline, PowerShell sends everything to **Out-Default**, which reroutes it right to the default output cmdlet, **Out-Host**. So, really, what you ran, even though you didn't realize it, is this:

```
Write-Output "Hello" | Out-Default | Out-Host
```

And that's what resulted in the word "Hello" being displayed on the command line. **Write-Host** does something similar, although it explicitly sends objects to **Out-Host**. So, this:

```
Write-Host Hello
```

Is actually running this:

```
Write-Host Hello | Out-Host
```

Generally speaking, the output cmdlets (those beginning with "Out") are designed to have things piped to them. They then take care of turning that output into strings of text and getting the text to whatever output device—file, screen, printer, and so forth—that you've specified.

### Here's Another Way to Think About Writing and Output

All of the Write cmdlets, with the exception of Write-Host, are writing to a *stream*, or, more properly, a *pipeline*. For example, **Write-Output** writes to the success pipeline, which is the pipeline that cmdlets run on and is what we're generally referring to when we use the term *pipeline* generically. **Write-Debug** writes to the debug pipeline, **Write-Error** writes to the error pipeline, and so forth.

As we've already discussed, when PowerShell comes to the end of a pipeline, its default action is to render whatever's in the pipeline into text and display it. More specifically, all of the pipelines are connected to the **Out-Default** cmdlet. So, anything left at the end of a pipeline goes to **Out-Default**, which, as we've described, sends the objects along to **Out-Host**. **Out-Host** then renders the objects into text and displays the result.

All of the pipelines except the success pipeline can be suppressed by using the various Preference variables we described earlier in this section. Essentially, the Preference variables put a "plug" into the associated pipeline so that the content in that pipeline never reaches **Out-Default**, and, therefore, never displays.

The **Write-Host** cmdlet is an exception: It does *not* write to a pipeline. Instead, it implicitly pipes its output directly to **Out-Host**, displaying the output in the console window as text.

So, to summarize: The Write cmdlets (except **Write-Host**) put objects into a pipeline. Preference variables determine whether or not a given pipeline (except the success pipeline) is connected to **Out-Default**. The Out cmdlets are responsible for rendering pipeline objects into text and sending the text to the associated output device, such as a printer, file, or the console window.

Because **Out-File**, **Out-Printer**, and the other Out cmdlets aren't directly connected to a pipeline, the only way to use them is to explicitly send objects their way. *Technically*, when you pipe objects to a cmdlet such as **Out-File**, that pipeline is *still connected to **Out-Default***, because the main success pipeline *always* ends in **Out-Default** (which then sends whatever it received on to **Out-Host**). However, **Out-File**, **Out-Printer**, **Out-Host**, and **Out-Null** don't pass anything down the pipeline. So, even though **Out-Default** is always implicitly called after every **Out-Printer** (for example), **Out-Default** is given no objects to work with, and so it doesn't create any visible result.

## Clearing the Console

PowerShell also has a cmdlet named **Clear-Host**, which simply clears the hosting application's window. Its alias, **Cls**, is one you may be familiar with from the Cmd.exe console or versions of MS-DOS.

**Clear-Host** doesn't have any parameters, and most people just run the **Cls** alias instead.

## Accepting Input

PowerShell offers one cmdlet for accepting text input from the command line: **Read-Host**. You can specify a text prompt, and whatever the user types is returned from the cmdlet and can be stored in a variable, if you like, as follows:

```
PS C:\> $username = Read-Host "Type your username"
```

You can add the **-asSecureString** parameter to have whatever the user types encrypted as a secure string—this is useful when you're asking them to type a password or other sensitive information. Whatever they type will be obscured by * characters on the screen, as shown here:

```
PS C:\> $var = read-host "Password" -assecurestring
Password: *********
PS C:\>
```

Secure strings are a bit more difficult to work with than normal strings of text. For example, you can't simply output the contents of a secure string, as shown here. Instead, PowerShell simply informs you that the variable contains a secure string:

```
PS C:\> $var
System.Security.SecureString
```

The **ConvertFrom-SecureString** cmdlet can convert a secure string into an encrypted string, but all you wind up with is the encrypted version, not the original cleartext that was typed:

```
PS C:\> convertfrom-securestring $var
01000000d08c9ddf0115d1118c7a00c04fc297eb01000000c3fa04e02c086948b8384ff78af7b2a0000000000
2000000000003660000a80000001000000099bf997ab82c7d2ed347fbc67cab7ed20000000004800000a00000
0010000000a91c2fa70a5ed0080b523499a48bc4f718000000a89c92a8fd1d1596f07c70c5c799b3bab1befd7
722a0b19514000000a15e2a9e566a7bb748a542080fa89b0aec580e5f
```

The purpose of secure strings is just that: They're *secure*. They can be stored in files and retrieved for later use (and certain PowerShell cmdlets *accept* a secure string as input and know how to retrieve the cleartext version of the string).

## Working with Variables

You don't *need* to use cmdlets to work with variables. Creating a new variable is as easy as assigning a value to it (and there's currently no way to make PowerShell insist on advance variable declaration, as some programming languages can do). For example:

```
PS C:\> $var = 5
```

Retrieving a variable is just as easy: Type it, and hit Enter. The default **Out-Host** cmdlet will display the variable's contents:

```
PS C:\> $var
5
```

But PowerShell does provide cmdlets for working with variables. In fact, it also has a PSDrive, since PowerShell's variable storage is exposed as a "disk drive" within the shell:

```
PS C:\> cd variable:
PS Variable:\> dir

Name                     Value
----                     -----
Error                    {RuntimeException, RuntimeException, RuntimeException, ...
DebugPreference             SilentlyContinue
PROFILE                     C:\Users\Don\Documents\WindowsPowerShell\Microsoft.Powe...
HOME                     C:\Users\Don
Host                     System.Management.Automation.Internal.Host.InternalHost
MaximumHistoryCount         64
MaximumAliasCount           4096
foreach
input                    System.Array+SZArrayEnumerator
StackTrace                  at System.Number.StringToNumber(String str, NumberSt...
names                    {computers.txt, computers.txt, computers.txt}
ReportErrorShowSource       1
ExecutionContext            System.Management.Automation.EngineIntrinsics
true                     True
VerbosePreference           SilentlyContinue
var                      5
ShellId                   Microsoft.PowerShell
name                     DON-PC
false                    False
```

The variable-manipulation cmdlets are:

- **Clear-Variable** removes a variable's value.

- **Get-Variable** retrieves the contents of a variable.

- **New-Variable** creates a new variable. Optionally, using parameters, you can assign a specific data type to the variable and assign an initial value.

- **Remove-Variable** deletes a variable.

- **Set-Variable** changes the value of a variable.

Again, however, it's unusual to see these cmdlets being used, since you can manipulate variables directly, just as with most programming languages.

## Working with Commands

PowerShell provides a few cmdlets for working *with* cmdlets, or commands. They are:

- **Get-Command** retrieves basic information about a cmdlet. If you don't provide a cmdlet name, then it retrieves a list of all cmdlets. You can use the **-verb** or **-noun** parameters to just retrieve cmdlets related to a specific verb, such as "Get", or a specific noun, such as "Variable." You can also just retrieve the cmdlets contained within a particular snap-in by using the **-pSSnapIn** parameter.

- **Measure-Command** allows you to measure the time it takes to run script blocks or cmdlets. Simply give it the command or script block you want to run, and it'll output the execute time.

- **Trace-Command** traces the execution of a specific command. It has a wealth of parameters, which you can review in the built-in help. This is primarily useful in debugging short script blocks that contain a few cmdlets, so that you can trace the progress of the block's execution.

## Working with Command-Line History

As you may know, PowerShell maintains a history of everything you type into the command line. Normally, you access this history using the up and down arrow keys on your keyboard (we'll cover that and other tips in "Command History"). PowerShell also provides three cmdlets used to manipulate the shell's command-line history:

- **Add-History** adds a command to the command-line history. You can read a text file containing a command-line history, for example, and pipe that to **Add-History** to re-create the command-line history for a past PowerShell session.

- **Get-History** retrieves a list of what's in the command-line history buffer. You could pipe this list to one of the "Out" cmdlets to save the command-line history into a file, or, even better, use one of the "Export" cmdlets (which we cover in Chapter 5) to create a CSV or XML file.

- **Invoke-History** runs commands from the session history. You specify the desired command by using its history ID (viewable with **Get-History**). You can use the **-whatif** or **-confirm** parameters to review what would happen and get confirmation, if desired.

## Working with PSDrives

Finally, PowerShell provides three cmdlets for working with PSDrives:

- **Get-PSDrive** retrieves information about a specific PSDrive or, if you don't specify one, lists all available drives.

- **New-PSDrive** creates a new drive using the specified provider. Use this to, for example, map network drives, as we showed you in the "PowerShell Drives" chapter.

- **Remove-PSDrive** removes an existing drive from the shell.

# Chapter 4
# **The PowerShell Pipeline**

Perhaps the most powerful concept in Windows PowerShell is its rich, object-oriented pipeline. You may already be familiar with pipelines from the Cmd.exe console, or from MS-DOS. For example, one common use was to pipe a long text file to the **More** utility, creating a paged display of text:

```
C:\> type myfile.txt | more
```

This technique evolved directly from *nix shells, which have used pipelines for years to pass, or *pipe*, text from one command to another. In PowerShell, this concept takes on whole new meaning as cmdlets work with rich *objects* rather than text, and pipe those objects to one another for great effect. For example, consider this cmdlet:

```
PS C:\> get-process
```

Run that, and you get a list of processes. It's easy to assume that what you're seeing is the actual output of the cmdlet; that is, it's easy to think that the cmdlet simply produces a text list. But it doesn't. The cmdlet produces a set of Process objects. Because there's nothing else in the pipeline waiting for those objects, PowerShell sends them to the default output cmdlet (**Out-Default**, as we discussed in the previous chapter). That cmdlet calls one of PowerShell's formatting cmdlets, which examines various properties of the objects—in the case of a Process, the Handles, Nonpaged Memory, Paged Memory, Working Set, Virtual Memory, CPU, ID, and ProcessName properties—and creates a table of information. So, the result that you *see* is certainly a text list, but you're not seeing the intermediate steps that created that text list from a collection of objects.

**By the Way...**

How does PowerShell decide what properties to use when it converts objects into a text-based listing? It's not arbitrary: For most object types, Microsoft has pre-defined the "interesting" properties that PowerShell uses. These pre-defined formats are in a file called DotNetTypes.format.ps1xml, located in the PowerShell installation folder. Other pre-defined types are defined in other files, such as FileSystem.format.ps1xml, Certificate.format.ps1xml, and so forth. These files are digitally signed by Microsoft, so you can't modify them unless you're prepared to re-sign them using your own code-signing certificate. However, you can build custom formats, a topic we cover in the chapter "Creating Custom Formats."

# Piping Objects from Cmdlet to Cmdlet

Once you have a collection of objects, however, you can do a lot more than let PowerShell create text lists. For example, take a look at the help for the **Stop-Process** cmdlet:

```
PS C:\> help stop-process

NAME
    Stop-Process

SYNOPSIS
    Stops one or more running processes.


SYNTAX
    Stop-Process [-id] <Int32[]> [-passThru] [-whatIf] [-confirm] [<CommonParameters>]

    Stop-Process -name <string[]> [-passThru] [-whatIf] [-confirm] [<CommonParameters>]

    Stop-Process -inputObject <Process[]> [-passThru] [-whatIf] [-confirm] [<CommonParame
    ters>]


DETAILED DESCRIPTION
    The Stop-Process cmdlet stops one or more running processes. You can specify a proces
    s by process name or process ID (PID), or pass a process object to Stop-Process. For
    Get-Process, the default method is by process name. For Stop-Process, the default met
    hod is by process ID.


RELATED LINKS
    Get-Process, Start-Process

REMARKS
    For more information, type: "get-help Stop-Process -detailed".
    For technical information, type: "get-help Stop-Process -full".
```

Notice that there are *three* ways in which **Stop-Process** can be used? If the first parameter is an integer, the cmdlet assumes you've given it a process ID, and it tries to stop that process ID. If you give it a string, it tries to stop a process with that name. Or, if you give it a Process object, it will try to stop the process represented by that object. The help indicates that the **-id** parameter name is optional, but that **-name** or **-inputObject**, should you use those, are required. In other words, you can do this:

```
PS C:\> stop-process 505
```

But you can't do this:

```
PS C:\> stop-process notepad
```

Instead, if you're providing a string, you need to provide the parameter name:

```
PS C:\> stop-process -name notepad
```

That's because only the **-id** parameter is *positional*; any other parameter, like **-name**, needs to be specified, which is easy enough to do from the command line.

## Finding Cmdlets That Accept Pipeline Input

That's all well and good from the command line, but from within the pipeline, things are somewhat different. Inside the pipeline, only certain parameters can accept input. To see this, you need to ask for full help (using the **-full** parameter of the **help** command). Here's an excerpt:

```
PARAMETERS
    -id <Int32[]>
        Specifies the process IDs of the processes to be stopped. To specify multiple IDs
        , use commas to separate the IDs. To find the PID of a process, type "get-process
        ". The parameter name ("-Id") is optional.

        Required?                   true
        Position?                   1
        Default value               Null
        Accept pipeline input?      true (ByPropertyName)
        Accept wildcard characters? false

    -inputObject <Process[]>
        Stops the processes represented by the specified process objects. Enter a variabl
        e that contains the objects or type a command or expression that gets the objects
        .

        Required?                   true
        Position?                   named
        Default value
        Accept pipeline input?      true (ByValue)
        Accept wildcard characters? False
```

Notice that the **-id** parameter can accept input from the pipeline, *as can the -inputObject parameter.* That means these parameters can accept pipeline input without specifying a parameter name. More importantly, **-inputObject** can accept pipeline input "ByValue", meaning it can accept entire Process objects. The **-id** parameter can only accept pipeline input if that input is actually a property *named* "ID"—that's what "ByPropertyName" means. In other words, if you can produce an object that has an ID property (other than a Process object), and that ID property's value corresponds to the ID of a process you want stopped, then you can pipeline that object into **Stop-Process**. Sound confusing? It is.

The practical upshot of this is that, when you're reading the full help, look for parameters that can accept pipeline input "ByValue". Those are the ones you want to work with. In this case, it tells us that we can pipe a bunch of Process objects to **Stop-Process**, and it'll stop those processes. But where do we get a collection of Process objects?

```
PS C:\> get-process
```

So, all we have to do is pipe those to **Stop-Process**:

> **Caution:** Don't run the following on your computer.

```
PS C:\> get-process | stop-process
```

And the computer will crash as its critical processes are stopped in their tracks. Oops. It's a good demonstration, though, right? The point is that you can continue piping objects down the pipeline to keep doing things with them. For example, most cmdlets that do something with an object also have a **-passthru** parameter, which tells the cmdlet to do whatever it's going to do, and then continue passing the objects down the pipeline. So, you could do this:

```
PS C:\> Get-service | stop-service -passthru | out-file c:\stopped.txt
```

This will retrieve a collection of Service objects, stop them, and then output a text list to a file named C:\Stopped.txt. Yes, it's unlikely you'd want to stop *all* of a server's services all at once—so how about just the ones start with the letter "A"?

```
PS C:\> Get-service -include a* | stop-service -passthru | out-file c:\stopped.txt
```

True, this technique would be more useful if you had a more powerful way of filtering the objects that **Get-Service** retrieves—and we'll discuss more powerful ways in the very next chapter, in fact—but this example serves the illustrate what the pipeline can do for you. By stringing together cmdlets that successively refine a collection of objects, you can accomplish extremely powerful administrative tasks with a *single line*—what the PowerShell community has taken to calling *one-liners*. One-liners can literally replace hundreds of lines of VBScript code, or tens of hours of manual effort.

## The Pipeline Enables Powerful One-Liners

Okay, we'll jump ahead of ourselves a bit and give you a *really* good example:

```
PS C:\ > get-wmiobject -query "Select Name,StartMode,State from win32_service
>> where startmode<>'disabled' AND state='Stopped'" | select Name | start-service
>>
```

This retrieves all services using **Get-Wmiobject** that have not been disabled and are not running. The names of the services are extracted using the **Select** cmdlet and then the list of stopped services is passed to **Start-Service**. Here's another one:

```
PS C:\>$svcname=Read-Host "Enter a service name" ; get-process | where {$_.id -eq (Get-WmiObject
win32_service | where {$_.name -eq $svcname}).ProcessID} | select -property StartTime
```

Yes, that's all one line of text. It asks you for a service name, and then gets a list of all processes. It filters out all the processes *except* the one that matches the service name you typed—it actually executes **Get-WmiObject** to get the process ID of the service you specified). Then it retrieves just the StartTime property—the practical upshot is that you can see exactly when the specified service started. Yes, it's pretty complicated, but you assemble these things one step at a time. For example, the first task is to get a service name:

```
PS C:\> $svcname=Read-Host "Enter a service name"
```

Easy enough. That stores the service name in the variable $svcname. Next, we want to start a new pipeline: Notice in the original command where the semicolon occurs? That tells PowerShell to begin a new logical line, as if you'd hit Enter. So, *technically*, this is a two-liner. Given the service name in $svcname, though, the rest occurs on one line. So, we know we need to get a Process object in order to get a start time, so how do we get Process objects?

```
PS C:> get-process
```

Now, we only want the process that represents the specified service. So, we need to make a call to **Get-WmiObject** (we cover that in an upcoming chapter—we said we were getting ahead of ourselves, here!) to retrieve the desired service:

```
PS C:\> Get-WmiObject win32_service
```

Well, okay, that gets *all* the services. Let's filter that down to get just the one we want:

```
PS C:\> Get-WmiObject win32_service | where { $_.name -eq $svcname }
```

That $_ variable, by the way, is a placeholder for "the current pipeline object." So, **Get-WmiObject** will retrieve all instances of the win32_service class, or services, and then **Where-Object** (or its alias, **Where**) will look at each one to see if its ID property matches the process ID of the service we retrieved from WMI. Don't worry if this a little confusing. We'll go over the **Where** cmdlet in the next chapter.

The upshot is that the **Where** cmdlet gets rid of all services except the one we're looking for. Specifically, what we're interested in from our service is its process ID. So, the entire call to **Get-WmiObject** will result in only one object being returned. Therefore, we can bundle that whole call into parentheses to treat it as a standalone object, and just refer to the process ID property:

```
PS C:\> (Get-WmiObject win32_service | where { $_.name -eq $svcname }).ProcessID
```

And now we combine that with our original call to **Get-Process** so that we can filter out the processes that don't have the process ID we're after.

```
PS C:\> get-process | where {$_.ID -eq (Get-WmiObject win32_service | where { $_.name -eq $svcname
}).ProcessID}
```

Once we've gotten the process we're after, we'll just select the StartTime property using **Select-Object**, or its alias, **Select**:

```
PS C:\> get-process | where {$_.ID -eq (Get-WmiObject win32_service | where { $_.name -eq $svcname
}).ProcessID} | select -property StartTime
```

And that's it. Yes, it's a bit funny-looking, and it definitely takes some time to wrap your head around it. Not to mention the fact that we haven't really explored some of these cmdlets yet! But the point is that complex one-liners are constructed on cmdlet at a time, which is a pretty easy way to work, since you can immediately see your results and decide what step will be next in order to get to your final goal.

## The Pipeline Enables Simple Output Redirection

For now, don't worry about complex one-liners. They'll come to you naturally enough as you learn more of PowerShell's cmdlets. For now, remember that the pipeline can be a great way to create output. For example, in the previous chapter, we mentioned that you could export a command-line history to a text file. Well, here's how:

```
PS C:\> Get-History | Out-File C:\History.txt
```

That retrieved the command history and *piped* it to the **Out-File** cmdlet. See, as you learn more cmdlets, you'll learn more techniques for making the pipeline useful! And the next chapter is all about some cmdlets designed to work almost entirely within the pipeline.

## The End of the (Pipe)line

What you rarely see is the *end* of the pipeline. Invisibly connected to the end of the pipeline is the **Out-Default** cmdlet, which basically does nothing except transfer objects to **Out-Host**. The **Out-Host** cmdlet is both clever and stupid: It's stupid, in that the only thing it knows how to deal with are formatting directives which tell it what text to display; it's smart in that, if it doesn't *get* formatting directives, it'll send whatever it *does* get to a Format cmdlet first.

So, here's a set of basic rules to remember about the end of the pipeline:

- If you end a pipeline by using an Out cmdlet (like **Out-File**), then the Out cmdlet doesn't pass anything else down the pipeline (unless it's **Out-String**, which is definitely an exception). So, **Out-Default** is still there at the end, but it has nothing to work with and so nothing else happens.

- If you end a pipeline with a Format cmdlet, then the pipeline contains formatting directives. **Out-Default** passes them to **Out-Host**, which loves formatting directives—it does whatever the directives say, thus producing text.

- If you don't end the pipeline with either a Format cmdlet or an Out cmdlet, then whatever's in the pipeline goes to **Out-Default**, which turns right around and sends them to **Out-Host**. Because **Out-Host** doesn't see formatting directives, it gets scared and calls on PowerShell's formatting system to format the pipeline objects. **Out-Host** then gets the formatting directives it wants, and displays whatever they tell it to.

In other words, *all* pipelines end in **Out-Default** (which, practically speaking, means they end in **Out-Host**). The various Out cmdlets all work with formatting directives, so if they see "raw" objects, they'll ask PowerShell to format them, first. That means even a simple cmdlet:

```
PS C:\> Get-Process
```

This is really running *four* cmdlets: First, **Get-Process**. Then, **Out-Default**. Then, **Out-Host**. Then, a formatting cmdlet—PowerShell would choose **Format-Table** in this case.

Chapter 5
# Cmdlets to Group, Sort, Format, Export, and More

Because PowerShell's output is almost entirely text-based, it's easy to mistake it for a text-based shell. However, what is really happening behind the scenes is that PowerShell is using .NET and cmdlets to carry out your commands and manipulate data as needed. Only when all processing is complete is the final data formatted for textual presentation. However, there are many things you can do to control how the data is ultimately presented.

## Formatting

Just about every PowerShell cmdlet is designed to produce textual output. The cmdlet developer creates a default output format based on the information to be delivered. For example, the output of **Get-Process** is a horizontal table. However, if you need a different output format, PowerShell has a few choices that are discussed below.

**Formatting Rules**
PowerShell uses a fairly clever system of priorities to determine which formats it uses. Refer to "Formatting Rules" for more information on these rules, if you're interested. You don't *need* to know these rules in order to use PowerShell's formatting capabilities.

## Format-List

This cmdlet produces a columnar list. Here's a sample using **Get-Process**:

```
PS C:\> get-process | format-list
Id      : 720
Handles : 63
CPU     : 0.1301872
Name    : ApntEx

Id      : 584
Handles : 105
CPU     : 0.5107344
Name    : Apoint

Id      : 404
Handles : 130
CPU     : 0.4706768
Name    : avgamsvr

Id      : 444
Handles : 205
CPU     : 2.1130384
Name    : avgcc
...
```

Even though we've truncated the output, you get the idea. Instead of the regular horizontal table, each process and its properties is listed in a column. As we've pointed when this cmdlet has been used in other examples, the **Format-List** doesn't use all the properties of an object; PowerShell instead follows its internal formatting rules, which may include using a *view*, which is essentially a set of pre-selected properties. Microsoft provides views for most of the common types of information you'll work with, and in many cases provides both table- and list-style views so that PowerShell doesn't just pick random properties for its output.

If you prefer more control over what information is displayed, you can use the **-property** cmdlet parameter to specify the properties:

```
PS C:\> get-process winword |format-list -property '
>> name,workingset,id,path
>>


Name       : WINWORD
WorkingSet : 32522240
Id         : 564
Path       : C:\Program Files\Microsoft Office\OFFICE11\WINWORD.EXE

PS C:\>
```

In this example we've called **Get-Process** seeking specific information on the WinWord process.

**How Did You Know?**

You might wonder how we knew what properties can be displayed when we use the **-property** cmdlet. To review, it is important to get to know the **Get-Member** cmdlet. This command lists all the available properties for the process object:

```
get-process | get-member
```

Different cmdlets and objects have different properties, especially in WMI.

Note that if you don't specify any properties, **Format-List** either uses a pre-defined view, or if none exists, **Format-List** looks in PowerShell's Types.ps1xml type definition file to see if any properties are marked as "defaults." If some properties are marked as defaults, and then those properties are used to construct the list. Otherwise, all of the object's properties are used to construct the list. To force the cmdlet to list all of an object's properties, use * for the properties list:

```
PS C:\> get-process | format-list *
```

## Format-Table

Just as there are some cmdlets that use a list format as the default, there are some that use a table format. Of course, sometimes you may prefer a table. The format of this **Get-WmiObject** expression produces a list by default:

**Why a list?**

Why does this cmdlet produce a list by default? There are two possibilities: Microsoft provided a pre-defined view which happens to be a list, or Microsoft provided *no* pre-defined view. In the latter case, PowerShell selected the list type because the object has more than five properties—if it had fewer, PowerShell would select a table under the same circumstances.

```
PS C:\> Get-WmiObject -class win32_logicaldisk

DeviceID     : C:
DriveType    : 3
ProviderName :
FreeSpace    : 2815565824
Size         : 15726702592
VolumeName   : Server2003

DeviceID     : D:
DriveType    : 5
ProviderName :
FreeSpace    :
Size         :
VolumeName   :

DeviceID     : E:
DriveType    : 3
ProviderName :
FreeSpace    : 2891620352
Size         : 24280993792
VolumeName   : XP
```

This is not too hard to read. However, here's the same cmdlet using the **Format-Table**:

```
PS C:\> Get-WmiObject -class win32_logicaldisk |format-table

DeviceID    DriveType ProviderName FreeSpace          Size VolumeName
--------    --------- ------------ ---------          ---- ----------
C:                  3                2815565824 15726702592 Server2003
D:                  5
E:                  3                2891620352 24280993792 XP


PS C:\>
```

Since the ProviderName property is blank, we can clean-up this output even more by using -**property** as we did with **Format-List**:

```
PS C:\> Get-WmiObject -class win32_logicaldisk |format-table '
>> -property deviceID,freespace,size,volumename,drivetype
>>


deviceID        freespace        size volumename   drivetype
--------        ---------        ---- ----------   ---------
C:             2815565824  15726702592 Server2003          3
D:                                                         5
E:             2891239424  24280993792 XP                  3


PS C:\>
```

Notice that the property headings are in the same order that we specified in the expression. They also use the same case. You *can* use * for the property list. However, doing so will often create unreadable output, because PowerShell tries to squeeze all the properties into a single screen-width table, and most objects simply have too many properties for that to work out well. For example, you can see here how PowerShell has made the column headers vertical in an attempt to fit as much as possible, still dropped 20 columns, and still created essentially useless output. What you're seeing after the vertical-ized column headers are the first character of the value that would normally appear in each column—the columns, in other words, are only one character wide.

........................................................................................................

**Have fun**
Try this with PowerShell's colors set to a black background and a green text color. Looks a bit like a screen saver from "The Matrix."

```
PS C:\> get-process | ft *

WARNING: 20 columns do not fit into the display and were removed.

_ N H V W P N P C C F P D P I P H W P P V T B E H E H M M M M M M N N P P P P P P P P
_ a a M S M P a o P i r e r d r a o a r i o a x a x a a a a a i o o o a a a e e e e e e
N m n     M t m U l o s o   i n r g i r t s i s i n c i i i x n d n n g g g a a a a a a
o e d     h p   e d c d   o d k e v t a e t E t d h n n n W W u p p e e e k k k k k k
u   l       a   V u r u   r l i d a u l P C x T l i W W M o o l a a d d d P P W W V V
n   e       n   e c i c   i e n M t a P r o i i e n i i o r r e g g M S S a a o o i i
N   s       y   r t p t   t C g e e l r i d t m   e n n d k k s e e e y y g g r r r r
a           s V t   y o S m M M o o e e e   N d d u i i   d d m s s e e k k t t
m           i e i   C u e o e e c r   d     a o o l n n   S S o t t d d i i u u
e           o r o   l n t r m m e i         m w w e g g   y y r e e M M n n a a
            n s n   a t   y o o s t         e H T   S S   s s y m m e e g g l l
              i     s     S r r s y           a i   e e   t t S M M m m S S M M
              o     s     i y y o             n t   t t   e e i e e o o e e e e
              n           z S S r             d l       m m z m m r r t t m m
                          e i i T             l e       M M e o o y y 6 0 0
                            z z i             e         e e 6 r r S S 4 r r
                            e e m                       m m 4 y y i i     y y
                              e                         o o S S z z       S S
                                                        r r i i e e       i i
                                                        y y z z 6         z z
                                                        S S e e 4         e e
                                                        i i   6           6
                                                        z z   4           4
                                                        e e
                                                        6
                                                        4
- - - - - - - - - - - - - - - - - - - - - - - - - - - - - - - - - - - - - - - - - -
P A 5 0 4 0 2         4   5 4 0 0 0   8       . 0       2 2 0 6 6 4 4 4 4 4 4
P A 2 4 8 8 4         6   2 8 8 8 4   8       . 0       4 4 8 2 2 4 4 4 4 2 2
P A 6 6 6 0 8 C L 0 4 4 T T 4 N 6 6 0 0 6 0 8 F 1 . 0 S 1 2 { 8 8 0 6 6 8 8 6 6 0 0
P c 6 8 0 8 4         0   6 0 8 8 8   3       . 0       4 4 8 4 4 2 2 0 0 4 4
```

**Format-Table** lets you tweak the output by using **-autosize**, which automatically adjusts the table output based on the date:

```
PS C:\> Get-WmiObject -class win32_logicaldisk |format-table '
>> -property deviceID,freespace,size,volumename,drivetype -autosize
>>


deviceID freespace         size volumename drivetype
-------- ---------         ---- ---------- ---------
C:       2815565824 15726702592 Server2003         3
D:                                                 5
E:       2890489856 24280993792 XP                 3


PS C:\>
```

This is the same command as before, except it includes autosize. Notice how much neater the output is. Using **-autosize** eliminates the need to calculate how long lines will be, add padding manually, or use any scripting voodoo.

## Format-Wide

Some cmdlets, like **Get-Service**, produce a long list of information that scrolls off the console screen. Wouldn't it be nice to get this information in multiple columns across the console screen? We can accomplish this with the **Format-Wide** cmdlet:

```
PS C:\> get-service |format-wide


Alerter                            ALG
AppMgmt                            aspnet_state
AudioSrv                            Avg7Alrt
Avg7UpdSvc                          AVGEMS
BAsfIpM                            BITS
Browser                            CiSvc
ClipSrv                            clr_optimization_v2.0.50727_32
COMSysApp                           CryptSvc
CVPND                              DcomLaunch
Dhcp                               dmadmin
dmserver                            Dnscache
ERSvc                              Eventlog
EventSystem                         FastUserSwitchingCompatibility
GrooveAuditService                  GrooveInstallerService
GrooveRunOnceInstaller              helpsvc
HidServ                            HTTPFilter
...
```

If you prefer more than two columns, which is the default, use the **-column** parameter to specify the number of columns:

```
PS C:\> get-service |format-wide -column 3


Alerter                ALG                    AppMgmt
aspnet_state            AudioSrv                Avg7Alrt
Avg7UpdSvc             AVGEMS                 BAsfIpM
BITS                  Browser                CiSvc
ClipSrv               clr_optimization_v2.0.5... COMSysApp
CryptSvc              CVPND                  DcomLaunch
Dhcp                  dmadmin                dmserver
Dnscache              ERSvc                  Eventlog
...
```

However, don't get carried away. The more columns you specify, the more you'll find the output getting truncated.

The **Format-Wide** cmdlet also lets you specify which single property you would like to display:

```
PS C:\> get-service |format-wide displayname -column 3


Alerter                Application Layer Gatew... Application Man...
ASP.NET State Service   Windows Audio           AVG7 Alert Mana...
AVG7 Update Service     AVG E-mail Scanner       Broadcom ASF IP...
Background Intelligent . Computer Browser         Indexing Service
ClipBook               .NET Runtime Optimizati... COM+ System App...
Cryptographic Services  Cisco Systems, Inc. VPN... DCOM Server Pro...
DHCP Client             Logical Disk Manager Ad... Logical Disk Ma...
DNS Client             Error Reporting Service   Event Log
```

```
COM+ Event System      Fast User Switching Com... Groove Audit Serv
Groove Installer Service GrooveRunOnceInstaller   Help and Support
...
```

Unlike **Format-Table** and **Format-List** that allow multiple properties, **Format-Wide** permits only a single property. In this example, we've specified the service's display name.

## Format-Custom

PowerShell provides the ability for you to display data in a custom format; that is, in neither a list nor a table. Unfortunately it requires defining a new format in a custom XML file, then using the **Update-FormatData** cmdlet to register it in PowerShell. Frankly, for most administrators, this cmdlet requires more effort than it's worth since it requires a certain degree of knowledge about .NET classes. We do cover custom format creation in the chapter "Creating Custom Formats," in case you're interested (you can also create custom list, wide, and table formats, if you like).

If you don't specify a specific custom view using the -**view** parameter, then **Format-Custom** will default to a *class* view of an object. In this view, you can see the exact structure of the object you're trying to display, including any child objects. The -**depth** parameter can limit how deeply into an object hierarchy **Format-Custom** will go; for example, displaying your hard drive's root folder would normally generate a very large and deep list, since your root folder contains every other file and folder on that drive. Here's an excerpt:

```
PS C:\> dir \ | format-custom -depth 1

class DirectoryInfo
{
 PSPath = Microsoft.PowerShell.Core\FileSystem::C:\DRIVERS
 PSParentPath = Microsoft.PowerShell.Core\FileSystem::C:\
 PSChildName = DRIVERS
 PSDrive =
   class PSDriveInfo
   {
     CurrentLocation =
     Name = C
     Provider = Microsoft.PowerShell.Core\FileSystem
     Root = C:\
     Description = Local
     Credential = System.Management.Automation.PSCredential
   }
 PSProvider =
   class ProviderInfo
   {
     ImplementingType = Microsoft.PowerShell.Commands.FileSystemProvider
     HelpFile = System.Management.Automation.dll-Help.xml
     Name = FileSystem
     PSSnapIn = Microsoft.PowerShell.Core
     Description =
     Capabilities = Filter, ShouldProcess
     Home = C:\Users\Don
     Drives =
       [
        C
       ]

   }
 PSIsContainer = True
 Mode = d----
 Name = DRIVERS
```

```
Parent =
  class DirectoryInfo
  {
    Mode = d--hs
    Name = C:\
    Parent =
    Exists = True
    Root = C:\
    FullName = C:\
    Extension =
    CreationTime = 11/2/2006 5:18:56 AM
    CreationTimeUtc = 11/2/2006 10:18:56 AM
    LastAccessTime = 4/19/2007 10:26:56 AM
    LastAccessTimeUtc = 4/19/2007 3:26:56 PM
    LastWriteTime = 4/19/2007 10:26:56 AM
    LastWriteTimeUtc = 4/19/2007 3:26:56 PM
    Attributes = Hidden, System, Directory
  }
Exists = True
```

As you can see, the output indents child objects slightly and provides a very "under the hood" look at the objects you're viewing. Normally, there's little use for this view; in some instances it can be useful for debugging or what we call "object spelunking," but, for the most part, you'll only use **Format-Custom** if you have a custom view definition that you want the cmdlet to use.

### Formatting Rules Overview: When Does PowerShell Use a List or Table?

PowerShell will automatically format with one of the Format cmdlets, depending on a couple of things. First, if PowerShell has a custom output view for the first object in the pipeline, it'll use that view—and the view itself defines whether it's a table, list, custom, or wide view—and PowerShell comes with tons of custom views for many different types of objects.

If there is no custom view, however, PowerShell will use **Format-List** if the first object in the pipeline has five or more properties; otherwise, it'll send the output to **Format-Table**. If **Format-Table** is selected, then it'll use the properties *of the first object in the pipeline* to form the table columns. So, if the first object has three properties and every other object in the pipeline has ten properties, you'll get a three-column table.

Note that PowerShell's formatting files—or a custom formatting file you create—can contain *multiple* different possible views for a given type of data. We'll get into these files in more detail in "Creating Custom Formats." For now, though, you need to know that PowerShell's formatting files—or custom formatting files you create—can contain more than one "view" for a given data type. Normally, when you explicitly use **Format-Table**, **Format-List**, **Format-Wide**, or **Format-Custom**, PowerShell will select the first registered view that matches that layout option. That is, if you send data to **Format-Table**, PowerShell will find the first table-style view and use it.

All of the formatting cmdlets, however, support a -**view** parameter, which lets you specify an alternate view. For example, normally **Get-Process** returns a view like this:

```
PS C:\> get-process

Handles NPM(K)    PM(K)      WS(K) VM(M)   CPU(s)     Id ProcessName
------- ------    -----      ----- -----   ------     -- -----------
    135      5     2680       4296    56               584 AcPrfMgrSvc
    260      7     5856       6064    74              2476 AcSvc
     86      6    10140       4972    73     0.16     3044 ACTray
     82      6    10236       4836    72     0.16     3048 ACWLIcon
```

```
109      3   11300    9136   43           1236 audiodg
106      5    8700    4500   70      0.09 2892 AwaySch
```

That's a table view. Yes, it has more than five properties, but it's a view specifically registered for Process objects, and PowerShell will always use a registered, type-specific view if one is available. However, you could specify an alternate view:

```
PS C:\> get-process | ft -view priority

ProcessName            Id  HandleCount  WorkingSet
-----------            --  -----------  ----------
AcPrfMgrSvc           584          135     4399104
AcSvc                2476          260     6205440


   PriorityClass: Normal

ProcessName            Id  HandleCount  WorkingSet
-----------            --  -----------  ----------
ACTray               3044           86     5091328
ACWLIcon             3048           82     4952064
audiodg              1236          109     9355264
```

Notice that this particular view is grouping Process objects on their PriorityClass property, and it has defined a different list of columns. We had to explicitly use **Format-Table** (or rather its alias, **Ft**) because we needed to specify the view's name, Priority. If we'd used another formatting cmdlet, this wouldn't have worked, because the Priority view is defined as a table—it can't be selected by anything but **Format-Table**.

Unfortunately, there's no quick or easy way to determine what special formats are available in PowerShell's built-in formatting files, other than opening them up in Notepad and browsing them. You'll find them in PowerShell's installation folder, each with a .format.ps1xml filename extension.

## GroupBy

All the format cmdlets include a parameter called -**GroupBy** that allows you to group output based on a specified property. For example, here is a **Get-Service** expression that groups services by their status such as Running or Stopped. The output below has been edited for brevity.

```
PS C:\> get-service |format-table -groupby status


   Status: Stopped

Status  Name          DisplayName
------  ----          -----------
Stopped Alerter       Alerter
Stopped ALG           Application Layer Gateway Service
Stopped AppMgmt       Application Management
Stopped aspnet_state   ASP.NET State Service


   Status: Running

Status  Name          DisplayName
------  ----          -----------
Running AudioSrv      Windows Audio
Running Avg7Alrt      AVG7 Alert Manager Server
```

```
Running Avg7UpdSvc        AVG7 Update Service
Running AVGEMS            AVG E-mail Scanner


   Status: Stopped

Status  Name               DisplayName
------  ----               -----------
Stopped BAsfIpM            Broadcom ASF IP monitoring service ...
Stopped BITS               Background Intelligent Transfer Ser...
Stopped Browser            Computer Browser
Stopped CiSvc              Indexing Service
Stopped ClipSrv            ClipBook
Stopped clr_optimizatio... .NET Runtime Optimization Service v...
Stopped COMSysApp          COM+ System Application


   Status: Running

Status  Name               DisplayName
------  ----               -----------
Running CryptSvc           Cryptographic Services


   Status: Running

Status  Name               DisplayName
------  ----               -----------
Running wuauserv           Automatic Updates
Running WZCSVC             Wireless Zero Configuration


   Status: Stopped

Status  Name               DisplayName
------  ----               -----------
Stopped xmlprov            Network Provisioning Service

PS C:\>
```

As you can see, grouping helps a little bit. However, this is probably not what you expected, since the cmdlet basically just generates a new group header each time it encounters a new value for the specified property. Because the services weren't first *sorted* on that property, things aren't grouped like you might want them to be. So, the trick, prior to grouping, is to first *sort* them.

........................................................................................................

**By the Way...**
Using the **-groupBy** parameter is the same as piping object to the **Group-Object** cmdlet and then piping the objects to a Format cmdlet. In both cases, you'll want to sort the objects *first* by using **Sort-Object**.

# Sort-Object: Sorting Objects

The **Sort-Object** cmdlet does exactly what its name implies: it sorts objects based on property values.

```
PS C:\> get-process|sort-object handles
```

| Handles | NPM(K) | PM(K) | WS(K) | VM(M) | CPU(s) | Id | ProcessName |
|---|---|---|---|---|---|---|---|
| 0 | 0 | 0 | 16 | 0 | | 0 | Idle |
| 21 | 1 | 168 | 376 | 4 | 0.46 | 776 | smss |
| 30 | 2 | 1912 | 2436 | 29 | 0.11 | 1288 | cmd |
| 34 | 2 | 400 | 1524 | 15 | 0.21 | 2664 | WLTRYSVC |
| 43 | 2 | 376 | 1392 | 13 | 0.18 | 2932 | MsPMSPSv |
| 62 | 3 | 1820 | 4404 | 34 | 0.21 | 1456 | ApntEx |
| 64 | 3 | 1744 | 5628 | 37 | 0.24 | 324 | notepad |
| 65 | 2 | 1472 | 1600 | 14 | 0.17 | 2488 | wdfmgr |
| 69 | 3 | 632 | 2044 | 13 | 0.10 | 1580 | sqlbrowser |
| 72 | 3 | 828 | 2428 | 27 | 0.33 | 1208 | scardsvr |
| 76 | 2 | 524 | 2116 | 19 | 0.04 | 828 | avgupsvc |
| 91 | 5 | 1284 | 3184 | 29 | 2.16 | 300 | svchost |
| 95 | 4 | 1528 | 5852 | 39 | 0.83 | 844 | sqlmangr |

...

Here we've taken the output of **Get-Process** and sorted it by the Handles property. The default sort is ascending, but if you prefer, the cmdlet includes a **-descending** parameter:

```
PS C:\> get-process|sort-object handles -descending
```

| Handles | NPM(K) | PM(K) | WS(K) | VM(M) | CPU(s) | Id | ProcessName |
|---|---|---|---|---|---|---|---|
| 1290 | 49 | 14000 | 23608 | 127 | 38.52 | 1892 | svchost |
| 1076 | 0 | 0 | 220 | 2 | 47.18 | 4 | System |
| 817 | 78 | 15856 | 8436 | 136 | 15.55 | 1628 | Groove |
| 706 | 7 | 1888 | 4880 | 28 | 18.51 | 868 | csrss |
| 616 | 16 | 25680 | 41096 | 127 | 100.01 | 484 | explorer |
| 589 | 12 | 8076 | 1508 | 62 | 3.24 | 892 | winlogon |
| 538 | 11 | 15508 | 8864 | 95 | 126.88 | 1948 | Smc |
| 483 | 20 | 38092 | 63020 | 223 | 168.63 | 2308 | WINWORD |

...

Let's return to our earlier example in which we tried to group the output of **Get-Service** by status. Now we can pipe the **Get-Service** cmdlet to **Sort-Object**, specifying primary sort on status, then on name. Next we send the object to **Format-Table** and group by status. Here's the output we get:

```
PS C:\> get-service|sort-object status,name |format-table -groupby status
```

```
  Status: Stopped
```

| Status | Name | DisplayName |
|---|---|---|
| Stopped | Alerter | Alerter |
| Stopped | ALG | Application Layer Gateway Service |
| Stopped | AppMgmt | Application Management |
| Stopped | aspnet_state | ASP.NET State Service |
| Stopped | BAsfIpM | Broadcom ASF IP monitoring service ... |
| Stopped | BITS | Background Intelligent Transfer Ser... |
| Stopped | Browser | Computer Browser |
| Stopped | CiSvc | Indexing Service |

```
...
  Status: Running

Status  Name              DisplayName
------  ----              -----------
Running AudioSrv          Windows Audio
Running Avg7Alrt          AVG7 Alert Manager Server
Running Avg7UpdSvc        AVG7 Update Service
Running AVGEMS            AVG E-mail Scanner
Running CryptSvc          Cryptographic Services
Running DcomLaunch        DCOM Server Process Launcher
Running Dhcp              DHCP Client
Running Dnscache          DNS Client
Running EventSystem        COM+ Event System
Running IISADMIN          IIS Admin
Running lanmanserver       Server
Running lanmanworkstation Workstation
...

PS C:\>
```

Again, we've edited the output for brevity, but you get the picture. And, by the way, we should point out that the "Format" cmdlets, which we've already discussed, also have a -**groupBy** parameter. Here's an example:

```
PS C:\> get-service | sort status | format-table -groupby status


  Status: Stopped

Status  Name              DisplayName
------  ----              -----------
Stopped napagent          Network Access Protection Agent
Stopped Netlogon          Netlogon
Stopped msvsmon80         Visual Studio 2005 Remote Debugger
Stopped MSiSCSI           Microsoft iSCSI Initiator Service
Stopped msiserver         Windows Installer
Stopped TBS               TPM Base Services
Stopped odserv            Microsoft Office Diagnostics Service
...


  Status: Running

Status  Name              DisplayName
------  ----              -----------
Running wudfsvc           Windows Driver Foundation - User-mo...
Running wuauserv          Windows Update
Running SSDPSRV           SSDP Discovery
Running UleadBurningHelper Ulead Burning Helper
...
```

So, which do you use, **Group-Object** or the -**groupby** parameter of a "format" cmdlet? Your choice. The **Group-Object** cmdlet has a few other options, such as specifying a case-sensitive grouping and specifying a different culture's sorting rules, but for the most part you'll get the same results, and you should use whichever one you like best.

Getting back to **Sort-Object**: One final parameter is -**Unique**, which not only gives sorted output, but also displays only the unique values:

```
PS C:\> $var=@(7,3,4,4,4,2,5,5,4,8,43,54)
PS C:\> $var|sort
2
3
4
4
4
4
5
5
7
8
43
54

PS C:\> $var|sort -unique
2
3
4
5
7
8
43
54
PS C:\>
```

In the first example, we've defined an array of numbers and first pipe it through a regular **Sort-Object** cmdlet. Compare that to the second expression that uses -**Unique**. Now the output is sorted and only unique objects are returned.

........................................................................................................................

**Alias Alert**
You will probably find it easier to use the alias for Sort-Object, which is Sort, as we did in the last example.

PowerShell also has a **Get-Unique** cmdlet that functions essentially the same as **Sort** -Unique, but without the sorting feature. However, its functionality is limited if you don't sort. Here's the array we just used piped through **Get-Unique**:

```
PS C:\> $var|get-unique
7
3
4
2
5
4
8
43
54
PS C:\>
```

The list is not 100% unique, as you'll see the number 4 repeated. This is because **Get-Unique** compares consecutive items and returns the next item only if it is different. This is why you need to sort the object before using **Get-Unique**:

```
PS C:\ > $var | sort | get-unique
2
```

```
3
4
5
7
8
43
54
```

This is the same result we got with **Sort** -Unique.

By the way, **Sort-Object** is perfectly happy to sort less complicated objects, too. For example:

```
$names = @("Don","Jeff","Alex")
```

The $names variable is now a collection (or array) of three String objects. Asking **Sort-Object** to put these in order is easy—we can even assign the sorted array right back to the same variable:

```
$names = $names | sort
```

Notice that we didn't have to tell **Sort-Object** *what* to sort on; since these are simple objects, it was able to figure it out on its own.

## Where-Object: Filtering Objects

In addition to sorting, you may need to limit or filter the output. The **Where-Object** cmdlet is a filter that lets you control what data is ultimately displayed. This cmdlet is almost always used in a pipeline expression where output from one cmdlet is piped to this cmdlet. The **Where-Object** cmdlet requires a code block enclosed in braces that is executed as the filter. Any input objects that match your criteria are passed down the pipeline; any objects that don't match your criteria are dropped.

Here's an expression to get all instances of the Win32_Service class where the state property of each object equals stopped.

```
Get-WmiObject -class win32_service | where {$_.state -eq "Stopped"}
```

Notice the use of the special $_ variable, which represents "the current pipeline object." So, that expression reads, "'where the current object's State property is equal to the value "Stopped."'" You may want to further refine this expression and format the output by piping to yet another cmdlet:

```
PS C:\> Get-WmiObject -class win32_service | where {$_.state -eq "Stopped"} | format-wide

Alerter                             ALG
AppMgmt                             aspnet_state
BAsfIpM                             Browser
CiSvc                               ClipSrv
clr_optimization_v2.0.50727_32          COMSysApp
CVPND                               dmadmin
dmserver                             ERSvc
FastUserSwitchingCompatibility        GrooveAuditService
GrooveInstallerService                GrooveRunOnceInstaller
helpsvc                             HidServ
NetDDE                              NetDDEdsdm
Netlogon                             NtLmSsp
NtmsSvc                             ose
PDEngine                            Pml Driver HPZ12
```

· · ·

In this example we've taken the same **Get-WmiObject** expression and piped it through **Format-Wide** to get a nice two-column report.

The key is recognizing that the script block in braces is what filters the object. If nothing matches the filter, then nothing will be displayed.

## ForEach-Object: Performing Actions Against Each Object

The **ForEach-Object** cmdlet actually straddles a line between interactive use and scripting. Its alias, **Foreach**, acts as a scripting construct, and we'll cover it as such. However, when used as a cmdlet its syntax is somewhat different, so we'll cover it here.

In its simplest form, **ForEach-Object** accepts a collection of objects from the pipeline and then executes a script block that you provide. The script block is executed once for each pipeline object, and within the script block you can use the special $_ variable to refer to the current pipeline object. For example, this command:

```
Get-WmiObject Win32_LogicalDisk
```

Will display a list of logical disks on your system. If you only wanted the free space on each disk, and if you wanted that value expressed in gigabytes, rather than bytes, you could use **ForEach-Object** as follows:

```
Get-WmiObject Win32_LogicalDisk | ForEach-Object { $_.FreeSpace / 1GB }
```

The script block shown will take the FreeSpace property of the current pipeline object, divide it by the special 1GB variable, and output the result to the pipeline. That script block is actually passed to a parameter named -**process**, which is positional; we don't *need* to supply the parameter name, but the following is functionally identical:

```
Get-WmiObject Win32_LogicalDisk | ForEach-Object -process { $_.FreeSpace / 1GB }
```

Resulting in output much like the following:

```
PS C:\> Get-WmiObject win32_logicaldisk | foreach-object -process { $_.FreeSpace / 1GB }
0
117.766156288
162.83420672
0
27.855847424
```

**ForEach-Object** has several aliases, including **%**. Condensing this line to use all aliases looks like this:

```
gwmi Win32_LogicalDisk | % -pr { $_.FreeSpace / 1GB }
```

The cmdlet also supports two other parameters: -**begin** and -**end**. These parameters accept script blocks just as -**process** does, but they work slightly differently. The script block given to -**begin** will run only once, before any pipeline objects are processed. Similarly, the script block given to -**end** will also run only once, but will do so after all pipeline objects have been processed. Here's an example:

```
PS C:\> gwmi win32_logicaldisk | % -process { $_.FreeSpace / 1GB } -begin { write " '
>> Disk Space Inventory" } -end { Write "Complete" }
>>
>>
Disk Space Inventory
0
117.7658368
162.83420672
0
27.855847424
Complete
```

You can see where the -**begin** and -**end** script blocks executed, displaying their information before and after the -**process** script block executed.

**ForEach-Object** can seem limited, since it would appear that only a single command can appear within each script block. However, PowerShell uses the **;** character to separate statements that appear on a single physical line. For example, if we wanted our -**process** script block to output the DeviceID property first, we'd do something like this:

```
PS C:\> gwmi Win32_LogicalDisk | % -pr { $_.DeviceID; $_.FreeSpace / 1GB }
```

Now, the -**process** script block contains two actual statements. Although they're contained on a single physical line, PowerShell will treat them, and execute them, independently. The results:

```
A:
0
C:
117.765771264
D:
162.83420672
F:
0
G:
27.855847424
```

**But wait, there's more**
The **ForEach-Object** cmdlet provides functionality similar to a filter or a function, which we cover in the chapter "Script Blocks, Functions, and Filters." And, as we've already mentioned, the cmdlet finds use as the scripting statement **foreach**.

# Select-Object: Choosing Specific Object Properties

**Select-Object**, or its alias, **Select**, takes a bit of work to understand. First, let's look at what we get when we pass a particular object to **Get-Member** (or its alias, **Gm**), to see what properties and methods the object has:

```
PS C:\> Get-WmiObject win32_bios | gm
```

```
   TypeName: System.Management.ManagementObject#root\cimv2\Win32_BIOS

Name              MemberType   Definition
```

```
----             ----------  -----------
BiosCharacteristics  Property     System.UInt16[] BiosCharacteristics {get;set;}
BIOSVersion          Property     System.String[] BIOSVersion {get;set;}
BuildNumber          Property     System.String BuildNumber {get;set;}
Caption              Property     System.String Caption {get;set;}
CodeSet              Property     System.String CodeSet {get;set;}
CurrentLanguage      Property      System.String CurrentLanguage {get;set;}
Description          Property     System.String Description {get;set;}
IdentificationCode   Property     System.String IdentificationCode {get;set;}
InstallableLanguages Property      System.UInt16 InstallableLanguages {get;set;}
InstallDate          Property     System.String InstallDate {get;set;}
LanguageEdition      Property      System.String LanguageEdition {get;set;}
ListOfLanguages      Property     System.String[] ListOfLanguages {get;set;}
```

Once you know what properties you are interested in, you can use **Select-Object** to limit the results:

```
PS C:\ > Get-WmiObject win32_bios | select Description,Manufacturer,version

Description                         Manufacturer             version
-----------                         ------------             -------
Phoenix ROM BIOS PLUS Version 1.10 A13 Dell Computer Corporation    DELL  - 27d5061e
```

The ability to return selected properties is especially helpful when it comes to exporting information.

# Exporting

PowerShell's ability to manipulate objects is pretty formidable. We've seen how PowerShell permits you to control the output format of an expression or cmdlet. However, PowerShell even has the ability to change or export the object into something else.

## Export-CSV

A comma-separated value (CSV) file is a mainstay of administrative scripting. It's a text-based database that can be parsed into an array or opened in a spreadsheet program like Microsoft Excel. The cmdlet requires an input object that is typically the result of a piped cmdlet:

```
Get-process | export-csv processes.csv
```

When you run this command on your system, it creates a text file called processes.csv. When the file is opened in a spreadsheet program, you'll be amazed by the amount of information that is available. In fact, it's probably overkill for most situations.

Here's another version of basically the same expression except this time we're using **Select-Object** to specify the properties we want returned:

```
PS C:\> get-process |select-object name,id,workingset,cpu| export-csv processes.csv
PS C:\> get-content processes.csv
#TYPE System.Management.Automation.PSCustomObject
Name,Id,WorkingSet,CPU
acrotray,3996,6574080,0.7110224
ApntEx,1456,4718592,6.5894752
Apoint,1592,7147520,6.0787408
avgamsvr,436,7389184,4.155976
avgcc,1684,12288000,10.4550336
avgemc,860,22593536,9.5036656
avgupsvc,828,3182592,1.6824192
```

```
BCMWLTRY,2948,6508544,16.2333424
Client,1084,1019904,140.6121904
cmd,1288,1093632,0.5207488
csrss,868,3440640,82.7790304
cvpnd,4000,8015872,9.6538816
EXCEL,2452,6545408,6.6996336
explorer,484,35528704,801.6427056
firefox,3028,71385088,881.2872288
Groove,2032,11628544,25.3264176
Idle,0,16384,
inetinfo,3012,5357568,1.4420736
Microsoft.Crm.Application.Hoster,1796,28168192,14.7812544
MSASCui,1732,10907648,7.310512
MsMpEng,1832,14114816,107.8951456
MsPMSPSv,2932,1425408,1.0114544
nvsvc32,1788,3522560,2.5236288
powershell,1560,53522432,7.9314048
procexp,588,10452992,86.1438688
PS C:\>
```

This produces a raw data report that we can further process any way we want. For example, if the **Out-File** already exists, it will be overwritten unless you use
-**NoClobber**. If you don't want the #TYPE header, which we find distracting, specify
-**NoTypeInformation** as part of the **Export-CSV** cmdlet.

On a related note, PowerShell also has an **Import-CSV** cmdlet that reads the contents of the csv file and displays the data as a table. Here's an example with abbreviated output:

```
PS C:\> import-csv processes.csv

Name              Id               WorkingSet        CPU
----              --               ----------        ---
acrotray          3996             6574080           0.7110224
ApntEx            1456             4718592           6.5894752
Apoint            1592             7147520           6.0787408
avgamsvr          436              7389184           4.155976
avgcc             1684             12288000          10.4550336
avgemc            860              22593536          9.5036656
avgupsvc          828              3182592           1.6824192
cmd               1288             1093632           0.5207488
csrss             868              3440640           82.7790304
cvpnd             4000             8015872           9.6538816
EXCEL             2452             6545408           6.6996336
...
```

By the way, in actuality **Import-CSV** reads a CSV file and assumes that the first line consists of column names. It then creates a collection of objects based upon the contents of the CSV file. For example, if you have a simple text file that looks like this:

```
name,type
notepad,process
calc,process
```

Then **Import-CSV** would create two objects, each with a Name and a Type property. For example:

```
PS C:\> $file = import-csv c:\yserver.txt
PS C:\> $file | gm
```

```
    TypeName: System.Management.Automation.PSCustomObject

Name          MemberType   Definition
----          ----------   ----------
Equals        Method       System.Boolean Equals(Object obj)
GetHashCode   Method        System.Int32 GetHashCode()
GetType       Method       System.Type GetType()
ToString      Method       System.String ToString()
name          NoteProperty System.String name=notepad
type          NoteProperty System.String type=process
```

As you can see, $file is a collection of objects, each of which have a Name and a Type property. This collection can be accessed like any other:

```
PS C:\> $file[0].name
notepad
PS C:\> $file[1].type
Process
```

Above, we've grabbed the Name property of the first object in the collection, and the Type property of the second.

## Export-CliXML

If you prefer to store results as an XML file, perhaps for processing by other tools, you can use PowerShell's **Export-CliXML** cmdlet. It works much the same way as **Export-CSV**:

```
PS C:\>Get-WmiObject -class win32_processor |export-clixml wmiproc.xml
```

This creates an XML file called wmiproc.xml, which can be imported back into PowerShell using **Import-CliXML**:

```
PS C:\> import-clixml wmiproc.xml


AddressWidth            : 32
Architecture            : 0
Availability            : 3
Caption                 : x86 Family 6 Model 9 Stepping 5
ConfigManagerErrorCode  :
ConfigManagerUserConfig :
CpuStatus               : 1
CreationClassName       : Win32_Processor
CurrentClockSpeed       : 1598
CurrentVoltage          : 33
DataWidth               : 32
Description             : x86 Family 6 Model 9 Stepping 5
DeviceID                : CPU0
ErrorCleared            :
ErrorDescription        :
ExtClock                : 133
Family                  : 2
InstallDate             :
L2CacheSize             : 1024

L2CacheSpeed            :
LastErrorCode           :
```

```
Level                       : 6
LoadPercentage              :
Manufacturer                : GenuineIntel
MaxClockSpeed               : 1598
Name                        :         Intel(R) Pentium(R) M processor 1600MHz
OtherFamilyDescription      :
PNPDeviceID                 :
PowerManagementCapabilities :
PowerManagementSupported    : False
ProcessorId                 : A7E9F9BF00000695
ProcessorType               : 3
Revision                    : 2309
Role                        : CPU
SocketDesignation           : Microprocessor
Status                      : OK
StatusInfo                  : 3
Stepping                    : 5
SystemCreationClassName     : Win32_ComputerSystem
SystemName                  : GODOT
UniqueId                    :
UpgradeMethod               : 6
Version                     : Model 9, Stepping 5
VoltageCaps                 : 2
__GENUS                     : 2
__CLASS                     : Win32_Processor
...
PS C:\>
```

As with the other exporting cmdlets, you can use **-NoClobber** to avoid overwriting an existing file. This can be a useful technique when used with command-line history. First, export it to an XML file:

```
PS C:\> get-history | export-clixml c:\history.xml
```

Later, when you want to re-import that command history into the shell, use **Import-CliXML** and pipe the results to **Add-History**:

```
PS C:\> import-clixml c:\history.xml | add-history
```

*Most* simple objects can be exported into the CliXML format, and then re-imported at a later date to approximately re-create those objects. The technique works best for objects that only have properties, where those properties only contain simple values such as strings, numbers, and Boolean values.

## ConvertTo-HTML

Finally, PowerShell includes a cmdlet to convert text output to an HTML table with the **ConvertTo-HTML** cmdlet. At its simplest, you can run an expression like this:

```
PS C:\> Get-Service | ConvertTo-HTML
```

If you execute this expression you'll see HTML code fly across the console, which doesn't do you much good. This can be changed by piping the HTML output to a file using **Out-File**, specifying a file name:

```
PS C:\> Get-Service | ConvertTo-HTML |out-file services.html
```

Now when you open services.html in a Web browser, you'll see a pretty complete table of running services and their properties. By default, the cmdlet lists all properties. However, you can specify the properties by name and in whatever order you prefer:

```
PS C:\> Get-Service | ConvertTo-HTML Name,DisplayName,Status | out-file services.html
```

Now when you open services.html, it's a little easier to work with. If you want to dress up the page a bit, **ConvertTo-HTML** has some additional parameters as shown in the following table:

### ConvertTo-HTML Optional Parameters

| Parameter | Description |
|---|---|
| Head | Inserts text into the <head> tag of the html page. You might want to include metadata or style sheet references. |
| Title | Inserts text into the <title> tag of the html page. This lets you have a more meaningful title to the page other than the default HTMLTABLE. |
| Body | Inserts text within the <body></body> tag. This lets you specify body specify formatting like fonts and colors as well as any text you want to appear before the table. |

Here's a script where we put it all together.

### Service2HTML.ps1

```
#Service2HTML.ps1
# a style sheet, style.css, should be in the same directory
# as the saved html file.

$server=hostname
$body="Services Report for "+$server.ToUpper()+"<HR>"
$file="c:\"+$server+"-services.html"

write-host "Generating Services Report for "$server.ToUpper()

 get-service |sort -property status -descending | ConvertTo-HTML `
 Name,DisplayName,Status -Title "Service Report" `
 -Head "<link rel=stylesheet type=text/css href=style.css>" `
 -Body $body | out-file $file

write-host "Report Generation Complete! Open" $file "for results."
```

This script uses the **Get-Service** cmdlet to generate a formatted HTML page. The script starts by defining some variables. First, we want the computer name to use in the report and other variables. Then we define a variable for the **-Body** parameter. If just text is being used, we don't have to bother with this. However, the **ConvertTo-HTML** cmdlet is a little finicky and doesn't handle the results of embedded cmdlets very well. By defining a variable, we can ensure its value is a string. We also specify the location and name of the saved file. We're using the server name as part of the filename.

After a message is sent to the user informing him the report is being generated, the heart of the script is reached. We take the **Get-Service** cmdlet and first pipe it to the **Sort-Object** cmdlet, sorting on service status and returning the results in descending order. This puts Running services at the top of the page and Stopped services at the bottom. Next we pipe that to **ConvertTo-HTML**, specifying the properties we want in the table. We include a **-head** parameter so we can reference a style sheet and then the **-body** parameter using the $body variable we defined at the beginning of the script. All of this is piped to **Out-File**, which saves the result to an HTML file. The results can be seen in the following figure.

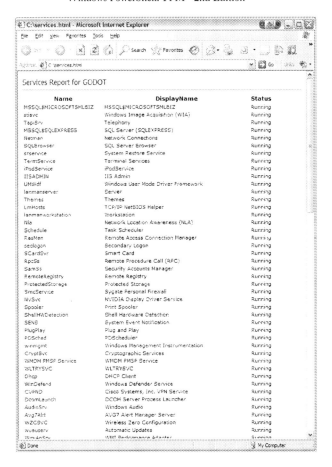

## Comparing Objects and Collections

Occasionally, you may have need to compare complex objects or collections—with text files perhaps being the most common and easily explained example. PowerShell provides a **Compare-Object** cmdlet, which can perform object comparisons. Now, before we get started, we have to remind you: *PowerShell deals in objects, not text.* A text file is technically a *collection* of individual *string objects*; that is, each line of the file is a unique, independent object, and the text file serves to "collect" them together.

When comparing objects, you start with two *sets*: The *reference set* and the *difference* set. In the case of two text files, these would simply be the two files. Which one is the reference and which one is the difference often doesn't matter; **Compare-Object** will show you which objects—that is, which lines of text—exist in one set but not the other, or which are present in both sets but different. That last bit—showing you objects which are present in both sets, but different—can get confusing, so we won't deal with it at first.

To begin, we're going to use two text files named Set1.txt and Set2.txt, which each contain some simple lines of text.

We'll use **Get-Content** to load each file into a variable, which we'll name $set1 and $set2:

```
PS C:\> $set1 = get-content c:\set1.txt
PS C:\> $set2 = get-content c:\set2.txt
```

And here's our first test:

```
PS C:\> compare-object -reference $set1 -difference $set2

InputObject                      SideIndicator
-----------                      -------------
LEAPED                                =>
THE                                   =>
JAUNDICED                             =>
THIS                                  <=
JUMPED                                <=
LAZY                                  <=
```

The SideIndicator tells us which "side" of the comparison was unequal. The reference set is always thought of as being on the left, while the difference set is thought of as being on the right—exactly as we showed in our screen shot of the two Notepad windows. And remember, we're seeing the *differences*, here. So, the first difference is LEAPED, which existed in the right file, but not the left. We also see that THE existed on the right but not the left, along with JAUNDICED. The words THIS, JUMPED, and LAZY appeared on the left, but not in the right. These differences don't appear in the same order as the actual differences within the file, which is important to keep in mind.

And notice, too, how two different lines of text always show as *missing*, rather than *different*. For example, the first lines of our two files are different—THIS and THE—but both THIS and THE are listed separately as "missing" from the other file. That's because the string objects THIS and THE are different objects, so PowerShell can't "match them up" as being the same object with a different property value. Were we to rearrange the text in one file completely, moving different words to different lines, **Compare-Object** would yield the exact same results. For example, these two files:

Produce exactly the same results:

```
PS C:\> compare-object -reference $set1 -difference $set2

InputObject                          SideIndicator
-----------                          -------------
LEAPED                                    =>
THE                                       =>
JAUNDICED                                 =>
THIS                                      <=
JUMPED                                    <=
LAZY                                      <=
```

This behavior reveals that PowerShell isn't doing a line-by-line comparison. Rather, it's asking itself, "do any of the objects in these files not exist in the other file?" The word THE is the best example of this: Set1 contains the word THE just once; Set2 contains THE twice. So, THE is shown as existing in Set2 at least one time when it doesn't exist somewhere in Set1. Try this: At the bottom of Set2.text, add two more lines containing THE and THE:

Once you've made that change, re-run **Compare-Object** and you'll get the *exact same results again.* This type of comparison can be very difficult to understand if you're used to text-based difference utilities, but it's a perfect example of how PowerShell cares about *objects.* That makes **Compare-Object** of limited use for classic text file comparisons, but comparison text files line-for-line was never really the purpose of this cmdlet.

So, let's focus on what **Compare-Object** is really intended for, as implied by its name: *Objects.* Here's a quick example where we'll query our local computer's Win32_LogicalDisk WMI class into two sets, and then compare them. As expected, when you compare the exact same two things, you get no differences:

```
PS C:\> $set1 = gwmi win32_logicaldisk
PS C:\> $set2 = gwmi win32_logicaldisk
PS C:\> compare-object -ref $set1 -diff $set2
```

So, now we'll change $set2 to be another computer's logical disks:

```
PS C:\> $set2 = gwmi win32_logicaldisk -computer mediaserver
```

Now we'll re-run our comparison. This time we're piping the results to **Format-Table** so that we can use its -**autosize** parameter to generate more easily read results:

```
PS C:\> compare-object -ref $set1 -diff $set2 | ft -auto

InputObject                                          SideIndicator
-----------                                          -------------
\\MEDIASERVER\root\cimv2:Win32_LogicalDisk.DeviceID="A:" =>
\\MEDIASERVER\root\cimv2:Win32_LogicalDisk.DeviceID="C:" =>
\\MEDIASERVER\root\cimv2:Win32_LogicalDisk.DeviceID="D:" =>
\\MEDIASERVER\root\cimv2:Win32_LogicalDisk.DeviceID="E:" =>
\\DON-PC\root\cimv2:Win32_LogicalDisk.DeviceID="A:"      <=
\\DON-PC\root\cimv2:Win32_LogicalDisk.DeviceID="C:"      <=
\\DON-PC\root\cimv2:Win32_LogicalDisk.DeviceID="D:"      <=
\\DON-PC\root\cimv2:Win32_LogicalDisk.DeviceID="F:"      <=
\\DON-PC\root\cimv2:Win32_LogicalDisk.DeviceID="G:"      <=
```

This is showing that our $set2 computer has an A, C, D, and E drive, while our local computer has A, C, D, F, and G. They are indeed different objects, and so they're all listed as such. But now let's have **Compare-Object** only look at a specific object property, rather than the entire object:

```
PS C:\> compare-object -ref $set1 -diff $set2 -property deviceid | ft -auto

deviceid SideIndicator
-------- -------------
E:          =>
F:          <=
G:          <=
```

By adding the -**property** parameter and specifying DeviceID as the property, we're now comparing *just that property* in the two sets. Now, the A, C, and D drives are gone because they're present in both sets. We're left with an E drive in $set2, and an F and G drive in $set1. This is truly showing us the *difference in the logical disk device IDs* between the two computers. But what if we wanted to also see the matching device IDs?

```
PS C:\> compare-object -ref $set1 -diff $set2 -property deviceid -include | ft -auto

deviceid SideIndicator
-------- -------------
A:          ==
C:          ==
D:          ==
E:          =>
F:          <=
G:          <=
```

Now, the matching properties are also included, with an indicator that they're present in both sets. We accomplished this by adding the -**includeEqual** parameter in the command. Another parameter, -**excludeDifference**, will remove the difference items, leaving just those that are the same in both sets:

```
PS C:\> compare-object -ref $set1 -diff $set2 -property deviceid -include -exclude | ft -auto

deviceid SideIndicator
-------- -------------
A:       ==
C:       ==
D:       ==
```

Perhaps a more practical example involves the use of the **Get-Process** cmdlet. Try this sometime in the morning:

```
PS C:\> $set1 = Get-Process
```

Leave PowerShell running all day s that $set1 will remain in memory. Then, later in the day, run this:

```
PS C:\> $set2 = Get-Process
```

Now you can use **Compare-Object** to see the different processes that were running during the morning and the afternoon. Taken to a more practical level, you could use this as an auditing technique for servers. For example, you could verify that a server is running exactly the processes that it *should* be running all the time:

```
PS C:\> gwmi win32_process -computer mediaserver | export-clixml c:\allowed.xml
```

We've chosen to save this list of "allowed" processes in an XML file, which PowerShell can later use to re-construct the process objects—meaning we don't need to leave the shell running. Whenever we want to conduct an audit of the server's processes:

```
PS C:\> $allowed = import-clixml c:\allowed.xml
PS C:\> $running = gwmi win32_process -computer mediaserver
PS C:\> compare-object -ref $allowed -diff $running -property name

name                            SideIndicator
----                            -------------
iexplore.exe                       =>
notepad.exe                        =>
```

We imported the original "allowed" process objects by using **Import-CliXML**; we then retrieved the current list of processes and compared the two sets by process name, revealing Internet Explorer and Notepad in use. Hey, is someone on that server console surfing the Web?

# Chapter 6
# Practical Tips and Tricks

## Using the Command Line

PowerShell's command line offers a number of shortcuts and features to help making typing faster. After all, just because this is the command line doesn't mean it needs to be primitive! By training yourself to use these shortcuts, you'll become much more efficient.

## Command History

Like Cmd.exe and most other command-line environments, PowerShell maintains a history, or "buffer," of commands you've typed (this is different from the command history that the **Get-History** and **Add-History** cmdlets can manipulate). Pressing the Up and Down arrow keys on your keyboard provides access to this history, recalling past commands so that you can either easily run them again, or allowing you to quickly change a previous command and run the new version.

A little-known shortcut is the F7 key, which pops up a command-line history window, allowing you to scroll through the window and select the command you want. If your press Enter, the selected command executes immediately. If you press the right or left arrow key, the command will be inserted but not executed. This is helpful when you want to recall a complicated command but need to tweak it. Press Esc to close the window without choosing a command.

By default only 50 commands will be stored in this buffer. To increase the command buffer, right-click the system menu of your PowerShell window and select Properties. On the Options tab, you can increase the buffer size from the default of 50. While you're at it, make sure the boxes for QuickEdit Mode and Insert Mode are checked. We'll show you how to take advantage of these later. Feel free to change the font size and colors as well.

Finally, one last trick for the command history: Type the beginning of a command that you've recently used, and press F8. PowerShell will fill in the rest of the command, and you can press F8 again to find the next "match" to what you'd typed. This is a quick way to recall a command that's further in the past than the arrow keys provide convenient access to.

## Line Editing

While PowerShell doesn't provide a full-screen editor (if you need that, then it may be time in investigate a visual development environment that supports PowerShell, such as SAPIEN PrimalScript—www. primalscript.com), it does provide basic editing capabilities for the current line:

- The Left and Right arrow keys move the cursor left and right on the current line.
- Pressing Ctrl+Left arrow and Ctrl+Right arrow moves left and right one word at a time, much as it does in Microsoft Word.
- The Home and End keys move to the beginning and end of the current line, respectively.
- The Insert key toggles between insert and overwrite mode.
- The Delete key deletes the character under the cursor; the Backspace key deletes the character "behind," or to the left of, the cursor.
- The Esc key clears the current line.

## Copy and Paste

- If you've enabled QuickEdit and Insert Mode for your PowerShell window, you can easily copy and paste between PowerShell and Windows. To copy from PowerShell, merely select the text and press Enter. You can then paste it into another application like Notepad. To paste something into PowerShell, position your cursor in the PowerShell window and use the mouse right button. The copied text will be inserted at the command prompt.

## Tab Completion

Also called *command completion,* this feature exists to help you complete command names and even parameter values more quickly. Pressing Tab on a blank line will insert an actual tab character; any other time—if you've already typed something on the line, that is—the Tab key kicks in command completion mode. Here's how it works:

- If you've just typed a period, then command completion will cycle through the properties and methods of whatever object is to the left of the period. For example, if $wmi represents a WMI object, typing **$wmi.** and pressing Tab will call up the first property or method from that WMI object.
- If you've typed a period and one or more letters, pressing Tab will cycle through the properties and methods that *match what you've already typed.* For example, if $wmi is an instance of the Win32_ OperatingSystem WMI class, typing **$wmi.re** and pressing Tab will display "$wmi.Reboot(", which is the first property or method that begins with "re".
- If you've just typed a few characters, and no punctuation other than a hyphen ("-"), command-completion will cycle through matching cmdlet names. For example, typing **get-w** and pressing Tab will result in "Get-WmiObject", the first cmdlet that begins with "get-w." Note that this does not work for aliases, only cmdlet names.

- If you've typed a command and a partial parameter name, you can hit Tab to cycle through matching parameter names. For example, you can type **gwmi -comp** and press Tab to get "gwmi -computerName".

- If none of the above conditions is true, then PowerShell will default to cycling through file and folder names. For example, type **cd**, a space, and press Tab. You'll see the first folder or file name in the current folder. Type a partial name, like **cd Doc**, and press Tab to have PowerShell cycle through matching file and folder names. Wildcards work, too: Type **cd pro*files** and press tab to get "cd 'Program Files'", for example.

## Instant Expressions

PowerShell can evaluate expressions at the command line. The easiest examples are mathematical expressions:

```
PS C:\> 2 + 2
4
PS C:\> 4 * 4
16
PS C:\> 16 / 16
1
PS C:\> 1 - 1
0
PS C:\>
```

PowerShell recognizes the characters "kb," "mb," and "gb" as having special purpose. It uses these characters to represent a *kibibyte*, *mibibyte*, and *gibibyte*, units of measurement for computer memory.

> **Kibi-what?**
>
> Does kilo equal 1,000 or 1,024? When measuring storage—such as hard drive space—or nearly anything else, kilo means 1,000, while mega means one million and giga means one billion. These three terms have long been used improperly to refer to computer memory measurements, as well. We say "improperly" because a "kilobyte" of computer memory—RAM—is actually 1,024, not an even thousand.
>
> In 2000, the International Electrotechnical Commission (of which the United States' American National Standards Institute is a member) created a new set of measurements specifically for computer memory, ending the 1,000-or-1,024 confusion. The term *kilo* therefore *always* means 1,000; since RAM is measured in powers of two, the term *kibi* was created to represent 1,024. This is all documented in IEEE 1541, a standard of the Institute of Electrical and Electronics Engineers, the European Union legalized these units of measurement in HD60027-2:2003-03.
>
> Technically, the abbreviation *kb* still means *kilobyte;* a kibibyte is properly abbreviated as *KiB* instead. However, PowerShell recognizes *kb* as meaning 1,024; therefore, it's a *kibibyte.*

For example, to add one mibibyte to one kibibyte:

```
PS C:\> 1kb + 1mb
1049600
```

These expression evaluation capabilities allow you to quickly perform basic calculations without having to pull up Windows Calculator, and to provide a built-in means of working with binary values. Here's one last example:

```
PS C:\> (gwmi win32_computersystem).TotalPhysicalmemory/1mb
2037.25
PS C:\>
```

The TotalPhysicalMemory property is displayed by default in bytes, but by dividing the value by 1mb, we can represent the value in MB.

## Pausing a Script

Use the **Start-Sleep** cmdlet to make your script pause for a specified number of seconds (or milliseconds, if you prefer; seconds is the default measurement):

```
PS C:\> Start-Sleep 10
```

## Displaying a Progress Meter

PowerShell's **Write-Progress** cmdlet allows you to display a sort of text-based progress bar in the PowerShell window. During long-running tasks, this can be a useful way of telling the user (or yourself) that PowerShell isn't "locked up," it's just busy. Here's a quick example of how the cmdlet works:

```
for ($i=0; $i -lt 100; $i++) {
        Start-Sleep 1
  Write-Progress -activity "Waiting..." -status "STATUS" -id 1 -percentComplete $i

}
```

This results in a progress bar as shown here:

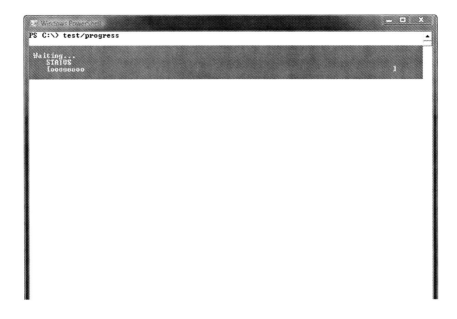

There are a couple of key parameters for **Write-Progress**:

- **-ID** specifies a unique numeric ID number for your progress bar. You can use whatever number you like for this, but you should specify it so that you can refer back to your progress bar.

- **-percentComplete** is the percentage of the bar that should be filled in, on a scale of 1 to 100. In our example, this was easy to provide, because we were using a loop that counted from 1 to 100. If you're using other values, you'll need to divide, multiply, or whatever to ensure that this property receives a value of 1 to 100.

- **-secondsRemaining** is an alternative to **-percentComplete** and simply specifies the number of seconds that the user should expect before the operation will be complete.

- **-activity** and **-status** display text labels, as shown in our example. Typically, the "activity" is whatever broad operation is being conducted, such as "Querying computers." Status is more specified, such as "Querying Server2" or "Querying Server3." You can also specify **-CurrentOperation**, which is even more specific and which appears below the progress bar.

Both **-secondsRemaining** and **-percentComplete** are optional; if you don't specify them, then no progress bar will be displayed. Instead, just the activity and status messages—which are both mandatory—will be displayed.

Here's an extended example. This assumes we have a file named C:\Computers.txt, which contains one computer name per line. Pay close attention to the use of **Write-Progress**: You can see that each time, we're updating the information and, in some cases, displaying a bit more information about what's going on. The current computer name is used for the "status" label, while the current operation—service pack or logical disk inventory—is displayed for the **-currentOperation** parameter.

**InventoryProgress.ps1**

```
# initial status bar
Write-Progress -activity "Getting inventory" -status "Starting" -id 1

# get computer names
$computers = Get-Content c:\computers.txt

# how many computers?
$qty = $computers | Measure-Object
$currentComputer = 1

foreach ($computer in $computers) {
        # calculate status
        [int]$pct = ($currentComputer / $qty.count) * 100

        # update status bar
  Write-Progress -activity "Getting inventory" -status $computer -id 1 -percent $pct

        # get service pack
  Write-Progress -activity "Getting inventory" -status $computer -id 1 -percent $pct `
      -current "Service Pack"
        $wmi = gwmi win32_operatingsystem -computer $computer
  write `n
        write $computer
  write "Service Pack: " $wmi.servicepackmajorversion

        # get disks
  Write-Progress -activity "Getting inventory" -status $computer -id 1 -percent $pct `
      -current "Disks"
        $wmi = gwmi win32_logicaldisk -computer $computer
```

```
Write-Host "Logical disks: "
    foreach ($disk in $wmi) {
            write $disk.deviceid
    }

    # next computer...
    $currentComputer++
}
```

Also note that we didn't add any error checking, just to keep this sample clearer. It will result in errors if any of the computer names specified in C:\Computers.txt aren't available, or if we don't have permission to query a computer's WMI information.

When the progress bar finishes, it should automatically go away. If for some reason the progress bar remains on the screen, you can call **Write-Progress –completed $True** to dismiss it.

## Keeping a Transcript

Sometimes, it can be useful to keep track of exactly what you're doing in PowerShell. For example, if you're experimenting a bit, going back and reviewing your work can help you spot things that worked correctly. You could then copy and paste those command lines into a script for future use. PowerShell offers a way to keep track of your work through a *transcript*. You start a new one with the **Start-Transcript** cmdlet:

```
PS C:\> Start-Transcript C:\MyWork.txt
```

A transcript is just a simple text file that contains everything shown in the PowerShell console window. A downside to it is that, if you *do* want to copy and paste your work into a script, you first have to edit out all the command prompts, your mistakes, and so forth. Once started, a transcript will continue recording your work until you either close the shell, or run the **Stop-Transcript** cmdlet:

```
PS C:\> Stop-Transcript
```

The **Start-Transcript** has additional parameters (which you can look up by using **Help**) that append to an existing file, force an existing file to be overwritten, and so forth.

# Chapter 7
# PowerShell Command-Line Parsing

In an attempt to be all things to all people, and to maintain backward compatibility with external executables and the way Cmd.exe worked, PowerShell has a rather complex command-line parser. A *parser* is a piece of software that takes the entire command line you've entered, breaks it down, and tries to figure out what you want PowerShell to do. For example, PowerShell's parser looks for spaces as command delimiters, uses hyphens to indicate cmdlet parameters, and uses other standards. Knowing what the parser is doing under the hood can provide some useful insight into why certain commands don't seem to work as expected, and can give you an idea of how to work around any oddities you come across.

Parsing would be simple if it weren't for us humans. For example, nobody wants to type **cd** "\" to change to the root of their hard drive—we just want to type **cd** \. Yet \ is clearly a string (well, a character, in any event), and not a number, and in programming languages, strings are usually enclosed in quotation marks. So, there's a lot of complex stuff under the hood in PowerShell, working to figure out what the heck you mean every time you hit Enter. Fortunately, the eggheads up at Microsoft had to write all that complex stuff; you just need to know how it affects you. String handling is a major part of the parser's complexity. The other major part is that the parser can actually operate in one of two distinct modes.

## Quotation Marks

Quotation marks are usually used to set off a string of characters that should be treated *just* as a string of characters and not as part of a command or other keyword. For example, consider this:

```
PS C:\> write-host "Hello" -fore cyan
Hello
```

You can't see it, but "Hello" is displayed in the color cyan. You'll have to trust us, because even printing this one page in color would have doubled the price of this book. But that command is very different from:

```
PS C:\> write-host "Hello -fore cyan"
Hello -fore cyan
```

See, the quotation marks are telling PowerShell that "-fore cyan" isn't intended to be a parameter. It's just a string of characters, so PowerShell shouldn't try to interpret it as a command.

PowerShell actually treats single and double quotation marks somewhat differently. Double quotation marks are still subject to a quick review by the parser, to see if any variables are lurking in there. Any variables that PowerShell finds are replaced with their contents. Watch:

```
PS C:\> $hello = "Greeting"
PS C:\> Write-host "What a $hello"
What a Greeting
PS C:\> Write-host 'What a $hello'
What a $hello
```

See the difference between the two? Because PowerShell always looks for spaces to separate different keywords, any string that contains an embedded space needs to be enclosed in *some* kind of quotation mark:

```
PS C:\> cd \program files
Set-Location : A parameter cannot be found that matches parameter name 'files'.
At line:1 char:3
+ cd <<<< \program files
PS C:\> cd "\program files"
PS C:\Program Files>
```

The first command failed, because PowerShell thought "files" was supposed to be a separate parameter, and it couldn't find one named "files," so it got upset. By enclosing everything in quotation marks, we told PowerShell to treat the entire string as a single parameter—the folder we wanted to change to.

PowerShell does support a weird alternative when you only need to quote *one* character, like the space between "Program" and "Files":

```
PS C:\> cd \program' files
PS C:\Program Files>
```

The *backtick*, or *backquote*, is PowerShell's escape character. By "escaping" the space, we're telling PowerShell that the space isn't really a space; it's to be treated literally, as part of a string, not as a keyword separator. But, honestly, that way just looks too strange, and only saves you one keystroke. But that escaping trick works well elsewhere, too. Consider this:

```
PS C:\Program Files> $saying = "Peace"
PS C:\Program Files> write-host "say $saying"
say Peace
PS C:\Program Files> write-host "say '$saying"
say $saying
```

In the second example, by "escaping" the dollar sign, we forced PowerShell to treat it as a literal dollar sign, not as the beginning of a variable name. This prevents PowerShell from "expanding" the variable, even though we used double quotes.

## Parsing Modes

PowerShell's parser supports two distinct parsing modes: *Expression mode* and *command mode*. In expression mode, strings must be quoted, numbers aren't quoted, and so forth. In command mode, numbers are still numbers, but anything else is treated as a string unless it starts with $, @, ', ", or ( - all special characters that denote the start of a variable, array, string, or sub-expression.

Expression mode is active whenever you *don't* type a PowerShell cmdlet name or alias at the start of a line. For example:

```
PS C:\> 2 + 2
4
```

That's expression mode. Command mode kicks in when you *do* start off with a PowerShell cmdlet or alias:

```
PS C:\> Write-Host 2+2
2+2
```

Different output in this case, because you're in command mode and that "+" forces PowerShell to treat "2+2" as a string, and not a number. However, remember that "(" at the start of a string forces expression mode for it:

```
PS C:\> write-host (2+2)
4
```

By forcing into expression mode, "2+2" is evaluated as an expression rather than a string, and you get the output you were probably expecting. The differences between these modes can be subtle, but by remembering these basic rules you'll usually be able to keep yourself out of trouble.

## Line Termination

PowerShell needs to know when you've reached the end of a line, so that it can process what you've given it. When you've typed a complete command, a carriage return (technically, a "newline" character) indicates the end of the line. So, if you type something like this, you get a result:

```
PS C:\> write-host "2+2"
2+2
```

However, if you type something that's not *complete*, PowerShell treats the new line character as another form of whitespace, like a tab or space character. At the command line, you'll get a special prompt, telling you that PowerShell is waiting for you to finish:

```
PS C:\> write-host "2+2
>> "
>>
>>
2+2
```

Here, we left off the closing quotation mark, and so PowerShell figured we weren't done yet. It prompted us, and we completed the quotation mark, and hit Enter again to complete the command and display the result. If you purposely want to break a long line and use the nested >> prompt, use the back-tick character at the end of your line:

```
PS C:\ > get-wmiobject win32_computersystem | select-object Caption,Name,Manufacturer, '
>> model | format-list
>>
```

The semicolon is also an "end of line" character. By using it, you can put two logical lines onto a single physical line:

```
PS C:\> 2+2 ; 4+4
4
8
```

Understanding PowerShell's line termination rules can help keep you out of trouble, and help you understand what's going on when you get that strange ">>" prompt.

## Chapter 8
# Working with the PowerShell Host

Whenever we're using PowerShell interactively, we're working with what's called the *PowerShell hosting application*, or just *PowerShell host*. As we explained in Chapter 1, PowerShell's engine can be *hosted* by many different applications, such as Exchange Server 2007's management GUI, applications like SAPIEN PrimalScript, and more. When using the PowerShell.exe console host, the special variable $host provides access to some of this host's unique capabilities.

It is important that you understand the $host will vary depending on which application is hosting PowerShell. For many of you, the Windows PowerShell that you downloaded from Microsoft may be the only host you ever work with. To illustrate the concept of different hosts, look at the different values you get for each host. Here is $host from a Windows PowerShell session running on Windows Vista:

```
PS C:\ > $host


Name            : ConsoleHost
Version         : 1.0.0.0
InstanceId      : 9f47e1dc-2bf9-45d8-8110-95568aabd014
UI              : System.Management.Automation.Internal.Host.InternalHostUserInterface
CurrentCulture  : en-US
CurrentUICulture : en-US
PrivateData     : Microsoft.PowerShell.ConsoleHost+ConsoleColorProxy
```

We've mentioned that PrimalScript can host PowerShell. Here is the information for that host:

```
Name            : PrimalScriptHostImplementation
Version         : 1.0.0.0
```

```
InstanceId      : d75b566f-7658-4cac-bd71-de08a4d358be
UI              : System.Management.Automation.Internal.Host.InternalHostUserInterface
CurrentCulture  : en-US
CurrentUICulture : en-US
PrivateData     :
```

Finally, here is $host from Exchange 2007:

```
Name            : ConsoleHost
Version         : 1.0.0.0
InstanceId      : efd45da6-65a4-45ae-b221-ae3317c2b402
UI              : System.Management.Automation.Internal.Host.InternalHostUserInterface
CurrentCulture  : en-US
CurrentUICulture : en-US
PrivateData     : Microsoft.PowerShell.ConsoleHost+ConsoleColorProxy
```

For the most part, these hosts have identical functionality, but that's not to say that some other future host might have additional functionality. One way to check what your host can do is to pipe $host to **Get-Member**:

```
PS C:\ > $host | get-member


   TypeName: System.Management.Automation.Internal.Host.InternalHost

Name                   MemberType  Definition
----                   ----------  ----------
EnterNestedPrompt      Method      System.Void EnterNestedPrompt()
Equals                 Method      System.Boolean Equals(Object obj)
ExitNestedPrompt       Method      System.Void ExitNestedPrompt()
GetHashCode            Method      System.Int32 GetHashCode()
GetType                Method      System.Type GetType()
get_CurrentCulture     Method      System.Globalization.CultureInfo g
get_CurrentUICulture   Method      System.Globalization.CultureInfo g
get_InstanceId         Method      System.Guid get_InstanceId()
get_Name               Method      System.String get_Name()
get_PrivateData        Method      System.Management.Automation.PSObj
get_UI                 Method      System.Management.Automation.Host.
get_Version            Method      System.Version get_Version()
NotifyBeginApplication Method      System.Void NotifyBeginApplication
NotifyEndApplication   Method      System.Void NotifyEndApplication()
SetShouldExit          Method      System.Void SetShouldExit(Int32 ex
ToString               Method      System.String ToString()
CurrentCulture         Property    System.Globalization.CultureInfo C
CurrentUICulture       Property    System.Globalization.CultureInfo C
InstanceId             Property    System.Guid InstanceId {get;}
Name                   Property    System.String Name {get;}
PrivateData            Property    System.Management.Automation.PSObj
UI                     Property    System.Management.Automation.Host.
Version                Property    System.Version Version {get;}
```

You see most of the properties when you invoke $host. But what else is there?

# Culture Clash

Given that Windows is an international platform, it should come as no surprise that different versions have different regional and language settings. In PowerShell, this is referred to as the Culture, which is a property of $host:

```
PS C:\ > $host.currentculture

LCID            Name            DisplayName
----            ----            -----------
1033            en-US           English (United States)
```

You get the same result if you use the **Get-Culture** cmdlet. However, there may be situations where you need to execute a command or expression in another culture setting. Usually, the situation is with non-US users who are running a command or application that fails to execute properly unless they use the EN-US culture. Even though PowerShell has a cmdlet to get the current culture, there are no cmdlets for changing it system wide, which isn't very practical anyway. Culture settings are thread level. But what if you really, really had to change the culture setting temporarily? The Microsoft PowerShell team posted a function a while ago on their blog. The entry was based on pre-release code so we've updated it a bit:

```
Function Using-Culture (
[System.Globalization.CultureInfo]$culture = (throw "USAGE: Using-Culture -Culture culture -Script
{scriptblock}"),
[String]$script= (throw "USAGE: Using-Culture -Culture culture -Script {scriptblock}"))
{
    $OldCulture = [System.Threading.Thread]::CurrentThread.CurrentCulture
    trap
    {
        [System.Threading.Thread]::CurrentThread.CurrentCulture = $OldCulture
    }
    [System.Threading.Thread]::CurrentThread.CurrentCulture = $culture
    Invoke-Expression $script
    [System.Threading.Thread]::CurrentThread.CurrentCulture = $OldCulture
}
```

Using this function, you can execute any expression or command under the guise of a different culture:

```
PS C:\ > using-culture en-GB {get-date}

29 August 2007 17:06:27
```

The function executes **Get-Date** using the British culture settings, which have a different date format than the United States settings.

# Using the UI and RawUI

The $host object also gives you access to the underlying user interface (UI). You shouldn't need to access these properties and methods often. There are cmdlets for much of the functionality you are likely to need. Still, there may be situations where you'd like to tweak the PowerShell window or take advantage of a feature that doesn't have a ready cmdlet.

## Reading Lines and Keys

The best way to get user input is by using the **Read-Host** cmdlet:

```
PS C:\ > $name=Read-Host "What is your name?"
What is your name?: Jon
PS C:\ > $name
Jon
```

You can use the **ReadLine()** method from $host.ui, but it's a little primitive:

```
PS C:\ > write-host "What is your name?";$name=$host.ui.Readline()
What is your name?
Jon
PS C:\ > $name
Jon
```

The **ReadLine()** method has no provision for a prompt like **Read-Host**, so we used **Write-Host** to display something. The **ReadLine()** method simply waits for the user to type a line and press Enter. Off hand, we can't think of a situation where this would be preferable to using **Read-Host**. But there is another $host method that you might find helpful for which there is no PowerShell cmdlet.

The $host.ui.rawui object has a method called **ReadKey()** that works like the **ReadLine()** method, except it only accepts a single key:

```
PS C:\ > $host.ui.rawui.readkey()
y
```

| VirtualKeyCode | Character | ControlKeyState | KeyDown |
| --- | --- | --- | --- |
| 89 | y | NumLockOn | True |

```
PS C:\ >
```

You can fine tune this method by specifying some **Readkey()** options. You'll likely not need to echo the typed character:

```
PS C:\ > $host.ui.rawui.readkey("NoEcho,IncludeKeyUp,IncludeKeyDown")
```

You need to use either IncludeKeyUp or IncludeKeyDown, or both. We always use both. To use this method in a script or function, you'll also need to include the *KeyAvailable* property. This is a Boolean value that indicates whether a keystroke is waiting in the keyboard input buffer.

```
$ESCkey = 27
Write-Host "Press the ESC key to continue"

$Running=$True

while ($Running) {
 if ($host.ui.RawUi.KeyAvailable)
 { $key = $host.ui.RawUI.ReadKey("NoEcho,IncludeKeyUp,IncludeKeyDown")
  if ($key.VirtualKeyCode -eq $ESCkey)
 {
   $Running=$False
 }
 }
}
```

In this code example, we use a While loop that runs until the value of $Running is changed to $False. The outer If statement checks to see if a key is in the buffer:

```
if ($host.ui.RawUi.KeyAvailable)
```

If so, then the code uses the **ReadKey()** method:

```
{ $key = $host.ui.RawUI.ReadKey("NoEcho,IncludeKeyUp,IncludeKeyDown")
```

If the value of the entered key is 27, which is the key value of the ESC key, then $Running is set to $False and the next time through the While loop, the code will exit the loop.

## Changing the Window Title

You can access the title of your Windows PowerShell window very easily by accessing the *WindowTitle* property:

```
PS C:\ > $host.ui.rawui.WindowTitle
Windows PowerShell
```

You can just as easily change the window title. Here's an example:

### Create-ServerReport.ps1

```
function Set-Title {
Param ([string]$NewTitle)
$host.ui.rawui.WindowTitle=$NewTitle
}

Set-Alias title Set-Title

function Save-Title {
$Global:SavedTitle=$host.ui.rawui.WindowTitle
}

Save-Title
$report="c:\test\report.txt"

"REPORT CREATED "+(get-date).ToString() | Out-File $report

foreach ($server in @(Get-Content c:\test\servers.txt)) {
#skip blank lines
 if (($server).length -gt 0)
  {
  $newtitle="Checking " + $server.ToUpper()
    title $newtitle
    $server.ToUpper() | Out-File $report -append
    "PageFile" | Out-File $report -append
    Get-WmiObject win32_pagefile -computer $server.Trim() `
    | Out-File $report -append
    "OS" | Out-File $report -append
    Get-WmiObject win32_operatingsystem -computer $server.Trim()`
     | Out-File $report -append
    "ComputerSystem" | Out-File $report -append
    Get-WmiObject win32_computersystem -computer $server.Trim()`
     | Out-File $report -append
    #pause for a few seconds just to show title in action
    #not really required.
    sleep 5
 }
}

#revert back to old title
Title $savedtitle
#view report
Notepad $report
```

This script processes a list of servers, gets information about each server from WMI and saves the results to a text file. Since this script could run for a long time, we modify the title to reflect what server the script is working on. You can then minimize your PowerShell window yet still be able to monitor the script's progress.

The script defines functions to set the window title as well as save the current one. We also define an alias, Title, for the Set-Title function. Thus as each server is processed from the list, the window title is changed to reflect the current server:

```
$newtitle="Checking " + $server.ToUpper()
  title $newtitle
```

At the end of the script we change the title back to the saved, original window title:

```
Title $savedtitle
```

## Changing Colors

We can also modify the color settings of PowerShell windows. First, let's look at the current settings:

```
PS C:\ > $host.ui.rawui
```

```
ForegroundColor        : DarkYellow
BackgroundColor        : DarkMagenta
CursorPosition         : 0,2999
WindowPosition         : 0,2950
CursorSize             : 25
BufferSize             : 120,3000
WindowSize             : 120,50
MaxWindowSize          : 120,81
MaxPhysicalWindowSize  : 160,81
KeyAvailable           : False
WindowTitle            : Windows PowerShell
```

You might prefer something like this:

```
PS C:\ > $host.ui.rawui.backgroundcolor="green"
PS C:\ > $host.ui.rawui.foregroundcolor="black"
```

These changes last only for as long as your PowerShell session is running. If you want a more permanent change, then add lines like these to your profile script.

## Changing Window Size and Buffer

The raw UI also lets you control position and size of your PowerShell windows. To see the current size, you can use this expression:

```
PS C:\ > $host.ui.rawui.Windowsize | format-list
```

```
Width : 120
Height : 50
```

The WindowSize cannot be larger than the value of MaxPhysicalWindowSize. To simplify changing the console window size, you can use this function:

```
Function Set-WindowSize {
Param([int]$width=$host.ui.rawui.windowsize.width,
    [int]$height=$host.ui.rawui.windowsize.height)

    $size=New-Object System.Management.Automation.Host.Size($width,$height)

    $host.ui.rawui.WindowSize=$size

}
```

To dynamically change your console window to 60 columns wide and 30 rows, use the following command:

```
PS C:\> Set-windowsize 60 30.
```

If you don't specify a width or height value, the function will use the value of the current window size. We can take a similar approach to console's buffer.

The buffer controls how much of the window can be scrolled either vertically or horizontally. Setting a large vertical buffer lets you see more output from previous commands. If you have a script that will produce a lot of information, you may want to modify the buffer size so you can scroll up to see it all. Here's a function that might help:

```
Function Set-WindowBuffer {
Param([int]$width=$host.ui.rawui.BufferSize.width,
    [int]$height=$host.ui.rawui.BufferSize.height)

    $buffer=New-Object System.Management.Automation.Host.Size($width,$height)

    $host.ui.rawui.Buffersize=$buffer

}
```

You cannot set a buffer size that is less than the window size. But suppose your current window and buffer size is 120 X 50, if run this command:

```
PS C:\ > set-windowbuffer 120 500
```

You'll see a vertical scroll bar appear in your PowerShell window. Now you'll be able to scroll back to see more of your previous commands and output.

# Nested Prompts

One of the most interesting features about the console host is its *nested prompts*. This is a bit difficult to see in action, so let's walk through an example. Be *very* careful if you're following along! One wrong keystroke could crash your computer.

First, open several instances of Windows Notepad. Then, in PowerShell, run this:

```
PS C:\> get-process notepad | stop-process -confirm
```

You should see something like this:

```
Confirm
Are you sure you want to perform this action?
Performing operation "Stop-Process" on Target "notepad (2072)".
[Y] Yes [A] Yes to All [N] No [L] No to All [S] Suspend [?] Help (default is "Y"):
```

If you hit **S**, you'll suspend the pipeline operation and enter a *nested prompt*. Your original command is still pending, but you've sort of entered a side conversation with Windows PowerShell. In it, you can do whatever you want—check variables, run cmdlets, and so forth. By default, the PowerShell prompt reflects this nested state:

```
PS C:\>>>
```

Typing **Exit** ends the nested prompt and takes you back up one level:

```
PS C:\>>> exit
```

```
Confirm
Are you sure you want to perform this action?
Performing operation "Stop-Process" on Target "notepad (2072)".
[Y] Yes [A] Yes to All [N] No [L] No to All [S] Suspend [?] Help (default is "Y"):
```

Here, you'll see your original command still in action. Select **L** to abort. You can manually create a new nested prompt by running **$host.EnterNestedPrompt()**. There's not much use in this from the command line, perhaps, but when you're writing a script you can have a new prompt created for certain conditions, such as an error occurring. The nested prompt runs "inside" the script, so it'll have access to all the variables and so forth within a script. Again, running **Exit** ends the nested prompt, and would return to your script.

Note that you can't have more than 128 nested prompts (we can't imagine why you'd need even that many, to be honest). A built-in variable, $NestedPromptLevel, tells you how deeply you're already nested, and you can check it to see if it's safe to launch a new nested prompt.

........................................................................................................................

**By the Way...**
Instead of running **Exit**, you can also run **$host.ExitNestedPrompt()** to exit a nested prompt.

## Quitting PowerShell

Of course, running **Exit** from a non-nested prompt will exit the shell. But you can also run **$host. SetShouldExit(*xxx*)** to exit the shell, passing a number for *xxx*. This number will be returned as an error code to the Windows environment.

## Prompting the User to Make a Choice

The $host interface provides some access to PowerShell's underlying user interface capabilities. For example, suppose you want to provide a simple "Yes or No" text prompt. First, you would need to construct the prompt in an array:

```
PS C:\> $no = ([System.Management.Automation.Host.ChoiceDescription]"&No")
PS C:\> $no.helpmessage = "Do not continue"
PS C:\> $yes = ([System.Management.Automation.Host.ChoiceDescription]"&Yes")
PS C:\> $yes.helpmessage = "Continue"
PS C:\> $prompts = ($yes,$no)
```

What we've done is created two new prompts. Use the & character before whichever letter will be the "answer" for that prompt. In other words, in our example, you'd press "N" for "No" and "Y" for "Yes." We also specified a "help message" for each prompt, and then assembled them into an array in the $prompts variable. Next, you ask the host to display the prompt:

```
PS C:\> $host.ui.promptforchoice("Continue?","Do you want to continue?",'
>>[System.Management.Automation.Host.ChoiceDescription[]]$prompts,0)
>>

Continue?
Do you want to continue?
[Y] Yes [N] No [?] Help (default is "Y"):
```

Notice that the prompt does not display our "help message" text—that's only displayed if you select ? from the prompt. Also, as you can see, you can provide a title, a description, and then your array of choices. Those choices have to be of a specific .NET Framework type, System.Management. Automation.Host.ChoiceDescription, which is why you see that long class name enclosed in square brackets in there. The **PromptForChoice()** method will return whatever choice the user made. This is perhaps best wrapped up into a reusable function:

```
Function ChoicePrompt($caption, $message, $choices,$default=0) {
 $host.ui.promptforchoice($caption,$message, `
 [System.Management.Automation.Host.ChoiceDescription[]]$choices,$default)
}
```

You'd then call this function, passing it your desired caption, message, prompt array, and the index number of the default prompt choice. The function would return the index number—0 for the first choice, 1 for the second, and so forth—that the user picked. Here's how you might use it in a PowerShell session:

```
PS C:\ > $message="Please make a selection"
PS C:\ > $caption="Continue?"
PS C:\ > $yes = ([System.Management.Automation.Host.ChoiceDescription]"&Yes")
PS C:\ > $yes.helpmessage = "Continue"
PS C:\ > $no = ([System.Management.Automation.Host.ChoiceDescription]"&No")
PS C:\ > $no.helpmessage = "Do not continue"
PS C:\ > $choices = ($yes,$no)
PS C:\ > choiceprompt $caption $message $choices

Continue?
Please make a selection
[Y] Yes [N] No [?] Help (default is "Y"):
0
PS C:\
```

Chapter 9
# Security Features

PowerShell has some interesting challenges to meet in terms of security. The last time Microsoft produced a scripting shell, it produced the Windows Script Host (WSH) that is commonly used to run VBScript scripts. When WSH was produced, security wasn't much of a concern. As a result, VBScript probably became one of the biggest attack points within Windows. As a result, it was used to write and execute a number of viruses and other malicious attacks. Microsoft certainly didn't want to repeat that with PowerShell, and so a number of security features have been built-in.

## Why Won't My Scripts Run?

The first thing you may notice is that files having a .ps1 filename extension don't do anything automatically when double-clicked. The PowerShell window might not even open, since by default the .ps1 filename extension is associated with Notepad! But even if you manually open PowerShell and type a script name, it doesn't run. What good is PowerShell if it can't run scripts?

## When Scripts Don't Run

There are two reasons why a PowerShell script might not run. The first is the script's location. PowerShell won't run scripts that are located in the current directory—it's as if it simply can't see them. For example, we created a script named Test.ps1 in a folder named C:\Test. With PowerShell set to that folder, we type the script name— it isn't found:

```
PS C:\test> test
The term 'test' is not recognized as a Cmdlet, function, operable program,or script file.
Verify the term and try again.
At line:1 char:4
+ test <<<<
PS C:\test>
```

This is a security precaution to help prevent a malicious script from intercepting cmdlet and command names and then running. In other words, if we named our script Dir.ps1, it still wouldn't run—the **Dir** command would run instead. So, the only way to run a script is to explicitly refer to that folder:

```
PS C:\test> cd ..
PS C:\> test\test
Ok
PS C:\>
```

By moving up to the C:\ folder on the first line, we are able to run the script by referring to its folder (test) and filename (test, or test\test for the complete relative path).

Actually, you *can* have PowerShell execute scripts in the same directory if you *specify* the directory. For example, running **.\test.ps1** will run the Test.ps1 script in the current directory, which is specified by the .\ part. However, by specifying a directory you're eliminating the possibility of your script being confused for a command or cmdlet, which makes it safer.

The second reason is the most likely reason your script won't run—the execution policy. For security purposes, PowerShell defaults to a very restrictive *execution policy* that says the shell can only be used *interactively*, which occurs when you type in commands directly and have them execute immediately. This helps ensure that PowerShell can't be used to run script-based viruses by default. In order to run scripts, you'll need to change PowerShell to a different execution policy. However, first we need to talk a bit about how PowerShell identifies and decides whether to trust scripts.

---

**Note**

When considering security issues, keep in mind that PowerShell *may* eventually be a core part of Windows that is included with new installations. It is already included as an optional component of Windows Server 2008, for example.

## Digital Signatures

Digital signatures are an important part of how PowerShell's security works. A digital signature is created by using a code-signing certificate, sometimes referred to as a "Class 3" digital certificate or an Authenticode certificate, which is a Microsoft brand name. These certificates are sold by commercial certification authorities (CAs). The certificates can also be issued by company's own private CAs.

The CA is where the trust process starts. All Windows computers have a list of *trusted root CAs* that is configured in the Internet Options control panel applet as shown in the following figure. To access this window, open Internet Options, and click **Publishers...** on the **Content** tab. Then, select the **Trusted Root Certification Authorities** tab. This list, which is pre-populated by Microsoft and can be customized by administrators, determines the CAs that your computer *trusts*. By definition, your computer will trust any certificates issued by these CAs or any lower-level CA that a trusted CA has authorized. For example, if you trust CA 1, and they authorize CA 2 to issue certificates, then you'll trust certificates issued by CA 1 and by CA 2—your trust of CA 2 comes because it was authorized by the trusted CA 1.

When a CA issues a code-signing certificate, it consists of two halves: a private key and a public key. You usually install the entire certificate on your local computer and use it to digitally sign code including PowerShell scripts. A digital signature is created by calculating a *cryptographic hash*, which is a kind of complex checksum, on the script's contents. The hash is the result of a complex mathematical algorithm that is designed so that no two different scripts can ever produce the same hash value. In other words, the hash acts as a sort of electronic fingerprint for your script. The hash is then encrypted using your certificate's *private* key. This encrypted hash, which is referred to as the *signature*, is appended to the script.

Because the hash portion of the digital signature is unique to your script, it will change if your script changes in the slightest. Even an extra blank line somewhere in your script will invalidate the old checksum and digital signature. After making *any* changes to your script, you'll need to re-sign it. Tools like SAPIEN PrimalScript can be configured to automatically sign scripts each time they're saved, which can save *you* a lot of hassle.

## Trusted Scripts

When PowerShell tries to run a script, it first looks for a signature. If it doesn't find one, then the script is considered *untrusted*. If PowerShell does find a signature, it looks at the unencrypted part of the signature that contains information about the author of the script. PowerShell uses this information to retrieve the author's *public key*, which is always available from the CA that issued the code-signing certificate that was used to sign the script. If the CA isn't trusted, then the script isn't trusted. In this case, PowerShell doesn't do anything else with the script or signature.

If the CA is trusted, and PowerShell is able to retrieve the public key, then PowerShell tries to decrypt the signature using that public key. If it's unsuccessful, then the signature isn't valid, and the script is untrusted. If the signature can be decrypted, then PowerShell knows the script is *conditionally trusted*, which means it's been digitally signed by a trusted certificate issued by a trusted CA. Finally, PowerShell computes the same hash on the script to see if it matches the previously encrypted hash from the signature. If the two match, then PowerShell knows the script hasn't been modified since it was signed, and the script is fully trusted. If the hashes do not match, then the script *has* been modified, and the script is untrusted because the signature is "broken."

PowerShell uses the script's status as trusted or untrusted to decide whether or not the script can be executed in accordance with its current execution policy.

## Execution Policies

Within PowerShell, you can run **help about_signing** to learn more about PowerShell's four execution policies that are listed below.

- **AllSigned.** In this mode, PowerShell executes scripts that are trusted, which means they must be properly signed. Malicious scripts can execute, but you can use their signature to track down the author.

- **Restricted.** This is the default policy. The restricted mode means that no scripts are executed, whether signed or not.

- **RemoteSigned.** In this mode, PowerShell will run local scripts without them being signed. Remote scripts that are downloaded through Microsoft Outlook, Internet Explorer, and so forth must be trusted in order to run.

- **Unrestricted.** PowerShell runs all scripts, whether signed or not. Downloaded scripts will prompt before executing to be sure you really want to run them.

We highly recommend that you sign your scripts since it creates a more secure and trustworthy environment. If you plan to sign your scripts as recommended, then the AllSigned execution policy is appropriate. Otherwise, use RemoteSigned. The Unrestricted policy is overly generous and leaves your computer open to a range of attacks, therefore it shouldn't be used.

To check the current execution policy from within PowerShell, run:

```
PS C:\> Get-executionpolicy
```

You'll get back information about the current execution policy. If it's Restricted, then you'll know why your scripts won't run.

The execution policy can be changed within PowerShell. Keep in mind that this is changing a value in the system registry, to which only administrators may have access. Therefore, if you're not an administrator on your computer, then you may not be able to modify the execution policy. To change the execution policy, run the following within PowerShell:

```
PS C:\> set-executionpolicy RemoteSigned
```

This will set the execution policy to RemoteSigned. This change takes effect immediately without restarting PowerShell.

## Signing Scripts

Because code-signing certificates can be expensive ($300 per year or more is the current going rate), you may wish to create a *self-signed* certificate for your own local testing purposes. This certificate will be trusted only by your personal computer, but it costs you nothing to create. To create a self-signed certificate, you'll need a program called Makecert.exe that is available in the downloadable Microsoft .NET

Framework Software Development Kit (SDK) at http://msdn.microsoft.com/netframework/ downloads/updates/default.aspx. This file is also downloadable from the Windows Platform SDK. Documentation, including examples for this utility, can be found at http://msdn2.microsoft.com/en-us/ library/aa386968.aspx.

After downloading and installing this file, you can use the Makecert.exe file to create the certificate by running the following from a Cmd.exe shell:

```
C:\> Makecert -n "CN=PowerShell Local Certificate Root" -a sha1
 -eku 1.3.6.1.5.5.7.3.3 -r -sv root.pvk root.cer
 -ss Root -sr localMachine
```

> **Note:** If you have problems running Makecert, run **Makecert /?** to verify the correct syntax. Different versions of Makecert (a version might be included in your Microsoft Office installation, for example) require slightly different command-line arguments.

Note that this is all one long line of instructions. Next run:

```
C:\> Makecert -pe -n "CN=PowerShell User" -ss MY -a sha1
 -eku 1.3.6.1.5.5.7.3.3 -iv root.pvk -ic root.cer
```

Again, this is all one long line of typed instructions. These lines create two temporary files, root.pvk and root.cer, that you can save as backups. The actual certificate will be installed into your local certificate store where it can be used to sign scripts. Within PowerShell, run:

```
PS C:\> Set-authenticodeSignature "filename.ps1" '
>>@(get-childitem cert:\CurrentUser\My -codesigning)[0]
>>
PS C:\>
```

This is also one long line. This line retrieves your code-signing certificate and signs the file named filename.ps1, which should be an existing, unsigned PowerShell script. You can run **help set-authenticodesignature** for additional help with signing scripts. You can also use high-end script development environments, such as SAPIEN PrimalScript, to sign scripts using a graphical user interface.

We need to emphasize that a certificate made with Makecert is *only* useful for testing on your local computer. If you want to distribute your scripts internally or externally, you'll need to acquire a real code-signing certificate.

## Alternate Credentials

Whenever you start a new instance of the PowerShell shell, it runs under your *security context*. This means that PowerShell uses your logon credentials to run whatever scripts and commands you need to run. If your credentials do not have permissions to perform a particular command, such as retrieving a WMI object from a remote computer, then PowerShell will not be able to perform that task. One way to run PowerShell under alternate credentials is to use the Windows **RunAs** command. In this case, PowerShell will run under whatever credentials you provide to **RunAs**. However, sometimes this option might not work for what you need to do. For example, suppose you want to retrieve a WMI object from a computer on which you're not a local administrator. By default, WMI only permits local administrators to access WMI remotely. You *could* launch PowerShell using **RunAs**, if you can provide RunAs with credentials, such as a domain administrator account that is a local administrator on the computer in question. However, if that computer is not a domain member, there is no way to provide **RunAs** with the credentials of *another* computer's local accounts. If this situation arises, it appears that you're stuck.

However, it may only seem that way. Many PowerShell cmdlets support an optional parameter named -credential, which allows you to specify an alternate username and password that this one cmdlet will use to execute. For example, the **Get-WmiObject** cmdlet has a -credential parameter. Running **Help Get-WmiObject** indicates that the -credential parameter takes a value of the type PSCredential. This means you'll need to learn how to make one of those credentials.

The task, then, is to use PowerShell to get something called a *security principal*, which in English is a user or security group. PowerShell provides a cmdlet named **Get-Credential** that does just that. The cmdlet prompts you for the appropriate password and returns a PSCredential object that you can store in a variable. For example:

```
PS:> $cred = get-credential MYDOMAIN\Administrator
```

Note that the username is specified in the DOMAIN\USER format. For a local computer, use COMPUTER\USER instead. Always specify the short (NetBIOS) domain or computer name rather than the longer DNS domain name. If you prefer, you can also enter the username in the user@domain format, in which case you'll use the complete DNS domain name.

If you try this, there are two really important things to note:

- A dialog box will pop up, prompting you for the specified user's password.

- PowerShell *does not check the user*. Instead, it prompts you for a password. Keep in mind that it doesn't see if it's correct, and it doesn't check to see if the specified user exists. That's your responsibility.

Now you can run a command like this:

```
PS:> Get-wmiobject -class Win32_Process -computername Client32 -credential $cred
```

This script first utilizes the credential stored in the variable $cred to connect to a machine named Client32 and then attempts to retrieve all instances of the WMI Win32_Process class. Note that not *all* cmdlets support the -credential parameter as shown here. Run **Help** *cmdlet-name* to view a particular cmdlet's help file to see if it offers this functionality. In many cases, the ability to utilize alternate credentials isn't dependent on whether or not the cmdlets can accomplish this. Instead, it depends on whether or not the underlying Windows functionality, which the cmdlet is calling upon, can pass along alternate credentials.

## Is PowerShell Dangerous?

The answer is that PowerShell is no more dangerous than any other application. Certainly, PowerShell has the potential for great destruction, since it can delete files, modify the registry, etc. However, so can any other application. If you run PowerShell as a local administrator, then it will have full access to your system—just like any other application. If you follow the *principle of least privilege*, which means you *don't* routinely log on to your computer as a local administrator, and you don't routinely run PowerShell as a local administrator, then its potential for damage is minimized—just like any other application. In fact, when set to its AllSigned execution policy, PowerShell is arguably *safer* than many applications, since you can ensure that only scripts signed by an identifiable author will actually be able to run.

Naturally, much of PowerShell's security begins and ends with *you*. Microsoft has configured it to be *very* safe out-of-the-box. Therefore, anything you do from there can potentially loosen PowerShell's security. For this reason, you need to understand that your actions could have consequences before you do anything.

## Safer Scripts from the Internet

One potential danger point is downloading PowerShell scripts from the Internet or acquiring them from other untrusted sources. While these scripts are a great way to quickly expand your scripting skills, they present a danger if you don't know *exactly* what they do. Fortunately, Microsoft has provided the -**whatif** parameter, which is a very cool way to find out what scripts do.

All PowerShell cmdlets are built from the same basic *class,* or template, which allows them to have a -**whatif** parameter. Not every cmdlet actually implements this, but then not *every* cmdlet does something potentially damaging. Let's look at a good example of how you might use the -**whatif** parameter.

Say you download a script from the Internet, and in it you find the following:

```
PS:> Get-process | stop-process
```

> **Note:** Did you know that **Get-Process**, with no other arguments, returns a list of all processes?

This runs the **Get-Process** cmdlet and pipes its output to the **Stop-Process** cmdlet. So, this script will have the effect of *stopping every process* on your computer. Not good. However, if you weren't sure of this output, you could just add -**whatif**:

```
PS:> Get-Process | stop-process -whatif
```

The output listed below is what you'd get, which is a portion of the actual list:

```
What if: Performing operation "stop-process" on Target "acrotray (4092)".
What if: Performing operation "stop-process" on Target "alg (1480)".
What if: Performing operation "stop-process" on Target "ati2evxx (1356)".
What if: Performing operation "stop-process" on Target "ati2evxx (1672)".
What if: Performing operation "stop-process" on Target "BTStackServer (3668)".
What if: Performing operation "stop-process" on Target "BTTray (1252)".
What if: Performing operation "stop-process" on Target "btwdins (168)".
What if: Performing operation "stop-process" on Target "csrss (1084)".
What if: Performing operation "stop-process" on Target "explorer (3380)".
What if: Performing operation "stop-process" on Target "Groove (1232)".
What if: Performing operation "stop-process" on Target "hpqgalry (3260)".
What if: Performing operation "stop-process" on Target "hpqtra08 (1556)".
What if: Performing operation "stop-process" on Target "hpwuSchd2 (3956)".
What if: Performing operation "stop-process" on Target "HPZipm12 (1004)".
What if: Performing operation "stop-process" on Target "Idle (0)".
What if: Performing operation "stop-process" on Target "inetinfo (236)".
What if: Performing operation "stop-process" on Target "iPodService (1136)".
```

Other than getting this output, nothing would happen. The -**whatif** parameter tells PowerShell (or more specifically, the **Stop-Process** cmdlet) to display what it *would* do, without actually *doing* it. This allows you to see what the downloaded script would have done without taking the risk of running it. That's one way to make those downloaded scripts a bit safer in your environment—or at least see what they'd do. *Most* cmdlets that change the system in some way support -**whatif**, and you can check individual cmdlets' built-in help to be sure.

Note that -**whatif** doesn't take the place of a signature. For example, if your PowerShell execution policy is set to only run trusted (signed) scripts, and you download a script from the Internet that isn't signed, then you'll have to sign the script before you can add **-whatif** and run the script to see what it would do.

............................................................................................................................................................

**Our scripts aren't signed!**

We've deliberately *not* signed any of the sample scripts in this book (which are downloadable from www.SAPIENPress.com). If you decide to run any of our scripts, you need to evaluate them first to make sure they're suitable for you, and then sign them or configure PowerShell to not require a signature on scripts in order to execute them. We don't want you running any of our scripts until you've determined that they're appropriate for your environment, free of typos, and so forth.

You should also bear in mind the differences between the AllSigned and RemoteSigned execution policies. When you download a file with Microsoft Outlook or Microsoft Internet Explorer, Windows "marks" the file as having come from a potentially untrustworthy source, the Internet. Files "marked" in this fashion won't run under the RemoteSigned execution policy unless they've been signed. While we still encourage the use of the AllSigned execution policy, RemoteSigned at least lets you run unsigned scripts that you write yourself, while providing a modicum of protection against potentially malicious scripts you acquire from somewhere else.

# Passwords and Secure Strings

In certain situations, you may need to have a script prompt for a string that you need to keep safe and secure such as a password. PowerShell provides a special object called SecureString that is designed to securely work with string data. Three cmdlets are available for working with SecureString objects: **Read-Host**, **ConvertFrom-Securestring**, and **ConvertTo-Securestring**.

**Read-Host** prompts for input and masks whatever is typed. The typed input then returns as the result of the cmdlet that can be stored in a variable. For example:

```
PS C:\> $password = read-host -assecurestring
********
PS C:\>
```

The password is stored in the variable $password. However, unlike a regular variable, you can't just display the contents of a SecureString:

```
PS C:\> $password
System.Security.SecureString
PS C:\>
```

As you can see, the contents of $password weren't displayed. Instead, the *type* of $password—"System.Security.SecureString"—was displayed. So, how can you get the password? Well, you can't exactly. It's intended to be passed directly to other cmdlets that accept a SecureString as their input.

However, there's another way in which SecureString is useful. You may have already realized that hardcoding passwords into a script is a bad idea. Anyone with permission to run the script also has permission to read it, which means they can read the hard-coded password. SecureString provides a *slight* amount of additional security when you *must* hard-code a password. You start by creating a new SecureString like the ones we've shown you. Then you use **ConvertFrom-SecureString** to export your encrypted password in a format that can be hard-coded into a script:

```
PS C:\> $password = read-host -assecurestring
********

PS C:\> $password = ConvertFrom-SecureString $password
PS C:\> $password
01000000d08c9ddf0115d1118c7a00c04fc297eb010000009c0d9c7fe8c37b439faf
e000000000200000000000003660000a80000001000000093aaa18edf6f108b6222559
00000004800000a00000001000000098e4c93b57f59ff35110960a80b248a2180000
10ef82f30674ca4beea5df77c556388e95238b2140000002735d16881363c9c7b385
c7aea529
PS C:\>
```

That string of letters and numbers can be hard-coded into your script, assigning them to a variable. When you're ready to actually use the password, such as passing it as a parameter to a cmdlet that accepts a SecureString, then use **ConvertTo-SecureString** to turn the letters and numbers back into a SecureString:

```
PS C:\> $password = read-host -assecurestring
********

PS C:\> $password = ConvertFrom-SecureString $password
PS C:\> $password
01000000d08c9ddf0115d1118c7a00c04fc297eb010000009c0d9c7fe8c37b439faf
e000000000200000000000003660000a80000001000000093aaa18edf6f108b6222559
00000004800000a00000001000000098e4c93b57f59ff35110960a80b248a2180000
10ef82f30674ca4beea5df77c556388e95238b2140000002735d16881363c9c7b385
c7aea529
PS C:\> $password= ConvertTo-SecureString $password
PS C:\> $password
System.Security.SecureString
PS C:\>
```

The last four lines show **ConvertTo-SecureString** being used. As you can see, once again $password is a SecureString. So, here's how this works: A SecureString can be used in your script as a normal variable; only the various "Output" and "Write" cmdlets will be unable to display it. If a cmdlet needs a password, and you send the password in a SecureString, the cmdlet will be able to read the password.

When you need to store a SecureString in a file or in a script, convert it from a SecureString into an encrypted string; convert it back to a SecureString to actually use it.

Here's the only problem—the encryption algorithm used by **CovertFrom-SecureString** is *deterministic*, which means any given input always results in the same output. This makes the encrypted password vulnerable to a dictionary attack, which occurs when the encrypted password is compared to a *huge* list of pre-encrypted passwords. When a match is found, the dictionary knows the cleartext password used to produce that particular encrypted password, which means the password, is compromised. You *can* specify an encryption key when you use **CovertFrom-SecureString**; however, that key has to be used with **ConvertTo-SecureString**, and if you store the key in a file or in the script, then the key is essentially compromised and offers no particular security. And, no matter what, the output of **CovertFrom-SecureString** can be cracked by a dictionary attack.

Dictionary attacks are not particularly time-consuming once the dictionary itself is created. Pre-created dictionaries exist that contain every possible character combination for 6-, 7-, and 8-character passwords. A good dictionary will fit on a stack of DVD-ROM discs, and there are places on the Internet where you can buy such a stack—essentially, a ready-to-use password cracking tool. If you plan to use this SecureString technique to hard-code passwords into your script, be sure they're *very* long passwords—think pass*phrases*—to help avoid the possibility of an easy dictionary attack.

You should also be aware that a clever .NET developer or PowerShell scripter *can* decrypt the contents of a SecureString and display the cleartext result:

```
PS C:\> $Secret = read-host -assecurestring
********

PS>$Secret
System.Security.SecureString
PS>$BSTR = [System.Runtime.InteropServices.marshal]::SecureStringToBSTR($Secret)
PS>$ClearString = [System.Runtime.InteropServices.marshal]::PtrToStringAuto($BSTR)
PS>[System.Runtime.InteropServices.marshal]::ZeroFreeBSTR($BSTR)
PS>$ClearString
The password
PS>
```

What happened, here? A new SecureString was created and stored in the variable $secret. This might be a password, for example. Then, .NET's COM interoperability services were used to convert the SecureString to a binary string (BSTR). It is then used to output the cleartext version into the variable $ClearString. This isn't exactly the huge security leak it looks like, since it can only be done with the original SecureString object created by **Read-Host**, and only on the computer on which the SecureString was created. So, really, the only person who could use this trick is the person who typed the password in the first place. In essence, your personal login credentials are used to encrypt the SecureString in memory. So, without those, it can't be decrypted.

Chapter 10
# The Microsoft .NET Framework:
# An Overview for PowerShell Users

You probably don't *feel* as if you need to know much about the .NET Framework. Or maybe you're just *hoping* that's the case. Well, you're almost right. You certainly don't need to know *much* about the .NET Framework. However, you need to know a little so that all of PowerShell's features make sense to you. The good news is that what you need to know about the .NET Framework is summarized in this short chapter.

## Microsoft .NET Framework Essentials

.NET is Microsoft's leading-edge software development framework. Traditional .NET development begins inside a development environment like Microsoft Visual Studio, SAPIEN PrimalScript Enterprise, or even Windows Notepad. After applications are written in languages like Visual Basic .NET or Visual C#, they're compiled to a special language called the Microsoft Intermediate Language (MSIL). This is important, because it's different from how other things such as Visual Basic 6 compiled programs into a native, binary executable.

When you double-click a .NET executable, it doesn't run right away because it contains MSIL, not actual binary code. Instead, Windows fires up the .NET Common Language Runtime (CLR), which is what reads the MSIL and compiles it into executable, binary code that will run on your system. This makes .NET applications inherently portable, since they can (more or less) run on any platform for which a CLR is available. This is all a bit of an oversimplification, but it's more than close enough for Windows administrative work.

The point of all this is that PowerShell is built on .NET, as are the cmdlets you'll be running. .NET is what's called an *object-oriented* framework, which is a fancy way of saying it is kind of template-based. For example, all PowerShell cmdlets start out as copies of a standardized cmdlet *base class* or template. In programmer terms, you'd say that all cmdlets *inherit from* that cmdlet base class. This is important because it's what makes all cmdlets pretty consistent with one another, which allows them to share certain ubiquitous parameters, etc.

The object-oriented stuff plays heavily into how PowerShell works, which is why you need to know a bit more about what an object *is*. At the simplest level, perhaps a level suitable for cocktail parties, an object is a bunch of computer code bundled into a "black box." The black box has buttons you can push to make things happen, and it has little blinking lights to tell you what's going on inside. You don't actually know how the box works—inside it could be anything from a particle accelerator to a cheese sandwich. But that doesn't really matter since the point is that you only interact with the box through its blinking lights and buttons while everything inside remains a big mystery. You can build your own black box that incorporates another black box, which is called *inheritance*. Essentially inheritance occurs when you install box number one inside box number two, so box number two can take full advantage of box number one's functionality without knowing much about what goes on inside.

*Everything* is an object in .NET and in PowerShell. Every variable you create, every WMI class you return—*everything* is an object. All of these objects have buttons called *methods* and blinking lights called *properties*. For example, when you run the code listed below, the **Get-WmiObject** cmdlet gets all the instances of the Win32_Process WMI class.

```
PS C:\> $stuff = Get-WmiObject -class Win32_Process -namespace root\cimv2
```

Each instance of the Win32_Process WMI class is an object. Together, the instances are bundled into a *collection* of objects that is stored in $stuff. The collection *itself* is an object.

> **Note:** You can think of a collection as a bucket that is an object you can do things to. This bucket can also contain other independent objects. Sometimes a collection is referred to as a *list* or *array*.

So, the variable $stuff is now a collection of Win32_Process instances. Even a simple string of text "like this one" is really an object—specifically a *string* object—as far as PowerShell and .NET are concerned.

## Reflection

Microsoft's Component Object Model (COM) is the pre-PowerShell way of managing Windows, often through a language like VBScript. Part of what made COM so difficult was that objects had to take special steps to define their functionality ahead of time. In other words, when someone at Microsoft created a DLL that allowed your scripts to work with files and folders, they also had to create a little file called a *type library* that explained the capabilities of the DLL. That made COM difficult to extend in certain ways, and certainly made it tough to use.

On the other hand, with .NET there's a nifty feature called *reflection*. Basically, reflection is a way for one application like PowerShell to discover something about an object at runtime without being told in advance what the object can do. Reflection makes PowerShell infinitely extensible because you can add new cmdlets. PowerShell can also, more or less, ask the cmdlets what they do and how they work.

Reflection makes PowerShell easier for you to use. For example, if you don't know what capabilities an object has, just pipe an instance of it to the **Get-Member** cmdlet. This cmdlet uses reflection to display all the known properties and methods of the object within PowerShell.

## Assemblies

In .NET, everything eventually gets packaged into an *assembly*, which is a fancy word for what we otherwise call an executable, DLL, or some other file-that-contains-executable-code. You'll find assemblies distributed with PowerShell by default in the shell's installation folder.

> **Note:** One assembly can contain or *implement* multiple objects or *interfaces*—each one being a separate cmdlet, for example).

For example, System.Management.Automation.Commands.Management.dll is a file containing bunches of different cmdlets.

## Classes

The .NET Framework, and also PowerShell, treats almost everything as an object. However, different objects can be expected to have different functionality. For example, a car object has different capabilities than an airplane object. The Framework defines *classes* to distinguish between object types. A class is an abstract description of an object's capabilities. The name of a class is often referred to as its *type*. So, a string variable is more accurately referred to as "an object of the System.String type" or "an object of the System.String class." String objects have some distinct capabilities, such as the ability to return an uppercase version as shown in the following code:

```
PS C:\> $a = "hello"
PS C:\> $a.ToUpper()
HELLO
PS C:\>
```

Or the ability to display their length:

```
PS C:\> $a = "world"
PS C:\> $a.Length
5
PS C:\>
```

> **Don't Forget the ()**
> This is a great time to point out a difference between methods and properties. In the above two examples, notice that the method **ToUpper()** must be executed with parentheses, even though it doesn't have any arguments. The property **Length**, on the other hand, doesn't use parentheses. If you forget to add the parentheses to a method, it won't run properly. We forget all the time, and it can be very frustrating until you develop the proper typing habits!

The Framework exposes most of Windows' functionality, such as the ability to display graphical dialog boxes as classes. For example, if you create a new instance of the Windows.Forms.Form class, you're creating a new blank window or dialog box. You'll see how to use this in the next section. The important thing to remember right now is that the .NET Framework is comprised entirely of these classes. Knowing how to work with them can give you a lot of capabilities in PowerShell. Even if you don't work with advanced classes like Windows forms, you can still work with basic classes like String, Int32 that let your scripts manipulate data more easily.

## Variables as Objects

Earlier, we mentioned that even variables are objects. In particular, string variables in .NET are extremely robust and have a number of methods. One of them is **Split**, which is a method that takes a string and creates an array (or list) out of it by breaking the list up on some character like a comma or a space. Try this in PowerShell:

```
PS C:\> "1,2,3,4".Split(",")
```

What you're telling PowerShell is "take this string and execute its Split method." Use a comma for the method's input argument. When PowerShell does this, the method returns an array of four elements that each contains a number. PowerShell gets that array and displays it in a textual fashion with one array element per line:

```
1
2
3
4
```

There are other ways to use this technique. For example, we've already referred to **Get-Member**, a cmdlet that displays the methods and variables (which are collectively referred to as *members* in programmer-speak) associated with a given object instance. So, take a string like "Hello, World"—which, remember, is an instance of a String object—and pipe it to the **Get-Member** cmdlet to display information about that String object:

```
PS C:\> "Hello, World" | get-member


   TypeName: System.String

Name               MemberType           Definition
----               ----------           ----------
Clone              Method               System.Object Clone()
CompareTo          Method                System.Int32 CompareTo(Objec
Contains           Method               System.Boolean Contains(Stri
CopyTo             Method               System.Void CopyTo(Int32 sou
EndsWith           Method               System.Boolean EndsWith(Stri
Equals             Method               System.Boolean Equals(Object
get_Chars          Method                System.Char get_Chars(Int32
get_Length         Method                System.Int32 get_Length()
IndexOf            Method               System.Int32 IndexOf(Char va
IndexOfAny         Method                System.Int32 IndexOfAny(Char
Insert             Method               System.String Insert(Int32 s
LastIndexOf        Method                System.Int32 LastIndexOf(Cha
LastIndexOfAny     Method                System.Int32 LastIndexOfAny(
PadLeft            Method               System.String PadLeft(Int32
PadRight           Method               System.String PadRight(Int32
Remove             Method               System.String Remove(Int32 s
Replace            Method               System.String Replace(Char o
Split              Method               System.String[] Split(Params
StartsWith         Method                System.Boolean StartsWith(St
Substring          Method                System.String Substring(Int3
ToCharArray        Method                System.Char[] ToCharArray(),
ToLower            Method               System.String ToLower(), Sys
ToLowerInvariant   Method                 System.String ToLowerInvaria
ToString           Method               System.String ToString(), Sy
ToUpper            Method               System.String ToUpper(), Sys
ToUpperInvariant   Method                 System.String ToUpperInvaria
```

```
Trim              Method               System.String Trim(Params Ch
TrimEnd           Method               System.String TrimEnd(Params
TrimStart          Method                System.String TrimStart(Para
Chars           ParameterizedProperty System.Char Chars(Int32 inde
Length            Property             System.Int32 Length {get;}
```

This output is truncated a bit to fit in this book. However, you can see it includes every method and property of the String and correctly identifies "Hello, World" as a "System.String" type, which is the unique *type name* that describes what we informally call a *String object*. You can pipe nearly anything to **Get-Member** to learn more about that particular object and its capabilities.

## Variable Types

The fact that PowerShell is built on and around .NET gives PowerShell tremendous power, which isn't always obvious. For example, in the first chapter, we explained that any PowerShell variable can contain any type of data. This occurs because *all* types of data—strings, integers, dates, etc—are .NET classes that inherit from the base class named Object. A PowerShell variable can contain anything that inherits from Object. However, as in the previous example with a string, PowerShell can certainly tell the difference between different classes that inherit from Object.

You can force PowerShell to treat objects as a more specific type. For example, take a look at this sequence:

```
PS C:\> $one = 5
PS C:\> $two = "5"
PS C:\> $one + $two
10
PS C:\> $one = 5
PS C:\> $two = "5"
PS C:\> $one + $two
10
PS C:\> $two + $one
55
```

In this example, we gave PowerShell two variables: one contained the number five, and the other contained the string character "5". Even though this might look the same to you, it's a big difference to a computer! However, we didn't specify what type of data they were, so PowerShell assumed they were both of the generic Object type. PowerShell also decided it would figure out something more specific when the variables are actually used.

When we added $one and $two, or 5 + "5", PowerShell said, "Aha, this is addition: The first character is definitely not a string because it wasn't in double quotes. The second character one *was* in double quotes, but… well, if I take the quotes away it looks like a number, so I'll add them." This is why we correctly got ten as the result.

However, when we added $two and $one—reversing the order—PowerShell had a different decision to make. This time PowerShell said, "I see addition, but this first operand is clearly a string. The second one is a generic Object. So, let's treat it like a string too and concatenate the two." This is how we got the string "55", which is the first five tacked onto the second five.

But what about:

```
PS C:\> [int]$two + $one
10
```

Same order as the example that got "55", but in this type we specifically told PowerShell that the generic object in $two was an [Int], or integer, which is a type PowerShell knows about. So, this time PowerShell used the same logic as in the first example. When it added the two, it came up with "10".

You can force PowerShell to treat anything as a specific type. For example:

```
PS C:\> $int = [int]"5"
PS C:\> $int | get-member


   TypeName: System.Int32

Name        MemberType Definition
----        ---------- ----------
CompareTo   Method     System.Int32 CompareTo(Int32 value), System.Int
Equals      Method     System.Boolean Equals(Object obj), System.Boole
GetHashCode Method      System.Int32 GetHashCode()
GetType     Method     System.Type GetType()
GetTypeCode Method      System.TypeCode GetTypeCode()
ToString    Method     System.String ToString(), System.String ToStrin
```

Here, the value "5" would normally be either a String object or, at best, a generic Object. But by specifying the type [int], we forced PowerShell to try and convert "5" into an integer before storing it in the variable $int. The conversion was successful, which you can see when we piped $int to **Get-Member** revealing the object's type: System.Int32.

Note that once you apply a specific type to a variable, it stays that way until you specifically change it. For example:

```
PS C:\> [int]$int = 1
```

This creates a variable named $int as an integer and assigns it the value 1. The $int variable will be treated as an integer from now on, even if you don't include the type:

```
PS C:\> $int = 2
```

It is still using $int as an integer because it was already cast into a specific type. Once set up to be an integer, you can't put other types of data into it. Here's an example of an error that occurred when we tried to put a string into a variable that was already specifically cast as an integer:

```
PS C:\> [int]$int = 1
PS C:\> $int = 2
PS C:\> $int = "hello"
Cannot convert value "hello" to type "System.Int32". Error: "Input string was not in a correct
 format."
At line:1 char:5
+ $int <<<< = "hello"
PS C:\>
```

However, you can recast a variable by reassigning a new, specific type:

```
[string]$int = "Hello"
```

That works just fine, and $int will *now* be treated as a string by PowerShell.

PowerShell isn't a miracle worker: For example, if you try to force it to convert something that doesn't make sense, it will complain:

```
PS C:\> $int = [int]"Hello"
Cannot convert "Hello" to "System.Int32". Error: "Input string was not in a correct format."
At line:1 char:13
+ $int = [int]" <<<< Hello"
```

This occurred because "Hello" can't sensibly be made into a number.

This one's even more fun because it illustrates some of the advanced data types:

```
PS C:\> $xml = [xml]"<users><user name='joe' /></users>"
PS C:\> $xml.users.user

name
----
joe
```

In this example we created a string, but told PowerShell it was of the type XML, which is another data type that PowerShell knows. XML data works sort of like an object: We defined a parent object named Users and a child object named User. The child object had an attribute called Name, with a value of Joe. So, when we asked PowerShell to display $xml.users.user, it displays all the attributes for that user. We can prove that PowerShell treated $xml as XML data by using **Get-Member**:

```
PS C:\> $xml | get-member


    TypeName: System.Xml.XmlDocument

Name                           MemberType   Definition
----                           ----------   ----------
ToString                       CodeMethod   static System.Stri
add_NodeChanged                Method        System.Void add_No
add_NodeChanging               Method        System.Void add_No
add_NodeInserted               Method        System.Void add_No
add_NodeInserting              Method        System.Void add_No
add_NodeRemoved                Method        System.Void add_No
add_NodeRemoving               Method        System.Void add_No
AppendChild                    Method       System.Xml.XmlNode
Clone                          Method       System.Xml.XmlNode
CloneNode                      Method       System.Xml.XmlNode
CreateAttribute                Method       System.Xml.XmlAttr
CreateCDataSection             Method       System.Xml.XmlCDat
CreateComment                  Method       System.Xml.XmlComm
CreateDocumentFragment         Method        System.Xml.XmlDocu
CreateDocumentType             Method       System.Xml.XmlDocu
CreateElement                  Method       System.Xml.XmlElem
CreateEntityReference          Method        System.Xml.XmlEnti
CreateNavigator                Method       System.Xml.XPath.X
CreateNode                     Method       System.Xml.XmlNode
CreateProcessingInstruction Method             System.Xml.XmlProc
...
```

This demonstrates not only that variables *are* objects, but also that PowerShell understands different types of data, and provides different capabilities for the various types of data.

Curious about what object types are available? Here's a quick list of more common types (although there are more than this):

- Array
- Bool (Boolean)
- Byte
- Char (a single character)
- Char[] (Character array)
- Decimal
- Double
- Float
- Int (Integer)
- Int[] (Integer array)
- Long (Long integer)
- Long[] (Long integer array)
- Regex (Regular expression)
- Scriptblock
- Single
- String
- XML

You will learn more about variables in the chapter "Variables, Arrays, and Escape Characters" (where, because repetition is a *good thing* when you're learning, we'll repeat a lot of this information with new examples). We'll also be popping in with details on these other types as appropriate throughout this book. Some of the types aren't frequently used in administrative scripting, so we will not arbitrarily hit you with all of them at once. Instead, we'll cover them in a context where they're accomplishing something useful.

## Variable Precautions

One thing to be careful of is PowerShell's ability to change the type of a variable if you haven't explicitly selected a type. For example:

```
Write-host $a.ToUpper()
```

This works fine if $a contains a string, as shown here:

```
PS C:\> $a = "Hello"
PS C:\> write-host $a.ToUpper()
HELLO
PS C:\>
```

However, if $a was already set to an integer value, you'll get an error:

```
PS C:\> $a = 1
PS C:\> write-host $a.toupper()
Method invocation failed because [System.Int32] doesn't contain a method named 'toupper'.
At line:1 char:22
+ write-host $a.toupper( <<<< )
```

This occurs because, as an integer, $a doesn't have a **ToUpper()** method. You need to watch out for this when you're writing scripts that take input from other sources. For example, this might occur with a user or a file, since this type of error can be tricky to troubleshoot. One way around it is to force PowerShell to treat the variable as the string you're expecting it to be:

```
PS C:\> $a = 1
PS C:\> $a = [string]$a
PS C:\> write-host $a.ToUpper()
1
PS C:\>
```

You don't necessarily need to select a type up-front for every variable you use. However, you should be aware of situations that can make a variable contain a type of data other than what you originally expected.

## .NET Conclusion

PowerShell is built on and around the .NET Framework, which means everything in PowerShell has a distinctly .NET flavor to it. On one level, you can ignore this and use PowerShell at a more simple level. For example, you can let it treat everything as a generic Object. However, as you grow with PowerShell, and want to leverage more powerful features, you'll find yourself gradually learning more about .NET.

This chapter wasn't meant to be a comprehensive look at .NET—that's another book entirely! Instead, the purpose of this chapter is to provide a rather a quick look at how .NET impacts the way PowerShell is built and the way PowerShell works. You'll see a *lot* more details about these topics, especially variables and their capabilities, throughout the remaining chapters.

.

## Chapter 11
# Using WMI in Windows PowerShell

## WMI Fundamentals

Like PowerShell, Windows Management Instrumentation (WMI) was created to solve a problem with Windows management: Every different part of Windows made management information available through a different means. WMI is an attempt to make all of that more consistent. As a result, WMI is more or less a "one stop shop" for obtaining management information.

It is important to understand that WMI is completely separate from PowerShell. WMI can be used from within PowerShell, but it can also be used from VBScript, C++, VB.NET, and nearly any other Windows-based language. There's even **Wmic.exe**, a command-line tool that can access WMI from the old Cmd shell. WMI is important to you because, from within PowerShell, you can work with WMI to retrieve and manipulate information related to various aspects of Windows. PowerShell *doesn't* replace WMI, it *uses* it.

### WMI Architecture

WMI is built around *classes*, which are abstract descriptions of computer-related things. For example, the Win32_Volume class describes what a logical disk volume looks like. The class includes properties like size and serial number and can perform tasks like defragmenting. However, the class doesn't represent an *actual* volume; it's just a description of what a volume might look like. When you actually have a volume, you have an *instance* of the class. For example, if your computer has two volumes, you have two *instances* of the Win32_Volume class. Actually, only Windows Server 2003 exposes the Win32_Volume class, but we'll discuss this in more detail in a bit. Each instance has properties such as size and name. It might also have methods such as Defragment that you can use to manage that instance.

There are *lots* of WMI classes. Windows itself has hundreds, and Windows Server System products like SQL Server and Microsoft Exchange Server can each add hundreds more. To keep things organized, Microsoft files classes into *namespaces.* The main namespace for the core Windows classes is root\cimv2. Incidentally, most of the core classes' names start with Win32_. Internet Information Services 6.0 (IIS) installs the root\MicrosoftIISv2 namespace, along with lots of classes related to IIS management. The Windows XP SP2 Security Center can be accessed by the root\SecurityCenter namespace. In fact, nearly any recent Microsoft product installs a WMI namespace and several classes that can be used to manage that product.

## WMI Documentation

When you're working with classes, it's useful to know where the documentation is. Fortunately, Microsoft provides it free online. Unfortunately, they change the URLs almost constantly, so it's tough to publish a useful one. Instead, we suggest that you go to http://msdn.microsoft.com/library. In the "Search" box, type **Win32_OperatingSystem**. Make sure the search scope is set to "MSDN Library," then hit the **Search** button. In the search results, one of the first hits should be something like "Win32_ OperatingSystem class [WMI]," which is what you want, so click it. Then, right above the contents tree view on the left, click the "sync toc" link. This will take you into the WMI table of contents in Internet Explorer. You can browse from there. In other browsers, you'll need to click "Up One Level" in the contents—do this twice—to navigate up to where the WMI class documentation starts.

The documentation provides important information. For example, under the Operating System Classes category, locate the Win32_Volume class. You should see something similar to what was shown in the following figure. Notice that the table of contents on the left reveals several methods for this class that are actions you can perform, including **Defrag** and **AddMountPoint**. The main pane includes a brief description of the class, along with a list of its properties such as **DeviceID**, **FreeSpace**, **FileSystem**, and so on. When you scroll all the way to the bottom, you'll see a section labeled **Requirements**. This is where you will find documentation about operating systems, including the one this class exists on— Windows Server 2003 and later. This is important! If you're planning to use this class with a Windows XP computer, you now know that it won't work. From this example you can see why it is important to always check these requirements before you assume a class is universally supported on all versions of Windows.

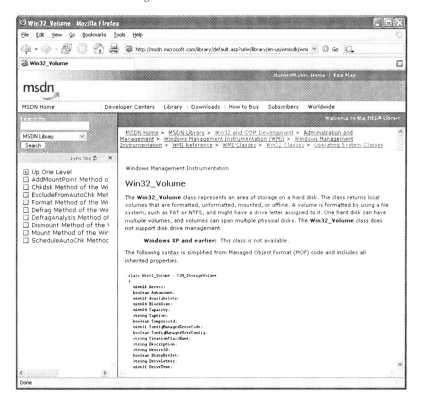

## Working with WMI Classes

Something you need to keep in mind about WMI is that while its goal is to present management information in a consistent fashion…well, it doesn't, really. The problem is that the actual implementation of WMI in any given Microsoft product is a decision left up to that product's development group. For example, the classes related to the core Windows operating system live in the root\cimv2 namespace. Those classes are all fairly consistent in the way they work: You query classes, the properties are read-only, and you execute methods to make changes. For example, if you query the Win32_Service class, you can examine the StartMode and StartName properties to determine if the service starts automatically, and to determine the account that the services uses to log on. However, to *change* those items, you execute the **Change()** method, passing parameters with the new information.

There are still inconsistencies. For example, you can connect to a remote computer's WMI service and start a new instance of the Win32_Process class, and that starts a new process running on the remote computer. However, you can't simply create a new instance of the Win32_LogicalDisk class in order to create a new hard disk partition.

Other product teams have taken different approaches. For example, the root\MicrosoftIISv2 namespace contains classes related to Internet Information Services (IIS) 6. In that namespace, one set of classes is provided for read-only information; a second set of classes has read-write properties that allow you to make configuration changes. *No* class in root\cimv2, however, has writable properties. This sort of inconsistency in how different products can be managed through WMI is unfortunate, but it's something you'll have to become accustomed to—it's just the way Microsoft built things.

## Remote Computers, Security, and WMI

WMI runs as a background service on Windows computers. When you connect to a remote computer, some kind of credentials must be provided so you can connect to the remote computer's WMI service. Normally, *your* credentials are passed along to execute whatever WMI actions you specify. So, if *you* have permission to perform the action, WMI will be able to perform it on your behalf. However, by default, only local administrators have permission to remotely utilize WMI in any way. This is configured in the WMI console. To view it, open a blank Microsoft Management Console (MMC) by running Mmc.exe.

From the File menu, select Add/Remove Snap-In. Click Add and scroll to the bottom to add the WMI Control snap-in. Focus the snap-in on whatever computer you want to view, such as the local computer, and then close the open dialogs to go back to the main console. Right-click WMI Control and then select Properties. If Properties isn't available, left-click WMI Control first, and then right-click it. On the Security tab, select Root and click Security. As shown here, by default only administrators have the Remote Enable permission, which allows them to remotely utilize WMI on this computer.

**Caution!**
Do not modify the WMI permissions unless you know what you're doing and are being very careful. A number of Microsoft and third-party applications rely on WMI. So, if you change the permissions, those applications might stop working.

## Using Wbemtest

Windows includes a built-in tool, called Wbemtest, which can be used to test WMI and interactively examine the WMI repository. To run it, select Run from the Start menu, type **Wbemtest**, and click the OK button.

When the application appears, the first thing you'll do is connect to a computer and a WMI namespace. For example, click the Connect button and type \\.\**root\cimv2** to connect to your local computer's root\cimv2 namespace, where the core Windows operating system classes are installed.

Next, you'll issue a WMI query. The easiest type of query takes the pattern **SELECT * FROM <WMI**

**Class Name>**, such as **SELECT \* FROM Win32_LogicalDisk**. Click the Apply button to execute the query, and you'll get a window containing the query's results—a collection of WMI instances. You can double-click an instance to examine its properties (when doing so, we always select the Hide System Properties checkbox to hide the properties that aren't actually very useful). For each instance, you can review the available property names, see the type of data each property holds, and see the property values associated with that particular instance.

The WMI Query Language (WQL) is similar to the Structured Query Language (SQL) used in most relational database management systems like Microsoft SQL Server, Oracle, or MySQL. You can use a WHERE clause to filter results. For example, to only get *local* drives, you'd issue the query **SELECT \* FROM Win32_LogicalDisk WHERE DriveType = 3**. If all you cared about was the DeviceID, you could just select that property by issuing **SELECT DeviceID FROM Win32_LogicalDisk**. We'll have some more WQL examples in the next chapter, but hopefully this gives you an idea of what WQL looks like.

We *strongly* recommend that you play with WMI in Wbemtest before doing so in PowerShell. While PowerShell does make it easy to work with WMI, Wbemtest provides a way of graphically exploring the WMI repository. If you're after a way to *browse* the WMI repository, visit www.PrimalScript.com/free-tools and download the free WMI Explorer.

## So What Can You Do with WMI?

WMI makes all things possible. Well, many things. The challenge with WMI is learning what class will get you the information you need or do the thing you want, and then figuring out which namespace the class lives in. We can't really offer any shortcuts apart from "browse the documentation." Be sure that you scroll to the bottom of a WMI class' documentation page, though, because some classes don't exist in older versions of Windows—each new version of Windows adds new stuff. Even some class properties get added over time, so don't go crazy if a WMI query on Windows Vista has properties that Windows XP doesn't—that's just progress.

If you're totally stuck trying to figure out what WMI class will do what you need, drop on by www.ScriptingAnswers.com and post a question in the Windows PowerShell forum—we'll try and get you pointed in the right direction.

## Retrieving WMI Objects

We need to point out that PowerShell actually offers two or three different ways of working with WMI. If you're perusing samples that you find in other books or on the Internet, in fact, you may see some of the other techniques. However, of the various ways PowerShell has to work with WMI, only one way—the way we're going to show you—can do *everything*. That is, we're going to show you the one technique PowerShell has for working with WMI that will do *everything* you'll need.

The first step in working with WMI is to get one or more instances of a WMI class; that is, to get a "WMI object." You might retrieve these instances from your local computer's WMI service, or you might get them from a remote machine's WMI service; either way, what you want is to get a collection of WMI instances (or objects) to work with. PowerShell provides an easy way to do this: The **Get-WmiObject** cmdlet. In its simplest form, you simply tell it which WMI class you want, and it'll retrieve all the instances of that class:

```
PS C:\> Get-WmiObject win32_service
```

If you find that typing **Get-WmiObject** over and over becomes tiresome, try the alias **Gwmi** instead:

```
PS C:\> gwmi win32_service
```

Retrieving instances from a remote computer is just as easy:

```
PS C:\> gwmi win32_service -computerName Server2
```

And, remember, you don't need to type the entire parameter name—you just need to type enough to distinguish the parameter from any others. For example:

```
PS C:\> gwmi win32_service -computer Server2
```

Or even:

```
PS C:\> gwmi win32_service -comp Server2
```

Sometimes, the user credentials you used to run PowerShell won't have the appropriate permissions (generally, local Administrator) on the remote computer. In those cases, the **Get-WmiObject** cmdlet can accept alternate credentials. Note that this *only* works with connections to remote computers! WMI itself is designed to not permit alternate credentials when you're connecting to the local WMI service. There are a couple of ways to specify alternate credentials. This is probably the easiest to type for a quick, one-time connection:

```
PS C:\> gwmi win32_service -computerName Server2 -credential DOMAIN\Username
```

PowerShell will automatically prompt you for the password. However, if you plan to use that same credential over and over, repeatedly typing in the username and the password can be a pain in the neck. PowerShell does provide a way for you to save the credential in a variable, and then pass that variable to the -**credential** parameter:

```
PS C:\> $cred = get-credential DOMAIN\Username
PS C:\> gwmi win32_service -comp Server2 -cred $cred
```

The **Get-Credential** cmdlet will prompt you for the password, and then securely store the credential in the variable $cred. That variable will last for the duration of your PowerShell session and can be passed to the -**credential** parameter of any cmdlet that supports the parameter, including **Get-WmiObject**.

The techniques we've just shown you assume that you're querying classes from the default root\cimv2 namespace. If you aren't, then you'll need to specify the WMI namespace:

```
PS C:\> gwmi AntiVirusProduct -namespace root\SecurityCenter
```

In the section Using Wbemtest, we made a big deal of using Wbemtest to test your WMI queries before using them in PowerShell. So, where exactly do you use a WQL query? **Get-WmiObject** supports an alternate syntax that accepts a complete WQL query, rather than just a class name:

```
PS C:\> gwmi -query "SELECT * FROM Win32_Service WHERE StartName = 'LocalSystem'"
```

The same -**computerName**, -**credential**, and -**namespace** parameters can be used with this syntax to specify a remote computer to connect to, an alternate set of credentials, and a namespace other than root\cimv2, if necessary.

An alternative approach is to use the -filter parameter. This parameter, which is available on a number of cmdlets, will filter output. The format depends on the cmdlet. For **Get-Wmiobject**, the filter value is the Where component of a WMI query. For example, you could use an expression like this:

```
PS C:\ > gwmi -query "select * from win32_logicaldisk where drivetype=3"
```

Or you can use -filter:

```
PS C:\ > gwmi win32_logicaldisk -filter "drivetype=3"
```

```
DeviceID    : C:
DriveType   : 3
ProviderName :
FreeSpace   : 44984381440
Size        : 80024170496
VolumeName  :
```

The output will be the same in either situation. So, when do you use a filter and when do you use a query? It's really up to you and the situation. If you are only selecting a subset of properties, then a query is more appropriate:

```
PS C:\ > gwmi -query "Select DeviceID,Freespace,Size from win32_logicaldisk"
```

What you cannot do though is combine **-query** and **-filter**. You can only use one or the other in a **Get-WmiObject** expression.

**Get-WmiObject** can even help you figure out what classes are available to you. Simply specify the -**namespace** parameter by itself, and add the -**list** parameter to list the classes available in that namespace:

```
PS C:\> gwmi -namespace root\securitycenter -list
```

```
__NotifyStatus                        __ExtendedStatus
__SecurityRelatedClass                __Trustee
__NTLMUser9X                          __ACE
__SecurityDescriptor                  __PARAMETERS
__SystemClass                         __ProviderRegistration
__EventProviderRegistration           __ObjectProviderRegistration
__ClassProviderRegistration           __InstanceProviderRegistration
__MethodProviderRegistration          __PropertyProviderRegistration
__EventConsumerProviderRegistration   __thisNAMESPACE
__NAMESPACE                           __IndicationRelated
__FilterToConsumerBinding             __EventConsumer
__AggregateEvent                      __TimerNextFiring
__EventFilter                         __Event
__NamespaceOperationEvent             __NamespaceModificationEvent
__NamespaceDeletionEvent              __NamespaceCreationEvent
__ClassOperationEvent                 __ClassDeletionEvent
__ClassModificationEvent              __ClassCreationEvent
__InstanceOperationEvent              __InstanceCreationEvent
__MethodInvocationEvent               __InstanceModificationEvent
__InstanceDeletionEvent               __TimerEvent
__ExtrinsicEvent                      __SystemEvent
__EventDroppedEvent                   __EventQueueOverflowEvent
__QOSFailureEvent                     __ConsumerFailureEvent
```

```
__EventGenerator                        __TimerInstruction
__AbsoluteTimerInstruction               __IntervalTimerInstruction
__Provider                              __Win32Provider
__SystemSecurity                        AntiSpywareProduct
AntiVirusProduct                        FirewallProduct
```

Class names that begin with a double underscore ("__") are *system classes* and you won't usually utilize these directly. Instead, focus on the classes at the end of the list, which don't start with a double underscore.

# Working with WMI Objects

So far, what we've shown you only displays the results of your WMI query. That is, PowerShell retrieves the objects you requested, but since you haven't told it what else to do with them, it converts them into a text list. That's fine if that's all you need, but you can do a lot more. For example, you can pipe those objects to other PowerShell cmdlets to refine and filter your list, such as filtering so that only running services are shown:

```
PS C:\> gwmi win32_service | where { $_.State -eq "Running" }
```

You can further refine that to perhaps list the running services in reverse alphabetical order:

```
PS C:\> gwmi win32_service | where { $_.State -eq "Running" } | sort name -desc
```

This is where the cmdlets introduced in the "Key Cmdlets for Windows Administration" chapter really come in handy to help you further refine that result set. However, you should be aware of one thing: When you run a command line like the one above, PowerShell has to retrieve *all* instances of the specified class. In the case of the Win32_Service class, that's not a big deal because there aren't *that* many. However, it does have to go get them all, and *then* filter them through the **Where-Object** cmdlet. A more efficient technique would be to issue a WQL query that filters the results *at the origin*—that is, on the computer you're connecting to. WQL is capable of filtering results much more quickly than PowerShell, so using the following technique will yield better performance:

```
PS C:\> gwmi -query "SELECT * FROM Win32_Service WHERE State = 'Running'" | sort name -desc
```

Note that we still have to have PowerShell perform the sort, because the WQL language doesn't support any keywords for sorting (there's no equivalent to the SQL language's ORDER BY clause).

All of this, however, still results in PowerShell reaching the end of the pipeline and generating a text list of whatever WMI objects are in the pipeline at that point. Sometimes you might need to place those objects into a variable, so that you can persist your results and actually do other things with them. Here's an example:

```
PS C:\> $wmi = gwmi win32_operatingsystem -computer Server2
PS C:\> $wmi.Reboot()
```

This example retrieves the Win32_OperatingSystem class from a remote machine, Server2. It saves the resulting collection (which contains just one instance) in the variable $wmi. Because the collection only has one object in it (that particular WMI class can *only* ever return one object), I can just pretend that the $wmi variable represents that object directly, and on the second line execute the object's **Reboot()** method—remotely restarting that server. If your WMI query returns more than one object, however, you have to use a slightly different technique:

```
PS C:\> $wmi = gwmi win32_service
PS C:\> $wmi[0]

ExitCode : 0
Name      : AcrSch2Svc
ProcessId : 340
StartMode : Auto
State     : Running
Status    : OK

PS C:\> $wmi[0].StopService()
```

Here, we've retrieved all instances of Win32_Service and put them into the variable $wmi. Next, we display the first instance in the collection—index number zero—by typing **$wmi[0]**. That lets us verify that the first instance is the one we're after by examining its name and other properties. Finally, we take the first instance and execute its **StopService()** method to stop that instance.

........................................................................................................................................

**Wait a second...**
Did we have to use WMI in this example? Couldn't we have just used the **Get-Service** and **Stop-Service** cmdlets? Well, yes, in this case—but only because we chose services to work with, and only because we're working with the local machine. Neither of those cmdlets work with remote machines, although WMI does. In addition, WMI works with a broader range of manageable components, although services are a great example.

If you're having trouble figuring out which properties and methods a given WMI class has, remember to consult the documentation—or just ask PowerShell by piping the WMI object to **Get-Member**:

```
PS C:\> gwmi win32_bios | get-member


  TypeName: System.Management.ManagementObject#root\cimv2\Win32_BIOS

Name                 MemberType  Definition
----                 ----------  ----------
BIOSVersion          Property    System.String[] BIOSVersion {get;set;}
BuildNumber          Property    System.String BuildNumber {get;set;}
CurrentLanguage      Property     System.String CurrentLanguage {get;set;}
Description          Property    System.String Description {get;set;}
Manufacturer         Property    System.String Manufacturer {get;set;}
Name                 Property    System.String Name {get;set;}
OtherTargetOS        Property    System.String OtherTargetOS {get;set;}
PrimaryBIOS          Property    System.Boolean PrimaryBIOS {get;set;}
ReleaseDate          Property    System.String ReleaseDate {get;set;}
SerialNumber         Property    System.String SerialNumber {get;set;}
SMBIOSBIOSVersion    Property     System.String SMBIOSBIOSVersion {get;set;}
SMBIOSMajorVersion   Property    System.UInt16 SMBIOSMajorVersion {get;set;}
SMBIOSMinorVersion   Property    System.UInt16 SMBIOSMinorVersion {get;set;}
SMBIOSPresent        Property    System.Boolean SMBIOSPresent {get;set;}
SoftwareElementID    Property    System.String SoftwareElementID {get;set;}
SoftwareElementState Property     System.UInt16 SoftwareElementState {get;set;}
Status               Property    System.String Status {get;set;}
TargetOperatingSystem Property     System.UInt16 TargetOperatingSystem {get;set;}
```

Properties and methods will be listed so that you can see them, and figure out what that particular WMI class is capable of doing for you.

Some WMI properties contain multiple values—that is, they're *arrays*. Those can be a bit trickier to work with. For example, the Win32_NetworkAdapterConfiguration class exposes a property named IPAddress, which contains the hardware addresses of a particular network adapter. However, since any given network adapter can have *multiple* IP addresses bound to it, this property must be an array so that it can contain all the possible IP addresses. For the *most part*, PowerShell can just display the property directly. That is, PowerShell detects that the property contains an array and deals with it accordingly. For example:

```
PS C:\> $nics = gwmi win32_networkadapterconfiguration
PS C:\> $nics[4].ipaddress
192.168.4.102
fe80::e468:3091:f2fc:8deb
```

Here you can see that two IP addresses—an IPv4 and IPv6 address (because this was executed on Microsoft Vista)—are returned. If you just wanted *one* of those, you'd treat the IPAddress property like any other PowerShell array or collection:

```
PS C:\> $nics = gwmi win32_networkadapterconfiguration
PS C:\> $nics[4].ipaddress[0]
192.168.4.102
PS C:\> $nics[4].ipaddress[1]
fe80::e468:3091:f2fc:8deb
```

Simply referring to the appropriate array element by its index number allows you to access *just* that element.

## Working Directly with Classes

So far, everything we've shown you has been about retrieving and working with instances of WMI classes. But did you know that you can do some cool stuff *directly* with classes, too? For example, let's retrieve a list of WMI classes, and then filter it so that we're just getting the Win32_Process class. We'll format the output in a list form:

```
PS C:\> $class = gwmi -list | where { $_.Name -eq "Win32_Process" }
PS C:\> $class | format-list
```

```
Name              : Win32_Process
__GENUS           : 1
__CLASS           : Win32_Process
__SUPERCLASS      : CIM_Process
__DYNASTY         : CIM_ManagedSystemElement
__RELPATH         : Win32_Process
__PROPERTY_COUNT  : 45
__DERIVATION      : {CIM_Process, CIM_LogicalElement, CIM_ManagedSystemElement}
__SERVER          : DON-PC
__NAMESPACE       : ROOT\cimv2
__PATH            : \\DON-PC\ROOT\cimv2:Win32_Process
```

We can see the methods of the class by piping the class itself to **Get-Member**. We'll actually ask that cmdlet to *just* display the methods, so that the list is shorter. Remember, we're not working with any particular running process at this point; we're working with the *class*—the abstract description of what a process looks like this:

```
PS C:\> $class | get-member -membertype method


   TypeName: System.Management.ManagementClass#ROOT\cimv2\Win32_Process

Name   MemberType Definition
----   ---------- ----------
Create Method     System.Management.ManagementBaseObject Create(System.String CommandL...
```

Only one method of the class itself: **Create()**. Which we're guessing creates a new process—let's try it:

```
PS C:\> $class.create("calc.exe")


__GENUS          : 2
__CLASS          : __PARAMETERS
__SUPERCLASS     :
__DYNASTY        : __PARAMETERS
__RELPATH        :
__PROPERTY_COUNT : 2
__DERIVATION     : {}
__SERVER         :
__NAMESPACE      :
__PATH           :
ProcessId        : 4676
ReturnValue      : 0
```

Of course, you can't see it unless you try it, but when we ran this we not only got the output shown, but a new Calculator window also popped up. And remember: If the original **Get-WmiObject()** call had been to a remote computer, *we would be starting the process on that computer.* That doesn't mean the process would be visible to other users on that computer (it normally wouldn't), but you *can* use this technique to start background processes remotely!

There's a quicker way to get a WMI class, using the [WMICLASS] type accelerator:

```
PS C:\> $wc = [WMICLASS]"\\.\root\cimv2:Win32_Process"
```

This retrieves the local computer's (represented by the special computername ".") Win32_Process class. And, by the way, if you're wondering how a particular method works, try running it *without* the (). For example:

```
PS C:\Users\Don> $wc.create


MemberType          : Method
OverloadDefinitions : {System.Management.ManagementBaseObject Create(System.String Comman
                      dLine, System.String CurrentDirectory, System.Management.Management
                      Object#Win32_ProcessStartup ProcessStartupInformation)}
TypeNameOfValue     : System.Management.Automation.PSMethod
Value               : System.Management.ManagementBaseObject Create(System.String Command
                      Line, System.String CurrentDirectory, System.Management.ManagementO
                      bject#Win32_ProcessStartup ProcessStartupInformation)
Name                : Create
IsInstance          : True
```

This detailed output shows us that the **Create()** method accepts a string, which is the command line we want to run, another string that is the working directory to set, and then a Win32_ProcessStartup object that contains options for starting the new process. Obviously, all but the first argument is optional, since we were able to use just the first argument in our previous example—you'll need to turn to the documentation, or just recklessly experiment, to see which arguments are required.

## Chapter 12
# Using ADSI in Windows PowerShell

Before we get started, we need to make sure you have some realistic expectations about ADSI in PowerShell. First, understand that ADSI support was always planned to be a part of PowerShell. Then, as PowerShell's ship date approached and the ADSI stuff wasn't up to the quality the team wanted from it, they decided to drop those features and move them to a future version (which, just to have something to call it, we'll refer to as version 2). Then, very close to PowerShell's final release, the team realized that *some* kind of directory services support was absolutely necessary—and so they added the support that we have today. To be honest, that support's pretty minimal; ADSI isn't the first-class citizen that, say, WMI is in version 1 of PowerShell. You can still do some great things with it, but in many cases you're working with the raw, underlying .NET Framework classes, and not an "adapted" view like PowerShell usually gives you with complex objects. Our goal in this chapter, then, is to show you what you *can* do, and to try and help you understand what's needlessly complex.

**There's Hope!**
Quest Software has created a set of cmdlets, and the PowerShell Community Extensions a PSDrive provider, that both help make Active Directory management easier. We cover them, briefly, in the chapter "The PowerShell Ecosystem: Third-Party Extensions." For this chapter, we're sticking with what's built into PowerShell.

# ADSI Fundamentals

Active Directory Services Interface, or ADSI, is an extremely misleading name. Rather than reading it as "Active Directory…Services Interface," which is what most administrators think it is, you should think of it as "Active…Directory Services Interface." ADSI was named at a time when Microsoft slapped the word "Active" on everything that wasn't bolted down: ActiveX Data Objects, Active Directory, Active Documents, and more. The thing to remember, though, is that ADSI *isn't just for Active Directory*. It works great with old Windows NT 4.0 domains, and even works with the local security accounts on standalone and member computers running modern versions of Windows.

ADSI is built around a system of *providers*. Each provider is capable of connecting to a particular type of directory: Windows NT (which includes local security accounts on standalone and member computers), Lightweight Directory Access Protocol (LDAP—this is what Active Directory, or AD, uses), and even Novell Directory Services, if you still have that in your environment somewhere.

## ADSI Queries

The primary way to access directory objects—that is, users, groups, and so forth—is by issuing an *ADSI query*. A query starts with an ADSI provider, so that ADSI knows which type of directory you're trying to talk to. The two providers you'll use most are **WinNT://** and **LDAP://**—and note that, unlike most things in PowerShell, *these provider names are case-sensitive*, and that *they use forward slashes, not backslashes*. Those two caveats mess us up every time!

The format of an ADSI query depends on the provider. For the WinNT:// provider, queries look something like this:

```
WinNT://NAMESPACE/OBJECT,class
```

The NAMESPACE portion of the query can either be a computer name or a NetBIOS domain name—including AD domains! Remember that AD is backward-compatible with Windows NT, and by using the WinNT:// provider to access AD, you'll be able to refer to directory objects—users and groups—without needing to know what organizational unit (OU) they're in, because Windows NT didn't have OUs. The OBJECT portion of the query is the object name—that is, the user name, group name, or whatever—that you're after. The class part of the query is technically optional, but we recommend always including it: It should be "user" if you're querying a user object, "group" for a group object, and so forth. So, a complete query for our test machine's local Administrator account would look like this:

```
WinNT://TESTBED/Administrator,user
```

An LDAP query is much different. These queries require a *fully qualified distinguished name,* or FQDN. For example, if you need to get the SalesUsers group, which is in the East OU, which is in the Sales OU of the MyDomain.com domain, your query would look like this:

```
LDAP://cn=SalesUsers,ou=East,ou=Sales,dc=MyDomain,dc=com
```

Definitely a bit more complicated. LDAP queries don't directly support wildcards, either; you need to know exactly which object you're after (PowerShell does provide a somewhat cumbersome .NET Framework-based means of searching for directory objects, which we'll outline in "Managing Directory Services").

## Using ADSI Objects

Once you've queried the correct object, you can work with its properties and methods. Objects queried through the WinNT:// provider generally have several useful properties. Although be aware that if you're accessing an AD object through the WinNT:// provider, you won't have access to all of the object's properties. You'll only see the ones that the older WinNT:// provider "understands." A few methods are available, too, such as **SetPassword()** and **SetInfo()**. The **SetInfo()** method is especially important: It must be executed after you change any object properties, so that the changes you made will be saved back to the directory correctly.

Objects retrieved through the LDAP:// provider don't directly support many properties. Instead, you execute the **Get()** and **GetEx()** methods, passing the property name you want, to retrieve properties. For example, assuming the variable $user represented a user, you'd retrieve the Description property as follows:

```
$user.Get("Description")
```

**Get()** is used to retrieve properties that have only a single value, such as Description. **GetEx()** is used for properties that can contain multiple values, such as AD's otherHomePhone property. The opposites of these two methods are **Put()** and **PutEx()**, which are used like this:

```
$user.Put("Description","New Value")
```

After you finish all the **Put()** and **PutEx()** calls you want, you must execute the **SetInfo()** method to save the changes back to the directory. As with the WinNT:// provider, security principals retrieved through the LDAP:// provider also have a **SetPassword()** method you can use.

We'll explore the actual use of ADSI within PowerShell in the chapter "Using ADSI in Windows PowerShell." We find, however, that the real trick with ADSI—especially with the LDAP:// provider—is in figuring out which properties do what. For example, in AD, a user's last name is stored in the "sn" property. Their city is in the property named "l." That's hardly intuitive—we strongly recommend picking up a copy of *ADSI Scripting: TFM* (SAPIEN Press, www.SAPIENPress.com), which contains an exhaustive reference of directory properties, including a cross-reference that maps the graphical administration tools' input fields to the underlying property names that you'll use when working with ADSI.

# Retrieving ADSI Objects

Unfortunately, there's no built-in "Get-DirectoryObject" cmdlet built into PowerShell, which is a shame. Instead, you have to use the [ADSI] type accelerator to retrieve objects. You'll need to start with an ADSI query string, which we showed you how to build in "ADSI Queries." Then, just feed that to the type accelerator:

```
PS C:\> $user = [ADSI]"WinNT://TESTBEST/Administrator,user"
```

This will retrieve the local Administrator user account from the computer named TESTBED, using the WinNT:// provider. You can then pipe the resulting object—which we've stored in the $user variable—to **Get-Member** (or its alias, **Gm**) to see what properties and methods the object contains:

```
PS C:\> $user | gm
```

```
   TypeName: System.DirectoryServices.DirectoryEntry

Name                     MemberType Definition
----                     ---------- ----------
AutoUnlockInterval        Property   System.DirectoryServices.PropertyValueCollection...
BadPasswordAttempts       Property   System.DirectoryServices.PropertyValueCollection...
Description               Property   System.DirectoryServices.PropertyValueCollection...
FullName                 Property   System.DirectoryServices.PropertyValueCollection...
HomeDirDrive              Property   System.DirectoryServices.PropertyValueCollection...
HomeDirectory             Property   System.DirectoryServices.PropertyValueCollection...
LockoutObservationInterval Property  System.DirectoryServices.PropertyValueCollection...
LoginHours                Property   System.DirectoryServices.PropertyValueCollection...
LoginScript               Property   System.DirectoryServices.PropertyValueCollection...
MaxBadPasswordsAllowed    Property   System.DirectoryServices.PropertyValueCollection...
MaxPasswordAge            Property   System.DirectoryServices.PropertyValueCollection...
MaxStorage               Property   System.DirectoryServices.PropertyValueCollection...
MinPasswordAge            Property   System.DirectoryServices.PropertyValueCollection...
MinPasswordLength         Property   System.DirectoryServices.PropertyValueCollection...
Name                      Property   System.DirectoryServices.PropertyValueCollection...
objectSid                 Property   System.DirectoryServices.PropertyValueCollection...
Parameters                Property   System.DirectoryServices.PropertyValueCollection...
PasswordAge               Property   System.DirectoryServices.PropertyValueCollection...
PasswordExpired           Property   System.DirectoryServices.PropertyValueCollection...
PasswordHistoryLength     Property   System.DirectoryServices.PropertyValueCollection...
PrimaryGroupID            Property   System.DirectoryServices.PropertyValueCollection...
Profile                  Property   System.DirectoryServices.PropertyValueCollection...
UserFlags                 Property   System.DirectoryServices.PropertyValueCollection...
```

We started with a WinNT:// provider example because these are perhaps the easiest objects to work with: You get nice, clearly defined properties. However, remember in "Using ADSI Objects" that we said you have to execute the object's **SetInfo()** method whenever you change any properties? Do you see the **SetInfo()** method listed above? Nope. And that's because a major problem with the [ADSI] type accelerator is that it doesn't pass in the object's methods—only its properties. You *can* still use the **SetInfo()** method, though:

```
PS C:\> $user.description = "Local Admin"
PS C:\> $user.SetInfo()
PS C:\> $user.description
Local Admin
```

It's just that the method doesn't show up in **Get-Member**, so you'll have to remember the method on your own. Basically, though, that's how you work with objects from the WinNT:// provider: Query the object, view or modify properties, and call **SetInfo()** if you've changed any properties. Use **SetPassword()** to change the password of a user object.

Although it isn't shown in the output of **Get-Member**, you can also use the **Get()**, **Put()**, **GetEx()**, and **PutEx()** methods we discussed in "Working with ADSI Objects:"

```
PS C:\> $user.get("description")
Local Admin
```

This isn't really useful with local computer accounts, since the object has direct properties you can access.

Here, you can see the WinNT:// provider being used to access an AD user named DonJ from the COMPANY domain (note that you have to use the domain's "short," or NetBIOS name, not its full DNS name):

```
PS C:\> $user = [ADSI]"WinNT://COMPANY/DonJ,user"
PS C:\> $user | gm


    TypeName: System.DirectoryServices.DirectoryEntry

Name                     MemberType Definition
----                     ---------- ----------
AutoUnlockInterval        Property  System.DirectoryServices.PropertyValueCollection...
BadPasswordAttempts        Property  System.DirectoryServices.PropertyValueCollection...
Description               Property  System.DirectoryServices.PropertyValueCollection...
FullName                  Property  System.DirectoryServices.PropertyValueCollection...
HomeDirDrive              Property  System.DirectoryServices.PropertyValueCollection...
HomeDirectory             Property  System.DirectoryServices.PropertyValueCollection...
LockoutObservationInterval Property  System.DirectoryServices.PropertyValueCollection...
LoginHours                Property  System.DirectoryServices.PropertyValueCollection...
LoginScript               Property  System.DirectoryServices.PropertyValueCollection...
MaxBadPasswordsAllowed     Property  System.DirectoryServices.PropertyValueCollection...
MaxPasswordAge            Property  System.DirectoryServices.PropertyValueCollection...
MaxStorage                Property  System.DirectoryServices.PropertyValueCollection...
MinPasswordAge            Property  System.DirectoryServices.PropertyValueCollection...
MinPasswordLength         Property  System.DirectoryServices.PropertyValueCollection...
Name                      Property  System.DirectoryServices.PropertyValueCollection...
objectSid                 Property  System.DirectoryServices.PropertyValueCollection...
Parameters                Property  System.DirectoryServices.PropertyValueCollection...
PasswordAge               Property  System.DirectoryServices.PropertyValueCollection...
PasswordExpired           Property  System.DirectoryServices.PropertyValueCollection...
PasswordHistoryLength      Property  System.DirectoryServices.PropertyValueCollection...
PrimaryGroupID            Property  System.DirectoryServices.PropertyValueCollection...
Profile                  Property  System.DirectoryServices.PropertyValueCollection...
UserFlags                 Property  System.DirectoryServices.PropertyValueCollection...
```

So, where are all the AD-specific properties, like otherHomePhone, and sn? Well, perhaps we could use the **Get()** method to retrieve one of them:

```
PS C:\> $user.get("sn")
Exception calling "get" with "1" argument(s): "The directory property cannot be found in
the cache.
"
At line:1 char:10
+ $user.get( <<<< "sn")
```

Nope. It turns out that the WinNT:// provider can't "see" any additional properties from AD; it can only see those properties that are backward-compatible with Windows NT 4.0 domains. So, when you're using the WinNT:// provider to access AD, you're giving up a lot of AD's extended capabilities.

Which brings us to AD's native provider, LDAP://. You'll retrieve objects in pretty much the same way as you did for the WinNT:// provider: Use the [ADSI] type accelerator, and provide an LDAP query string. Take a look:

```
PS C:\> $domain = [adsi]"LDAP://dc=company,dc=com"
PS C:\> $domain | gm


    TypeName: System.DirectoryServices.DirectoryEntry

Name                     MemberType Definition
----                     ---------- ----------
auditingPolicy            Property  System.DirectoryServices.PropertyValueColl...
creationTime              Property  System.DirectoryServices.PropertyValueColl...
```

```
dc                                Property  System.DirectoryServices.PropertyValueColl...
distinguishedName                 Property  System.DirectoryServices.PropertyValueColl...
forceLogoff                       Property  System.DirectoryServices.PropertyValueColl...
fSMORoleOwner                     Property  System.DirectoryServices.PropertyValueColl...
gPLink                            Property  System.DirectoryServices.PropertyValueColl...
instanceType                      Property  System.DirectoryServices.PropertyValueColl...
isCriticalSystemObject            Property  System.DirectoryServices.PropertyValueColl...
lockoutDuration                   Property  System.DirectoryServices.PropertyValueColl...
lockOutObservationWindow          Property  System.DirectoryServices.PropertyValueColl...
lockoutThreshold                  Property  System.DirectoryServices.PropertyValueColl...
masteredBy                        Property  System.DirectoryServices.PropertyValueColl...
maxPwdAge                         Property  System.DirectoryServices.PropertyValueColl...
minPwdAge                         Property  System.DirectoryServices.PropertyValueColl...
minPwdLength                      Property  System.DirectoryServices.PropertyValueColl...
modifiedCount                     Property  System.DirectoryServices.PropertyValueColl...
modifiedCountAtLastProm           Property  System.DirectoryServices.PropertyValueColl...
ms-DS-MachineAccountQuota         Property  System.DirectoryServices.PropertyValueColl...
msDS-AllUsersTrustQuota           Property  System.DirectoryServices.PropertyValueColl...
msDS-Behavior-Version             Property  System.DirectoryServices.PropertyValueColl...
msDs-masteredBy                   Property  System.DirectoryServices.PropertyValueColl...
msDS-PerUserTrustQuota            Property  System.DirectoryServices.PropertyValueColl...
msDS-PerUserTrustTombstonesQuota Property  System.DirectoryServices.PropertyValueColl...
name                              Property  System.DirectoryServices.PropertyValueColl...
nextRid                           Property  System.DirectoryServices.PropertyValueColl...
```

We've truncated the results a bit, but you can see that we've retrieved the domain object and displayed its properties—but not methods, because those won't be shown—by using the LDAP:// provider and the **Get-Member** cmdlet. We can retrieve the built-in Users container in a similar fashion:

```
PS C:\> $container = [adsi]"LDAP://cn=users,dc=company,dc=com"
PS C:\> $container | gm


   TypeName: System.DirectoryServices.DirectoryEntry

Name                   MemberType Definition
----                   ---------- ----------
cn                     Property  System.DirectoryServices.PropertyValueCollection cn ...
description            Property  System.DirectoryServices.PropertyValueCollection des...
distinguishedName      Property  System.DirectoryServices.PropertyValueCollection dis...
instanceType           Property  System.DirectoryServices.PropertyValueCollection ins...
isCriticalSystemObject Property  System.DirectoryServices.PropertyValueCollection isC...
name                   Property  System.DirectoryServices.PropertyValueCollection nam...
nTSecurityDescriptor   Property  System.DirectoryServices.PropertyValueCollection nTS...
objectCategory         Property  System.DirectoryServices.PropertyValueCollection obj...
objectClass            Property  System.DirectoryServices.PropertyValueCollection obj...
objectGUID             Property  System.DirectoryServices.PropertyValueCollection obj...
showInAdvancedViewOnly Property  System.DirectoryServices.PropertyValueCollection sho...
systemFlags            Property  System.DirectoryServices.PropertyValueCollection sys...
uSNChanged             Property  System.DirectoryServices.PropertyValueCollection uSN...
uSNCreated             Property  System.DirectoryServices.PropertyValueCollection uSN...
whenChanged            Property  System.DirectoryServices.PropertyValueCollection whe...
whenCreated            Property  System.DirectoryServices.PropertyValueCollection whe...
```

Notice anything similar about the container and the domain? They're both a "System.DirectoryServices. DirectoryEntry" object, even though they're very different objects. This is one of the things that make PowerShell's current ADSI support a bit complicated: PowerShell relies on this underlying .NET Framework class, "DirectoryEntry," to represent *all* directory objects. Obviously, different types of objects—containers, users, groups, and so forth—have different properties and capabilities, but this class represents them all generically. PowerShell and the Framework try to represent the object's properties as best it can, but it can't always show you *everything* that's available. This becomes especially apparent when you view the *untruncated* output of **Get-Member** for an AD user object:

```
PS C:\> $user = [adsi]"LDAP://cn=don jones,cn=users,dc=company,dc=com"
PS C:\> $user | gm


   TypeName: System.DirectoryServices.DirectoryEntry

Name                   MemberType Definition
----                   ---------- ----------
accountExpires          Property  System.DirectoryServices.PropertyValueCollection accou...
badPasswordTime         Property  System.DirectoryServices.PropertyValueCollection badPa...
badPwdCount             Property  System.DirectoryServices.PropertyValueCollection badPw...
cn                      Property  System.DirectoryServices.PropertyValueCollection cn {g...
codePage                Property  System.DirectoryServices.PropertyValueCollection codeP...
countryCode             Property  System.DirectoryServices.PropertyValueCollection count...
displayName             Property  System.DirectoryServices.PropertyValueCollection displ...
distinguishedName       Property  System.DirectoryServices.PropertyValueCollection disti...
givenName               Property  System.DirectoryServices.PropertyValueCollection given...
instanceType            Property  System.DirectoryServices.PropertyValueCollection insta...
lastLogoff              Property  System.DirectoryServices.PropertyValueCollection lastL...
lastLogon               Property  System.DirectoryServices.PropertyValueCollection lastL...
logonCount              Property  System.DirectoryServices.PropertyValueCollection logon...
name                    Property  System.DirectoryServices.PropertyValueCollection name ...
nTSecurityDescriptor    Property  System.DirectoryServices.PropertyValueCollection nTSec...
objectCategory          Property  System.DirectoryServices.PropertyValueCollection objec...
objectClass             Property  System.DirectoryServices.PropertyValueCollection objec...
objectGUID              Property  System.DirectoryServices.PropertyValueCollection objec...
objectSid               Property  System.DirectoryServices.PropertyValueCollection objec...
primaryGroupID          Property  System.DirectoryServices.PropertyValueCollection prima...
pwdLastSet              Property  System.DirectoryServices.PropertyValueCollection pwdLa...
sAMAccountName          Property  System.DirectoryServices.PropertyValueCollection sAMAc...
sAMAccountType          Property  System.DirectoryServices.PropertyValueCollection sAMAc...
sn                      Property  System.DirectoryServices.PropertyValueCollection sn {g...
userAccountControl      Property  System.DirectoryServices.PropertyValueCollection userA...
userPrincipalName       Property  System.DirectoryServices.PropertyValueCollection userP...
uSNChanged              Property  System.DirectoryServices.PropertyValueCollection uSNCh...
uSNCreated              Property  System.DirectoryServices.PropertyValueCollection uSNCr...
whenChanged             Property  System.DirectoryServices.PropertyValueCollection whenC...
whenCreated             Property  System.DirectoryServices.PropertyValueCollection whenC...
```

Active Directory Users and Computers uses a dialog box to display user properties, and it definitely displays more than these! For example, where is the Description property? Well, it turns out that the particular user we retrieved doesn't *have* a Description property—that is, it was never filled in when the user was created. So, the property isn't shown. We *can* set the property—provided we know the property name already, since **Get-Member** won't show it to us. We'll set the property, use **SetInfo()** to save the change, and then re-query the user to see if the property shows up:

```
PS C:\> $user.put("description","This is a test user.")
PS C:\> $user.setinfo()
PS C:\> $user = [adsi]"LDAP://cn=don jones,cn=users,dc=company,dc=com"
PS C:\> $user | gm


   TypeName: System.DirectoryServices.DirectoryEntry

Name                   MemberType Definition
----                   ---------- ----------
accountExpires          Property  System.DirectoryServices.PropertyValueCollection accou...
```

```
badPasswordTime      Property   System.DirectoryServices.PropertyValueCollection badPa...
badPwdCount          Property   System.DirectoryServices.PropertyValueCollection badPw...
cn                   Property   System.DirectoryServices.PropertyValueCollection cn {g...
codePage             Property   System.DirectoryServices.PropertyValueCollection codeP...
countryCode          Property   System.DirectoryServices.PropertyValueCollection count...
description          Property   System.DirectoryServices.PropertyValueCollection descr...
displayName          Property   System.DirectoryServices.PropertyValueCollection displ...
```

As you can see, the Description property now appears, because it has a value. This is an important caveat of working with ADSI in PowerShell: You can't rely on **Get-Member** to discover objects' capabilities. Instead, you'll need an external reference, such as a book like *ADSI Scripting: TFM* (SAPIEN Press), which lists *all* the available attributes for any given type of AD object.

## Searching for ADSI Objects

Sometimes you need to retrieve an object from Active Directory without knowing exactly where it is or what its FQDN is. PowerShell relies on the .NET Framework and the DirectoryServices. DirectorySearcher class. This type of object is used to find objects in a directory service such as Active Directory. Here's a sample function that uses the class to find a user object in Active Directory based on the user's SAM account name:

```
Function Find-User
{
Param ($sam=$(throw "you must enter a sAMAccountname"))
$searcher=New-Object DirectoryServices.DirectorySearcher
$searcher.Filter="(&(objectcategory=person)(objectclass=user)(sAMAccountname="+$sam+"))"
$results=$searcher.FindOne()
if ($results.path.length -gt 1)
    {
    return $results
    }
  else
    {
    return "Not Found"
    }
 }
```

You use the **New-Object** cmdlet to create the DirectorySearcher object:

```
$searcher=New-Object DirectoryServices.DirectorySearcher
```

The searcher will by default search the current domain, although you can specify a location such as an OU, which we'll show in a little bit. What you will need to do, however, is specify a LDAP search filter:

```
$searcher.Filter="(&(objectcategory=person)(objectclass=user)(sAMAccountname="+$sam+"))"
```

The filter instructs the searcher to find user objects where the *sAMAccountname* property matches that passed as a function parameter. The function calls the searcher's **FindOne()** method:

```
$results=$searcher.FindOne()
```

Assuming a user is found, the resulting object will be stored in $results. The script checks the length of the *Path* property of $results. If a user object was found, the *Path* property will be the user's distinguishedname and will have a length greater than 1. Otherwise, the user was not found and the function returns and error message:

```
if ($results.path.length -gt 1)
  {
  return $results
  }
  else
  {
  return "Not Found"
  }
```

Here's how you can use the function:

```
PS C:\> find-user jhicks

Path                                Properties
----                                ----------
LDAP://CN=Jeff Hicks,OU=IT,DC=MYCOMPANY,... {homemdb, distinguishedname, countrycode, cn...}


PS C:\>
```

The *Path* property shows the user's distinguished name. The *Properties* property is a collection of all the user properties. Here's another way you might use this function:

```
PS C:\> $user=find-user jhicks
PS C:\> $user.properties.description
Company admin
PS C:\> $user.properties.userprincipalname
jhicks@MYCOMPANY.LOCAL
PS C:\>
```

The results of the Find-User function are stored in the $user variable. This means we can access its properties directly, such as *Description* and *UserPrincipalName*. If you want to see all of user's defined properties, simply use:

```
PS C:\> $user.properties
```

You can also use the searcher object to search from a specific container and to find more than one object:

```
PS C:\> $Searcher = New-Object DirectoryServices.DirectorySearcher
PS C:\> $Root = New-Object DirectoryServices.DirectoryEntry `
>> 'LDAP://OU=Sales,OU=Employees,DC=mycompany,DC=local'
>>
PS C:\> $Searcher.SearchRoot = $Root
PS C:\> $searcher.Filter="(&(objectcategory=person)(objectclass=user))"
PS C:\> $Searcher.FindAll()

Path                                Properties
----                                ----------
LDAP://CN=Sales User1,OU=Sales,OU=Employees,DC=MYCOMPANY... {homemdb, distinguishedname, cou…
LDAP://CN=Sales User2,OU=Sales,OU=Employees,DC=MYCOMPANY... {homemdb, distinguishedname, cou…
LDAP://CN=Sales User3,OU=Sales,OU=Employees,DC=MYCOMPANY... {homemdb, distinguishedname, cou…
LDAP://CN=Sales User4,OU=Sales,OU=Employees,DC=MYCOMPANY... {homemdb, distinguishedname, cou…
LDAP://CN=Sales User5,OU=Sales,OU=Employees,DC=MYCOMPANY... {homemdb, distinguishedname, cou…
```

```
LDAP://CN=Sales User6,OU=Sales,OU=Employees,DC=MYCOMPANY... {homemdb, distinguishedname, cou…
LDAP://CN=Sales User7,OU=Sales,OU=Employees,DC=MYCOMPANY... {homemdb, distinguishedname, cou…
LDAP://CN=Sales User8,OU=Sales,OU=Employees,DC=MYCOMPANY... {homemdb, distinguishedname, cou…
LDAP://CN=Sales User9,OU=Sales,OU=Employees,DC=MYCOMPANY... {homemdb, distinguishedname, cou…
LDAP://CN=Sales User10,OU=Sales,OU=Employees,DC=MYCOMPAN... {homemdb, distinguishedname, cou…

PS C:\>
```

In this example, we create a new object type called a DirectoryEntry:

```
PS C:\> $Root = New-Object DirectoryServices.DirectoryEntry `
>> 'LDAP://OU=Sales,OU=Employees,DC=mycompany;DC=local'
>>
```

This object can be used for the *Root* property of the searcher object:

```
PS C:\> $Searcher.SearchRoot = $Root
```

Again, we're going to search for user objects:

```
PS C:\> $searcher.Filter="(&(objectcategory=person)(objectclass=user))"
```

Only this time, we'll use the **FindAll()** method to return all objects that match the search pattern:

```
PS C:\> $Searcher.FindAll()
```

## Working with ADSI Objects

You've actually already seen a quick example of working with AD objects when we set the Description property of our test user account back in the Using ADSI Objects section.

Here's how to change a password:

```
PS C:\> $user.setpassword("P@ssw0rd!")
```

Retrieve the object into a variable, and then call its **SetPassword()** method, passing the desired new password as an argument.

Creating new objects is straightforward: You'll need to retrieve the *parent container* that you want the new object created in, and then call the parent's **Create()** method. Doing so will return an object that represents the new directory object; you'll need to set any mandatory properties and then save the object to the directory. Here's an example:

```
PS C:\> $container = [adsi]"LDAP://cn=users,dc=company,dc=com"
PS C:\> $user = $container.create("user","cn=JefferyH")
PS C:\> $user.put("sAMAccountName","JefferyH")
PS C:\> $user.setinfo()
```

If you're familiar with VBScript, you may be thinking, "wow, this looks a lot like what we did in VBScript." It sure does—it's almost *exactly* the same, in fact. We'll present additional directory-related tasks in the "Managing Directory Services" chapter, but hopefully this gives you a quick idea of what

PowerShell can do with ADSI.

We should show you one more thing before we go on: Some AD properties, like WMI properties, are *arrays*, meaning they contain multiple values. For example, the Member property of an AD group object contains an array of FQDNs, with each FQDN representing one group member. Here's an example of retrieving the FQDN of the first member of a domain's Domain Admins group:

```
PS C:\> $user.setinfo()
PS C:\> $group = [adsi]"LDAP://cn=Domain Admins,cn=Users,dc=company,dc=com"
PS C:\> $group.member[0]
CN=Administrator,CN=Users,DC=company,DC=com
```

Modifying these properties is a bit complicated, since you have to use the **PutEx()** method, and pass it a parameter indicating if you're clearing the property completely, updating a value, adding a value, or deleting a value. The special parameter values are:

- 1: Clear the property

- 2: Change an existing value within the property

- 3: Add a new value to the property

- 4: Delete a value from the property

So, to add a new user to the Domain Admins group, which we've already retrieved into the $group variable, do this:

```
PS C:\> $group.PutEx(3, "member", @("cn=Don Jones,cn=Users,dc=company,dc=com"))
PS C:\> $group.setinfo()
```

We used the value 3, so we're adding a value to the array. We have to actually add an array, even though we only need to have one item—the user we want to add to the group—in the array. So, we use PowerShell's @ operator to create a new, one-element array containing the FQDN of the new group member. **SetInfo()** is needed to save the information back to the directory.

We hope this quick overview gives you a good start in using ADSI from within PowerShell. As you can see, the actual mechanics of it all aren't that complicated; the tough part is understanding what's going on inside the directory, including the property names that let you view and modify the information you need.

# Part II

# Windows PowerShell Scripting

# Chapter 13
# Scripting Overview

With many shells—particularly some *nix shells—using the shell interactively is a very different experience than scripting with the shell. Typically, shells offer a complete scripting language that is *only* available when you're running a script. Not so with PowerShell: The shell behaves exactly the same, and offers exactly the same features and functionality, whether you're writing a script or using the shell interactively. In fact, a PowerShell script is a *true* script—simply a text file listing the things you'd type interactively. The only reason to write a script is because you're tired of typing those things interactively and want to be able to run them again and again with less effort.

## Script Files

PowerShell recognizes the .PS1 filename extension as a PowerShell script. Notice the "1" in there? That indicates a script designed to work with PowerShell version 1; future versions of PowerShell will presumably be able to use that as an indicator for backward-compatibility. Script files are simple text files; they can be edited with Windows Notepad or any other text editor. In fact, by default, the .PS1 filename extension is associated with Notepad, not PowerShell, so double-clicking a script file opens it in Notepad rather than executing it in PowerShell. Of course, we're a bit biased against Notepad as a script editor: Notepad was certainly never designed for that task, and better options exist. We're obviously keen on SAPIEN PrimalScript (www.primalscript.com) because it offers a full visual development environment with PowerShell-specific support, such as the ability to package a PowerShell script in a standalone executable that runs under alternate credentials.

# Profiles

PowerShell supports four special scripts called *profiles*. These scripts are physically identical to any other script; what makes them special is that PowerShell looks for them when it starts and, if it finds them, executes them. Think of them as a sort of "auto-run" set of scripts, allowing you to define custom aliases, functions, and so forth. For example, by defining custom aliases in your profile, those aliases will be defined every time PowerShell runs, making your aliases available to you anytime you're using the shell.

PowerShell looks for profiles using a specific path and filename. It looks for them—and executes them, if they're present—in the following order:

- %windir%\system32\WindowsPowerShell\v1.0\profile.ps1
  This applies to all users and to all shells.

- %windir\system32\WindowsPowerShell\v1.0\Microsoft.PowerShell_profile.ps1
  This applies to all users but only to the PowerShell.exe shell.

- %UserDocuments%\WindowsPowerShell\profile.ps1
  This applies to the current user but affects all shells.

- %UserDocuments%\WindowsPowerShell\Microsoft.PowerShell_profile.ps1
  This applies to the current user and only to the PowerShell.exe shell.

........................................................................................

**By the way…**
%UserDocuments% isn't a valid environment variable; we're using it to represent the user's "Documents" folder. On Windows XP, for example, this would be under %UserProfile%\My Documents; on Windows Vista it's under %UserProfile%\Documents.

Notice the references to "all shells." In this book, we're primarily working with the PowerShell.exe shell. However, other shells exist: The Exchange Management Shell (which ships with Exchange Server 2007) is a different shell. So, if you have things you want defined in *all* the shells you use—such as custom aliases—you'd put them in one of the "all shells" profiles.

........................................................................................

**A Note on Shells**
Note that you don't *have* to use custom shells. For example, you don't need to use the Exchange Management Shell to manage Exchange Server 2007. Instead, you could simply add the Exchange snap-in to PowerShell.exe, using **Add-PSSnapIn**. Doing so would give you access to the Exchange cmdlets from the PowerShell.exe shell. This trick allows you to create a shell environment that has *all* the cmdlets you need to manage *all* your PowerShell-manageable products.

None of these profile files are created by default. You should also remember that these are *just PowerShell scripts*, so they won't run unless they meet your shell's execution policy—in other words, your profiles need to be signed if your execution policy is AllSigned.

# Scripting Basics

In the next several chapters, we'll cover the various elements of PowerShell scripting. These aren't necessarily covered in any particular order; that is, you don't necessarily need to know one thing before another thing. And keep in mind that everything we're covering related to scripting *works fine when you're using the shell interactively*. So, you can use everything we're about to show you even if you're not planning on writing scripts at all. Here's what we'll cover:

- Variables, arrays, and escape sequences, including associative arrays (also called dictionaries or hash tables). We've covered some of this information in earlier chapters, but a review will help you master these concepts, and we'll dive into a bit more depth with them.

- Objects, which are the basis of PowerShell's functionality. Again, we've touched on objects already, but now we'll take the time to completely define them.

- Operators, which allow PowerShell to manipulate and compare data. You've seen some operators in action already, but we'll be covering more operators, and in more depth, than we have previously.

- Regular expressions are a technique used for pattern-matching, and are often used to validate input—for example, making sure an e-mail address *looks like* an e-mail address.

- Loops and decision-making constructs form the bulk of PowerShell's scripting language, and allow your scripts to make decisions based on conditions you specify, and to repeat a given task over and over.

- Error handling is a key skill that allows you to anticipate and deal with errors that occur when your scripts run.

- The PowerShell Debugger provides a simple way to debug scripts by following their execution line by line and examining the contents of variables and object properties as you go.

- Finally, PowerShell for VB Scripters will introduce PowerShell using concepts familiar to VBScript developers. Think of this as kind of a "jump start" for using PowerShell, where you'll be able to leverage what you already know about VBScript to understand PowerShell more quickly.

# Scope

Now that you're going to begin working with scripts, you're going to run up against a concept called *scope*, which is very important in Windows PowerShell. So far, we've just been working interactively in the shell, which is referred to as the *global scope*. When you're just working interactively in the shell, *everything* occurs in the global scope, so it's like there's no scope at all.

However, when you run a script, PowerShell creates a new *script scope*, which contains the script. The script scope is a *child* of the global scope; the global scope is referred to as the script scope's *parent*. Some special rules govern interaction between the two scopes:

- The parent scope cannot see "inside" of the child scope.

- The child scope can *read* elements of the parent scope but can modify them only if a special syntax is used.

- If a child scope attempts to modify a parent scope element *without* using the special syntax, then a new element of the same name is created within the child scope, and the child scope effectively "loses" access to the parent scope element of that name.

*Elements*, in the above rules, refer primarily to variables and functions. So, to reiterate these rules in a variable-centric sense:

- The parent scope cannot access variables, which are defined in a child scope.

- The child scope can *read* variables defined in the parent scope but can modify them only if a special syntax is used.

- If a child scope attempts to modify a parent scope variable *without* using the special syntax, then a new variable of the same name is created within the child scope, and the child scope effectively "loses" access to the parent scope variable of that name.

When you create a function—either by defining it in the global scope or, more commonly, within a script—the function itself is a *local scope*, and is considered a child of whatever scope it was created in. Here's a quick example—we haven't discussed functions, yet, but this one isn't complicated so we hope it'll help illustrate this scope stuff:

```
$var1 = "Hello"
   1.    Function MyFunction {
   2.     Write-Host $var1
$var1 = "Goodbye"
   3.     Write-Host $var1
   4.    }
   5.    Write-Host $var1
   6.    MyFunction
   7.    Write-Host $var1
```

If you were to run this script, here's the output you'd see:

```
Hello
Hello
Goodbye
Hello
```

Why is this true? The first executable line in this script is the first line, which sets the variable $var1 equal to the value "Hello". Next, a function is defined—but not executed, yet. PowerShell skips over the function definition to line 7, where the contents of $var1 are displayed—our first line of output. Next, line 8 calls MyFunction. This enters the function, which is a child scope of the script scope. Line 3 displays the contents of $var1. Since $var1 hasn't been defined in this scope, PowerShell looks to the parent scope to see if $var1 exists there. It does, and so our second line of output is also "Hello". Line 4 assigns a new value to $var1. Because a scope cannot directly modify its parent's variables, however, line 4 is actually creating a *new* variable called $var1. When line 5 runs, $var1 now exists in the local scope, and so our third line of output is "Goodbye". When we exit the function, its scope is discarded. When line 9 runs, $var1 still contains its original value—the function never modified *this* $var1—and so our last line of output is "Hello" again.

Now take a look at this slight revision:

```
$var1 = "Hello"
Function MyFunction {
 Write-Host $var1
 $script:var1 = "Goodbye"
 Write-Host $var1
}
Write-Host $var1
MyFunction
Write-Host $var1
```

We boldfaced the one line we changed. This time, all four lines of output will be "Hello", because inside the function we've used the special syntax that allows a child scope to explicitly modify its parent's variables. There are four of these scope identifiers that PowerShell recognizes:

- $global: works with objects in the global scope

- $script: works with objects in the parent script scope

- $local: works with objects in the local scope

- $private: works with objects in a private scope

There's another technique, called *dot sourcing*, which impacts scope. Take a look at our original example script, this time with another modification:

```
$var1 = "Hello"
Function MyFunction {
 Write-Host $var1
 $var1 = "Goodbye"
 Write-Host $var1
}
Write-Host $var1
. MyFunction
Write-Host $var1
```

Notice how we're calling the function on the second-to-last line of code? We've typed a period, followed by a space, and then the function name. This is called dot sourcing, and it forces the function to run, not in its own scope but rather *right within the script scope*. In other words, when you run something—a script or a function—using dot sourcing, you tell PowerShell to forgo the step of creating a new scope and to instead run all the commands in the current scope. In this revised example, all four lines of output will be "Hello", because the function *runs in the script scope* where $var1 was defined. So, when the function tries to modify $var1, it's able to do so because $var1 exists in the same scope that the function is running in.

Dot sourcing is a useful trick. For example, you could write a script that does nothing but define a bunch of utility functions—that is, functions that do some useful tasks that you use from time to time (almost like cmdlets). By dot sourcing that script into the global scope, those functions become defined within the global scope, making them available to you just like a cmdlet or global variable.

We'll touch on scope more as appropriate in the following few chapters; if you're confused about it then, refer back to this chapter and walk through these short examples again to refresh your memory. Scope in PowerShell is actually a lot more expansive than we've covered here; our goal in this chapter was to introduce you to the concept, as it will impact most of your scripts. In the chapter "Scope in Windows PowerShell," we'll dive into scope in much more detail.

# Chapter 14
# Variables, Arrays, and Escape Characters

PowerShell's power lies in its ability to manipulate objects and command output, parameters, strings, variables, and more. By understanding how PowerShell accomplishes this, you'll be better prepared to manage your systems with PowerShell either straight from the command line or in a PowerShell script. If you're familiar with Microsoft Windows Cmd.exe shell, this power and flexibility will be new and exciting because PowerShell is an object-oriented shell, while Cmd is text-oriented, which makes it much more limited.

## Variables

Variables play a key role in PowerShell as they do in most scripting technologies. A *variable* is a place-holder for some value. The value of the placeholder might change based on script actions or intentional changes. In other words, the value is *variable*.

In VBScript, variables are typically set with string values. Consider the following code fragment:

```
Set objNetwork=CreateObject("wscript.network")
strUserName=objNetwork.UserName
wscript.echo "Current user is " & strUsername
```

The variable strUserName contains the string value that is returned from the Username property of the objNetwork object. It is often easier to use the variable strUserName instead of constantly calling objNetwork.Username. We can use variables in PowerShell the same way.

PowerShell variable names must begin with $:

```
PS C:\> $name="SAPIEN Technologies, Inc."
PS C:\> $name
SAPIEN Technologies, Inc.
PS C:\>
```

In this example, we have created a variable, $name, with a value of "SAPIEN Technologies, Inc." We can display the value of the variable by invoking the variable name. This variable will maintain this value until we close the shell or set $name to something else.

There are two important things to note in this example.

1. We never had to formally *declare* the variable.

2. We're not writing a script.

PowerShell allows variables to be used "within the shell" or *interactively* without requiring you to write a script. Variables used interactively stay in memory for the duration of the PowerShell session.

Variables can contain numbers as the following example demonstrates:

```
PS C:\> $pi=3.1416
PS C:\> [decimal]$R=Read-host "Enter a radius value"
Enter a radius value: 4
PS C:\> $Area=$pi*($R*$R)
PS C:\> Write-host "The Area of a circle with a radius of $R is $Area"
The Area of a circle with a radius of 4 is 50.2656
PS C:\>
```

The example is pretty straightforward. We begin by defining a variable called $pi. A value for the radius variable, $R, is set by calling **Read-Host**. We specifically cast it as a decimal type otherwise $R will be treated as a string, which would cause the mathematical expressions to not be properly interpreted. A variable, $Area, is set with the appropriate mathematical formula. Finally, we use **Write-Host** to display the results.

> **Note**
> If you've been coding VBScript for a while, you might get a little confused. PowerShell doesn't require any concatenation symbols like & or + to join strings and variables together. With PowerShell, you simply wrap anything you want displayed in quotes and type out the expression.

If we want to run this again, all we need to do is press the up arrow a few times to reset $R and rerun the **Write-Host** cmdlet. If you're thinking this is a cumbersome method to use variables and repeat code, then you're right! A better approach would be to create a function, which we'll cover in the "Script Blocks, Functions, and Filters" chapter.

We can also set a variable to hold the results of a cmdlet:

```
PS C:\> $proc500=get-process | where {$_.handles -gt 500}
PS C:\> $proc500
```

| Handles | NPM(K) | PM(K) | WS(K) | VS(M) | CPU(s) | Id | ProcessName |
|---------|--------|-------|-------|-------|--------|-----|-------------|
| 684 | 7 | 1680 | 4580 | 27 | 3.96 | 868 | csrss |
| 578 | 13 | 26112 | 38372 | 104 | 33.44 | 2024 | explorer |
| 680 | 76 | 12024 | 4896 | 114 | 4.39 | 3916 | Groove |
| 1926 | 54 | 47988 | 9536 | 187 | 39.28 | 1228 | iTunes |
| 541 | 12 | 15092 | 9892 | 91 | 79.01 | 1896 | Smc |

```
 1228      42   12900      19756   88   15.61  1860 svchost
 1141       0       0        220    2   23.15     4 System
  527      21    6716       3488   52    2.04   892 winlogon
PS C:\>
```

In this example, we create a variable called $proc500. The value of this variable is created by taking the object output of a **Get-Process** cmdlet and piping it to the **Where** cmdlet. The **Where** cmdlet (technically, **Where** is an alias to **Where-Object**) filters any process with a handle count that is less than or equal to 500 (that is, it "keeps" any processes with a handle count greater than 500). When you type **$proc500** at the next prompt, PowerShell displays the variable's contents in formatted output. It is important to remember that this is not a function or a cmdlet. The value of $proc500 is not reevaluated every time it is invoked.

However, the value of $proc500 is more than a collection of strings. In fact, it is an object that can be further manipulated. For example, if you run $proc500.count, PowerShell returns a value of 8, which is the number of processes in $proc500. We'll cover variables as objects in more detail later in this chapter.

PowerShell includes several cmdlets for working with variables that you can see by asking for help:

```
PS C:\> help *var*

Name                          Category              Synopsis
----                          --------              --------
Get-Variable                    Cmdlet               Gets the variables in the curren
New-Variable                    Cmdlet               Creates a new variable.
Set-Variable                    Cmdlet               Sets the value of a variable. Cr
Remove-Variable                 Cmdlet               Deletes a variable and its value
Clear-Variable                  Cmdlet               Deletes the value of a variable.
Variable                       Provider             Provides access to the Windows P
about_Automatic_Variables      HelpFile              Variables automatically set by t
about_Environment_Variable     HelpFile              How to access Windows environmen
about_Shell_Variable           HelpFile              Variables that are created and d
PS C:\>
```

## Get-Variable

Recall that you can get a variable's value by typing out the variable name. But what if you forgot the variable name? If you can remember at least part of it, you can use **Get-Variable** to list all matching variables and their values:

```
PS C:\> get-variable v*

Name                          Value
----                          -----
var                           9.42
VerbosePreference                SilentlyContinue

PS C:\>
```

In this example, we are finding all the variables that begin with the letter "v". Notice we didn't' need to use $v*. The $ symbol is used in conjunction with the variable name when used in the shell.

Run **Get-Variable \*** to see all the defined variables:

```
PS C:\> get-variable *

Name                      Value
----                      -----
Error                     {System.Management.Automation.ParseExce
DebugPreference              SilentlyContinue
PROFILE                    C:\Documents and Settings\admin\My
HOME                      C:\Documents and Settings\admin
Host                      System.Management.Automation.Internal.H
MaximumHistoryCount          64
MaximumAliasCount           4096
pi                        3.1416
input                     System.Array+SZArrayEnumerator
var                       9.42
StackTrace                    at System.Number.StringToNumber(Stri
ReportErrorShowSource        1
proc                      {csrss, explorer, Groove,..
ExecutionContext             System.Management.Automation.EngineIntr
true                      True
VerbosePreference            SilentlyContinue
PSHOME                    C:\Program Files\Windows PowerShell\v1.
ShellId                    Microsoft.PowerShell
false                     False
null
MaximumFunctionCount        4096
ErrorActionPreference        Continue
ConsoleFileName
ReportErrorShowStackTrace    0
r                         5
?                         True
PWD                       C:\
^                         get-variable
_
ReportErrorShowExceptionClass 0
ProgressPreference           Continue
MyInvocation                 System.Management.Automation.Invocation
args                      {}
MaximumErrorCount           256
Area                      13961.2704
WhatIfPreference            0


PS C:\>
```

You will recognize some of these variables from our earlier examples. However, note that variables such as MaximumErrorCount or PSHOME are PowerShell's *automatic* variables that are set by the shell. The following table lists these variables. Keep in mind that you should not create a variable that uses one of these default automatic variable names.

### PowerShell Automatic Variables

| Variable | Description |
| --- | --- |
| $$ | Contains the last token of the last line received by the shell. |
| $? | Contains the success/fail status of the last operation. |
| $^ | Contains the first token of the last line received by the shell. |
| $_ | Contains the current pipeline object, used in script blocks, filters, and the Where statement. |
| $Args | Contains an array of the parameters passed to a function. |

| Variable | Description |
|---|---|
| $DebugPreference | Specifies the action to take when data is written using write-debug in a script or WriteDebug in a cmdlet or provider. |
| $Error | Contains objects for which an error occurred while being processed in a cmdlet. |
| $ErrorActionPreference | Specifies the action to take when data is written using write-error in a script or WriteError in a cmdlet or provider. |
| $foreach | Refers to the enumerator in a foreach loop. |
| $Home | Specifies the user's home directory. Equivalent of %homedrive%%homepath%. |
| $Input | Use in script blocks that are in the middle of a pipeline. |
| $LASTEXITCODE | Contains the exit code of the last Win32 executable execution. |
| $MaximumAliasCount | Contains the maximum number of aliases available to the session. |
| $MaximumDriveCount | Contains the maximum number of drives available, excluding those provided by the underlying operating system. |
| $MaximumFunctionCount | Contains the maximum number of functions available to the session. |
| $MaximumHistoryCount | Specifies the maximum number of entries saved in the command history. |
| $MaximumVariableCount | Contains the maximum number of variables available to the session. |
| $PsHome | The directory where Windows PowerShell is installed. |
| $Host | Contains information about the current host. |
| $OFS | Output Field Separator, used when converting an array to a string. By default, this is set to the space character. The following example illustrates the default setting and setting OFS to a different value: &{ $a = 1,2,3; "$a"} 1 2 3 &{ $OFS="-"; $a = 1,2,3; "$a"} 1-2-3 |
| $ReportErrorShowExceptionClass | When set to TRUE, shows the class names of displayed exceptions. |
| $ReportErrorShowInnerException | When set to TRUE, shows the chain of inner exceptions. The display Of each exception is governed by the same options as the root Exception, that is, the options dictated by $ReportErrorShow* will be used to display each exception. |
| $ReportErrorShowSource | When set to TRUE, shows the assembly names of displayed exceptions. |
| $ReportErrorShowStackTrace | When set to TRUE, emits the stack traces of exceptions. |
| $StackTrace | Contains detailed stack trace information about the last error. |
| $VerbosePolicy | Specifies the action to take when data is written using Write-verbose in a script or WriteVerbose in a cmdlet or provider. |
| $WarningPolicy | Specifies the action to take when data is written using Write-warning in a script or WriteWarning in a cmdlet or provider. |

## Set-Variable

PowerShell has a specific cmdlet for creating variables called Set-Variable, which has an alias of Set. The syntax is as follows:

```
PS C:\> set-variable var "Computername"
PS C:\> $var
Computername
PS C:>
```

This is the same as typing **$var="Computername"**. This cmdlet has several parameters for which you might find some need. For one thing, you can define a read-only, or constant, variable:

```
PS C:\> set-variable -option "constant" -name pi -value 3.1416
PS C:\> get-variable pi

Name                    Value
----                    -----
pi                      3.1416

PS C:\> $pi=0
Cannot overwrite variable pi because it is read-only or constant.
At line:1 char:4
+ $pi= <<<< 0
PS C:\>
```

By using the **-option** parameter, we specified that we wanted the variable to be a constant. Once set, you cannot change the value or clear or remove the variable. It will exist for as long your PowerShell session is running. If you close the shell and reopen it, the constant no longer exists.

........................................................................................................................................

**Variable Already Exists**

If you've been following along with the chapter in your own PowerShell session, you may already have a variable called pi. If so, when you try to run the previous code, you'll get an error that an existing variable cannot be made constant. You can only set the constant option when the variable is first created. In this instance, use Remove-Variable to delete pi and try to run this code again. It should now work with no errors.

The **-scope** parameter allows you to define the variable's scope or where it can be used. Typically, you will set the scope to global, local, or script.

```
PS C:\>set-variable -scope "global" -name var -value 1
```

Although it is not required, you can create variables with additional parameters, such as **-option** and **-scope**. We also recommend that you use **-name** and **-value**, which help remove any ambiguity about your intentions.

Normally, you can assign the results of a PowerShell expression to a variable:

```
PS C:\>$stoppedServices= get-service |where {$_.status -EQ "stopped"}
```

However, if you want to specify additional **Set-Variable** parameters, such as its scope, then you need to the expression to **Set-Variable**:

```
PS C:\> get-service |where {$_.status -EQ "stopped"} | set-variable
-scope "global" -name StoppedServices
PS C:\> get-variable stoppedServices
```

```
Name                           Value
----                           -----
StoppedServices                 {Alerter, ALG, AppMgmt, aspnet_state,…
PS C:\>
```

## New-Variable

PowerShell does not have the equivalent of the VBScript **Dim** statement, nor is anything like it required in PowerShell. However, you can use **New-Variable** to explicitly define a variable. This cmdlet is almost identical to **Set-Variable**. You can specify the variable's scope and option as follows:

```
PS C:\> new-variable -option "constant" -name myZip -value 13078
PS C:\> get-variable myzip

Name                           Value
----                           -----
myZip                          13078
```

However, if you attempt to use **New-Variable** again to create the same variable but with a different value, PowerShell will refuse:

```
PS C:\> new-variable myZip 89123
new-variable : A variable with name 'myZip' already exists.
At line:1 char:13
+ new-variable <<<< myZip 89123
```

If you needed to change the variable value, you need to use **Set-Variable**. However, even that will not work in this example because myZip was created as a constant.

You might wonder how you will know when various cmdlets should be used. The answer is that it probably depends on what type of variables you are creating and how they will be used. For example, you may want to create all the empty variables you will need at the beginning of a script with **New-Variable**, and then use **Set-Variable** to define them as needed. Using different cmdlets may help you keep track of what is happening to a variable throughout the script.

## Clear-Variable

The process of retaining a variable while changing its value is straightforward:

```
PS C:\> $var="apple"
PS C:\> $var
apple
PS C:\> $var="orange"
PS C:\> $var
orange
PS C:\>
```

This example creates the variable, $var, and then sets it to a value. In this case, the value was set it to "apple." Changing the value to "orange" is just as easy. If for some reason you want to retain the variable but remove the value, you can use the **Clear-Variable** cmdlet:

```
PS C:\> clear-variable var
PS C:\> $var
PS C:\>
```

Notice we didn't need to use $var, just var. We also could have set $var="":

```
PS C:\> $var
orange
PS C:\> $var=""
PS C:\> $var

PS C:\>
```

···························································································································································

**Technically Speaking**
Technically, setting $var="" is not the same thing as using the Clear-Variable cmdlet. The cmdlet actually erases the value. The expression $var="" is really setting the value of $var to a string object with a length of 0. In most instances this shouldn't be an issue, but if in doubt, use Clear-Variable.

You can also clear multiple variables with a single command:

```
PS C:\> $var=1
PS C:\> $var2=2
PS C:\> $var3=3
PS C:\> get-variable var*

Name                    Value
----                    -----
var                     1
var3                    3
var2                    2


PS C:\> clear-variable var*
PS C:\> get-variable var*

Name                    Value
----                    -----
var
var3
var2

PS C:\>
```

In this example, we created variables var, var2, and var3. We used **Get-Variable** to display the values, followed by **Clear-Variable var\*** to clear the values of any variables that started with var.

The last item to understand about **Clear-Variable**, is that invoking **Clear-Variable** in a child scope has no effect on variables in the parent scope. In fact, this is typically true of most cmdlets. Refer back to the chapter "Scripting Overview" for a refresher on PowerShell scopes.

```
PS C:\> $var=3
PS C:\> &{clear-variable var}
PS C:\> $var
3
PS C:\>
```

The first line of this example is considered the parent scope. Using the ampersand character invokes a child scope and attempts to clear var. But as you can see, that cmdlet had no effect. Var remains untouched.

## Remove-Variable

When you want to remove the variable and its value, then call the **Remove-Variable** cmdlet. The syntax is essentially the same as **Clear-Variable**. You can remove a single variable:

```
PS C:\> $var="foobar"
PS C:\> $var
foobar
PS C:\> remove-variable var
PS C:\> $var
PS C:\>
```

Alternatively, you can remove multiple variables with a wildcard:

```
PS C:\> get-variable var*

Name                    Value
----                    -----
var                     5
var3                    980
var2                    78

PS C:\> remove-variable var*
PS C:\> get-variable var*
PS C:\>
```

# Environment Variables

Windows has its own set of environmental variables, such as %Path% and %Windir%. You can access these variables with the **env** provider in PowerShell. A *provider* acts as an interface between PowerShell and an internal data source. In this case, you can access the environmental variables that are stored in the registry. When accessing a variable in expression mode, you type **$env:*variablename***. Don't let this confuse you—we're just using the $ character to prefix the **env:** provider; PowerShell has a built-in variable, $env, which is pre-set to connect to the **env:** provider. Note the colon at the end of the provider name.

Here is an example of how to use the provider:

```
PS C:\> $env:systemroot
E:\WINDOWS
PS C:\> $env:path
E:\Program Files\Windows Resource Kits\Tools\;E:\WINDOWS\system32;E:\WINDOWS;E:
\WINDOWS\System32\Wbem;E:\Program Files\Support Tools\;E:\Program
Files\Common Files\Roxio Shared\DLLShared;E:\Program Files\Common
Files\GTK\2.0\bin;E:\Program Files\Windows Power Shell\v1.0\
PS C:\>
```

When used with a cmdlet, you only need to use just **env:** instead of **$env:**.

If you want to see all of the current Windows environmental variables in PowerShell, type:

```
Get-Childitem env:
```

This is the equivalent of the **SET** command in the traditional Cmd.exe shell. If you want the variables sorted by name use:

```
Get-Childitem env: | sort {$_.key}
```

# Variable Types

The fact that PowerShell is built on .NET gives it tremendous versatility that isn't always obvious. Keep in mind that any PowerShell variable can contain any *type* of data. This is true because *all* types of data such as strings, integers, and dates are .NET classes, which means they all inherit from the base class named Object. A PowerShell variable can contain anything that inherits from Object. However, as you saw in earlier examples with a string, PowerShell can tell the difference between different classes that inherit from Object.

You can force PowerShell to treat objects as a more specific type. When you do this, you are asking PowerShell to *cast* a variable to a specific type. We've already done this with the [ADSI] type, in the chapter "Using ADSI in Windows PowerShell." For a simpler example, take a look at this sequence:

```
PS C:\> $one = 5
PS C:\> $two = "5"
PS C:\> $one + $two
10
PS C:\> $two + $one
55
```

Here we give PowerShell two variables. One variable contains the number five, while the other variable contains the string character "5." This might look the same to you, but this is a big difference to a computer! Since we didn't specify what type of data these variables are, PowerShell assumes they are both the generic Object type. This caused PowerShell to decide it would figure out something more specific when the variables are used.

When we added $one and $two or 5 + "5," PowerShell said, "Aha, this must be addition. The first character is definitely not a string because it's not in double quotes. The second character *is* in double quotes but... Well, if I take the quotes away it looks like a number, so I'll add them." PowerShell's logic correctly gave 10 as the result.

However, when we add $two and $one, reversing the order, PowerShell has a different decision to make. In this case PowerShell said, "I see addition, but this first operand is clearly a string. The second one is a generic Object, so let's also treat it like a string, and concatenate the two." This PowerShell logic gave us the string "55," which is just the first five tacked onto the second.

But what about:

```
PS C:\> [int]$two + $one
10
```

This is the same order as the example that resulted in "55." However, this time we specifically told PowerShell to cast the generic object in $two as an Int or integer, which is a type PowerShell knows. So, it used the same logic as in the first example. It added the two to come up with 10.

You can force PowerShell to treat anything as a specific type. For example:

```
PS C:\> int = [int]$"5"
PS C:\> $int | get-member


  TypeName: System.Int32

Name          MemberType Definition
----          ---------- ----------
CompareTo     Method     System.Int32 CompareTo(Int32 value), System.Int
Equals        Method     System.Boolean Equals(Object obj), System.Boole
GetHashCode   Method      System.Int32 GetHashCode()
GetType       Method     System.Type GetType()
GetTypeCode   Method      System.TypeCode GetTypeCode()
ToString      Method     System.String ToString(), System.String ToStrin
```

Here the value "5" would normally be either a String object or, at best, a generic Object. However, by specifying the type [int], we forced PowerShell to try to convert "5" into an integer before storing it in the variable $int. The conversion was successful because we can see where we piped $int to **Get-Member**, which revealed the object's type: System.Int32.

Note that once you apply a specific type to a variable, it stays that way until you specifically change it. For example:

```
PS C:\> [int]$int = 1
```

This creates a variable named $int as an integer, and assigns it the value 1. The $int variable will be treated as an integer from now on, even if you don't include the type:

```
PS C:\> $int = 2
```

It is still using $int as an integer because it was already cast into a specific type. Once set up to be an integer, you can't put other types of data into it. Here's an example of an error because we tried to put a string into a variable that was already specifically cast as an integer:

```
PS C:\> [int]$int = 1
PS C:\> $int = 2
PS C:\> $int = "hello"
Cannot convert value "hello" to type "System.Int32". Error: "Input
string was not in a correct format."
At line:1 char:5
+ $int <<<< = "hello"
PS C:\>
```

However, you can recast a variable by reassigning a new, specific type:

```
PS C:\> [string]$int = "Hello"
```

That works fine, and $int will *now* be treated as a string by PowerShell.

PowerShell isn't a miracle worker. For example, PowerShell will complain if you try to force it to convert something that doesn't make sense:

```
PS C:\> [int]$int = "Hello"
Cannot convert "Hello" to "System.Int32". Error: "Input string was
not in a correct format."
```

```
At line:1 char:13
+ $int = [int]" <<<< Hello"
```

This occurred because "Hello" can't sensibly be made into a number. The next example is even more fun since it illustrates some of the advanced data types:

```
PS C:\> [xml]$xml = "<users><user name='joe' /></users>"
PS C:\> $xml.users.user

name
----
joe
```

Here we created a string, but told PowerShell it was of the type XML, which is another data type with which PowerShell is familiar. XML data works sort of like an object in that we define a parent object named Users, and a child object named User. The child object has an attribute called Name, with a value of Joe. So, when we ask PowerShell to display $xml.users.user, it displays all the attributes for that user. We can prove that PowerShell treated $xml as XML data by using **Get-Member**:

```
PS C:\> $xml | get-member


   TypeName: System.Xml.XmlDocument

Name                      MemberType      Definition
----                      ----------      ----------
ToString                  CodeMethod      static System.Stri
add_NodeChanged           Method            System.Void add_No
add_NodeChanging          Method            System.Void add_No
add_NodeInserted          Method            System.Void add_No
add_NodeInserting         Method            System.Void add_No
add_NodeRemoved           Method            System.Void add_No
add_NodeRemoving          Method            System.Void add_No
AppendChild               Method          System.Xml.XmlNode
Clone                     Method          System.Xml.XmlNode
CloneNode                 Method          System.Xml.XmlNode
CreateAttribute           Method            System.Xml.XmlAttr
CreateCDataSection        Method            System.Xml.XmlCDat
CreateComment             Method            System.Xml.XmlComm
CreateDocumentFragment     Method             System.Xml.XmlDocu
CreateDocumentType        Method            System.Xml.XmlDocu
CreateElement             Method            System.Xml.XmlElem
...
```

This demonstrates not only that variables *are* objects, but also that PowerShell *does* understand different types of data and provides different capabilities for them.

If you're curious about what object types are available, here's a quick list of more common types:

| | |
|---|---|
| Array | Bool (Boolean) |
| Byte | Char (a single character) |
| Char[] (Character array) | Decimal |
| Double | Float |
| Int (Integer) | Int[] (Integer array) |
| Long (Long integer) | Long[] (Long integer array) |
| Regex (Regular expression) | Single |
| Scriptblock | String |
| WMI | XML |

There are more types than those listed above. In fact, we'll be popping in with details on the other types as appropriate throughout this book. Some of them aren't frequently used in administrative scripting, so we don't want to arbitrarily hit you with all of them at once. Instead, we'll cover them in a context where they're used for something practical. Just remember that, unlike other scripting languages with which you may be familiar, a PowerShell variable can contain more than a number or string.

## Variable Precautions

One thing to be careful of is PowerShell's ability to change the type of a variable if you haven't explicitly selected a type. For example:

```
PS C:\> Write-host $a.ToUpper()
```

This works fine if $a contains a string, as shown here:

```
PS C:\> $a = "Hello"
PS C:\> write-host $a.ToUpper()
HELLO
PS C:\>
```

However, you'll get an error if $a was already set to an integer value:

```
PS C:\> $a = 1
PS C:\> write-host $a.ToUpper()
Method invocation failed because [System.Int32] doesn't contain a
method named 'ToUpper'.
At line:1 char:22
+ write-host $a.ToUpper( <<<< )
PS C:\>
```

This occurs because, as an integer, $a doesn't have a **ToUpper()** method. Since this type of error can be tricky to troubleshoot, you need to watch out for this when you're writing scripts that take input from other sources, such as a user or a file.

One way around it is to force PowerShell to treat the variable as the string you're expecting it to be:

```
PS C:\> $a = 1
PS C:\> $a = [string]$a
PS C:\> write-host $a.ToUpper()
1
```

```
PS C:\>
```

You don't necessarily need to select a type up front for every variable you use, but you should be aware of situations that can make a variable contain a type of data other than what you originally expected.

You should also take precautions with variable naming. PowerShell is pretty forgiving and will let you use just about anything as a variable name:

```
PS C:\> $$="apple"
PS C:\> $$
apple
PS C:\> ${var}=100
PS C:\> ${var}
100
PS C:\>
PS C:\> $7="PowerShell Scripting"
PS C:\> $7
PowerShell Scripting
PS C:\>
```

However, if you attempt to create a variable with anything other than a number or letter, PowerShell will complain:

```
PS C:\> $(j)="SAPIEN"
Invalid assignment expression. The left hand side of an assignment operator nee
ds to be something that can be assigned to like a variable or a property.
At line:1 char:6
+ $(j)=" <<<< SAPIEN"
PS C:\>
```

Using these types of variables names isn't very practical or recommended. Instead, you should use variable names that are meaningful to you. So, instead of:

```
PS C:\> $g=Get-Process
```

Use something like:

```
PS C:\> $Processes=Get-Process
```

It may require a bit more typing, but using meaningful variable names will definitely make it easier to troubleshoot and maintain your PowerShell scripts.

# Arrays

An *array* is essentially a container for storing things. For almost all administrative scripts, *simple arrays* will suffice. When you think about a simple array, picture an egg carton with a single row. You can make the egg carton as long as you want. With a simple array, you can put numbers, strings, or objects in each compartment. Multi-dimensional arrays exist, but they are beyond the scope of what we want to cover here.

**Array or Collection**

When reading technical material, you may also come across the term *collection*, which is a type of array that is usually created as the result of some query. For example, you might execute a query to return all instances of logical drives on a remote server using Windows Management Instrumentation (WMI). The resulting object will hold information about all logical drives in a collection. This collection object is handled in the much same way as an array when it comes time to enumerate the contents. For now, remember that when you see the term collection, think array. Or vice-versa; it doesn't really matter which term you use.

You can create an array by defining a variable and specifying the contents as delimited values:

```
PS C:\> $a=9,5,6,3
```

To view the contents of $a, all you need to do is type $a:

```
PS C:\> $a
9
5
6
3
```

The other technique you are more likely to use is the **ForEach** cmdlet:

```
PS C:\> foreach ($i in $a) {Write-host $i}
9
5
6
3
PS C:\>
```

This cmdlet looks inside the parentheses for what it should process. For every item in the parentheses, the **ForEach** statement does whatever commands are in the curly braces. In the previous example we used a variable name of $i. This example instructs the **ForEach** statement that for every $i variable in the $a variable, our array, it should echo back the value of $i.

When we run this command the first time, the cmdlet gets the first value of the array ($a) and sets it to $i. The cmdlet writes the value of $i to the console, and then runs through the array again getting the next array element, 5. This process is repeated until the end of the array is reached.

If you want to create an array with a range of numbers, you should use the range operator (..):

```
PS C:\> $a=2..7
PS C:\> $a
2
3
4
5
6
7
PS C:\>
```

To create an array with strings, each element must be enclosed in quotes:

```
PS C:\> $servers="dc1","app02","print1","file3"
PS C:\> foreach ($c in $servers) {$c}
dc1
app02
print1
file3
PS C:\>
```

If you used **$servers="dc1,app02,print1,file3"** then the only element of the array would be dc1,app02,print1,file3, because PowerShell only sees one set of double quotes. Therefore, there would be only one item to make into an array.

PowerShell arrays can also contain objects. Consider this example:

```
PS C:\> $svc=get-service | where {$_.status -eq "running"}
PS C:\> $svc

Status  Name             DisplayName
------  ----             -----------
Running AudioSrv         Windows Audio
Running Avg7Alrt         AVG7 Alert Manager Server
Running Avg7UpdSvc       AVG7 Update Service
Running AVGEMS           AVG E-mail Scanner
Running CryptSvc         Cryptographic Services
Running DcomLaunch       DCOM Server Process Launcher
Running Dhcp             DHCP Client
Running Dnscache         DNS Client
Running Eventlog         Event Log
Running EventSystem       COM+ Event System
Running IISADMIN         IIS Admin
Running iPodService       iPodService
Running lanmanserver      Server
...
```

We've created an array called $svc that contains all running services. We'll work with this more a little later.

When you work with individual elements in an array, the first important thing to remember is that arrays start counting at 0. To reference a specific element the syntax is *$arrayname[index]*:

```
PS C:\> write-host $servers[0]
dc1
PS C:\> write-host $servers[3]
file3
PS C:\>
```

You can use the length property of the array to determine how many elements are in the array:

```
PS C:\> $servers.length
4
PS C:\>
```

If you go back and look at the contents, you'll see that file3 is the last element of the array, yet it has an index of [3]. What gives? Remember to start counting at 0.

It's also easy to create an array from an existing source instead of manually typing a list of names. If you already have a list of server names such as Servers.txt, you could read that file with the **Get-Content** cmdlet and populate the array:

```
PS C:\> $Serverlist =get-content servers.txt
PS C:\> $serverlist
Seattle1
Vegas02
XPLAP01
PS C:\>
```

In this example, servers.txt is a simple text file with a list of computer names. We create the array $serverlist by invoking **Get-Content**. Invoking $serverlist merely displays the array's contents. Armed with this array, it's a relatively simple matter to parse the array and pass the computer name as the parameter for any number of commands:

```
PS C:\> foreach ($srv in $serverlist) {
>> write-host "Examining" $srv
>> #calling Get-WmiObject
>> Get-WmiObject -class win32_operatingsystem -computername $srv
>> }
>>
Examining Seattle1


SystemDirectory : C:\WINDOWS\system32
Organization    : MyCompany
BuildNumber     : 3790
RegisteredUser : MyCompany
SerialNumber    : 69713-640-3403486-45904
Version         : 5.2.3790


Examining Vegas02


SystemDirectory : C:\WINDOWS\system32
Organization    : MyCompany.com
BuildNumber     : 3790
RegisteredUser :
SerialNumber    : 69723-540-7598465-549822
Version         : 5.2.3790


Examining XPLAP01


SystemDirectory : C:\WINDOWS\system32
Organization    : MyCo
BuildNumber     : 2600
RegisteredUser : Admin
SerialNumber    : 55274-640-1714466-23528
Version         : 5.1.2600
PS C:\>
```

Using **ForEach**, we enumerate each element of the array and execute two cmdlets. **Write-Host** is called to display a message about what PowerShell is doing. Then we call the **Get-WmiObject** cmdlet to return operating system information from the specified server using WMI.

# $OFS

PowerShell has a special variable called $OFS which defines the Output Field Separator. By default this is a space. When you convert an array into a string, be default you will get something like this:

```
PS C:\ > $a="Jeff","Don","Chris","Alex"
PS C:\ > [string]$a
Jeff Don Chris Alex
```

However, what if you preferred to separate the values with a comma?

```
PS C:\ > $ofs=","
PS C:\ > [string]$a
Jeff,Don,Chris,Alex
```

Here's another way you might use this:

```
Function Get-LargeProcessList {
$ps=Get-Process | Where {$_.workingset -ge 50000000}

$ofs=","
$results=@()

foreach ($p in $ps) {$results+=$p.name + " (" +$p.id +")"}

return [string]$results

}
```

This function creates a variable of all processes where the workingset is greater or equal to 5000000 bytes:

```
$ps=Get-Process | Where {$_.workingset -ge 50000000}
```

The function defines a new Output Field Separator:

```
$ofs=","
```

It also defines an empty array object we'll use a bit later:

```
$results=@()
```

The function then goes through each item in the process collection and populates the $results array with the name and process id:

```
foreach ($p in $ps) {$results+=$p.name + " (" +$p.id +")"}
```

Finally, the function returns a string version of the results array:

```
return [string]$results
```

The end result is something like this:

```
audiodg (1420),avgrssvc (1236),csrss (816),dwm (3720),explorer (3856),firefox
(13480),GROOVE (4248),msnmsgr (3300),OUTOOK (7936),POWERPNT (12284),powershell
(29160),PrimalScript (30332),procexp (1136),SearchIndexer (2708),sidebar (1588)
spoolsv (1996),sqlservr (2204),svchost (1148),svchost (1216),svchost (1252),svchost
(1296),svchost (1604),svchost (172),svchost (2028),TabTip (3476),WINWORD (12204),
WmiPrvSE (19612)
```

# Associative Arrays

*Associative arrays* are special types of arrays. Think of them as a way of relating, or associating one piece of data with another piece of data. For example, they're useful for performing certain types of data lookup that we'll see in this chapter. You may also see associative arrays referred to as *dictionaries* or *hash tables*.

An associative array is a data structure that stores multiple *key-value* pairs:

| Key | Value |
|-----|-------|
| Don | Blue |
| Chris | Pink |
| Jeffery | Blue |

The *key* is usually some piece of well-known or easily obtained information, while the *value* is the data you want to look up. Keys are unique in the array, while values can be repeated as necessary. In our table example, the associative array keys are a person's name, while each corresponding value is the person's favorite color. Notice that the key names are unique while data values can be duplicated.

PowerShell uses the *hash table* data type to store the contents of an associative array because that data type provides fast performance when looking up data. What's really neat about associative arrays is that the individual values can be of different types. In other words, one key might be connected to a string, while another is connected to an XML document. This lets you store any kind of arbitrary data you want in an array.

## Creating an Associative Array

The @ operator is used to create an associative array as follows:

```
$aa = @{"Don"="Blue"; "Chris"="Pink"; "Jeffery"="Blue"}
```

This creates an associative array with three keys and three values, exactly as shown in the previous table. Of course, the values don't have to be simple strings. They can be numbers, the output from a cmdlet, or even other associative arrays. We'll take a closer look at this later in the chapter.

By the way, the @ operator can also be used to create a normal array:

```
PS C:\> $a = @(1,2,3,4,5)
PS C:\> $a
1
2
3
4
5
```

The difference is that only values were given to the @ operator; we didn't give it key=value pairs, so it created a normal one-dimensional array for us.

Want to just create an empty hash table so that you can use a script or other process to add data to it?

```
PS C:\> $ht = new-object System.Collections.Hashtable
```

## Using an Associative Array

You can display the entire contents of an associative array by calling its name:

```
PS C:\> $aa = @{"Don"="Blue"; "Chris"="Pink"; "Jeffery"="Blue"}
PS C:\> $aa

Name                    Value
----                    -----
Jeffery                  Blue
Chris                    Pink
Don                      Blue


PS C:\>
```

However, normally you'd want to access a single element:

```
PS C:\> $aa."Don"
Blue
PS C:\>
```

Type the associative array variable name, a period, and then the key you want to retrieve. PowerShell will respond by displaying the associated value. Note that keys and values, if the values are strings, can be contained in single or double quotes just like any other string. Keys are always expected to be strings, and so usually need to be enclosed in quotes.

However, the quotes can be omitted if the key doesn't contain any spaces, periods, or other word-breaking characters:

```
PS C:\> $aa.Don
Blue
PS C:\>
```

To check and see what data type a particular key's value is:

```
PS C:\> $aa.Don.GetType()

IsPublic IsSerial Name                           BaseType
-------- -------- ----                           --------
True     True     String                         System.Object
```

A single value within an associative array can actually be *another* associative array:

```
PS C:\> $aa2 = @{Key1="Value1"; Colors=$aa}
PS C:\> $aa2.Colors

Name                    Value
----                    -----
Jeffery                  Blue
```

```
Chris                   Pink
Don                     Blue


PS C:\> $aa2.Colors.Don
Blue
PS C:\>
```

In this example, a new associative array is named $aa2. It has two keys: 1) Key1, which has a value of "Value1"; and 2) Colors, which is assigned the associative array $aa we used earlier as its value. Displaying **$aa2.Colors** displays the entire $aa associative array, while **$aa2.Colors.Don** accesses a single key within the $aa associative array.

Let's take a look at a more practical example. First, we'll demonstrate that an associative array can contain just about any type of value:

```
PS C:\> $systems=@{"XPLAP01"=Get-WmiObject -class win32_computersystem}

PS C:\> $systems

Name                    Value
----                    -----
XPLAP01                     \\XPLAP01\root\cimv2:Win32_ComputerSy


PS C:\> $systems.XPLAP01


Domain             : myit.local
Manufacturer        : Dell Computer Corporation
Model              : Latitude D800
Name               : XPLAP01
PrimaryOwnerName    : Admin
TotalPhysicalMemory : 1609805824
```

Here we've created an associative array called $systems with a single element. The key is XPLAP01 and the data value is a WMI object representing an instance of the Win32_Computersystem class. Invoking just the array name displays the contents, which in this case is a single computer. If we want to see the value of the XPLAP01 key we use **$systems.XPLAP01**.

If the key name has a space you will have to use:

```
PS C:\> $myArray.'Test User'
```

Alternatively, you can use:

```
PS C:\> $myArray.['Test User']
```

If we know the name of a specific WMI object attribute, we can return its value with a command like this:

```
PS C:\> $systems.xplap01.totalphysicalmemory
1609805824
PS C:\>
```

This works because the value associated with key XPLAP01 is a WMI object. Therefore, we can use dotted notation to display a specific property value.

Let's add a second system to the array:

```
PS C:\> $systems.DC01=Get-WmiObject -class "win32_computersystem"
-computername "MYIT-DC01"
```

We can easily define a new key and value by setting the value for the new key using dotted notation. If you were to run **$systems.count**, it would return a value of 2. How did we know about the Count property? We asked. Pipe an associative array to **Get-Member** to get a complete list of an associative array's methods and properties.

Now that we have more than one item in the array, we can use the **Keys** and **Values** properties to get more than one key or value:

```
PS C:\> $systems.keys
DC01
XPLAP01
PS C:\> $systems.values


Domain            : myit.local
Manufacturer       : MICRO-STAR INTERNATIONAL CO., LTD
Model             : KM400-8235
Name              : DC01
PrimaryOwnerName   : ADMIN
TotalPhysicalMemory : 1073168384

Domain            : myit.local
Manufacturer       : Dell Computer Corporation
Model             : Latitude D800
Name              : XPLAP01
PrimaryOwnerName   : Admin
TotalPhysicalMemory : 1609805824
PS C:\>
```

Suppose we read a text list of computers and build the associative array. As we've shown, with this type of array, you can get the associated data by specifying the key.

However, if we want to enumerate the array and display only the computer's model as part of a hardware inventory, we would use code like this:

```
PS C:\> $keys=$systems.Get_Keys()
```

This code stores the keys in a yet another array called $keys. Technically, $keys is a *collection* that is basically a list. We can now use the **ForEach** cmdlet to iterate through the associative array:

```
PS C:\> foreach ($key in $keys) {write-host $key $systems.$key.Model}
DC01 KM400-8235
XPLAP01 Latitude D800
PS C:\>
```

There's a lot going on in this single command, so let's take it apart. We start with the basic **ForEach** cmdlet that says for each item in the $keys collection, set it to the $key variable. As we loop through, $key becomes DC01 and XPLAP01 and so on, assuming we had a larger array. Then for each pass, **ForEach** runs the code in the curly braces. The brace code calls the **Write-Host** cmdlet that displays the value of $key and the model property from the WMI object value of the corresponding key in $systems.

That last part can get a little confusing. Remember, the first time through the value of $key is DC01. So, $systems.$key.model is the equivalent of typing $systems.dc01.model. As we discussed earlier, $systems. dc01 returns the corresponding value that is a WMI Win32_Computersystem object. Since this is an object, we can get the model property value merely by asking for it. This process is repeated for every item in $keys.

In the traditional text-based shell, this type of coding would be complicated and involve a lot of string parsing and manipulation. However, because PowerShell works with objects, even if they are in arrays, we can manipulate the object and let PowerShell display the final results in just about whatever text format we want.

## Programmatically Modifying and Enumerating an Associative Array

Even though we haven't covered scripting, yet, we're going to use a script for a quick example—you can always refer back to this later, if you need it. What we want to do is create a new, blank associative array. Next, we want to retrieve a list of local logical disks and add each drive letter as a key to the array, and then add each drive's free space to the array. Finally, we then want to enumerate through the array and display all of that information. Here's the script:

```
$ht = New-Object system.Collections.Hashtable

# add drives to array
$drives = gwmi -query "SELECT * FROM Win32_LogicalDisk WHERE DriveType = 3"
foreach ($drive in $drives) {
    $ht.add($drive.deviceid, $drive.freespace)
}

# enumerate through array
foreach ($key in $ht.keys) {
    Write-Host "$key has..."$ht.item($key) "bytes free"
}
```

We started by creating a new, blank associative array, or hash table. We execute a WMI query (see the chapter "Using WMI in Windows PowerShell" for more information on that) to get a list of local drives (the DriveType restriction in our query eliminates network drives, removable drives, and optical drives). Then, we used the array's **Add()** method to add new elements, simply specifying the key and value as the method's arguments. To enumerate through the array, we chose to enumerate through its Keys collection. Each key is a single drive letter; we use the Item property, specifying the key we're interested in, to retrieve that key's value.

Removing a single key works similarly. For example, if we wanted to remove the C: drive from our array, we'd do this:

```
$ht.Remove("C:")
```

We just specify the key we want removed. The **Contains()** method tells us whether the array contains a particular key. For example, if we hadn't removed our C: drive, we could do this:

```
PS C:\> $ht.contains("C:")
True
```

Finally, the **Clear()** method completely empties the array so that we can start over.

# Escape Characters

In PowerShell, if you aren't executing a cmdlet, script, or executable, then you are displaying an *expression*. Remember from the "PowerShell Command-Line Parsing" chapter that PowerShell parses what you type in either *command mode* or *expression mode*. Numbers are treated as numbers and strings should be places in quotes. When you enter a string in quotes, PowerShell echoes it back to you:

```
PS C:\> "Hello, Reader"
Hello, Reader
```

If you don't use quotes, PowerShell assumes you are trying to execute something, so it generates an error:

```
PS C:\> Hello,Reader
'Hello' is not recognized as a Cmdlet, function, operable program, or
script file.
At line:1 char:6
+ Hello, <<<< Reader
```

You can also use **Write-Host** to echo what you've typed back to the console. See if you can spot the subtle differences in these two expressions:

```
PS C:\> write-host "Hello, Reader"
Hello, Reader
PS C:\> write-host Hello, Reader
Hello Reader
PS C:\>
```

In the first expression, the phrase "Hello, Reader" is written to the console screen exactly as you typed it into the expression. In the second expression, PowerShell is smart enough to figure out that Hello and Reader are both strings. However, it only writes back the two strings. Notice what's missing. PowerShell thinks the comma is a separator, so it writes back the two strings, which at first glance looks like the first expression. We think you'll be better served, though, if you use quotes for strings that you want to display. It will make it easier to separate text you have specified versus cmdlet results or expressions.

Occasionally you may want to display a *literal* value in a string such as the quotes. To accomplish this, you need to insert a special escape character, the backward apostrophe, before the quote characters so they are treated as literal values. The backward apostrophe is technically known as the grace accent but often referred to as a back tick.

```
PS C:\> write-host '"Hello', Reader'"
"Hello, Reader"
```

In this example, we also escaped the comma since that's part of the string expression and not a PowerShell character. You are more likely to use this technique with folder paths. If you try to run this:

```
PS C:\ > get-childitem program files
```

You'll get an error. Now, you could enclose the folder name in quotes, "program files", or you can use the escape character:

```
PS C:\ > get-childitem program` files
```

Which method you use is up to you. If you need something special, such as a beep or a tab, simply use one of PowerShell's escape characters shown in this table:

## Escape Characters

| Sequence | Result |
| --- | --- |
| `0 | (null) |
| `a | (alert) |
| `b | (backspace) |
| `f | (form feed) |
| `n | (new line) |
| `r | (carriage return) |
| `t | (tab) |
| `v | (vertical quote) |

To see how this works, open a PowerShell window and run the following command:

```
PS C:\> Write-Host `a
```

Depending on your computer's configuration, a beep should be emitted.

# Chapter 15
# Objects

An object is essentially a black box that has been designed by a developer to fill a certain need. The Microsoft Windows operating system contains hundreds of objects. From an administrative scripting or automation perspective, many of these objects can be exploited through scripting.

We've stressed many times that PowerShell is an object-oriented shell based on .NET. This means you will manipulate objects in the shell and in PowerShell scripts.

## Properties

All objects have properties. Some objects have more properties than other objects. The properties depend on the object. Consider an automobile as an object. For many people, an automobile is essentially a "black box." Many people don't fully understand how it works, but they do know how to use it. An automobile "object" may have properties such as model, color, horsepower, and maximum speed. These properties will have values such as Ferrari, red, 450, and 180.

Object properties that can be changed are called *read-write* properties. In the automobile example, the color property might be read-write because you can change the color of the car by painting it. Other properties that can't be changed by the user are considered *read-only* properties. In the automobile object example, horsepower and maximum speed are read-only properties because they can't be changed by the user.

## Methods

An object's methods are actions that the object can take. Depending on the object, some methods are executed from the object, while other methods are executed on the object, usually to make a change to the object.

Continuing with the automobile object, it may have an Accelerate method that makes it do something. Or it may have a ChangeTire method that makes a change to the object itself. Some methods can take parameters to fine tune what the method will do. For example, the automobile's accelerate method may require two parameters: 1) a start speed; and 2) end speed.

Generally, an object's methods and properties are specified using a dotted notation. Let's say we created a car object called objMyCar. We could set some properties using the dotted notation:

objMyCar.color="blue"

objMyCar.horsepower=300

objMyCar.MaxSpeed=120

Calling a method can be as simple as:

objMyCar.Accelerate(0,60)

This pseudo-command calls the Accelerate method of the car object with a start speed parameter of 0 and an end speed parameter of 60.

That's all fine with a metaphorical object, but you are probably wondering how this applies to things you care about, like WMI or file system objects. So, let's begin by discussing how you find out about the properties and methods of objects. One way is to review the online documentation from Web sites such as MSDN or by using solid reference books.

With the addition of .NET, PowerShell reflection can make this even easier. Now you can use the **Get-Member** cmdlet to ask the object what it can do and how it can be configured. Once you have a reference to an object, pass it to **Get-Member** through a pipeline:

```
PS C:\> $host |get-member


   TypeName: System.Management.Automation.Internal.Host.InternalHost

Name                   MemberType Definition
----                   ---------- ----------
EnterNestedPrompt      Method      System.Void EnterNestedPrompt()
Equals                 Method     System.Boolean Equals(Object obj)
ExitNestedPrompt       Method      System.Void ExitNestedPrompt()
GetHashCode            Method     System.Int32 GetHashCode()
GetType                Method     System.Type GetType()
get_CurrentCulture     Method      System.Globalization.CultureInfo get
get_CurrentUICulture   Method      System.Globalization.CultureInfo get
get_InstanceId         Method     System.Guid get_InstanceId()
get_Name               Method     System.String get_Name()
get_PrivateData        Method      System.Management.Automation.PSObjec
get_UI                 Method     System.Management.Automation.Host.PS
get_Version            Method     System.Version get_Version()
NotifyBeginApplication Method      System.Void NotifyBeginApplication()
NotifyEndApplication   Method      System.Void NotifyEndApplication()
SetShouldExit          Method     System.Void SetShouldExit(Int32 exit
ToString               Method     System.String ToString()
CurrentCulture         Property   System.Globalization.CultureInfo Cur
CurrentUICulture       Property   System.Globalization.CultureInfo Cur
InstanceId             Property   System.Guid InstanceId {get;}
Name                   Property   System.String Name {get;}
PrivateData            Property   System.Management.Automation.PSObjec
UI                     Property   System.Management.Automation.Host.PS
```

```
Version                Property  System.Version Version {get;}
```

PS C:\>

If you only want to see an object's properties, you can use **Get-Member -membertype properties**. You still may need to refer to documentation to fully understand what all the output means. However, at least you have an idea of what you're looking for when you read the documentation.

With a little clever coding, you can even see what the values are for a given property. This can often help when learning about a particular object:

```
PS C:\> $props=$host|get-member -membertype properties
PS C:\> foreach ($p in $props) {
>> Write-host "Property:" $p.name
>> $host.($p.name)
>> }
>>
Property: CurrentCulture

LCID            Name            DisplayName
----            ----            -----------
1033            en-US           English (United States)
Property: CurrentUICulture
1033            en-US           English (United States)
Property: InstanceId

Property: Name
ConsoleHost
Property: PrivateData

ErrorForegroundColor    : Red
ErrorBackgroundColor    : Black
WarningForegroundColor  : Yellow
WarningBackgroundColor  : Black
DebugForegroundColor    : Yellow
DebugBackgroundColor    : Black
VerboseForegroundColor  : Yellow
VerboseBackgroundColor  : Black
ProgressForegroundColor : Yellow
ProgressBackgroundColor : DarkCyan

Property: UI

RawUI : System.Management.Automation.Internal.Host.InternalHostRawUse

Property: Version

Major       : 1
Minor       : 0
Build       : 0
Revision    : 0
MajorRevision : 0
MinorRevision : 0

PS C:\>
```

In this example, we create a variable called $props that contains all the properties of the $host object. Next we use **ForEach** to enumerate $props, displaying the name of each property $p.name, and then displaying the value of each property with $host.($p.name). Putting $p.name in parentheses lets us create the equivalent of $host.version or $host.name.

## Variables as Objects

Earlier we mentioned that PowerShell variables are actually objects. In .NET, string variables are extremely robust and have a number of methods and properties. Take, for example, **Split()**, which is a method that takes a string and creates an array (or list) by breaking the list on some character such as comma or a space. Try this in PowerShell:

```
PS C\:> "1,2,3,4".Split(",")
```

This tells PowerShell to "take this string, and execute its **Split()** method. Use a comma for the method's input argument." When PowerShell executes this commend, the method returns an array of four elements, each element containing a number. PowerShell displays the array it in a textual fashion, with one array element per line:

```
1
2
3
4
```

There are other ways to use this. For example, PowerShell has a cmdlet called **Get-Member** that displays the methods and variables associated with a given object instance. Taking a string like "Hello, World", which is a String object, and piping it to the **Get-Member** cmdlet, displays information about that String object:

```
PS C:\> "Hello, World" | get-member
```

```
   TypeName: System.String
Name               MemberType             Definition
----               ----------             ----------
Clone              Method                 System.Objcct Clone()
CompareTo          Method                  System.Int32 CompareTo(Object v
Contains           Method                 System.Boolean Contains(String
CopyTo             Method                 System.Void CopyTo(Int32 source
EndsWith           Method                 System.Boolean EndsWith(String
Equals             Method                 System.Boolean Equals(Object ob
IndexOf            Method                 System.Int32 IndexOf(Char value
IndexOfAny         Method                  System.Int32 IndexOfAny(Char[]
Insert             Method                 System.String Insert(Int32 star
LastIndexOf        Method                  System.Int32 LastIndexOf(Char v
LastIndexOfAny     Method                  System.Int32 LastIndexOfAny
PadLeft            Method                 System.String PadLeft(Int32 tot
PadRight           Method                 System.String PadRight(Int32 to
Remove             Method                 System.String Remove(Int32 star
Replace            Method                 System.String Replace(Char oldC
Split              Method                 System.String[] Split(Params Ch
StartsWith         Method                  System.Boolean StartsWith(Strin
Substring          Method                  System.String Substring(Int32 s
ToCharArray        Method                  System.Char[] TSystem.Char[] To
ToLower            Method                 System.String ToLower(), Syste
ToString           Method                 System.String ToString(), Syste
ToUpper            Method                 System.String ToUpper(), System
Trim               Method                 System.String Trim(Params Char[
TrimEnd            Method                 System.String TrimEnd(Params Ch
TrimStart          Method                 System.String TrimStart(Params
Chars              ParameterizedProperty System.Char Chars(Int32 inde
Length             Property               System.Int32 Length {get;}
```

Even though this output is truncated a bit to fit in this book, you can see that it includes every method and property of the String. It also correctly identifies "Hello, World" as a "System.String" type, which is the unique *type name* that describes what we informally call a String object. You can pipe nearly *anything* to **Get-Member** to learn more about that particular object and its capabilities.

One of the most frequently used object variables is the $_ variable. We've used it repeatedly in our examples. $_ is an automatic variable that stands for the current object. Here's an example:

```
PS C:\> get-process | where {$_.workingset -gt 10000*1024}

Handles NPM(K)    PM(K)    WS(K) VS(M)   CPU(s)      Id ProcessName
------- ------    -----    ----- -----   ------      -- -----------
    604     14    23856    37308   112    32.26    2236 explorer
    114      5     6540    12380    52     3.12    2444 i_view32
    617     10    56252    52784   172     7.02     632 PS
    246      5     8672    12300    45     3.02    1512 MsMpEng
    201     12    11528    19400    71     1.24    3452 Skype
    198      6    26016    12816  1584     1.07     544 sqlservr
   1416     49    17768    26312   131     5.25    1556 svchost
    405     14    37140    58236   287   111.07    3900 WINWORD
```

This pipes the output of **Get-Process** to the **Where** cmdlet and only displays those processes where the workingset property of the current object ($_) is greater than 10240000. We use dotted notation to define the object and property: **$_.workingset**.

> ........................................................................................................................................
> ### How Did We Know That?
> The output of the Get-Process cmdlet is a System.Diagnostic.Process object. One of this object's properties is workingset. You can find the properties yourself by running:
> ```
> PS C:\> get-process | get-member -membertype property
> ```

Let's go back and look at the array of service objects we created earlier in this chapter. We used the following expression to create the object:

```
PS C:\> $svc=get-service | where {$_.status -eq "running"}
```

Since we know the array contains service objects, it might help to know more about these objects. Let's look at the first element of the array:

```
PS C:\> $svc[0]

Status   Name              DisplayName
------   ----              -----------
Running  AudioSrv          Windows Audio
```

We know the first running service in the array is Windows Audio. We're going to learn about this object using this service as an example, even if we're not interested in that specific service. We'll pass the first element of the array to **Get-Member** and display the object's properties.

```
PS C:\> $svc[0] |get-member -membertype properties
```

```
TypeName: System.ServiceProcess.ServiceController

Name                    MemberType    Definition
----                    ----------    ----------
Name                    AliasProperty Name = ServiceName
CanPauseAndContinue       Property      System.Boolean CanPauseAndCont
CanShutdown               Property      System.Boolean CanShutdown {ge
CanStop                   Property    System.Boolean CanStop {get;}
Container                 Property    System.ComponentModel.IContain
DependentServices         Property      System.ServiceProcess.ServiceC
DisplayName               Property      System.String DisplayName {get
MachineName               Property      System.String MachineName {get
ServiceHandle             Property      System.Runtime.InteropServices
ServiceName               Property      System.String ServiceName {get
ServicesDependedOn        Property       System.ServiceProcess.ServiceC
ServiceType               Property      System.ServiceProcess.ServiceT
Site                      Property    System.ComponentModel.ISite Si
Status                    Property    System.ServiceProcess.ServiceC
```

Not every property is necessarily populated, nor is it of interest. However, we want to show you where this information comes from and how it is connected to the object.

The easier way to learn property names is by sending the output of the array element to **Format-List**:

```
PS C:\> $svc[0] |format-list


Name             : AudioSrv
DisplayName      : Windows Audio
Status           : Running
DependentServices : {}
ServicesDependedOn : {RpcSs, PlugPlay}
CanPauseAndContinue : False
CanShutdown      : False
CanStop          : True
ServiceType      : Win32ShareProcess
```

As you can see, *everything* in PowerShell is an object, with properties and methods that you can use directly—you don't necessarily need a cmdlet to do everything, since many objects have their own built-in capabilities that you can call upon. If an object is stored in a variable, then the variable *represents* that object and has the same properties and methods as the object itself.

# Chapter 16
# Operators

As with any shell or scripting language, you need a set of operators to do stuff. You need to be able to compare objects, perform arithmetic operations, perform logical operations, and more.

## Assignment Operators

PowerShell uses assignment operators to set values to variables. We've been using the equal sign, but there are many other operators as well. The following table lists PowerShell assignment operators:

**PowerShell Assignment Operators**

| <u>Operator</u> | <u>Description</u> |
|---|---|
| = | Sets a value of a variable to the specified value |
| += | Increases the value of a variable by the specified value or appends to the existing value |
| -= | Decreases the value of a variable by the specified value |
| *= | Multiplies the value of a variable by the specified value or appends to the existing value |
| /= | Divides the value of a variable by the specified value |
| %= | Divides the value of a variable by the specified value and assigns the remainder (modulus) to the variable |

In addition to the traditional uses of =, in PowerShell this operator has a few extra bells and whistles that might be of interest to you. First, when you assign a hexadecimal value to a variable, it is stored as its decimal equivalent:

```
PS C:\> $var=0x10
PS C:\> $var
16
PS C:\>
```

You can also use a type of shorthand to assign a variable a multiple byte value. By using **kb, mb,** and **gb,** which are known as numeric constants, you store actual kilobyte, megabyte, and gigabyte values respectively:

```
PS C:\> $var=10KB
PS C:\> $var
10240
PS C:\> $var=2MB
PS C:\> $var
2097152
PS C:\> $var=.75GB
PS C:\> $var
805306368
PS C:\>
```

In the first example, we set $var to 10KB or 10 kilobytes. Displaying the contents of $var shows the actual byte value of 10 kilobytes. We repeat the process by setting $var to 2 megabytes and then .75 gigabytes. In each example, we display the value of $var. By the way, there is no numeric constant for anything greater than a gigabyte.

The += operator increases the value of a given variable by a specified amount:

```
PS C:\> $var=7
PS C:\> $var
7
PS C:\> $var+=3
PS C:\> $var
10
PS C:\>
```

The variable $var begins with a value of 7. We then use += to increment it by 3, which changes the value of $var to 10.

The -= operator decreases the value of a given variable by a specified amount. Let's continue with the previous example:

```
PS C:\> $var-=3
PS C:\> $var
7
PS C:\>
```

$var starts out with a value of 10. Using the -= operator, we decrease its value by 3, which returns us to 7.

What if we want to multiply a variable value by a specific number? This calls for the *= operator. Let's continue with the same $var that currently has a value of 7:

```
PS C:\> $var*=3
PS C:\> $var
21
PS C:\>
```

We can also divide by use the /= operator:

```
PS C:\> $var/=7
PS C:\> $var
3
PS C:\>
```

Finally, we can use %= to divide the variable value by the assigned value and return the modulus or remainder:

```
PS C:\> $var=9
PS C:\> $var%=4
PS C:\> $var
1
PS C:\>
```

In this example, we start with a $var value of 9. Using the modulus assignment operator with a value of 4 means we're diving 9 into 4. The remainder value is then assigned to $var, which in this example is 1.

You need to be careful with assignment operators and variable values. Remember PowerShell does a pretty good job at deciding if what you typed is a number or a string. If you put something in quotes, PowerShell treats it as a string. If you're not careful, you can get some odd results:

```
PS C:\> $var="3"
PS C:\> $var+=7
PS C:\> $var
37
PS C:\>
```

In this example, we think we set $var to 3 and increased it by 7 using the += operator. However, "3" is a string, so the += operator simply concatenates instead of adds, which is why we end up with a $var value of 37. If you are ever unsure about what type of object you're working with, you can use the **GetType()** method:

```
PS C:\> $var.gettype()

IsPublic IsSerial Name                     BaseType
-------- -------- ----                     --------
True     True     String                   System.Object


PS C:\>
```

One final comment on assignment operators: It is possible to assign values to multiple variables with a single statement:

```
PS C:\> $varA,$varB,$varC="Apple",3.1416,"Windows"
PS C:\> get-variable var?

Name                 Value
----                 -----
varC                 Windows
varB                 3.1416
varA                 Apple
```

```
PS C:\>
```

The assigned values are set to their respective variables. If you have more values than variables, then the extra values are assigned to the last variable:

```
PS C:\> $varA,$varB,$varC="Apple",3.1416,"Windows","Linux"
PS C:\> get-variable var?

Name                    Value
----                    -----
varC                    {Windows, Linux}
varB                    3.1416
varA                    Apple


PS C:\>
```

Our recommendation is to be careful with this type of statement because you can end up with unintentional variable values. PowerShell will wait, so set and modify variables one at a time.

## Arithmetic Operators

Arithmetic operators allow you to perform mathematical calculations with numeric values from variables or parameters. With these operators, you can add, subtract, multiply, and divide. You can then pass the result as a parameter to another process or cmdlet. The following table lists these operators.

**PowerShell Arithmetic Operators**

| Operator | Description | Example |
|---|---|---|
| + | Adds two values together. | `PS C:\> 5+4`<br>`9` |
| - | Subtracts one value from another. | `PS C:\> 134-90`<br>`44` |
| - | Changes a value to a negative number. | `PS C:\>-6`<br>`-6` |
| * | Multiplies two values together. | `PS C:\> 3*4.5`<br>`13.5` |
| / | Divides one value by another. | `PS C:\> 6/4`<br>`1.5` |
| % | Returns the remainder from a division. This is also known as the modulus. | `PS C:\Temp> 6%4`<br>`2` |

As you see from the examples in the table, results are not limited to integer values. In fact, you can obtain some pretty detailed results:

```
PS C:\> 3.1416*3
9.4248
PS C:\> 3.1416/12345
0.000254483596597813
PS C:\>
```

**Extra Credit**

In PowerShell, you also have access to the .NET Framework Math class. If you need more sophisticated mathematical operations such as square root or raising a number to a power, those methods can be invoked like this:

```
PS C:\> [system.math]::pow(2,16)
65536
PS C:\> [system.math]::sqrt(5)
2.23606797749979
```

See http://msdn2.microsoft.com/en-us/library/xaz41263.aspx for a full list of available methods for the Math class.

## Precedence

As you probably learned in elementary school, there is an order for evaluating arithmetic operators. Suppose you have an expression like 5+1/2*3. Would you be surprised that the answer is 6.5? Take a moment and look at the order of precedence:

- - (for a negative number)

- *, /, %

- +, - (for subtraction)

Expressions are evaluated left to right following the order above. So, when 5+1/2*3 is evaluated, 1 divided by 2 is first, which gives us .5. This value is then multiplied by 3, which equals 1.5. Next, 1.5 is added to 5 for a result of 6.5.

We use parentheses to override the precedence. In this case, (5+1)/(2*3) will equal 1. Parenthetical elements are evaluated first, and then the rest of the expression is evaluated. In the new example, 5+1=6 and 2*3=6, then 6 divided by 6 equals 1.

## Variables

Using arithmetic operators with variables is no different from using numbers, as long as the variable contains a number:

```
PS C:\> $var1="Windows"
PS C:\> $var2=100
PS C:\> $var1+var2
You must provide a value expression on the right-hand side of the '+' operator.
At line:1 char:7
+ $var1+v <<<< ar2
PS C:\>
```

In this example, we set two variables, but one of them is a string. When we try to use the + operator, PowerShell throws an error. Here is a valid example:

```
PS C:\> $var1=5
PS C:\> $var2=1
PS C:\> $var3=2
PS C:\> $var4=3
PS C:\> ($var1+$var2)/($var3*$var4)
```

```
1
PS C:\>
```

This is essentially the same example we used earlier, except that we substituted variables. Here's a more practical example:

```
PS C:\> $proc=Get-process
PS C:\> $total=0
PS C:\> foreach ($p in $proc) {$total+=$p.workingset}
PS C:\> $total
584568832
PS C:\>
```

This example gets the total number of bytes for all running processes allocated to processes working set. First we send the output of **Get-Process** to a variable and initialize the total variable to zero. We then use a simple **foreach** loop and add the working set size of each process object to the running total. Finally, we display the value of $total.

Since the value of $total is in bytes, we might want to display it in KB or MB:

```
PS C:\> $total/1KB
570868
PS C:\> $total/1MB
557.48828125
PS C:\>
```

Be careful when trying to mix numbers and text, such as when using **Write-Host**. This cmdlet will expand variables but not perform any arithmetic operations:

```
PS C:\> write-host "Total working set size="$total/1KB "KB"
Total working set size= 584568832/1KB KB

PS C:\>
```

That's not really what we're after. By enclosing $total/1024 in parenthesis, the expression is evaluated and written to the screen as expected:

```
PS C:\> write-host "Total working set size="($total/1KB) "KB"
Total working set size= 570868 KB
PS C:\> write-host "Total working set size="($total/1MB) "MB"
Total working set size= 557.48828125 MB
PS C:\>
```

## Unary Operators

A subtype of the arithmetic operator is a unary operator, which is used to increment or decrement a variable's value. PowerShell uses ++ to increase a value by one and to decrease it:

```
PS C:\> $var=10
PS C:\> $var++
PS C:\> $var
11
PS C:\> $var--
PS C:\> $var
```

```
10
PS C:\>
```

$var starts with a value of 10. Using the ++ operator doesn't appear to do anything, but it actually increased the value of $var by 1. Using the - operator decreases the value by 1.

## Logical Operators

PowerShell logical operators are used to test or validate an expression. Typically, the result of these operations is TRUE or FALSE. Here are the operators:

### PowerShell Logical Operators

| Operator | Description | Example |
|---|---|---|
| -and | All expressions must evaluate as TRUE. | (1 -eq 1) -and (2 -eq 2) returns TRUE |
| -or | At least one expression must evaluate as TRUE. | (1 -eq 1) -or (2 -eq 4) returns TRUE |
| -not | Evaluates the inverse of one of the expressions. | (1 -eq 1) -and -not (2 -gt 2) returns TRUE |
| ! | The same as -not. | (1 -eq 1) -and ! (2 -gt 2) returns TRUE |

Logical operators should be used when you want to evaluate multiple conditions. While you can evaluate several expressions, your scripts and code will be easier to debug or troubleshoot if you limit the operation to two expressions:

```
PS C:\> $varA=5
PS C:\> $varB=5
PS C:\> if (($varA -eq $varB) -and ($varB -gt 20))
>>{
>>Write-Host "Both conditions are true."
>>}
>>else
>>{
>>Write-Host "One or both conditions are false."
>>}
>>
One or both conditions are false.
PS C:\>
```

Here's the same example using -**or**:

```
PS C:\> if (($varA -eq $varB) -or ($varB -gt 20))
>> {
>> Write-Host "At least one condition is true."
>> }
>> else
>> {
>> Write-Host "Both conditions are false."
>> }
>>
At least one condition is true.
PS C:\>
```

We get a different result if we change $varA to 20:

```
PS C:\> $varA=20
PS C:\> if (($varA -eq $varB) -or ($varB -gt 20))
>> {
>> Write-Host "At least one condition is true."
>> }
>> else
>> {
>> Write-Host "Both conditions are false."
>> }
>>
Both conditions are false.
PS C:\>
```

# Bitwise Operators

If you find yourself needing binary or bitwise operations, PowerShell has the requisite operators as shown:

## PowerShell Bitwise Operators

| Operator | Definition |
|----------|------------|
| -band    | binary and |
| -bor     | binary or  |
| -bnot    | binary not |

The underlying binary math is beyond the scope of this book. However, here are some examples if you need to perform a bitwise comparison:

```
PS C:\> 255 -band 255
255
PS C:\> 255 -band 150
150
PS C:\> 32 -bor 16
48
PS C:\>
```

In each case, the value that is returned from the comparison is the digital equivalent of the underlying bitwise operation.

# Special Operators

PowerShell has several special operators that are capable of specialized tasks that can't be easily accomplished any other way.

## Replace Operator

The -**replace** operator can be used to substitute characters in a string. The operator essentially uses pattern matching to find a target string or character. If it is found, the substitution is made. The -**replace** syntax is:

```
"String-to-search" -replace "Search-for","Replace-with"
```

You can search and replace a single character or part of a word:

```
PS C:\> "PowerShell" -replace "e","3"
Pow3rSh3ll
PS C:\> "PowerShell" -replace "shell","tool"
Powertool
PS C:\> "PowerShell" -replace "k","m"
PowerShell
PS C:\>
```

In the first example, all instances of the letter e are replaced with the number 3. In the second, the string "shell" is replaced with "tool". The last example shows that if no successful match is made, the string remains untouched. You can use the **-replace** operator with variables, but be careful:

```
PS C:\> $var="PowerShell"
PS C:\> $var -replace "p","sh"
showerShell
PS C:\> $var
PowerShell
PS C:\>
```

The **-replace** operator doesn't change the original variable—instead, it only displays the replaced result. When we look at $var again, we see it hasn't changed. If you want to change the variable value, you should use something like this:

```
PS C:\> $var=$var -replace "p","sh"
PS C:\> $var
showerShell
PS C:\>
```

All we need to do is redefine $var by setting its value to the output of the **-replace** operation. The operator can also make replacements within collections and arrays:

```
PS C:\> $var=@("aaa","bbb","abab","ccc")
PS C:\> $var
aaa
bbb
abab
ccc
PS C:\> $var=$var -replace "a","z"
PS C:\> $var
zzz
bbb
zbzb
ccc
PS C:\>
```

We start with a simple array, then redefine $var using the **-replace** operator to change all occurrences of a to z.

There's really no limit when using this operator. You can even use it to make changes to text files:

```
PS C:\> $var=get-content "boot.ini"
PS C:\> $var -replace "windows","WIN"
[boot loader]
timeout=15
default=multi(0)disk(0)rdisk(0)partition(2)\WIN
[operating systems]
multi(0)disk(0)rdisk(0)partition(2)\WIN="Microsoft WIN XP
```

```
Professional" /fastdetect /NoExecute=OptIn
multi(0)disk(0)rdisk(0)partition(1)\WIN="WIN Server 2003, Enterprise"
/noexecute=optout /fastdetect
C:\CMDCONS\BOOTSECT.DAT="Microsoft WIN Recovery Console" /cmdcons
PS C:\>
```

Here we dumped the contents of our boot.ini file to $var and then replaced all instances of "Windows" with "WIN". Granted, this may not be the best production-oriented example, but it demonstrates the point.

Keep in mind that the **-replace** operator is case-insensitive. However, if you want to use this operator to make a case-sensitive search and replace, you can use the -**creplace** operator. The next table lists the replace special operators.

### PowerShell Replace Operators

| Operator | Definition | Example |
|---|---|---|
| -replace | Replace. | "PowerShell" -replace "s","$" |
| -ireplace | Case-insensitive replace. Essentially the same as -replace. | "PowerShell" -replace "s","$" |
| -creplace | Case-sensitive replace. | "PowerShell" -creplace "p","t" |

When using -**creplace**, the replacement is only made when a case-sensitive match is made:

```
PS C:\> "PowerShell" -creplace "p","t"
PowerShell
PS C:\> "PowerShell" -creplace "P","t"
towerShell
PS C:\>
```

In the first example, since no lower case "p" is found, no replacement is made. However, in the second example a match is made, so the operator replaces "P" with "t".

In the "Regular Expressions" chapter, we will discuss how you can also use regular expressions for matching and replacing.

## Type

If you've been following along, by now you surely know that PowerShell is an object-oriented shell. As such, we may need to check if a variable is a particular type of object. PowerShell includes three type operators, as shown:

### PowerShell Type Operators

| Operator | Definition | Example |
|---|---|---|
| -is | Checks if object IS a specific type. | $var -is [string] |
| -isnot | Checks if object IS NOT a specific type. | $var -isnot [string] |
| -as | Converts object to specified type. | 3.1416 -as string |

The operation result will be either TRUE or FALSE for -**is** and -**isnot**.

```
PS C:\> $now=get-date
PS C:\> $now -is [datetime]
True
PS C:\> 1024 -is [int]
True
PS C:\> "Microsoft" -isnot [string]
False
PS C:\>
```

In the first example, we create the variable $now from the output of the **Get-Date** cmdlet. Now we can use **-is** to validate that it is DateTime object. We do the same thing by verifying that 1024 is an integer. Both operations return TRUE. In the last example, we checked to see if "Microsoft" is not a string. Since it is a strong, the operation returns FALSE.

The **-as** operator converts the object to the specified type:

```
PS C:\> $var=get-date
PS C:\> $var.gettype()

IsPublic IsSerial Name                                BaseType
-------- -------- ----                                --------
True     True     DateTime                            System.ValueType


PS C:\> if ($var -isnot [string]) {
>> $var=$var -as [string]
>> $var.gettype()
>> $var.PadLeft(25)
>> }
>>

IsPublic IsSerial Name                                BaseType
-------- -------- ----                                --------
True     True     String                              System.Object
    5/21/2006 7:53:02 PM
PS C:\>
```

In this example, we created a DateTime object. To do this, we called the **GetType()** method to show we have nothing hidden up our sleeves. However, we want to call the Padleft method of the string object. We check to see if $var is not a string. If so, then we use the **-as** operator to recreate $var as a string object. Again, we call **GetType()** to show the successful change and finally the **Padleft()** method.

........................................................................................................................

**ToString**
It is easier to convert an object to a string by using the **ToString()** method. Most objects have this method. The end result is essentially the same as using the -as operator.

## Range Operator (..)

The Range operator (..) is used to indicate a range of values. Keep in mind that you must specify the beginning and end points of the range:

```
PS C:\> $var=@(1..5)
PS C:\> $var
1
2
```

```
3
4
5
PS C:\>
```

Here, we created an array variable whose contents are 1 through 5 inclusive. The range operator only works with integer values. If you try this with string characters, PowerShell will complain:

```
PS C:\> $var=@("a".."j")
Cannot convert value "a" to type "System.Int32". Error: "Input string
was not in a correct format."
At line:1 char:13
+ $var=@("a".." <<<< j")
PS C:\>
```

## Call Operators (&)

Call operators are used when you want to execute a command. Sometimes PowerShell can't tell if what you typed is a command. To force PowerShell to execute a statement, use the ampersand (&) character. For example, we might want to execute all PowerShell scripts in the current directory:

```
PS C:\> $all=get-childitem *.ps1
PS C:\> foreach ($s in $all) {&$s}
PS C:\> #each Powershell script executes
```

You can also use the call operator to create a variable that holds the results of a cmdlet:

```
PS C:\> $j=get-process | where {$_.workingset -gt 5000000}
PS C:\> &$j
PS C:\> #an array of all processes with a workingset size greater than 5000 is returned.
```

In this example, when we force $j to run the output is little unfriendly. We can get a nicer output from $j using a command like this:

```
PS C:\> foreach ($item in $j) {$item.name}
```

In both of these examples, the variable we are creating is the output of the cmdlet we ran. In a significant manner, this is slightly different than the following:

```
PS C:\> $j="get-process"
PS C:\> $j
get-process
PS C:\> &$j | where {$_.workingset -gt 5000000}

Handles NPM(K)    PM(K)      WS(K) VM(M)   CPU(s)      Id ProcessName
------- ------    -----      ----- -----   ------      -- -----------
    209      6     3696       6768    56    25.65     416 avgcc
    873     21    34840      16820   161 1,282.25    1256 explorer
   1056     24    97188     116708   464   247.16    4972 firefox
    806     81    16636      21764   143    17.18    5264 Groove
    659     20    28224       5284   264    75.64    1488 iexplore
    234     10    10912       6116    68    17.09    1420 mmc
    251      5     9308       4920    47   251.73    1552 MsMpEng
     63      3     1696       5604    37     0.54    1372 notepad
```

```
1772    69  112832    31536  712   200.94  2304  OUTLOOK
 553    11   49156    48388  163     7.16   532  powershell
 393    61   15164     9952   89    94.55   596  Skype
 559    12   16192    12808   97  5,118.91  1676  Smc
 298    13   14816     6464   88   177.96   576  StatBar
1549    51   24640    15220  166   366.55  1596  svchost
 351    30   14612   551216  653  3,497.73  5412  vmware-vmx
 446    17   33656    53764  282    25.21  2600  WINWORD
 592    21   21564    15984  106    11.52  4636  wmplayer

PS C:\>
```

In this instance, we set $j to a string of a cmdlet name. When we use the call operator, the value of $j is evaluated and executed. Notice that we added our workingset filter to the line where $j is executed. This is because the $_ variable doesn't exist until the cmdlet is run. All we've really done here is essentially create another alias for the **Get-Process** cmdlet.

Don't get too hung up on this operator. The only time you are likely to use it is when calling a PowerShell command from outside of PowerShell:

```
C:\powershell &c:\scripts\showservices.ps1
```

This command is run from a Windows Cmd.exe prompt. Using the **&** operator tells PowerShell to execute c:\scripts\showservices.ps1. This is one way you can integrate your PowerShell scripts into your Windows Cmd.exe environment.

## Format Operator (-f)

The PowerShell format operator (-f) let's you format strings using the .NET string object format method. The syntax is a little backwards compared to what we worked with so far:

```
PS C:\ > FormatString -f "string to format"
```

.NET formatting is a way of specifying the format of a particular object. For example, a DateTime object could be formatted as a short date (5/22/2007) or a long date (Monday, May 22, 2007). You can format a number as currency, number, or percent. To get the most out of this operator, you need to become very familiar with .NET formatting, most of which is outside the scope of this book. However, we'll provide a few examples that you will find useful.

```
PS C:\ > $now=get-date
PS C:\> $now

Monday, May 22, 2007 1:10:59 PM
PS C:\> "{0:d}" -f $now
5/22/2007
PS C:\> "{0:D}" -f $now
Monday, May 22, 2007
PS C:\> "{0:t}" -f $now
1:10 PM
PS C:\> "{0:T}" -f $now
1:10:59 PM
PS C:\>
```

In this example, we created the variable $now that holds the current date and time. We can format this variable in a number of ways. First, we can use the format pattern {0:d} to display $now as a short date. Alternatively, we can use {0:D} to format $now as a long date. This is another example where PowerShell is case-sensitive. Using {0:t} or {0:T} will format for short or long time, respectively. Let's look at the examples of numeric formatting that are included below.

```
PS C:\> $var=12345.6789
PS C:\> "{0:N}" -f $var
12,345.68
PS C:\> "{0:N3}" -f $var
12,345.679
PS C:\> "{0:F}" -f $var
12345.68
PS C:\> "{0:F3}" -f $var
12345.679
PS C:\>
```

The numeric variable is being formatted in these examples. In the first example, the formatting patter {0:N} formats the variable as a number with a thousands separator. The default for this formatter for most English language systems is to specify two decimal places. This can be changed by using a precision modifier. In the second example, {0:N3} instructs PowerShell to format $var as a number to three decimal places. Using the F formatting string tells PowerShell to format the number in a fixed format. {0:F} is practically the same as {0:N}, except there is no thousands separator. We can also specify a precision modifier, such as {0:F3}, to control the number of decimals. Here's a practical example:

```
PS C:\> $proc=get-process | where {$_.workingset -gt 5000000}
PS C:\> foreach ($p in $proc) {
>> $ws="{0:N4}" -f ($p.workingset/1MB)
>> write-host $p.name 't $ws "MB"
>> }
>> $n=get-date
>> $d="{0:T}" -f $n
>> write-host "run at" $d
>>
avgcc    6.8984 MB
avgemc   17.5781 MB
explorer       32.0117 MB
firefox        216.0430 MB
Groove   11.1250 MB
iexplore       76.4063 MB
MsMpEng        5.0898 MB
powershell     21.6094 MB
Skype    11.8594 MB
Smc      9.3828 MB
StatBar        6.7344 MB
svchost        30.1836 MB
THUNDE~1       49.9141 MB
WINWORD        54.8281 MB
wmplayer       17.7539 MB
wuauclt        19.0352 MB
run at 10:07:47 PM
PS C:\>
```

In this example, we looped through $proc and displayed the process name, set its workingset size in MB to four decimal places, and end with a time stamp. You will find it easier to create new variables when formatting. In the example below, we create $ws as the value of the working set size divided by 1MB and formatted to four decimal places:

```
$ws="{0:N4}" -f ($p.workingset/1MB)
```

We perform a similar formatting task by setting $n to the current date and time, and then formatting $n in a short time pattern:

```
$d="{0:T}" -f $n
```

So, exactly how does the formatting operator work? Or, more specifically, how do those .NET Framework formatting strings work?

The examples we've used so far all look something like "{0:N4}", which is composed of two distinct parts: The *argument number*, and the *formatting directive*. Essentially, this example says, "take the argument in the first position, and format it according to the N4 style." N4 means numeric, with 4 digits after the decimal. The first position is numbered zero, which is where the zero comes from in the formatting string. Here's another example:

```
PS C:\> $v1 = 1.23456
PS C:\> $v2 = 6.54321
PS C:\> "{0:N4} {1:N3}" -f $v1,$v2
1.2346 6.543
```

Here, we've created two variables, each with decimal values. This time, our formatting string is taking the first item and formatting it in the N4 style, and the second item is being numbered in the N3 style—that is, numeric, with three digits after the decimal. After the -**f** operator, we've provided a comma-separated list (technically, an array) with our two values. And, as you can see in the output, each was formatted according to the strings: Position one (index number zero) has four decimal places, and position two (index number one) has three.

So, if the first part of a formatting directive indicates which input value is to be formatted, and the second indicates what type of formatting to use, then what types of formatting are available? Here's a list:

Numeric Formats

- C or c – Currency; C2 would include two digits after the decimal
- D or d – Decimal; D2 would indicate at least two digits, with zeros added to the beginning if necessary
- E or e – Scientific notation; E2 indicates two digits after the decimal
- F or f – Fixed-point; F2 indicates two digits after the decimal
- G or g – Uses the most compact available method—either fixed-point or scientific notation
- N or n – Basic number; N2 indicates two digits after the decimal
- P or p – Percentage; P2 indicates two digits after the decimal
- R or r – Round-trip; only supported for [single] and [double] numbers
- X or x – Hexadecimal; H2 indicates a minimum of 2 digits in the output; the case (X or x) determines the case of the output

Date and Time Formats

- d – Short date
- D – Long date

- f – Full date/time (short)

- F – Full date/time (long)

- g – General date/time (short)

- G – General date/time (long)

- M or m – Month-day pattern (MMMM dd)

- o – Round-trip day/time

- R or r – RFC1123 date (ddd, dd MMM yyyy HH:mm:ss GMT)

- s – Sortable (ISO 8601)

- t – Short time

- u – Universal sortable date/time (no timezone conversion)

- U – Universal sortable date/time (uses Coordinated Universal Time, or UTC)

- Y or y – Year-month pattern (yyyy MMMM)

Note that the "round trip" formats are intended to produce output that can be successfully converted back into its original non-string data type. In the case of a date, for example, it includes a time zone indicator. Also note that these are just the standard formats; it's possible to create custom formats, but doing so generally requires specialized .NET Framework programming and is beyond the scope of this book.

........................................................................................................................................

**Online Help**
Microsoft's official documentation on .NET formatting is available at http://msdn2.microsoft.com/en-us/library/26etazsy.aspx.

## Comparison Operators

PowerShell has several types of comparison operators that you can use to evaluate expressions. These operators are listed in the following table.

**PowerShell Comparison Operators**

| Operator | Description | Algebraic Equivalent |
|---|---|---|
| -eq | Equals | A=B |
| -ne | Not equal | A<>B |
| -gt | Greater than | A>B |
| -ge | Greater than or equal to | A>=B |
| -lt | Less than | A<B |
| -le | Less than or equal to | A<=B |

**Note**

These operators are all case-insensitive, meaning that "HELLO" is the same as "hello", as far as PowerShell is concerned. Case-sensitive operators are available: -ceq, -cne, -cgt, -cge, -clt, and -cle all perform case-sensitive comparisons when you're comparing strings.

You are probably familiar with most of these operators or at least their algebraic equivalent. In PowerShell, these operators are used to evaluate an expression and return either TRUE or FALSE.

```
PS C:\> $varA=100
PS C:\> $varB=200
PS C:\> $varA -eq $varB
False
PS C:\> $varA -ne $varB
True
PS C:\> $varA -lt $varB
True
PS C:\>
```

After we define some variables, we compare them with a few of the comparison operators that return either TRUE or FALSE.

These comparison operators work just fine for simple numeric comparisons. For string comparisons we can use **-like** and **-match**. If your comparison needs are simple, the **-like** operator may be all you need:

```
PS C:\> "10.10.10.1" -like "10.10.10.*"
True
PS C:\> "10.10.10.25" -like "10.10.10.*"
True
PS C:\> "10.10.11.1" -like "10.10.10.*"
False
PS C:\>
```

**Note**

The -like and -match operators are also case-insensitive; -clike and -cmatch are their case-sensitive counterparts.

In this example, we're comparing an IP address (10.10.10.1) to a pattern that uses the wildcard character (*). This comparison returns the Boolean value TRUE. The second comparison also matches, but the third fails. The operator returns FALSE because the third octet no longer matches the pattern.

Depending on the logic of your script, you may want to check the inverse. In other words, you may want to determine whether the address is not like the pattern. For an inverse type of comparison, use the **-notlike** operator.

```
PS C:\> "10.10.11.1" -notlike "10.10.10.*"
True
PS C:\>
```

This is essentially the same comparison, except this operator returns TRUE because 10.10.11.1 is not like 10.10.10.*.

The asterisk is a multiple character wildcard that can be used if we need something more granular. For example, we can use the "?" operator if we want to match any subnet of 10.10.10.x to 10.10.19.x.

```
PS C:\> "10.10.11.1" -like "10.10.1?.*"
True
PS C:\> "10.10.15.1" -like "10.10.1?.*"
True
PS C:\> "10.10.25.1" -like "10.10.1?.*"
False
PS C:\>
```

In this example, you can see the first two comparisons are TRUE, but the last one does not meet the pattern so it returns FALSE.

**Text Comparison only**
Make sure you understand the IP address comparisons are merely looking at the IP address string. We are not calculating or comparing network address with subnet masks or the like.

Let's look at some text comparison examples.

```
PS C:\> "sapien" -like "SAPIEN"
True
PS C:\> "sapien" -like "sap*"
True
PS C:\> "sapien" -like "sap?"
False
PS C:\> "sapien" -like "sapie[a-p]"
True
PS C:\>
```

The first example is a pretty basic comparison that also demonstrates that the **-like** operator is not case-sensitive. The second example uses the wildcard character, which means it will return TRUE for a string like "sapien". However, it will also return TRUE for "sapsucker" and "sapling". The third example returns FALSE because the "?" character means any single character after "sap". The last example is a bit different. We can use brackets to denote a range of characters with which to compare. In this case, the **-like** operator will return TRUE for anything that starts with "sapie" and ends with any character between "a" and "p".

The **-like** operator limits your comparisons essentially to a few wildcards. If you need something that will compare a pattern, then use the **-match** operator. This operator also returns TRUE if the string matches the specified pattern.

At its simplest, **-match** returns TRUE if any part of the string matches the pattern:

```
PS C:\> $var="XPDesktop01"
PS C:\> $var -match "XP"
True
PS C:\> $var -match "desk"
True
PS C:\> $var -match "01"
True
PS C:\>
```

In this example, we set a variable to the value "XPDesktop01" and compared it with a variety of patterns using -**match**. As you can see, they all return TRUE because pattern such as "desk" exist somewhere in the string. However, sometimes we need to be more particular such as only returning TRUE if the name starts with "XP". In this case, we can use "^" to indicate we want to match the beginning characters:

```
PS C:\> $var -match "^XP"
True
PS C:\> $var -match "^Win2K"
False
PS C:\>
```

If we want to match something at the end of the string, then we use the $ character:

```
PS C:\> $var -match "01$"
True
PS C:\> $var -match "02$"
False
PS C:\>
```

In the first example, we get a positive match because $var, which is XPDesktop01, ends in 01. The second attempt is FALSE because $var does not end in 02.

Other times, we may be looking for something in between such as a range of characters. In this case, we can use brackets and match anything that falls within the range:

```
PS C:\> "hat" -match "h[aeiou]t"
True
PS C:\> "hit" -match "h[aeiou]t"
True
PS C:\> "hyt" -match "h[aeiou]t"
False
PS C:\>
```

In this example, "hat" and "hit" match the pattern because the middle character is included in the bracketed set. The last example fails to match because "y" is not in the set.

One final comment on -**match** is that the matching results are automatically stored in an array called $matches:

```
PS C:\> "CHI-SRV-02" -match "^chi"
True
PS C:\> $matches

Name                    Value
----                    -----
0                       CHI
PS C:\> "NYD-SRV-03" -match "^NY[a-d]"
True
PS C:\> $matches

Name                    Value
----                    -----
0                       NYD
PS C:\>
```

In the first example, the match pattern is looking for a string that begins with "chi". Since the string includes "chi", it returns TRUE. The $matches array is automatically populated with the matching text.

In the second example, we're looking for something that starts with NY and the third character can be a, b, c, or d. The $matches array shows us that NYD matched.

The 0 element of the array always returns the matched string. However, it is also possible to group results and save them as named groups:

```
PS C:\> "Computer system=XPDesk02" -match "^comp.*=(?<sysname>.*)"
True
PS C:\> $matches

Name                          Value
----                          -----
sysname                        XPDesk02
0                             Computer system=XPDesk02
PS C:\> $matches.sysname
XPDesk02
PS C:\>
```

In this example, we have a string, "Computer system=XPDesk02" that is being matched against a pattern that will match up with "Computer system=". To create a named group, we enclose the name of our group in parentheses. In this case, sysname and a matching pattern (.*) will be enclosed in parentheses. The syntax for defining the named group is ?*<name>*. If we have a match, then the $matches array will not only have element 0, but also our named element sysname. Until we use -**match** again, this array remains intact, and we can get the sysname property with dotted notation as we did with $matches.sysname in the example above.

Almost all of our examples have been fairly basic and theoretical. Here's an example of how we might use -**match** in a production setting:

```
PS C:\> $sys=Get-WmiObject -class "win32_computersystem"
PS C:\> $sys.name
XPDESK01
PS C:\> if ($sys.name -match "^xp") {
>> write-host "Running audit code"
>> #audit code can run here
>> }
>> else
>> {
>> write-host "Skipping system"
>> }
>>
Running audit code
PS C:\>
```

This code could be part of a larger script. Essentially, it sets the variable $sys to an instance of the Win32_ComputerSystem WMI object. We're displaying the object's name property so you'll understand how the rest of the code works. Next we build an IF statement that says, "If the name property starts with XP, then display a message and run something. Otherwise, just display a message that the system is being skipped". At this point, do not be concerned about understanding the IF statement since it will be covered in the chapter "Loops and Decision-Making Constructs." As you see, the name matches so the appropriate message is displayed.

The -**match** operator is also used with regular expressions, which will be discussed in the "Regular Expressions" chapter.

# Chapter 17
# Regular Expressions

How often have you tried searching through log files looking for a particular piece of information or searching for all information that meets a certain format like an IP address? A regular expression is a text pattern that is used to compare against a string of text. If the string of text matches the pattern, then you've found what you're looking for. For example, we know that an IP address has the format *xxx.xxx.xxx.xxx*. We don't know how many integers each octet has, only that there should be four sets of three numbers that are separated by periods. Conceptually, *xxx.xxx.xxx.xxx* is our pattern, and if it's found in the string we are examining, a match is made. Regular expressions can be very complex and confusing at first. We don't have space in this chapter for an exhaustive review of this topic, but we will give you enough information to use basic regular expressions in your PowerShell scripts.

Up to this point, pattern matching has been pretty simple and straightforward. But what if we want to validate that a string was in a particular format such as a UNC path or an IP address? In this case, we can use special regular expression characters to validate a string. The following table lists several of the more common special characters.

**Regular Expression Special Characters**

| Character | Description |
|---|---|
| \w | Matches a word (alpha-numeric and the underscore character) |
| \d | Matches any digit (0-9) |
| \t | Matches any tab |
| \s | Matches any whitespace, tab, or newline |

There are additional special characters, but these are the ones you are most likely to use. By the way, each of these characters has an inverse option you can use simply by using the capital letter version. For example, if you want to match a pattern for anything that was not a digit, you would use \D. This is an example of when PowerShell is case-sensitive.

PowerShell supports the quantifiers available in .NET regular expressions, as shown in the next table:

**Regular Expression Qualifiers**

| Format | Description |
| --- | --- |
| Value | Matches exact characters anywhere in the original value |
| . | Matches any single character |
| [value] | Matches at least one of the characters in the brackets |
| [range] | Matches at least one of the characters within the range; the Use of a hyphen (-) allows specification of contiguous character |
| [^] | Matches any character except those in brackets |
| ^ | Matches the beginning characters |
| $ | Matches the end characters |
| * | Matches zero or more instances of the preceding character |
| ? | Matches zero or more instances of the preceding character |
| \ | Matches the character that follows as an escaped character |
| + | Matches repeating instances of the specified pattern such as abc+ |
| {n} | Specifies exactly n matches |
| {n,} | Specifies *at least* n matches |
| {n,m} | Specifies at least n, but no more than m, matches. |

By combining pattern matching characters with these quantifiers, it is possible to construct some very complex regular expressions.

# Writing Regular Expressions

Let's look at some simple regular expression examples:

```
PS C:\> "SAPIEN Press" -match "\w"
True
PS C:\> $matches

Name                    Value
----                    -----
0                       S


PS C:\> "SAPIEN Press" -match "\w*"
True
PS C:\> $matches

Name                    Value
----                    -----
0                       SAPIEN


PS C:\> "SAPIEN Press" -match "\w+"
True
PS C:\> $matches
```

```
Name                    Value
----                    -----
0                       SAPIEN


PS C:\> "SAPIEN Press" -match "\w* \w*"
True
PS C:\> $matches

Name                    Value
----                    -----
0                       SAPIEN Press


PS C:\>
```

The first example compares the string "SAPIEN Press" to the pattern \w. Recall that comparison results are automatically stored in the $matches variable. As you can see, \w matches "S". Why doesn't it match "SAPIEN" or "SAPIEN Press"? The \w pattern means any word, even a single-character word. If we want to match a complete word, then we need to use one of the regular expression qualifiers. For example, you can see the second and third examples use \w* and \w+ respectively. In this particular example, these patterns return the same results.

If we want to match a two word phrase, then we would use an example like the last one using \w* \w*. If we were testing a match for "SAPIEN Press PowerShell", then we'd use something like this:

```
PS C:\> "SAPIEN Press Powershell" -match "\w* \w*"
True
PS C:\> $matches

Name                    Value
----                    -----
0                       SAPIEN Press


PS C:\>
```

This also matches, but as you can see it only matches the first two words. If we want to specifically match a two-word pattern, then we need to qualify our regular expression so it starts and ends with a word:

```
PS C:\> "SAPIEN Press Powershell" -match "^\w* \w*$"
False
PS C:\> "SAPIEN Press" -match "^\w* \w*$"
True
PS C:\>
```

The recommended best practice for strict regular expression evaluation is to use the ^ and $ qualifiers to denote the beginning and end of the matching pattern.

Here's another example:

```
PS C:\> "1001" -match "\d"
True
PS C:\> $matches

Name                    Value
```

```
----                     -----
0                        1


PS C:\> "1001" -match "\d+"
True
PS C:\> $matches

Name                     Value
----                     -----
0                        1001


PS C:\>
```

In the first example, the digit matching pattern is used to get a TRUE result. However, $matches shows it only matched the first digit. Using \d+ in the second example returns the full value.

If we want the number to be four digits, then we can use a qualifier like this:

```
PS C:\> "1001" -match "\d{4,4}"
True
PS C:\> "101" -match "\d{4,4}"
False
PS C:\>
```

The qualifier {4,4} indicates that we want to find a string with at least four matches. In this case, that would be an integer (\d) and no more than 4. When we use the regular expression to evaluate 101, it returns TRUE.

The following example shows a regular expression that is evaluating a simple UNC path string:

```
PS C:\> "\\file01\public" -match "^\\\\\w*\\\w*$"
True
PS C:\> $matches

Name                     Value
----                     -----
0                        \\file01\public


PS C:\>
```

This example looks a little confusing, so let's break it apart. First, we want an exact match so we're using ^ and $ to denote the beginning and end of the regular expression. We know the server name and path will be alphanumeric words, so we can use \w. Because we want the entire word, we'll use the * qualifier. All that's left are the \\ and \ characters in the UNC path. Remember that \ is a special character in regular expressions. If we want to match the \ character itself, then we need to "escape" it using another \ character. In other words, each \ will become \\. So, the elements of the regular expression break down to:

^ (beginning of expression)

\\    becomes \\\\

\w* (servername)

\    becomes \\

\w* (sharename)

$ (end of expression)

Putting this all together, we end up with ^\\\\\w*\\\w*$. As you can see in the example, this is exactly what we get.

Notice that $matches indicates the match at index 0, which is fine assuming we want a complete match. But we can also use regular expressions to match individual components by grouping each pattern:

```
PS C:\ > "\\server01\public" -match "(\\\\\w*)\\(\w*)"
True
PS C:\ > $matches

Name                     Value
----                     -----
2                        public
1                        \\server01
0                        \\server01\public
```

You're probably thinking, "So what?" Well, regular expressions in PowerShell support a feature called *named captures*. This allows us to define a name for the capture instead of relying on the index number. The format is to use "?<capturename>" inside parentheses of each pattern.

```
PS C:\ > "\\server01\public" -match "(?<server>\\\\\w*)\\(?<share>\w*)"
True
PS C:\ > $matches

Name                     Value
----                     -----
server                   \\server01
share                    public
0                        \\server01\public
```

We still have the complete match at index 0, but notice there are now names associated with the other matches. Now I can reference these elements directly by name:

```
PS C:\ > $matches.server
\\server01
PS C:\ > $matches.share
public
```

Using named captures makes it much easier to work with the matches object. One final note on this particular pattern is that it will not match a longer UNC like \\File01\Public\Scripts.

Let's look at another example. Here's a regular expression pattern to match an IP address:

```
PS C:\> "192.168.100.2" -match "^\d+\.\d+\.\d+\.\d+$"
True
PS C:\> $matches

Name                     Value
----                     -----
0                        192.168.100.2


PS C:\> "192.168.100" -match "^\d+\.\d+\.\d+\.\d+$"
```

```
False
PS C:\>
```

This should begin to look familiar. We're matching digits and using the \ character to escape the period character, since the period is a special regular expression character. By using the beginning and end of expression characters, we also know that we'll only get a successful match on a string with four numbers that are separated by periods. Of course, there's more to an IP address than four numbers. Each set of numbers can't be greater than three digits long. Here's how we can construct a regular expression to validate that:

```
PS C:\> "192.168.100.2" -match "^\d{1,3}\.\d{1,3}\.\d{1,3}\.\d{1,3}$"
True
PS C:\> "172.16.1.2543" -match "^\d{1,3}\.\d{1,3}\.\d{1,3}\.\d{1,3}$"
False
PS C:\>
```

The first example matches because each dotted octet is between 1 and 3 digits. The second example fails because the last octet is 4 digits.

PowerShell regular expressions also support named character sets, using a named character set:

```
PS C:\ > "powershell" -match "\p{Ll}"
True
PS C:\ > $matches

Name                    Value
----                    -----
0                       p
```

The named character set syntax is to use \p and the set name, in this case {Ll} to indicate all lowercase letters. This functionally the same as:

```
PS C:\ > "powershell" -match "[a-z]"
```

This may not seem like much of an improvement, but using character classes can simplify your regular expression:

```
PS C:\ > "PowerShell" -match "\p{L}+"
True
PS C:\ > $matches

Name                    Value
----                    -----
PowerShell
```

The {L} character class indicates any upper or lowercase character. We could get the same result with this:

```
PS C:\ > "PowerShell" -match "[a-zA-z]+"
```

The character set requires a little less typing. As your expressions grow in length and complexity, you will appreciate this.

You can use any of these Unicode character sets:

## Regular Expression Unicode Character Sets

| **Character Set** | **Description** |
|---|---|
| Cc | Other, Control |
| Cf | Other, Format |
| Cn | Other, Not Assigned (no characters have this property) |
| Co | Other, Private Use |
| Cs | Other, Surrogate |
| Ll | Letter, Lowercase |
| Lm | Letter, Modifier |
| Lo | Letter, Other |
| Lt | Letter, Titlecase (ie Microsoft Windows) |
| Lu | Letter, Uppercase |
| Mc | Mark, Spacing Combining |
| Me | Mark, Enclosing |
| Mn | Mark, Nonspacing |
| Nd | Number, Decimal Digit |
| Nl | Number, Letter |
| No | Number, Other |
| Pc | Punctuation, Connector |
| Pd | Punctuation, Dash |
| Pe | Punctuation, Close |
| Pf | Punctuation, Final quote |
| Pi | Punctuation, Initial quote |
| Po | Punctuation, Other |
| Ps | Punctuation, Open |
| Sc | Symbol, Currency |
| Sk | Symbol, Modifier |
| Sm | Symbol, Math |
| So | Symbol, Other |
| Zl | Separator, Line |
| Zp | Separator, Paragraph |
| Zs | Separator, Space |

The .NET Framework also provides other grouping categories for the character sets shown above.

**Additional Regular Expression Groupings**

| Character Set | Grouping |
|---|---|
| C | All control characters Cc, Cf, Cs, Co, and Cn. |
| L | All letters Lu, Ll, Lt, Lm, and Lo. |
| M | All diacritic marks Mn, Mc, and Me. |
| N | All numbers Nd, Nl, and No. |
| P | All punctuation Pc, Pd, Ps, Pe, Pi, Pf, and Po. |
| S | All symbols Sm, Sc, Sk, and So. |
| Z | All separators Zs, Zl, and Zp. |

You might have to experiment with these sets because they may not all be self-evident. For example:

```
PS C:\ > "<tag>" -match "\p{P}"
```

Will return FALSE because < is not considered but rather a symbol:

```
PS C:\ > "<tag>" -match "\p{S}"
```

This expression will return TRUE.

# Select-String

PowerShell includes a pattern matching cmdlet called **Select-String**. The intent is that you'll be able to select strings from text files that match pattern. The pattern can be as simple as "ABC" or a regular expression like "\d{1,3}\.\d{1,3}\.\d{1,3}\.\d{1,3}".

```
SYNTAX
   Select-String [-pattern] <string[]> -inputObject <psobject> [-include <string[]>] [-
exclude <string[]>] [-simpleMatch] [-caseSensitive] [-quiet] [-list] [<CommonParameters>]

   Select-String [-pattern] <string[]> [-path] <string[]> [-include <string[]>] [-exclude
 <string[]>] [-simpleMatch] [caseSensitive] [-quiet] [-list] [<CommonParameters>]
```

This cmdlet is like the grep and findstr commands.

For example, you might have an audit file of user activity and you want to find all lines that include the user account for Tybald Rouble:

```
PS C:\ > get-content audit.txt | select-string -pattern "mydomain\trouble"
```

Every line with the pattern "mydomain\trouble" would be displayed.

When used with **Get-ChildItem**, you can quickly search an entire directory of files for specific strings. Jeff finds this especially useful. Despite his best efforts, Jeff's script library is a little disorganized. Often, Jeff will know he has code to do something but can't remember what script or scripts might include it. Using a command like this, he can quickly find what scripts include the code snippet he's after:

```
PS C:\ > get-childitem s:\*.* -include *.vbs | Select-String "Security_.AuthenticationLevel"
```

A list of every script and line number, including the matching text, will be displayed. These results are stored in a MatchInfo object:

```
TypeName: Microsoft.PowerShell.Commands.MatchInfo

Name            MemberType Definition
----            ---------- ----------
Equals          Method     System.Boolean Equals(Object obj)
GetHashCode     Method      System.Int32 GetHashCode()
GetType         Method     System.Type GetType()
get_Filename    Method     System.String get_Filename()
get_IgnoreCase  Method      System.Boolean get_IgnoreCase()
get_Line        Method     System.String get_Line()
get_LineNumber  Method      System.Int32 get_LineNumber()
get_Path        Method     System.String get_Path()
get_Pattern     Method     System.String get_Pattern()
RelativePath    Method     System.String RelativePath(String directory)
set_IgnoreCase  Method      System.Void set_IgnoreCase(Boolean value)
set_Line        Method     System.Void set_Line(String value)
set_LineNumber  Method      System.Void set_LineNumber(Int32 value)
set_Path        Method     System.Void set_Path(String value)
set_Pattern     Method     System.Void set_Pattern(String value)
ToString        Method     System.String ToString(), System.String ToString(String directory)
Filename        Property   System.String Filename {get;}
IgnoreCase      Property   System.Boolean IgnoreCase {get;set;}
Line            Property   System.String Line {get;set;}
LineNumber      Property   System.Int32 LineNumber {get;set;}
Path            Property   System.String Path {get;set;}
Pattern         Property   System.String Pattern {get;set;}
```

Knowing the outgoing object allows us to accomplish tasks like this:

```
PS C:\ > get-childitem s:\*.* -include *.vbs | Select-String "Security_.AuthenticationLevel" '
| select filename,LineNumber | format-table -auto

Filename                        LineNumber
--------                        ----------
CompSysClass.vbs                        15
DiskClass.vbs                           84
DiskUsagetoXML.vbs                      95
GetEventsLogsAsynch-Msg.vbs             39
GetEventsLogsAsynch.vbs                 23
GetPercentFreeDrive.vbs                 25
MailstoreFileSizeReport.vbs            151
ScriptFunctionLibrary.vbs               30
ScriptFunctionLibrary.vbs               60
wmiphysicalmemquery-v2.vbs              26
```

Now Jeff can open each file and jump right to the line with his "missing" code sample. But if you look at the results closely, you'll see that one file made two matches. For a short example like this, it is trivial, but it might make a difference when searching thousands of lines of text in a directory. The **Select-String** cmdlet has a -**List** parameter that will stop searching a file at the first match. This is very handy when you don't need every match in file.

By the way, if you're using PrimalScript, you don't need to use this technique because the "Find In Files" feature returns the same type of results.

What about something more administrative?

```
PS C:\ > get-eventlog -logname system -newest 100 | select message,timewritten '
|select-string -pattern "Windows Installer"
```

This example will search the local event log for the last 100 events and display those with the pattern "Windows Installer" in the message.

**Select-String** can also use regular expression patterns:

```
PS C:\ > cat c:\iplist.txt | select-string "(172.16.)\d{2,3}\.\d{1,3}"
```

This expression will select all strings from IPList.txt that start with 172.16 and where the third octet has either two or three digits. This pattern will match on strings like 172.16.20.124, but not on 172.16.2.124.

# Regex Object

When you use the **-match** operator, even with a regular expression pattern, the operation only returns the first match found:

```
PS C:\> $var="Sapien Press PowerShell TFM"
PS C:\> $var -match "\w+"
True
PS C:\> $matches

Name                    Value
----                    -----
0                       Sapien
PS C:\>
```

To match all instances of the pattern, you need to use the Regex object. In this example, notice that the match method returns all matches in $var:

```
PS C:\> $regex=[regex]"\w+"
PS C:\> $regex.matches($var)

Groups   : {Sapien}
Success : True
Captures : {Sapien}
Index    : 0
Length   : 6
Value    : Sapien

Groups   : {Press}
Success : True
Captures : {Press}
Index    : 7
Length   : 5
Value    : Press

Groups   : {PowerShell}
Success : True
Captures : {PowerShell}
Index    : 13
Length   : 10
Value    : PowerShell

Groups   : {TFM}
```

```
Success : True
Captures : {TFM}
Index    : 24
Length   : 3
Value    : TFM
PS C:\>
```

We create an object variable called $regex and cast it to a regex object using [regex], specifying the regular expression pattern. We can now call the matches method of the regex object using $var as a parameter. The method returns all instances where the pattern matches, as well as where they were found in $var.

A more direct way to see all the matches is to use the Value property:

```
PS C:\> foreach ($i in $regex.matches($var)) {$i.value}
Sapien
Press
PowerShell
TFM
PS C:\>
```

The results of $regex.matches($var) is a *collection*. Using a **ForEach** loop, we can enumerate the collection and display the Value property for each item in the collection.

This object has several methods and properties with which you will want to become familiar:

```
PS C:\> $regex|get-member


   TypeName: System.Text.RegularExpressions.Regex

Name                MemberType Definition
----                ---------- ----------
Equals              Method     System.Boolean Equals(Object obj)
get_Options         Method     System.Text.RegularExpressions.RegexOpt
get_RightToLeft     Method      System.Boolean get_RightToLeft()
GetGroupNames       Method      System.String[] GetGroupNames()
GetGroupNumbers     Method      System.Int32[] GetGroupNumbers()
GetHashCode         Method     System.Int32 GetHashCode()
GetType             Method     System.Type GetType()
GroupNameFromNumber Method      System.String GroupNameFromNumber(Int32
GroupNumberFromName Method      System.Int32 GroupNumberFromName(String
IsMatch             Method     System.Boolean IsMatch(String input), S
Match               Method     System.Text.RegularExpressions.Match Ma
Matches             Method     System.Text.RegularExpressions.MatchCol
Replace             Method     System.String Replace(String input, Str
Split               Method     System.String[] Split(String input), Sy
ToString            Method     System.String ToString()
Options             Property   System.Text.RegularExpressions.RegexOpt
RightToLeft         Property   System.Boolean RightToLeft {get;}


PS C:\>
```

In order to see the current value of $regex , we need to use the **ToString()** method:

```
PS C:\> $regex.ToString()
\w+
PC C:\>
```

223

**IsMatch()**will return either TRUE or FALSE if any match is made:

```
PS C:\> if ($regex.IsMatch($var)) {
>> write-host "found" ($regex.Matches($var)).Count "matches"
>> }
>>
found 4 matches
PS C:\>
```

In this example, we check to see if **IsMatch()** is TRUE. If it is TRUE, the number of matches found in the string will be displayed. By the way, the **Count()** method is not a property of the $regex object, but the result of evaluating $regex.Matches($var), which returns a collection object:

```
PS C:\> ($regex.Matches($var)).gettype()

IsPublic IsSerial Name                              BaseType
-------- -------- ----                              --------
True     True     MatchCollection                   System.Object

PS C:\>
```

You can also use regular expressions to perform a find and replace operation. Simple operations can be done with the -Replace operator:

```
PS C:\ > $text="The quick brown fox jumped over the lazy cat"
PS C:\ > $text=$text -replace "cat","dog"
PS C:\ > $text
The quick brown fox jumped over the lazy dog
```

In this example, I've replaced all patterns of "cat" with "dog". We can also use this operator with the Regex object:

```
PS C:\ > [regex]$regex="timeout=\d{1,3}"
PS C:\ > $boot=get-content c:\boot.ini
PS C:\ > $boot -match $regex
timeout=30
PS C:\ > $boot=$boot -replace $regex,"timeout=10"
```

In this example, my regular expression pattern is looking for the phrase "timeout=", followed by 1 to 3 digits. To see how this might work, I save the contents of my boot.ini to $boot and attempt a regular expression match.

```
PS C:\ > $boot -match $regex
timeout=30
```

There is a match on the line "timeout=30". Now I can replace that line with a new line:

```
PS C:\ > $boot=$boot -replace $regex,"timeout=10"
```

$Boot will now have an updated version of my boot.ini, which I could then write back to a file.

But this example doesn't' really take advantage of the Regex object because there was only one match.

Consider this:

```
PS C:\ > [regex]$regex="[\s:]"
PS C:\ > $c=(get-date).ToLongTimeString()
PS C:\t > $c
3:20:07 PM
PS C:\ > $d=$regex.replace($c,"_")
PS C:\ > $d
3_20_07_PM
```

The regular expression pattern is searching for any space character or colon (:). We're going to use it against a variable that holds the result of **Get-Date**. The idea is that we want to use the time stamp as a filename, but this means we need to replace the colon character with a legal filename character. For the sake of consistency, we'll replace all instances with the underscore character:

```
PS C:\ > $d=$regex.replace($c,"_")
```

The value of $d can now be used as part of a filename.

With regular expressions it is critical that you are comparing apples to apples. In order for a regular expression pattern to match, it must match the pattern but also *not* match something else. For example, consider this variable:

```
PS C:\ > $a="Windows 2003 PowerShell 101"
```

Suppose we want to match a number:

```
PS C:\ > [regex]$regex="\d+"
```

The Regex object will match all numbers in $a:

```
PS C:\> $regex.matches($a)


Groups    : {2003}
Success   : True
Captures  : {2003}
Index     : 8
Length    : 4
Value     : 2003

Groups    : {101}
Success   : True
Captures  : {101}
Index     : 24
Length    : 3
Value     : 101
```

But if the only number we want to match is at the end, then we need a more specific regular expression pattern like this:

```
PS C:\ > [regex]$regex="\d+$
PS C:\ > $regex.matches($a)
```

```
Groups   : {101}
Success  : True
Captures : {101}
Index    : 24
Length   : 3
Value    : 101
```

Now, we are only obtaining a match at the end of the string. Let's go through one more example to drive this point home. Here's a regular expression pattern that matches a domain credential:

```
PS C:\ > [regex]$regex="\w+\\\w+"
```

This will return TRUE for expressions like these:

```
PS C:\ > $regex.IsMatch("sapien\jeff")
True
PS C:\ > $regex.IsMatch("sapien\jeff\oops")
True
```

Clearly the second string is not a valid credential. To get a proper match we need a regular expression like this:

```
PS C:\ > [regex]$regex="^\w+\\\w+$"
PS C:\ > $regex.IsMatch("sapien\jeff")
True
PS C:\ > $regex.IsMatch("sapien\jeff\oops")
False
```

Now the match is more accurate because the pattern uses ^ to match at the beginning of the string and $ to match at the end.

# Regular Expression Examples

Before we wrap up this quick introduction to regular expressions, let's review of regular expressions that you're likely to need and use.

## E-mail Address

It's not unreasonable that you might want to search for a string of text that matches an email address pattern. Here is one such regular expression:

```
^([\w-]+)(\.[\w-]+)*@([\w-]+\.)+[a-zA-Z]{2,7}$
```

The selection is a sequence consisting of:

A start anchor (^).

The expression ([\w-]+) that matches any word string and the dash character.

The expression (\.[\w-]+)* that matches a period and then any word string and the dash.

The @ character.

The expression ([\w-]+\.)+ that matches any word string that ends in a period.

The expression [a-zA-Z]{2,7} that matches any string of letters and numbers at least two characters long and no more than seven. This should match domain names like .ca and .museum.

An end anchor ($).

The expression [a-zA-Z]{2,7} will return any character string that is at least two characters and no more than seven. This should allow domain names such as .ca and .museum.

........................................................................................................................................

**There's More than One Way**
There are many different regular expression patterns for an e-mail address. Even though this particular pattern should work for just about any address, it is not 100% guaranteed. We used this pattern because it is relatively simple to follow.

Here's how we might use this expression:

```
PS C:\> $regex=[regex]"^([\w-]+)(\.[\w-]+)*@([\w-]+\.)+[a-zA-Z]{2,7}$"
PS C:\> $var= ("j.hicks@sapien.com","oops@ca",`
>> "don@sapien.com","alex@dev.sapien.com")
PS C:\> $var
j.hicks@sapien.com
oops@ca
don@sapien.com
alex@dev.sapien.com
PS C:\> $var -match $regex
j.hicks@sapien.com
don@sapien.com
alex@dev.sapien.com
PS C:\> $var.count
4
PS C:\>
```

We start by creating a regex object with our e-mail pattern and define an object variable with some e-mail names to check. We've introduced one entry that we know will fail to match. The easiest way to list the matches is to use the **-match** operator that returns all the valid email addresses.

If you try expressions like these:

```
PS C:\> $regex.matches($var)
PS C:\> $regex.IsMatch($var)
False
PS C:\>
```

You will see that nothing or FALSE is returned. This occurs because $var is an array. We need to enumerate the array and evaluate each element against the regular expression pattern:

```
PS C:\> foreach ($item in $var) {
>> if ($regex.IsMatch($item)) {
>> write-host $item "is a valid address"
>> }
>> else {
>> write-host "$item is NOT a valid address" }
>> }
>>
j.hicks@sapien.com is a valid address
oops@ca is NOT a valid address
don@sapien.com is a valid address
alex@dev.sapien.com is a valid address
```

```
PS C:\>
```

In this example ,we're enumerating each item in $var. If the current variable item matches the regular expression pattern, then we display a message confirming the match. Otherwise, we display a non-matching message.

## String with No Spaces

Up to now, we've been using regular expressions to match alphanumeric characters. However, we can also match whitespaces such as a space, tab, new line, or the lack of whitespace. Here's a regex object that uses \S that is looking to match non-whitespace characters:

```
PS C:\> $regex=[regex]"\S"
PS C:\> $var="The-quick-brown-fox-jumped-over-the-lazy-dog."
PS C:\> $var2="The quick brown fox jumped over the lazy dog."
PS C:\>
```

In this example, we have two variables—one with whitespaces and the other without. Which one will return TRUE when evaluated with IsMatch?

```
PS C:\> $regex.IsMatch($var)
True
PS C:\> $regex.IsMatch($var2)
True
PS C:\>
```

Actually, this is a trick question because both return TRUE. This happens because \S is looking for any non-whitespace character. Since each letter or the dash is a non-whitespace character, the pattern matches. If our aim is to check a string to find out if it contains any spaces, then we really need to use a different regular expression and understand that a finding of FALSE is what we're seeking:

```
PS C:\> $regex=[regex]"\s{1}"
PS C:\> $regex.Ismatch($var)
False
PS C:\> $regex.Ismatch($var2)
True
PS C:\>
```

The regular expression \s{1} is looking for a whitespace character that occurs only one time. Evaluating $var with IsMatch returns FALSE because there are no spaces in the string. The same execution with $var2 returns TRUE because there are spaces in the string. So, if we wanted to take some action based on this type of negative matching, we might use something like this:

## NegativeMatchingTest.ps1

```
$var="The-quick-brown-fox-jumped-over-the-lazy-dog."
$var2="The quick brown fox jumped over the lazy dog."
$regex=[regex]"\s{1}"
$var
if (($regex.IsMatch($var)) -eq "False")
{
write-host "Expression has spaces"
}
else
```

```
{
write-host "Expression has no spaces" }

$var2
if (($regex.IsMatch($var2)) -eq "False")
{
write-host "Expression has spaces"
}
else
{
write-host "Expression has no spaces" }
```

This action produces the following output:

```
The-quick-brown-fox-jumped-over-the-lazy-dog.
Expression has no spaces
The quick brown fox jumped over the lazy dog.
Expression has spaces
PS C:\>
```

The purpose of this example is to illustrate that there may be times when you want to match on something that is missing or a negative pattern.

## Domain Credential

Let's look at a regular expression example to match a Windows domain name that is in the format *Domain\username*:

```
PS C:\> $regex=[regex]("\w+\\\w+")

PS C:\> $var=@("sapien\jeff","sapien\don","sapien\alex")
PS C:\> $regex.matches($var)


Groups    : {sapien\jeff}
Success : True
Captures : {sapien\jeff}
Index    : 0
Length   : 11
Value    : sapien\jeff

Groups    : {sapien\don}
Success : True
Captures : {sapien\don}
Index    : 12
Length   : 10
Value    : sapien\don

Groups    : {sapien\alex}
Success : True
Captures : {sapien\alex}
Index    : 23
Length   : 11
Value    : sapien\alex


PS C:\>
```

Again, we create our regex object and an object variable with some domain names. Invoking the **Matches()** method shows the results. As we've demonstrated earlier, you can display the match values in at least two different ways:

```
PS C:\> foreach ($m in $regex.matches($var)) {$m.value}
sapien\jeff
sapien\don
sapien\alex


PS C:\> $var -match $regex
sapien\jeff
sapien\don
sapien\alex
PS C:\>
```

Which method you choose will depend on what you want to do with the information.

## Telephone Number

Matching a phone number is pretty straightforward. We can use the pattern \d{3}-\d{4} to match any basic phone number without the area code:

```
PS C:\> $regex=[regex]"\d{3}-\d{4}"
PS C:\> "555-1234" -match $regex
True
PS C:\> $matches

Name                     Value
----                     -----
0                        555-1234

PS C:\> "5551-234" -match $regex
False
PS C:\> $regex.IsMatch("abc-defg")
False
PS C:\> $regex.IsMatch("123-0987")
True
PS C:\>
```

We hope these examples are looking familiar. First, we defined a regular expression object and then we test different strings to see if there is a match. You can see that only three digits (\d{3}) plus a dash (-) plus four digits (\d{4}) make a match.

## IP Address

For our final example, let's look at a likely use for a regular expression. We want to examine a Web log and pull out all the IP addresses. Here's the complete set of commands. We'll go through them at the end:

```
PS C:\Logs> $var=get-content "ex060211.log"
PS C:\Logs> $regex=[regex]"\d{1,3}\.\d{1,3}\.\d{1,3}\.\d{1,3}"
PS C:\Logs> $regex.Matches($var)
Groups   : {192.168.10.1}
Success : True
Captures : {192.168.10.1}
```

```
Index    : 15679
Length   : 12
Value    : 192.168.10.1

Groups   : {217.58.174.3}
Success  : True
Captures : {217.58.174.3}
Index    : 15728
Length   : 12
Value    : 217.58.174.3

PS C:\Logs> $regex.Matches($var)| select-object -unique -property "value"

Value
-----
192.168.10.1
69.207.16.195
61.77.118.73
69.207.43.227
59.16.161.193
221.248.23.251
202.196.222.222
216.127.66.128
64.252.96.72
213.97.113.25
85.124.110.222
59.11.81.103
59.13.34.109
220.195.3.86
38.119.239.197
217.58.174.3
220.135.88.151
69.241.39.66
213.152.142.15


PS C:\Logs>
```

The first thing we do is dump the contents of the log file to the variable $var. Next we create an object variable that will be a regular expression object by casting it as type regex and specifying the matching pattern.

```
PS C:\Logs> $regex=[regex]"\d{1,3}\.\d{1,3}\.\d{1,3}\.\d{1,3}"
```

Remember, we need to use a regular expression object because the **-match** operator only checks for the first instance of a match. In an IIS log, the first IP listed is usually the host Web server and we want the visitor's IP address that comes second. Everything we've covered up to now about patterns and regular expressions is still valid. We're just going to use an object with built-in regular expression functionality. You'll also notice that our IP address pattern does not use ^ and $. That's because the IP addresses we're looking for don't start or end each line of the log file.

Invoking the **Matches()** method of the regex object essentially takes our matching pattern and compares it to the contents of $var:

```
PS C:\Logs> $regex.Matches($var)
```

Whenever a match is found, it will be displayed. We've edited the output to only show a few representative examples.

Alone that might be sufficient. But we'll take this one step further and send the output of the **Matches()** method to the **Select-Object** cmdlet.

```
PS C:\Logs> $regex.Matches($var)| select-object -unique -property "value"
```

With this cmdlet we can select only the value property of each regular expression match and also return a list of unique values.

# Regular Expression Reference

We've only scratched the surface on regular expressions. This is a very complex topic that extends well beyond the scope of this book. Even so, we want to make sure you know where you can go quench your thirst for more information on regular expressions.

In PowerShell, you can run `Help about_regular_expression` to view PowerShell's documentation on the topic. If you'd like a book recommendation, *Mastering Regular Expressions* by Jeffrey Friedl (O'Reilly) is now in its third edition and is considered by many to be a definitive reference.

As you might expect, there are many excellent online resources. Here is a short list of our favorites:

- The official Microsoft documentation can be found at http://msdn2.microsoft.com/en-us/library/az24scfc(vs.71).aspx.

- Regexlib.com has an online regular expression tester and a terrific one page "cheat sheet".

- Wikipedia has a great article on regular expressions including historical background at http://en.wikipedia.org/wiki/Regular_expression.

- http://www.regular-expressions.info offers some nice tutorials and general information about regular expressions.

Finally, there are a number of free tools you can download that will help you evaluate and test regular expressions:

- Regex Coach (http://www.weitz.de/regex-coach/)

- Regular Expression Workbench 3.1 (http://www.gotdotnet.com/Community/UserSamples/Details.aspx?SampleGuid=BC2B09E3-7E83-4B0A-93D9-A2EC8B207849)

- Expresso (http://www.codeproject.com/dotnet/expresso.asp)

- RegEx Buddy (http://www.regexbuddy.com)—this is a commercial tool, meaning you'll have to purchase it if you like it.

# Chapter 18
# Loops and Decision-Making Constructs

One advantage PowerShell has over the traditional Cmd.exe shell is that you can create loops and logic structures directly from the console. If you've read this book from the beginning, you've seen examples like this:

```
PS C:\> foreach ($i in (1,2,3,4,5)) {
>> write-host "Current value is "$i
>> }
>>
Current value is 1
Current value is 2
Current value is 3
Current value is 4
Current value is 5
PS C:\>
```

The curly brace { at the end of the first line tells PowerShell there is more to the **ForEach** command. When we press Enter, PowerShell changes the prompt to >>, which indicates it is waiting for the rest of command. Once we enter the last element and press Enter for a new line, the command is parsed and executed.

We mention this because many of our examples in this chapter are presented as PowerShell scripts. The benefit is that it is easier to edit and re-run a script than to retype an entire logic construct, since that provides another opportunity for you to make a typing mistake.

Let's start our exploration with the logic construct we just used.

# If

The **If** statement also executes a block of code if some condition is met. However, this construct can also execute a block of code if the condition is not met. For this reason, **If** is more of a decision-making construct instead of a looping one:

```
if (<condition>)
  {<code_block1>}
[else
  {<code_block2>}]
```

The Else section is optional. Here's a quick one line example:

```
PS C:\> $i=1
PS C:\> if ($i -le 10) {write-host "less than 10"}
less than 10
PS C:\>
```

This example says that if the condition contained within the parentheses is TRUE, then execute the code in the braces. Since $i is less than 10, the code is executed.

If we want a block of code to run if the condition is not TRUE, then we introduce the **Else** operator.

```
PS C:\> $i=11
PS C:\> if ($i-le 10) {
>> "Less than 10"
>. }
>> else
>. {
>>"Greater than 10"
>> }
>>
```

In simple English, if $i is less than 10, then execute the first block of code; otherwise, execute the second block of code. By the way, you are very likely to see code snippets where the **If Else** statement is all on a single line like this:

```
PS C:\> $var=Get-WmiObject -class win32_logicaldisk | '
>> where {$_.deviceid -eq "C:"}
>>
PS C:\> if ($var.freespace -le 5GB) {"Low space"} else {"OK"}
Low space
PS C:\> if ($var.freespace -le 1GB) {"Low space"} else {"OK"}
OK
PS C:\>
```

The **If** statement in this example is checking if the free space on drive C:, which we obtained through WMI, is less than some value. If so, then a "Low Space" message is displayed. Otherwise, an "OK" message is displayed.

**Formatting the Expression**
As long as you have the proper syntax with parentheses and braces, it is up to you on how you format the expression. You can either break it into different lines as we did in IfTest.ps1 or stick to a single line as we did in the example above. If you have several lines of code or commands that you want to execute, you'll find it easier to write and troubleshoot by breaking the statement into multiple lines.

But what about a situation where if a condition is not true you want it to check for other conditions before resorting to an **Else** statement? PowerShell supports an **ElseIf** component to the **If** statement:

```
if (<condition>)
  {<code_block1>}
Elseif (<condition2>)
  {<code_block2>)
else
  {<code_block3>}
```

Here, our previous example is expanded to demonstrate:

```
PS C:\> $i=45
PS C:\> if ($i -le 10) {
>> write-host "Less than 25"
>> }
>> elseif ($i -le 50)
>> {
>> write-host "Less than 50"
>> }
>> else
>> {
>> write-host "Greater than 50"
>>}
>>
```

The logic of this example is that if $i is less than 10, and then execute the first block of code. If it is not, then the **ElseIf** condition is evaluated. If this condition is TRUE, then the second block of code is executed. If even this condition is FALSE, then the last **Else** statement is reached and the last block of code is run.

You can have as many **ElseIf** statements as you want. However, from a practical perspective more than one or two will make your code a little harder to troubleshoot. If you want to evaluate multiple conditions, a better operator to use is **Switch**, which is discussed below.

Finally, even though it may not be technically required, if you include **ElseIf**, you should end your **If** statement with an **Else** clause. Let's look at a practical example that combines several logic constructs in a single script. The script checks the CPU time for each running process. If the CPU time is less than 300 seconds, the script displays the process name and CPU time in green. If the CPU time is greater than 301 and less than 1000, the process displays the information with no color coding. Otherwise, the process information is displayed in red:

## ProcessCPU.ps1

```
#ProcessCPU.ps1
$process=get-process
$low=0 #counter for low cpu processes
$med=0 #counter for medium cpu processes
$high=0 #counter for high cpu processes
foreach ($p in $process) {
[int]$cpuseconds="{0:F0}" -f $p.cpu

 if ($cpuseconds -le 300) {
 write-host $p.name $cpuseconds "seconds" -foregroundcolor "Green"
 $low++
 }
 elseif (($cpuseconds -ge 301) -AND ($cpuseconds -le 1000)) {
 write-host $p.name $cpuseconds "seconds"
 $med++
 }
 else
 {
 write-host $p.name $cpuseconds "seconds" -foregroundcolor "Red"
 $high++
 }
}
#display a summary message
write-host `n"Process Summary"
write-host "-->" $low "low CPU processes"
write-host "-->" $med "medium CPU processes"
write-host "-->" $high "high CPU processes"
```

This script uses a number of PowerShell elements that we've covered up to this point. The script begins by initializing some variables, including one that holds the output of the **Get-Process** cmdlet. We then use **ForEach** to enumerate each element of the $process object. Remember, it is a collection. Within this construct, we use **If** and **ElseIf** statements to evaluate a condition as follows. Determine whether the value of $cpuseconds is greater or less than some value. For example, if the value of $cpuseconds is less than or equal to 300, then we display a message in green and increase the $low variable by one. If that isn't true, then the **ElseIf** statement is evaluated. If this condition is true, then the number of CPU seconds is between 301 and 1000, which means the process information is displayed. Otherwise, the **Else** clause is reached and the number of CPU seconds is greater than 1000, so we display the message in red.

........................................................................................................................................

**Formatting Details**

We want to point out some special characters that were used in the `ProcessCPU.ps1` script. First, we specifically cast $cpuseconds as an integer type by using [int]. We did this so that our comparisons with **-le** and **-ge** would work as expected. We also used **-f** to format the value of $p.cpu that contains the number of seconds, and then format it to a fixed type with no decimal places. This changes a value like 180.7899632 to 181. Finally, the `n instructs PowerShell to write a blank line to the console. It helps separate the summary section from the rest of the output.

Here's an excerpt of the script's output:

```
svchost 73 seconds
svchost 47 seconds
svchost 1133 seconds
svchost 27 seconds
```

```
svchost 261 seconds
svchost 24 seconds
System 5645 seconds
wcescomm 12747 seconds
wdfmgr 9 seconds
winlogon 55 seconds
WINWORD 71 seconds
WISPTIS 4 seconds
WLTRAY 168 seconds
WLTRYSVC 9 seconds
wmiapsrv 654 seconds

Process Summary
--> 42 low CPU processes
--> 4 medium CPU processes
--> 15 high CPU processes
PS C:\>
```

You'll have to run the full script on your system to see the actual colorized output.

## Switch

If you find yourself needing to check multiple conditions or otherwise create a lengthy **If** and **ElseIf** statement, then you need to use PowerShell's **Switch** statement. This statement acts like many **If** statements. If you have experience with VBScript, you'll recognize this construct as a Select Case statement. By default, **Switch** is not case-sensitive. Here's a quick example:

```
PS C:\> $var=5
PS C:\> switch ($var) {
>> 1 {"Option 1"}
>> 2 {"Option 2"}
>> 3 {"Option 3"}
>> 4 {"Option 4"}
>> 5 {"Option 5"}
>> }
>>
Option 5
PS C:\>
```

The **Switch** statement evaluates the contents contained within parentheses, and then the condition or value is matched against a set of expressions contained within braces. Each expression has a corresponding block of code in braces. If the expression matches, then command processing *switches* to the corresponding code.

In this example, the code that corresponds to the matching expression is executed, since the value of $var is 5. If there is no match, then nothing will be displayed. However, you can use **default** at the end of the **Switch** statement to execute code in the event that no other matches are made:

```
PS C:\> $var=5
PS C:\> switch ($var) {
>> 1 {"Option 1"}
>> 2 {"Option 2"}
>> 3 {"Option 3"}
>> Default {"No match"}
>> }
>>
No match
PS C:\>
```

In this variation, the default code block is executed since there is no matching expression for the value of $var.

Typically, you will write out **Switch** statements in separate lines to make it easier to read and trouble-shoot. However, you could just as easily write a statement like this:

```
Switch ($i) {1 {"Option 1"} 2 {"Option 2"} 3{"Option 3"}}
```

This statement will evaluate $i by looking for 1, 2, or 3, and then executing the corresponding code.

The **Switch** statement also supports additional options that are outlined in the following table:

### Switch Options

| Option | Description |
|--------|-------------|
| -casesensitive | If the match clause is a string, modify it to be case-sensitive. If the variable to be evaluated is not a string, this option is ignored. |
| -exact | Indicates that if the match clause is a string, it must match exactly. Use of this parameter disables -wildcard and -regex. If the variable to be evaluated is not a string, this option is ignored. |
| -file | Take input from a file (or representative) rather than statement. If multiple -file parameters are used, the last one is be used. Each line of the file is read and passed through the switch block. |
| -regex | Indicates that the match clause, if a string, is treated as a regular expression string. Using this parameter disables -wildcard and -exact. If the variable to be evaluated is not a string, this option is ignored. |
| -wildcard | Indicates that if the match clause is a string, it is treated as a -wildcard string. Use of this parameter disables -regex and -exact. If the variable to be evaluated is not a string, this option is ignored. |

The complete **switch** syntax can be one of the following:

```
switch [-regex|-wildcard|-exact][-casesensitive] ( pipeline )
```

or

```
switch [-regex|-wildcard|-exact][-casesensitive] -file filename {
"string"|number|variable|{ expression } { statementlist }
default { statementlist
}
```

Let's look at a quick example.

```
PS C:\> $var="PowerShell123","PowerShell","123","PowerShell 123"
PS C:\> Switch -regex ($var) {
>> "^\w+[a-zA-Z]$" {write-host $_" is a word"}
>>"^\d+$" {write-host $_" is a number"}
>>"\s" {write-host $_" has a space"}
>>Default {write-host "No match found for"$_}
>>}
>>
```

In this script, we set a variable with several different values. The **Switch** statement uses the regex option, which tells PowerShell we will be matching based on regular expressions. A different message is displayed, depending on the match:

```
No match found for PowerShell123
PowerShell is a word
123 is a number
PowerShell 123 has a space
PS C:\>
```

If a Switch statement will result in multiple matches, then each match block of code will be executed. If this is not your intention, then you need to use the **Break** or **Continue** keywords, which are covered below.

# For

The **For** loop is similar to the **ForEach** loop. With this statement, we can keep looping while some condition is met and execute a block of code each time through the loop. The condition could be a counter. For example, we might need a loop that says, "Start counting at one and execute some block of code each time until you reach ten." Or we might need a loop that says, "As long as some statement is true, keep looping and execute a block of code each time."

If you've used the **For** loop in VBScript, conceptually PowerShell's implementation is no different. However, the syntax of PowerShell's **For** loop may confuse you at first:

```
for (<init>; <condition>; <repeat>) {<command block>}
```

This syntax essentially instructs PowerShell that *for (some set of conditions) {do this block of commands}*.

Let's break this down. The <init> element is one or more sets of commands that are separated by commas. These commands are run before the loop begins. Typically, this is where you initialize a variable with some starting value. This variable is usually checked by some statement or code, <condition>, that returns a Boolean value of TRUE or FALSE. If the condition is TRUE, then the code in the command block code that is enclosed in braces, <command block>, is executed. The <repeat> element is one or more sets of commands that are separated by commas, and are run each time through the loop.

Traditionally, these commands are used to modify the init variable. Each element in parentheses is separated by a semicolon or a carriage return. Thus, you could have a **For** statement that looks like this:

```
for (<init>
    <condition>
    <repeat>){
    <command_block>
    }
```

Here's a very basic example:

```
PS C:\> for ($i=1;$i -le 10;$i++) {write-host "loop #"$i}
loop # 1
loop # 2
loop # 3
loop # 4
loop # 5
loop # 6
```

```
loop # 7
loop # 8
loop # 9
loop # 10
PS C:\>
```

The initial command sets $i to a value of 1. The condition that is checked each time is to see if $i is less than 10. If it is, then we use the **Write-Host** cmdlet to display a message. Each time the loop is executed, $i is incremented by 1 by using $i++.

This is a very complete example. However, it's possible to reference other variables from within the same scope. The following command is essentially the same, except $i is defined outside of the **For** statement.

```
PS C:\> $i=1
PS C:\> for (;$i -le 10;$i++) {write-host "loop #"$i}
loop # 1
loop # 2
loop # 3
loop # 4
loop # 5
loop # 6
loop # 7
loop # 8
loop # 9
loop # 10
PS C:\>
```

Notice the **For** statement's condition, which is the portion in parentheses, has an empty init value. Even so, we still include the semi-colon delimiter.

........................................................................................................................

**Runaway Loop**
Be careful with the **For** syntax. If you do not properly specify an expression to evaluate each time through the loop, it will run an infinite number of times until you press Ctrl-Break or Ctrl-C, or kill the PowerShell process.

# While

The **While** statement is similar to the **For** statement. This logical construct also executes a block of code as long as some condition is TRUE:

```
while (<condition>){<command_block>}
```

However, the syntax is a little more direct. Here's essentially the same loop as we used before, only it has been rewritten to use the **While** operator:

```
PS C:\> $i=1
PS C:\> while ($i -le 10)
>> {
>> write-host "loop #"$i
>> $i++
>> }
>>
loop # 1
```

```
loop # 2
loop # 3
loop # 4
loop # 5
loop # 6
loop # 7
loop # 8
loop # 9
loop # 10
PS C:\>
```

In this example, we've broken the **While** operation into separate lines to make it easier to follow. However, this could have been written as one line:

```
while ($i -le 10){write-host "loop #"$i;$i++}
```

## Do While

A variation on **While** is **Do While**. In the **While** operation, the condition is checked at the beginning of the statement. In the **Do While** operation, it is checked at the end:

```
PS C:\> $i=0
PS C:\> do {
>> $i++
>> write-host "`$i="$i
>> }
>> while ($i -le 5)
>>
$i= 1
$i= 2
$i= 3
$i= 4
$i= 5
$i= 6
PS C:\>
```

In this example, you can see what happens when you check at the end. The loop essentially says, "Increase $i by one and display the current value as long as $ is less than or equal to 5."

However, notice that we end up with a sixth pass. This occurs because when $i=5, the while condition is still TRUE, so the loop repeats, including running the increment and display code. But now when the while clause is evaluated, it is FALSE, which causes the loop to end. This is not necessarily a bad thing. This type of loop will always run at least once until the While clause is evaluated. It will continue looping for as long as the condition is TRUE.

## Do Until

A similar loop is **Do Until**. Like **Do While**, the expression is evaluated at the bottom of the loop. This construct will keep looping *until* the expression is TRUE:

```
PS C:\> do {
>> $i++
>> write-host "`$i="$i
>> }
>> until ($i -ge 5)
>>
```

```
$i= 1
$i= 2
$i= 3
$i= 4
$i= 5
PS C:\>
```

This is almost the same code block that we used with **Do While**. However, the conditional expression uses **-ge** instead of **-le**. The advantage of using **Do Until** is that the loop ends when we expect it to, because when one $i equals 5, the loop exits. Again, we want to stress that there is nothing wrong with using **Do** loops instead of **While**. It all depends on what you are trying to achieve.

# ForEach

The **ForEach** statement is used for stepping through a collection of objects. Usually, some block of code is executed for each step when the **ForEach** statement is used. In other words, "take these steps for each thing in the collection of things." Here's the syntax for this statement:

```
foreach ($<item> in $<collection>){<command_block>}
```

This statement is expecting a variable and a collection in parenthesis. The command block that is contained in the braces will be executed for each variable, each time it goes through the collection. The command block can be as simple as something like this:

```
PS C:\> $var=("apple","banana","pineapple","orange")
PS C:\> foreach ($fruit in $var) {$fruit}
apple
banana
pineapple
orange
PS C:\>
```

We first create an array of fruits. Remember that an array is a collection. The **ForEach** statement says that for each fruit variable in the fruit collection ($var), display the value of the fruit variable.

Here's a slightly more involved example:

### ForEachFruit.ps1

```
#ForEachFruit.ps1
$var=("apple","banana","pineapple","orange")
foreach ($fruit in $var) {
$i++ #this is a counter that is incremented by one each time through
write-host "Adding" $fruit
}
write-host "Added" $i "pieces of fruit"
```

When this script is run, it produces the following output:

```
Adding apple
Adding banana
Adding pineapple
Adding orange
Added 4 pieces of fruit
PS C:\>
```

242

We can even nest other logic constructs within a **ForEach** statement:

## ForEachFile.ps1

```
#ForEachFile.ps1
set-location "C:\"
$sum=0
foreach ($file in get-childitem) {
#$file.GetType()
 if (($file.GetType()).Name -eq "FileInfo") {
  write-host $file.fullname `t $file.length "bytes"
  $sum=$sum+$file.length
  $i++
  }
}
write-host "Counted" $i "file for a total of" $sum "bytes."
```

In this script, we're using the **Get-ChildItem** cmdlet to return all items in C:\. We can do this because the results of the **Get-ChildItem** cmdlet return a collection object. So, even though we don't know the contents of the collection, we can still enumerate on the fly. For each $file variable in the collection, if the object type name is FileInfo, then we display the name and file size (using the length property). We've also added code to calculate a running total of the sum of all the files using $sum, and we use $i as a counter that increases by one each time.

When the script is run, it generates the following output:

```
C:\AUTOEXEC.BAT         0 bytes
C:\AVG7QT.DAT    12283633 bytes
C:\COMLOG.txt    0 bytes
C:\CONFIG.SYS    0 bytes
C:\docs.csv      24938 bytes
C:\DVDPATH.TXT   55 bytes
C:\EventCombMT_Debug.log        854 bytes
C:\hpfr5550.xml         488 bytes
C:\IALog.txt     271 bytes
C:\log.csv       10734 bytes
C:\Log.txt       72 bytes
C:\mtaedt22.exe         2650696 bytes
C:\netdom.exe    142848 bytes
C:\new-object.txt        10240 bytes
C:\out-grid.ps1         811 bytes
C:\out-propertyGrid.ps1         1330 bytes
C:\processes.html        118828 bytes
C:\servers.txt   19 bytes
C:\showprocessinfo.ps1  710 bytes
C:\showservices.ps1     477 bytes
C:\test.ps1      88 bytes
C:\txt.csv       22995 bytes
Counted 22 file for a total of 15270087 bytes.
PS C:\>
```

**Alias Alert**
The **ForEach** statement is also an alias for the **ForEach-Object** cmdlet. We're pointing this out in case you find examples using the cmdlet, because this particular alias works a bit differently than the cmdlet. PowerShell has a special parsing mode that detects the alias and lets you use it as we're showing. If you were to simply replace "foreach" in the examples above with "foreach-object", the script wouldn't run.

We covered the use of **ForEach-Object**—the cmdlet, not the alias—earlier. Typically, you'll use **ForEach** (the alias) in a script and **ForEach-Object** (the cmdlet) in a one-liner at the command line.

To make things more confusing, PowerShell defines another alias, **%** (just the percent sign). It is interchangeable with the **ForEach-Object** cmdlet, but not with **ForEach**. For that reason, we'll often refer to **ForEach** as a *statement* rather than a cmdlet—but you'll see other folks refer to it however *they* prefer, so be prepared.

# Break

The **Break** statement very simply terminates just about any logic construct we've covered in this chapter, including **For**, **ForEach**, **While**, and **Switch**. When a **Break** statement is encountered, PowerShell exits the loop and runs the next command in the command block or script:

```
PS C:\> $i=0
PS C:\> $var=10,20,30,40
PS C:\> foreach ($val in $var)
>> {
>> $i++
>> if ($val -eq 30){break}
>> }
>> write-host "found a match at item $i"

found a match at item 3
PS C:\>
```

In this example, we're searching an array of numbers for 30. When it is found, we want to stop looking, exit the **ForEach** loop, and display the message. Even though the **Switch** statement is not a loop, **Break** also is used within a code block to force an exit from the entire **Switch** statement.

# Continue

The **Continue** statement is essentially the opposite of **Break**. When the **Break** statement is encountered, PowerShell returns immediately to the beginning of a loop like **For**, **ForEach**, and **While**. You can also use **Continue** with **Switch**.

Here's a script that doesn't use **Continue**:

**SwitchNoContinue.ps1**

```
#SwitchNoContinue.ps1
$var="PowerShell123","PowerShell","123","PowerShell 123"
Switch -regex ($var) {
```

```
"\w" {write-host $_" matches \w"}
"\d" {write-host $_" matches \d"}
"\s" {write-host $_" matches \s"}
Default {write-host "No match found for"$_ }
}
```

When this script is run, all matching code blocks are run, since there are multiple possible matches:

```
PowerShell123 matches \w
PowerShell123 matches \d
PowerShell matches \w
123 matches \w
123 matches \d
PowerShell 123 matches \w
PowerShell 123 matches \d
PowerShell 123 matches \s
PS C:\>
```

If we want the switch statement to only run code after the first match, then we can use **Continue**, which will keep processing each element in $var:

## SwitchContinue.ps1

```
#SwitchContinue.ps1
$var="PowerShell123","PowerShell","123","PowerShell 123"
Switch -regex ($var) {
"\w" {write-host $_" matches \w" ;
    continue}
"\d" {write-host $_" matches \d" ;
    continue}
"\s" {write-host $_" matches \s" ;
    continue}
Default {write-host "No match found for"$_ ;
    }
}
```

This is the same script except with the addition of **Continue**. When run, the script produces the following output:

```
PowerShell123 matches \w
PowerShell matches \w
123 matches \w
PowerShell 123 matches \w
PS C:\ >
```

Because each element of $var matches the \w regular expression, only the block of code associated with that part of the **Switch** statement is executed.

245

# Chapter 19
# Script Blocks, Functions, and Filters

*Modularization* is generally thought of as a way to break code down into discrete, more or less self-contained segments. These segments, or *modules*, can be transported between scripts so they can be reused again and again with minimal modification. In this chapter, we'll look at some of the ways PowerShell code can be modularized.

## Script Blocks

A *script block* is a series of PowerShell statements enclosed in curly braces. A script block can be assigned to a variable as shown here:

```
PS C:\> $sb = {
>> $x = 10
>> $y = 10
>> $x * $y }
>>
```

Note that this script was typed interactively. When it saw the { character, PowerShell knew we were typing a script block. The special >> prompt indicated that PowerShell was waiting for additional input. Pressing Enter on a blank >> prompt ended the input. You can prove that the script block text is in the $sb variable by checking it as follows:

```
PS C:\> $sb
$x = 10
$y = 10
$x * $y
```

```
PS C:\>
```

The script block can be executed with the invoke operator, which is an ampersand "&":

```
PS C:\> &$sb
100
PS C:\>
```

When invoked as part of a pipeline, a script block has access to a special variable called *$input* that contains all of the objects passed through the pipeline. For example, the **Get-Process** cmdlet returns an object for each running process. These objects are all stored in $input and can be enumerated with a **foreach** construct:

```
PS C:\> $sb = {
>> foreach ($process in $input ) {
>> $process.ProcessName }
>> }
>>
PS C:\> get-process | &$sb
acrotray
alg
ati2evxx
ati2evxx
BTSTAC~1
BTTray
btwdins
csrss
dllhost
explorer
firefox
Groove
Hpqgalry
```

Again, this was all typed interactively. Notice that when the **Get-Process** is called, its output is piped to $sb, which was invoked using the & operator. This may be clearer in the following script:

**Blocktest.ps1**

```
$sb = {
 foreach ($process in $input) {
   $process.ProcessName
 }
}

get-process | &$sb
```

Running this script produces the same output:

```
PS C:\> test\blocktest
acrotray
alg
ati2evxx
ati2evxx
BTSTAC~1
BTTray
btwdins
csrss
```

```
dllhost
explorer
firefox
Groove
Hpqgalry
```

Script blocks are a simple way to modularize code and allow it to be reused. However, script blocks become more important when used in conjunction with other modularization techniques, such as functions and filters.

# Functions

Functions are a construct common to most programming languages that provide the basic modularization programmers have used for decades. PowerShell allows you to create a function by *declaring* it as follows:

1. Use the **Function** keyword.

2. Provide the name of your function.

3. Enclose the function's code within {curly braces}.

A very basic function might look like this:

```
function myFunction {
 write-host "Hello"
}
```

Functions are nearly identical to script blocks except for two differences: 1) functions are explicitly declared using the **Function** keyword, and 2) functions have a name. Otherwise, functions are practically the same as a script block.

This particular function doesn't accept any input arguments, nor does it really return any kind of value. It simply displays "Hello" on the screen. In languages like VBScript, this function might have been written as a Sub, since functions typically return some value in VBScript. However, in PowerShell, there is not a separate construct if a value isn't being returned. Instead, you simply have the function not return anything if you don't need it to.

Note that you can interactively declare functions without writing a script. Try typing the following into PowerShell at the prompt:

```
PS C:\> function myFunction { write-host "Hello" }
```

This is the same function as the first example, but it is declared all on one line. Because it was entered into the command prompt within PowerShell, this function becomes available globally. In other words, it lives within the global *scope*. Scope controls the availability of functions, and it applies to the availability of variables (we covered scope for the first time in the chapter "Scripting Overview"). With myFunction declared globally, any child scopes such as scripts will be able to call the function. However, if you declare a function within a script, then only that script and *its* child scopes will be able to "see" the function and use it.

Functions can also be nested:

```
Function Outer1 {
 Function Inner1 {
   #code A here
 }
 Function Inner2 {
   #code B here
 }
 #code C here
}
Function Outer2 {
 Function Inner3 {
   #code D here
 }
 Function Inner4 {
   #code E here
 }
 #code F here
}
```

If this were included in a script, then the entire script would be able to call either Outer1 or Outer2. However, the script would not be able to directly call any of the Inner functions, since those exist within the Outer functions' private scopes. Any code within Outer1 (code C) is be able to call Inner1 and Inner2. However, the code within Outer2 (code F) is not be able to access Inner1 and Inner2 because those two functions are contained within the private scope of Outer1.

## Input Arguments

Functions have two ways of accepting input arguments. Here's the first:

```
Function add2 {
 [int]$args[0] + [int]$args[1]
}
```

This could be called like this:

```
PS C:\> Add2 10 20
30
```

This output shows that the two input arguments, 10 and 20, were successfully added. Inside the function these arguments were accessed by using the special $args variable. The $args variable is an array in which each element in the array represents one argument passed to the function. Even though this is a fairly informal technique for accepting input arguments, it may be difficult to follow when you read the script months later. A more formal, easier-to-maintain way to work with input arguments looks like this:

```
Function add2 ([int]$x, [int]$y) {
 $x + $y
}
```

You would call this in exactly the same way. Up front, it defines that two input arguments of the Integer type are required.

A third way to declare this function is as follows:

```
Function add2 {
 Param ([int]$x, [int]$y)
```

```
 $x + $y
}
```

This is the same idea; however, the parameters are defined in a special **Param** section that must be the first line of code in the function, instead of defining the arguments as a part of the function declaration itself.

Once again, you can call the function as follows:

```
PS C:\> Add2 10 20
30
```

However, when you specifically define and name arguments using either of the above techniques, you can also call the function by naming the arguments as you pass them in:

```
PS C:\> Add2 -x 10 -y 20
30
```

This passes the value 10 specifically to the $x argument, and 20 to the $y arguments. It does not make a difference in the math, but for more complex functions, this technique provides more control and allows you to pass in arguments out of order, if necessary.

You can also declare a default value for an argument. In this case, if the function is called without a value for the argument, the function may be able to proceed using a default value:

```
Function add2 {
 Param ([int]$x = 10, [int]$y = 10)
 $x + $y
}
```

Calling the function with no input arguments results in a value:

```
PS C:\> Add2
20
```

## Returning a Value

Returning a value from a function is fairly easy—whatever the function outputs *to the default output stream* (typically using **Write**-Output) is also its return. So, really, all of the sample functions we've looked at so far *have* returned a value. For example:

```
PS C:\> $result = add2 10 10
PS C:\> $result
20
```

Here, our Add2 function was called with 10 and 10 as input arguments. The result of the function was stored in $result. *Anything* output from the function becomes part of its result, not just the last thing it outputs. For example:

**Functiontest.ps1**

```
$a = "Hello"

function foo ($b) {
 $b.ToUpper()
 $b.ToLower()
}
$x = foo $a
$x
```

The function foo outputs both the uppercase and lowercase versions of the input argument. $x is set equal to foo's output. Notice that the function doesn't explicitly use **Write-Output**; instead, it's simply allowing the default cmdlet to write to the default output stream. The result of this is:

```
PS C:\> test\functiontest
HELLO
Hello
```

This shows that $x contains both pieces of information output by the function.

You can also use the **Return** keyword to explicitly return a value:

```
$a = "Hello"

function foo ($b) {
 return $b.ToUpper()
 $b.ToLower()
}
$x = foo $a
$x
```

There's a caveat, though: Once you use **Return**, the function exits immediately. So, in the above example, **$b.ToLower()** would never execute, because it comes *after* the **Return**.

If a function produces output and uses **Return**, the value on the **Return** line is simply appended to any other output. Consider this function:

```
$a = "Hello"

function foo ($b) {
 $b.ToUpper()
 Return $b.ToLower()
}
$x = foo $a
$x
```

The result is identical to the first version of this function:

```
PS C:\> test\functiontest
HELLO
Hello
```

The idea of having a function return *anything* output from that function is neat, but it can also be confusing. We recommend that you concatenate all of your intended output into a variable and use the **Return** keyword to return that value from the function. That way your function is only returning data through one technique, and it's a technique that's easy to spot when you're reviewing the code later.

## Piping to Functions

The examples you've seen so far in this chapter have demonstrated that you can call functions outright. However, you can also pipe the output of other commands into a function. When you do this, the piped-in data is stored in the special $input variable. If multiple objects are piped to a function, then the function is called only once. In this case, all of the objects are placed into $input at the same time. Here's a very simple example of a function that simply outputs whatever's piped in:

```
function foo {
 $input
}
```

Piping this function generates same output for the **Get-Process** cmdlet as the **Get-Process** generates by itself:

```
PS C:\> get-process | foo

Handles NPM(K)    PM(K)    WS(K) VM(M)   CPU(s)     Id ProcessName
------- ------    -----    ----- -----   ------     -- -----------
     37      3     1080     3624    31     0.05   2208 acrotray
    104      5     1144     3384    32     0.02    492 alg
     61      2      548     2136    19     0.52   1076 ati2evxx
     90      3     1152     4664    31     0.72   3960 ati2evxx
    228      7     6316     8688    65     0.64   3216 BTSTAC~1
    182      5     4004     7420    56    98.94   2216 BTTray
     55      3     2060     3044    31     0.16   1508 btwdins
   1093      9     2020     3964    31    51.44    816 csrss
    218      5     2896     7716    45     0.30   5836 dllhost
    697     15    18696     7036   108   160.30    604 explorer
```

However, consider this revised function:

```
function foo {
 $input | get-member
}
```

The function is now piping its input to the **Get-Member** cmdlet, which changes the output as follows:

```
PS C:\> get-process | foo


   TypeName: System.Diagnostics.Process

Name                 MemberType    Definition
----                 ----------    ----------
Handles              AliasProperty Handles = Handlecount
Name                 AliasProperty Name = ProcessName
```

Even though this output is truncated, it shows that $input was recognized as an object of the System. Diagnostics.Process type.

Here's another example:

```
function foo {
 foreach ($i in $input) {
   $i.ProcessName
 }
}
```

Below is the partial output from this function when **Get-Process** is piped to it:

```
PS C:\> get-process | foo
acrotray
alg
ati2evxx
ati2evxx
BTSTAC~1
BTTray
btwdins
csrss
dllhost
```

The function takes the output of **Get-Process** into the $input variable. It then goes through each object in $input and displays just the ProcessName property of each.

## Function Phases

Functions can include up to three special script blocks that execute during different phases of execution. When filters are discussed in the next section, you'll see this applies to filters also. These script blocks use special names to identify themselves:

- **Begin:** This script block is executed only once when the function or filter is first called.

- **Process:** If multiple objects are passed into the function or filter through the pipeline, this script block is executed once for each object.

- **End:** This script block is executed after all pipeline objects have been dealt with by the Process script block.

Understanding how these script blocks work might take a little time. With a function, everything in the pipeline is normally lumped together into the $input variable. However, if the function contains a Process block, then $input is null. Instead, the Process block uses the special $_ variable to access the current pipeline object. Here's an example:

```
function foo {
 Begin {
   "Running processes:"
 }
 Process {
   $_.ProcessName
 }
 End {
   "Complete"
 }
}
```

This produces the following output when **Get-Process** is piped to it:

```
PS C:\> get-process | foo
Running processes:
```

```
acrotray
alg
ati2evxx
ati2evxx
BTSTAC~1
BTTray
btwdins
csrss
dllhost
explorer
firefox
Groove
hpqgalry
hpqtra08
hpwuSchd2
HPZipm12
Complete
```

The Begin block runs first. For each object in the pipeline, Process is executed once, with the current object being put into the $_ variable. End is executed when all objects have been processed. Note that when using any of these blocks, *no code can appear outside a block.* Any code within the function that's not within a block will result in an error. For example:

```
function foo {
 "Starting function foo"
 Begin {
   "Running processes:"
 }
 Process {
   $_.ProcessName
 }
 End {
   "Complete"
 }
}
```

Results in this:

```
PS C:\> get-process | foo
Starting function foo
'begin' is not recognized as a cmdlet, function, operable program,
or script file.
At C:\test\blocktest.ps1:3 char:8
+  Begin <<<< {
Get-Process : Cannot evaluate parameter 'Name' because its argument
is specified as a script block and there is no input. A script
block cannot be evaluated without input.
At C:\test\blocktest.ps1:6 char:10
+  Process <<<< {
'end' is not recognized as a cmdlet, function, operable program,
or script file.
At C:\test\blocktest.ps1:9 char:6
+  End <<<< {
PS C:\>
```

This occurs because code exists outside a script block when script blocks are in use.

# Filters

Filters are *essentially* the same as functions. The big differences are that: 1) filters are declared using the **Filter** keyword, and 2) when objects are piped to a filter, the filter executes one time for each object in the pipeline, rather than just one time for the entire pipeline. Basically, a filter is like a function that contains only a Process script block.

Filters make use of the special $_ variable that represents the current pipeline object. Here's an example:

```
filter foo {
    $_.ProcessName
}
```

When the output of **Get-Process** is piped to this filter, the filter executes one time for each object that **Get-Process** produces. You can see how this differs from a function, which gets *all* of the objects in one big chunk through the $input variable. The filter can be used just like you might use a function:

```
PS C:\> get-process | foo
acrotray
alg
ati2evxx
ati2evxx
BTSTAC~1
BTTray
btwdins
```

Because the filter only gets one object at a time from the pipeline, it doesn't need to use a foreach construct the way our earlier function example did.

## Functions vs. Filters

The differences between a function and a filter can be summarized as follows:

- When something is piped to a function, the piped data goes into the special $input variable and the function is executed once.

- When something is piped to a filter, the filter is executed one time for each object in the piped data. The current object is available in the special $_ variable, and there's no $input variable.

One thing that can make it difficult to understand these differences is that you can write functions that behave exactly the same way filters behave. For example, consider this filter:

```
filter ext {
    $_.Extension
}
```

Now, use **Get-ChildItem** to retrieve the child items (files) of the C: drive, and pipe the child items (files) to the newly-created **Ext** filter:

```
PS C:\> get-childitem c: | ext
.wsf
.sql
.BAT
.txt
.SYS
.pdf
```

```
.log
.xml
.Log
.wsf
.log
.wsf
.log
.txt
```

As you can see, the **Get-ChildItems** cmdlet returns several child objects—all files—that were piped to **Ext**. The **Ext** filter executed *one time* for each item in the pipeline. For each item in the pipeline, **Ext** displayed its **Extension** property.

Let's try the exact same thing with a function:

```
function ext2 {
    $_.Extension
}
```

Now run it the same way:

```
PS C:\> get-childitem c: | ext2
PS C:\>
```

Why is there no output? The answer is because it's a function, so it's executed only *one time*. It's not passed each child item one at a time. Instead, it's passed an entire *collection* of child objects in one big chunk. So, using $_ to access the pipeline object is really accessing that collection, which doesn't have an **Extension** property.

With this in mind, let's revise our function:

```
function ext2 {
 foreach ($file in $input) {
    $file.Extension
 }
}
```

Now we'll get the same output as with the original filter:

```
PS C:\> get-childitem c: | ext2
.wsf
.sql
.BAT
.txt
.SYS
.pdf
.log
.xml
.Log
.wsf
.log
.wsf
.log
.txt
```

This time the function is taking $input and going through each item *inside the function*.

Here's another way to write the function to get the exact same result:

```
function ext2 {
 Process {
   $_.Extension
 }
}
```

This time the function is using the special Process script block, which means the function *itself* is called only once:

```
PS C:\> get-childitem c: | ext2
.wsf
.sql
.BAT
.txt
.SYS
.pdf
.log
.xml
.Log
.wsf
.log
.wsf
.log
.txt
```

The special Process script block automatically takes $input and executes the script block one time for each object within $input, making each object accessible via the $_ variable, which is exactly the same as a filter would do.

So, you may be wondering how to know when you should write a filter and when you should use a function that uses script blocks. Really, it's up to you. Whatever is easier for you to understand and use, then that's the one you should use. A function containing a Process script block is functionally identical to a filter.

## Cmdlets and Snap-ins

Cmdlets are the basic commands available within PowerShell. As such, they encapsulate code that performs useful work. This code is normally written by Microsoft. Cmdlets are normally written in a higher-level .NET Framework language such as VB.NET or C#. For example, the PowerShell documentation provides this C# example of a cmdlet that generates a random number:

```
using System;
using System.Management.Automation;
// GetRandom.cs
/// <summary>
/// an implementation of a random number generator
/// </summary>
[Cmdlet("get", "random")]
public class GetRandomCommand : Cmdlet
{
    protected override void EndProcessing()
    {
        Random r = new Random();
        WriteObject(r.Next());
    }
```

```
}
```

This code would then be compiled using **Csc.exe**, which is the C# compiler provided with the .NET Framework Software Development Kit (SDK). Once compiled, it would be called from within PowerShell as follows:

```
PS C:\> (new-object random).next()
```

As explained in the first chapter, snap-ins are more or less collections of cmdlets. You can see which snap-ins, if any, are available but not active by running **Get-PSSnapin** and using the **-registered** parameter; in a base installation of PowerShell. Nothing will be shown because only the core PowerShell snap-ins exists that were loaded into the shell by default. However, if you've installed third-party snap-ins, they'll be displayed. You can subsequently load them into the shell using **Add-PSSnapIn**:

```
PS C:\> Add-pssnapin MySnapInName
```

Creating new snap-ins is fairly complex and typically requires a high-level .NET language, such as VB.NET or C#. It's beyond the scope of this book to cover cmdlet or snap-in creation. However, these examples are provided so you can see a bit of what goes into them and how they're used to encapsulate more complex, high-level code for use within PowerShell.

## Modularization Tricks

While it's useful to have script blocks, functions, and filters available for copying and pasting between scripts, you can also make them a persistent part of your global shell environment by adding them to your profile. For example, if you've created a function that performs some useful task that you're calling on again and again, simply add the function into your profile to make it available as soon as PowerShell starts. In fact, Microsoft uses this trick. The PowerShell **Help** command is actually a function that is predefined in the default profile that ships with PowerShell. To add a function to your profile, just open your profile, which is a text file, and paste the function into your profile.

# Chapter 20
# Error Handling

*Error handling* is sort of proactive debugging: Using special techniques, you build scripts that anticipate certain errors and deal with them on the fly, instead of just crashing. PowerShell divides errors into two categories:

- **Terminating**. Causes your script or command to stop executing.

- **Non-terminating**. Even though a problem still exists, the script or command is allowed to continue running.

When an error occurs, the error itself is represented by an object called **ErrorRecord**. This object contains an *exception*, which is essentially a fancy word for *error*. An exception also includes other information about why and where the error occurred. Like any other object, **ErrorRecord** has properties that you can examine:

- **Exception**. This is the error that occurred. It's an object in and of itself. For example, Exception. Message contains an English description of the error.

- **TargetObject**. This is the object that was being operated when the error occurred. This may be Null if there was no particular object involved.

- **CategoryInfo**. This divides all errors into a few dozen broad categories.

- **FullyQualifiedErrorId.** This property identifies the error more specifically. In fact, it is the most specific identifier.

- **ErrorDetails.** May be Null, but when present contains additional information. It's actually a subobject called ErrorDetails.Message. One of its properties is the most specific possible English description of the error.

- **InvocationInfo.** Tells you the context in which the error occurred, such as a cmdlet name or script line. May be Null.

A special variable, $error, is used to store the most recent **ErrorRecord** objects. In fact, by default the most recent 256 errors are stored. The $error variable is an array. For example, $error[0] contains the most recent error and $error[1] is the one before that. Each element of $error is an ErrorRecord object. For example, to see the error text for the most recent error, you would examine:

```
PS C:\> $error[0].Exception.Message
```

When an error occurs, you can examine $error to determine whether your script can do anything about the error. However, before your script has the opportunity to do so, you will have to *trap* the error.

## Error Actions

Most cmdlets support the ubiquitous **-ErrorAction** argument, which is aliased as just **EA**. This argument specifies what should happen if the cmdlet encounters a non-terminating error. The default behavior is Continue, which means the cmdlet displays the error and tries and continue executing the cmdlet or script. Other options include:

**Stop**. Makes the cmdlet stop executing

**Inquire**. Asks the user what to do

**SilentlyContinue**. Continues without displaying any clues as to what went wrong

Here's an example of SilentlyContinue:

```
PS C:\> $a = Get-WmiObject Win32_OperatingSystem -ea stop
```

This executes **Get-WmiObject**. If something goes wrong, it will stop rather than continuing. However, if you've defined a *trap handler*, which we'll discuss next, then the trap handler will still execute after the cmdlet stops. Essentially, the **-ea stop** is telling the cmdlet, "Hey, if an error occurs, raise an exception for me." This exception is the key to making error trapping work: When an exception is raised, PowerShell will look for a trap handler that's set up to handle that particular type of exception. If it finds one, it will execute the handler. So, without an exception, you can't trap errors in PowerShell.

Note that if you tell a cmdlet to "SilentlyContinue", then no exception is raised when a problem occurs; without an exception, PowerShell won't try to look for a trap handler, and you'll never be able to "handle" the problem.

## Trapping Errors

Trapping in PowerShell can be fairly complicated. When an error occurs in a script, an exception is "thrown" or "raised." That exception is delivered to an exception handler, which is called the *trap handler*. Following the execution of the handler, the session state established by ErrorPolicy settings is checked to determine whether or not the script should continue running. If a specific trap handler has not been defined, the exception will simply be delivered to the output mechanism. This usually means the exception will be displayed and the script will halt. If a trap handler is defined, it may reset the ErrorPolicy, which determines whether or not the script will continue after the error is resolved.

Let's briefly summarize how this works. If a *trap handler* has been defined, the handler is executed when an error occurs. The handler has access to $error to see what went wrong. It can also set the ErrorPolicy to determine whether or not the script continues. Defining the trap handler looks a bit like this:

```
Trap [ExceptionType] {
 # statements go here
 # $_ represents the ErrorRecord that was thrown
 Return [argument] | break | continue
}
```

The [ExceptionType] is the type of exception you want to trap. This allows you to define a different trap handler for different types of errors or exceptions. However, you do not *have* to include [ExceptionType]. If you don't, the trap handler will handle any exceptions that occur. You can actually define multiple traps for the same exception. If that exception occurs, all of the traps will execute in the order in which they're defined.

Within the trap handler, the special $_ variable represents the ErrorRecord that caused the trap handler to be executed in the first place.

At the end of the trap handler, you have three options:

- **Continue**. This causes script execution to continue at the line of code following the line that caused the error.

- **Break**. This causes the current scope to stop executing.

- **Return** [argument]. This exits the current scope, optionally returning whatever argument you specify.

If multiple trap handlers are executed, then the Continue/Break/Return of the *last-executed handler* is the one that takes effect.

Understanding how these three options work requires you to understand a bit about trap scope. If you don't specify any of these three options, then the trap handler will exit returning $_, which is the error that caused the trap handler to be called in the first place.

# Trap Scope

Remember that PowerShell supports *scopes* (which we discussed in the chapter "Scripting Overview"). Essentially, the shell is the global scope. Running a script begins a new scope in which the script itself runs. In addition, each function that's executed is a unique scope. You can define a unique trap handler within each of these scopes. Scripts can have trap handlers, while functions can have self-contained trap handlers that are private to the function. When an exception is thrown, a trap handler in the *current scope* is executed if one is available. For example, if an error occurs in a script, PowerShell looks for a trap handler defined within the script. If it can't find one, the error is raised to the parent scope, and PowerShell looks for a trap handler there.

When you exit a trap handler using **Continue**, the next line of code *in the same scope as the trap handler* is executed. The **Break** keyword exits the current scope and goes up one level to the parent scope, passing the exception up to the parent scope. If another trap handler is defined in the parent scope, it can be called at this point.

The **Return** keyword does more or less the same thing, except that the specified argument is passed to the parent scope and no exception is thrown. So, if the trap handler lives inside a function, the **Return** keyword will append to the function's return value and the function exits normally as if nothing bad occurred.

## Throwing Your Own Exceptions

You can use the **Throw** keyword to throw an exception. This is basically the same thing that happens when a line of script causes an error, except you're sort of causing the error on purpose. This can be used to pass the error up to a parent scope for handling. For example:

**Script1.ps1**

```
trap {
 write-host "YIKES!!!"
 throw $_
}
script2
```

**Script2.ps1**

```
trap {
 write-host "In Script2"
 break
}
$a = get-content C:\nofile.txt -erroraction stop
```

Here, Script1 calls Script2. Script2 defines a trap handler and then attempts to get the content of a non-existent file. Note that the **Get-Content** cmdlet is run with the -**erroraction** argument, specifying that should an error occur, the cmdlet should stop. The default action is to Continue. Other choices would be SilentlyContinue or Inquire (e.g., ask the user what to do). So, when an error occurs, since C:\nofile.txt doesn't exist, an exception is thrown by **Get-Content**. It stops running, and the exception is picked up by the trap handler in Script2. This trap handler outputs "In Script2" and then breaks. This break causes execution of Script2 to stop, and execution to return to the parent scope, which is Script1.

The **Break** keyword passes the exception up to Script1, which has its own trap handler defined. It outputs "YIKES!!!" and then throws an exception. The exception it throws is $_, which is the exception that caused the trap handler to run. Throwing an exception is kind of like using **Break**—the current scope exits and the specified exception is passed to the calling scope. Assuming Script1 was launched interactively from within PowerShell, then the global scope is the calling scope and will receive the exception in $_.

The output looks like this:

```
PS C:\> script1
In Script2
YIKES!!!
The path 'nofile.txt' does not exist.

At c:\ps\scripts\script2.ps1:6 char:17
+ $a = get-content <<<< C:\nofile.txt -erroraction stop
```

You can see where Script1 was executed from a PowerShell prompt. Script2 was called, and its trap handler output "In Script2" before passing the exception back to Script1. Script1's trap handler outputs "YIKES!!!" before passing the exception back up the line to the global scope. PowerShell's behavior is to display the error, "The path 'nofile.txt' does not exist" and then list the original location where the error occurred.

You can also use **Throw** to throw a text error:

```
Throw "this is my error"
```

PowerShell constructs an actual ErrorRecord object out of this. The exception is a generic RuntimeException, the ErrorID is the string you provided (which will also go into the exception's Message property), the ErrorCategory is OperationStopped, and the targetObject is the string you provided.

If you just call **Throw** with no argument, the ErrorRecord's exception is RuntimeException. The ErrorID is "ScriptHalted," which also goes into the exception's Message property. The ErrorCategory is OperationStopped, and the targetObject property is Null.

# Tips for Error Trapping

Take a look at TrapTest.ps1:

### TrapTest.ps1

```
function CheckWMI ($computer) {

 trap {
   write-host "An error occured: "
   write-host "ID: " $_.ErrorID
   write-host "Message: "$_.Exception.Message
   throw "Couldn't check $computer"
 }

 $a = Get-WmiObject Win32_OperatingSystem `
  -property ServicePackMajorVersion `
  -computer $computer -ea stop
 write-host "$computer : " $a.ServicePackMajorVersion

}

write-host "Service Pack Versions:"
CheckWMI("DON-PC")
CheckWMI("TESTBED")
```

Assuming DON-PC exists and TESTBED doesn't, this produces the following output:

```
PS C:\> test\traptest
Service Pack Versions:
DON-PC : 2
An error occured:
ID:
Message: Command execution stopped because the shell variable
"ErrorActionPreference" is set to Stop: The RPC server is unavailable.
(Exception from HRESULT: 0x800706BA)
Couldn't check TESTBED
```

```
At C:\test\traptest.ps1:8 char:10
+     throw <<<< "Couldn't check $computer"
```

Notice that -ea stop was specified for the cmdlet, ensuring that it would stop execution and allow the trap to execute. Let's make one small change to the original script: Remove the -ea argument, allowing the default of Continue to take place.

Here's the revised output:

```
PS C:\> test\traptest
Service Pack Versions:
DON-PC : 2
Get-WmiObject : The RPC server is unavailable. (Exception from
HRESULT: 0x800706BA)
At C:\test\traptest.ps1:11 char:21
+ $a = Get-WmiObject <<<< Win32_OperatingSystem `
TESTBED :
PS C:\>
```

See the difference? The trap didn't get to execute in this case—the error occurred right at the cmdlet. So, whenever possible, make sure you're executing cmdlets with an appropriate ErrorAction argument, and defining a trap to handle whatever errors might crop up.

Chapter 21
# The PowerShell Debugger and Debugging Techniques

Debugging is the process of removing bugs, or errors, from your script. There are really two types of errors: Simple *syntax errors*, which are usually just typos, and *logic errors*, which mean your script won't behave like you think it should—even though it might not actually give you any error messages. In this chapter, we'll show you a few different types of errors, and walk you through a methodology that helps locate the error quickly, so that you can fix it and move on.

## The Debugging Process

Debugging can be tricky. The best way to debug is to have a thorough understanding of what your script is doing and how PowerShell is executing it. Let's work with an example: Without actually *running* this script, can you predict where the error will occur?

### TrickyDebugging.ps1

```
$foo = "this is the original text"
1.
2.   function f1($str)
3.   {
"Calling f1..."
4.   $str.toUpper()
5.   }
6.
7.   function f2($value)
8.   {
"Calling f2... what is value?"
9.   $value | get-member
```

```
""
"Before f1 value is: " + $value
"Before f1 foo is: " + $script:foo
10. $script:foo = f1 $value
"after f1 value is: " + $value
"after f1 foo is: " + $script:foo
11. }
12.
""
"BEFORE PASS 1, WHAT IS FOO?"
13. $foo | get-member
""
14.
"PASS 1"
15. f2 $foo
16.
""
"AFTER PASS 1, WHAT IS FOO?"
17. $foo | get-member
""
18.
""
"PASS 2"
19. f2 $foo
20.
""
"global value"
21. $foo
```

......................................................................................................................................................

**Here's What We Do**
When we're trying to follow a script like this, we take a piece of paper and a pen, and a printout of the script, and start reading. We use the paper to keep track of the values inside variables, in much the same way that PowerShell keeps track of them in memory. Usually, a methodical approach like that reveals the bug in no time.

After you read through this script, try running it in PowerShell. Then, load the script into an editor like PrimalScript that offers line numbering, and let's walk through *exactly* what's happening. This is the process you'll have to do anytime you want to debug something.

First the variable, $foo, is assigned a value. This occurs in the script's scope, which is a child of the shell's global scope. Then, two functions, f1 and f2, are defined but not yet executed.

The action starts on line 21, where two literal strings are output and $foo is piped to the **Get-Member** cmdlet. This displays the type of object $foo is. If you've run the script, you'll see that it's a System. String. Remember this piece of information.

Next, on line 24, a blank line is output. On line 27, $foo is passed to the fg2 function. That function is defined on line 9; you can see it's accepting input—whatever was in $foo—into the variable $value. Line 12 passes $value to **Get-Member**. Notice anything? The $value variable isn't recognized as a string since it's a generic System.Object. On line 14, $value is output, as is the script-level $foo variable. You'll notice in the script's output that these two match. This is exactly what should occur at this point.

The f1 function is called, passing $value as its input argument. The function places that input into the $str variable. It outputs "Calling f1…" and then outputs the result of $str.toUpper. We didn't check, but we can expect that $str was received as a System.Object, but that PowerShell was able to coerce it into being a System.String so the **ToUpper()** method would work. *Everything* output by function f1 becomes its "return value," which is placed into the script-level $foo object back on line 16. Lines 17 and 18 confirm that $value and $foo are now different, since $foo has been replaced with an uppercase version of $value.

So far so good. However, on line 31, the output indicates that $foo isn't a System.String anymore; it's now a System.Object. Line 36 repeats the whole process, but gets an error on line 6 when f1 is called a second time, because $str is now an Object that can't be coerced into a String. As such, it has no **ToUpper()** method to call, which is what the error indicates if you run the script.

So, the problem is that at some point PowerShell stopped coercing $str into a String and left it as an Object. Why? The answer is on the *first call* to f1. Remember, f1's output was "Calling f1…" followed by a carriage return, followed by the result of $str.toUpper. That carriage return is the culprit since it prevents PowerShell from recognizing a string. Instead the carriage return causes it to recognize an *array* of two strings. This means the second time f1 is called, $str appears to contain an array, which doesn't have a **ToUpper()** method.

The *proper* way to have a function output text without having that text become part of the function's return value is to use **Write-Host.** Modify line 5 as follows:

```
Write-Host "Calling f1..."
```

When you run the script again, you'll see it works fine! That's because the output of f1 never contains a carriage return, which allows the string to be recognized as a System.String by PowerShell.

Another fix would be to modify line 1 as follows:

```
[string]$foo = "this is the original text"
```

Again, *just* this change makes the script work because the decision on whether or not the string is a String or an Object is no longer PowerShell's choice. In fact, $foo is explicitly declared as a String and stays that way throughout. Strings *can* contain carriage returns. However, keep in mind when something is not specifically declared as a string that contains a carriage return, it will be interpreted as an Object.

This is just one example of how nitty-gritty you need to get when you're debugging. Walk through every line of code. As in this example, add extra code to help you figure out what's what, such as when we used **Get-Member** to see how data type variables were being treated. This isn't to say that debugging is *simple*. However, the best way to debug is by following your script one line at a time and *seeing* what PowerShell is doing.

> **Please, Believe Us**
> Nobody believes us when we say, "walk through your script one line at a time." Invariably, we'll watch administrators struggle with a script, glancing at it, thinking they know what the problem is, and making a change that doesn't help. You can't debug like that—we call it "shotgun debugging," because your "fixes" are all over the place, and you wind up blasting holes in your script. *Trust us,* a methodical, line-by-line approach might seem more time-consuming, but in the end, it isn't.

# Debug Mode and Tracing

As the previous debugging example illustrated, it's critical to understand what your script is doing and with what data it's working. The contents of variables change as your script jumps in and out of functions. So, knowing exactly what's going on allows you to mentally follow the script's progress and spot the problems that are causing bugs. Unfortunately, PowerShell v1 lacks a full debugger. In fact, v1 lacks any means for a third-party debugging to "plug in" and help you. That means you're more or less on your own when it comes to figuring out what your scripts are doing.

Fortunately, PowerShell *does* include a "debug mode" that gives you some ability to see what's going on inside your script. Your primary tool is the **Set-PSDebug** cmdlet that allows you to trace the execution of your script. This means that by writing status information throughout the script, you can see what's happening as your script executes.

**Set-PSDebug** is a fairly complicated cmdlet that allows you to control the *trace level* of script execution. It also allows you to turn on line-by-line script execution, pausing execution after each line so you can examine the contents of variables to see what your script is doing. We'll use the DebugTest.ps1 script in the following example to see how this works:

### DebugTest.ps1

```
function F1 {
 param ($n, $a)
 if (F2($a)) {
   "$n is old enough to vote"
 } else {
   "$n is too young to vote"
 }
}

function F2 {
 param ($var)
 if ($var -gt 17) {
   $true
 } else {
   $false
 }
}

[string]$name = "Joe"
[int]$age = 25

F1 $name, $age
```

Looking at this script, you'd expect it to display "Joe is old enough to vote." Walk through the script in your head to make sure you agree with that before you proceed.

However, running the script produces this output:

```
PS C:\> test\debugtest
Joe 25 is too young to vote
```

Clearly this output is not correct. So, what went wrong? The best way to find out is to start debugging in order to find out what's in the variables and what execution path the script is taking.

We'll start by running **Set-PSDebug** and specifying a trace level. We'll also turn on step-by-step execution. There are three possible trace levels:

- 0: No tracing.

- 1: Trace script lines as they execute.

- 2: Also trace variable assignments, function calls, and scripts.

Level 2 is the most detailed, which is what we want. Actually, specifying the -step argument implies -trace 1, so we'll need to explicitly specify -trace 2 to get the detail we want. After running **Set-PSDebug**, we'll run our script.

As you can see, PowerShell now asks on a line-by-line basis if we're ready to execute that line:

```
PS C:\> set-psdebug -trace 2 -step
PS C:\> test\debugtest

Continue with this operation?
  1+ test\debugtest
[Y] Yes [A] Yes to All [N] No [L] No to All [S] Suspend [?] Help
(default is "Y"):
```

If you're following along, hit "Y" for each of the following lines as we move through this script one line at a time:

- You'll notice that the first three lines are merely asking for permission to execute the script itself, and to recognize the two functions. Press Enter three times to move to line 19 of the script.

- After setting a variable, PowerShell confirms the value that's gone into the variable. This is shown by default in yellow text after the line of script is run:

```
Continue with this operation?
 19+ [string]$name = "Joe"
[Y] Yes [A] Yes to All [N] No [L] No to All [S] Suspend [?] Help
(default is "Y"):
DEBUG:  19+ [string]$name = "Joe"
DEBUG:     ! SET $name = 'Joe'.

Continue with this operation?
 20+ [int]$age = 25
[Y] Yes [A] Yes to All [N] No [L] No to All [S] Suspend [?] Help
(default is "Y"):
```

- We then set the $age variable, which is confirmed.

- Next we call the F1 function.

- Now we're on line 3 inside of function F1, which calls function F2.

- This is a good point to see what actually got passed into F1 for input arguments. Press "S" and hit Enter to suspend the script. Notice that PowerShell drops to a special prompt so we can examine the values of the $n and $a variables. Notice that $n contains "Joe," a carriage return, and "25," which is not what we expected. Also notice that $a does not contain anything, which is why our script isn't working properly.

```
Continue with this operation?
  3+  if (F2($a)) {
[Y] Yes [A] Yes to All [N] No [L] No to All [S] Suspend [?] Help
(default is "Y"):S
PS C:\>>> $n
Joe
25
PS C:\>>> $a
PS C:\>>>
```

- Since we've spotted a problem, there's no point in continuing until this problem is fixed. We'll enter EXIT to return to the script, and then reply with "L" to abandon execution of further lines of code:

```
PS C:\>>> exit

Continue with this operation?
  3+  if (F2($a)) {
[Y] Yes [A] Yes to All [N] No [L] No to All [S] Suspend [?] Help
(default is "Y"):1
WriteDebug stopped because the DebugPreference was 'Stop'.
At C:\test\debugtest.ps1:22 char:1
+ F <<<< 1 $name, $age
PS C:\>
```

So, our problem is that both the name and age are being passed into the $n argument of function F1, while $a isn't getting a value at all. The problem? Our initial call to F1:

```
F1 $name, $age
```

PowerShell doesn't use a comma to separate arguments. This line should be:

```
F1 $name $age
```

After making this modification, let's debug the script again. To begin, hit Enter at the debug prompts until you get to line 3 again. Then, hit S to suspend the script and check the values in $n and $a:

```
PS C:\> test\debugtest

Continue with this operation?
  1+ test\debugtest
[Y] Yes [A] Yes to All [N] No [L] No to All [S] Suspend [?] Help
(default is "Y"):
DEBUG:    1+ test\debugtest
DEBUG:     ! CALL script 'debugtest.ps1'

Continue with this operation?
  1+ function F1 {
[Y] Yes [A] Yes to All [N] No [L] No to All [S] Suspend [?] Help
(default is "Y"):
DEBUG:    1+ function F1 {

Continue with this operation?
 10+ function F2 {
[Y] Yes [A] Yes to All [N] No [L] No to All [S] Suspend [?] Help
(default is "Y"):
DEBUG:  10+ function F2 {

Continue with this operation?
 19+ [string]$name = "Joe"
[Y] Yes [A] Yes to All [N] No [L] No to All [S] Suspend [?] Help
(default is "Y"):
DEBUG:  19+ [string]$name = "Joe"
DEBUG:     ! SET $name = 'Joe'.

Continue with this operation?
 20+ [int]$age = 25
```

```
[Y] Yes [A] Yes to All [N] No [L] No to All [S] Suspend [?] Help
(default is "Y"):
DEBUG:   20+ [int]$age = 25
DEBUG:    ! SET $age = '25'.

Continue with this operation?
 22+ F1 $name $age
[Y] Yes [A] Yes to All [N] No [L] No to All [S] Suspend [?] Help
(default is "Y"):
DEBUG:   22+ F1 $name $age
DEBUG:    ! CALL function 'F1' (defined in file 'C:\test\debugtest.ps1')

Continue with this operation?
  3+  if (F2($a)) {
[Y] Yes [A] Yes to All [N] No [L] No to All [S] Suspend [?] Help
(default is "Y"):s
PS C:\>>> $n
Joe
PS C:\>>> $a
25
PS C:\>>>
```

Now we can see that $n contains "Joe" and $a contains "25", which is what we want. We'll type EXIT to return to the script, and hit A to execute all remaining lines without stopping one line at a time.

```
PS C:\>>> exit

Continue with this operation?
  3+  if (F2($a)) {
[Y] Yes [A] Yes to All [N] No [L] No to All [S] Suspend [?] Help
(default is "Y"):a
DEBUG:    3+  if (F2($a)) {
DEBUG:     ! CALL function 'F2' (defined in file 'C:\test\debugtest.ps1')
DEBUG:   12+  if ($var -gt 17) {
DEBUG:   13+    $true
DEBUG:    4+    "$n is old enough to vote"
Joe is old enough to vote
PS C:\>
```

You can see that trace messages are still output for each line of code that executes, but we're not prompted to run each line. Line 3 calls function F2, which starts on line 12. We can see that the If construct was true because it executed line 13, which returned the value $true. That resulted in a true comparison for line 3, which resulted in line 4 executing, producing our script's output. We'll disable tracing by running:

```
Set-PSDebug -off
```

### Tracing Your Work
PowerShell also provides the **Trace-Command** cmdlet, which is pretty complicated but provides insight into PowerShell's internal workings. Because it provides such a deep view of PowerShell, it requires significant programming experience to use and understand. Therefore, it will not be covered, since we consider it a bit beyond the scope of this book.

One good technique for using **Set-PSDebug** is to either have a printed copy of your script or have your script up in a script development environment, such as SAPIEN PrimalScript, as you execute the script line-by-line. That way you can see each line of script code in the context of the full script, which allows you to follow PowerShell's execution of your script one line at a time. As you debug, keep a piece of scratch paper handy so you can jot down variables' contents. You'll also frequently suspend the script to check variables' contents. When PowerShell displays each line of code prior to executing it, ask yourself what *should* happen. That way, when you hit Enter to execute that line, you'll either get the result you expected indicating all is well, or you won't, meaning you'll know where the problem occurred.

## Debugging Techniques

In addition to knowing how to use the debugger, there's a lot to be said for having some good debugging tricks up your sleeve. In the next few sections, we'll share some of our favorite tips for making debugging go a bit smoother.

Remember that our goal with debugging is *always* to get a better idea of what our script *is actually doing*, and then compare that to our expectations. If you don't have any expectations for your script, then you won't know if it's doing anything wrong! Always follow this basic methodology:

1.  Print your script. Seriously, this seems archaic today, but until you get to be a really skilled debugger, this is a huge help.

2.  Next to each line of the script, jot down a note about what the line does. For example, "queries two classes from WMI." Be specific. If you've already put these types of comments into your script—good for you! See how much time it saves, now that you're debugging?

3.  Walk through your script *one line at a time* and predict what each will do. Keep two pieces of scratch paper: One for variables, and one for output. On each, write down what you think PowerShell will do. This lets you keep track of variables' values, and predict the output.

With the above pieces of paper in hand, you're ready to start debugging. In many cases, you can use the built-in debugger and compare its line-by-line results to your own to see if there's any difference (difference = bug). In other cases, you may wish to "beef up" your script by using some of the following techniques. For each of these, we're going to be starting with the following script:

```
#Test-Debug.ps1
$computers = Get-Content c:\computers.txt
foreach ($computer in $computers) {
    Write-Output `n$computer
    $wmi = gwmi -query "select * from win32_logicaldisk where drivetype=3" `
        -computer $computer
        foreach ($drive in $wmi) {
                $device = $drive.deviceid
                $space = $drive.freespace / 1MB
    Write-Output "$device has $space MB free"
        }
}
```

As-is, this script produces output like this:

```
zLOCALHOST
C: has 113432.03515625 MB free
D: has 155298.8046875 MB free
G: has 32439.875 MB free


MEDIASERVER
C: has 136600.62109375 MB free
D: has 194455.5390625 MB free
```

## Writing Verbose Information

Our short sample script above produces useful information: an inventory of free drive space on local drives for a list of computers. However, if something goes wrong, then we just get error messages mixed into the output and may have to guess at the cause. Sometimes, having the option to see more detailed information—that is, more *verbose* information—is useful. PowerShell's **Write-Verbose** cmdlet gives us this capability. For example, consider this revision:

```
#Test-Debug.ps1
$computers = Get-Content c:\computers.txt
$qty = $computers | Measure-Object
$qty = $qty.count
Write-Verbose "Inventorying $qty computers"

foreach ($computer in $computers) {
   Write-Output `n$computer
   Write-Verbose "Connecting..."
   $wmi = gwmi -query "select * from win32_logicaldisk where drivetype=3" `
         -computer $computer

   Write-Verbose "Free space on local drives..."
        foreach ($drive in $wmi) {
               $device = $drive.deviceid
               $space = $drive.freespace / 1MB
     Write-Output "$device has $space MB free"
         }
}
```

You can see in the beginning of the script that we've actually calculated information specifically to be written "verbosely:" the number of computers in the list. When we run this, here's what we get:

```
LOCALHOST
C: has 113432.015625 MB free
D: has 155298.8046875 MB free
G: has 32439.875 MB free


MEDIASERVER
C: has 136577.55859375 MB free
D: has 194455.5390625 MB free
```

Um, wait a minute… that's the same thing. The trick to **Write-Verbose**, you see, is that it writes to the *verbose* pipeline—which, by default, is turned off. We can turn it on by setting the $VerbosePreference variable from its default value of "SilentlyContinue" to "Continue," and rerunning our script:

```
PS C:\> $verbosepreference = "Continue"
PS C:\> .\test-debug.ps1
```

```
VERBOSE: Inventorying 3 computers


LOCALHOST
VERBOSE: Connecting...
VERBOSE: Free space on local drives...
C: has 113431.640625 MB free
D: has 155298.8046875 MB free
G: has 32439.875 MB free


MEDIASERVER
VERBOSE: Connecting...
VERBOSE: Free space on local drives...
C: has 136573.43359375 MB free
D: has 194455.5390625 MB free
```

Of course, you can't see it here, but the verbose information it not only prefaced by "VERBOSE:" but also displayed in an alternate color so that it stands out. Now we can watch our script run with a lot more detail about what's happening at each step. This is useful when you're not necessarily debugging, too, just to help track down exactly what's going on in the script.

## Writing Debugging Information

Debugging information is often much less attractively formatted, and typically includes "inside" information. Here's a modified script that includes this information, using the **Write-Debug** cmdlet:

```
#Test-Debug.ps1
$computers = Get-Content c:\computers.txt
$qty = $computers | Measure-Object
Write-Debug "`$qty is $qty"

$qty = $qty.count
Write-Debug "`$qty is $qty"
Write-Verbose "Inventorying $qty computers"

foreach ($computer in $computers) {
   Write-Debug "`$computer is $computer"
   Write-Output `n$computer

   Write-Verbose "Connecting..."
   $wmi = gwmi -query "select * from win32_logicaldisk where drivetype=3" `
       -computer $computer

       $wmi | Measure-Object | write-debug

   Write-Verbose "Free space on local drives..."
       foreach ($drive in $wmi) {
               $device = $drive.deviceid
     Write-Debug "`$device is $device"

               $space = $drive.freespace / 1MB
     Write-Debug "`$space is $space"
     Write-Output "$device has $space MB free"
       }
}
```

Our strategy is to put a **Write-Debug** after every variable assignment or change, outputting the new variable value. This lets us keep close tabs on what the script is doing. You'll notice that we wrote strings like "`$qty is $qty" a lot. The first $qty will be displayed literally, because we've *escaped* the dollar sign. The second $qty will be replaced with the variable's actual value.

**Write-Debug** writes to PowerShell's *debug* pipeline, and the $DebugPreference variable controls whether or not that pipeline is on or off. By default, it's set to "SilentlyContinue", which means "don't display." We'll set it to "Continue" to see our debug output.

```
PS C:\> $debugpreference = "continue"
PS C:\> .\test-debug.ps1
DEBUG: $qty is Microsoft.PowerShell.Commands.GenericMeasureInfo
DEBUG: $qty is 3
VERBOSE: Inventorying 3 computers
DEBUG: $computer is LOCALHOST


LOCALHOST
VERBOSE: Connecting...
DEBUG: Microsoft.PowerShell.Commands.GenericMeasureInfo
VERBOSE: Free space on local drives...
DEBUG: $device is C:
DEBUG: $space is 113431.625
C: has 113431.625 MB free
DEBUG: $device is D:
DEBUG: $space is 155298.8046875
D: has 155298.8046875 MB free
DEBUG: $device is G:
DEBUG: $space is 32439.875
G: has 32439.875 MB free
DEBUG: $computer is MEDIASERVER


MEDIASERVER
VERBOSE: Connecting...
DEBUG: Microsoft.PowerShell.Commands.GenericMeasureInfo
VERBOSE: Free space on local drives...
DEBUG: $device is C:
DEBUG: $space is 136542.49609375
C: has 136542.49609375 MB free
DEBUG: $device is D:
DEBUG: $space is 194455.5390625
D: has 194455.5390625 MB free
```

Wow, that's a lot of extra information! As you can see, it's a bit poorly formatted, but that's okay because this information is just for us, so we can follow our script. We can now see "inside" the script, looking at every value as it changes and following the script's execution with great precision.

The *best* part about **Write-Debug** and **Write-Preference** is that you can use them in your script from the very start, before you every have to debug. By default, their output isn't displayed, but you can turn them on whenever you need them and turn them off again when you're finished. A *really* cool part about these cmdlets is a development environment like PrimalScript: If you set the $DebugPreference variable *in your script*, say as the first line, then PrimalScript captures this debug information to a separate pane, which allows you to review the debug information separately from your script's primary output.

## Using Nested Prompts

We talked about nested prompts first in the chapter "Working with the PowerShell Host." A *nested prompt* is one which occurs inside an existing pipeline. For debugging purposes, it's pure gold: You can have your script "pause" in mid-execution, open a new nested prompt, and then use the shell interactively *inside your script's scope*. That means all your script variables and so forth will be completely available. We're going to go back to our original example script and throw in a nested prompt:

```
#Test-Debug.ps1
$computers = Get-Content c:\computers.txt
foreach ($computer in $computers) {
   Write-Output `n$computer
   $wmi = gwmi -query "select * from win32_logicaldisk where drivetype=3" `
        -computer $computer
        $host.EnterNestedPrompt()
        foreach ($drive in $wmi) {
               $device = $drive.deviceid
               $space = $drive.freespace / 1MB
     Write-Output "$device has $space MB free"
        }
}
```

........................................................................................................................

**Important!**
Keep in mind that the capabilities of the $Host variable are typically available only within the PowerShell.exe console host. If you're running your script from PrimalScript, configure it to *not* capture script output. This will launch your script in a new instance of PowerShell.exe.

When we run this script, as soon as it hits the $Host.EnterNestedPrompt() line, a new nested prompt is opened. We can then examine variables, such as the $wmi variable we just created, to see if they contain what we expect. When we're done, entering **Exit** will exit the nested prompt, returning control to the script. Here's what it looks like from the shell:

```
PS C:\> .\test-debug.ps1


LOCALHOST
PS C:\>>> $wmi


DeviceID    : C:
DriveType   : 3
ProviderName :
FreeSpace   : 118939058176
Size        : 250056704000
VolumeName  :

DeviceID    : D:
DriveType   : 3
ProviderName :
FreeSpace   : 162842599424
Size        : 250056704000
VolumeName  : Storage

DeviceID    : G:
DriveType   : 3
ProviderName :
FreeSpace   : 34015674368
Size        : 163913347072
VolumeName  : Backup
```

```
PS C:\>>> exit
C: has 113429.125 MB free
D: has 155298.8046875 MB free
G: has 32439.875 MB free


MEDIASERVER
PS C:\>>>
```

Nested prompts can be used to "break" or "pause" your script at a specific point, let you examine and change things, and then pick right back up where you left off—an invaluable debugging technique.

# Chapter 22
# PowerShell for VBScript, Cmd.exe, and *nix Users

PowerShell can seem intimidating for VBScript users and familiar for *nix users—and both types of user would be wrong, in a way! In reality, PowerShell's a lot more like VBScript (well, in some ways, at least) than you might think, and although it's definitely inspired by *nix shells, its differences are significant and profound. In this chapter, we'll try to address some of the most common "migration points" that come up as folks start to learn PowerShell.

## If You're Used to VBScript...

Let's quickly clear up a potential point of confusion: There's no easy, set way to convert a VBScript to a PowerShell script. But why would you want to? If the VBScript works, keep it! After all, VBScript isn't going anywhere. However, in this chapter we will present a sort of "jump-start" guide to PowerShell using VBScript as a basis. That way, if you *do* know VBScript, you'll be able to start writing *new* scripts in PowerShell a bit more quickly. So, this chapter is about converting *you* to PowerShell, not your scripts.

Let's begin by acknowledging that PowerShell is *very* different from VBScript. You *will* need to learn new technologies and concepts to use PowerShell effectively. However, there are some similarities, especially in PowerShell's scripting language, that can be a bit easier to learn if you see them side by side with their VBScript counterparts. So, in this chapter we'll cover the similarities between PowerShell and VBScript.

As we begin, keep in mind that PowerShell is a *management* shell. It isn't intended for logon scripts (although it can definitely be used as a logon script processor), so there are a lot of topics, such as mapping drives and checking for group membership, that we will not cover in this chapter. PowerShell's best use is not as a logon script processor. For the time being, stick with VBScript or KiXtart for those scripts.

Perhaps most importantly is that PowerShell works in a way that is radically different from VBScript. So, we don't want you to try and "convert" your VBScript code to PowerShell. Instead, *rewrite* those scripts from scratch, if you must, using PowerShell's unique, and often easier, way of doing things.

## Variables

PowerShell variables do *not* need to be declared up front. That's true in VBScript, except VBScript *does* give you the option of doing so, while PowerShell does not. However, explicit variable declaration is *always* optional in PowerShell.

Variables in PowerShell, like those in VBScript, can contain any type of data. In VBScript, this is done by making all variables the Variant type. In PowerShell, variables are the more generic Object type. Unlike in VBScript, you can tell PowerShell to force a variable to be of a certain type:

```
[string]$var = "hello"
```

This creates a new variable, $var, and forces it to be a string. Notice that all variable names being with $. Apart from that, PowerShell variable naming rules are similar to the rules in VBScript.

Variable naming in VBScript typically uses Hungarian notation, where a three-letter prefix such as obj, str, or int is used to denote the type of data the variable is intended to hold. PowerShell does not require this. In fact, when working with PowerShell this isn't considered a best practice. However, you're welcome to name your variables in this fashion if you're accustomed to doing so.

## COM Objects

If you've used VBScript, KiXtart, or any similar scripting language for Windows administration, at some point you've almost certainly used a Component Object Model (COM) component. Windows is built on COM, and COM objects provide significant functionality for files, folders, WMI, and much more. Scripting without COM would be almost unthinkable.

However, PowerShell isn't built on COM; instead it's built on the .NET Framework. The Framework replaces *much* of the functionality you may have used COM for, but not *all*. As a result, there's often still a need to utilize an old COM component. Sometimes, that need might simply be that you know how to do something using a particular COM component and you don't have time to learn an alternative way in PowerShell. Fortunately, PowerShell includes an adaptation layer that permits you to utilize COM components.

### Instantiating Objects

If you've used VBScript, you may be familiar with syntax like this:

```
Dim objFSO
Set objFSO = CreateObject("Scripting.FileSystemObject")
```

In VBScript, this statement instantiates a COM component having the ProgID Scripting. FileSystemObject. When executed, VBScript asks Windows to instantiate the component. In turn, Windows looks up the ProgID in the registry to locate the actual DLL involved, loads the DLL into memory, and plugs it into the script. The variable objFSO represents the running DLL, providing an interface for working with it.

PowerShell can do nearly the same thing:

```
$fso = new-object -com Scripting.FileSystemObject
```

Using the same ProgID, PowerShell can instantiate the COM object and assign it to a variable so you can work with it. Notice the -com parameter, which is easy to forget. However, if you don't include it, PowerShell will not be able to "find" the COM object and instantiate it for you.

## Using Objects

Once instantiated, using a COM object's properties and methods is straightforward:

```
$file = $fso.OpenTextFile("C:\file.txt",8,True)
```

You can even pipe the COM object to the **Get-Member** cmdlet to see the available properties and methods of a COM object:

```
PS C:\> $fso | get-member


   TypeName: System.__ComObject#{2a0b9d10-4b87-11d3-a97a-00104b365c9

Name                    MemberType Definition
----                    ---------- ----------
BuildPath               Method     string BuildPath (string, string)
CopyFile                Method     void CopyFile (string, string, bool)
CopyFolder              Method     void CopyFolder (string, string, bool
CreateFolder            Method      IFolder CreateFolder (string)
CreateTextFile          Method      ITextStream CreateTextFile (string, b
DeleteFile              Method     void DeleteFile (string, bool)
DeleteFolder            Method      void DeleteFolder (string, bool)
DriveExists             Method     bool DriveExists (string)
FileExists              Method     bool FileExists (string)
FolderExists            Method      bool FolderExists (string)
GetAbsolutePathName Method      string GetAbsolutePathName (string)
GetBaseName             Method     string GetBaseName (string)
GetDrive                Method     IDrive GetDrive (string)
GetDriveName            Method      string GetDriveName (string)
GetExtensionName        Method      string GetExtensionName (string)
GetFile                 Method     IFile GetFile (string)
GetFileName             Method     string GetFileName (string)
GetFileVersion          Method      string GetFileVersion (string)
GetFolder               Method     IFolder GetFolder (string)
GetParentFolderName Method       string GetParentFolderName (string)
GetSpecialFolder        Method      IFolder GetSpecialFolder (SpecialFold
GetStandardStream       Method      ITextStream GetStandardStream (Standa
GetTempName             Method     string GetTempName ()
MoveFile                Method     void MoveFile (string, string)
MoveFolder              Method     void MoveFolder (string, string)
OpenTextFile            Method      ITextStream OpenTextFile (string, IOM
Drives                  Property   IDriveCollection Drives () {get}
```

However, there's an important caveat here. PowerShell creates this list by looking at the COM object's type library that is either embedded in the DLL or included in a separate TLB file. If PowerShell can't find the type library, then *it can't use the COM component*. Most COM components come with type libraries, especially the COM components written by Microsoft. However, some COM components don't have a type library, or if they do, the type library isn't properly registered with Windows. In these cases, the COM component won't be usable within PowerShell.

In addition, if a type library is *wrong*, which happens occasionally, PowerShell may not be able to utilize the entire COM object. For example, the Microsoft-supplied type library for the WshController COM object provides an incorrect spelling for the Execute method. This makes the object difficult to use properly. However, in the case of this particular object, there's little reason to use it inside PowerShell.

### GetObject

Another way you may have used COM in VBScript was with **GetObject()**, which often connects to an existing object or service. In VBScript, you could do this:

```
Set objUser = GetObject("WinNT://don-pc/administrator,user")
```

This example uses the ADSI WinNT provider to retrieve the local administrator user.

**GetObject()** in PowerShell is a bit more difficult. Unfortunately, PowerShell doesn't have a cmdlet that does exactly this. In fact, PowerShell doesn't even provide a cmdlet for ADSI; instead, as outlined in the "Using ADSI in Windows PowerShell" chapter, you use the [ADSI] type accelerator, which works similarly to GetObject() in VBScript. Had this GetObject() example been for WMI, we could use the **Get-WmiObject** cmdlet instead. In some cases, WMI offers an alternative to what you were doing in ADSI (especially with member and standalone computers), although certainly not always (as with domain controllers).

## Comments

VBScript uses a single quote (') to begin a comment, while PowerShell uses the hash (#) symbol.

## Loops and Constructs

As illustrated in the following table, there's nearly a one-to-one correspondence between VBScript and PowerShell constructs:

| In VBScript… | In PowerShell… |
|---|---|
| Exit Do, Exit For | Break |
| For…Next | For |
| For Each…Next | Foreach |
| Function | Function |
| Sub | (no equivalent; use Function) |
| If…Then | If |
| If…ElseIf…Else | If, ElseIf, and Else |
| Select…Case | Switch |
| Do…Loop Until, Do Until…Loop | Do…until, Do until |
| Do…Loop While, Do While…Loop | Do…While, While |

Refer to the chapter "Loops and Decision-Making Constructs" to review the discussion of these loops and constructs.

## Type Conversion

VBScript provides a number of specific functions to convert between data types including **CStr()**, **CInt()**, and **CDate()**. PowerShell uses a single operator, -as, to do the same thing:

```
$var = $var2 -as [string]
```

This example attempt to convert $var2 into a string and store the result in $var. Refer to the "Variables, Arrays, and Escape Characters" chapter for more information on variables and types.

## Operators and Special Values

In many cases, PowerShell uses different operators than VBScript, and it uses some operators differently. The following table provides a summary of these operators:

| In VBScript... | Purpose... | In PowerShell... |
|---|---|---|
| = | Assignment | = |
| = | Equality test | -eq |
| > | Greater than | -gt |
| < | Less than | -lt |
| >= | Greater than or equal to | -ge |
| <= | Less than or equal to | -le |
| True | Boolean True | $true |
| False | Boolean False | $false |
| AND | Boolean AND | -and |
| NOT | Boolean NOT | -not |
| OR | Boolean OR | -or |
| AND | Binary AND | -band |
| OR | Binary OR | -bor |
| NOT | Binary NOT | -bnot |
| &, + | String concatenation | + |

Refer to the chapter "Operators" to review the discussion of the additional operators offered in PowerShell.

## Functions and Subs

VBScript and PowerShell declare functions similarly. Here's a function in VBScript that returns TRUE if the input parameter is more than 5; otherwise, it returns FALSE:

```
Function IsMoreThan5(intValue)
 If intValue > 5 Then
   IsMoreThan5 = True
 Else
   IsMoreThan5 = False
 End if
End Function
```

Notice that VBScript returns a value by setting the function name equal to the return value. PowerShell works similarly:

```
Function IsMoreThan5($Value) {
 If ($Value -gt 5) {
   Return $true
 } Else {
   Return $false
 }
}
```

Notice that the **Return** keyword is used to return the function's value. In fact, *any* output of the function will be appended to the return value. The following is functionally identical:

```
Function IsMoreThan5($Value) {
 If ($Value -gt 5) {
   $true
 } Else {
   $false
 }
}
```

This example shows that outputting $true or $false into the pipeline makes those values the function's return value. Refer to the "Script Blocks, Functions, and Filters" chapter to review the discussion of how functions have significantly expanded capabilities in PowerShell.

PowerShell does not provide a separate Sub construct as VBScript does. However, a Function that returns no value is essentially the same as a Sub.

## Error Handling

VBScript's **On Error Resume Next** statement, and the corresponding **On Error Goto 0** statement, are used to implement error handling. Essentially, you execute **On Error Resume Next** before any operation that may result in an error, and then check the special **Err** object to see if an error did indeed occur. VBScript's error handling is actually quite primitive, while PowerShell's is much more advanced.

In brief, you declare a *trap*, which is what PowerShell executes when an error (or *exception*) occurs (or is *thrown*). You do whatever you need to do within the trap, and then tell PowerShell to either **continue**, which resumes execution on the line following whatever line caused the exception, or **break**, which halts execution. For example:

```
Trap {
 # handle error here
 Continue
}
```

Refer to the "Error Handling" chapter to review the discussion of how to define different trap blocks for different types of exceptions.

## Windows Management Instrumentation

This is an easy point of conversion. Any time you used **GetObject()** or some other means of retrieving WMI information, just use the **Get-WmiObject** cmdlet or its convenient alias, **Gwmi**, in PowerShell. However, notice that just running it with a class name won't return every property of the class by default:

```
PS C:\> gwmi win32_operatingsystem


SystemDirectory : C:\WINDOWS\system32
Organization    : SAPIEN Technologies, Inc.
BuildNumber     : 2600
RegisteredUser  : Don Jones
SerialNumber    : 76487-338-1820253-22242
Version         : 5.1.2600
```

Notice that this doesn't return every property for the class. Instead, the properties shown are defined by a special *view* within PowerShell. While you can update that view to list more properties, you can also use the -property parameter if there's a specific property you need:

```
PS C:\> gwmi win32_operatingsystem -property buildnumber


BuildNumber      : 2600
__GENUS          : 2
__CLASS          : Win32_OperatingSystem
__SUPERCLASS     :
__DYNASTY        :
__RELPATH        :
__PROPERTY_COUNT : 1
__DERIVATION     : {}
__SERVER         :
__NAMESPACE      :
__PATH           :
```

If necessary, you can assign that to a variable. However, notice that you get back a collection of multiple instances that can be referred to individually by number, as shown here:

```
PS C:\> $obj = gwmi win32_logicaldisk
PS C:\> $obj[0]


DeviceID     : A:
DriveType    : 2
ProviderName :
FreeSpace    :
Size         :
VolumeName   :

PS C:\> $obj[1]


DeviceID     : C:
DriveType    : 3
ProviderName :
FreeSpace    : 91841773568
Size         : 153006624768
VolumeName   :
```

If you just need a specific property from an instance:

```
PS C:\> $obj[1].DriveType
3
```

Run **Help Gwmi** to get a comprehensive list of parameters.

## Active Directory Services Interface

It's unfortunate that PowerShell doesn't come with a built-in "Get-ADSIObject" cmdlet. Undoubtedly a similar cmdlet will be available in the future, but it is not yet included in PowerShell v1.0. You *can* use WMI to perform some ADSI queries. You *can* also use the underlying .NET Framework directory services classes, and the [ADSI] type accelerator to manipulate AD. There are two chapters you can review for some examples of what you *can* do in PowerShell with ADSI: "Using ADSI in Windows PowerShell" and "Managing Directory Services." For now, however, you may want to continue using VBScript for more complex ADSI-related tasks.

## Common Tasks in VBScript

You are probably familiar with the VBScript items listed below. Therefore, we'll quickly point out how to do nearly the same thing in PowerShell:

- **WScript.Echo**. For producing output to the command line, use the Write-Host cmdlet.

- **MsgBox(), InputBox()**. No direct analog in PowerShell, since it's intended to be entirely command line. Use the **Read-Host** cmdlet to accept input from the command line.

- **WMI**. Use Get-WmiObject.

- **Working with text files.** Refer to the "Managing Files and Folders" chapter. Several PowerShell cmdlets are available to manipulate text files. The basic technique is to read the entire file into an object and then enumerate through each line of the file as a child object.

- **ADSI**. Tricky because there's not a direct equivalent in PowerShell v1. However, refer to the discussion earlier in this chapter for information on how to work with ADSI. You'll primarily use the [ADSI] type accelerator, which will accept the same ADSI queries that you used with **GetObject()** in VBScript.

- **Working with the registry.** Review the "Managing the Registry" chapter for more information. PowerShell provides a registry "drive" and cmdlets for working with the registry.

## PowerShell Paradigm Change

Probably the biggest mental leap you can make when moving from VBScript to PowerShell is that PowerShell is intended to deal with *objects* and not text. That's all well and good in theory, but it can be a confusing concept to implement until you get used to it. For example, look at ServicePack.vbs, which is a VBScript that reads a list of names from C:\Computers.txt (one name per line) and uses WMI to display the service pack version for each.

### ServicePack.vbs

```
Dim strFile
strFile = "C:\computers.txt"

Dim objFSO, objTS, strComputer
Set objFSO = CreateObject("Scripting.FileSystemObject")
If objFSO.FileExists(strFile) Then
   Set objTS = objFSO.OpenTextFile(strFile)
   Do Until objTS.AtEndOfStream
      strComputer = objTS.ReadLine
```

```
    Dim objWMI
    Set objWMI = GetObject("winmgmts:\\" & strComputer & _
    "\root\cimv2")

    Dim colResults, objResult, strWMIQuery

    strWMIQuery = "SELECT * FROM Win32_OperatingSystem"
    Set colResults = objWMI.ExecQuery(strWMIQuery)
    For Each objResult In colResults
        WScript.Echo strComputer & ":" & _
          objResult.ServicePackMajorVersion
    Next

  Loop
End If

objTS.Close
WScript.Echo "Complete"
```

As mentioned previously, you're probably familiar enough with VBScript to follow what this script is doing. However, take time to notice the methodology. Each time through the **Do** loop, a line is read from the text file, which is assumed to be a computer name. A WMI connection to that computer is created, and the Win32_OperatingSystem class retrieved. For each instance of the class, a loop displays the ServicePackMajorVersion property.

Now look at ServicePack.ps1, which does the same thing.

## ServicePack.ps1

```
$names = get-content "c:\computers.txt"
foreach ($name in $names) {
 $wmi = Get-WmiObject win32_operatingsystem `
  -property servicepackmajorversion `
  -computer $name
 $sp = $wmi.servicepackmajorversion
 write-host "$name : $sp"
}
```

First of all, notice how much shorter this is! It actually could be shorter, but we wrote it more for clarity than brevity. Again, the *real* thing to notice is the methodology. The **Get-Content** cmdlet is used to retrieve the entire contents of the text file into $names, all in one step. A **foreach** loop goes through each child item (or line) of the text file, pulling each child item into $name. The **Get-WmiObject** cmdlet retrieves just the desired property, placing the class instance into $wmi. The $sp variable is used to hold the actual property in which we're interested. The **Write-Host** is used to output the information to the screen.

Keep in mind that, where VBScript typically requires something to be done in a particular way, PowerShell is a lot more flexible. ServicePack2.ps1 demonstrates the same script, from a different approach.

## ServicePack2.ps1

```
filter getversion {
 $wmi = Get-WmiObject win32_operatingsystem `
  -property servicepackmajorversion `
  -computer $_
 $sp = $wmi.servicepackmajorversion
```

```
 write-host "$_ : $sp"
}

get-content "c:\computers.txt" | getversion
```

Here, the content of the text file is piped to "getversion", which is a custom filter. This filter is called once for each object or line of text in the text file. The special $_ variable refers to the current object, which would be a single computer name. ServicePack3.ps1 simplifies this even further.

### ServicePack3.ps1

```
filter getversion {
 $wmi = Get-WmiObject win32_operatingsystem `
  -property servicepackmajorversion `
  -computer $_
 write-host "$_ : " $wmi.servicepackmajorversion
}
get-content "c:\computers.txt" | getversion
```

All that's been done here is to remove the $sp variable. This was done because $wmi.servicepackma-jorversion is now output directly, which removes a line of code. This could be simplified even further. However, the VBScript example we started with has been simplified about as much as possible.

Getting used to PowerShell's way of working with objects takes some time. However, if you make the effort, these examples have demonstrated how much more quickly you can produce usable administrative scripts.

## If You're Used to Cmd.exe

By and large, almost everything you know and do in Cmd.exe works the same in Windows PowerShell, so jump right in and start working! There are, of course, exceptions, which can be frustrating as you're getting started.

First, remember that PowerShell uses a space to separate elements of a command. So, this consider this command from Cmd.exe:

```
C:\Test\> cd..
```

It isn't legal in PowerShell. Instead, you have to use this syntax, with a space between the command (or rather, the alias) and the argument:

```
PS C:\> cd ..
```

Spaces in file and folder paths can be frustrating, too. Simply remember to enclose them in quotes using one of the following methods:

- Enclose portions of a path that contain a space in quotation marks, as in cd \"program files"\ sapien.

- Use a backtick to escape the spaces, as in cd \program` files\sapien.

- Enclose the entire path in quotation marks, as in cd "\program files\sapien".

Which method you use is up to you. Also remember that whenever PowerShell sees a space followed by a dash, it assumes that you're giving it a command-line argument. That can be a problem sometimes, so you may need to enclose things in quotation marks to force PowerShell to behave in a certain way.

Perhaps the most useful utility for troubleshooting comes with the free PowerShell Community Extensions (http://www.codeplex.com/PowerShellCX): Echoargs.exe. This handy external utility will accept a command line and tell you how PowerShell interpreted it. Be sure to check it out if you're having difficulty getting a particular Cmd.exe-style command line to run properly from PowerShell.

## For

In the CMD shell, you can use the FOR command to process a text file or the results of a command. As an example, you might have an expression like this:

```
C:\>for /f %s in (servers.txt) do @wmic /node:%s os get csname,caption
```

This expression will go through the servers.txt file, presumably a list of server names, and then use Windows Management Instrumentation Command Line (WMIC) to return the caption from OS, which is an alias for the Win32_OperatingSystem class and the server name.

In PowerShell, you will use the **ForEach-Object** cmdlet. In this particular scenario, you will also use **Get-WmiObject**:

```
PS C:\>foreach ($s in (get-content servers.txt)) {
>> Get-WmiObject win32_operatingsystem -computer $s `
>> | format-table CSName,Caption -auto
>> }
>>
```

This will work, but in PowerShell you can simplify this further:

```
PS C:\>Get-WmiObject win32_operatingsystem -computer (get-content servers.txt) |
>> Format-Table CSName,Caption -auto
>>
```

In this example, the **ForEach** cmdlet is implied by:

```
(get-content servers.txt)
```

PowerShell understands that the **Get-Content** cmdlet is returning an array of strings and will automatically enumerate the array when used in this context.

Often, administrators need to parse out files:

```
C:\>for /f "tokens=1,2 delims=," %t in (tasks.csv) do @echo %t= %u
```

This example gets the first and second element of each line in tasks.csv, using the comma as the delimiter. In PowerShell, you would achieve the same result with an expression like this:

```
PS C:\> foreach ($line in (get-content tasks.csv)) {$a=$line.split(",");$a[0]+" = "+$a[1]}
```

As we did earlier, we're getting each line of the file, but instead of displaying it, we're using the **Split()** method, specifying the comma as the delimiter to create a temporary array:

```
{$a=$line.split(",")
```

In PowerShell, the first array element starts at 0, so to display the first two elements we use code like this:

```
$a[0]+" = "+$a[1]
```

## Working with Environment Variables

Not only does PowerShell have its own variables, but it can also access environmental variables through the Environment provider. To retrieve all environmental variables in a CMD shell, you would type:

```
C:\> set
```

In PowerShell, you can use the **DIR** command because the Environment provider presents the variables as a drive:

```
PS C:\> dir env:
```

To reference a specific environmental variable, use syntax like this:

```
PS C:\> $env:windir
C:\WINDOWS
```

You can modify the environmental variables or even add new ones, but they won't change environmental variables in your CMD shell nor will they be seen outside of PowerShell. You need to modify the registry if you want to make permanent changes. Once your PowerShell session terminates, environmental variable changes will also terminate.

## "If" Comparisons

In the CMD shell, the **If** statement is used frequently, especially in batch files. PowerShell also has an **If** statement that is not too dissimilar. Let's look at some of the ways you use **If** in a CMD shell and the corresponding PowerShell equivalent.

One common usage in a CMD session is to check for the existence of a file:

```
C:\> if exist %windir%\notepad.exe echo Found Notepad
```

In PowerShell:

```
PS C:\> if (dir $env:windir\notepad.exe) {write-host "Found Notepad"}
```

If the **Dir** command is successful, then the If statement will be TRUE and the **Write-Host** script block will be executed.

In the CMD shell, you might also have taken this to the next step:

```
C:\>if exist %windir%\notepad.exe (echo Found Notepad) ELSE echo Notepad not found
```

The PowerShell syntax is very similar:

```
PS C:\> if (dir $env:windir\notepad.exe) {write-host "Found Notepad"
>> } else {
>> write-host "Notepad not found"
>> }
>>
```

This code works fine when Notepad.exe exists, but if it doesn't, PowerShell will generate an error and the last part of the If statement will never run. To instruct PowerShell to continue so that your error handling will work, run this command first:

```
PS C:\> $erroractionpreference="SilentlyContinue"
```

This instructs to ignore any error and continue. To change back to PowerShell's default, use this command:

```
PS C:\> $erroractionpreference="Continue"
```

There is more information on using If in PowerShell in the "Loops and Decision Making Constructs" chapter.

## If You're Used to *nix

UNIX and Linux variants are *so* geared to text-based operations that they can take an act of will to wrench your mind out of the text-based way of doing things. The two most common question we're asked from *nix administrators is whether or not PowerShell has something like Grep or Awk—two text-parsing utilities that every *nix administrator relies upon as heavily as they do the oxygen they breathe. PowerShell does *not* have these utilities, because it does not *need* these utilities; PowerShell offers a profoundly better way of performing tasks that doesn't require text parsing. Because PowerShell often "looks" so much like a *nix shell (PowerShell was, after all, inspired by shells like Bash), *nix administrators unconsciously start applying their *nix know-how to the tasks they need to accomplish in PowerShell. If you find yourself doing that, stop and think about the *PowerShell* way to accomplish the task—using objects.

For example, we're often asked if there's a way to Grep the output of **Get-Alias** in order to locate all the available aliases for a given cmdlet. That's a classically *nix way of attacking the problem: You have a command that produces a list of aliases and their corresponding cmdlets, so you parse that text output looking for a specific cmdlet name—thus, locating all the aliases in the process.

But remember that things are different in PowerShell. An alias or a cmdlet, creates an object, complete with properties and methods. The output of **Get-Alias** *is not text:* It is a collection of Alias objects. Piping one to **Get-Member** reveals its properties:

```
PS C:\> get-alias | get-member


   TypeName: System.Management.Automation.AliasInfo

Name                   MemberType    Definition
----                   ----------    ----------
Equals                 Method        System.Boolean Equals(Object obj)
GetHashCode            Method        System.Int32 GetHashCode()
```

```
GetType                 Method          System.Type GetType()
get_CommandType         Method           System.Management.Automation.CommandTypes get_Com...
get_Definition          Method          System.String get_Definition()
get_Description         Method           System.String get_Description()
get_Name                Method          System.String get_Name()
get_Options             Method          System.Management.Automation.ScopedItemOptions ge...
get_ReferencedCommand Method             System.Management.Automation.CommandInfo get_Refe...
get_ResolvedCommand     Method           System.Management.Automation.CommandInfo get_Reso...
set_Description         Method           System.Void set_Description(String value)
set_Options             Method          System.Void set_Options(ScopedItemOptions value)
ToString                Method          System.String ToString()
CommandType             Property         System.Management.Automation.CommandTypes Command...
Definition              Property        System.String Definition {get;}
Description             Property         System.String Description {get;set;}
Name                    Property        System.String Name {get;}
Options                 Property         System.Management.Automation.ScopedItemOptions Op...
ReferencedCommand       Property         System.Management.Automation.CommandInfo Referenc...
ResolvedCommand         Property         System.Management.Automation.CommandInfo Resolved...
ResolvedCommandName   ScriptProperty System.Object ResolvedCommandName {get=$this.Reso...
```

Hmm, the ResolvedCommandName property might contain the name of the cmdlet that the alias resolves to. Let's test it by examining an alias to see what that property contains:

```
PS C:\> $aliases = get-alias
PS C:\> $aliases[0].resolvedcommandname
Add-Content
```

Sure enough! So, if we're looking for aliases of the **Get-ChildItem** cmdlet, for example, we could simply filter on the ResolvedCommandName property as follows:

```
PS C:\> get-alias | where { $_.ResolvedCommandName -eq "Get-ChildItem" }

CommandType     Name                    Definition
-----------     ----                    ----------
Alias           gci                     Get-ChildItem
Alias           ls                      Get-ChildItem
Alias           dir                     Get-ChildItem
```

Easy enough, and we didn't have to parse any text at all. Instead, we just used the objects' native properties.

Some *nix admins may wonder: What if I needed to find every instance of an object—say, a service—where one of the properties contains a specific substring? I don't know if what I'm looking for will be in the Name or DisplayName properties, for example, and I don't know the complete string I'm after, only a substring. Still not a problem—and still no need for something like Grep:

```
PS C:\> get-service | where { $_.Name -like "*Wind*" -or $_.DisplayName -like "*Wind*" }

Status  Name               DisplayName
------  ----               -----------
Running AudioEndpointBu... Windows Audio Endpoint Builder
Running Audiosrv           Windows Audio
Running Eventlog           Windows Event Log
Stopped FontCache3.0.0.0   Windows Presentation Foundation Fon...
Stopped idsvc              Windows CardSpace
Running MpsSvc             Windows Firewall
Stopped msiserver          Windows Installer
Stopped QWAVE              Quality Windows Audio Video Experience
Stopped SDRSVC             Windows Backup
```

It's unlikely that you'd ever need to do a search like this across *all* of an object's properties; bear in mind how many different properties exist, and how few of them actually contain text strings like this. In addition, because we're not just working with text, the output of the above command *is actual Service objects*, meaning they have methods like Stop and Start. So, once you've got the services you want, you don't have to re-parse the output of Grep to do something to those services: You've already got the actual services to work with!

In general, anytime you're approaching a problem and thinking, "How can I parse this text to get what I want?" stop yourself and instead ask, "What's an object-oriented way to do this so that I don't have to parse any text at all?" As you educate yourself about more and more of PowerShell's abilities, you're likely to discover easier and more efficient ways to accomplish many tasks (at least on Windows-based systems).

## Chapter 23
# Best Practices for Scripting

Now we come to the "Best Practices" chapter, a chapter that no self-respecting book on coding can be without. Please understand that, in administrative scripting, there are no points (or at least very few points) for style; that said, these best practices are intended to help make your scripts easier to read, easier to write, easier to maintain, and easier to debug. Feel free to use, modify, or disregard these practices as desired!

## Script Formatting

Apart from PowerShell's own basic formatting requirements—primarily that functions must appear in your script *before* those functions can be called—we simply recommend that you keep your scripts neat-looking. Here's how we recommend that functions, loops, and other constructs be formatted for clarity:

```
If ($x -eq 5) {
        # code
        # code
}
```

Notice that we've put the construct's starting { curly brace on the same line as the construct's opening keyword; the code within the construct is indented, and the construct's closing } curly brace is on its own line, vertically aligned with the start of the construct's opening keyword.

This formatting technique helps you visually identify constructs, the code within the construct, and visually verify that the construct has been properly closed.

We also recommend including a blank line before each construct's first line. This helps to visually separate the construct and makes your script easier to read.

## Comments

PowerShell uses the # character to start a comment line, and we *strongly* recommend commenting your scripts. We offer the following recommendations:

- Start your script with several comments that provide your name, the version of the script, and its overall purpose.

- Place a comment before each construct, indicating what the construct is doing. In multi-part constructs, including a comment within each part indicating what that part does. For example:

```
# Check to see if $x contains the key value 5
If ($x -eq 5) {

        # $x does contain 5
        # more code goes here
} else {

        # $x does not contain 5
        # more code goes here
}
```

- Place a comment before each cmdlet used, indicating in a general sense what you're doing. For example:

```
# Retrieve the logical disk WMI class
$wmi = Get-WmiObject win32_logicaldisk
```

Proper use of comments can make your scripts easier to read for someone else—or for *you*, several months later, when you've forgotten exactly why you wrote the script the way you did.

## Script and Function Naming

Although we don't follow this suggestion in many of the examples in this book (primarily for clarity when we're trying to make a quick point), we do agree with the PowerShell team's overall recommendation that scripts and functions follow cmdlet-style naming conventions. That is, use a *verb-noun* naming syntax, where nouns are singular ("Get-Process", not "Get-Processes"), and where verbs are selected from the official verb list:

Common Verbs

- **Add** – Add a resource to a container or attach an element to another element (use with Remove)

- **Clear** – Remove all elements from a container

- **Copy** – Copy a resource to another name or another container

- **Get** – Retrieve data (use with Set)

- **Hide** – Make not visible (use with Show)

- **Invoke** – Introduce or put into operation

- **Join** – Join two or more resources (use with Split)

- **Lock** – Lock a resource (use with Unlock)

- **Move** – Move a resource

- **New** – Create a new resource

- **Remove** – Remove a resource from a container (use with Add)

- **Rename** – Renames a resource

- **Select** – Identifies a subset of resources

- **Set** – Place some data (use with Get)

- **Show** – Make visible (use with Hide)

- **Split** – Splits a resource (use with Join)

- **Unlock** – Unlock a resource (use with Lock)

- **Wait** – Remain inactive until something expected happens

Communications Verbs

- **Connect** – Connect to a resource (use with Disconnect)

- **Disconnect** – Detach from a resource (use with Connect)

- **Read** – Read from a connected resource (use with Write)

- **Receive** – Acquire information from a connected resource (use with Send)

- **Send** – Write information to a destination (use with Receive)

- **Write** – Write information to a target (use with Read)

Data Verbs

- **Backup** – Back up data

- **Checkpoint** – Create a snapshot of the current state or configuration (use with Restore)

- **Compare** – Compare two resources and show a set of differences

- **Convert** – Changes data into a specific format or encoding

- **ConvertFrom** – Change data from one format to another, where the source format is described by the noun (e.g., ConvertFrom-Unicode); use Import if the data will be copied from a persistent storage form such as a file

- **ConvertTo** – Change data from one format to another, where the destination format is described by the noun (e.g., ConvertTo-HTML); use Export if the data will be copied to a persistent storage form such as a file

- **Dismount** – Detach an entity from a path

- **Export** – Copy a set of resources to a persistent data store, such as a file

- **Import** – Create a set of resources from a persistent data store, such as a file

- **Initialize** – Prepare a resource for use

- **Limit** – Limit the consumption or apply a constraint to a resource

- **Merge** – Combine resources into a single unit

- **Mount** – Attach an entity to a path
- **Publish** – Make known to another (use with Unpublish)
- **Restore** – Roll back the data state to a predefined set of conditions (use with Checkpoint)
- **Unpublish** – Make unknown to another (use with Publish)
- **Update** – Update or refresh a resource
- **Out** – Send data out of the environment

Diagnostic Verbs

- **Debug** – Examine operation or diagnose a problem
- **Measure** – Retrieve statistics or identify resources consumes
- **Ping** – Determine if a resource is responding to requests
- **Resolve** – Translate a shorthand name into its proper, full name
- **Test** – Verify operation or consistency
- **Trace** – Track activity

Lifecycle Verbs

- **Disable** – Make something unavailable (use with Enable)
- **Enable** – Make something available or active (use with Disable)
- **Install** – Place resources in a location and initialize it (use with Uninstall)
- **Uninstall** – Remove resources and de-initialize them (use with Install)
- **Restart** – Resume operation (use with Suspend)
- **Suspend** – Pause operation (use with Resume)
- **Start** – Start an activity (use with Stop)
- **Stop** – Stop an activity (use with Start)

Security Verbs

- **Block** – Prevent access to a resource (use with Unblock)
- **Grant** – Allow access to a resource (use with Revoke)
- **Revoke** – Remove access to a resource (use with Grant)
- **Unblock** – Permit access to a resource (use with Block)

**Stay up-to-date!**
The official list of allowed verbs is published in the PowerShell Software Development Kit, located at http://msdn2.microsoft.com/en-us/library/ms714428.aspx.

## Parameter Declaration

Although PowerShell is fairly flexible in how you declare parameters (arguments) for functions, we definitely prefer the use of a Param() block. For example, rather than this:

```
Function MyFunction($arg1, $arg2) {
}
```

We suggest:

```
Function MyFunction {
      Param (
            [int]$arg1 = 5,
            [string]$arg2 = "Hello"
            )
}
```

There are several reasons for this. First and foremost, this is the *only* way to declare input parameters for a *script* (and the Param() block must begin on the script's first line), and so using this technique for functions provides better consistency. Second, we think this method is easier to read, making functions more self-documenting.

You'll notice that we also provided a specific data type for each argument, and provided a default value for each—two additional best practices that can save you a great deal of debugging time, and which we heartily recommend that you *always* follow.

## Functions vs. Filters

A filter really isn't that different from a function. For example, this:

```
Filter Test1 {
      $_.Name
}
```

is functionally identical to this:

```
Function Test1 {
      PROCESS {
            $_.Name
            }
}
```

We prefer using a function with a PROCESS script block over filters. Our first reason is that functions can provide additional capabilities in the form of BEGIN and END blocks; filters cannot. Our second reason is that since you can get all the functionality you need from a function, why not just use them consistently for everything? We also think the use of the PROCESS script block is visually clearer, and is equivalent to the syntax of the **ForEach-Next** cmdlet (which uses **-process**, **-begin**, and **-end** parameters to accomplish something similar). Again, visual clarity and consistency are driving forces behind many of our best practices recommendations.

## Variable Naming

PowerShell doesn't enforce many restrictions on variable names, and in a simple script, you probably don't need to, either. Use variable names which are visually meaningful—$computername, for example, rather than $c—but otherwise, don't worry much about the names.

In more complicated scripts, however, you might find a naming convention that provides a clue as to a variable's scope to be useful. For example, a short prefix on each variable name can help make script- and function-scope variables more visually obvious, and help prevent you from accidentally using the exact same variable name in a nested scope (which, as we discussed in the "Scripting Overview" chapter, can cause unexpected behavior). For example:

- $s_computername represents a script-level variable.

- $1_computername represents a variable declared within a script's child scope, such as a function or filter.

- $12_computername might be a variable that exists within a nested function—that is, a function nested within another function.

There are no formal rules for this, and you should definitely adopt a naming practice that works for you. Having *some* kind of system in place can make it easier to keep track of what variables go where.

Similarly, it can be useful to develop a naming scheme that indicates what type of data a variable holds. Here are some suggestions:

- $s_computername is a script-level variable that hasn't been assigned a specific type.

- $s_intComputerNumber is a script-level variable that has been specifically cast to the [int] type.

- $1_strUserName is a function's local variable, which has been set as a [string] type.

You get the idea. If you decide to take this approach, you can consider using the Hungarian notation type prefixes, which were popularized in VBScript:

- Str for [string]

- Int for [int]

- Bol for [Boolean]

- Dat for [datetime]

- Xml for [xml]

- Sng for [single]

- Dbl for [double]

And so forth. While this form of notation is no longer popular amongst developers working in languages like C# or VB, that's primarily because those languages strongly enforce data types; if you try to put the wrong type of data into a variable, you get an error, so there's less need to remind yourself which type of data is "supposed" to be in a variable. PowerShell is less strict about enforcing types, unless you explicitly cast a variable as a specific type; using notations like this may help you keep track of variables' types more easily. It's your decision.

## Use Source Control

You've taken the time to write a script, debug it, and get it working—why would you not put it somewhere safe? This is especially true if you're working with other administrators on the same scripts. Source control solutions let you "check in" a script, retrieve read-only copies to run, and "check out" scripts for editing. When you "check in" a script, your version replaces the old version as the "newest," but old versions are retained and can be retrieved—in case you suddenly realize that some of the changes in the new version are incorrect.

SAPIEN PrimalScript integrates with popular source-control solutions like Microsoft Visual SourceSafe (and compatible solutions), as well as open-source systems like CVS/Subversion. There are even free, "personal" source control products that are SourceSafe-compatible, so you don't need to spend money to take advantage of these features (an example of one is IonForge). In many cases, the source control repository or database can be located on another computer, providing an additional level of backup in case the computer where you're working crashes.

# Part III

# Practical Examples for Windows Administration

# Chapter 24
# Managing Files and Folders

File and directory management is a pretty common administrative task. Here are some ways to accomplish typical tasks using PowerShell.

## Creating Text Files

We've already discussed how you can use console redirection to send output to a text file and how to using **Out-File**, so we won't go into detail. Instead, we'll provide a few examples for creating text files. First, let's look at a line of code that redirects output to a text file:

```
PS C:\> Get-WmiObject win32_share > myshares.txt
```

Remember > send output to the specified file, overwriting an existing file with the same name. Use >> to append to an existing file. The file will be created if it doesn't already exist.

Here's the same expression, but using the **Out-File** cmdlet:

```
PS C:\> Get-WmiObject win32_share | out-file myshares.txt -noclobber
```

We used **-NoClobber** to prevent **Out-File** from overwriting myshares.txt, if it already exists.

Finally, you can also use **New-Item** to create a file and even add some content to it:

```
PS C:\> $now=get-date
PS C:\> new-item audit.log -type File -value "Created $now" -force
```

```
   Directory: Microsoft.PowerShell.Core\FileSystem::C:\


Mode              LastWriteTime     Length Name
----              -------------     ------ ----
-a---        6/16/2006 10:40 AM         30 audit.log


PS C:\> get-content audit.log
Created 6/16/2006 10:40:30 AM
PS C:\>
```

In this example, we use **New-Item** to create a file called audit.log and give it some content.

# Reading Text Files

Reading text files is pretty straightforward with **Get-Content**:

```
PS C:\> get-content boot.ini
[boot loader]
timeout=15
default=multi(0)disk(0)rdisk(0)partition(2)\WINDOWS
[operating systems]
multi(0)disk(0)rdisk(0)partition(2)\WINDOWS="Microsoft Windows XP
Professional"
 /fastdetect /NoExecute=OptIn
multi(0)disk(0)rdisk(0)partition(1)\WINDOWS="Windows Server 2003,
Enterprise" /
noexecute=optout /fastdetect
C:\CMDCONS\BOOTSECT.DAT="Microsoft Windows Recovery Console" /cmdcons
PS C:\>
```

We can use **-TotalCount** to display a specified number of lines from a text file:

```
PS C:\> get-content ADOXEXCEPTION.LOG -TotalCount 5
CADOXCatalog Error
      Code = 80040e4d
      Code meaning = IDispatch error #3149
      Source = Microsoft OLE DB Provider for SQL Server
      Description = Login failed for user 'scriptaccess'.
PS C:\>
```

In this example, the first five lines of a log file are displayed. You can get the same result with this expression:

```
PS C:\> get-content ADOXEXCEPTION.LOG |select-object -first 5
```

An advantage to this approach is that **Select-Object** also has a **-Last** parameter that you can use to display a specified number of lines from the end of the file.

# Parsing Text Files

While PowerShell might be a highly object-oriented shell, that doesn't mean *you* don't need to work with pure text now and again. Log files and INI files are perhaps two of the most common examples of text files Windows administrators need to work with on a regular basis.

Typically, in a text file, you are looking to extract pieces of information. PowerShell offers several techniques. The simplest approach is to use the **-Match** operator:

```
PS C:\ > (get-content foo.txt) -match "bar"
```

More complicated parsing and matching might require regular expressions and the regex object:

```
PS C:\ > [regex]$regex="\d{1,3}\.\d{1,3}\.\d{1,3}\.\d{1,3}"
PS C:\ > $regex.Matches((get-content ex070517.log))|select value

Value
-----
172.16.10.1
172.16.10.101
172.16.10.1
172.16.10.2
```

You might also use the **Select-String** cmdlet to extract complete lines from a text file:

```
PS C:\ > gc C:\temp\teched.txt | select-string "server 2008"
```

If you need a refresher, take a look back at the chapter "Regular Expressions."

## Parsing IIS Log Files

Using **Select-String**, it is very easy to extract information from IIS log files. Suppose you want to find all the 404 errors that occurred during May 2007. You could use an expression like this:

```
get-childitem ex0705* | select-string " - 404"
```

You'll a listing of every matching line. Use console redirection or **Out-File** to save the results:

```
get-childitem ex0705* | select-string " - 404" | out-file May07-404.txt
```

Let's take this a step further and find the IP addresses for the computers that received the 404 error. To accomplish this, we will use a combination of **Select-String** and a regular expression:

```
PS C:\system32\LogFiles\W3SVC1 > [regex]$regex="\d{1,3}\.\d{1,3}\.\d{1,3}\.\d{1,3}"
PS C:\system32\LogFiles\W3SVC1 > $(foreach ($found in (get-childitem ex0705* | `
>> select-string " - 404")) {
>> ($regex.matches($found.ToString()))[1].value} ) | select -unique
>>
64.34.179.85
69.207.43.227
69.207.92.234
69.207.4.215
71.98.99.72
207.36.196.127
210.253.120.121
203.17.208.78
```

We'll break this apart from the inside out so you can see what is happening. First, we know that an expression like this:

```
get-childitem ex0705* | select-string " - 404"
```

will return all the strings from log files that start with ex0705 that match on " - 404". We want to examine each matched line, so we'll nest the previous command in a **ForEach** construct:

```
Foreach($found in (get-childitem ex0705* | select-string " - 404"))
```

For every line in the file, we first need to convert it into a string:

```
$found.ToString()
```

We have a regex object, with a pattern that should match an IP address:

```
[regex]$regex="\d{1,3}\.\d{1,3}\.\d{1,3}\.\d{1,3}"
```

The **Matches()** method of the Regex object will return all matching instances in the line:

```
$regex.matches($found.ToString())
```

But we only need to see the value of the second match. The first match will be the web server's IP address:

```
($regex.matches($found.ToString()))[1].value
```

If we ran what we have so far:

```
PS c:\system32\LogFiles\W3SVC1 > foreach ($found in (get-childitem ex0705* | '
>> select-string " - 404")) {($regex.matches($found.ToString()))[1].value}
```

Every client IP address would be listed, probably in duplicate. Because this is PowerShell, we'll add one final tweak by piping the output of this command to **Select-Object**, specifying the -**Unique** parameter:

```
PS C:\system32\LogFiles\W3SVC1 > $(foreach ($found in (get-childitem ex0705* | '
>> select-string " - 404")) {
>> ($regex.matches($found.ToString()))[1].value} ) | select -unique
```

Notice that the main filtering expression is enclosed in parentheses and preceded by a $ sign. This indicates that PowerShell should treat it as an expression and execute it in its entirety. The results of that expression are then piped to **Select-Object**, leaving us with a list of unique IP addresses.

## Parsing INI Files

Another common administrative task is parsing information from ini files like this:

```
;MyApp.ini
;last updated 2:28 PM 6/13/2007
[Parameters]
```

```
Password=P@ssw0rd
Secure=Yes
Encryption=Yes
UseExtendedSyntax=No

[Open_Path]
path=\\server01\files\results.txt

[mail]
server=MAIL01
from=admin@mycompany.com

[Win2003]
foo=bar
```

If all the settings are unique in the entire file, you can use **Select-String** to extract the value for a particular setting with a PowerShell one-liner:

```
PS C:\ > ((cat myapp.ini | select-string -pattern "password=").ToString()).Split("=")[1]
P@ssw0rd
```

Here's how this works. First, this example is using **cat**, which is an alias for **Get-Content**, which keeps a long expression from having to be any longer. Piping the contents of myapp.ini to **Select-String** will return a MatchInfo object when a match is made:

```
cat myapp.ini | select-string -pattern "password="
```

However, we need to convert the result to a string object, so we use the **ToString()** method:

```
(cat myapp.ini | select-string -pattern "password=").ToString()
```

If we were to look at the returned value thus far, we would get:

```
Password=P@ssw0rd
```

Since we now have a string, we can use the **Split()** method to split the string at the = sign:

```
((cat myapp.ini | select-string -pattern "password=").ToString()).Split("=")
```

This expression results in a small 0-based array, meaning the first element has an index number of 0. All that remains is to display the second array element, which has an index number of 1:

```
((cat myapp.ini | select-string -pattern "password=").ToString()).Split("=")[1]
```

In my sample ini file, this technique would work since all of my values are unique. But what about situations where I need a specific value under a specific heading? This is a little more complicated, but can be achieved with some extra parsing. Here's a function we wrote to retrieve the value from a particular section on an ini file:

```
Function Get-INIValue {

# $ini is the name of the ini file
```

```
# $section is the name of the section head like [Mail]
# Specify the name without the brackets
# $prop is the property you want under the section
# sample usage: $from=Get-inivalue myapp.ini mail from

Param ([string]$ini,[string]$section,[string]$prop)

#get the line number to start searching from
$LineNum=(Get-Content myapp.ini | Select-String "\[$section\]").Linenumber
$limit=(Get-Content myapp.ini).length #total number of lines in the ini file

for ($i=$LineNum;$i -le $limit;$i++) {
 $line=(Get-Content myapp.ini)[$i]
     if ($line -match $prop+"=") {
        $value=($line.split("="))[1]
        return $value
        Break
        }
   }
return "NotFound"
}
```

The function is expecting the name of the ini file, the section name, and the name of the value. Once this file is loaded, you can use it like this:

```
PS C:\ > $smtp=Get-inivalue myapp.ini mail server
```

The function will return the value the "server" setting under the [Mail] section of myapp.ini. The function first obtains the number of the line in the ini file that contains the section heading:

```
$LineNum=(Get-Content myapp.ini | Select-String "\[$section\]").Linenumber
```

The function also gets the total number of lines in the ini file that it will use later:

```
$limit=(Get-Content myapp.ini).length #total number of lines in the ini file
```

Now that we know where to start searching, we can loop through each line of the ini file until we reach the end:

```
for ($i=$LineNum;$i -le $limit;$i++) {
```

Because the ini file will be treated as a 0-based array, the value of $LineNum will actually return the first line after the heading:

```
 $line=(Get-Content myapp.ini)[$i]
```

The function examines each line using the -**Match** operator to see if it contains the property value we are seeking:

```
    if ($line -match $prop+"=") {
```

If not, the function will keep looping until it reaches the end of the file, at which point the function will return "NotFound".

When a match is made, the line is split at the = sign and the second item (index number of 1) is returned:

```
$value=($line.split("="))[1]
```

The function returns this value, and since there's no longer any need to keep looping through the ini file, the function stops by using the **Break** statement.

```
return $value
Break
```

# Copying Files

Copying files in PowerShell is not much different than copying files in Cmd.exe. In fact, by default PowerShell uses the alias **Copy** for the **Copy-Item** cmdlet.

```
PS C:\> copy *.ps1 c:\temp
PS C:\> get-childitem c:\temp


    Directory: Microsoft.PowerShell.Core\FileSystem::C:\temp


Mode                LastWriteTime     Length Name
----                -------------     ------ ----
-a---      5/17/2006   8:31 PM         863 brace.ps1
-a---      5/29/2006  12:18 PM          15 demo.txt
-a---      2/11/2006   6:26 PM       19817 ex060211.log
-a---      5/29/2006  10:58 AM          16 j.txt
-a---      5/23/2006   1:03 PM         811 out-grid.ps1
-a---      5/23/2006   1:06 PM        1330 out-propertyGrid.ps1
-a---      5/19/2006  11:17 AM         710 showprocessinfo.ps1
-a---      5/19/2006  11:04 AM         477 showservices.ps1
-a---       5/1/2006   8:10 PM          88 test.ps1


PS C:\>
```

This example copies all ps1 files in C: to C:\temp. You can also recurse and force files to be overwritten:

```
PS C:\>copy-item C:\Logs C:\Backup -recurse -force
```

This expression copies all files and subdirectories from C:\Logs to C:\Backup, overwriting any existing files and directories with the same name.

As you work with PowerShell, you'll discover that not every command you can execute in Cmd.exe is valid in PowerShell. For example, the following is a valid command in Cmd.exe:

```
C:\logs> copy *.log *.old
```

When you try this in PowerShell, you'll get a message about an invalid character. It appears the **Copy-Item** cmdlet works fine when copying between directories, but it can't handle a wildcard copy within the same directory.

Here's a workaround:

**BulkCopy.ps1**

```
#BulkCopy.ps1
Set-Location "C:\Logs"

$files=Get-ChildItem |where {$_.extension -eq ".log"}

foreach ($file in $files) {
 $filename=($file.FullName).ToString()
 $arr=@($filename.split("."))
 $newname=$arr[0]+".old"

 Write-Host "copying "$file.Fullname "to"$newname
 copy $file.fullname $newname -force
}
```

With this script, we first define a variable that contains all the files we want to copy by extension. Next we iterate through the variable using **ForEach**. Within the loop, we break apart the filename using **Split** so we can get everything to the left of the period. We need this name so we can define what the new filename will be with the new extension, including the path. Then it's a matter of calling **Copy-Item**. Notice that in the script, we're using the **copy** alias.

> ...........................................................................................................................................................
>
> **Provider Alert**
> If you look through the Help for **Copy-Item** and some of the other Item cmdlets, you will see a -**Credential** parameter. This might lead you to believe that you could use the -**Credential** parameter to copy files to a network and share and specify alternate credentials. Unfortunately, in the first version of PowerShell, the file system and registry providers do not support this parameter. Hopefully this will change in later versions of PowerShell. In the meantime, start a PowerShell session using the RunAs command if you need to specify alternate credentials.

## Deleting Files

The **Remove-Item** cmdlet has aliases of **del** and **erase**, and functions essentially the same as these commands in Cmd.exe:

```
PS C:\> remove-item c:\temp\*.txt
```

The cmdlet comes in handy when you want to recurse through a directory structure or exclude certain files.

```
PS C:\> remove-item c:\backup\*.* - recurse -exclude 2006*.log
```

This expression will recurse through c:\backup, deleting all files except those that match the pattern 2006*.log. Like **Copy-Item**, you can also use -**Include** and -**Credential**.

# Renaming Files

Renaming files is also very straightforward:

```
PS C:\Temp> rename-item foo.txt bar.txt
```

This cmdlet has aliases of **rni** and **ren**, and like the other item cmdlets, it lets you specify credentials and force an overwrite of an existing file. You have to be a little more creative if you need to rename multiple files:

### BulkRename.ps1

```
#BulkRename.ps1
Set-Location "C:\Logs"

$files=get-childitem -recurse |where {$_.extension -eq ".Log"}

foreach ($file in $files) {
 $filename=($file.name).ToString()
 $arr=@($filename.split("."))
 $newname=$arr[0]+".old"

 Write-Host "renaming"$file.Fullname "to"$newname
 ren $file.fullname $newname -force
}
```

This is a legitimate command in Cmd.exe:

```
C:\ ren *.log *.old
```

Since this doesn't work in PowerShell, we use something like the BulkRename script instead. This is a variation on our BulkCopy script from above. Instead of **copy**, we call **ren**. By the way, as the script is written above, it will recurse through subdirectories starting in C:\Logs, renaming every file it finds that ends in .log to .old.

# File Attributes and Properties

Earlier in this chapter, we worked with file attributes to work around some issues copying files in PowerShell. Often times, you may need to know if a file is marked as ReadOnly or set as such. This is easily accomplished by checking the **IsReadOnly** property of the file object:

```
PS C:\ > (Get-childitem file.txt).IsReadonly
False
```

You can enable ReadOnly by calling the **Set-ReadOnly()** method.

```
PS C:\ > (Get-childitem file.txt).Set_IsReadonly($TRUE)
PS C:\ > (Get-childitem file.txt).IsReadonly
True
```

Specify $TRUE to enable it and $FALSE to turn it off:

```
PS C:\ > (Get-childitem file.txt).Set_IsReadonly($False)
PS C:\ > (Get-childitem file.txt).IsReadonly
False
```

To display other attributes, you can use the **Attributes** property:

```
PS C:\ > (get-childitem boot.ini -force).Attributes
Hidden, System, Archive
```

We use the **-Force** parameter so that **Get-ChildItem** will ignore the Hidden attribute and display file information. To set other file attributes you can use the **Set_Attributes()** method:

```
PS C:\ > (get-childitem file.txt).Attributes
Archive
PS C:\ > (get-childitem file.txt).Set_Attributes("Archive,Hidden")
PS C:\ > (get-childitem file.txt -force).Attributes
Hidden, Archive
```

In this snippet, you can see the file.txt only has the Archive attribute set. Using **Set_Attributes()**, we set the file attributes to Archive and Hidden, which is confirmed with the last expression. This is also another way of setting the ReadOnly attribute.

Setting the file attribute to Normal will clear all basic file attributes:

```
PS C:\ > (get-childitem file.txt -force).Set_Attributes("Normal")
PS C:\ > (get-childitem file.txt -force).Attributes
Normal
PS C:\ > attrib file.txt
        C:\file.txt
PS C: \ >
```

Because everything is an object in PowerShell, working with file properties such as when a file was created or last modified is very simple. Here's an abbreviated output that gets all files from F:\SAPIEN and displays when the file was created, last accessed and last modified:

```
PS C:\ > get-childitem f:\sapien | Select Name,CreationTime,LastAccessTime,LastWriteTime '
>>| format-table -auto
>>

Name                    CreationTime         LastAccessTime         LastWriteTime
----                    ------------         --------------         -------------
Add2LocalAdmin.bat        6/12/2007 1:17:34 PM 6/15/2007 9:04:01 AM 6/12/2007 1:20:23 PM
Add2LocalAdmin.txt        6/14/2007 9:28:43 PM 6/15/2007 9:04:01 AM 6/12/2007 1:20:23 PM
AddToGroup.txt            6/14/2007 9:28:43 PM 6/15/2007 9:04:01 AM 6/12/2007 1:22:38 PM
AddToGroup.Wsf            6/12/2007 1:21:43 PM 6/15/2007 9:04:02 AM 6/12/2007 1:22:38 PM
AddUsertoGroup.txt        6/14/2007 9:28:43 PM 6/15/2007 9:04:02 AM 6/12/2007 4:18:54 PM
AddUsertoGroup.vbs        6/12/2007 4:18:54 PM 6/15/2007 4:29:51 PM 6/12/2007 4:18:54 PM
```

**It Isn't Necessarily What You Think**
The **LastAccessTime** property will indicate the last time a particular file as accessed, but this doesn't mean by a user. Many other processes and applications, such as anti-virus programs and defragmentation utilities, can affect this file property. Do not rely on this property as an indication of the last time user accessed a file. You would need to enable auditing to obtain that information.

PowerShell makes it very easy to change the value of any of these properties. This is similar to the Touch command:

```
PS C:\ > (get-childitem file.txt).Set_LastAccessTime("12/31/2007 01:23:45")
PS C:\ > (get-childitem file.txt).Set_LastWriteTime("12/31/2007 01:23:45")
PS C:\ > (get-childitem file.txt).Set_CreationTime("12/31/2007 01:23:45")
PS C:\ > get-childitem file.txt |select Name,CreationTime,LastWriteTime,LastAccessTime | `
>> format-table -auto
>>

Name      CreationTime          LastWriteTime         LastAccessTime
----      ------------          -------------         --------------
file.txt 12/31/2007 1:23:45 AM 12/31/2007 1:23:45 AM 12/31/2007 1:23:45 AM
```

Here, we've set all the time stamps to 12/31/2007 1:23:45 AM. Obviously, use this power with caution.

Another property that you can easily set from the console is file encryption. This is accomplished with the **Encrypt()** method.

```
PS C:\ > (get-childitem file.txt).Attributes
Archive
PS C:\ > (get-childitem file.txt).Encrypt()
PS C:\ > (get-childitem file.txt).Attributes
Archive, Encrypted
```

You can still open the file because it was encrypted with your private key, but anyone else attempting to open the file will fail. To reverse the process, simply use the **Decrypt()** method:

```
PS C:\ > (get-childitem file.txt).Decrypt()
PS C:\ > (get-childitem file.txt).Attributes
Archive
```

**Proceed with Caution**
Before you get carried away and start encrypting everything—stop. Using the encrypting file system requires some serious planning and testing. You have to plan for recovery agents, lost keys, and more. This is not a task to undertake lightly. You will need to research the topic and test thoroughly in a non-production environment.

What about compression? Even though compression can be indicated as file attribute, you cannot compress a file simply by setting the attribute. Nor does the .NET file object have a compression method. The easy solution is to use Compact.exe to compress files and folders.

The other approach is to use WMI:

```
PS C:\ > $wmifile=Get-WmiObject -query "Select * from CIM_DATAFILE where name='c:\\file.txt'"
PS C:\ > $wmifile


Compressed : False
Encrypted  : False
Size       :
Hidden     : False
Name       : c:\file.txt
Readable   : True
System File :
Version    :
Writeable  : True
```

You would think all you need to do is set the Compressed property to TRUE:

```
PS C:\ > $wmifile.Compressed=$TRUE
PS C:\ > $wmifile.Compressed
True
```

It looks like it works, but when you examine the file in Windows Explorer, you'll see that it isn't actually compressed.

```
PS C:\ > (get-childitem file.txt).Attributes
Archive
```

You need to use the **Compress()** method:

```
PS C:\ > $wmifile.Compress()


__GENUS          : 2
__CLASS          : __PARAMETERS
__SUPERCLASS     :
__DYNASTY        : __PARAMETERS
__RELPATH        :
__PROPERTY_COUNT : 1
__DERIVATION     : {}
__SERVER         :
__NAMESPACE      :
__PATH           :
ReturnValue      : 0



PS C:\ > (get-childitem file.txt).Attributes
Archive, Compressed
```

This is also confirmed in Windows Explorer. To reverse the process use the **Uncompress()** method:

```
PS C:\ > $wmifile.Uncompress()
```

## Working with Paths

When working with folders in PowerShell, you are also working with paths. A path, as the name suggests, is the "direction" to reach a particular destination. For a short path and likely known path like C:\

Windows, working with paths isn't critical. But as your scripts grow in complexity or you are dealing with path variables, you'll want to be familiar with PowerShell's path cmdlets. These cmdlets work with any provider that uses paths, such as the registry and certificate store.

## Test-Path

Adding error handling to a script is always helpful, especially when dealing with folders that may not exist. You can use **Test-Path** to validate the existence of a given path. The cmdlet returns TRUE if the path exists:

```
PS C:\ > test-path c:\windows
True
```

You can also use this cmdlet to verify the existence of registry keys:

```
PS C:\ > test-path hklm:\software\Microsoft\Windows\CurrentVersion
True
PS C:\ > test-path hklm:\software\MyCompany\MyApp\Settings
False
```

## Convert-Path

Before PowerShell can work with paths, they also need to be properly formatted. The **Convert-Path** cmdlet will take paths or path variables and convert them to a format PowerShell can understand. For example, the ~ character represents your user profile path. Using **Convert-Path** will return the explicit path:

```
PS C:\ > convert-path ~
C:\Documents and Settings\jhicks
```

Here are some other ways you might use this cmdlet:

```
PS C:\windows\system32 > convert-path .
C:\windows\system32
PS C:\windows\system32 > convert-path hklm:\system\currentcontrolset
HKEY_LOCAL_MACHINE\system\currentcontrolset
PS C:\windows\system32 > convert-path ..\
C:\windows
PS C:\windows\system32 > convert-path ..\..\
C:\
PS C:\windows\system32 >
```

The last two examples could also be achieved using **Split-Path**.

## Split-Path

This cmdlet will split a given path into its parent or leaf components. You can use this cmdlet to display or reference different components of a given path. The default is to split the path and return the parent path component:

```
PS C:\ > split-path c:\folderA\FolderB
c:\folderA
```

This cmdlet also works with other providers such as the registry:

```
PS C:\ > split-path hklm:\system\currentcontrolset
hklm:\system
```

**Split-Path** will include specified path's qualifier, which is the provider path's drive such as D:\ or HKLM:. If you wanted to get just the qualifier, in essence the root, use the -**Qualifier** parameter:

```
PS C:\ > split-path f:\folderA\FolderB\FolderC -qualifier
f:
```

You can use -**NoQualifier** to return a path without the root:

```
PS C:\ > split-path f:\folderA\FolderB\FolderC -noqualifier
\folderA\FolderB\FolderC
PS C:\ > split-path hklm:\system\currentcontrolset -noqualifier
\system\currentcontrolset
```

However, if you need the last part of the path and not the parent, use the -**Leaf** parameter:

```
PS C:\ > split-path c:\folderA\FolderB -leaf
FolderB
```

You're not limited to folder paths. You can use -**Leaf** to parse out a filename from a path:

```
PS C:\ > split-path "C:\program files\SAPIEN\PrimalScript 2007 Enterprise\PrimalScript.exe" '
>>-leaf
PrimalScript.exe
```

When using path variables, you may need to include the -**Resolve** parameter to expand the variable to its full path:

```
PS C:\ > split-path $pshome\*.xml -leaf -resolve
microsoft.powershell.commands.management.dll-help.xml
microsoft.powershell.commands.utility.dll-help.xml
microsoft.powershell.consolehost.dll-help.xml
microsoft.powershell.security.dll-help.xml
PshX-SAPIEN.dll-Help.xml
system.management.automation.dll-help.xml
```

This parameter is also useful in confirming that a path component exists:

```
PS C:\ > split-path C:\Windows\system33 -leaf -resolve
Split-Path : Cannot find path 'C:\Windows\system33' because it does not exist.
At line:1 char:11
+ split-path <<<< C:\Windows\system33 -leaf -resolve
```

PowerShell also has a specific cmdlet for resolving path names.

## Resolve-Path

The **Resolve-Path** cmdlet is primarily intended to resolve wildcards or variables that might be part of a path:

```
PS C:\ > resolve-path $env:windir

Path
----
C:\WINDOWS
```

The cmdlet's output is a PathInfo object. This object provides additional PowerShell information about the path:

```
PS C:\ > resolve-path $env:windir | format-list


Drive        : C
Provider     : Microsoft.PowerShell.Core\FileSystem
ProviderPath : C:\WINDOWS
Path         : C:\WINDOWS
```

You can also use the cmdlet with wildcards:

```
PS C:\ > resolve-path c:\windows\*.exe

Path
----
C:\windows\dbplugin.exe
C:\windows\explorer.exe
C:\windows\hh.exe
C:\windows\IsUninst.exe
C:\windows\notepad.exe
C:\windows\regedit.exe
C:\windows\slrundll.exe
C:\windows\TASKMAN.EXE
C:\windows\twunk_16.exe
C:\windows\twunk_32.exe
C:\windows\winhelp.exe
C:\windows\winhlp32.exe
```

## Join-Path

Occasionally, you need to construct a path from disparate elements, and **Join-Path** will create a PowerShell-ready path:

```
PS C:\ > join-path -path c:\scripts -childpath "My PowerShell Projects"
c:\scripts\My PowerShell Projects
```

The **-Path** and **-Childpath** parameters are positional, so you don't need to specify the parameter names. You can get the same result as the example above like this:

```
PS C:\ > join-path c:\scripts "My PowerShell Projects"
c:\scripts\My PowerShell Projects
```

The path name doesn't have to be explicit. You can also use variables like this:

```
PS C:\ > join-path $env:userprofile "Scripts\PowerShell"
C:\Documents and Settings\jhicks\Scripts\PowerShell
```

The cmdlet can also work with wildcards and the -**Resolve** parameter to expand the wildcard and create a complete path:

```
PS C:\ > join-path c:\prog* "microsoft*" -resolve
C:\Program Files\Microsoft ActiveSync
C:\Program Files\Microsoft CAPICOM 2.1.0.2
C:\Program Files\Microsoft Expression
C:\Program Files\microsoft frontpage
C:\Program Files\Microsoft IntelliPoint
C:\Program Files\Microsoft Money
C:\Program Files\Microsoft Office
C:\Program Files\Microsoft SQL Server
C:\Program Files\Microsoft Visual Studio
C:\Program Files\Microsoft Visual Studio 8
C:\Program Files\Microsoft Works
C:\Program Files\Microsoft.NET
```

## Creating Directories

Creating directories in PowerShell is nearly the same as it is in Cmd.exe:

```
PS C:\Temp> mkdir "NewFiles"
```

Alternatively, you can use the New-Item cmdlet that offers a few more features:

```
PS C:\Temp> new-item -type directory \\File01\public\sapien
```

The cmdlet also creates nested directories. In other words, like **mkdir** in Cmd.exe, it creates any intermediate directories:

```
PS C:\Temp> new-item -type directory c:\temp\1\2\3


    Directory: Microsoft.PowerShell.Core\FileSystem::C:\temp\1\2


Mode                LastWriteTime     Length Name
----                -------------     ------ ----
d----         6/16/2006  1:56 PM             3
PS C:\Temp> tree /a
Folder PATH listing for volume Server2003
Volume serial number is 0006EEA4 34AB:AD37
C:.
+---1
|   \---2
|       \---3
+---jdh
+---sapien
\---temp2
PS C:\Temp>
```

## Listing Directories

Even though you can use dir in PowerShell to list directories and files, it is really an alias for **Get-ChildItem**. However, you can specify files to include or exclude in the search and also recurse through subdirectories:

```
PS C:\> dir -exclude *.old -recurse
```

Remember: even though PowerShell is displaying text, it is really working with objects. This means you can get creative in how you display information:

```
PS C:\Temp> dir -exclude *.old,*.bak,*.tmp -recurse | select-object '
>>FullName,Length,LastWriteTime | format-table -auto
>>
FullName                    Length LastWriteTime
--------                    ------ -------------
C:\Temp\1                          6/16/2006 1:56:45 PM
C:\Temp\1\2                        6/16/2006 1:56:45 PM
C:\Temp\1\2\3                      6/16/2006 1:56:45 PM
C:\Temp\jdh                        6/16/2006 1:09:41 PM
C:\Temp\sapien                     6/16/2006 1:05:41 PM
C:\Temp\temp2                      6/16/2006 12:48:44 PM
C:\Temp\temp2\bar.Log           11 6/16/2006 11:09:27 AM
C:\Temp\showservices.ps1       477 5/19/2006 11:04:29 AM
C:\Temp\test.abc                88 5/1/2006 8:10:10 PM
C:\Temp\test.Log                88 5/1/2006 8:10:10 PM
C:\Temp\test.ps1                88 5/1/2006 8:10:10 PM


PS C:\Temp>
```

This expression recurses from the starting directory, listing all files that don't end in .old, .bak, or .tmp. Using the **dir** alias, the output from **Get-ChildItem** is piped to **Select-Object** because we want to display only certain information formatted as a table.

## Deleting Directories

Deleting a directory is essentially the same as deleting a file. You can use the **rmdir** alias for **Remove-Item**:

```
PS C:\Temp> rmdir sapien
```

PowerShell gives you a warning if you attempt to remove a directory that isn't empty:

```
PS C:\Temp> rmdir files

Confirm
The item at C:\Temp\files has children and the -recurse parameter was
not specified. If you continue, all children will be removed with the
item. Are you sure you want to continue?
[Y] Yes [A] Yes to All [N] No [L] No to All [S] Suspend [?] Help
(default is "Y"):n
PS C:\Temp>
```

As you can see, the solution is to use the **-Recurse** parameter:

```
PS C:\Temp> rmdir files -recurse
PS C:\Temp>
```

# Chapter 25
# Managing Systems by Using WMI

Using WMI in administrative scripts is a common practice. WMI is an extremely powerful way to manage just about every aspect of a system including hardware, software, and configuration. It can also be used to remotely manage systems.

PowerShell has the **Get-WmiObject** cmdlet that acts as an interface to WMI. This cmdlet lets you access any WMI class in any WMI namespace. For our purposes, we'll stick to the default namespace of Root\Cimv2 and the Win32 classes, since you'll use these classes in 95% of your scripts.

## Retrieving Basic Information

At its simplest, all you have to do is specify a class and run **Get-WmiObject** in order for the cmdlet to find all instances of that class and return a page of information:

```
PS C:\> Get-WmiObject win32_share

Name                   Path                  Description
----                   ----                  -----------
E$                     E:\                   Default share
IPC$                                         Remote IPC
downloads$             e:\downloads
ADMIN$                 E:\WINDOWS             Remote Admin
C$                     C:\                   Default share


PS C:\>
```

In this example, we asked PowerShell to display WMI information about all instances of the Win32_
Share class on the local computer. With this particular class, there are other properties that by default
are not displayed. Depending on the class, you might get different results. For example, the following
expression displays a long list of properties and values:

```
PS C:\> Get-WmiObject win32_Processor
```

## Listing Available Classes

You're probably saying, "That's great, but how do I find out what Win32 classes are available?" All
you have to do is ask. The **Get-WmiObject** cmdlet has a -**List** parameter you can invoke. Open a
PowerShell prompt and try this:

```
PS C:\> Get-WmiObject -list | where {$_.name -like "win32*"}
```

You should get a long, two column list of all the available Win32 classes. You can query any of these
classes using **Get-WmiObject**.

The **Get-WmiObject** cmdlet defaults to the root\CIMv2 namespace, but you can query available
classes in any namespace:

```
PS C:\> Get-WmiObject -namespace root\securitycenter -list


__SystemClass                               __thisNAMESPACE
...
__InstanceOperationEvent                    __MethodInvocationEvent
__InstanceCreationEvent                     __InstanceModificationEvent
__InstanceDeletionEvent                     __ExtrinsicEvent
__SystemEvent                               __EventDroppedEvent
__ConsumerFailureEvent                      __QOSFailureEvent
__EventQueueOverflowEvent                   __ClassOperationEvent
__ClassModificationEvent                    __ClassCreationEvent
__ClassDeletionEvent                        __TimerEvent
__AggregateEvent                            __EventConsumer
__FilterToConsumerBinding                   __TimerNextFiring
__EventFilter                               __ProviderRegistration
__EventProviderRegistration                 __EventConsumerProviderRegistratio
__PropertyProviderRegistration               __ObjectProviderRegistration
__ClassProviderRegistration                 __InstanceProviderRegistration
__MethodProviderRegistration                 __SystemSecurity
__SecurityRelatedClass                      __NTLMUser9X
__PARAMETERS                                __NotifyStatus
__ExtendedStatus                            FirewallProduct
AntiVirusProduct
PS C:\>
```

**Note**

All those classes starting with __ are WMI system classes; you can't really hide them, but you're
not going to really use them, either. You want the classes that *don't* start with __.

Here we've queried for a list of classes in the Root\SecurityCenter namespace.

# Listing Properties of a Class

The next question most of you are asking is, "How can I find out the properties for a given class?" As we discussed previously, you can use **Get-Member** to list all the properties for a WMI object. Take a look at the following script:

### ListWMIProperties.ps1

```
#ListWMIProperties.ps1
$class=Read-Host "Enter a Win32 WMI Class that you are interested in"
$var=get-WMIObject -class $class -namespace "root\Cimv2"
$properties=$var | get-member -membertype Property
Write-Host "Properties for "$Class.ToUpper()
foreach ($property in $properties) {$property.name}
```

This script prompts you for a Win32 WMI class and defines a variable using **Get-WmiObject** for that class. We define a second variable that is the result of piping the first variable to **Get-Member**. All that's left is to loop through $properties and list each one. Here's what you get when you run the script:

```
Enter a Win32 WMI Class that you are interested in: win32_logicaldisk
Properties for WIN32_LOGICALDISK
Access
Availability
BlockSize
Caption
Compressed
ConfigManagerErrorCode
ConfigManagerUserConfig
CreationClassName
Description
DeviceID
DriveType
ErrorCleared
ErrorDescription
ErrorMethodology
FileSystem
FreeSpace
InstallDate
LastErrorCode
MaximumComponentLength
MediaType
...
PS C:\>
```

Usually, there are only a handful of properties in which you are interested. In this case, you can use the -**Property** parameter to specify which properties you want to display:

```
PS C:\> Get-WmiObject -class win32_processor '
>>-property name,caption,L2CacheSize
>>


__GENUS          : 2
__CLASS          : Win32_Processor
__SUPERCLASS     :
__DYNASTY        :
__RELPATH        :
__PROPERTY_COUNT : 3
```

```
__DERIVATION    : {}
__SERVER        :
__NAMESPACE     :
__PATH          :
Caption         : x86 Family 6 Model 9 Stepping 5
L2CacheSize     : 1024
Name            :        Intel(R) Pentium(R) M processor 1600MHz


PS C:\>
```

Here, we've asked for the Win32_Processor class, and specifically the name, caption, and L2CacheSize properties. Unfortunately, the cmdlet also insists on displaying system properties, such as __Genus.

Since you don't care about those properties most of the time, a neater approach is something like this:

```
PS C:\> Get-WmiObject -class win32_processor | `
>> select-object name,caption,L2CacheSize | `
>> format-list
>>


name       :        Intel(R) Pentium(R) M processor 1600MHz
caption    : x86 Family 6 Model 9 Stepping 5
L2CacheSize : 1024


PS C:\>
```

Here, we're calling the same cmdlet, except we use **Select-Object** to pick the properties in which we're interested.

## Examining Existing Values

As you learn to work with WMI, it's helpful to look at what information is populated on a system. This is a great way to learn the different properties and what values you can expect. The more you work with WMI, you'll realize that not every property is always populated. There's no reason to spend time querying empty properties. With this in mind, we've put together a helpful script that enumerates all the properties for all the instances of a particular WMI class. However, the script only display properties with a value and it won't display any of the system class properties like __Genus:

### ListWMIValues.ps1

```
#ListWMIValues.ps1
$class=Read-Host "Enter a Win32 WMI Class that you are interested in"
$var=get-WMIObject -class $class -namespace "root\CimV2"

$properties=$var | get-member -membertype Property
Write-Host -foregroundcolor "Yellow" "Properties for "$Class.ToUpper()
# if more than one instance was returned then $var will be an array
# and we need to loop through it
$i=0

if ($var.Count -ge 2) {
 do {
 foreach ($property in $properties) {
 #only display values that aren't null and don't display system
```

```
#properties that start with __
  if ($var[$i].($property.name) -ne $Null -AND `
$property.name -notlike "__*") { write-Host -foregroundcolor "Green" `
$property.name"="$var[$i].($property.name)
  }
 }
 Write-Host "*********************************"
#divider between instances
 $i++
 }while($i -le ($var.count-1))
}
# else $var has only one instance
else {
 foreach ($property in $properties) {
  if ($var.($property.name) -ne $Null -AND `
$property.name -notlike "__*") {
  write-Host -foregroundcolor "Green" `
$property.name"="$var.($property.name)
  }
 }
}
```

This script is based on our earlier ListWMIProperties script. Once we have the variable with all the properties, we iterate through all the instances of the specified WMI class. If the property value isn't null and the property name is not like __*, then the property name and its value are displayed. We've even thrown in a little color to spice up the display.

## Remote Management

Now that you know about WMI classes and properties, we'll take a closer look at what you do with it. While you can make some system configuration changes with WMI, most of the WMI properties are read-only, which makes for terrific management reports. The **Get-WmiObject** cmdlet even has two parameters that make this easy to do on your network.

You *can* use -**Computername** to specify a remote computer that you want to connect to and -**Credential** to specify alternate credentials. However, you *can't* use alternate credentials when querying the local system. Here's an example:

```
PS C:\> Get-WmiObject win32_operatingsystem `
>>-computer dc01 -credential (get-credential)
>>

cmdlet get-credential at command pipeline position 1
Supply values for the following parameters:
Credential


SystemDirectory : C:\WINDOWS\system32
Organization    : SAPIEN Press
BuildNumber     : 3790
RegisteredUser  : Staff
SerialNumber    : 69713-640-3403486-45904
Version         : 5.2.3790


PS C:\>
```

329

This example connects to computer DC01 and gets information on the Win32_Operatingsystem WMI object. For alternate credentials, we call the **Get-Credential** cmdlet that presents a standard Windows authentication box.

**VBScript Alert**

If you have a library of WMI scripts written in VBScript, don't delete them yet! With a little tweaking, you can take the essential WMI queries from your VBScripts and put them into PowerShell scripts. Use the **Where** cmdlet for your WMI queries. For example, you may have a WMI query like:

```
Select deviceID,drivetype,size,freespace
from Win32_LogicalDisk where drivetype='3'
```

In PowerShell this can be rewritten as:

```
Get-WmiObject win32_logicaldisk | Select
deviceid,drivetype,size,freespace | where
{drivetype -eq 3}
```

Of course, you can also simply pass the original WQL query to **Get-WmiObject** by using its **-query** parameter. Once you have the core query, you can tweak your PowerShell script and use the filtering, formatting, sorting, and exporting options that are available in PowerShell. If you don't have a script library, there are many, many WMI scripts available on the Internet that you can leverage and turn into PowerShell scripts.

The **Get-WmiObject** cmdlet does not allow you to specify multiple classes. So, if you want information from different Win32 classes, you'll have to call the cmdlet several times and store information in variables:

**WMIReport.ps1**

```
#WMIReport.ps1
$OS=Get-WmiObject -class win32_operatingsystem `
| Select-Object Caption,CSDVersion

#select fixed drives only by specifying a drive type of 3
$Drives=Get-WmiObject -class win32_logicaldisk | `
where {$_.DriveType -eq 3}
Write-Host "Operating System:" $OS.Caption $OS.CSDVersion

Write-Host "Drive Summary:"
write-Host "Drive"`t"Size (MB)"`t"FreeSpace (MB)"
foreach ($d in $Drives) {
 $free="{0:N2}" -f ($d.FreeSpace/1048576)
 $size="{0:N0}" -f ($d.size/1048576)
 Write-Host $d.deviceID `t $size `t $free
}
```

This script reports system information from two WMI Win32 classes. We first define a variable to hold operating system information, specifically the Caption and CSDVersion, which is the service pack. The second class, Win32_LogicalDisk, is captured in $Drives. Since we're only interested in fixed drives, we use the **Where** cmdlet to filter by drive type.

Once we have this information we can display it any way we choose. Here's what you might see when the script runs:

```
Operating System: Microsoft(R) Windows(R) Server 2003, Enterprise
Edition Service Pack 1
Drive Summary:
Drive  Size (MB)      FreeSpace (MB)
C:      8,095  2,417.88
E:     15,006      4,696.01
PS C:\>
```

# The [WMI] Type

If you prefer a different approach to working with WMI and have some experience working with it, you may prefer to use PowerShell's [WMI] type:

```
PS C:\> [WMI]$srv="root\cimv2:win32_computersystem.Name='Godot'"
PS C:\> $srv


Domain           : WORKGROUP
Manufacturer     : Dell Computer Corporation
Model            : Latitude D800
Name             : Godot
PrimaryOwnerName  : Administrator
TotalPhysicalMemory : 1609805824
```

By creating a new object of type [WMI], we can directly access the WMI instance. PowerShell returns a pre-determined subset of information when you call object as we did above. However, you have access to all the WMI properties, which you can see by piping the object to **Get-Member**:

```
PS C:\> $srv|Get-Member
```

If we want additional information, all we have to do is check the object's property:

```
PS C:\> $srv.Status
OK
PS C:\> $srv.Roles
LM_Workstation
LM_Server
SQLServer
Print
NT
PS C:\>
```

While you can't specify alternate credentials using the [WMI] type, you can specify a remote system like this:

```
PS C:\> [WMI]$srv="\\DC01\root\cimv2:win32_computersystem.Name='DC01'"
```

To use the [WMI] type, you must create a reference to a specific instance of a WMI object. For example, you can't create a WMI object to return all instances of Win32_LogicalDisk:

```
PS C:\> [WMI]$disk="root\cimv2:win32_logicaldisk"
Cannot convert value "root\cimv2:win32_logicaldisk" to type
"System.Management.ManagementObject". Error: "Specified
argument was out of the range of valid values.
Parameter name: path"
At line:1 char:11
+ [WMI]$disk= <<<< "root\cimv2:win32_logicaldisk"
PS C:\>
```

Instead, you must specify a single instance by using the WMI object's primary key and querying for a certain value:

```
PS C:\> [WMI]$disk="root\cimv2:win32_logicaldisk.DeviceID='C:'"
PS C:\> $disk


DeviceID     : C:
DriveType    : 3
ProviderName :
FreeSpace    : 2797834240
Size         : 15726702592
VolumeName   : Server2003


PS C:\>
```

That's great, but how do you figure out an object's primary key? The easiest way is to run Wbemtest and query for a Win32 class. The results are the format you need to use with the [WMI] type in PowerShell.

In this screen shot you can see that we've queried for all instances of the Win32_logicaldisk class. Each instance is displayed using the default key, which in this case is DeviceID. Here's another example:

We can tell from this screenshot that the default key is Handle. The Handle is the same as the ProcessID. If you need a refresher on Wbemtest, see the section Using Wbemtest.

Once we know this piece of information, we can write PowerShell code like this:

```
PS C:\> [wmi]$ps="root\cimv2:win32_process.handle='4536'"
PS C:\> $ps | Select Name,VirtualSize,WorkingSetSize,PageFileUsage,ExecutablePath


Name          : PrimalScript.exe
VirtualSize   : 320835584
WorkingSetSize : 38825984
PageFileUsage : 64581632
ExecutablePath : C:\Program Files\SAPIEN\PrimalScript 2007 Enterprise\PrimalScript.exe
PS C:\>
```

## The [WMISearcher] Type

Finally, PowerShell also has a [WMISearcher] type. This allows you to submit a query to WMI and return a collection of objects.

```
PS C:\> $d = [WmiSearcher]"Select * from Win32_Logicaldisk where drivetype = 3'
PS C:\> $d.get()


DeviceID     : C:
DriveType    : 3
ProviderName :
FreeSpace    : 3007844352
Size         : 15726702592
VolumeName   : Server2003

DeviceID     : E:
DriveType    : 3
```

```
ProviderName :
FreeSpace    : 3738099712
Size         : 24280993792
VolumeName   : XP
```

The object, $d, is a collection of all Win32_LogicalDisk instances where drive type is equal to 3. To access to collection we call the **Get()** method. This technique is very helpful when you want to find dynamic information that might include multiple instances of a given WMI class.

```
PS C:\> $s=[WMISearcher]"Select * from win32_Service `
>> where StartMode='Disabled'"
>>
PS C:\> $s.Get()|format-table -autosize

ExitCode Name                          ProcessId StartMode State Stat
-------- ----                          --------- --------- ----- --
    1077 Alerter                            0 Disabled Stopped OK
    1077 ALG                                0 Disabled Stopped OK
    1077 ClipSrv                            0 Disabled Stopped OK
    1077 FastUserSwitchingCompatibility     0 Disabled Stopped OK
    1077 HidServ                            0 Disabled Stopped OK
    1077 Irmon                              0 Disabled Stopped OK
    1077 Messenger                          0 Disabled Stopped OK
    1077 msvsmon80                          0 Disabled Stopped OK
    1077 NetDDE                             0 Disabled Stopped OK
    1077 NetDDEdsdm                         0 Disabled Stopped OK
    1077 RemoteAccess                       0 Disabled Stopped OK
    1077 RemoteRegistry                     0 Disabled Stopped OK
    1077 SCardSvr                           0 Disabled Stopped OK
    1077 SharedAccess                       0 Disabled Stopped OK
    1077 TermService                        0 Disabled Stopped OK
    1077 TlntSvr                            0 Disabled Stopped OK
    1077 WMDM PMSP Service                  0 Disabled Stopped OK


PS C:\>
```

You cannot use the WMISearcher type to query a remote system. If you need to do that, then you'll have to continue using the **Get-WmiObject** cmdlet.

So, when should you use **Get-WmiObject** and when should you use the WMI type? If you know exactly the WMI object and instance you want to work with, and don't need to specify alternate credentials, then WMI type is the best and fastest approach. Otherwise, use the **Get-wmiObject** cmdlet.

## Practical Examples

Let's look at a few practical examples of using WMI and PowerShell. If you are like most administrators, you have a list or two of server names. Often, you want to obtain information from all of the servers in a list or perform some action against each of them, such as restarting a service.

There are a few ways you can "process" multiple computers from a list. Here's one approach:

```
foreach ($server in (get-content servers.txt)) {
  # do something else to each computer
  Get-WmiObject <WMIClass or query> -computer $server
  }
```

With this approach, you can run multiple commands on each server, passing the servername as the

-**computer** parameter for the **Get-wmiObject** cmdlet. Here's how this might look in a script:

```
foreach ($server in (get-content servers.txt)) {
   Write-Host $server.ToUpper() -fore Black -back Green
   Get-WmiObject Win32_Operatingsystem -computer $server |`
   Format-Table Caption,BuildNumber,ServicePackMajorVersion
   Get-WmiObject Win32_Computersystem -computer $server |`
   Format-Table Model,TotalPhysicalMemory
   }
```

The code snippet takes each computer name from servers.txt using **Get-Content**. Each time through the list the computer name is assigned to the $server variable and first displayed using **Write-Host**.

```
Write-Host $server.ToUpper() -fore Black -back Green
```

Then two different **Get-WmiObject** expressions are executed with the results of each piped to **Format-Table**. The end result is information about each operating system, including its name and service pack version, as well as information about the server model and the total amount of physical memory.

If you are only executing a single command for each server, a more efficient approach is something like this:

```
Get-WmiObject <WMI Query or Class> -computer (Get-Content servers.txt)
```

You can use whatever syntax variation you want for **Get-WmiObject**. The trick here is that the result of the **Get-Content** command will implicitly be processed as if you were using **ForEach**. Here's a variation on something we tried above:

```
PS C:\> Get-WmiObject Win32_Computersystem -computer (Get-Content servers.txt) |`
>> Format-Table Model,TotalPhysicalMemory
>>
```

We will get a table with hardware model and total physical memory for each computer in the list. But if you run this yourself, you'll notice something is missing. How you can tell what information belongs to which computer? Easy. Have WMI tell you. Most WMI classes have a property, usually CSName, that will return the name of the computer. Testing your WMI expression will let you know what you can use. If nothing else, you can always use the __SERVER property. This is always populated. Here's our previous example revised to include the server name:

```
PS C:\> Get-WmiObject Win32_Computersystem -computer (Get-Content servers.txt) |`
>> Format-Table __Server,Model,TotalPhysicalMemory
>>
```

Now you will get a more meaningful report.

Here's one more slightly complex example, but something you are likely to need. This code sample could be used in a script to return drive utilization information:

```
Get-WmiObject -query "Select * from win32_logicaldisk where drivetype=3" `
-computer (Get-Content servers.txt) -credential $cred | `
Format-Table @{Label="Server";Expression={$_.SystemName}},DeviceID,`
@{Label="Size (MB)";Expression={"{0:N2}" -f ($_.Size/1MB)}}, `
@{Label="Free (MB)";Expression={"{0:N2}" -f ($_.FreeSpace/1MB)}}
```

The **Get-WmiObject** cmdlet is using the query parameter to return all logical disks of drive type 3, which indicates a fixed local disk. This query is run against each computer listed in servers.txt. Our example also passes a stored set of alternate credentials, which has been saved ahead of time in the $cred variable.

The results of the query are then piped to **Format-Table**, which creates a few custom table headers. Because the Size and FreeSpace properties are returned in bytes, we'll format them using the format operator, -f, to megabytes. The result is a table showing every server name, its fixed drives, and their size and free space in MB to two decimal places.

# WMI Events and PowerShell

A particular useful feature of WMI is the ability to subscribe to Windows events and execute code in response to each event. For example, you could run a WMI script that would check every five seconds to verify that a specific service had not stopped. Or you might need to monitor a folder and be notified when a new file is created. WMI events are used to meet these needs. This can be a complicated process and is definitely an advanced WMI topic.

PowerShell does not have any cmdlets designed explicitly for working with WMI events. The **Get-wmiObject** cmdlet also doesn't support WMI events. Fortunately, the .NET Framework has a few classes you can use in PowerShell.

You will use the System.Management.ManagementEventWatcher class to watch for new events. Before you can create the object, you will need to create System.Management.ManagementScope and System.Management.WQLEventQuery objects. But these are pretty easy to define. The scope will be the WMI namespace, typically root\cimv2. Use the **New-Object** cmdlet:

```
PS C:\ > $path="root\cimv2"
PS C:\ > $scope  = New-Object System.Management.ManagementScope $path
```

The event query is a little more complicated. The query is written like any other WMI query. The difference is that you need to specify an event class. But what events can you work with? Have PowerShell tell you:

```
PS C:\> Get-WmiObject -list -namespace root\cimv2 | where '
>> {$_.__derivation -match "event"} | sort
>>
```

This will generate a long list that we won't reprint here. But we will use some of the event classes you are likely to see. Suppose you want to know when a new process has started. You would use a query like "Select* from Win32_ProcessStartTrace". To create the appropriate object, type this:

```
PS C:\> $query="Select * from win32_processStartTrace"
PS C:\> $EventQuery  = New-Object System.Management.WQLEventQuery $query
```

Once you have the scope and query objects, you can create the watcher object:

```
PS C:\> $watcher = New-Object System.Management.ManagementEventWatcher $scope,$EventQuery
```

The watcher object has some options you can set by modifying a System.Management.EventWatcherOptions object. One item you will likely want to set is a timeout value. This value determines how long WMI will wait before timing out.

```
PS C:\> $options = New-Object System.Management.EventWatcherOptions
PS C:\> $options.TimeOut = [timespan]"0.0:0:1"
PS C:\> $watcher.Options = $options
```

The event watcher object is now ready to start. If you look at the object's properties, you'll see a **Start()** method. This method ties your event query to the watcher object, but the event notification is asynchronous. You also need to call the **WaitForNextEvent()** method to instruct PowerShell to wait for the next event:

```
PS C:\> $watcher.WaitFornextevent()
Exception calling "WaitForNextEvent" with "0" argument(s): "Timed out "
At line:1 char:26
+ $watcher.WaitFornextevent( <<<< )
```

Wait a moment. This timed out. Well, we told it to wait only for a second before timing out. We could have set a longer timeout value, but you'll never really know how long it might be before a specific event occurs. With WMI events, your script needs to keep running so that it can "receive" notifications about events. Here's a better way:

```
PS C:\> while ($true) {
>>          trap [System.Management.ManagementException] {continue}
>>          $watcher.WaitForNextEvent()
>>      }
>>
```

At this point, PowerShell will wait until the event, which, if you've been following from the beginning of this section, is when a new process starts. As soon as we launch Notepad, PowerShell will display this:

```
__GENUS             : 2
__CLASS             : Win32_ProcessStartTrace
__SUPERCLASS        : Win32_ProcessTrace
__DYNASTY           : __SystemClass
__RELPATH           :
__PROPERTY_COUNT    : 8
__DERIVATION        : {Win32_ProcessTrace, Win32_SystemTrace, __ExtrinsicEvent, __Event...}
__SERVER            :
__NAMESPACE         :
__PATH              :
PageDirectoryBase   : 49667
ParentProcessID     : 2460
ProcessID           : 16952
ProcessName         : notepad.exe
SECURITY_DESCRIPTOR :
SessionID           : 0
Sid                 : {1, 5, 0, 0...}
TIME_CREATED        : 128293441418864430
```

Every new process will be listed here as it starts. To quit simply type Ctrl-C, although you may need to wait a bit depending on the timeout value specified. By the way, the reason for the trap line is so that when the WMI event times out, the error message will be suppressed. It makes your event monitoring a little cleaner.

Let's take everything we have so far and wrap it up in a function:

```
Function Get-WmiEvent ($query){
 $path="root\cimv2"
```

```
$EventQuery = New-Object System.Management.WQLEventQuery $query
$scope      = New-Object System.Management.ManagementScope $path
$watcher    = New-Object System.Management.ManagementEventWatcher $scope,$EventQuery
$options    = New-Object System.Management.EventWatcherOptions
$options.TimeOut = [timespan]"0.0:0:1"
cls
Write-Host Waiting for events in response to: $EventQuery.querystring `
-back darkgreen -fore black
$watcher.Options = $options
$watcher.Start()
while ($true) {
   trap [System.Management.ManagementException] {continue}
$watcher.WaitForNextEvent()
 }
}
```

Once the function is loaded, the only argument is the event query:

```
PS C:\> get-wmievent "select * from Win32_ProcessStartTrace"
```

The screen will clear and the query will be displayed with a dark green background. This gives you more screen real estate for all the events plus you'll be able to see what type of events you are monitoring. As new processes are started you'll see information, but perhaps you would prefer to see less information. The output shows you the properties, so let's create a new function for monitoring new processes that only displays pertinent information.

```
Function Get-NewProcessEvent {
 $path="root\cimv2"
 $query="Select * from Win32_ProcessStartTrace"
 $EventQuery = New-Object System.Management.WQLEventQuery $query
 $scope      = New-Object System.Management.ManagementScope $path
 $watcher    = New-Object System.Management.ManagementEventWatcher $scope,$EventQuery
 $options    = New-Object System.Management.EventWatcherOptions
 $options.TimeOut = [timespan]"0.0:0:1"
 $watcher.Options = $options
 cls
 Write-Host Waiting for events in response to: $EventQuery.querystring `
 -back darkgreen -fore black
 $watcher.Start()
 while ($true) {
    trap [System.Management.ManagementException] {continue}
 $watcher.WaitForNextEvent() | select ProcessName,ProcessID,ParentProcessID
 }
}
```

This is very similar to our previous function, except we've hard coded in the query. Because we know this function will be used to watch for new processes, we can select process specific properties:

```
$watcher.WaitForNextEvent() | select ProcessName,ProcessID,ParentProcessID
```

When the event fires, the returned object is piped to the **Select** cmdlet, which returns the ProcessName, ProcessID and PartentProcessID properties. Now we have a simpler display of information.

As you work with WMI events, especially as you look at VBScript examples you might find online or in books, you'll come across queries like this:

```
"Select * from __InstanceCreationEvent Within 5 where TargetInstance ISA 'CIM_datafile' AND
TargetInstance.drive='c:' AND TargetInstance.Path='\\files\\'"
```

We don't have space to cover WMI events in detail, but a query like this returns a TargetInstance object whenever a corresponding event fires. In this query, any time a new file is created in C:\Files, an event will fire. The query will check every five seconds. The returned object will be a CIM_Datafile.

We could pass this query string to our Get-wmiEvent function, and it will work. When a new file is created, this will be returned to PowerShell:

```
__GENUS               : 2
__CLASS               : __InstanceCreationEvent
__SUPERCLASS          : __InstanceOperationEvent
__DYNASTY             : __SystemClass
__RELPATH             :
__PROPERTY_COUNT      : 3
__DERIVATION          : {__InstanceOperationEvent, __Event, __IndicationRelated, __SystemClass}
__SERVER              : GODOT
__NAMESPACE           : //./root/CIMV2
__PATH                :
SECURITY_DESCRIPTOR   :
TargetInstance        : System.Management.ManagementBaseObject
TIME_CREATED          : 128294215675296404
```

In this situation, we need a little more processing to get the details of the TargetInstance. Here's a function designed to watch for the creation of a new file:

```
Function Get-NewFileEvent {
# $folderpath is the full path to the folder you
# want to monitor like C:\files\PowerShell

# $interval is the polling interval in seconds.

Param([string]$folderpath,[int32]$interval)
 $path="root\cimv2"
 $drive=Split-Path $folderpath -Qualifier
 $Folder=(Split-Path $folderpath -NoQualifier).Replace("\","\\")+"\\"
 $query="Select * from __InstanceCreationEvent Within `
 $interval where TargetInstance ISA 'CIM_datafile' AND `
 TargetInstance.drive='$drive' AND TargetInstance.Path='$folder'"
 $EventQuery = New-Object System.Management.WQLEventQuery $query
 $scope       = New-Object System.Management.ManagementScope $path
 $watcher     = New-Object System.Management.ManagementEventWatcher $scope,$EventQuery
 $options     = New-Object System.Management.EventWatcherOptions
 $options.TimeOut = [timespan]"0.0:0:1"
 $watcher.Options = $options
 cls
 Write-Host Waiting for events in response to: $EventQuery.querystring `
 -back darkgreen -fore black
 $watcher.Start()
 while ($true) {
    trap [System.Management.ManagementException] {continue}
      $evt=$watcher.WaitForNextEvent()
      if ($evt) {
        $evt.TargetInstance | select Name,FileSize,CreationDate
      Clear-Variable evt }
 }
}
```

This function takes a parameter for the folder to monitor and a polling interval in seconds. The WMI event query needs the drive and folder, so we used the **Split-Path** cmdlet to parse the folder path:

```
$drive=Split-Path $folderpath -Qualifier
$Folder=(Split-Path $folderpath -NoQualifier).Replace("\","\\")+"\\"
```

The WMI query also expects the folder path to use \\ in place of \, so we use the **Replace()** method to make the change.

The function loops repeatedly waiting for the next event to fire:

```
while ($true) {
    trap [System.Management.ManagementException] {continue}
    $evt=$watcher.WaitForNextEvent()
```

If an event fires, then $evt will become defined, which we can test for:

```
    if ($evt) {
```

If the object exists, we get the TargetInstance property and pipe that to the **Select** cmdlet to display the filename, its size, and when it was created:

```
        $evt.TargetInstance | select Name,FileSize,CreationDate
```

Thus, when a file is created, you will see something like this:

```
Name                                        FileSize CreationDate
----                                        -------- ------------
c:\files\file.txt                               1193 20070720134955.005960-240
```

After the information has been displayed, we clear the variable so that the function doesn't continue to repeat the same information until a new event fires:

```
    Clear-Variable evt }
```

As you can see, there is no single approach to working with WMI events in PowerShell. It all depends on the type of events you want to monitor and what type of information or action you want to take.

**The PowerShell Team Rocks**
We want to give proper credit and thanks to the Microsoft PowerShell team for providing some terrific examples on this topic, which we've shamelessly "borrowed." We strongly recommend reading the team blog at http://blogs.msdn.com/powershell/default.aspx on regular basis.

What about connecting to events on remote computers and using alternate credentials? Here's our function to watch for new processes, rewritten to support connecting to a remote machine and specifying alternate credentials:

```
Function Get-NewRemoteProcessEvent {
Param([string]$computer=".",[System.Management.Automation.PSCredential]$credential)
```

```
$path="\\$computer\root\cimv2"
$query="Select * from Win32_ProcessStartTrace"
$EventQuery = New-Object System.Management.WQLEventQuery $query
$scope      = New-Object System.Management.ManagementScope $path

if ($Credential) {
#use alternate credentials if passed
  $scope.options.Username = $credential.GetNetworkCredential().Username
  $scope.options.Password = $credential.GetNetworkCredential().Password
}

$watcher     = New-Object System.Management.ManagementEventWatcher $scope,$EventQuery
$options     = New-Object System.Management.EventWatcherOptions
$options.TimeOut = [timespan]"0.0:0:1"
$watcher.Options = $options
cls
Write-Host Connected to $path. Waiting for events in response to: $EventQuery.querystring `
-back darkgreen -fore black
$watcher.Start()
while ($true) {
   trap [System.Management.ManagementException] {continue}
$watcher.WaitForNextEvent() | select ProcessName,ProcessID,ParentProcessID
}
}
```

There are really only a few differences. First, we've set the default computer name to the local system. If you specify a computer name, then the path will include the computer name:

```
$path="\\$computer\root\cimv2"
```

The second parameter is a set of alternate credentials. The function is expecting an object created from an earlier **Get-Credential** command. If a credential is passed, the username and password are extracted with the **GetNetworkCredential()** method and assigned to the management scope:

```
if ($Credential) {
#use alternate credentials if passed
  $scope.options.Username = $credential.GetNetworkCredential().Username
  $scope.options.Password = $credential.GetNetworkCredential().Password
}
```

After that, everything else is the same. As soon as a new process is started on the remote machine, the ProcessName, ProcessID, and ParentProcessID properties are displayed.

As you see, there is very little difference between monitoring events locally versus a remote machine. In fact, you should be able to create functions and scripts that will work both locally and with remote systems and alternate credentials. There is no reason to have separate functions. One function can do it all.

**Read More About It**
Our book, *Advanced VBScript for Microsoft Windows Administrators* (Microsoft Press 2006), has a chapter devoted to scripting events with WMI. Even though the topic is covered from a VBScript point of view, it should still give you some helpful information. You should be able to use the examples as starting points for your PowerShell script development.

## Chapter 26
# Managing Services

PowerShell offers several cmdlets that make managing Windows servers a breeze. The cmdlets you will use most often are briefly discussed in the following sections.

## Listing Services

We've used the **Get-Service** cmdlet in many examples throughout this book. Here's a standard expression to list all running services:

```
PS C:\> get-service | Where {$_.status -eq "Running"}
```

This is an important expression because you need to know either the service's real name or its display name to manage the service.

## Starting Services

It should come as no surprise that PowerShell uses the **Start-Service** cmdlet to start a service. You can specify the service by its real name:

```
PS C:\> start-service -name "spooler"
```

Alternatively, you can specify the service by its display name:

```
PS C:\> start-service -Displayname "Print spooler"
```

Be sure to use quotes for the display name, since it usually contains spaces. Because the cmdlet doesn't display a result unless there is an error, you can use the
-**Passthru** parameter to force the cmdlet to pass objects down the pipeline.

```
PS C:\> start-service -displayname "print spooler" -passthru

Status  Name            DisplayName
------  ----            -----------
Running Spooler         Print Spooler


PS C:\>
```

## Stopping Services

Stopping services is just as easy. Everything we discussed about starting services applies to stopping services. The only difference is, we use the **Stop-Service** cmdlet.

```
PS C:\> stop-service webclient -passthru

Status  Name            DisplayName
------  ----            -----------
Stopped WebClient       WebClient


PS C:\>
```

## Suspending and Resuming Services

Some services can be suspended or paused. This doesn't stop the service completely; it only prevents it from doing anything. Be aware that not all services support suspension:

```
PS C:\> suspend-service spooler
Suspend-Service : Service 'Print Spooler (Spooler)' cannot be
suspended because the service does not support being suspended or
resumed.
At line:1 char:16
+ suspend-service <<<< spooler
PS C:\>
```

If you can suspend a service, you'll see something like this:

```
PS C:\> suspend-service w3svc -passthru

Status  Name            DisplayName
------  ----            -----------
Paused  W3SVC           World Wide Web Publishing


PS C:\>
```

Use the **Resume-Service** cmdlet to resume a suspended service:

```
PS C:\> resume-service w3svc -passthru

Status  Name           DisplayName
------  ----           -----------
Running W3SVC          World Wide Web Publishing


PS C:\>
```

# Restarting-Services

If you want to restart a service, you could use the combination of **Stop-Service** and **Start-Service**. But the simpler approach would be to use **Restart-Service**:

```
PS C:\> restart-service spooler
WARNING: Waiting for service 'Print Spooler (Spooler)' to finish starting...
PS C:\> get-service spooler

Status  Name           DisplayName
------  ----           -----------
Running Spooler        Print Spooler
```

For services with dependencies, you'll need to use the **-Force** parameter, otherwise PowerShell will object:

```
PS C:\> restart-service lanmanserver
Restart-Service : Cannot stop service 'Server (lanmanserver)' because it has dependent
services. It can only be stopped
 if the Force flag is set.
At line:1 char:16
+ restart-service <<<< lanmanserver
PS C:\> (get-service lanmanserver).DependentServices

Status  Name           DisplayName
------  ----           -----------
Running Browser        Computer Browser
```

The solution is to use the **-Force** parameter:

```
PS C:\> restart-service lanmanserver -force -passthru

Status  Name           DisplayName
------  ----           -----------
Running lanmanserver    Server
```

# Managing Services

The **Set-Service** cmdlet is used to change a service's start mode, say from Auto to Manual. You can either specify the service by name or display name.

```
PS C:\> set-service -name spooler -StartupType Manual
```

You can change the Startup Type to Automatic, Manual, or Disabled. Unfortunately, there are no provisions in **Get-Service** to see the start-mode.

345

PowerShell has no built-in method for changing the service account or its password; instead, you'll have to use WMI—the Win32_Service class has much broader capabilities—to perform these and additional service-related tasks. If you need to work with services on remote systems, then this is the only way you can accomplish these tasks.

## Get Service Information with Get-WmiObject

This basic command:

```
PS C:\> Get-WmiObject win32_service
```

will provide a list of service information on the local system. There are several ways to filter WMI information. Here's one approach:

```
PS C:\> Get-WmiObject win32_service -filter {state='running'}| Select Name,State,StartMode
Name                              State                     StartMode
----                              -----                     ---------
AcrSch2Svc                        Running                      Auto
ALG                               Running                     Manual
AppMgmt                           Running                     Manual
AudioSrv                          Running                      Auto
Avg7Alrt                          Running                      Auto
Avg7UpdSvc                        Running                      Auto
AVGEMS                            Running                      Auto
BITS                              Running                     Manual
CryptSvc                          Running                      Auto
DcomLaunch                        Running                      Auto
Dhcp                              Running                      Auto
Dnscache                          Running                      Auto
```

We've truncated the output to save space. Because we can't do it with the basic service cmdlets, let's find services where the StartUp type is not 'Auto':

```
PS C:\> Get-WmiObject win32_service -filter {StartMode != 'Auto' }| Select Name,StartMode '
>>| sort StartMode | format-table
>>

Name                                    StartMode
----                                    ---------
MSSQLServerADHelper                      Disabled
NetDDE                                   Disabled
Messenger                                Disabled
FastUserSwitchingCompatibility            Disabled
Irmon                                    Disabled
SQLBrowser                               Disabled
TlntSvr                                  Disabled
RemoteAccess                              Disabled
NetDDEdsdm                               Disabled
NetTcpPortSharing                         Disabled
Alerter                                  Disabled
ClipSrv                                  Disabled
ALG                                      Manual
SCardSvr                                 Manual
SSDPSRV                                  Manual
SwPrv                                    Manual
SysmonLog                                Manual
RasMan                                   Manual
RasAuto                                  Manual
```

Again, we've truncated the output. One thing to be aware of is that even though we are working with services, there are two different objects. The objects returned by **Get-Service** are ServiceController objects and the objects from **Get-WmiObject** are Win32_Service objects. Each object may have a different name for the same property. For example, the ServiceController object's property name is "State" and it is "Status" for Win32_Service. But both will indicate whether a service is running, stopped, or whatever. But this doesn't mean we can't combine the best of both worlds:

```
PS C:\> Get-WmiObject win32_service -filter {StartMode = 'Disabled' } '
>>| set-service -startuptype Manual -confirm
>>

Confirm
Are you sure you want to perform this action?
Performing operation "Set-Service" on Target "Alerter (Alerter)".
```

This snippet takes the output of the **Get-WmiObject** cmdlet that will return all disabled services and pipes it to **Set-Service**, which changes the startup type to Manual. We've also added the -**Confirm** parameter to prompt you before changing each service.

## Change Service Logon Account

To change the logon account for a service requires WMI. Suppose you want to change the logon account for the Alerter service. We'll start by creating an object for the Alerter service:

```
PS C:\> [wmi]$svc=Get-wmiobject -query "Select * from win32_service where name='Alerter'"
```

We can check the StartName property to see the current service account:

```
PS C:\> $svc.StartName
NT AUTHORITY\LocalService
```

To change the service configuration requires us to invoke the **Change()** method. Reading the MSDN documentation for this method at http://msdn2.microsoft.com/en-us/library/aa384901.aspx, we see that the method requires multiple parameters:

```
Change(DisplayName, PathName, ServiceType, ErrorControl, StartMode,
DesktopInteract, StartName, StartPassword, LoadOrderGroup,
LoadOrderGroupDependencies, ServiceDependencies)
```

Even though we only want to change the **StartName** and **StartPassword** parameters, we still have to provide information for the other parameters. In PowerShell, we can pass $Null. This will keep existing settings for the service:

```
PS C:\> $svc.Change($Null,$Null,$Null,$Null,$Null,$Null,"MyDomain\svcAccount","P@ssw0rd123")
```

We use $Null for the first six parameters, then specify the new account and password. We don't have to specify the service parameters after the password since they aren't changing. They will assumed to be $Null. If you are successful, WMI will return a value of 0:

```
__GENUS          : 2
__CLASS          : __PARAMETERS
__SUPERCLASS     :
__DYNASTY        : __PARAMETERS
__RELPATH        :
__PROPERTY_COUNT : 1
__DERIVATION     : {}
__SERVER         :
__NAMESPACE      :
__PATH           :
ReturnValue      : 0
```

If you get any other error, check the MSDN documentation for the error code.

Of course, the new settings won't take effect until the service is restarted:

```
PS C:\> restart-service "Alerter"
```

Because we are using **Get-WmiObject**, you could also do this for services on remote computers:

```
PS C:\> [wmi]$svc=Get-wmiobject -query "Select * from win32_service where name='Alerter'" '
>> -computer "FILE01" -credential "mydomain\administrator"
>>
PS C:\>
```

From this point, everything else is the same, except for restarting the service.

## Controlling Services on Remote Computers

To control services on remote computers, such as starting stopping or pausing, you can't use the PowerShell cmdlets. You will have to use the WMI methods. WMI does not have a restart method, but we can achieve the same result like this:

```
PS C:\> $svc.StopService()
PS C:\> $svc.StartService()
```

You would use these commands at the end of our change service account process. In fact, there's no reason you couldn't use them for managing services on the local system as well. If you want to pause or resume a service, the methods are **PauseService()** and **ResumeService()**.

## Change Service Logon Account Password

Changing the service account password uses essentially the same approach as changing the **Startname** parameter. The only service parameter that is changing is **StartPassword**:

```
PS C:\> [wmi]$svc=Get-wmiobject -query "Select * from win32_service where name='Alerter'"
PS C:\> $rc=$svc.Change($Null,$Null,$Null,$Null,$Null,$Null,$Null,"N3wP@ssw")
PS C:\> if ($rc -eq 0) {restart-service "Alerter"} else {
>> write-host -foreground "RED" "Changing password failed with a return value of $rc."}
>>
PS C:\>
```

As we did with changing the service account on a remote computer, you can use the same techniques for changing the service account password as well, by specifying a remote computer name and alternate credentials.

> **Note**
> The WMI Win32_Service class isn't compatible with cmdlets like **Stop-Service** and **Start-Service**. That is, you can't get a bunch of Win32_Service objects and pipe them to **Start-Service**; the *-Service cmdlets only accept service objects generated by the **Get-Service** cmdlet.

# Chapter 27
# Managing Permissions

Managing file permissions with scripting has always been a popular and challenging task. Even though PowerShell provides new ways to access and work with access control lists (ACLs), you still may find more familiar command-line utilities—Cacls.exe, Xcacls.exe, Dsacls.exe, and forth—easier to use. And the good news is that you can use them right from within PowerShell! In this chapter, we'll also take a look at PowerShell's native abilities to work with permissions.

## Viewing Permissions

The **Get-Acl** cmdlet can be used in PowerShell to obtain security descriptor information for files, folders, printers, registry keys, and more. By default, all information is displayed in a table format:

```
PS C:\> get-acl c:\boot.ini


    Directory: Microsoft.PowerShell.Core\FileSystem::C:\


Path               Owner                   Access
----               -----                   ------
boot.ini           BUILTIN\Administrators    NT AUTHORITY\SYSTEM Al...
PS C:\>
```

The problem is that some of the information is truncated. Therefore, you'll probably prefer to use something like this:

```
PS C:\> get-acl boot.ini |format-list


Path   : Microsoft.PowerShell.Core\FileSystem::C:\boot.ini
Owner  : BUILTIN\Administrators
Group  : NT AUTHORITY\SYSTEM
Access : NT AUTHORITY\SYSTEM Allow FullControl
         BUILTIN\Administrators Allow FullControl
         BUILTIN\Power Users Allow ReadAndExecute, Synchronize
Audit  :
Sddl   : O:BAG:SYD:PAI(A;;FA;;;SY)(A;;FA;;;BA)(A;;0x1200a9;;;PU)


PS C:\>
```

The **Get-Acl** cmdlet also works for directories:

```
PS C:\> get-acl c:\users |format-list


Path   : Microsoft.PowerShell.Core\FileSystem::C:\users
Owner  : COMPANY\administrator
Group  : COMPANY\None
Access : BUILTIN\Administrators Allow FullControl
         NT AUTHORITY\SYSTEM Allow FullControl
         COMPANY\administrator Allow FullControl
         CREATOR OWNER Allow 268435456
         BUILTIN\Users Allow ReadAndExecute, Synchronize
         BUILTIN\Users Allow AppendData
         BUILTIN\Users Allow CreateFiles



PS C:\>
```

It will even work on registry keys:

```
PS C:\> get-acl '
>> HKLM:\software\microsoft\windows\CurrentVersion\run|format-list
>>


Path   : Microsoft.PowerShell.Core\Registry::HKEY_LOCAL_MACHINE\software\micros
         oft\windows\CurrentVersion\run
Owner  : BUILTIN\Administrators
Group  : NT AUTHORITY\SYSTEM
Access : BUILTIN\Users Allow ReadKey
         BUILTIN\Users Allow -2147483648
         BUILTIN\Power Users Allow SetValue, CreateSubKey, Delete, ReadKey
         BUILTIN\Power Users Allow -1073676288
         BUILTIN\Administrators Allow FullControl
         BUILTIN\Administrators Allow 268435456
         NT AUTHORITY\SYSTEM Allow FullControl
         NT AUTHORITY\SYSTEM Allow 268435456
         CREATOR OWNER Allow 268435456
Audit  :
Sddl   : O:BAG:SYD:AI(A;ID;KR;;;BU)(A;CIIOID;GR;;;BU)(A;ID;CCDCLCSWRPSDRC;;;PU)
         (A;CIIOID;SDGWGR;;;PU)(A;ID;KA;;;BA)(A;CIIOID;GA;;;BA)(A;ID;KA;;;SY)(A
         ;CIIOID;GA;;;SY)(A;CIIOID;GA;;;CO)
```

```
PS C:\>
```

Notice that the cmdlet returns the owner. You can create a **Get-Acl** expression to display just that information:

```
PS C:\> get-acl c:\* |format-table Path,Owner -autosize

Path                                          Owner
----                                          -----
Microsoft.PowerShell.Core\FileSystem::C:\backinfo     BUILTIN\Admi...
Microsoft.PowerShell.Core\FileSystem::C:\backups      MYCO\ATech
Microsoft.PowerShell.Core\FileSystem::C:\deploy2000   MYCO\ATech
Microsoft.PowerShell.Core\FileSystem::C:\deploy2003   MYCO\ATech
Microsoft.PowerShell.Core\FileSystem::C:\Desktop Sna  MYCO\ATech
Microsoft.PowerShell.Core\FileSystem::C:\Documents and BUILTI
Microsoft.PowerShell.Core\FileSystem::C:\HPAiOScrubber MYCO\ATech
Microsoft.PowerShell.Core\FileSystem::C:\IALog        BUILTIN\Admi..
...
```

We've truncated and edited the output to fit the page, but you get the idea.

---

**What about Active Directory?**

The first version of PowerShell does not have terrific support for Active Directory. There are no cmdlets designed to work with permissions in Active Directory. The best approach would be to continue using command-line tools like Dsacls.exe.

---

## Viewing Permissions for an Entire Object Hierarchy

The **Get-Acl** cmdlet doesn't have a recurse method, but we won't let that slow us down. If you want a report to show owners for a directory structure, you can use a script like this:

### GetOwnerReport.ps1

```
#GetOwnerReport
$report="C:\OwnerReport.csv"
$StartingDir=Read-Host "What directory do you want to start at?"
Get-ChildItem $StartingDir -recurse |Get-Acl `
| select Path,Owner | Export-Csv $report -NoTypeInformation

#send two beeps when report is finished
write-Host 'a 'a 'n"Report finished. See "$report
```

The script prompts you for a starting directory. It then uses **Get-ChildItem** to pass every item to **Get-Acl** and recurse through subdirectories. You'll notice that we piped output to Select-Object to get just the Path and Owner properties. Finally, we send the data to a CSV file. The script beeps a few times to let you know it is finished and displays a message.

## Changing Permissions

Getting access control lists is half the job. You might still want to reset permissions through PowerShell. To be honest, this is not the easiest task to do in PowerShell, mainly because permissions in Windows are *complicated*, and there's only so much a shell can do to simplify that situation.

To get really detailed with permissions, you need to understand .NET security objects and NTFS security descriptors. However, we're just going to start with some simpler examples. Setting an access control rule is a matter of bit-masking access rights against a security token. The bits that match a security principal's account determine whether you can view a file, make changes to a file, or take ownership.

You can use **Set-Acl** to update an object's access rule. However, you first have to construct a .NET security descriptor, or get the security descriptor from an existing object, modify the security descriptor appropriately, and apply it to the desired object. This is not an insurmountable task, just very tedious. The script ChangeACL.ps1 takes a simplified approach and grants permissions you specify to the specified security principal on all objects in the specified starting directory and subdirectories.

## ChangeACL.ps1

```
#ChangeACL.ps1
$Right="FullControl"

#The possible values for Rights are
# ListDirectory
# ReadData
# WriteData
# CreateFiles
# CreateDirectories
# AppendData
# ReadExtendedAttributes
# WriteExtendedAttributes
# Traverse
# ExecuteFile
# DeleteSubdirectoriesAndFiles
# ReadAttributes
# WriteAttributes
# Write
# Delete
# ReadPermissions
# Read
# ReadAndExecute
# Modify
# ChangePermissions
# TakeOwnership
# Synchronize
# FullControl

$StartingDir=Read-Host " What directory do you want to start at?"
$Principal=Read-Host " What security principal do you want to grant" `
"$Right to? `n Use format domain\username or domain\group"

#define a new access rule
#the $rule line has been artificially broken for print purposes
#It needs to be one line. The online version of the script is properly
#formatted.
$rule=new-object System.Security.AccessControl.FileSystemAccessRule
($Principal,$Right,"Allow")

foreach ($file in $(Get-ChildItem $StartingDir -recurse)) {
 $acl=get-acl $file.FullName
 #display filename and old permissions
 write-Host -foregroundcolor Yellow $file.FullName
 #uncomment if you want to see old permissions
 #write-Host $acl.AccessToString `n
```

```
#Add this access rule to the ACL
$acl.SetAccessRule($rule)

#Write the changes to the object
set-acl $File.Fullname $acl

#display new permissions
$acl=get-acl $file.FullName
Write-Host -foregroundcolor Green "New Permissions"
Write-Host $acl.AccessToString `n
}
```

This script creates a simple access rule that allows a specific right. If you can use a broad right, such as Modify or Full Control, you'll find it easy to work with the script. We've hard coded in the $Right variable. The script prompts you for directory path and the name of the security principal to which you wish to apply the right.

The real work of the script is creating a new FileSystemAccess rule object. Creating the object requires that we specify the name of the security principal, the right to be applied, and whether to allow or deny the right. With this rule, we can recurse through the file system starting at the specified directory. For each file, we get the current access control list using **Get-Acl**:

```
$acl=get-acl $file.FullName
```

Next we add the new access rule to the ACL:

```
$acl.SetAccessRule($rule)
```

Now we call Set-Acl to write the new and modified ACL back to the object.

```
set-acl $File.Fullname $acl
```

The script finishes the loop by displaying the new ACL so you can see the change.

# Automating Cacls.exe to Change Permissions

As you've seen, using **Set-Acl** is not simple, especially if you have complex permissions. Therefore, you may find it easier to use Cacls.exe from within a PowerShell script:

### SetPermswithCACLS.ps1

```
#SetPermsWithCACLS.ps1
# CACLS rights are usually
# F = FullControl
# C = Change
# R = Readonly
# W = Write

$StartingDir=Read-Host " What directory do you want to start at?"
$Right=Read-Host " What CALCS right do you want to grant? Valid choices are F, C, R or W"
Switch ($Right) {
 "F" {$Null}
 "C" {$Null}
 "R" {$Null}
 "W" {$Null}
```

```
  default {
    Write-Host -foregroundcolor "Red" `
    `n $Right.ToUpper() "is an invalid choice. Please Try again."`n
    exit
  }
}

$Principal=Read-Host " What security principal do you want to grant" `
"CACLS right"$Right.ToUpper()"to?" `n `
"Use format domain\username or domain\group"

$Verify=Read-Host `n "You are about to change permissions on all" `
"files starting at"$StartingDir.ToUpper() `n "for security"`
"principal"$Principal.ToUpper() `
"with new right of"$Right.ToUpper()"."`n `
"Do you want to continue ? [Y,N]"

if ($Verify -eq "Y") {

  foreach ($file in $(Get-ChildItem $StartingDir -recurse)) {
  #display filename and old permissions
  write-Host -foregroundcolor Yellow $file.FullName
  #uncomment if you want to see old permissions
  #CACLS $file.FullName

  #ADD new permission with CACLS
  CACLS $file.FullName /E /P "${Principal}:${Right}" >$NULL

  #display new permissions
  Write-Host -foregroundcolor Green "New Permissions"
  CACLS $file.FullName
  }
}
```

This script first prompts you for a starting directory and a permission right you want to grant. We've used a **Switch** statement to make sure a valid parameter for Cacls.exe is entered. As long as the user has entered F, C, W, or R, the script continues and prompts you for the name of a security principal you want to add to the access control list. Because this is a major operation, we've included a prompt using **Read-Host** to provide a summary of what the script is about to do. If anything other than Y is entered, the script ends with no changes being made. Otherwise, the **ForEach** loop is executed.

Within this **ForEach** loop, we use **Get-ChildItem** to enumerate all the files in the starting directory path and recurse through all subdirectories. The script displays the current file as a progress indicator, and then calls Cacls.exe. Because of the way PowerShell processes Win32 commands such as Cacls.exe, we need to enclose the program's parameters in quotes. You'll also notice that instead of using:

```
CACLS $file.FullName /e /p "$Principal:$Right"
```

we used:

```
CACLS $file.FullName /e /p "${Principal}:${Right}"
```

In PowerShell, an expression like Foo:Bar is treated as <namespace>:<name>, which is like $global:profile or $env:windir. In order for PowerShell to treat the Cacls.exe parameter as a command line parameter, we must delimit the variable name using braces, as we've done in this example. The script finishes by displaying the new access control permissions for each file.

If you've used Cacls.exe before, you may have noticed that we used /E /P to assign permissions.

According to Cacls' Help screen, /P is used to modify permissions for an existing entry. You would use /G to grant permissions to a new user. In Cmd.exe, either /G or /P will work regardless of whether or not the user already existed in the access control list.

This is not the case in PowerShell. PowerShell actually appears to enforce the Cacls.exe parameters. You can use /G if a user does not exist in the file's access control list. However, you must use /P if the user already exists. When you attempt to use /G to modify an existing user's permission, Cacls.exe will run, but no change will be made.

So, how do you know if you should use /P or /G without checking every file first? Not to worry. You can use /P regardless of whether or not the user exists in the access control list, which is what we've done here. The moral is, don't assume that every single Cmd.exe tool and command works identically in PowerShell. Most should, but if it doesn't, you have to look at how PowerShell is interpreting the expression.

One final note about the script: we could have used /T with Cacls.exe to change permissions on all files and subdirectories. The end result would have been the same, but then we couldn't have demonstrated some of PowerShell's output features.

# Complex Permissions in PowerShell

By now you've seen that managing permissions with PowerShell can be done, although it is not for the faint of heart. That said, let's look at a few more situations where you can use PowerShell.

## Get Owner

We showed you earlier how you can use **Get-Acl** to display the owner of a file. You may prefer to create a function that takes a filename as a parameter:

```
Function Get-Owner {
param([string]$file)

$var=(Get-Acl $file).Owner
write $var

}
```

With this function loaded, you can use an expression like:

```
PS C:\> Get-Owner c:\file.txt
```

To return the owners on a group of files, you have to enumerate the file collection like this:

```
PS C:\> foreach ($f in (get-childitem c:\temp\*.txt)) {write-host $f =(get-owner $f)}
```

This approach is fine for reporting purposes. However, this function can't leverage the pipeline. You might consider rewriting it as a filtering function:

```
Filter Get-Owner {
   [string]$file=$_.FullName
   $var=(Get-Acl $file).Owner
   return $var
}
```

357

Armed with this filter, you can accomplish something like this:

```
PS C:\c> get-childitem c:\public -recurse | get-owner | group | Select Name,Count

Name                                                 Count
----                                                 -----
SAPIEN\jhicks                                          70
BUILTIN\Administrators                                 35
SAPIEN\don                                             10
```

The **Get-Owner** filter returns a collection of owner names, which is then processed by the **Group** cmdlet, which in turn passes the results to **Select** to give us the final report.

## Set Owner

Unfortunately, PowerShell does not provide a mechanism for setting the owner of a file other an administrator or the Administrators group. Even though Windows 2003 now allows you to assign ownership, it cannot be done through PowerShell. Use this technique to set a new owner on a file:

```
PS C:\> [System.Security.Principal.NTAccount]$newOwner="Administrators"
PS C:\> $var=get-childitem c:\file.txt
PS C:\> $acl=$var.GetAccessControl()
PS C:\> $acl.SetOwner($NewOwner)
PS C:\> $var.SetAccessControl($acl)
```

The important step is to cast the $NewOwner object as a security principal:

```
PS C:\> [System.Security.Principal.NTAccount]$newOwner="Administrators"
```

After we get the current access control list, we call the **SetOwner()** method, specifying the new owner:

```
PS C:\> $acl.SetOwner($NewOwner)
```

This change will not take effect until we call the **SetAccessControl()** method on the file and apply the modified access control list with the new owner:

```
PS C:\> $var.SetAccessControl($acl)
```

## Retrieving Access Control

We showed you at the beginning of the chapter how to use **Get-Acl** to retrieve file permissions. One approach you might take is to wrap the code into a function:

```
Function Get-Access {
param([string]$file)
   $var=(Get-Acl $file).Access
   write $file.ToUpper()
   write $var
 }
```

Once it's loaded, you can use it to quickly get the access control for a given file:

```
PS C:\> get-access boot.ini
BOOT.INI


FileSystemRights : FullControl
AccessControlType : Allow
IdentityReference : NT AUTHORITY\SYSTEM
IsInherited       : False
InheritanceFlags : None
PropagationFlags : None

FileSystemRights : FullControl
AccessControlType : Allow
IdentityReference : BUILTIN\Administrators
IsInherited       : False
InheritanceFlags : None
PropagationFlags : None

FileSystemRights : ReadAndExecute, Synchronize
AccessControlType : Allow
IdentityReference : BUILTIN\Power Users
IsInherited       : False
InheritanceFlags : None
PropagationFlags : None
```

The downside to this approach is that it can't easily be used in the pipeline. Take an expression like this:

```
PS C:\> get-childitem c:\files\*.txt | get-access | format-table
```

It will fail to enumerate all the files. A better approach is a filtering function:

```
Filter Get-AccessControl {
 [string]$file=$input
 $var=(Get-Acl $file).Access
 $obj=New-Object Object

 Add-Member -inputobject $obj -membertype Noteproperty -Name FileName -value $file.ToUpper()
 Add-Member -inputobject $obj -membertype Noteproperty -Name AccessControl -value $var

 Return $obj
}
```

We've used the **New-Object** cmdlet to create a custom object to return file and access information. Because the **AccessControl** property of our custom object is a collection of access rules,
you need to use an expression like this in order to expand them:

```
PS C:\> (get-childitem c:\file.txt | Get-AccessControl).AccessControl
```

Or use an expression like this to look at a group of files:

```
PS C:\> foreach ($a in (get-childitem c:\temp\*.pdf | Get-AccessControl)) '
>> {$a.filename;$a.AccessControl}
>>
C:\TEMP\COMPARE2.PDF


FileSystemRights : FullControl
AccessControlType : Allow
IdentityReference : BUILTIN\Administrators
```

```
IsInherited       : True
InheritanceFlags : None
PropagationFlags : None

FileSystemRights : FullControl
AccessControlType : Allow
IdentityReference : NT AUTHORITY\SYSTEM
IsInherited       : True
InheritanceFlags : None
PropagationFlags : None

FileSystemRights : FullControl
AccessControlType : Allow
IdentityReference : SAPIEN\jhicks
IsInherited       : True
InheritanceFlags : None
PropagationFlags : None

FileSystemRights : ReadAndExecute, Synchronize
AccessControlType : Allow
IdentityReference : BUILTIN\Users
IsInherited       : True
InheritanceFlags : None
PropagationFlags : None

C:\TEMP\COMPARETEST.PDF
FileSystemRights : FullControl
AccessControlType : Allow
IdentityReference : BUILTIN\Administrators
IsInherited       : True
InheritanceFlags : None
PropagationFlags : None

FileSystemRights : FullControl
AccessControlType : Allow
IdentityReference : NT AUTHORITY\SYSTEM
IsInherited       : True
InheritanceFlags : None
PropagationFlags : None

FileSystemRights : FullControl
AccessControlType : Allow
IdentityReference : SAPIEN\jhicks
IsInherited       : True
InheritanceFlags : None
PropagationFlags : None

FileSystemRights : ReadAndExecute, Synchronize
AccessControlType : Allow
IdentityReference : BUILTIN\Users
IsInherited       : True
InheritanceFlags : None
PropagationFlags : None


PS C:\>
```

But what if you want to find a particular security principal? Use this function to enumerate the **AccessControl** property, searching for the particular user or group:

```
Filter Get-Principal {

Param([string]$Principal,[Object]$ac)
```

```
  foreach ($rule in $ac.AccessControl) {
   if ($rule.IdentityReference -eq $Principal) {
     $ac.filename,$rule
     }
  }
}
```

Use this filter in conjunction with the **Get-AccessControl** filter to display files and access rules that apply to a given user:

```
PS C:\> foreach ($a in (get-childitem c:\temp\ -include *.zip -recurse| '
>> Get-AccessControl)) {get-principal sapien\don $a}
>>
C:\TEMP\ZTEST\WSHVBSCRIPTCORE.ZIP


FileSystemRights : FullControl
AccessControlType : Allow
IdentityReference : SAPIEN\don
IsInherited      : False
InheritanceFlags : None
PropagationFlags : None

C:\TEMP\IPDEMO.ZIP
FileSystemRights : FullControl
AccessControlType : Allow
IdentityReference : SAPIEN\don
IsInherited      : False
InheritanceFlags : None
PropagationFlags : None
```

## Removing a rule

Removing access for a user or group is relatively straightforward:

```
$file="file.txt"
[System.Security.Principal.NTAccount]$principal="SAPIEN\rgbiv"
$acl=Get-Acl $file
$access=(Get-Acl $file).Access
$rule=$access | where {$_.IdentityReference -eq $principal}
$acl.RemoveAccessRuleSpecific($rule)
Set-Acl $file $acl
```

Obviously, we need to know what file and user or group we are working with:

```
$file="file.txt"
[System.Security.Principal.NTAccount]$principal="SAPIEN\rgbiv"
```

As we did when adding a rule, we need to use **Get-Acl** to retrieve the current access control list:

```
$acl=Get-Acl $file
```

To find a specific access rule, we need to filter the existing rules with **Where**:

```
$access=(Get-Acl $file).Access
$rule=$access | where {$_.IdentityReference -eq $principal}
```

The variable, $rule, will hold all the rules that apply to the specified security principal. To remove the rule, we call the **RemoveAccessRuleSpecific()** method:

```
$acl.RemoveAccessRuleSpecific($rule)
```

Finally, to apply the new access control list, we call **Set-Acl**:

```
Set-Acl $file $acl
```

# Chapter 28
# Managing Event Logs

PowerShell has a terrific cmdlet in **Get-Eventlog** that makes it easy to find information in a system's event log. Since different systems may have different event logs, one of the first commands you'll want to use is this:

```
PS C:\> get-eventlog -list

Max(K) Retain OverflowAction      Entries Name
------ ------ --------------      ------- ----
   512      7 OverwriteOlder        2,125 Application
15,360      0 OverwriteAsNeeded     5,485 Windows PowerShell
   512      7 OverwriteOlder        1,829 Security
   512      7 OverwriteOlder        2,139 System

PS C:\>
```

If you run something like the following script, every single entry in the log will scroll by:

```
Get-Eventlog "Windows Powershell"
```

That's probably not very practical, unless you're dumping the contents to another file.

Fortunately, the cmdlet has a parameter, **-Newest**, that will display the last (or newest) number of log entries that you specify:

```
PS C:\> get-eventlog "windows powershell" -newest 5

Index Time         Type Source            EventID Message
----- ----         ---- ------            ------- -------
 5485 Jun 25 19:31 Info PowerShell            400 Engine state is cha
 5484 Jun 25 19:31 Info PowerShell            600 Provider "Certifica
 5483 Jun 25 19:31 Info PowerShell            600 Provider "Variable"
 5482 Jun 25 19:31 Info PowerShell            600 Provider "Registry"
 5481 Jun 25 19:31 Info PowerShell            600 Provider "Function"


PS C:\>
```

The default table format usually ends up truncating the event message. If that happens, you can try something like:

```
PS C:\> get-eventlog "windows powershell" -newest 5 |format-list
```

Alternatively, you can try something like this:

```
PS C:\> get-eventlog "windows powershell" -newest 5 | `
>> select EntryType,TimeGenerated,EventID,Message | `
>> format-list
>>


EntryType     : Information
TimeGenerated : 6/25/2006 7:31:42 PM
EventID       : 400
Message       : Engine state is changed from None to Available.

                Details:
                    NewEngineState=Available
                    PreviousEngineState=None

                    SequenceNumber=8
                    HostName=ConsoleHost
                    HostVersion=1.0.9567.1
                    HostId=577b95e7-1182-47df-9797-71058b592014
                    EngineVersion=1.0.9567.1
                    RunspaceId=6fc71134-8871-4b50-bc47-53fc5942b4ed
                    PipelineId=
                    CommandName=
                    CommandType=
                    ScriptName=
                    CommandPath=
                    CommandLine=
...
```

We've truncated the output, but you get the idea. If you're interested in a specific event ID, use the **Where-object** cmdlet:

```
PS C:\> get-eventlog System -newest 5 |where {$_.EventID -eq 7036}

Index Time         Type Source            EventID Message
----- ----         ---- ------            ------- -------
11218 Jun 24 23:06 Info Service Control M...   7036 The PDEngine service ...
11217 Jun 24 23:00 Info Service Control M...   7036 The PDEngine service ...
```

```
PS C:\>
```

Here, we're looking for event log entries with an EventID of 7036. Notice we used -**Newest** to look for the last five entries. You might wonder why only two entries were returned. The answer is because the -**Newest** parameter is processed first and returns the last five entries. From within those five entries, only two had an EventID of 7036.

If you want to see the last five entries of EventID 7036, regardless of when they were logged, you have to get a little more creative:

```
PS C:\> $logs=get-eventlog System |where {$_.EventID -eq 7036}
PS C:\> for ($i=0; $i -lt 5; $i++) {$logs[$i]}

Index Time          Type Source             EventID Message
----- ----          ---- ------             ------- -------
11218 Jun 24 23:06 Info Service Control M...7036 The PDEngine service
11217 Jun 24 23:00 Info Service Control M...7036 The PDEngine service
11215 Jun 24 20:19 Info Service Control M...7036 The IMAPI CD-Burning
11214 Jun 24 20:19 Info Service Control M...7036 The IMAPI CD-Burning
11212 Jun 24 20:18 Info Service Control M...7036 The IMAPI CD-Burning


PS C:\>
```

We first dump all the logs that match our query to a variable, $logs. Then we use **For** to get the first five entries. Curious about where all your errors are coming from? Try something like this:

```
PS C:\> get-eventlog -log system | group source | Select Count,Name '
>> | sort count |format-table -auto

Count Name
----- ----
    1 WgaNotify
    1 Wdf01005
    1 WGA
    1 KB929969
    1 Internet Explorer 7 Disk
    1 Wudf01000
    1 Windows Installer 3.1
    1 Setup
    1 Serial
    1 Workstation
    1 USER32
    1 NetBT
    1 SRService
    2 WMPNetworkSvc
    4 Removable Storage Service
    4 WPDClassInstaller
    6 Application Popup
    6 HTTP
    7 WindowsMedia
    8 Ftdisk
   12 Dhcp
   16 VMnetAdapter
   18 SideBySide
   25 BROWSER
   28 DCOM
   30 VMnetuserif
   81 Tcpip
```

```
 84 Print
 95 EventLog
 99 NtServicePack
103 b57w2k
114 W32Time
207 WinDefend
246 Windows Update Agent
1380 Service Control Manager
```

Every event log includes a source indicating where the event originated. All we've done is look at the System event log, grouping the event records by the **Source** property, piping that result to **Select** so that we only get the **Count** and **Name** properties, which in turn in sorted by the **Sort** cmdlet and finally the result is presented by **Format-Table**. This is a terrific example of leveraging the pipeline.

You can use the same technique to get a summary breakdown of error types:

```
PS C:\> get-eventlog -log system | group EntryType | Select Count,Name | sort count '
>> |format-table -auto
>>

Count Name
----- ----
 167 Error
 262 Warning
 2159 Information
```

If you want results for all logs, it takes a little more finesse:

```
foreach ($log in (Get-EventLog -list)) {
    #only display logs with records
    if ($log.Entries.Count -gt 0) {
      Write-Host -background DarkGreen -foreground Black $log.log
      Get-EventLog -log $log.log | group EntryType | Select Count,Name | sort count `
      |Format-Table -auto
    }
}
```

This snippet uses the **ForEach** cmdlet to get every event log on the local system. If the number of entries in each log is greater than 0:

```
if ($log.Entries.Count -gt 0) {
```

Then we'll display the log name and then use the same code from earlier to return a count of each error type.

Let's combine both of our efforts and get a listing of event types for each source from every event log with records:

```
foreach ($log in (Get-EventLog -list)) {
    #only display logs with records
    if ($log.Entries.Count -gt 0) {
      Write-Host -background DarkGreen -foreground Black $log.log
      Get-EventLog -log $log.log | group source,entrytype | sort count | `
      select Count,Name |format-table -auto
    }
}
```

We'll get a listing like this for every event log:

```
Application

Count Name
----- ----
    1 Windows Product Activation, Warning
    1 WSH, 0
    1 Winlogon, Information
    1 MPSampleSubmission, Information
    1 WmdmPmSp, Information
    1 Windows Product Activation, Information
    1 WLTRYSVC, Information
    1 SceCli, Information
    2 NTBackup, Error
    2 WSH, Information
    2 WmdmPmSN, Information
    2 MsiInstaller, Error
    2 ESENT, Error
    2 Userenv, Information
    3 ASP.NET 2.0.50727.0, Warning
    3 System.ServiceModel.Install 3.0.0.0, Information
    3 MSDTC, Information
    4 HHCTRL, Information
    4 COM+, Information
    4 crypt32, Information
    5 MPSampleSubmission, Error
    6 ASP.NET 2.0.50727.0, Information
    9 System.ServiceModel.Install 3.0.0.0, Warning
    9 DrWatson, Information
   10 NTBackup, Information
   14 usnjsvc, 0
   14 VMware Virtual Mount Service Extended, Information
   14 WinMgmt, Warning
```

# Working with Remote Event Logs

While the **Get-Eventlog** cmdlet is easy to use, it can only be used on the local system. If you want to query event logs on remote systems, you'll need to use WMI and the **Get-WmiObject** cmdlet:

```
PS C:\> $credential=get-credential

cmdlet get-credential at command pipeline position 1
Supply values for the following parameters:
Credential
PS C:\> Get-WmiObject win32_NTEventlogfile `
>> -computer DC01 -credential $credential | `
>> select-object FileSize,LogFileName,NumberOfRecords |`
>> format-table -autosize
>>


 FileSize LogFileName               NumberOfRecords
 -------- -----------               ---------------
   720896 Application                          3617
   524288 Directory Service                    2712
  6291456 DNS Server                          32861
    65536 File Replication Service              124
134217728 Security                           331683
  5177344 System                              22345
```

```
PS C:\>
```

In this example, we use alternate credentials and create a variable to hold them. We then run **Get-WmiObject** for the remote system and get instances of Win32_NTEventlogfile. We selected a few properties and formatted the output. The expression above is similar to **Get-Eventlog -list**.

Event log entries belong to the **Win32_NTLogEvent** WMI class. To query logs via WMI, you need specify at least the logfile name and preferably more. Here's our earlier event log query rewritten to use **Get-WmiObject** on a remote system:

```
PS C:\> Get-WmiObject win32_NTLogEvent -computer DC01 -credential `
>> $credential | where `
>> {$_.logfile -eq "System" -AND $_.EventCode -eq "7036"} |`
>> select-object TimeGenerated,Message | format-table -autosize
>>
#output truncated for display purposes
20050331092522.000000-300 The Network Location Awareness (NLA) service
20050331092522.000000-300 The Distributed File System service entered
20050331085717.000000-300 The WinHTTP Web Proxy Auto-Discovery Service
20050331085320.000000-300 The Windows Installer service entered the st
20050331084607.000000-300 The World Wide Web Publishing Service servic
20050331084606.000000-300 The World Wide Web Publishing Service servic
20050331084047.000000-300 The WinHTTP Web Proxy Auto-Discovery Service
20050331083404.000000-300 The Windows Installer service entered the ru
20050331082950.000000-300 The Network Connections service entered the
20050330172042.000000-300 The Network Location Awareness (NLA) service


PS C:\>
```

Depending on the number of log entries, this expression may take several minutes to run before anything appears. The drawback to the technique we just showed is that *all* the event log records must first be retrieved. Then those records are piped to the **Where** cmdlet. For a small event log, this approach is reasonable. But there is a better way. Do you remember the -**Query** parameter? This parameter will instruct the **Get-WmiObject** cmdlet to filter records in place before we send the results on through the pipeline:

```
PS C:\> Get-WmiObject -query "Select Logfile,Eventcode,TimeGenerated,Message from `
>> win32_NTLogEvent Where logfile='System' AND EventCode='7036'" -computer "DC01" `
>> -credential $credential| Format-Table TimeGenerated,Message -autosize
>>
#output truncated for display purposes
20050331092522.000000-300 The Network Location Awareness (NLA) service
20050331092522.000000-300 The Distributed File System service entered
20050331085717.000000-300 The WinHTTP Web Proxy Auto-Discovery Service
20050331085320.000000-300 The Windows Installer service entered the st
20050331084607.000000-300 The World Wide Web Publishing Service servic
20050331084606.000000-300 The World Wide Web Publishing Service servic
20050331084047.000000-300 The WinHTTP Web Proxy Auto-Discovery Service
20050331083404.000000-300 The Windows Installer service entered the ru
20050331082950.000000-300 The Network Connections service entered the
20050330172042.000000-300 The Network Location Awareness (NLA) service


PS C:\Backing Up Event Logs
```

This example is querying a remote computer, but you could just as easily use it to query the local system.

# Event Log Information

To get more detailed information about event logs, you'll need to use the **Get-WmiObject** cmdlet. Here's an example that shows you event log information on your computer:

```
PS C:\> Get-WmiObject -query "Select * from win32_NTEventLogFile" `
>> | select LogFileName,Name,FileSize,MaxFileSize,NumberofRecords,Status,`
>> @{Name="Created";Expression={$_.ConvertToDateTime($_.CreationDate)}},`
>> @{Name="Modified";Expression={$_.ConvertToDateTime($_.LastModified)}}`
>> | Format-List
>>


LogFileName      : Application
Name             : C:\WINDOWS\system32\config\AppEvent.Evt
FileSize         : 1703936
MaxFileSize      : 2097152
NumberofRecords  : 2759
Status           : OK
Created          : 5/17/2007 12:36:24 PM
Modified         : 6/19/2007 3:42:38 PM

LogFileName      : Security
Name             : C:\WINDOWS\System32\config\SecEvent.Evt
FileSize         : 65536
MaxFileSize      : 524288
NumberofRecords  :
Status           : OK
Created          : 5/17/2007 12:36:24 PM
Modified         : 5/17/2007 12:36:24 PM

LogFileName      : System
Name             : C:\WINDOWS\system32\config\SysEvent.Evt
FileSize         : 851968
MaxFileSize      : 2097152
NumberofRecords  : 2588
Status           : OK
Created          : 5/17/2007 12:36:24 PM
Modified         : 6/19/2007 3:45:46 PM

LogFileName      : Windows PowerShell
Name             : C:\WINDOWS\System32\config\WindowsPowerShell.evt
FileSize         : 10747904
MaxFileSize      : 15728640
NumberofRecords  : 14771
Status           : OK
Created          : 5/17/2007 9:59:06 PM
Modified         : 6/21/2007 3:12:05 PM


PS C:\>
```

The PowerShell expression takes the result of the **Get-WmiObject** cmdlet and pipes it to the **Select-Object** cmdlet. With this cmdlet, we are choosing only a few parameters like **Name** and **FileSize**. But you probably noticed these expressions:

```
>> @{Name="Created";Expression={$_.ConvertToDateTime($_.CreationDate)}},`
>> @{Name="Modified";Expression={$_.ConvertToDateTime($_.LastModified)}}'
```

We wanted to display the event logs' creation and last modified dates. However, in WMI, they are presented in a special format like this: 20070517123624.166841-240. Hardly user-friendly. What we've done is create custom properties called **Created** and **Modified**. The values are the result of the corresponding expression. In the expression, we are calling the **ConvertToDateTime()** method of the current object in the pipeline, passing it the **CreationDate** property as a parameter. The result is a more familiar date time format. Finally, everything is piped to **Format-List** to make it a little easier to read.

## Backup Event Logs

Backing up event logs is relatively straightforward in PowerShell. If you use the [WMI] type adapter, you'll have access to the **BackupEventLog()** method. Although there is a required and not-so-obvious step:

```
PS C:\> [wmi]$syslog=Get-WMiobject -query "Select * from win32_NTEventLogFile where '
>> LogFileName='system'"
>>
PS C:\> $backup=(get-date -format yyyyMMdd)+"_"+$syslog.CSName+"_"+$syslog.logfilename+".evt"

PS C:\> $syslog.psbase.scope.options.enablePrivileges=$TRUE
PS C:\> $syslog.backupeventlog("F:\backups\$backup")


__GENUS         : 2
__CLASS         : __PARAMETERS
__SUPERCLASS    :
__DYNASTY       : __PARAMETERS
__RELPATH       :
__PROPERTY_COUNT : 1
__DERIVATION    : {}
__SERVER        :
__NAMESPACE     :
__PATH          :
ReturnValue     : 0



PS C:\>
```

Here's how this works. In this example, we going to backup the System Eventlog on the local computer:

```
PS C:\> [wmi]$syslog=Get-WMiobject -query "Select * from win32_NTEventLogFile where '
>> LogFileName='system'"
```

We need a name for the backup file, which we calculate using the current date, the name of the computer, and the log file name:

```
PS C:\> $backup=(get-date -format yyyyMMdd)+"_"+$syslog.CSName+"_"+$syslog.logfilename+".evt"
```

This expression will return a value like 20070622_XPDESK01_System.evt. The advantage to using the **CSName** property is that if we back up a remote server, we can automatically capture the name.

Now comes the not-so-obvious part. In order to backup event logs, you need to specify the Backup privilege. If you don't, you'll get an Access Denied message when you try to backup the log.

In VBscript, you can include this privilege in your connection string like this:

```
Set oWMIService = GetObject("winmgmts:" _
 & "{impersonationLevel=impersonate,(Backup,Security)}!\\" & strComputer & "\root\cimv2")
```

The **Get-WmiObject** cmdlet doesn't have a similar option. However, you can access the underlying .NET management object and configure it to enable all privileges:

```
PS C:\> $syslog.psbase.scope.options.enablePrivileges=$TRUE
```

With privileges enabled, we can now back up the event log:

```
PS C:\> $syslog.backupeventlog("F:\backups\$backup")
```

....................................................................................................

**Location, Location, Location**
There is a very subtle but important detail about the **BackupEventLog()** method, especially when using **Get-WmiObject** to access event logs on remote computers. Even though you are running a script and remotely accessing a computer, the backup method is actually executing on the remote system. This means that the path you specify is relative to the remote system. If you back up the event log to drive C:\, it will be backed up to drive C:\ of the remote computer, not the computer where you are executing the script. Verify that the destination folder is accessible from the remote computer, and you won't have any surprises.

If you want to back up all event logs, you can use code like this:

```
$path="F:\Backups"
foreach ($log in (Get-WmiObject win32_nteventlogfile)) {
    $backup=(Get-Date -format yyyyMMdd)+"_"+$log.CSName+"_"+$log.logfilename+".evt"
    Write-Host "Backing up"$log.LogFileName"to $path\$backup"
    $log.psbase.scope.options.enablePrivileges=$TRUE
    $rc=$log.backupeventlog($path+"\"+$backup)
    if ($rc.ReturnValue -eq 0) {
        Write-Host -foreground GREEN "Backup successful" }
        else {
        Write-Host -foreground RED `
        "Backup failed with a return value of"$rc.ReturnValue
    }
}
```

The $path variable is the backup directory we want to use. Using **ForEach**, we get every event log on the computer:

```
foreach ($log in (Get-WmiObject win32_nteventlogfile)) {
```

As we did before, we define a backup file name and enable all privileges:

```
$backup=(Get-Date -format yyyyMMdd)+"_"+$log.CSName+"_"+$log.logfilename+".evt"
Write-Host "Backing up"$log.LogFileName"to $path\$backup"
$log.psbase.scope.options.enablePrivileges=$TRUE
```

When we call the **BackupEventLog()** method, we save the results to a variable:

```
$rc=$log.backupeventlog($path+"\"+$backup)
```

With this variable, we can check if the backup was successful or not. If it wasn't, we display the **ReturnValue** property:

```
if ($rc.ReturnValue -eq 0) {
    Write-Host -foreground GREEN "Backup successful" }
    else {
    Write-Host -foreground RED `
    "Backup failed with a return value of"$rc.ReturnValue
}
```

One thing to be aware of is that if the backup file already exists, it will not be overwritten and you will get a return value of 183.

# Clearing Event Logs

Clearing an event log follows the same approach we used for backing up event logs that we covered in the previous section:

```
PS C:\> [wmi]$evtlog=Get-WMiobject -query "Select * from win32_NTEventLogFile `
>> where LogFileName='Application'"
>>
PS C:\> $evtlog.ClearEventLog()


__GENUS         : 2
__CLASS         : __PARAMETERS
__SUPERCLASS    :
__DYNASTY       : __PARAMETERS
__RELPATH       :
__PROPERTY_COUNT : 1
__DERIVATION    : {}
__SERVER        :
__NAMESPACE     :
__PATH          :
ReturnValue     : 0
```

Once we have a reference to the event log file, all we need to do is call the **ClearEventLog()** method. You do not need any additional privileges, unless you are clearing the Security event log. Even if you have administrative credentials, you will still need this command before you can clear the log:

```
PS C:\> $evtlog.psbase.scope.options.EnablePrivileges=$true
```

Unlike the Event Viewer management console, this method will not warn you first about backing up the log, so use with caution.

Let's wrap up our exploration of backing up and clearing event logs by looking at a way to back up and clear multiple logs on a remote computer:

### Backup-EventLogs.ps1

```
$path=\\file01\backup\eventlogs #the folder where backups will be saved

$computer="file03"  #the name of a remote computer
```

```
$iLimit=10 #threshhold size in MB

foreach ($log in (Get-WmiObject win32_nteventlogfile -computer $computer)) {
    if ($log.FileSize/1MB -gt $iLimit) {
        Write-Host $log.LogFileName"="($log.FileSize/1MB)"MB"
        $reply=Read-Host "Do you want to backup and clear the event log?[YN]"

        if ($reply -eq "y") {
            $log.psbase.scope.options.enablePrivileges=$TRUE
            $backup=(Get-Date -format yyyyMMdd)+"_"+$log.CSName+"_"+`
            $log.logfilename+".evt"
            Write-Host "Backing up"$log.LogFileName"to $path\$backup"
            $rc=$log.BackupEventLog($path+"\"+$backup)

            if ($rc.ReturnValue -eq 0) {
                Write-Host -foreground GREEN "Backup successful. Clearing Event log."
                $rc2=$log.ClearEventLog()

                    if ($rc2.ReturnValue -eq 0) {
                    Write-Host -foreground GREEN "ClearEventLog successful."
                    }
                    else {
                    Write-Host -foreground RED `
                    "ClearEventLog failed with a return value of"$rc2.ReturnValue
                    } #end if rc2.return value
                 }
                else {
                Write-Host -foreground RED `
                "Backup failed with a return value of"$rc.ReturnValue
            } #end if rc.returnValue
        } #end if reply
    } #end if logfile > limit
 } #end foreach
```

This script defines some values we will need. The script's goal is to check every event log on the remote computer, and, if the size is greater than the threshold, then the event log will be backed up and cleared.

We loop through every event log on the remote computer:

```
foreach ($log in (Get-WmiObject win32_nteventlogfile -computer $computer)) {
```

If the **FileSize** property is greater than the threshold, then we'll display a message and prompt if the user wants to back up and clear the log:

```
if ($log.FileSize/1MB -gt $iLimit) {
    Write-Host $log.LogFileName"="($log.FileSize/1MB)"MB"
    $reply=Read-Host "Do you want to backup and clear the event log?[YN]"
```

Assuming the user answered yes, the script then enables privileges, defines a backup file name and backs up the log:

```
$log.psbase.scope.options.enablePrivileges=$TRUE
$backup=(Get-Date -format yyyyMMdd)+"_"+$log.CSName+"_"+`
$log.logfilename+".evt"
Write-Host "Backing up"$log.LogFileName"to $path\$backup"
$rc=$log.BackupEventLog($path+"\"+$backup)
```

We can check the **ReturnValue** property from the **BackupEventLog()** method to verify a successful backup:

```
if ($rc.ReturnValue -eq 0) {
```

If it was successful, then we can clear the event log:

```
Write-Host -foreground GREEN "Backup successful. Clearing Event log."
$rc2=$log.ClearEventLog()
```

Again, we check the **ReturnValue** to verify a successful operation and display an appropriate message:

```
if ($rc2.ReturnValue -eq 0) {
Write-Host -foreground GREEN "ClearEventLog successful."
}
else {
Write-Host -foreground RED `
"ClearEventLog failed with a return value of"$rc2.ReturnValue
} #end if rc2.return value
```

If the backup failed, then none of the above happens and an error message is displayed instead:

```
else {
Write-Host -foreground RED `
"Backup failed with a return value of"$rc.ReturnValue
```

For simple and local event log management, the **Get-Eventlog** cmdlet should suffice. For anything more complex or involving remote systems, you will need to use the **Get-WmiObject** cmdlet.

# Chapter 29
# Managing Processes

If you've been with us from the beginning, you're familiar with **Get-Process**. This cmdlet lists all running processes on your system.

```
PS C:\> get-process

Handles NPM(K)    PM(K)      WS(K) VM(M)   CPU(s)     Id ProcessName
------- ------    -----      ----- -----   ------     -- -----------
     33      2      800       3128    23     0.44   3580 ApntEx
     79      3     1768       5668    36     4.61   3852 Apoint
    128      4     2388       5752    45     1.40   1732 avgamsvr
    180      6     3500      10852    53     3.65   4016 avgcc
    168      7     2084       6708    50     2.29   1760 avgemc
     77      2      536       2128    20     0.48   1748 avgupsvc
    155      4     2700       6288    47     6.77   1604 BCMWLTRY
...
```

If you're interested in a specific process, you can reference it by name or by ID:

```
PS C:\> get-process winword

Handles NPM(K)    PM(K)      WS(K) VM(M)   CPU(s)     Id ProcessName
------- ------    -----      ----- -----   ------     -- -----------
    403     16    34340      53644   188    10.77   3032 WINWORD
PS C:\> get-process -id 3032

Handles NPM(K)    PM(K)      WS(K) VM(M)   CPU(s)     Id ProcessName
------- ------    -----      ----- -----   ------     -- -----------
```

```
    408      17    34384      53788  188   13.46  3032 WINWORD


PS C:\>
```

As you can see, either expression returns the same information. The reason you need to know either the process name or ID is so you can terminate the process with **Stop-Process**:

```
PS C:\> notepad
PS C:\> get-process notepad

Handles NPM(K)    PM(K)     WS(K) VM(M)  CPU(s)     Id ProcessName
------- ------    -----     ----- -----  ------     -- -----------
     33      3     1180      3812    32    0.11   3868 notepad


PS C:\> stop-process 3868
PS C:\>
```

We started Notepad and found the process ID with **Get-Process**.

Because **Get-Process** produces object output like all other cmdlets, you can use it in the pipeline. Here's one example:

```
PS C:\> get-process | where {$_.handles -gt 1000} | sort handles -desc

Handles NPM(K)    PM(K)     WS(K) VM(M)  CPU(s)     Id ProcessName
------- ------    -----     ----- -----  ------     -- -----------
   4218     25   163156     57408  406 5,073.57   4832 firefox
   3111     17   130808    144644  363  808.68    1284 thunderbird
   2344     33    41108     19944  191   48.27    3700 msnmsgr
   1882     90    56308     12332  285  330.66    3084 GROOVE
   1858     65    34520     45848  176  115.58    1180 svchost
   1507     14    80784     20948  249   58.50    2972 powershell
   1462     28    63000     82512  302   21.70    9448 PrimalScript
   1092     14     2276      5624   39    4.91    1064 svchost
```

This expression takes the output of **Get-Process** and filters it with the **Where** cmdlet looking for processes with a handle count greater than 1000. The results of **Where** cmdlet are then piped to the **Sort** cmdlet, which sorts the output by the **Handles** property in descending order.

## Starting a Process

On the local system, the easiest and most obvious way to start a process is to simply run a program. However, it can also be done with WMI:

```
PS C:\> [wmiclass]$newproc="root\cimv2:Win32_Process"
PS C:\> $spawn=$newproc.Create("calc.exe")
```

We use the [wmiclass] type adapter to specify we're going to work with the Win32_Process class. The object, $newproc, is a generic and undefined Win32_Process, but we can call the **Create()** method to start the Windows calculator. The syntax for **Create()** allows you to specify a working directory, should that be required:

```
$spawn=$newproc.Create("notepad","c:\windows")
```

We created an object, $spawn, so that we can check if the command was successful or not by examining the **Returnvalue** property:

```
PS C:\> [wmiclass]$newproc="root\cimv2:Win32_Process"
PS C:\>
PS C:\> $spawn=$newproc.Create("calc.exe")
PS C:\> if ($spawn.returnvalue -eq 0) {
>> Write-Host "Process is now running with process id"$spawn.ProcessID
>> } else {
>>   Write-Host "Process failed to start. Return value ="$spawn.ReturnValue
>> }
>>
Process is now running with process id 9564
PS C:\>
```

Of course, if you don't need all the error checking, you can accomplish this with a simple one-line expression:

```
PS C:\> ([wmiclass]"root\cimv2:Win32_Process").Create("calc.exe")
```

# Stopping Local Processes

We can kill a process with **Stop-Process** by specifying the ID:

```
PS C:\> stop-process 1676
```

If we didn't know the process ID, we can also use:

```
Stop-process -name notepad
```

Because terminating a process could have a significant effect on your system, you may want to take advantage of the **-Confirm** parameter to make verify you're killing the correct process:

```
PS C:\> stop-process 1676 -confirm
```

```
Confirm
Are you sure you want to perform this action?
Performing operation "Stop-Process" on Target "schedul2 (1676)".
[Y] Yes [A] Yes to All [N] No [L] No to All [S] Suspend [?] Help (default is "Y"):
```

We'll explain how to stop processes on remote servers a little bit later.

# Process Tasks

Here are some examples of using PowerShell for some common process management tasks.

### Find Top 10 Processes by CPU Usage

```
PS C:\> Get-process | sort cpu -desc | select -first 10

Handles NPM(K)    PM(K)     WS(K) VM(M)  CPU(s)     Id ProcessName
```

| Handles | NPM(K) | PM(K) | WS(K) | VM(M) | CPU(s) | Id | ProcessName |
|---|---|---|---|---|---|---|---|
| 3951 | 31 | 304104 | 208512 | 571 | 3,822.30 | 4832 | firefox |
| 305 | 9 | 35384 | 6328 | 1496 | 601.85 | 1888 | sqlservr |
| 1419 | 29 | 62120 | 41964 | 307 | 549.94 | 4520 | PrimalScript |
| 1880 | 17 | 118824 | 132564 | 364 | 499.01 | 1284 | thunderbird |
| 365 | 9 | 1908 | 4520 | 32 | 480.17 | 796 | services |
| 294 | 8 | 21304 | 26324 | 73 | 442.37 | 3560 | procexp |
| 796 | 0 | 0 | 220 | 2 | 361.70 | 4 | System |
| 786 | 22 | 33384 | 23772 | 149 | 286.46 | 2528 | explorer |
| 1816 | 90 | 52576 | 17280 | 264 | 232.18 | 3084 | GROOVE |
| 340 | 8 | 8832 | 14912 | 76 | 211.08 | 3536 | xfilter |

Here's another example of leveraging the pipeline. The **Get-Process** cmdlet output is sorted by the CPU property in descending order. That output is then piped to the **Select-Object** cmdlet, which only returns the first 10 items in the list.

## Find Top 10 Processes by Memory Usage

To find the top 10 processes with the largest working set, we can use a similar expression as above:

```
PS C:\> Get-Process | sort workingset -desc | select -first 10
```

| Handles | NPM(K) | PM(K) | WS(K) | VM(M) | CPU(s) | Id | ProcessName |
|---|---|---|---|---|---|---|---|
| 3948 | 31 | 304092 | 208512 | 570 | 3,828.01 | 4832 | firefox |
| 1879 | 17 | 118828 | 132568 | 364 | 499.05 | 1284 | thunderbird |
| 671 | 14 | 64684 | 70508 | 224 | 20.16 | 2972 | powershell |
| 1425 | 29 | 62120 | 41968 | 307 | 550.99 | 4520 | PrimalScript |
| 1788 | 65 | 30316 | 41632 | 174 | 65.83 | 1180 | svchost |
| 724 | 21 | 43384 | 33896 | 258 | 176.05 | 2900 | WINWORD |
| 294 | 8 | 21304 | 26324 | 73 | 442.52 | 3560 | procexp |
| 786 | 22 | 33384 | 23772 | 149 | 286.74 | 2528 | explorer |
| 1841 | 33 | 40888 | 22572 | 191 | 36.65 | 3700 | msnmsgr |
| 270 | 7 | 19080 | 21904 | 63 | 147.00 | 1136 | MsMpEng |

The only difference from the previous example is that we are sorting on the **Workingset** property.

## Find Top 10 Longest Running Processes

```
PS C:\> Get-process | where {($_.name -ne "System") -and ($_.name -ne "Idle")} '
>> | sort starttime | select -first 10
>>
```

| Handles | NPM(K) | PM(K) | WS(K) | VM(M) | CPU(s) | Id | ProcessName |
|---|---|---|---|---|---|---|---|
| 21 | 1 | 172 | 388 | 4 | 0.44 | 600 | smss |
| 824 | 9 | 3356 | 5708 | 69 | 47.87 | 724 | csrss |
| 583 | 74 | 8172 | 2808 | 63 | 1.69 | 748 | winlogon |
| 366 | 9 | 1908 | 4520 | 32 | 487.66 | 796 | services |
| 552 | 11 | 5176 | 1092 | 46 | 3.66 | 808 | lsass |
| 221 | 6 | 3440 | 5432 | 63 | 1.08 | 960 | svchost |
| 626 | 14 | 2256 | 5604 | 39 | 2.69 | 1064 | svchost |
| 276 | 8 | 19128 | 21932 | 64 | 147.06 | 1136 | MsMpEng |
| 1788 | 65 | 30292 | 41624 | 174 | 65.88 | 1180 | svchost |
| 111 | 6 | 1732 | 4236 | 32 | 0.96 | 1292 | svchost |

This example is a little more complex because we want to filter out the Idle and System processes using the **Where** cmdlet:

```
where {($_.name -ne "System") -and ($_.name -ne "Idle")}
```

This expression is a compound filter using the -**And** operator to return process objects where the name is not "System" and not "Idle". The remaining process objects are sorted on the **StartTime** property. The **Select** cmdlet finally returns the first 10 objects in the list.

How did we know about the **StartTime** property? We used **Get-Member** to see all the possible process object properties:

```
PS C:\> get-process | get-member
```

## Find Process Details

Once you know what type of process information you can get, you can execute expressions like this:

```
PS C:\> get-process | Select Name,ID,Company,FileVersion,Path


Name        : alg
Id          : 1380
Company     : Microsoft Corporation
FileVersion : 5.1.2600.2180 (xpsp_sp2_rtm.040803-2158)
Path        : C:\WINDOWS\System32\alg.exe

Name        : ApntEx
Id          : 3432
Company     : Alps Electric Co., Ltd.
FileVersion : 5.0.1.13
Path        : C:\Program Files\Apoint\Apntex.exe

Name        : Apoint
Id          : 2960
Company     : Alps Electric Co., Ltd.
FileVersion : 5.4.101.113
Path        : C:\Program Files\Apoint\Apoint.exe
...
```

In addition to the **Name** and **ID** properties, we've selected the **Company, FileVersion**, and **Path** information for each process. Now you can be better informed about exactly what is running on your server.

## Find Process Owners

Another piece of process information you might find valuable is the process owner. Unfortunately, the **Get-Process** cmdlet doesn't provide access to this information. But we can use **Get-WmiObject**:

```
PS C:\> $n=Get-wmiobject -query "Select * from win32_process where name='notepad.exe'"
PS C:\> $n.GetOwner().user
PS C:\> jhicks
```

The **Get-WmiObject** expression creates a WMI object which has a **GetOwner()** method. The method returns an object with properties of **Domain** and **User**. Once you understand the concept, you can put this together as a one-line expression:

```
PS C:\> (Get-WmiObject -query "Select * from win32_process where `
>> name='notepad.exe'").GetOwner().User
```

```
>>
jhicks
```

We've broken the expression up for printing, but you can type it as one line.

Here's an example of how to show the owners of all running processes:

```
PS C:\> Get-WmiObject -query "Select * from win32_Process" | `
Select ProcessID,Name,@{Name="Owner";Expression={$_.GetOwner().User}}`
|sort owner | Format-Table ProcessID,Name,Owner -autosize
```

This example is pretty straightforward until we get to the **Select** cmdlet. In addition to selecting the **ProcessID** and **Name** properties, we're also defining a custom property called **Owner**. The value will be the result of calling the **GetOwner()** method of the current object in the pipeline:

```
Expression={$_.GetOwner().User}
```

This property can be passed through the pipeline to the **Sort** cmdlet, which in turn sends the output to **Format-Table** for presentation. We'll let you run this on your own to see the results.

## Remote Processes

As with most PowerShell cmdlets, the process management tools only work on the local system. WMI is required to manage processes on remote systems.

```
PS C:\> Get-wmiobject -class win32_process -computer DC01 '
>> -credential $cred|select Name,Handle,VirtualSize,WorkingSetSize `
>> | format-table
>>

Name                   Handle       VirtualSize    WorkingSetSize
----                   ------       -----------    --------------
System Idle Process 0                         0             16384
System                 4              1921024            225280
smss.exe               832            3891200            385024
csrss.exe              928           30216192           3166208
winlogon.exe           956           65359872           1617920
services.exe           1000          42635264          10158080
lsass.exe              1012          43880448           2850816
svchost.exe            1176          65966080           5095424
svchost.exe            1236          39313408           4874240
MsMpEng.exe            1880          49737728          12865536
...
```

This example assumes we've defined $cred earlier with the **Get-Credential** cmdlet. When using **Get-WmiObject**, you'll get back some additional WMI properties like **__Class** that generally aren't needed so use the **Select** cmdlet or choose properties with **Format-Table** to present only the information you want. It is also possible, with **Get-WmiObject**, to query for specify processes:

```
PS C:\> Get-WmiObject -query "Select * from win32_process where workingsetsize > '
>> 10248000" -computer "DESK61"| >> format-table Name,ProcessID,WorkingSetSize -autosize
>>

Name            ProcessID WorkingSetSize
----            --------- --------------
```

```
MsMpEng.exe          1136        21778432
svchost.exe          1180        47415296
explorer.exe         2528        30642176
xfilter.exe          3536        15269888
procexp.exe          3560        28946432
msnmsgr.exe          3700        20414464
SnagIt32.exe         2472        15695872
powershell.exe       2972        17870848
thunderbird.exe      1284       146759680
firefox.exe          4832        58589184
WINWORD.EXE          9588        83107840
PrimalScript.exe     9448        90677248
```

After using **Get-Process** for awhile, you may come to expect the same results when querying a remote computer using **Get-WmiObject**. You can get the same information with an expression like this:

```
Get-WmiObject -Query "Select * from win32_process" | `
Format-Table HandleCount,QuotaNonPagedPoolUsage,PageFileUsage,`
WorkingSetSize,VirtualSize,KernelModeTime,ProcessID,Name | `
Format-Table -autosize
```

But if you execute this code, you'll see the formatting isn't quite what you might expect. This is because PowerShell has defined a default view for the **Get-Process** cmdlet that handles all the formatting. You can achieve a similar result with an expression like this:

```
Get-WmiObject -Query "Select * from win32_process" | sort Name | Format-Table `
@{Label="Handles";Expression={$_.HandleCount}},`
@{Label="NPM(K)";Expression={"{0:F0}" -f ($_.QuotaNonPagedPoolUsage/1KB)}},`
@{Label="PM(K)";Expression={"{0:F0}" -f ($_.PageFileUsage/1KB)}},`
@{Label="WS(K)";Expression={"{0:F0}" -f ($_.WorkingSetSize/1KB)}},`
@{Label="VM(M)";Expression={"{0:F0}" -f ($_.VirtualSize/1MB)}},`
@{Label="CPU(s)";Expression={"{0:N2}" -f (($_.KernelModeTime/10000000)+`
($_.UserModeTime/10000000))}},`
@{Label="ID";Expression={$_.ProcessID}},`
@{Label="ProcessName";Expression={$_.Name}} `
-autosize
```

The results of the **Get-WmiObject** cmdlet are sorted and then sent to **Format-Table**. We then define custom labels and values using script blocks that will give us the same results as the **Get-Process** cmdlet. The added benefit is that we can specify a remote computer. Since this is a lot to type each time you want to use it, we recommend creating a script block:

```
$pswmi={Get-WmiObject -Query "Select * from win32_process" | sort Name | `
Format-Table `
@{Label="Handles";Expression={$_.HandleCount}},`
@{Label="NPM(K)";Expression={"{0:F0}" -f ($_.QuotaNonPagedPoolUsage/1KB)}},`
@{Label="PM(K)";Expression={"{0:F0}" -f ($_.PageFileUsage/1KB)}},`
@{Label="WS(K)";Expression={"{0:F0}" -f ($_.WorkingSetSize/1KB)}},`
@{Label="VM(M)";Expression={"{0:F0}" -f ($_.VirtualSize/1MB)}},`
@{Label="CPU(s)";Expression={"{0:N2}" -f (($_.KernelModeTime/10000000)+`
($_.UserModeTime/10000000))}},`
@{Label="ID";Expression={$_.ProcessID}},`
@{Label="ProcessName";Expression={$_.Name}} `
-autosize}
```

Anytime you want to run this simply type:

```
&$pswmi
```

An even better approach would be to add the **-Computer** parameter:

```
$pswmi={Get-WmiObject -Query "Select * from win32_process" -computer $computer `
 | sort Name | Format-Table `
@{Label="Handles";Expression={$_.HandleCount}},`
@{Label="NPM(K)";Expression={"{0:F0}" -f ($_.QuotaNonPagedPoolUsage/1KB)}},`
@{Label="PM(K)";Expression={"{0:F0}" -f ($_.PageFileUsage/1KB)}},`
@{Label="WS(K)";Expression={"{0:F0}" -f ($_.WorkingSetSize/1KB)}},`
@{Label="VM(M)";Expression={"{0:F0}" -f ($_.VirtualSize/1MB)}},`
@{Label="CPU(s)";Expression={"{0:N2}" -f (($_.KernelModeTime/10000000)+`
($_.UserModeTime/10000000))}},`
@{Label="ID";Expression={$_.ProcessID}},`
@{Label="ProcessName";Expression={$_.Name}} `
-autosize}
```

As long as $computer has been defined, we can successfully run this script block. Need a refresher on script blocks, take a look at the Script Blocks section.

Finally, here's one more approach:

```
Function Get-PS {
Param([string]$computer="localhost",`
[System.Management.Automation.PSCredential]$credential)

if ($credential)
   {#use alternate credentials if supplied

 Get-WmiObject -Query "Select * from win32_process" -computer $computer `
 -credential $credential | sort Name | Format-Table `
 @{Label="Handles";Expression={$_.HandleCount}},`
 @{Label="NPM(K)";Expression={"{0:F0}" -f ($_.QuotaNonPagedPoolUsage/1KB)}},`
 @{Label="PM(K)";Expression={"{0:F0}" -f ($_.PageFileUsage/1KB)}},`
 @{Label="WS(K)";Expression={"{0:F0}" -f ($_.WorkingSetSize/1KB)}},`
 @{Label="VM(M)";Expression={"{0:F0}" -f ($_.VirtualSize/1MB)}},`
 @{Label="CPU(s)";Expression={"{0:N2}" -f (($_.KernelModeTime/10000000)+`
 ($_.UserModeTime/10000000))}},`
 @{Label="ID";Expression={$_.ProcessID}},`
 @{Label="ProcessName";Expression={$_.Name}}`
 -autosize

   } else {

Get-WmiObject -Query "Select * from win32_process" -computer $computer `
 | sort Name | Format-Table `
@{Label="Handles";Expression={$_.HandleCount}},`
@{Label="NPM(K)";Expression={"{0:F0}" -f ($_.QuotaNonPagedPoolUsage/1KB)}},`
@{Label="PM(K)";Expression={"{0:F0}" -f ($_.PageFileUsage/1KB)}},`
@{Label="WS(K)";Expression={"{0:F0}" -f ($_.WorkingSetSize/1KB)}},`
@{Label="VM(M)";Expression={"{0:F0}" -f ($_.VirtualSize/1MB)}},`
@{Label="CPU(s)";Expression={"{0:N2}" -f (($_.KernelModeTime/10000000)+`
($_.UserModeTime/10000000))}},`
@{Label="ID";Expression={$_.ProcessID}},`
@{Label="ProcessName";Expression={$_.Name}} `
 -autosize
 }
}
```

This function takes parameters for the computer name and alternate credentials.

```
Get-PS file02 (get-credential SAPIEN\administrator)
```

If a computer name is not passed the default will be Localhost:

```
Param([string]$computer="localhost",`
```

If the user passes an alternate credential object, then a version of the **Get-WmiObject** script block that uses -**Credential** will be called:

```
Get-WmiObject -Query "Select * from win32_process" -computer $computer `
-credential $credential | sort Name | Format-Table '
```

Otherwise, the function executes **Get-WmiObject** with the current credentials:

```
Get-WmiObject -Query "Select * from win32_process" -computer $computer `
```

There are many variations on this you might want to consider. The right approach will depend on your needs.

## Creating a Remote Process

To create a process on a remote computer, we need to use WMI and the [wmiclass] type adapter in the same way we created a local process:

```
$computer="Exch01"
[wmiclass]$remoteproc="\\$computer\root\cimv2:Win32_Process"
$spawn=$remoteproc.Create("calc.exe")
if ($spawn.returnvalue -eq 0) {
Write-Host "Process is now running with process id"$spawn.ProcessID
} else {
 Write-Host "Process failed to start. Return value ="$spawn.ReturnValue
}
```

The primary difference is that we need to specify a complete path, including the computer name to the Win32_class:

```
[wmiclass]$remoteproc="\\$computer\root\cimv2:Win32_Process"
```

After that, everything is the same except that the remote process is not interactive. In our example, the Windows calculator will not automatically appear on the desktop on Exch01, but it can be seen in Task Manager. If you launch remote processes, you need to realize they will run until someone stops them or they complete on their own.

## Stopping Remote Process

To stop a remote process, you need to obtain a reference to it using **Get-WmiObject**:

```
PS C:\> $calc=Get-Wmiobject -query "Select * from win32_Process where name='calc.exe'" `
>> -computer FILE02
>>
PS C:\> $calc.Terminate()
```

This expression will terminate the Windows calculator running on FILE02. As with starting processes, the **Terminate()** method will return an object with a **ReturnValue** property. A value of 0 will indicate success. This command can be executed as a one-liner as well:

```
PS C:\ (Get-Wmiobject -query "Select * from win32_Process where name='calc.exe'" '
>> -computerFILE02).Terminate()
>>

__GENUS          : 2
__CLASS          : __PARAMETERS
__SUPERCLASS     :
__DYNASTY        : __PARAMETERS
__RELPATH        :
__PROPERTY_COUNT : 1
__DERIVATION     : {}
__SERVER         :
__NAMESPACE      :
__PATH           :
ReturnValue      : 0


PS C:\>
```

The **Get-Process** cmdlet is terrific for working with local processes and has a wealth of information. However, it cannot get process information on remote systems. But, as you've seen, using **Get-WmiObject** is easy to use and can achieve the same results. You might even consider writing functions for process management tasks using **Get-WmiObject** that replicate the functionality of **Get-Process**. If you do, we hope you'll share.

# Chapter 30
# Managing the Registry

One of the great features in PowerShell is its ability to treat the registry like a file system. Now you can connect to the registry and navigate it just as you would a directory. This is because PowerShell has a Registry provider that presents the registry as a drive. That shouldn't come as too much of a surprise because the registry is a hierarchical storage system much like a file system. So, why not present it as such?

In fact, PowerShell accomplishes this feat for other hierarchical storage types. If you run **Get-Psdrive**, you can see the available "drives" and their providers:

```
PS C:\> get-psdrive

Name       Provider     Root
----       --------     ----
Alias      Alias
C          FileSystem   C:\
cert       Certificate  \
D          FileSystem   D:\
Env        Environment
F          FileSystem   F:\
Function   Function
G          FileSystem   G:\
HKCU       Registry     HKEY_CURRENT_USER
HKLM       Registry     HKEY_LOCAL_MACHINE
M          FileSystem   M:\
N          FileSystem   N:\
P          FileSystem   P:\
Variable   Variable
Z          FileSystem   Z:\
```

Even though the list shows drives mapped to network shares, you cannot access remote registries. We'll show you later how to use **Get-WmiObject** to accomplish that task. In the meantime, you can use **Set-Location** or its alias **cd** to change to any of these PSDrives just as if they were another hard drive in your computer:

```
PS C:\> cd HKLM:System
PS HKLM:\System> dir


  Hive: Microsoft.PowerShell.Core\Registry::HKEY_LOCAL_MACHINE\System

SKC VC Name                      Property
--- -- ----                      --------
  4  0 ControlSet001             {}
  4  0 ControlSet003             {}
  0  0 LastKnownGoodRecovery      {}
  0 32 MountedDevices            {\??\Volume{1edc8241-c4b6-11d9-8
  0  4 Select                    {Current, Default, Failed, LastK
  2  6 Setup                     {SetupType, SystemSetupInProgres
  7  0 WPA                       {}
  4  0 CurrentControlSet          {}

PS HKLM:\> cd currentcontrolset\services\tcpip
PS HKLM:\system\currentcontrolset\services\tcpip> dir


  Hive: Microsoft.PowerShell.Core\Registry::HKEY_LOCAL_MACHINE\system\currentc
ontrolset\services\tcpip

SKC VC Name                      Property
--- -- ----                      --------
  0  3 Linkage                   {Bind, Route, Export}
  5 16 Parameters                {NV Hostname, DataBasePath, Name
  0  6 Performance               {Close, Collect, Library, Open.
  0  1 Security                  {Security}
  0  7 ServiceProvider            {Class, DnsPriority, HostsPriori
  0  3 Enum                      {0, Count, NextInstance}


PS HKLM:\system\currentcontrolset\services\tcpip>
```

For example, if we want to see the keys in our current registry location, we would use an expression like this:

```
PS HKLM:\system\currentcontrolset\services\tcpip> get-itemproperty .


PSPath        : Microsoft.PowerShell.Core\Registry::HKEY_LOCAL_MACHINE\system
                \currentcontrolset\services\tcpip
PSParentPath  : Microsoft.PowerShell.Core\Registry::HKEY_LOCAL_MACHINE\system
                \currentcontrolset\services
PSChildName   : tcpip
PSDrive       : HKLM
PSProvider    : Microsoft.PowerShell.Core\Registry
Type          : 1
Start         : 1
ErrorControl  : 1
Tag           : 5
ImagePath     : System32\DRIVERS\tcpip.sys
DisplayName   : TCP/IP Protocol Driver
Group         : PNP_TDI
```

```
DependOnService : {IPSec}
DependOnGroup   : {}
Description     : TCP/IP Protocol Driver


PS HKLM:\system\currentcontrolset\services\tcpip>
```

In fact, you have to use **Get-Itemproperty** to retrieve any registry keys. You can use this cmdlet without even having to change your location to the registry:

```
PS C:\> get-itemproperty HKLM:\software\microsoft\windows\currentversion\run


PSPath                      : Microsoft.PowerShell.Core\Registry::HKEY_LOCAL_MACHINE\softwar…
                              tversion\run
PSParentPath                : Microsoft.PowerShell.Core\Registry::HKEY_LOCAL_MACHINE\softwar…
                              tversion
PSChildName                 : run
PSDrive                     : HKLM
PSProvider                  : Microsoft.PowerShell.Core\Registry
Apoint                      : C:\Program Files\Apoint\Apoint.exe
NvCplDaemon                 : RUNDLL32.EXE C:\WINDOWS\system32\NvCpl.dll,NvStartup
nwiz                        : nwiz.exe /installquiet
Broadcom Wireless Manager UI : C:\WINDOWS\system32\WLTRAY.exe
IntelliPoint                : "C:\Program Files\Microsoft IntelliPoint\point32.exe"
Windows Defender            : "C:\Program Files\Windows Defender\MSASCui.exe" -hide
SunJavaUpdateSched          : "C:\Program Files\Java\jre1.6.0_01\bin\jusched.exe"
TrueImageMonitor.exe        : C:\Program Files\Acronis\TrueImageWorkstation\TrueImageMonitor…
AcronisTimounterMonitor     : C:\Program Files\Acronis\TrueImageWorkstation\TimounterMonito….
Acronis Scheduler2 Service  : "C:\Program Files\Common Files\Acronis\Schedule2\schedhlp.exe"
GrooveMonitor               : "C:\Program Files\Microsoft Office\Office12\GrooveMonitor.exe"
AVG7_CC                     : C:\PROGRA~1\Grisoft\AVGFRE~1\avgcc.exe /STARTUP
ProcExp                     : "c:\windows\procexp.exe" /t
NeroFilterCheck             : C:\Program Files\Common Files\Ahead\Lib\NeroCheck.exe
QuickTime Task              : "C:\Program Files\QuickTime\qttask.exe" -atboottime
iTunesHelper                : "C:\Program Files\iTunes\iTunesHelper.exe"
```

This expression lists registry keys that indicate what programs are set to run when the computer starts up. We didn't have to change our location to the registry; we only had to specify the registry location as if it were a folder.

You can also create a variable for an item's properties. Here we get the registry keys for **Parameters** from our current location using the **Get-Itemproperty** cmdlet:

```
PS HKLM:\system\currentcontrolset\services\tcpip> '
>>$ipparams=get-itemproperty Parameters
>>
PS HKLM:\system\currentcontrolset\services\tcpip>$ipparams


PSPath                      : Microsoft.PowerShell.Core\Registry::HKEY_LOCAL_M
                              ACHINE\system\currentcontrolset\services\tcpip\P
                              arameters
PSParentPath                : Microsoft.PowerShell.Core\Registry::HKEY_LOCAL_M
                              ACHINE\system\currentcontrolset\services\tcpip
PSChildName                 : Parameters
PSDrive                     : HKLM
PSProvider                  : Microsoft.PowerShell.Core\Registry
NV Hostname                 : godot
```

```
DataBasePath               : E:\WINDOWS\System32\drivers\etc
NameServer                 :
ForwardBroadcasts          : 0
IPEnableRouter             : 0
Domain                     :
Hostname                   : godot
SearchList                 :
UseDomainNameDevolution    : 1
EnableICMPRedirect         : 1
DeadGWDetectDefault        : 1
DontAddDefaultGatewayDefault : 0
EnableSecurityFilters      : 0
TcpWindowSize              : 64512
DisableTaskOffload         : 1
ReservedPorts              : {1433-1434}


PS HKLM:\system\currentcontrolset\services\tcpip>

PS HKLM:\system\currentcontrolset\services\tcpip> `
>> $ipparams.tcpwindowsize
>>
64512
PS HKLM:\system\currentcontrolset\services\tcpip>
```

We defined $ipparams to hold the registry keys from HKLM\System\CurrentControlSet\Services\
Tcpip\Parameters. Invoking the variable $ipparams, lists all the keys and their values. Alternatively, we
can get a specific key and value by using a property name:

```
$ipparams.tcpwindowsize
```

We can set a registry value using **Set-Itemproperty**. Here we changed the Domain key under parameters that had no value, to a value of SAPIEN:

```
PS HKLM:\system\currentcontrolset\services\tcpip\parameters> `
>> set-itemproperty -path . -name Domain -value SAPIEN
>>
PS HKLM:\system\currentcontrolset\services\tcpip\parameters> `
>> (get-itemproperty .).Domain
>>
SAPIEN
PS HKLM:\system\currentcontrolset\services\tcpip\parameters>
```

To properly use **Set-Itemproperty**, you should specify a path. In this example, we used a "." to indicate
the current location, the name of the key, and its new value.

Because accessing the registry in PowerShell is like accessing a file system, you can recurse through it,
search for specific items, or do a massive search and replace.

You can use **New-Item** and **New-Itemproperty** to create new registry keys and properties. Let's change
our location to HKEY_Current_User and look at the current items in the root:

```
PS HKCU:\> dir


  Hive: Microsoft.PowerShell.Core\Registry::HKEY_CURRENT_USER

SKC VC Name                      Property
```

```
--- -- ----                          --------
 2  0 AppEvents                       {}
 3 32 Console                         {ColorTable00, ColorTable01, ColorTab..
26  1 Control Panel                    {Opened}
 0  4 Environment                     {TEMP, TMP, USERNAME, EnvironmentVari..
 1  6 Identities                      {Identity Ordinal, Migrated5, Last Us..
 2  0 Keyboard Layout                  {}
 0  0 Network                         {}
 4  1 Printers                        {DeviceOld}
 1  0 S                              {}
77  0 Software                        {}
 1  0 SYSTEM                         {}
 0  0 UNICODE Program Groups          {}
 2  0 Windows 3.1 Migration Status   {}
 0  1 SessionInformation             {ProgramCount}
 0  7 Volatile Environment            {LOGONSERVER, CLIENTNAME, SESSIONNAME..


PS HKCU:\>
```

## Creating Registry Items

In PowerShell it is very easy to create new registry keys and values. We'll create a new sub key called PowerShell TFM under HKCU using the **New-Item** cmdlet:

```
PS HKCU:\> new-item "PowerShell TFM"


  Hive: Microsoft.PowerShell.Core\Registry::HKEY_CURRENT_USER

SKC VC Name                          Property
--- -- ----                          --------
  0  0 PowerShell TFM                  {}


PS HKCU:\> cd "PowerShell TFM"
PS HKCU:\PowerShell TFM>
```

The **New-Item** cmdlet creates the appropriate type of object because it realizes we are in the registry. To create registry values we use **New-Itemproperty**:

```
PS HKCU:\PowerShell TFM> new-itemproperty -path .'
>> -name "Pub" -value "SAPIEN"
>>


PSPath       : Microsoft.PowerShell.Core\Registry::HKEY_CURRENT_...
PSParentPath : Microsoft.PowerShell.Core\Registry::HKEY_CURRENT_USER
PSChildName : PowerShell TFM
PSDrive      : HKCU
PSProvider  : Microsoft.PowerShell.Core\Registry
Pub          : SAPIEN


PS HKCU:\PowerShell TFM>
```

We now have a String entry called Pub with a value of SAPIEN. If you want to create a different registry entry, such as a DWORD, then use the **-PropertyType** parameter:

```
PS HKCU:\PowerShell TFM> new-itemproperty -path . '
>> -PropertyType DWORD -name "Recommend" -value 1
>>


PSPath        : Microsoft.PowerShell.Core\Registry::HKEY_CURRENT_USE...
PSParentPath  : Microsoft.PowerShell.Core\Registry::HKEY_CURRENT_USER
PSChildName   : PowerShell TFM
PSDrive       : HKCU
PSProvider    : Microsoft.PowerShell.Core\Registry
Recommend     : 1


PS HKCU:\PowerShell TFM>
```

## Removing Registry Items

To remove an item, we call **Remove-Itemproperty**:

```
PS HKCU:\PowerShell TFM> remove-itemproperty -path . -name Recommend
```

We use **Remove-Item** to remove the sub key we created:

```
PS HKCU:\> remove-item "PowerShell TFM"
```

**Standard Registry Rules Apply**
Since PowerShell takes a new approach to managing the registry, take great care in modifying the registry. Be sure to test your registry editing skills with these new expressions and cmdlets on a test system before even thinking about touching a production server or desktop.

## Searching the Registry

Searching the registry for information is not that much different from searching any other file system. However, because there is so much information, you'll want to filter it in some way. Here's one example:

```
PS HKLM:\software> dir . | where {$_.name -match "Sapien"}


  Hive: Microsoft.PowerShell.Core\Registry::HKEY_LOCAL_MACHINE\software

SKC VC Name                      Property
--- -- ----                      --------
  2  0 SAPIEN                     {}
  2  0 SAPIEN Technologies, Inc.    {}


PS HKLM:\software>
```

From the current location, we're searching for any child keys that match the word "Sapien". We could take this a step further and enumerate all the matching registry keys:

```
PS HKLM:\software> dir . | where {$_.name -match "Sapien"} | dir -recurse
```

As you work with the registry in PowerShell, you will realize that you need to use **Get-ChildItem** to enumerate child keys and **Get-Itemproperty** to retrieve values, sometimes you need to combine the two cmdlets:

```
PS HKLM:\software> foreach ($item in (dir . | where {$_.name -match "Sapien"} | `
>> dir -recurse)) {$item;Get-ItemProperty $item.pspath | select * -exclude `
>> PSDrive,PS*Path,PSChild*,PSProv*
>> }
>>
```

This snippet is a little trickier, so follow along carefully. First, we will search from the current location for registry key with the word "Sapien".

```
dir . | where {$_.name -match "Sapien"}
```

The results of this expression are then processed by the **dir** alias recursively:

```
| dir -recurse
```

Each of the results is a registry location that we want to enumerate using **Get-Itemproperty.** Therefore, everything we've done so far is part of a larger **foreach** expression. For every matching registry key found, the key name will be displayed and then **Get-Itemproperty** is called:

```
{$item;Get-ItemProperty $item.pspath
```

The resulting object is a custom object that includes some PowerShell properties, like PSDrive and PSPath, that we can ignore. We pipe everything to the **Select** cmdlet, excluding the properties we aren't interested in:

```
select * -exclude PSDrive,PS*Path,PSChild*,PSProv*
```

When executed, we get information like this:

```
  Hive: Microsoft.PowerShell.Core\Registry::HKEY_LOCAL_MACHINE\software\SAPIEN Technologies…

SKC VC Name                      Property
--- -- ----                      --------
  0  1 2007                      {(default)}

(default) : C:\Program Files\SAPIEN\PrimalScript 2007 Enterprise\PrimalScript.exe

  0  2 Wizards                   {WMI Wizard, ADSI Wizard}

WMI Wizard : WMIWizard.WMIWiz
ADSI Wizard : ADSIWizard.ADSIWiz
```

Finally, suppose you recall part of registry value but not sure the exact location. We might use a process like this:

```
PS HKLM:\software\microsoft> $errorActionPreference="SilentlyContinue"
PS HKLM:\software\microsoft> foreach ($item in dir . -recurse) {
>> if (($item.GetValueNames()) -eq "RegisteredOwner") {
>>$item.name;$item.GetValue("RegisteredOwner")}}

HKEY_LOCAL_MACHINE\software\microsoft\Windows NT\CurrentVersion
SAPIEN Scripting Guru
PS HKLM:\software\microsoft> $errorActionPreference="Continue"
PS HKLM:\software\microsoft>
```

We first set our error action preference to "SilentlyContinue" so that all the errors about non-existing keys will be ignored. The main expression evaluates each result of the **dir** command:

```
PS HKLM:\software\microsoft> foreach ($item in dir . -recurse) {
```

If the result of the **GetValueNames()** method equals "RegisteredOwner", we'll return the item name as well as getting the value of the "RegisteredOwner" key using the **GetValue()** method:

```
>> if (($item.GetValueNames()) -eq "RegisteredOwner") {
>>$item.name;$item.GetValue("RegisteredOwner")}}
```

The result is the registry key and the value of the "RegisteredOwner" key. When finished we set our error action preference back to "Continue".

## Working with Remote Registries

To access remote registries, you need to use WMI and the StdReg provider:

```
$Reg = [WMIClass]"root\default:StdRegProv"
```

This will connect you to the local registry via WMI. We recommend you test things locally first. When you are ready, you can connect to a remote registry by specifying a computer name in the path:

```
$Reg = [WMIClass]\\Computername\root\default:StdRegProv
```

You must be running PowerShell with credentials that have administrative rights on the remote computer. There is no mechanism to specify alternate credentials.

Once you have this object, you can use its methods as shown in the following table:

**StdRegProv Class**

| Name | MemberType |
|---|---|
| Name | AliasProperty |
| CheckAccess | Method |
| CreateKey | Method |
| DeleteKey | Method |
| DeleteValue | Method |
| EnumKey | Method |

| Name | MemberType |
|---|---|
| EnumValues | Method |
| GetBinaryValue | Method |
| GetDWORDValue | Method |
| GetExpandedStringValue | Method |
| GetMultiStringValue | Method |
| GetStringValue | Method |
| SetBinaryValue | Method |
| SetDWORDValue | Method |
| SetExpandedStringValue | Method |
| SetMultiStringValue | Method |
| SetStringValue | Method |
| ConvertFromDateTime | ScriptMethod |
| ConvertToDateTime | ScriptMethod |
| CreateInstance | ScriptMethod |
| Delete | ScriptMethod |
| GetRelatedClasses | ScriptMethod |
| GetRelationshipClasses | ScriptMethod |
| GetType | ScriptMethod |
| Put | ScriptMethod |

You can get this same information by piping $reg to the **Get-Member** cmdlet.

To use the WMI object, almost all the methods will require you to specify a hive constant. Add these commands to your profile or any remote registry scripts:

```
$HKLM=2147483650
$HKCU=2147483649
$HKCR=2147483648
$HKEY_USERS=2147483651
```

Due to the WMI architecture and security, you cannot access the HKEY_CURRENT_USER hive on a remote machine. We've included it here for any PowerShell scripts you plan to run locally that will use WMI to access the registry. Most of your remote registry commands will use the constant for HKEY_LOCAL_MACHINE.

## Enumerating Keys

The **EnumKey()** method is used to enumerate registry keys, starting from a given key:

```
PS C:\> $reg.EnumKey($HKLM,"Software")


__GENUS          : 2
__CLASS          : __PARAMETERS
__SUPERCLASS     :
__DYNASTY        : __PARAMETERS
__RELPATH        :
__PROPERTY_COUNT : 2
__DERIVATION     : {}
__SERVER         :
```

```
__NAMESPACE     :
__PATH          :
ReturnValue     : 0
sNames          : {Acronis, ahead, Alps, ALPS Electric Co., Ltd....}
```

You need to specify the hive constant and the name of registry key. In this example, we are enumerating the keys directly in HKEY_LOCAL_MACHINE\Software. The returned values are stored as an array in the **sNames** property. Thus, a more complete way to enumerate the keys would be something like this:

```
PS C:\> foreach ($app in ($reg.EnumKey($HKLM,"Software")).sNames) {$app}
```

If you wanted to recurse through sub keys, you would need an enumeration function. We'll show you one later.

## Enumerating Values

To enumerate values for registry keys use the **EnumValues()** method:

```
PS C:\> $regpath="SOFTWARE\Microsoft\Windows\CurrentVersion\Run"
PS C:\> $values=$reg.EnumValues($HKLM,$RegPath)
PS C:\> foreach ($value in $values.sNames) {$value}
Apoint
NvCplDaemon
nwiz
Broadcom Wireless Manager UI
IntelliPoint
Windows Defender
SunJavaUpdateSched
TrueImageMonitor.exe
AcronisTimounterMonitor
Acronis Scheduler2 Service
GrooveMonitor
AVG7_CC
XFILTER
ProcExp
NWEReboot
NeroFilterCheck
QuickTime Task
iTunesHelper
PS C:\>
```

As with the **EnumKeys()** method, you need to specify a hive and registry path. The returned values are stored in the **sNames** property, which is why we enumerate them like an array.

In this particular example, we are returning the values of the registry keys in HKEY_LOCAL_MACHINE\ SOFTWARE\Microsoft\Windows\CurrentVersion\Run. The semantics Microsoft chose are a little misleading. Even though we're getting values for registry keys, we don't know the data associated with each key. In this example, the value may be sufficient. But what about something like this:

```
PS C:\> $regpath="SOFTWARE\Microsoft\Windows NT\CurrentVersion"
PS C:\> $values=$reg.EnumValues($HKLM,$RegPath)
PS C:\> foreach ($value in $values.sNames) {$value}
SubVersionNumber
CurrentBuild
InstallDate
ProductName
RegDone
```

```
RegisteredOrganization
RegisteredOwner
SoftwareType
CurrentVersion
CurrentBuildNumber
BuildLab
CurrentType
CSDVersion
SystemRoot
SourcePath
PathName
ProductId
DigitalProductId
LicenseInfo
PS C:\>
```

We need the associated data for each of these key values. The registry provider has several methods for getting key data. But you need to know what type of data is in each key. We'll show you one way to get the type information a little bit later.

In our example above, we know that all the data are strings, so we will use the **GetStringValue()** method:

```
PS C:\> foreach ($value in $values.sNames) {$value+" = '
>> "+$reg.GetStringValue($HKLM,$regpath,$value).sValue}
>>
SubVersionNumber =
CurrentBuild = 1.511.1 () (Obsolete data - do not use)
InstallDate =
ProductName = Microsoft Windows XP
RegDone =
RegisteredOrganization = SAPIEN Technologies
RegisteredOwner = Scripting Guru
SoftwareType = SYSTEM
CurrentVersion = 5.1
CurrentBuildNumber = 2600
BuildLab = 2600.xpsp_sp2_qfe.070227-2300
CurrentType = Uniprocessor Free
CSDVersion = Service Pack 2
SystemRoot = C:\WINDOWS
SourcePath = D:\I386
PathName = C:\WINDOWS
ProductId = 55274-770-4022292-22510
DigitalProductId =
LicenseInfo =
PS C:\>
```

The method requires the registry hive, the path, and the value to get:

```
"+$reg.GetStringValue($HKLM,$regpath,$value)
```

The code is getting each value and passing it to the **GetStringValue()** method. You could manually get the value for a single value like this:

```
PS C:\> $reg.GetStringValue($hklm,"software\microsoft\windows nt\currentversion",'
>>"RegisteredOwner")
```

```
__GENUS          : 2
```

```
__CLASS          : __PARAMETERS
__SUPERCLASS     :
__DYNASTY        : __PARAMETERS
__RELPATH        :
__PROPERTY_COUNT : 2
__DERIVATION     : {}
__SERVER         :
__NAMESPACE      :
__PATH           :
ReturnValue      : 0
sValue           : Scripting Guru
```

As before, the data is stored in the **sValue** property. That's why in our snippet we use:

```
>> "+$reg.GetStringValue($HKLM,$regpath,$value).sValue}
```

to return the data.

## Searching the Registry

To search the registry with WMI requires a little fancy footwork. You have to get each key and its values, then repeat the process for every sub key. We've put together a few functions to make this easier. The first function is used to enumerate a registry path:

```
Function Get-RegistryPath {

Param([Management.ManagementObject]$Reg,[int64]$Hive,[string]$regpath)
#Get-RegistryPath $reg $HKLM "Software\Microsoft\Windows NT\CurrentVersion"

#$reg must previously defined
#$Reg = [WMIClass]"root\default:StdRegProv"
# or
#$Reg = [WMIClass]"\\servername\root\default:StdRegProv"
#$Hive is a numeric constant
# $HKLM=2147483650
# $HKCU=2147483649

#get values in root of current registry key
 $values=$Reg.enumValues($Hive,$regpath)
 if ($values.snames.count -gt 0) {
    for ($i=0;$i -lt $values.snames.count;$i++) {
       $iType = $values.types[$i]
       $value = $values.snames[$i]
       Get-RegistryValue $Reg $Hive $regpath $value $iType
    }
 }

$keys=$Reg.EnumKey($Hive,$regpath)

# enumerate any sub keys
if ($keys.snames.count -gt 0) {
   foreach ($item in $keys.snames) {

       #recursively call this function
       Get-RegistryPath $Reg $hive "$regpath\$item"

   }
 }
}
```

The function takes parameters for the WMI registry object, the hive constant and the starting registry path:

```
Get-RegistryPath $reg $HKLM "Software\Microsoft\Windows NT\CurrentVersion"
```

The function calls another function which returns key data for any keys in the starting location. Then it enumerates any sub keys, and if the count is greater than 0, the function recurses and calls itself. In this way, the entire registry key is recursively enumerated. To get the data for each key, we'll use this function:

```
Function Get-RegistryValue {

Param([Management.ManagementObject]$Reg,[int64]$Hive,[string]$regitem,[string]$value,`
[int32]$iType)

#$reg must previously defined
#$Reg = [WMIClass]"root\default:StdRegProv"
# or
# $Reg = [WMIClass]"\\servername\root\default:StdRegProv"
# $Hive is a numeric constant
# $HKLM=2147483650
# $HKCU=2147483649

# $regitem is a registry path like "software\microsoft\windows nt\currentversion"
# $Value is the registry key name like "registered owner

# iType is a numeric value that indicates what type of data is stored in the key.
# Type 1 = String
# Type 2 = ExpandedString
# Type 3 = Binary
# Type 4 = DWord
# Type 7 = MultiString
# sample usage:
# $regPath="software\microsoft\windows nt\currentversion"
# $regKey="RegisteredOwner"
# Get-RegistryValue $reg $hklm $regPath $regKey 1

    $obj=New-Object System.Object

  switch ($iType) {
    1 {
        $data=($reg.GetStringValue($Hive,$regitem,$value)).sValue
    }
    2 {
        $data=($reg.GetExpandedStringValue($Hive,$regitem,$value)).sValue
    }
    3 {
        $data="Binary Data"
    }
    4 {
        $data=($reg.GetDWordValue($Hive,$regitem,$value)).uValue
    }
    7 {
        $data=($reg.GetMultiStringValue($Hive,$regitem,$value)).sValue
    }
    default {
        $data="Unable to retrieve value"
    }
  } #end switch
```

```
        Add-Member -inputobject $obj -membertype "NoteProperty" -name Key -value $value
        Add-Member -inputobject $obj -membertype "NoteProperty" -name KeyValue -value $data
        Add-Member -inputobject $obj -membertype "NoteProperty" -name RegPath -value $regitem
        Add-Member -inputobject $obj -membertype "NoteProperty" -name Hive -value $hive
        Add-Member -inputobject $obj -membertype "NoteProperty" -name KeyType -value $iType
        return $obj
}
```

This function requires a registry provider, hive constant, registry path, and key name and data type as parameters. These are passed from the Get-RegistryPath function:

```
$values=$Reg.enumValues($Hive,$regpath)
  if ($values.snames.count -gt 0) {
     for ($i=0;$i -lt $values.snames.count;$i++) {
        $iType = $values.types[$i]
        $value = $values.snames[$i]
        Get-RegistryValue $Reg $Hive $regpath $value $iType
     }
  }
```

The collection of values is checked to see if there are any. Assuming there are values, the collection is enumerated. The $values object actually has two properties. The **snames** property is every key name and the **types** property is the corresponding data type. The WMI registry provider doesn't have a good mechanism for discovering what type of data might be in a given key. So, we have to match up the data type with the key name. These values are then passed to the Get-RegistryValue function.

This function evaluates the data type with the **Switch** statement and uses the appropriate method to read the data. Binary data is skipped and a message is returned instead. We then use a custom object to return information. The advantage is that we can use these object properties in formatting the output:

```
PS C:\> Get-RegistryPath $reg $hklm "software\microsoft\windows nt\currentversion" |'
>> Select Key,Keyvalue,RegPath
>>
```

Or you can run a command like this:

```
PS C:\> Get-RegistryPath $reg $hklm "software\microsoft\windows nt\currentversion" | '
>> where {$_.key -match "registeredown
>>
```

Enumerating or searching the registry with WMI is a slow process and over the network to a remote computer will be even slower. But if this is your business requirement, don't expect blazing results.

## Modifying the Registry

Creating a registry key with the WMI provider is pretty simple.

```
PS C:\> $reg.CreateKey($HKCU,"PowerShellTFM")
```

This will create a key called "PowerShellTFM" under HKEY_CURRENT_USER. You can even create a hierarchy with one command:

```
PS C:\> $reg.CreateKey($HKCU,"PowerShellTFM\Key1\Key2")
```

The command will create Key1 and then Key2. What about adding values to keys? It depends on the type of data you need to store:

```
#create a string value
PS C:\> $reg.SetStringValue($HKCU,"PowerShellTFM\Key1","SampleKey","I am a string")

#create a dword
PS C:\> $reg.SetDWORDValue($HKCU,"PowerShellTFM\Key1","Sample Dword",1024)

#create an expanded string value
PS C:\> $reg.SetExpandedStringValue($HKCU,"PowerShellTFM\Key1\Key2",`
>> "Sample Expandable","%Username%")
>>

#create multistring value
PS C:\> $reg.SetMultiStringValue($HKCU,"PowerShellTFM\Key1\Key2",`
>> "Sample Multi",(get-content c:\file.txt))
>>
PS C:\>
```

When creating a multi-string value, you can't have any blank lines. The WMI method will let you insert blank lines, but when you edit the value with Regedit.exe, it will remove them. Make sure you have no blank lines to begin with, and you should be fine. In all cases, you can check the Return value to verify success. A value of 0 indicates the value was successfully written to the registry.

To delete a value, specify the hive, the registry path and the key name:

```
PS C:\> $reg.DeleteValue($HKCU,"PowerShellTFM\Key1","SampleKey")
```

To delete a key, specify the hive and key path:

```
PS C:\> $reg.DeleteKey($HKCU,"PowerShellTFM\Key1\Key2")
```

You delete a key with values, but you can't delete a key with sub keys. If we had used this command instead:

```
PS C:\> $reg.DeleteKey($HKCU,"PowerShellTFM\Key1")
```

you would get a return value of 5, which tells you there are sub keys that must be removed first. In this case, that would be Key2. So, to cleanly delete the keys, we would first need to remove Key2 and then remove Key1.

Working with remote registries via WMI is possible, but it is not the easiest management task you'll face. Write functions and scripts to make it a little , but don't expect snappy performance. Hopefully, future versions of PowerShell will provide better mechanisms for remote registry management.

# Chapter 31
# Managing Directory Services

As we described in earlier chapters, PowerShell's current support for ADSI is pretty minimal in the first version of PowerShell. PowerShell relies primarily on the .NET Framework DirectoryService classes. If you are familiar with these classes, you can work with them using the **New-Object** cmdlet:

```
$Root = New-Object DirectoryServices.DirectoryEntry 'LDAP://DC=company,dc=local'
```

However, the PowerShell team realized most administrators won't have experience programming in .NET, so they developed an ADSI type adapter, which we cover in more detail a bit later in the chapter. This type adapter abstracts the underlying .NET Framework classes and makes it a little bit easier to work with Active Directory objects.

Even though the ADSI type adapter is helpful, there are limitations. Fortunately, Quest Software has developed a free set of cmdlets for managing Active Directory users and computers. These cmdlets can create and modify basic objects, such as users, groups, and computers. We provide a brief overview on these cmdlets in the Quest Cmdlets for Active Directory Management section.

We've covered PSDrives earlier in the book. Wouldn't it be nice to mount your Active Directory store like any other file system? PowerShell does not ship with a directory services provider, but the free PowerShell Community Extensions includes one. When installed, it will create a new PSDrive that is mapped to the root of your Active Directory domain. You can then navigate Active Directory just like any other drive. This PSDrive provider is compatible with the Quest cmdlets.

Depending on your needs, there are several approaches to working with Active Directory without resorting to third-party extensions. We'll show you several example tasks in this chapter. After working with these examples, you'll realize how valuable the third-party extensions are.

# Working with the Directory via WMI

If your directory service management needs are simple, say you want to be able to find users, you can actually use WMI and the **Get-WmiObject** cmdlet to query Active Directory:

## GetLDAPUsers.ps1

```
#GetLDAPUsers.ps1

$user=read-host "What user credentials do you want to use for" `
"authentication to the" `n `
"domain controller? Use format domain\username."
$cred=get-credential $user
$server=read-host "What domain controller do you want to connect to?"

$rc=read-host "Do you also want to save output to a text file? [YN]"
if ($rc -eq "Y") {
$file=read-host "Enter the filename and path"
write-host "Connecting to" $server "as" $user
Get-WmiObject -class ds_user -namespace root\directory\ldap `
-computername $server -credential $cred | `
select-object DS_Name,DS_distinguishedname,DS_sAMAccountname |`
tee-object -file $file
}
else
{
write-host "Connecting to" $server "as" $user
Get-WmiObject -class ds_user -namespace root\directory\ldap `
-computername $server -credential $cred | `
select-object DS_Name,DS_distinguishedname,DS_sAMAccountname
}
```

This script connects to an Active Directory domain controller and returns a list of all user accounts including their distinguished name and down-level SAM account name. You have the option of saving the output to a text file.

The core of the script is the **Get-WmiObject** expression. For most other WMI-related scripts, we've used the root\cimv2 namespace. However, in this script, we're going to connect to the root\directory\ldap namespace on the specified server. In this namespace, we are looking for objects that belong to the ds_user class. Once we have these objects, we can use the **Select-object** cmdlet to return just the properties in which we are interested. This is what you get when you run the script:

```
What user credentials do you want to use for authentication to the
domain controller? Use format domain\username.:
mycompany\administrator
What domain controller do you want to connect to?: dc01
Do you also want to save output to a text file? [YN]: n
Connecting to dc01 as mycompany\administrator s

DS_Name                 DS_distinguishedname      DS_sAMAccountname
-------                 --------------------      -----------------
Administrator           CN=Administrator,CN=Use... Administrator
Guest                   CN=Guest,CN=Users,DC=my... Guest
SUPPORT_388945a0        CN=SUPPORT_388945a0,CN=... SUPPORT_388945a0
krbtgt                  CN=krbtgt,CN=Users,DC=m... krbtgt
__vmware_user__         CN=__vmware_user__,CN=U... __vmware_user__
svcSharepoint           CN=svcSharepoint,CN=Use... svcSharepoint
Joe Hacker              CN=Joe Hacker,OU=Testin... jhacker
Jane Cracker            CN=Jane Cracker,OU=Test... jcracker
```

```
ldog                CN=ldog,OU=Testing,DC=m... ldog
test user1          CN=test user1,OU=omaha,... tuser1
Test User2          CN=Test User2,OU=Testin... tuser2
Test User3          CN=Test User3,OU=Testin... tuser3
Test User4          CN=Test User4,OU=Testin... tuser4
Lucky Dog           CN=Lucky Dog,OU=home,DC... lucky
Steve McQueen       CN=Steve McQueen,OU=Tes... smqueen
Bill Shakespeare    CN=Bill Shakespeare,OU=... bills
azygot              CN=azygot,OU=Testing,DC... azygot


PS C:\>
```

If you're interested in all properties for a specific account, such as Administrator, or if you want to learn what user properties are available, you can use an expression like this:

```
Get-WmiObject -class ds_user -namespace root\directory\ldap `
>> "-computername MYDC -Credential (get-credential) | `
>> where {$_.dssAMAccountname -eq "Administrator"}
>>
```

# Working with Users by Using the [ADSI] Type Accelerator

If you want to do more than just build Active Directory reports in PowerShell, then you need to use the [ADSI] type accelerator. This feature allows you to create, modify, display, and delete Active Directory objects such as users, groups, and computers. In order to use the type accelerator, you need to know the distinguished name of the object.

```
PS C:\> $admin=[ADSI]"LDAP://CN=Administrator,CN=Users,DC=MyCo,DC=com"
PS C:\> $admin

distinguishedName
-----------------
{CN=Administrator,CN=Users,DC=MyCo,DC=com}


PS C:\> $admin.memberof
CN=UnrestrictedUsers,OU=home,DC=MyCo,DC=com
CN=Group Policy Creator Owners,CN=Users,DC=MyCo,DC=com
CN=Domain Admins,CN=Users,DC=MyCo,DC=com
CN=Enterprise Admins,CN=Users,DC=MyCo,DC=com
CN=Schema Admins,CN=Users,DC=MyCo,DC=com
CN=Administrators,CN=Builtin,DC=MyCo,DC=com

PS C:\> $admin.WhenChanged

Tuesday, October 17, 2006 2:38:28 AM
```

Piping $admin to **Get-Member** will list what appear to be all the available ADSI properties of the object. If you are familiar with ADSI, you'll realize that some properties are missing. **Get-Member** only displays properties with defined values. You can modify other properties as long as you already know the property name, which we'll show you later. One other important reminder is that when you create an object, the property values are stored in a local cache. If the object is modified in Active Directory, you won't see the changes locally unless you refresh the cache. Here's how we would do it with our previous example:

```
$admin.psbase.refreshcache()
```

We can also use the ADSI type accelerator to create an object in Active Directory. Take a look at CreateUser.ps1:

## CreateUser.ps1

```
#CreateUser.ps1
#specify the OU where you want to create the account
$OU=[ADSI] "LDAP://OU=Testing,DC=MyCo,DC=Local"

#using the ADSI type specifier
#Add the user object as a child to the OU
$newUser=$OU.Create("user","CN=Francis Bacon")
$newUser.Put("sAMAccountName","fbacon")
#commit changes to Active Directory
$newUser.SetInfo()
#set a password
$newUser.SetPassword("P@ssw0rd")
$newUser.SetInfo()
#Define some other user properties
$newUser.Put("DisplayName","Francis Bacon")
$newUser.Put("UserPrincipalName","Fbacon@MyCo.com")
$newUser.Put("GivenName","Francis")
$newUser.Put("sn","Bacon")
#enable account = 544
#disable account = 546
$newUser.Put("UserAccountControl","544")
$newUser.Put("Description","Created by PowerShell "`
+(get-date).ToString())

#commit changes to Active Directory
$newUser.SetInfo()
#flag the account to force password change at next logon
$newUser.Put("pwdLastSet",0)
$newUser.SetInfo()
```

Before you can create an object, you first must create an object for the parent container. In this example, we're using the Testing organizational unit. To create a new user object, we simply invoke the parent object's **Create()** method and specify the type of child object and its name:

```
$newUser=$OU.Create("user","CN=Francis Bacon")
```

To define properties, we'll use the **Put()** method. When you create a user account, you have to also define the sAMAccountname:

```
$newUser.Put("sAMAccountName","fbacon")
```

Before we can set any other properties, the object needs to be written from the local cache to Active Directory. This is accomplished by calling the **SetInfo()** method:

```
$newUser.SetInfo()
```

To set the user's password, there is a **SetPassword()** method that takes the new password as a parameter:

```
$newUser.SetPassword("P@ssw0rd")
```

Once this is accomplished, we can define some additional properties by using the **Put()** method, as you can see in the remainder of the script.

To modify an existing user, it is merely a matter of creating an ADSI user object and using the **Put()** method to define user attributes. Don't forget to call **SetInfo()**, or none of your changes will be committed to Active Directory.

```
PS C:\> $user=[ADSI]"LDAP://CN=Bill Shakespeare,OU=Testing,DC=MyCo,dc=local"
PS C:\> $user.put("Title","Playwright")
PS C:\> $user.Setinfo()
PS C:\> $user.Title
Playwright
PS C:\>
```

To delete a user, we create an object for the parent container, typically an organizational unit, then simply call the **Delete()** method:

```
PS C:\> $ou=[ADSI]"OU=SAPIEN,DC=MyCo,DC=local"
PS C:\> $ou.psbase.get_children()

distinguishedName
-----------------
{CN=SAPIEN Authors,OU=SAPIEN,DC=MyCo,DC=local}
{CN=Test User2,OU=SAPIEN,DC=MyCo,DC=local}
PS C:\> $ou.delete("user","CN=Test User2")
PS C:\>
```

There is no need in this situation to call **SetInfo()**. As soon as you invoke the **Delete()** method, the object is gone. You can use this method to delete any object. All you have to do is specify the object class and its name.

## Getting Password Age

The easiest way to obtain the password age for a user or a computer is to use the WinNT provider and look at the PasswordAge property:

```
PS C:\> $user=[ADSI]"WinNT://Company/aSample,user"
PS C:\> "{0:N0}" -f ($user.passwordage[0]/84600)
78
PS C:\>
```

The first step is to create an ADSI object for the user employing the WinNT provider. In this example, we are getting the user object for Ann Sample in the Company domain.

The password age is stored in the password property, but PowerShell returns it as a single element array. Therefore, we reference it with an index number of 0. The value is in seconds, so we divide it by 86400 to obtain the number of days and use the -f format operator to display it as a simple integer. As you can see, her password was last changed 78 days ago.

The password age for a computer account can be used to identify obsolete computer accounts. If the password has not changed in, say, 45 days, it is very likely the computer account is no longer active.

```
PS C:\> $server=[ADSI]"WinNT://company/NTFile07$"
PS C:\> "{0:N0}" -f ($user.passwordage[0]/84600)
368
```

```
PS C:\>
```

The only difference with this code, compared to the code for a user account, is that we must specify the sAMAccountname of the computer, which should be the computer's NetBIOS name appended with the $ sign. The remaining code is the same. In this example, it is very clear that server NTFile07 is likely obsolete and no longer in use, since its password age is over a year old.

## Deleting Users

Deleting a user is a very straightforward task. All you need is the distinguished name of the container or organizational unit and the Active Directory name of the user object:

```
PS C:\> $ou=[adsi]"LDAP://OU=employees,DC=company,dc=local"
PS C:\> $ou.Delete("user","CN=Sam Hamm")
```

The first line creates an ADSI object that represents the parent container—in this case, the Employees OU. The second line calls the **Delete()** method, which requires the type of object and its canonical name.

## Bulk-Creating Users

With a little extra effort, we can expand the previous example to create a group of users in bulk. The following script will create a group of users based on information stored in a comma-separated value file:

### Import Users from a CSV File

```
#Import-Users.ps1

$data="newusers.csv"
$imported=Import-Csv $data

#retrieve list of csv column headings
#Each column heading should correspond to an
#ADSI user property name

$properties=$imported |Get-Member -type noteproperty | `
where {$_.name -ne "OU" -and $_.name -ne "Password" `
-and $_.name -ne "Name" -and $_.name -ne "sAMAccountName"}

 for ($i=0;$i -lt $imported.count;$i++) {
   Write-Host "Creating User" $imported[$i].Name "in" $imported[$i].OU
   $OU=[ADSI]("LDAP://"+$imported[$i].OU)

   $newUser=$OU.Create("user","CN="+$imported[$i].Name)
   $newUser.Put("sAMAccountName",$imported[$i].samAccountname)
   #commit changes to Active Directory
   $newUser.SetInfo()
   #set a password
   $newUser.SetPassword($imported[$i].Password)
   $newUser.SetInfo()

      foreach ($prop in $properties) {
       #set additional properties
       $value=$imported[$i].($prop.name)
       if ($value.length -gt 0) {
          #only set properties that have values
```

```
            $newUser.put($prop.name,$value)
            }
        }

    $newUser.SetInfo()
}
```

Our script assumes the CSV file will have required column headings of OU, Name, sAMAccountname, and Password. The OU column will contain the distinguished name of the organizational unit where the new user account will be created, such as OU=Employees,DC=Company,DC=Local. The Name property will the user's Active Directory name and the sAMAccountname property will be the user's down-level logon name. You can have as many other entries as you want. Each column heading must correspond to an ADSI property name. For example, use "SN" for the user's last name and "GivenName" for the user's first name. The script begins by using the **Import-CSV** cmdlet to import the CSV file:

```
$data="newusers.csv"
$imported=Import-Csv $data
```

Because the CSV file will likely contain column headings for additional user properties, we'll create an object to store those property names. We'll exclude the required columns by selecting all property names that don't match the required names:

```
$properties=$imported | Get-Member -type noteproperty | `
where {$_.name -ne "OU" -and $_.name -ne "Password" `
-and $_.name -ne "Name" -and $_.name -ne "sAMAccountName"}
```

Armed with this information, we can now run through the list of new user information using **For**:

```
for ($i=0;$i -lt $imported.count;$i++) {
    Write-Host "Creating User" $imported[$i].Name "in" $imported[$i].OU
```

The object, $imported, is an array, so we can access each array member by using the array index. We'll first create an object for the OU where the user will be created, using the ADSI type adapter:

```
$OU=[ADSI]("LDAP://"+$imported[$i].OU)
```

Now we can create the new user by referencing the required imported user properties:

```
$newUser=$OU.Create("user","CN="+$imported[$i].Name)
$newUser.Put("sAMAccountName",$imported[$i].samAccountname)
#commit changes to Active Directory
$newUser.SetInfo()
```

At this point, we can add any other user properties that are defined in the CSV file. We accomplish this by enumerating the property list object:

```
    foreach ($prop in $properties) {
```

For each property name, we'll get the corresponding value from the current user:

```
    $value=$imported[$i].($prop.name)
```

For example, if the property name is Title, then $value will be set to the value of $imported[$i].Title. We put $prop.name in parentheses to instruct PowerShell to evaluate the expression, so that, in this example, it will return Title.

This script, as written, can only set single valued properties that accept strings. The script checks the length of $value. A length of 0 means there is no value and there's no reason to attempt to set the property. So, if the length of $value is greater than 0, we know there is a value, and we'll set the user property with it:

```
if ($value.length -gt 0) {
    #only set properties that have values
    $newUser.put($prop.name,$value)
    }
```

After all the properties have been set, we call the **SetInfo()** method to write the new information to Active Directory:

```
$newUser.SetInfo()
```

This process is repeated for every user imported from the CSV file.

## Working with Computers

Creating a new computer account is very similar to creating a new user account, and, in many ways, it's much easier because there are very few properties you have to define. Here's a function you can use to create a new computer account:

```
Function New-Computer {
Param([string]$name=$(Throw "You must enter a computer name."),
[string]$Path="CN=computers,DC=company,DC=Local",
[string]$description="Company Server",
[boolean]$enabled=$TRUE)

$OU=[ADSI]("LDAP://"+$Path)
$computer=$OU.Create("computer","CN=$name")
$computer.Put("SamAccountName",$name)
$computer.put("Description",$description)
if ($enabled) {
    $computer.Put("UserAccountControl",544)
    } else {
    $computer.Put("UserAccountControl",546)
}

$computer.SetInfo()

}
```

The function requires the name of the new computer object and, optionally, the organizational unit path, a description, and whether or not the account should be enabled. Default values are specified for the optional parameters:

```
Function New-Computer {
Param([string]$name=Throw("You must enter a computer name."),
[string]$Path="CN=computers,DC=company,DC=Local",
[string]$description="Company Server",
```

```
[boolean]$enabled=$TRUE)
```

The function creates an ADSI object for the OU or container where you want to create the computer object.

```
$OU=[ADSI]("LDAP://"+$Path)
```

The function next creates the computer object in the container specifying the Active Directory name and the sAMAccountname.

```
$computer=$OU.Create("computer","CN=$name")
$computer.Put("SamAccountName",$name)
```

The description is defined:

```
$computer.put("Description",$description)
```

By default, the computer account is enabled, but if specified it can be disabled. The UserAccountControl property defines this setting:

```
if ($enabled) {
    $computer.Put("UserAccountControl",544)
    } else {
    $computer.Put("UserAccountControl",546)
}
```

Finally, we call the **Setinfo()** method to write the new account to the Active Directory database:

```
$computer.SetInfo()
```

## Delete Computer Accounts

Deleting a computer is essentially the same as with user accounts. All you need are the distinguished name of the container or organizational unit and the Active Directory name of the computer object:

```
PS C:\> $ou=[adsi]"LDAP://OU=Desktops,DC=company,dc=local"
PS C:\> $ou.Delete("computer","CN=XPDesk81")
```

The first line creates an ADSI object that represents the parent container—in this case ,the Desktops OU. The second line calls the **Delete()** method, which requires the type of object and its canonical name.

# Working with Groups

Creating a group is very similar to creating a user:

```
PS C:\> $OU=[ADSI]"LDAP://OU=SAPIEN,DC=MyCo,dc=local"
PS C:\> $newGroup=$OU.Create("group","CN=SAPIEN Authors")
PS C:\> $newGroup.Put("sAMAccountName","SAPIEN-Authors")
PS C:\> $newGroup.Put("Description","Contract Writers")
```

```
PS C:\> $newGroup.SetInfo()
PS C:\>
```

Modifying group membership is not especially difficult. If you are familiar with this task in ADSI, it's not too different conceptually in PowerShell. As with ADSI, you need a DirectoryEntry object for the group. You also need to know the distinguished name of the user object you want to add. Armed with that information, it's a matter of adding the user's distinguished name to the object's Member property. Here's a script that demonstrates how to modify group membership:

### AddToGroup.ps1

```
#AddToGroup.ps1

$Grp=[ADSI]"LDAP://CN=SAPIEN Authors,OU=SAPIEN,DC=MyCo,DC=local"
$NewUserDN="CN=Bill Shakespeare,OU=Testing,DC=MyCo,DC=local"

#create an array object from current group members
$grpMembers=@($Grp.Member)

#display current group membership
Write-Host "There are currently" $grpMembers.Count "members in" $Grp.Name
foreach ($user in $grpMembers) {$user}

Write-Host `n; Write-Host "Adding" $NewUserDN
($grp.Member).add($NewUserDN) > $NULL

#commit changes to Active Directory
$Grp.SetInfo()

#refresh object and display new membership list
$Grp.psbase.refreshCache()
$grpMembers=@($grp.Member)

#display new membership
Write-Host "There are now" $grpMembers.Count "members in" $grp.Name
foreach ($user in $grpMembers) {
 if ($user -eq $NewUserDN) {
 write-Host -foregroundcolor Green $user
 }
 else
 {
 write-Host $user
 }
}
```

This script creates an ADSI object for the SAPIEN Authors group and also creates an object for the current membership list that is displayed using **ForEach**. Adding the new user appears a little confusing at first:

```
($grp.Member).add($NewUserDN) > $NULL
```

What we need to do is to call the **Add()** method for the group's Member property, which is a collection, and specify the user's distinguished name. By the way, if we wanted to nest another group, we would specify that group's distinguished name. The reason we redirect output to $Null is purely cosmetic. Without the redirection, the expression returns the number of members currently in the group. In the course of running the script, displaying that number here serves no purpose and is distracting. We eliminate it by redirecting any output to $Null.

None of this work means anything until we commit the change to Active Directory using **SetInfo()**. The script finishes by refreshing the local cache and listing its new members, indicating the new user in a green font.

## Moving Objects

PowerShell and the .NET Framework use a slightly different method for moving objects in Active Directory. You should be able to call the **MoveTo()** method like this:

```
PS C:\> $obj=[ADSI]"LDAP://CN=Desk61,CN=Computers,DC=company,dc=local"
PS C:\> $obj.MoveTo([ADSI]"LDAP://OU=Desktops,DC=Company,dc=local")
```

All you have to do is specify the container where the object should be moved to. However, this code does not appear to work in the current version of PowerShell. PowerShell abstracts the .NET classes, but, in this situation, there appears to be a bug in the process. At some point, we expect this to be corrected, and then you can use code like this.

In the mean time, the Active Directory provider in the PowerShell Community Extensions can be used to move objects. Because the provider allows you to navigate your Active Directory domain as if it were a file system, you can use the **Move** command much the same way you would move a file:

```
PS COMPANY:\computers> move XPDesk02 company:\desktops
```

We discuss the PowerShell Community Extensions in more detail in the section, PowerShell Community Extensions.

## WinNT:// Provider

Even though we've been showing you how to use the ADSI type with the LDAP:// provider and Active Directory, it will also work with the WinNT:// provider. You can use this provider if you want a flat view of your domain or if you are working with member servers and desktops.

### ListWinNT.ps1

```
#ListWinNT.ps1
$member=[ADSI]"WinNT://MyServer"
 foreach ($item in $member.psbase.children) {
 if ($item.psbase.schemaclassname -eq "user") {
  Write-Host $item.Name
 }
 }
```

This script will list every object that is of the user schema class and display the user name. If MyServer is a member workstation, it will list local user accounts. If you substitute MyServer with the flat name of your domain, you will get a list of all user accounts, regardless of what organizational unit they might belong to. The displayed name will be the sAMAccountname.

## Searching for Users

We'll wrap up this chapter by showing you how easy it is to search in Active Directory with PowerShell. Because PowerShell is based on .NET, it can create a DirectorySearcher object using the **New-Object** cmdlet. Here's a short script that will return the distinguished name of every user account in an Active Directory domain:

## SearchForAllUsers.ps1

```
#SearchForAllUsers.ps1
$searcher=New-object DirectoryServices.DirectorySearcher
$searcher.Filter="(&(objectcategory=person)(objectclass=user))"
$users=$searcher.FindAll()
#display the number of users
Write-Host "There are "$users.count"users in this domain."
#display each user's distinguishedname
foreach ($user in $users) {
 Write-Host $user.properties.distinguishedname
}
```

After the Directory Searcher object is created, we define a search filter. The filter is an LDAP query string. In this case, we want to find all objects that are basically user accounts. The Directory Searcher has two methods you are most likely to use: **FindAll()** and **FindOne()**. The former will return all objects that match the query, and the latter will only return the first one it finds. In this script, we create a new object to hold the query results. We can then use the **For-Each** cmdlet to display the distinguishedname property of each user in the result collection.

........................................................................................................................................

### Fun with LDAP Filters
You don't have to have extensive knowledge about LDAP to build a complex query. If you are running Windows 2003, you already have a tool that will do it for you. In Active Directory Users and Computers, there is a Saved Queries feature. When you create a query, an LDAP query string is generated. All you need to do is copy the string and use it as the directory searcher filter. For example, we created a saved query to find all disabled users that created a LDAP query string of (&(objectCategory = person) (objectClass = user) (userAccountControl:1.2.840.113556.1.4.803: = 2)). When we substitute this string for the filter in SearchForAllUsers.ps1, we get a list of every disabled user. The tool is pretty powerful and can create some very complex query strings. Now, you can also use them in your PowerShell scripts.

There is a subtle but important fact to remember when using the Directory Searcher object. The objects returned by the query aren't really the Active Directory objects but are more like pointers. The search result can give you some property information like distinguishedname, but if you want more specific object information, you need to get the object itself. This script is slightly modified from SearchForAllUsers.ps1:

## SearchForAllUsersAdvanced.ps1

```
#SearchForAllUsersAdvanced.ps1
$searcher=New-object DirectoryServices.DirectorySearcher
$searcher.Filter="(&(objectcategory=person)(objectclass=user))"
$users=$searcher.FindAll()
#display the number of users
Write-Host "There are "$users.count"users in this domain."
foreach ($user in $users) {
 foreach ($user in $users) {
 $entry= $user.GetDirectoryEntry()
 $entry |Select displayname,samaccountname,description,distinguishedname
 }
```

}

In the **ForEach** loop, we create a new object called $entry by invoking the **GetDirectoryEntry()** method of the object that was returned by the query. This object gives us access to all the properties in Active Directory. In this script, we selected to show DisplayName, sAMAccountName,Description, and DistinguishedName. When executed we get a result like this:

```
displayname           samaccountname      description           distinguishedname
-----------           --------------      -----------           -----------------
{Administrator} {Administrator} {Built-in ac...   {CN=Administrat..
{Joe Hacker}      {jhacker}       {Another test user} CN=Joe Hacker...
{Jane Cracker}   {jcracker}       {Test user}       {CN=Jane Crack...
{Bill Shakespeare}{bills}          {Sample User Acc...{CN=Bill Shake...
{}                {azygot}        {}                {CN=azygot,OU=...
{Jack W. Frost} {jfrost}          {TFM}             {CN=Jack Frost...
{Francis Bacon} {fbacon}          {Created by Pow... {CN=Francis Ba...
```

We mentioned that the directory searcher also has a **FindOne()** method. This is very useful when you know there is only one result, such as finding the distinguishedname of a user when all you know is the user's sAMAccountname.

## FindUserDN.ps1

```
#FindUserDN.ps1
$sam=Read-Host "What user account do you want to find?"
$searcher=New-Object DirectoryServices.DirectorySearcher
$searcher.Filter="(&(objectcategory=person)(objectclass=user)"`
+"(sAMAccountname="+$sam+"))"
$results=$searcher.FindOne()
if ($results.path.length -gt 1)
 {write-host $results.path}
else
 {write-host "User" $sam "was not found."}
```

This script is very similar to the other searching scripts. The primary difference is that the search filter is looking for user objects where the sAMAccountname is equal to a value specified by the user with the **Read-Host** cmdlet. Since we know there will only be one result, the searcher can stop as soon as it finds a match. We've added some error checking in the script. If a match was found, then the length of the path property will be greater than one, so we can display it. Otherwise, there is no path, which means no match was found, and so we can display a message to that effect.

The ADSI type accelerator is really just a wrapper for .NET directory service objects. It hides a lot of the underlying functionality. You can create PowerShell scripts that directly create and manipulate the .NET objects, but in our opinion that process is more like systems programming than scripting. We believe you'll find it much easier to manage Active Directory with the free third-party snap-ins from Quest Software and the PowerShell Community Extensions.

---

**Read More About It**
The MSDN documentation for the .NET directory service objects and the System.
DirectoryServices.Namespace can be found at: http://msdn2.microsoft.com/en-us/library/system.
directoryservices(vs.80).aspx.

# Part IV

# Advanced Windows PowerShell

# Chapter 32
# Scope in Windows PowerShell

In the chapter "Scripting Overview," we touched on the concept of scope in PowerShell. In that chapter, we were primarily concerned with variables and functions, the two elements of PowerShell where scope is of most concern. But scope in PowerShell is much more flexible and functional than we let on in that earlier chapter, so we're taking the time in this chapter to explain it in all its gory detail.

First, the term *scope* is defined in the dictionary as "extent or range of view, outlook, application, effectiveness, etc." That's a good definition for our purposes, because PowerShell's scope does define the range of effectiveness for a number of elements, including variables, functions, aliases, and more.

## Types of Scope

PowerShell starts with one top-level scope: The *global* scope. This is the only scope that is not contained within any other scope; you can think of it as the ultimate "parent" scope, or the "root" scope. The command line itself exists within the global scope, and any variables, PSDrives, aliases, or functions that you define interactively all exist in the global scope.

Whenever you run a script, a new scope is created to contain the script. This *script scope* is a child of the scope that ran the script. In other words, if you run a script in the global scope, the new script scope is a child of the global scope. If one script runs another, then the second script's scope is a child of the first script's scope, and so forth. It's essentially a hierarchy, not unlike the file system's hierarchy of folders and subfolders.

The inside of a function, script block, or filter is a private scope as well, and it is a child of whatever scope contains it. A function within a script has a scope which is a child of the script's scope—again, similar to the hierarchy of folders on the file system.

## Scope-Aware Elements

Several elements of PowerShell are scope-aware:

- Variables

- Functions

- Aliases

- PSDrives

Those last two may be surprising, but, in fact, you can define an alias within a script—which has its own scope—and that alias *will exist only within that scope*. This plays directly into PowerShell's scoping rules, which we'll discuss next.

## Scope Rules

PowerShell's rules regarding scopes are simple: When you try to access an element, PowerShell first looks to see if it's defined in the current scope. If it is, then you'll be able to access it for both reading and writing—meaning you'll be able to *use* the element and *change* the element, if desired.

If the specified element isn't available in the current scope, then PowerShell starts looking up the hierarchy, starting with the parent of the current scope, then its parent, then its parent, and so forth, up to the top-level global scope. If the specified element is found at some point, then you'll have access to *use* it, but not *change* it—at least, not without using a special technique. A simple script is probably the easiest way to illustrate this:

```
function test1 {
  write-host $example    # line 2
  $example = "Two"       # line 3
  write-host $example    # line 4
}

$example = "One"         # line 7
Write-host $example       # line 8
test1                    # line 9
write-host $example       # line 10
```

This produces the following output:

```
One
One
Two
One
```

On line 7, the value "One" is placed into the variable $example. Line 8 writes this, resulting in the first line of output. Line 9 then calls the function, which is a new scope. Line 2 writes the current value of $example. This variable doesn't exist in the function's scope, so PowerShell looks up one scope to the function's parent, which is the script itself. The $example variable is found, and line 2 outputs it—resulting in our second line of output. Line 3 changes the value of the $example variable. However, by default a scope cannot *change* elements from its parent. Therefore, PowerShell creates a *new* $example variable *within the current scope*. Line 4 attempts to access $example, and *now* it does exist in the current scope, resulting in our third line of output. With the function complete, we execute line 10. Our last line of output is "One," because that's still the value of $example *within the current scope*. Parent scopes—the script, in this case—cannot "see" inside their child scopes; they cannot see the function.

*The same thing applies to functions, aliases, and PSDrives.* Here's another example:

```
function test1 {
 new-psdrive Z filesystem c:\test
 dir z:
}

test1
dir Z:
```

Try running this (assuming you have a folder named C:\Test). The function maps a new drive, Z:, to the C:\Test folder, and gets a directory listing. After the function exits, the script tries to get a directory listing of Z:, and fails because the Z: mapping *only exists* inside the function's scope.

Aliases work the same way:

```
function test1 {
 new-alias plist get-process
 plist
}

test1
plist
```

Again, the function defines a new alias and then uses it; the script is unable to use that alias because the alias definition only exists within the function's scope.

## Specifying Scope

When you look at these four elements—functions, aliases, PSDrives, and variables—you'll find that three of them have specific cmdlets used to create new elements:

- **New-Alias** is used to create new aliases.

- **New-Variable** is used to create new variables.

- **New-PSDrive** is used to create new PSDrives.

Each of these three cmdlets supports a **-scope** parameter, which allows you to create a new element *in a scope other than the current one*. The **Set-Variable** cmdlet, which allows you to change an existing variable, also has a **-scope** parameter, which allows you to change the value of a variable in a scope other than the current one.

> **By the Way...**
> Other cmdlets used to deal with aliases, variables, and PSDrives also support a **-scope** parameter, such as **Remove-Alias** and **Get-PSDrive**.

All of these -**scope** parameters can accept one of several values:

- "Global" references the global scope.

- "Script" references the first script that is a parent of the current scope.

- "Local" references the current scope.

- A numeric value, with 0 representing the current scope, 1 representing the current scope's parent, and so forth.

As a general rule, it's considered a poor practice to have one scope modify anything in its parent or parents. That's because, as an element—such as a script or function—is moved around and re-used in different ways, you can't be sure what the state of the parent scope will be. Modifying a parent scope involves a risk that you'll impact some other process or operation. However, sometimes it's necessary, which is why the -**scope** parameter exists. For example, to create a function that defines a new alias in the global scope, you'd do something like this:

```
Function test1 {
 New-Alias plist get-process -scope global
}
```

Or, to change the value of a global variable named $example:

```
Set-Variable $example "New Value" -scope global
```

Variables provide a shortcut reference, which may be easier to remember:

```
$global:example = "New Value"
```

Again, the keywords Global, Local, and Script can all be used with this syntax.

# Best Practices for Scope

As we've already mentioned, avoid modifying parent scopes unless there's absolutely no other way to accomplish what you need. Functions are a good example: A function should *never* do this:

```
Function example {
 $script:var = "New Value"
}

$var = "Old value"
example
```

Why? Well, for one, if this function is ever re-used in a different script, $var might not be the right variable name. By tying the function to this script, we've limited the function's reusability. Instead, functions should output their return values or collections:

```
Function example {
 return "New Value"
}

$var = "Old value"
$var = example
```

This way, the function can be easily dropped into any script, or even the global shell, and used safely.

Our second recommendation is to *always* assign a value to a variable before using it in the current scope. Consider this sample function:

```
Function sample {
 $var = $input1 + $input2
 Return $var
}
```

What will the function return? Well, we've no idea—it depends on what $input1 and $input2 contain. The script that this function lives in might have defined those variables, or it might not have. Instead, use variables only after they've been explicitly assigned a value in the current scope:

```
Function sample {
 $input1 = 1
 $input2 = 2
 $var = $input1 + $input2
 Return $var
}
```

Or, in the case of a function, define them as input arguments with default values:

```
Function sample ($input1 = 1, $input2 = 2) {
 $var = $input1 + $input2
 Return $var
}
```

This ensures that the function won't "pick up" a variable from a parent scope by accident. Another way to look at this best practice is that functions should *never* rely on a variable from a parent scope. If information needs to be used inside of a function, pass it into the function via arguments. So, the only way data gets *in* a function is via arguments, and the only way data gets *out* of a function is by being returned from the function. This makes functions self-contained and self-reliant, and you won't need to worry about their parent scope.

## Dot Sourcing

*Dot sourcing* is a clever technique that tells PowerShell to execute something—usually a script—in the current scope, rather than creating a new scope. For example, consider the following script, which we'll pretend is named Sample.ps1:

```
New-Alias PList Get-Process
PList
```

This simple script defines a new alias and then uses it. Just run this script:

```
PS C:\> test\sample
```

The alias is defined, executed, and then the script scope is discarded when the script ends, so the alias no longer exists. However, if you *dot source* the script:

```
PS C:\> . test\sample
```

Now the script runs *without creating a new scope.* Since it was run from the shell, which is the global scope, the script's commands all execute within the global scope. Now the PList alias will *remain* defined after the script runs, because the **New-Alias** cmdlet was executed within the global scope.

Dot-sourcing can be a useful technique for "including" a script library file. For example, suppose you have a script file named Library.ps1, which contains a function named Ping-Computer. You can easily reuse that across multiple scripts. Here's an example of a script that "includes" Library.ps1:

```
# include library functions
. path\library

# use library function
Ping-computer localhost
```

The script shown *dot sources* Library.ps1, so Library.ps1 executes in *this script's scope,* rather than launching in a new child scope. Therefore, everything defined in Library.ps1, including the Ping-Computer function, is now defined inside this script's scope, making those functions available for use. PowerShell doesn't include a dedicated "include" statement simply because dot-sourcing provides that functionality already.

**By the Way...**
PowerShell follows its execution policy when dot-sourcing scripts. For example, if we had located Library.ps1 on a network folder and accessed it via a UNC path, then Library.ps1 would have to be digitally signed *and* the execution policy in PowerShell would need to be set to RemoteSigned. If both of those conditions weren't true, PowerShell would pause the script execution and prompt you for permission to run Library.ps1.

# Nested Prompts

Earlier, we introduced you to the concept of nested prompts. A nested prompt exists *in the same scope as it was created*. In other words, imagine we have a script like this:

```
Function Test1 {
        $var = 3
        Function Test2 {
                $var = 5
                $host.EnterNestedPrompt()
        }
        Test2
}
$var = 1
Test1
```

When we run this, $var is set to 1, and function Test1 is called. It sets $var to 3, creating a new $var in this scope, and calls Test2. Test2 sets $var to 5, creating yet another version of $var in the local scope. Test2 then opens a nested prompt. If, within that nested prompt, we examined the value of $var, we would find it to be 5:

```
PS C:\> test\demo1
PS C:\>>> $var
5
PS C:\>>> exit
PS C:\>
```

This behavior ensures that nested prompts remain a useful debugging technique: The nested prompt exists *within* the scope in which the prompt is called, so it has access to all of that scope's PSDrives, variables, aliases, functions, and so forth.

# Tracing Complicated Nested Scopes

Dealing with scopes can become complicated when they're very deeply nested—in fact, that complication is just one more reason to observe our two main best practices: Don't use one scope to mess with another, and don't use variables without assigning them a value inside the current scope. Consider the following example, and assume that the script Library.ps1 (referred to in the example) contains a function named Four:

```
function One {
   $var1 = "One"

        function Two {
      $var2 = "Two"
```

```
            function Three {
    $var3 = "Three"
                    test/ExternalScript
                    . test/Library
            }

            $host.EnterNestedPrompt()
        }
    }
}
$var = "Zero"
```

Here are some statements regarding this code:

- The variable $var exists in the script scope, which is a child of the global scope.

- The variable $var2 exists in the scope of function Two, which is a child of function One, which is a child of the script, which is a child of the global scope—that means $var2 is four levels deep.

- Function Four, which we said is defined inside Library.ps1, exists five levels deep: It was dot-sourced into function Three. Inside function Four is a new scope, which is six levels deep.

- ExternalScript is running in its own scope, because it wasn't dot-sourced. The script scope for ExternalScript is six levels deep: It's a child of function Three, which is a child of function Two, which is a child of function One, which is a child of the script, which is a child of the global scope.

- Function Two creates a nested prompt, which is in the same scope—four levels deep—as function Two itself.

PowerShell doesn't provide any built-in means of determining how deeply nested the current scope is, so you have to pay close attention to scopes as you're writing and working with scripts. You have to remember the rules for scope use and dot-sourcing, and keep track of these things—on a piece of paper, if necessary!

# Chapter 33
# Working with COM Objects

Just because PowerShell is based on the .NET Framework doesn't mean you can't use older Component Object Model (COM) components in your scripts. For example, using **Add-PSDrive** to map a network drive in PowerShell *doesn't* add the drive mapping to Windows Explorer; you can, however, still use the WshNetwork COM component to perform this task. You'll use the **New-Object** cmdlet to instantiate the COM component, and then call its methods or access it properties much as you may have done in VBScript or some other language. Here's an example:

```
PS C:\> $network = new-object -com "WScript.Network"
PS C:\> $network.MapNetworkDrive("z:","\\localhost\c$")
PS C:\> z:
PS Z:\>
```

You'll need to know the unique ProgID ("WScript.Network," in this case) of the COM component you want to use. You'll notice that PowerShell's tab completion (which we covered in the "Practical Tips and Tricks" chapter) works for many COM components as well.

**Oops...**
Don't forget to add the **-comObject** parameter to **New-Object** (we've used a shortened version of the parameter name). If you do forget, **New-Object** won't work properly.

There's an incredible amount of trickery going on under the hood when PowerShell instantiates a COM component, and it can get complicated. For example, sometimes a COM component has what's called an *interop assembly,* which is a special .NET assembly that connects complex COM components to the

.NET Framework—and, thus, to PowerShell. Other COM components don't have an interop assembly available. Sometimes, when you try to instantiate a COM component that *does* have an interop assembly, PowerShell winds up "connected" to that interop assembly, and not the actual COM component, which means you won't have access to the properties and methods you need.

To force PowerShell to throw an error in this condition, you can add the **-strict** parameter to **New-Object**:

```
PS C:\> $network = new-object -com "WScript.Network" -strict
```

This way, if PowerShell "sees" an interop assembly, an exception will be raised that you can trap (read the "Error Handling" chapter for details), and your script will "know" that it has to work differently. This particular error still returns the COM component, but lets you know that you might have to take different steps to use it, because you'll actually be working with the interop wrapper. This technique is especially important when you're deploying a script to different machines. Some machines may have an interop assembly for your COM component, while other machines might not; the **-strict** parameter lets your script detect machines that do have an interop assembly and at least fail somewhat more gracefully.

Working with COM components can be frustrating sometimes, because in many cases, the COM components don't expose the full functionality available from a given piece of Windows. For example, the WshNetwork object gives you access to the current computer, user, and domain name, but not the site name or forest name. For that information, you'll have to use a different COM component, ADSysInfo. *That* component, however, won't map drives—you'll still need WshNetwork for that. So, COM scripting becomes a patchwork exercise, an exercise that PowerShell was actually designed to improve, actually, by having *all* functionality exposed through cmdlets. Until that happy day arrives, however, we're left with COM for many tasks.

A complete review of all the COM components available in Windows is far beyond the scope of this book—there are literally thousands. However, Bruce Payette's book, *Windows PowerShell in Action* (we're firm believers that you can't have too many PowerShell books), provides a number of fun examples for using COM to automate Internet Explorer, Windows Explorer, Microsoft Word, and other common applications. You can also pick up a copy of Don Jones' *VBScript, WMI, and ADSI Unleashed* (SAMS), which covers a number of COM components that are useful for scripting.

Finally, don't forget that if you want to learn more about a particular COM object, after you've created it in PowerShell, pipe the object to **Get-Member**. Most of the properties should be self-explanatory.

# Practical Examples of Using COM

We'd like to share a few valuable COM components that you may have use for in your administrative scripts. None of these examples are long or complicated, which means you can put them to use right away.

## Mapping Network Drives and Printers

When you use **New-PSDrive** to add a mapped drive—that is, a local drive mapped to a shared folder—to the shell, you're *only* adding that mapped drive to PowerShell. It won't show up in Windows Explorer at all, which means **New-PSDrive** isn't such a good technique for mapping drives in a logon script. But you do have two alternatives: First, you could simply run **Net Use**, the same command you'd run in Cmd.exe to map a drive. Or, you could use a COM object:

```
PS C:\> $net = new-object -com "WScript.Network"
$net.MapNetworkDrive("Z:\","\\Server\Share")
```

This is essentially the same thing you'd do to accomplish this task in VBScript, which brings up an excellent point: *PowerShell can do many of the same things as a VBScript, in the exact same way*. So, you don't necessarily have to learn a new technique for everything; while the "VBScript way" might not be the most efficient use of PowerShell, many times it'll still work.

## Accessing Local Domain, Site, Forest, and Logon Information

This is another task example where PowerShell doesn't contribute a lot of specific functionality, but where an old VBScript-style technique can address the problem perfectly. For example, to access the name of the local computer, the logged-on user, or the user's logon domain, do this:

```
PS C:\> $net = new-object -com "WScript.Network"
PS C:\> $net.UserName
JJones
PS C:\> $net.UserDomain
SAPIEN
PS C:\>$net.ComputerName
XPDESK02
PS C:\>
```

The WScript.Network object, however, is relatively old, and doesn't provide Active Directory-specific information. The ADSysInfo COM object could help with that; however, the object appears to be lacking a means of interoperating with the .NET framework. You can get this COM object to work in PowerShell, but it's frankly not worth the effort. This is another reminder that not all COM objects are readily usable in PowerShell.

## Automating Internet Explorer

One of our favorite uses for COM is to pop up an Internet Explorer window and direct it to a particular Web site. For example, if your company has an intranet Web server, you could post a "message of the day" Web page there. Then, in a PowerShell logon script, you could pop up Internet Explorer and navigate it to that page each time a user logs on. It's a great way to convey important information. Here's how to do it from the PowerShell command line:

```
PS C:\> $ie = new-object -com "InternetExplorer.Application"
PS C:\> $ie.navigate("www.microsoft.com")
PS C:\> $ie.visible = $true
```

Of course, doing this in a script uses exactly the same commands.

## Controlling an Interactive Character

This is another fun trick that might find its way into a logon script you write. PowerShell architect Jeffrey Snover uses this at the beginning of his talks on Windows PowerShell, and it's very attention-getting! The idea is to instantiate a Microsoft Agent character—a little cartoon person not unlike the old Office Assistant characters—and get it to say something. Here's how to do it:

```
PS C:\> $agent = new-object -com "Agent.Control.2"
PS C:\> $agent.connected = $true
PS C:\> $character = join-path $env:windir "msagent\chars\merlin.acs"
```

```
PS C:\> [void]$agent.characters.load("merlin",$character)
PS C:\> $merlin = $agent.characters.item("merlin")
PS C:\> $action = $merlin.moveto(100,100)
PS C:\> $action = $merlin.show()
PS C:\> $action= $merlin.speak("Hello, there, everybody!")
PS C:\> $action = $merlin.hide()
PS C:\> $agent.connected = $false
```

You can use the agent's **MoveTo()**, **Show()**, **Hide()**, and **Speak()** methods to control it. Notice that each of these methods returns a status code, which is why we've assigned the result of the method to the $action variable—we don't *need* the status code, but if we don't put it into a variable, PowerShell will try and display it. Merlin is the only character we found on our Windows Vista computer; Robbie the Robot, Peedy the Parrot, and Genie characters might be available on your system—check the folder we referenced above for the appropriate .ACS files.

## Making Your Computer Talk

In the previous example, we showed you an example of controlling Microsoft Agent, an interactive character that includes speech synthesis capabilities. But what if you *just* want the speech, without the cartoon character? No problem:

```
PS C:\> $voice = new-object -com "SAPI.SPVoice"
PS C:\> $voice.speak("This PowerShell stuff rocks!")
```

Feed it any text you like, and it'll say it. Not always the best pronunciation, perhaps, but usually comprehensible.

# Issues with COM in PowerShell

COM is not completely trouble-free when used in PowerShell. For one, not every COM component can be successfully adapted into PowerShell; sometimes, you'll have to figure out some strange techniques in order to get things to work properly. This is primarily due to the way the .NET Framework deals with COM components—that is, not always very well.

COM component threading also causes some issues. PowerShell is what's called a *multi-threaded apartment* application, or MTA application. Many COM components won't work unless the application using them is *single-threaded*, or STA, so the PowerShell COM adapter basically tries to fake it if need be. There's a workaround for COM components that don't work properly because of this threading issue, but it essentially requires .NET programming, and it's pretty hardcore, and frankly we don't understand it very well—it's a bit beyond the purview of a systems administrator.

Chapter 34
# Working with XML Documents

PowerShell has a very powerful and intuitive way of allowing you to work with complex XML documents. Essentially, PowerShell *adapts* the structure of the XML document itself into an object hierarchy, so that working with the XML document becomes as easy as referring to object properties and methods.

## What PowerShell Does with XML

When PowerShell converts text into XML, it parses the XML's document hierarchy and constructs a parallel object model. For example, take the following XML document (which you can type into a text file that has an XML filename extension):

```
<Pets>
 <Pet>
 <Breed>Ferret</Breed>
 <Age>3</Age>
 <Name>Patch</Name>
 </Pet>
 <Pet>
 <Breed>Bulldog</Breed>
 <Age>5</Age>
 <Name>Chesty</Name>
 </Pet>
</Pets>
```

You can load that XML into PowerShell as follows:

```
PS C:\> [xml]$xml = get-content c:\pets.xml
```

PowerShell then constructs the object hierarchy. For example, you could access the breed of the first pet as follows:

```
PS C:\> $xml.pets.pet[0].breed
Ferret
```

The $xml variable represents the XML document itself. From there, you simply specify the document elements as properties: The top-level <Pets> element, the first <Pet> element (indicated by pet[0], just like an array), and then the <Breed> element. If you don't specify a sub-element, PowerShell treats sub-elements as properties. For example, to view *all* of the properties—sub-elements, that is—of the second pet, you'd do this:

```
PS C:\> $xml.pets.pet[1]
```

```
Breed                   Age                     Name
-----                   ---                     ----
Bulldog                 5                       Chesty
```

This is a pretty creative way of working with XML and doesn't require you to use any of the more complex mechanisms that software developers usually have to deal with. Let's move on to a more complex example.

## Basic XML Manipulation

As an example, we went to our own blog's RSS feed—RSS just being an XML application, after all—located at http://blog.sapien.com/current/rss.xml, and saved the RSS XML as a local file so that we could work with it. The following page includes an excerpt; the remainder of the file just has additional <Item> nodes containing more blog entries. With this XML in a local file, our first step is to get this loaded into PowerShell and recognized as XML:

```
PS C:\> [xml]$rss = get-content c:\users\don\documents\rssfeed.xml
```

Simple enough: By specifically casting $rss as an [xml] type, we've let PowerShell know that some XML is coming its way. **Get-Content** loads the text from the file, and PowerShell does the rest.

```
<?xml version="1.0" encoding="UTF-8"?>
<rss xmlns:content="http://purl.org/rss/1.0/modules/content/" xmlns:wfw="http://wellformedweb.org/
CommentAPI/" xmlns:itunes="http://www.itunes.com/dtds/podcast-1.0.dtd" xmlns:dc="http://purl.org/
dc/elements/1.1/" version="2.0">
  <channel>
    <title>
      The SAPIEN Scripting Blog
    </title>
    <link>
      http://blog.sapien.com/current/
    </link>
    <description>
      Scripting news, Windows PowerShell, VBScript, PrimalScript software, scripting
      books, and more.
    </description>
    <copyright>
      Copyright ©2007 SAPIEN Technologies, Inc.
```

```
      </copyright>
      <language>
        en-US
      </language>
      <generator>
        Squarespace v3.5 (http://www.squarespace.com/)
      </generator>
      <item>
        <title>
          WSH and VBScript Core: TFM
        </title>
        <category>
          Books and Training
        </category>
        <category>
          VBScript
        </category>
        <dc:creator>
          Jeffery Hicks
        </dc:creator>
        <pubDate>
          Wed, 18 Apr 2007 13:01:45 +0000
        </pubDate>
        <link>
          http://blog.sapien.com/current/2007/4/18/wsh-and-vbscript-core-tfm.html
        </link>
        <guid isPermaLink="false">
          121527:1089428:1015063
        </guid>
        <description>
          <![CDATA[You know how in discussion forums, including ScriptingAnswers.com, people are
always referring you to Microsoft documentation for more information? Well, if you&#8217;ve looked
at the official WSH and VBScript documentation, you&#8217;ve probably found it lacking any real
meat. But we deserve better.
]]>
        </description>
        <wfw:commentRss>
          http://blog.sapien.com/current/rss-comments-entry-1015063.xml
        </wfw:commentRss>
      </item>
      <item>
        <title>
          Control Your PowerShell(s)!
        </title>
        <category>
          Windows PowerShell
        </category>
        <dc:creator>
          Don Jones
        </dc:creator>
        <pubDate>
          Sun, 15 Apr 2007 14:55:18 +0000
        </pubDate>
        <link>
          http://blog.sapien.com/current/2007/4/15/control-your-powershells.html
        </link>
        <guid isPermaLink="false">
          121527:1089428:1010385
        </guid>
        <description>
          <![CDATA[FYI: If you&#8217;ve been seeking to gain some centralized control over
PowerShell&#8217;s ExecutionPolicy, Microsoft has a downloadable ADM template that will allow you
to control the shell via Group Policy. It&#8217;s at http://www.microsoft.com/downloads/details.
aspx?familyid=2917A564-DBBC-4DA7-82C8-FE08B3EF4E6D&mg_id=10050&displaylang=en.
```

```
]]>
        </description>
        <wfw:commentRss>
            http://blog.sapien.com/current/rss-comments-entry-1010385.xml
        </wfw:commentRss>
      </item>
```

You may have noticed that the top-level element, which we've boldfaced in the excerpt, is the <rss> tag (the <xml> tag doesn't count; that's considered a *meta-tag* and simply defines the version of XML we're using). We can access this element in PowerShell very easily:

```
PS C:\> $rss.rss
```

```
content : http://purl.org/rss/1.0/modules/content/
wfw     : http://wellformedweb.org/CommentAPI/
itunes  : http://www.itunes.com/dtds/podcast-1.0.dtd
dc      : http://purl.org/dc/elements/1.1/
version : 2.0
channel : channel
```

What you're looking at here is the <rss> element of $rss, our XML document, and you're seeing the *attributes* of the <rss> tag—go back and refer to the XML excerpt, and you'll see where these values came from. We didn't have to do anything special to access them, though—PowerShell just knew how.

Underneath the <rss> tag is a <channel> tag, and underneath that is a <title> tag. We can access the feed's title as follows:

```
PS C:\> $rss.rss.channel.title
```

```
        The SAPIEN Scripting Blog
```

In other words, the object hierarchy—rss.channel.title—mirrors the hierarchy of tags in the XML document. Underneath the <channel> tag we'll also find multiple <item> tags, each one representing a blog posting. Each <item> tag has various sub-tags, including a <title> tag, which is the title of that blog posting. Because PowerShell will find more than one <item> section, it will create a collection out of them. So, to access the title of the first blog post:

```
PS C:\> $rss.rss.channel.item[0].title
```

```
        WSH and VBScript Core: TFM
```

Or, if we wanted to see all the post titles, we could enumerate through the <item> collection:

```
PS C:\> foreach ($post in $rss.rss.channel.item) { $post.title }
```

```
        WSH and VBScript Core: TFM

        Control Your PowerShell(s)!

        Techmentor Orlando 2007 Session Material

        I can name that OS in one note
```

What if we wanted to change the title of the second post?

```
PS C:\> $rss.rss.channel.item[1].title = "Alternate title"
```

We could, of course, pipe the $rss variable to **Out-File** to save the altered XML back to disk, if we wanted to. So, working with XML in PowerShell is fairly straightforward.

Our little example here illustrates how easily you can work with a fairly straightforward XML file; more complicated files simply create a deeper object hierarchy—more complex files don't really change how things work. It's a bit beyond the scope of this book to get into really complicated XML operations like XPath queries and so forth. However, we hope this quick look at XML has given you an idea of what PowerShell can do and offered some possibilities for parsing XML files that you may have in your environment.

# A Practical Example

So, what good is all this XML stuff? Let's look at a real-world example—one that will also introduce you to additional XML techniques. We're going to start with a basic XML file that contains computer names:

```
<Computers>
 <Computer Name="DON-LAPTOP" />
 <Computer Name="LOCALHOST" />
 <Computer Name="SERVER2" />
</Computers>
```

Our goal is to inventory some basic information from these computers (of course, you could add more to your list, if you wanted to), including their Windows build number, service pack version, and the amount of free space on their local disk drives. We want our final result to look something like this:

```
<Computers>
 <Computer Name="DON-LAPTOP">
   <Status>Complete</Status>
   <OS BuildNumber="6000" ServicePack="0" />
   <Disks>
       <Disk DeviceID="C:" FreeSpace="10MB" />
       <Disk DeviceID="E:" FreeSpace="22MB" />
   </Disks>
 </Computer>
 <Computer Name="LOCALHOST">
   <Status>Complete</Status>
   <OS BuildNumber="6000" ServicePack="0" />
   <Disks>
       <Disk DeviceID="C:" FreeSpace="10MB" />
       <Disk DeviceID="E:" FreeSpace="22MB" />
   </Disks>
 </Computer>
 <Computer Name="SERVER2">
   <Status>Unreachable</Status>
 </Computer>
</Computers>
```

Our goal is to build a PowerShell script not only capable of retrieving the necessary information, but also capable of putting it into this XML format and saving it all back to disk. We'll start by defining a GetStatus function, which we'll use to ensure WMI connectivity to a remote computer. This function simply makes an attempt to query a WMI class from the specified computer; its -**ErrorAction** parameter is set to SilentlyContinue, so that in the event of an error, no error message will be shown. The built-in $? variable contains a TRUE or FALSE value, depending on whether the previous command completed successfully or not, so we're simply outputting that variable as the result of the function.

```
function GetStatus([string]$computer) {
    gwmi win32_operatingsystem -computer $computer `
        -ea silentlycontinue
        Write-Output $?
}
```

Next, we write out a status message and load our inventory XML file from disk. Notice that we're explicitly declaring $xml as an [XML] data type, forcing PowerShell to parse the text file as XML.

```
Write-Host "Beginning inventory..."

# load XML
[xml]$xml = gc c:\test\inventory.xml
```

Next, we're going to repeat a large block of code once for each <computer> node found in the XML. We start by pulling the Name attribute of the <computer> tag into the variable $name. Be careful here because working with XML is case-sensitive. Make sure the attribute you are calling is the same case as the XML file.

```
for ($i=0; $i -lt $xml.computers.computer.count; $i++) {

        # get computername
    $name = $xml.computers.computer[$i].getattribute("Name")
```

We create a new XML node named <Status>. Notice that the main XML document, stored in $xml, has the capability of creating new nodes—we're specifically creating an *element*, which is basically an XLM tag. We're then executing our GetStatus function, passing it the current computer name to test.

```
        # create status node and get status
    $statusnode = $xml.CreateNode("element","Status","")
        $status = GetStatus $name
```

If the status comes back as FALSE—that is, not TRUE, as indicated by the ! operator—we set the <Status> node's inner text—the text appearing between <Status> and </Status>--to "Unreachable." Otherwise, we set the inner text to "Complete" and continue with the rest of our script.

```
        if (! $status) {
    $statusnode.set_innertext("Unreachable")
        } else {
    $statusnode.set_innertext("Complete")
```

If our status check was successful, we'll query the Win32_OperatingSystem class from the remote computer. We're also submitting a WMI query to retrieve all instances of Win32_LogicalDisk where the DriveType property is equal to 3, indicating a local disk. We issued the query this way because it'll actually be processed by the remote computer; we *could* have queried all instances of Win32_LogicalDisk and piped them to **Where-Object** to filter for the ones with a DriveType of 3, but that would have brought all the remote disks' data over to our computer first. This way, we're filtering out what we don't want right at the source.

```
# get OS info
$os = gwmi win32_operatingsystem -computer $name

# get local disks
$disks = gwmi -computer $name -query `
  "select * from win32_logicaldisk where drivetype=3" `
```

We'll ask the XML document, in $xml, to create an <OS> and <Disks> element. We'll continue work-ing with these elements to populate them with inventory data.

```
# create os node, disks node
$osnode = $xml.CreateNode("element","OS","")
$disksnode = $xml.CreateNode("element","Disks","")
```

Since we have the operating system build number and service pack information available, we can add those attributes to the <OS> element.

```
# append OS attrs to node
$osnode.setattribute("BuildNumber",$os.buildnumber)
$osnode.setattribute("ServicePack", `
        $os.servicepackmajorversion)
```

Now we append the complete <OS> element to the current <Computer> node. Notice that we're pip-ing the output of **AppendChild()** to the **Out-Null** cmdlet. That's because **AppendChild()** normally displays the node it just finished appending; that output looks messy when we run our script, so we're sending the output to **Out-Null** to get rid of it.

```
# append OS node to Computer node
$xml.computers.computer[$i].appendchild($osnode)`
        | Out-Null
```

Now it's time to enumerate through the logical disks we retrieved from WMI. We start by creating a new XML element named <Disk>, which will store our device ID and free space information.

```
# go through the logical disks
foreach ($disk in $disks) {
        # create disk node
   $disknode = $xml.CreateNode("element","Disk","")
```

Next we create the DeviceID attribute on the <Disk> node. We also convert the free space to megabytes, rather than bytes, by dividing the FreeSpace property by 1MB. We then use the .NET Framework's System.Math class to round the megabyte measurement to the nearest megabyte, so that we don't wind up with a decimal value. Finally, we convert the numeric free space measurement to a string, and concatenate the letters "MB" to provide a unit of measurement in our inventory file. We set the <Disk> node's FreeSpace attribute equal to our megabyte measurement.

```
#create deviceid and freespace attribs
$disknode.setattribute("DeviceID",$disk.deviceid)
        $freespace = $disk.freespace / 1MB
        $freespace = [system.math]::round($freespace)
   $freespace = $freespace.tostring() + "MB"
```

435

```
$disknode.setattribute(,"FreeSpace",$freespace)
```

We're now ready to append the current <Disk> node to the overall <Disks> node. After completing all of the available logical disks, we append the completed <Disks> node to the current <Computer> node. Again, we're using **Out-Null** to keep the output from **AppendChild()** from displaying.

```
                    # append Disk node to Disks node
                    $disksnode.appendchild($disknode) | Out-Null
        }

            # append disks node to Computer node
    $xml.computers.computer[$i].appendchild($disksnode) `
            | Out-Null
    }
```

We've reached the end of our If/Else construct, which had checked the result of our GetStatus function. We can, therefore, append the <Status> node, which will either contain "Complete" or "Unreachable", to the <Computer> node. Again, we're piping the output of the **AppendChild()** method to **Out-Null** in order to suppress the output text.

```
    # append status node to Computer node
$xml.computers.computer[$i].appendchild($statusnode) `
        | out-null
}
```

At this point, we've reached the end of our original For loop. We're ready to delete any existing output file and write our modified XML to a new filename, complete with all the inventory information we've added.

```
# output XML
del "c:\test\inventory-out.xml" -ea silentlycontinue
$xml.save("c:\test\inventory-out.xml")

Write-Host "...Inventory Complete."
```

The saved XML file can be opened and viewed in Internet Explorer or any other application that knows how to read XML files. Here's the full, final script:

## XMLInventory.ps1

```
function GetStatus([string]$computer) {
   gwmi win32_operatingsystem -computer $computer `
        -ea silentlycontinue
        Write-Output $?
}

Write-Host "Beginning inventory..."

# load XML
[xml]$xml = gc c:\test\inventory.xml

for ($i=0; $i -lt $xml.computers.computer.count; $i++) {

        # get computername
    $name = $xml.computers.computer[$i].getattribute("Name")
```

```
        # create status node and get status
$statusnode = $xml.CreateNode("element","Status","")
        $status = GetStatus $name
        if (! $status) {
  $statusnode.set_innertext("Unreachable")
        } else {
  $statusnode.set_innertext("Complete")

                # get OS info
                $os = gwmi win32_operatingsystem -computer $name

                # get local disks
  $disks = gwmi -computer $name -query `
   "select * from win32_logicaldisk where drivetype=3" `

                # create os node, disks node
  $osnode = $xml.CreateNode("element","OS","")
  $disksnode = $xml.CreateNode("element","Disks","")

                # append OS attrs to node
  $osnode.setattribute("BuildNumber",$os.buildnumber)
  $osnode.setattribute("ServicePack", `
            $os.servicepackmajorversion)

                # append OS node to Computer node
  $xml.computers.computer[$i].appendchild($osnode) `
             | Out-Null

                # go through the logical disks
                foreach ($disk in $disks) {
                        # create disk node
    $disknode = $xml.CreateNode("element","Disk","")

                        #create deviceid and freespace attribs
    $disknode.setattribute("DeviceID",$disk.deviceid)
                        $freespace = $disk.freespace / 1MB
                        $freespace = [system.math]::round($freespace)
    $freespace = $freespace.tostring() + "MB"
    $disknode.setattribute(,"FreeSpace",$freespace)

                        # append Disk node to Disks node
                        $disksnode.appendchild($disknode) | Out-Null
                }

                # append disks node to Computer node
    $xml.computers.computer[$i].appendchild($disksnode) `
             | Out-Null
        }

        # append status node to Computer node
  $xml.computers.computer[$i].appendchild($statusnode) `
        | out-null

}

# output XML
del "c:\test\inventory-out.xml" -ea silentlycontinue
$xml.save("c:\test\inventory-out.xml")

Write-Host "...Inventory Complete."
```

Chapter 35
# The PowerShell Extensible Type System

As you've no doubt picked up by now, PowerShell is entirely object-oriented. The objects that PowerShell works with are each of a particular *type*. That is, what we've loosely been calling a "string object" or "Process object" is more correctly referred to as "an object of the String type," or "an object of the Process type." Actually, even more specifically, we'd use the *complete* type name: System.String, or System.Diagnostic.Process.

While all of these types come straight from the .NET Framework, PowerShell doesn't expose us directly to them in most cases. Instead, it *adapts* the Framework objects into something a bit more administrator-friendly. For example, run:

```
PS C:\> Get-Process | Get-Member
```

You'll notice that the end of the member listing includes several items called a "ScriptProperty." These properties don't exist in the actual System.Diagnostic.Process type; rather, they're added, or adapted, onto the type by PowerShell. For example, the CPU ScriptProperty gives us an easier property name—CPU—to work with than the underlying type does. In other cases, PowerShell will create AliasProperties, perhaps substituting the property name "Count" for the less consistent "Length" that some Framework types use.

Most of PowerShell's additions, changes, and so forth are defined in Types.ps1xml, a file that's installed along with PowerShell, in the same folder as the PowerShell.exe console application. This XML-formatted file doesn't contain *every* type that PowerShell can use; rather, it contains those types that PowerShell's programmers wanted to extend, modify, or otherwise adapt for our ease of use.

Types.ps1xml is digitally signed using a Microsoft certificate; modifying the file would break the signature and render the entire file unusable. Fortunately, however, PowerShell's *extensible type system* permits us to create *our own* type extension files, using the same format and capabilities as Types.ps1xml. We can then import our files into PowerShell and take advantage of whatever capabilities we've built into our extended types.

In this chapter, we'll introduce you to several type extension features:

- Creating an AliasProperty

- Creating a ScriptProperty

- Creating a NoteProperty

- Creating a ScriptMethod

- Defining a set of default properties—the properties used by the **Format-List** cmdlet if you don't specify any properties

There are other capabilities in the type extension system, but most of them require a deeper understanding of .NET Framework programming than we can cover in this book.

---

**Type Trivia**

If you browse around the Types.ps1xml file included with PowerShell, you'll notice that many types, especially WMI classes, have a "PSStatus" property set defined, and you might wonder what this is for. During PowerShell's development, this property set was originally part of a concept to provide task-specific views—for example, a "status" view, a "capacity" view, and so forth, and these "PSStatus" property sets were to define the properties that would comprise a "status" view. Although the idea never made it further than defining these property sets for a few types, the concept is still a good one. Perhaps it will make a comeback in a future version of PowerShell!

## The Basic Type Extension File

The basic type extension file is simple—no more than three lines:

```
<?xml version="1.0" encoding="utf-8" ?>
<Types>
</Types>
```

All of your type extensions will be inserted between the <Types> and </Types> tags.

---

**Don't forget!**

All editions of PrimalScript provide good support for XML editing, including tag color-coding, auto-indentation, and so forth. Enterprise editions of PrimalScript also include a Visual XML Editor, which provides a graphically-based XML editing experience that some users greatly prefer.

## Creating Type Extensions

Within the <Types> and </Types> tags of your file, you'll place <Type> sections—one for each type that you're extending. A simple <Type> section looks like this:

```
<Type>
    <Name>type name</Name>
    <Members>
    </Members>
</Type>
```

Within the <Name> and </Name> tags, you'll place the *entire* .NET Framework type name of the type you're extending. The easiest way to find the type name is to retrieve one or more instances of the type and pipe them to **Get-Member**:

```
PS C:\> get-item test | gm


  TypeName: System.IO.DirectoryInfo
```

The **Get-Member** output will clearly list the TypeName, as shown here—simply copy it into the <Name> tag and you're done. Your actual type extensions, which will cover in the next several sections, will go within the <Members> and </Members> tags. That's an important convention to take note of.

---

**Remember!**
Every type extension we show you in the next section is intended to be inserted within the <Member> and </Member> tags, unless we explicitly state otherwise at the time.

---

Keep in mind that each new <Type> you define can have *as many* of the following extensions as you need, in any combination.

## AliasProperty

An AliasProperty simply assigns a new name to one of a type's existing properties. For example, if you find the built-in property name PerformanceOverOneHour to be too cumbersome, you could make an AliasProperty named POOH, and PowerShell would let you use the new property name. The original property name would be suppressed within PowerShell, not even showing up in **Get-Member** output. Here's how to do it:

```
<AliasProperty>
    <Name>property</Name>
    <ReferencedMemberName>original</ReferencedMemberName>
</AliasProperty>
```

You'd replace *property* with your new property name, and *original* with the original property name.

## ScriptProperty

A ScriptProperty allows you to create a new property *that contains PowerShell script code*. This means you're essentially creating a dynamically-valued property! Here's what one looks like:

```
<ScriptProperty>
    <Name>property</Name>
    <GetScriptBlock>
        code
    </GetScriptBlock>
</ScriptProperty>
```

You'd replace *property* with your new property name, and *code* indicates where your PowerShell script code would go. This code can use a special variable, $this, to refer to the current object instance. For example, suppose you have an object that has a TotalSpace and a FreeSpace property—not unlike the Win32_LogicalDisk class, perhaps. You decide you want to create a new PercentFree property, which will contain the percentage of free space, something which would need to be calculated based on the TotalSpace and FreeSpace values. Here's how it might look:

```
<ScriptProperty>
    <Name>PercentFree</Name>
    <GetScriptBlock>
        [system:math]::round($this.FreeSpace / $this.TotalSpace)
    </GetScriptBlock>
</ScriptProperty>
```

Remember that this script code works *exactly* as if you were in the PowerShell console or writing a script. Because we haven't started the line with a cmdlet—we just launched straight into our math expression—the **Write-Output** cmdlet is implied, meaning that output is being written to the success pipeline. Anything that your script outputs to the success pipeline will become the value for your ScriptProperty.

A ScriptProperty is a very valuable and powerful way to extend PowerShell's capabilities, using script code that's simpler to write than full .NET Framework code.

By the way: Notice that the script code is contained within a <GetScriptBlock> tag pair? That's important: This script is run whenever someone tries to *read* the property value. That is, if we're trying to display PercentFree, the <GetScriptBlock> is called. It wouldn't make sense to be able to put a value into PercentFree; we can't change the amount of free disk space just by sticking a new number into a property (although we sure wish we could, sometimes)! In theory, you could create a ScriptProperty that was *writable*—that is, which allowed changes to be made to the property. However, because you won't usually have a means of passing that property change through to the underlying .NET Framework type, there's not much use for such a capability.

## NoteProperty

A NoteProperty is an odd duck: It's essentially a property with a fixed, static value. Here's an example:

```
<NoteProperty>
    <Name>property</Name>
    <Value>value</Value>
</NoteProperty>
```

You'd replace *property* with the name for your NoteProperty, and replace *value* with the static value that you want the property to contain. PowerShell primarily uses specially named NoteProperties to contain fixed meta-data values, such as the serialization depth of certain types of objects; we haven't thought of a good use for a NoteProperty in a type extension file, but if we do, we'll make a point of blogging about it at http://blog.sapien.com (search the blog for NoteProperty to see if we've come up with anything since publishing this book).

## ScriptMethod

A ScriptMethod is a bit like a ScriptProperty. In fact, in many instances there isn't a great distinction between them. In programmer-speak, though, a property simply returns some value, such as our ScriptProperty example, which returned a value that was calculated from two other existing properties.

In other words, our ScriptProperty didn't *do* anything. A method, on the other hand, is expected to carry out some action, although it may also return a value as the result of that. Here's what a ScriptMethod looks like:

```
<ScriptMethod>
    <Name>property</Name>
    <Script>
        code
    </Script>
</ScriptMethod>
```

You'd replace **property** with your new property name, and **code** indicates where your PowerShell script code would go. That code can use a special variable, $this, to refer to the current object instance, just as you did with a ScriptProperty. And, as with a ScriptProperty, anything output to the success pipeline becomes a return value for your method.

## Default Property Set

When you use **Format-List** to format a set of objects—or when PowerShell automatically chooses **Format-List** according to its formatting rules—PowerShell will list *all* properties for the objects, unless a type extension has been registered that defines a *default property set*. If a default property set is defined, then only those properties will be included in the list, unless you explicitly use **Format-List** and specify a different set of properties for inclusion. A default property set is easy to create:

```
<MemberSet>
    <Name>PSStandardMembers</Name>
    <Members>
        <PropertySet>
            <Name>DefaultDisplayPropertySet</Name>
            <ReferencedProperties>
                <Name>property</Name>
                <Name>property</Name>
                <Name>property</Name>
            </ReferencedProperties>
        </PropertySet>
    </Members>
</MemberSet>
```

You would, of course, replace our **property** placeholders with the property names you want. You can include as many <Name> tag sets as desired within the <ReferencedProperties> section. Remember that each property you specify *must be an actual property of the type*; you can't just make up words! If you want to see a list of available properties, pipe an instance of the type to **Get-Member** and review the output.

## Importing Your Type Extensions

When you've finished your type extension file, you need to tell PowerShell to use it. To do so, you'll run the **Update-TypeData** cmdlet. You have the choice of having your extensions loaded *in front* of PowerShell's built-in extensions, or *after* the built-in ones; in case of a conflict, PowerShell uses the first type extension definition it finds, so having your extensions loaded first will let them "win" over PowerShell's built-in extensions.

- To load your extensions before PowerShell's, run **Update-TypeData -prependPath** *filename*.

- To load your extensions after PowerShell's, run **Update-TypeData -appendPath** *filename*.

In both instances, of course, provide the complete path and file of your .ps1xml type extension file. Your changes take effect immediately and last until you close the shell; there is no cmdlet for unloading a type data file. You also can't reload a file once it's been loaded into a PowerShell session. You have to exit and restart PowerShell. To have your changes take effect each time you open a new shell, add the **Update-TypeData** commands to your PowerShell profile.

## A Practical Example

For an example, we've decided to extend the System.String type. We're going to add an AliasProperty that renames the String's Length property to HowLong, and we're going to add a ScriptMethod that assumes the String contains a computer name or IP address and tells you if it can ping that address. We'll also add a ScriptProperty that returns a TRUE or FALSE, depending on whether or not the String's contents look like a Universal Naming Convention (UNC) path. These are perhaps not the *most* practical examples, but they will let us show you the breadth of the type extension system using a common, easy-to-experiment-with type.

Because the type extensions themselves are relatively simple and are well-described in the preceding sections, we're just going to show you the entire type extension file all at once. We'll import this using **Update-TypeData** and its **-prependPath** parameter, and then walk you through a test.

### StringTypeExtension.ps1xml

```xml
<?xml version="1.0" encoding="utf-8" ?>
<Types>
 <Type>
   <Name>System.String</Name>
   <Members>
     <AliasProperty>
       <Name>HowLong</Name>
       <ReferencedMemberName>Length</ReferencedMemberName>
     </AliasProperty>
     <ScriptProperty>
       <Name>IsUNC</Name>
       <GetScriptBlock>
        $this -match "^\\\\\w+\\\w+"
       </GetScriptBlock>
     </ScriptProperty>
     <ScriptMethod>
       <Script>
        $wmi = gwmi -query "select * from win32_pingstatus where address = '$this'"
        If ($wmi.statuscode -eq 0) { $true } else { $false }
       </Script>
     </ScriptMethod>
   </Members>
 </Type>
</Types>
```

For our ScriptProperty, we're using a regular expression, and the regular expression **-match** operator. Because the operator already returns a TRUE or FALSE value, we're just letting that output become the value of our ScriptProperty. Our ScriptMethod isn't much more complicated: It uses the Win32_ PingStatus WMI class to ping whatever's in the String (which we reference by using $this). If the resulting StatusCode property is zero, we output the Boolean $true value; if not, we output $false.

Let's see our new type extension in action:

```
PS C:\test> Update-TypeData -pre sample.ps1xml
PS C:\test> [string]$s = "localhost"
PS C:\test> $s.canping()
True
PS C:\test> $s = "\\Server\Share"
PS C:\test> $s.isunc
True
PS C:\test> $s.howlong
14
PS C:\test>
```

Perfect results!

# Chapter 36
# Creating Custom Objects

Why in the world would you need to create a custom object? Surely there are enough objects in the world already, right? Even a function returns objects. But usually there are limitations. Consider this example:

**PingFunction.ps1**

```
function Ping-Computer {
        PROCESS {
    $wmi = gwmi -query "SELECT StatusCode FROM Win32_PingStatus WHERE Address = '$_'"
                foreach ($result in $wmi) {
                        if ($result.statuscode -eq 0) {
                                Write-Output $_
                        }
                }
        }
}

Get-Content c:\computers.txt | Ping-Computer
```

When we run this script, it'll read computer names from a file named C:\Computers.txt, and pipe those to the Ping-Computer function. That function has a Process script block (which we discussed in the chapter "Script Blocks, Functions, and Filters"), which processes the names one at a time. For each name, it attempts to ping it using the Win32_PingStatus WMI class. If the ping is successful (a StatusCode of zero), the computer name is output back to the pipeline.

This is a useful function… but it's of *minimal* usefulness. For example, the Win32_PingStatus class can return other information, such as the address that the destination computer used to reply, or the resolved address, or the response time. Unfortunately, if we're just returning simple values from our function, we can't return *all* of that data—we're stuck with just returning the names of the computers we could ping.

And that's why we might want to create a custom object. For example, suppose we make up an object named PingResult. We'll give it several properties:

- Address – the address or computer name we attempted to ping

- ProtocolAddress – the address the destination used to reply

- ResponseTime – the time elapsed to handle the request

- Status – the English text that corresponds to the StatusCode

- StatusCode – a numeric code indicating whether or not the ping succeeded

PowerShell allows us to create such an object, on the fly. We can reprogram our Ping-Computer function to output these PingResult objects, allowing us to output a richer type of information than merely a list of successful computer names.

## Custom Object Creation

Creating a new object is straightforward: Use the **New-Object** cmdlet, and ask it to create a new generic object—that is, an object of the general Object type:

```
PS C:\> $obj = New-Object Object
```

From there, you can add *members*—properties, in this case—to the object. We're going to work with a special type of property called a *NoteProperty*, which is something PowerShell can add to almost any type of object, and which can be used to store simple values like strings, numbers, and so forth. To add a member to our object, we'll pipe our object to **Add-Member**, telling **Add-Member** what type of member to add, the name we want for the new member, and the value we want the member set to:

```
PS C:\> $obj | Add-Member NoteProperty MyProperty -value "Hello"
```

And that's it. We can pipe $obj to **Add-Member** again and again to add as many properties as we need.

## Using Custom Objects

So, let's get back to our Ping-Computer example. Here's a revised version of the function that utilizes custom objects:

### CustomObjectPing.ps1

```
function ping-computer {
    PROCESS {
        $wmi = gwmi -query "SELECT * FROM Win32_PingStatus WHERE Address = '$_'"
        foreach ($result in $wmi) {
            $pingresult = New-Object object
            $pingresult | Add-Member noteproperty ResponseTime -value $result.responsetime
            $pingresult | Add-Member noteproperty StatusCode -value $result.StatusCode
            $pingresult | Add-Member noteproperty ProtocolAddress -value $result.ProtocolAddress
            $pingresult | Add-Member noteproperty Address -value $result.Address
            switch ($result.statuscode) {
```

```
        0     { $status = "Success" }
        11001 { $status = "Buffer too small" }
        11002 { $status = "Dest net unreachable" }
        11003 { $status = "Dest host unreachable" }
        11004 { $status = "Dest protocol unreachable" }
        11005 { $status = "Dest port unreachable" }
        11006 { $status = "No resources" }
        11007 { $status = "Bad option" }
        11008 { $status = "Hardware err" }
        11009 { $status = "Packet too big" }
        11010 { $status = "Request timed out" }
        11011 { $status = "Bad request" }
        11012 { $status = "Bad route" }
        11013 { $status = "TTL expired transit" }
        11014 { $status = "TTL expired reass'y" }
        11015 { $status = "Paramater err" }
        11016 { $status = "Source quench" }
        11017 { $status = "Option too big" }
        11018 { $status = "Bad dest" }
        11032 { $status = "Negot IPSEC" }
        11050 { $status = "Failure" }
        default { $status = "No reply" }
      }
      $pingresult | Add-Member noteproperty Status -value $status
      Write-Output $pingresult
    }
  }
}

Get-Content c:\computers.txt | ping-computer | Format-Table
```

You can see that the last line of our script is getting our list of computer names from C:\Computers.txt, piping them to the Ping-Computer function and piping the function's output to **Format-Table**. Here's how the function works:

We've enclosed the entire function's contents in a Process script block. That makes the function usable from the pipeline. Remember that the Process block will be executed once for each input object passed in from the pipeline. The $_ variable will contain the current pipeline object.

First, we execute the Win32_PingStatus query, passing $_ as the address to ping. Note that this query executes *locally*; the remote computer is only contacted via ping, not via WMI. We examine the results (usually only one result) that we get back by using a Foreach loop.

Within the loop, we create a new object, $pingresult, by using **New-Object**. We add several properties using **Add-Member** and populate those properties with properties from the WMI instance: ResponseTime, StatusCode, ProtocolAddress, and Address. We then use a Switch construct to examine the StatusCode property and populate the $status variable with a text version of the status code. Notice that a Default condition in the Switch construct fills in the "no reply" status in the event that no reply was received. The $status variable is used to populate the last property that we added to the object. Finally, the finished $pingresult object is output to the pipeline using **Write-Output**. Here's our script's output:

```
ResponseTime    StatusCode     ProtocolAddress  Address       Status
------------    ----------     ---------------  -------       ------
                                                DON-LAPTOP    No reply
0               0              ::1              LOCALHOST     Success
0               0              fe80::e468:309... DON-PC       Success
                                                SERVER2       No reply
```

449

It's worth noting that on Windows Vista, the Win32_PingResult class will work with IPv6 and not just IPv4. You can see this in the ProtocolAddress property, where IPv6-style addresses are listed.

If we wanted to make this Ping-Computer function available in the global scope, we could dot-source it. We'll delete the last line of the script, just leaving the function, and then dot-source it:

```
PS C:\> . ./bigping
```

This defines the function in the global scope, rather than creating a new script scope for it. With the function defined in the global scope, we can use it at the command line, just like a cmdlet:

```
PS C:\> $results = get-content c:\computers.txt | ping-computer
PS C:\> $results


ResponseTime    :
StatusCode      :
ProtocolAddress :
Address         : DON-LAPTOP
Status          : No reply

ResponseTime    : 0
StatusCode      : 0
ProtocolAddress : ::1
Address         : LOCALHOST
Status          : Success

ResponseTime    : 0
StatusCode      : 0
ProtocolAddress : fe80::e468:3091:f2fc:8deb
Address         : DON-PC
Status          : Success

ResponseTime    :
StatusCode      :
ProtocolAddress :
Address         : SERVER2
Status          : No reply
```

Our $results variable contains the results of the pipeline we executed. Since it's a collection of our "PingResult" objects, we can treat $results like any other collection. For example, to examine the second object:

```
PS C:\> $results[1]


ResponseTime    : 0
StatusCode      : 0
ProtocolAddress : ::1
Address         : LOCALHOST
Status          : Success
```

Anytime you need a function to return *rich* results—that is, more than just a simple value—a custom object is a good option. In this case, we've created a useful utility function that not only lets us know what computers were pingable, but provides other useful information, as well. Because our function is returning a real object, we can pass those objects down the pipeline. For example, here's a command line that uses our function and only outputs the names of the computers which *were not* pingable. Further, we're only displaying the Address property of unresponsive computers:

```
PS C:\> get-content c:\computers.txt | ping-computer | where { $_.Status -eq "No reply" }'
>>| select Address

Address
-------
DON-LAPTOP
SERVER2
```

You can see how this sort of custom object lends itself well to filtering, sorting, and other functionality provided by PowerShell's other cmdlets.

# A Practical Example

Note that the example we showed you earlier isn't *practical*, but we thought you'd like to see another. For this example, we're going to create a custom function called Get-OSInfo. It'll accept a computer name—either a single string, or an array of strings—and for each one, it'll retrieve that computer's Win32_OperatingSystem class and output a custom object containing the computer's Windows build number, service pack version, and computer name.

Here's the script:

### GetOSInfo.ps1

```
function Get-OSInfo {
        param([string[]]$addresses)

        function OutputInfo {
                param (
                        [string]$computer,
                        [string]$build,
                        [string]$spver
                )
                $output = New-Object psobject
                $output | Add-Member NoteProperty ComputerName -value $computer
                $output | Add-Member NoteProperty BuildNumber -value $build
                $output | Add-Member NoteProperty SPVersion -value $spver
                $output
        }

        trap {
    OutputInfo $address,"Unknown","Unknown"
        }

        foreach ($address in $addresses) {
                $os = gwmi win32_operatingsystem -computer $address -ea continue
                OutputInfo $address $os.buildnumber $os.servicepackmajorversion
        }

}
```

**Remember!**
If you dot-source this or add it to your profile this function will be available from the command line and can be used almost like a simple cmdlet.

To use this function:

```
Get-OSInfo @("don-pc","server2") | format-table
```

So, what's going on? We start by declaring a function that accepts a string array (which, remember, can consist of only one element, if we're only interested in one computer). We declare a function named OutputInfo, which actually outputs our custom object: It creates a new object, adds three NoteProperty members, and then outputs the custom object to the success pipeline (using an implicit **Write-Output**).

We've defined an error handler in case WMI is unable to reach one of the computers we specified. If that happens, the trap handler calls OutputInfo, passing along "Unknown" values for the build number and service pack version number. The trap handler calls "continue," allowing the script to continue after the error.

Next is the main body of the script: A simple Foreach loop that contacts WMI and retrieves the Win32_OperatingSystem class. Notice the **-EA**, or **-errorAction**, parameter, which specifies that exceptions be raised (so we can trap them). If no errors occurred, then the OutputInfo function is called with the retrieved WMI information.

The beauty of building our own custom object is that we don't have to worry about formatting the output. Since our output values are in object properties, any of PowerShell's Format cmdlets can handle formatting for us:

```
Get-OSInfo @("don-pc","server2") | format-list
```

If we'd simply output string values, we would have needed to format them ourselves, which is much less efficient (anything that makes us do extra work is "inefficient" as far as we're concerned).

# Chapter 37
# Object Serialization

Occasionally, there's a need for objects to be represented in a more easily portable format, such as XML. Serialization is the process of taking an object and converting it into an XML representation. The reverse, *deserialization*, converts the XML back into an object—although the object is often less functional than it was prior to serialization, often including only property values and omitting methods since it is no longer "connected" to the real-world software that originally generated it. In other words, if you serialize a Windows service into an XML file, you can carry that to another computer and deserialize it back into an object. But that object won't be able to start and stop the original service; it'll simply be a way of examining the service's properties as they were at the time it was serialized. Serialized objects, then, are essentially a "snapshot" of an object at a specific point in time.

PowerShell primarily uses the **Export-CliXML** cmdlet to serialize objects and save the resulting XML in a text file. For example, run this command:

```
PS C:\> gwmi win32_operatingsystem | export-clixml c:\test\win32os.xml
```

It results in the following XML representation (which we've truncated to save space):

```
<Objs Version="1.1" xmlns="http://schemas.microsoft.com/powershell/2004/04">
  <Obj RefId="RefId-0">
    <TN RefId="RefId-0">
      <T>
        System.Management.ManagementObject#root\cimv2\Win32_OperatingSystem
      </T>
      <T>
        System.Management.ManagementObject
      </T>
```

453

```
        <T>
            System.Management.ManagementBaseObject
        </T>
        <T>
            System.ComponentModel.Component
        </T>
        <T>
            System.MarshalByRefObject
        </T>
        <T>
            System.Object
        </T>
    </TN>
    <Props>
      <S N="RegisteredUser">
          Don Jones
      </S>
      <S N="SerialNumber">
          89580-378-1205931-71241
      </S>
      <U16 N="ServicePackMajorVersion">
          0
      </U16>
      <S N="SystemDirectory">
          C:\Windows\system32
      </S>
      <S N="SystemDrive">
          C:
      </S>
      <Nil N="TotalSwapSpaceSize"/>
      <U64 N="TotalVirtualMemorySize">
          5963004
      </U64>
      <U64 N="TotalVisibleMemorySize">
          2882304
      </U64>
      <S N="Version">
          6.0.6000
      </S>
      <S N="WindowsDirectory">
          C:\Windows
      </S>
    </Props>
  </Obj>
</Objs>
```

The **Import-CliXML** cmdlet does the opposite, returning the XML to a static object inside the shell:

```
PS C:\> $os = import-clixml c:\test\win32os.xml
PS C:\> $os.servicepackmajorversion
0
PS C:\> $os.name
Microsoftr Windows VistaT Ultimate |C:\Windows|\Device\Harddisk0\Partition1
PS C:\>
```

PowerShell has a set of default rules used to serialize objects. However, you can customize the serialization by providing *serialization directives* in a type extension file (we first discussed these files in "The PowerShell Extensible Type System").

## Why Export Objects to XML?

Exporting, or serializing, objects to XML allows them to be persisted, or saved, as a static snapshot. One practical reason to do so is to share those objects with other PowerShell users. For example, you might want to export your command-line history to an XML file so that you can share it with another user—who could then import it to re-create your command-line history.

Another less obvious reason might be to get a snapshot of objects when you're not physically around. For example, suppose you have a long-running process that starts on one of your servers at 1:00am every morning. You know it should finish by 5:00am. You could write a very short PowerShell script, like this:

```
Get-Process | Export-CliXML c:\1am.xml
```

And you could schedule it to run at 1:15am, when the long-running process should be running. Later, at 5:30am, you could run a second script:

```
Get-Process | Export-CliXML c:\5am.xml
```

When you arrive for work, you could grab both of these files and re-import them, effectively reconstructing the objects *as they were* when the XML file was created. This would let you examine the objects from that point in time, even though you weren't physically present then. For example, to compare the two sets of objects:

```
PS C:\> $1 = import-clixml c:\1am.xml
PS C:\> $5 = import-clixml c:\5am.xml
PS C:\> compare-object $1 $5
```

Using this example, $1 contains all of the objects that were running at 1am. You can pipe $1 to any other cmdlet capable of working with objects, allowing you to sort, group, filter, or format the process objects in any way. This ability to easily persist objects—a result of PowerShell's serialization capabilities—has myriad uses.

# Creating Serialization Directives

Serialization directives are entered into the type extension file within the <MemberSet> tag. In other words, you're starting with the following basic template for a type:

```
<Type>
    <Name>type name</Name>
    <Members>
        <MemberSet>
            <Name>PSStandardMembers</Name>
            <Members>
               ...serialization directives go here...
            </Members>
        </MemberSet>
    </Members>
</Type>
```

Review the "The PowerShell Extensible Type System" chapter if you need a refresher on type extensions. Remember, when you provide this PSStandardMembers member set, you're *overriding* PowerShell's default serialization rules. That means *only* the method you specify will be used to serialize the class type you've specified.

For the following examples, we'll be using the output of our **Ping-Computer** cmdlet. This is available in the SAPIEN Extensions for Windows PowerShell (PshX-SAPIEN) snap-in, which is available for download at www.PrimalScript.com/freetools. This cmdlet outputs objects of the type SapienPshX. PingResult. For each of our examples, we'll serialize using the following command:

```
ping-computer "localhost" | export-clixml c:\test\export.xml
```

For your reference, PowerShell's default serialization behavior results in the following:

```
<Objs Version="1.1" xmlns="http://schemas.microsoft.com/powershell/2004/04">
  <Obj RefId="RefId-0">
    <TN RefId="RefId-0">
      <T>
        sapienPshX.PingResult
      </T>
      <T>
        System.Object
      </T>
    </TN>
    <Props>
      <S N="ComputerName">
        localhost
      </S>
      <I32 N="StatusCode">
        0
      </I32>
      <I32 N="ResponseTime">
        0
      </I32>
      <S N="ProtocolAddress">
        ::1
      </S>
    </Props>
  </Obj>
</Objs>
```

As you can see, this default output displays the object's type (in <T> tags), the type it inherits from (the second <T> tag set), and then the object's properties (<S> is a string, <I32> is an integer, and so forth). Had we generated a collection of these objects, one <Obj> tag section would have been generated for each.

## Serializing as a String

This technique allows you to serialize the object as a string:

```
<NoteProperty>
 <Name>SerializationMethod</Name>
 <Value>String</Value>
</NoteProperty>
```

Here's a complete example:

```
<Types>
   <Type>
       <Name>sapienPshX.PingResult</Name>
       <Members>
```

```
        <MemberSet>
            <Name>PSStandardMembers</Name>
            <Members>
              <NoteProperty>
                  <Name>SerializationMethod</Name>
                  <Value>String</Value>
              </NoteProperty>
            </Members>
        </MemberSet>
      </Members>
    </Type>
</Types>
```

And here's the result when we export **Ping-Computer localhost | Export-CliXML c:\test\export.xml**:

```
<Objs Version="1.1" xmlns="http://schemas.microsoft.com/powershell/2004/04">
  <S>
    sapienPshX.PingResult
  </S>
</Objs>
```

What this SerializationMethod is doing is telling PowerShell to call the object's built-in **ToString()** method. In the .NET Framework, pretty much *all* classes inherit (eventually) from System.Object (although most classes have several ancestors between them and the top-level SystemObject class). System.Object provides a simple **ToString()** method, which simply outputs the class' type name; many objects *override* this simple method and provide their own, more robust **ToString()**. However, as you can see here, our sapienPshX.PingResult class simply utilizes System.Object's simpler method, so our export result simply contains the type name as a string.

Specifying the String Serialization method is primarily useful when the type you're working with provides a useful and robust **ToString()** method of its own.

## Specifying a String Source

Our next SerializationMethod is similar to the previous one. We're still going to specify a String output, but this time we're going to add a source other than the object's **ToString()** method to get that string. Specifically, we're going to use a PowerShell script block, and its output will be used as the source for our final serialized XML. Here's a simple example:

```
<NoteProperty>
 <Name>SerializationMethod</Name>
 <Value>String</Value>
</NoteProperty>
<ScriptProperty>
 <Name>StringSerializationSource</Name>
 <GetScriptBlock>PowerShell Script Code Here</GetScriptBlock>
</ScriptProperty>
```

Here's a more complete example, where we're using a script to output only two of the object's four properties, along with a timestamp as a third property:

```
  <Type>
      <Name>sapienPshX.PingResult</Name>
      <Members>
        <MemberSet>
            <Name>PSStandardMembers</Name>
```

```
                  <Members>
                    <NoteProperty>
                       <Name>SerializationMethod</Name>
                       <Value>String</Value>
                    </NoteProperty>
                    <ScriptProperty>
                       <Name>StringSerializationSource</Name>
                       <GetScriptBlock>
                         $newobj = new-object PSObject
                             $timestamp = Get-Date
                             $newobj | add-member NoteProperty Timestamp -value $timestamp
                             $newobj | add-member NoteProperty Computer -value $this.ComputerName
                             $newobj | add-member NoteProperty StatusCode -value $this.StatusCode
                             $newobj
                       </GetScriptBlock>
                    </ScriptProperty>
                  </Members>
              </MemberSet>
          </Members>
     </Type>
</Types>
```

However, what we're doing is creating a new, blank object called $newobj (we covered the creation of custom objects in "Creating Custom Objects"). We're adding three properties—Timestamp, Computer, and StatusCode—and setting them to specific values. The special $this variable represents the original PingResult object, and we're accessing its ComputerName and StatusCode properties. Finally, we output $newobj, and that's what PowerShell uses to generate the string in our serialized XML:

```
<Objs Version="1.1" xmlns="http://schemas.microsoft.com/powershell/2004/04">
  <S>
     @{Timestamp=5/1/2007 10:15:12 AM; Computer=localhost; StatusCode=0}
  </S>
</Objs>
```

Remember, the three properties of our $newobj object aren't broken down, because we've specified that the final serialization be a single string.

You can use property types other than a ScriptProperty as the StringSerializationSource. In this next example, we'll use a NoteProperty, which is basically just a static text string:

```
<Types>
    <Type>
        <Name>sapienPshX.PingResult</Name>
        <Members>
            <MemberSet>
                <Name>PSStandardMembers</Name>
                <Members>
                  <NoteProperty>
                     <Name>SerializationMethod</Name>
                     <Value>String</Value>
                  </NoteProperty>
                  <NoteProperty>
                     <Name>StringSerializationSource</Name>
                     <Value>Static Text</Value>
                  </NoteProperty>
                </Members>
            </MemberSet>
        </Members>
    </Type>
</Types>
```

The result is the following:

```
<Objs Version="1.1" xmlns="http://schemas.microsoft.com/powershell/2004/04">
  <S>
     Static Text
  </S>
</Objs>
```

Not terribly useful, since every object of the specified type will always be serialized with this exact output, but it demonstrates that the StringSerializationSource can be something other than a ScriptProperty.

## Controlling Serialization Depth

When you're working with hierarchical objects—such as file system folders, where one folder can contain additional folders, which can contain additional folders, and so forth—you may want to control the *depth* to which PowerShell serializes that hierarchy. If you don't, then serializing a top-level object, such as the root folder of a drive, will automatically serialize *the entire object hierarchy*—in other words, the entire drive, which can be time-consuming and produce unexpectedly large results.

Adding a depth-control serialization directive does *not* require you to specify any properties to be serialized; PowerShell will still follow its default rules, but it will do so only for the specified depth within the object's hierarchy. In other words, this serialization directive can stand alone. Here it is:

```
<NoteProperty>
  <Name>SerializationDepth</Name>
  <Value>2</Value>
</NoteProperty>
```

## Serializing Only Specific Properties

Perhaps the most useful SerializationMethod is to export just specific properties of the object. Using this method, you can ensure that only the *useful* properties of an object are exported, meaning deserialized objects will contain only useful data. You may also wish to omit properties that won't have meaning later on, such as a constantly changing value like CPU utilization. The basic format is as follows:

```
<NoteProperty>
 <Name>SerializationMethod</Name>
 <Value>SpecificProperties</Value>
</NoteProperty>
<PropertySet>
 <Name>PropertySerializationSet</Name>
 <ReferencedProperties>
   <Name>property</Name>
 </ReferencedProperties>
</PropertySet>
```

You can include as many referenced properties as you want. Again, all of the properties you reference must already exist for the class you're working with; you'd use this technique mainly to "hide" properties of the class that you *don't* want to be serialized. Here's a full example:

```
<Types>
  <Type>
```

```
        <Name>sapienPshX.PingResult</Name>
        <Members>
            <MemberSet>
                <Name>PSStandardMembers</Name>
                <Members>
                  <NoteProperty>
                      <Name>SerializationMethod</Name>
                      <Value>SpecificProperties</Value>
                  </NoteProperty>
                  <PropertySet>
                    <Name>PropertySerializationSet</Name>
                    <ReferencedProperties>
                      <Name>ComputerName</Name>
                      <Name>StatusCode</Name>
                    </ReferencedProperties>
                  </PropertySet>
                </Members>
            </MemberSet>
        </Members>
    </Type>
</Types>
```

And here's the XML it creates:

```
<Objs Version="1.1" xmlns="http://schemas.microsoft.com/powershell/2004/04">
  <Obj RefId="RefId-0">
    <TN RefId="RefId-0">
      <T>
          sapienPshX.PingResult
      </T>
      <T>
          System.Object
      </T>
    </TN>
    <Props>
      <S N="ComputerName">
          localhost
      </S>
      <I32 N="StatusCode">
          0
      </I32>
    </Props>
  </Obj>
</Objs>
```

Notice that this output is identical to what PowerShell would create using its default rules, except that only two of our object's four properties are being serialized.

## Controlling the Inheritance of Serialization Directives

We mentioned earlier in this chapter that nearly all classes inherit from System.Object, which is the top-level and most generic class available in the .NET Framework. Our serialized object XML, as in the example we just showed you, reflects this inheritance by listing not only our type, but the type from which it inherits:

```
  <TN RefId="RefId-0">
    <T>
        sapienPshX.PingResult
    </T>
```

```
    <T>
        System.Object
    </T>
  </TN>
```

More complex objects have a more complex hierarchy in their serialized XML. For example, here's a service, obtained with **Get-Service**:

```
  <TN RefId="RefId-0">
    <T>
        System.ServiceProcess.ServiceController
    </T>
    <T>
        System.ComponentModel.Component
    </T>
    <T>
        System.MarshalByRefObject
    </T>
    <T>
        System.Object
    </T>
  </TN>
```

When defining a serialization method, class inheritance comes into play. For example, in our prior example (selecting specific properties), we showed you the sapienPshX.PingResult class, and we selected two of its four properties. The properties we selected will normally be serialized for that class *and for any classes that derive from it.* Suppose we have a second class, named sapienPshX.BetterPingResult, which inherits from sapienPshX.PingResult. Without any serialization directives, only the ComputerName and StatusCode properties would be serialized for that inherited type, because it inherits from a type that *has* a specific serialization directive registered.

Create a type extension like this:

```
<Types>
   <Type>
       <Name>sapienPshX.PingResult</Name>
       <Members>
          <MemberSet>
             <Name>PSStandardMembers</Name>
             <Members>
               <NoteProperty>
                  <Name>SerializationMethod</Name>
                  <Value>SpecificProperties</Value>
               </NoteProperty>
               <PropertySet>
                 <Name>PropertySerializationSet</Name>
                 <ReferencedProperties>
                    <Name>ComputerName</Name>
                    <Name>StatusCode</Name>
                 </ReferencedProperties>
               </PropertySet>
             </Members>
          </MemberSet>
       </Members>
   </Type>
   <Type>
       <Name>sapienPshX.BetterPingResult</Name>
       <Members>
          <MemberSet>
```

```
            <Name>PSStandardMembers</Name>
            <Members>
              <NoteProperty>
                 <Name>SerializationMethod</Name>
                 <Value>SpecificProperties</Value>
              </NoteProperty>
              <PropertySet>
                <Name>PropertySerializationSet</Name>
                <ReferencedProperties>
                   <Name>ResponseTime</Name>
                </ReferencedProperties>
              </PropertySet>
            </Members>
          </MemberSet>
        </Members>
    </Type>
</Types>
```

Now, our sapienPshX.BetterPingResult type will serialize with three properties: ComputerName and StatusCode (because its parent type, sapienPshX.PingResult, serializes with those properties), and ResponseTime, a property we've specifically selected for the type. You *can*, however, *block* this inheritance behavior in serialization directives. Here's the same example type extension file with a minor change, which we'll boldface:

```
<Types>
    <Type>
        <Name>sapienPshX.PingResult</Name>
        <Members>
          <MemberSet>
             <Name>PSStandardMembers</Name>
             <Members>
               <NoteProperty>
                  <Name>SerializationMethod</Name>
                  <Value>SpecificProperties</Value>
               </NoteProperty>
               <PropertySet>
                 <Name>PropertySerializationSet</Name>
                 <ReferencedProperties>
                    <Name>ComputerName</Name>
                    <Name>StatusCode</Name>
                 </ReferencedProperties>
               </PropertySet>
             </Members>
          </MemberSet>
        </Members>
    </Type>
    <Type>
        <Name>sapienPshX.BetterPingResult</Name>
        <Members>
          <MemberSet>
             <Name>PSStandardMembers</Name>
             <Members>
               <NoteProperty>
                  <Name>SerializationMethod</Name>
                  <Value>SpecificProperties</Value>
               </NoteProperty>
               <NoteProperty>
                  <Name>InheritPropertySerializationSet</Name>
                  <Value>false</Value>
               </NoteProperty>
               <PropertySet>
```

```
            <Name>PropertySerializationSet</Name>
            <ReferencedProperties>
              <Name>ResponseTime</Name>
            </ReferencedProperties>
          </PropertySet>
        </Members>
      </MemberSet>
    </Members>
  </Type>
</Types>
```

Now, objects of the sapienPshX.BetterPingResult type will *only* serialize with a ReponseTime property, because we've turned off the serialization directive inheritance. Any types that happen to inherit from sapienPshX.BetterPingResult will still inherit its serialization directives, unless they also have InheritPropertySerializationSet set to FALSE.

# Serialization: Now and Tomorrow

What's the purpose, then, of serialization, and why should you care about it? Today, serialization is a way of saving objects into a simplified, easily transportable format. For example, you might export a bunch of objects from one computer, move the XML file to another computer, and then import the objects from XML to work with them again. Saving objects is another good use of serialization: For example, by piping **Get-History** to **Export-CliXML**, you can save your command history in an XML file. You can then use **Import-CliXML** to import that file, pipe it to **Add-History**, and "reload" your command history. This is useful when giving demonstrations, or when conducting various repetitive tasks.

In the future, serialization will play an important role in remote management. A future version of Windows PowerShell will allow you to connect to remote copies of the shell, having them execute commands locally on the computer where they're installed. Those remote shells will then serialize the results of your commands, transmit the results—as a stream of XML text via an HTTP-like connection—back to you, where your shell will reconstruct the objects so that you can work with them. Being able to customize how objects are serialized will provide important capabilities at that time, in addition to the useful things you can do right now.

# Chapter 38
# Creating Custom Formats

Windows PowerShell uses XML-based files to define how various types of objects should be formatted. If you open the PowerShell installation folder, you'll see a number of files ending in ".format.ps1xml"; these files control the built-in formatting behavior that PowerShell ships with. You can create your own formats, as well.

## Examining the Formatting Format

One of the easiest ways to see how these XML files work is to examine an existing type's formatting. For example, running **Get-EventLog System | Format-List** produces output like the following (which we've seriously truncated to save space):

```
PS C:\> get-eventlog system | format-list


Index              : 1888
EntryType          : Information
EventID            : 1103
Message            : Your computer was successfully assigned an address from the network,
                     and it can now connect to other computers.
Category           : (0)
CategoryNumber     : 0
ReplacementStrings : {}
Source             : Dhcp
TimeGenerated      : 4/18/2007 9:06:18 PM
TimeWritten        : 4/18/2007 9:06:18 PM
UserName           :
```

How does PowerShell know to select these particular properties and display them in this particular fashion? Well, if we pipe **Get-EventLog** to **Get-Member**, we'll see what type of data the cmdlet is returning:

```
PS C:\Users\Don> get-eventlog system | get-member

  TypeName: System.Diagnostics.EventLogEntry
```

We can then open the DotNetTypes.format.ps1xml file (located in PowerShell's installation folder, which is in the Windows system folder—System32 or System64) and locate the formatting for that type. It starts off with a <View> tag, which contains the entire definition for how we want to view, or see, items of this particular type. The <Name> of the view is what you'll use with the **-view** parameter of a formatting cmdlet to manually select the view. Notice that <TypeName> is contained within a <ViewSelectedBy> tag: The <ViewSelectedBy> tag contains a list of things that will trigger PowerShell to use this view; any use of the System.Diagnostics.EventLogEntry type will trigger this view.

Next is the <ListControl> section, which actually defines the look of the view. Our list has one <ListEntry>, which consists of several <ListItems>. For each <ListItem>, the XML defines the property that will be shown: Index, EntryType, and so forth. These are the object properties that PowerShell selects when building the table we saw earlier. You'll notice that these properties are the columns that PowerShell displayed when we ran **Get-EventLog**. They weren't *all* displayed, though, because our PowerShell window wasn't wide enough. PowerShell displayed only as many columns as would fit, displaying columns in the exact order listed here in this XML.

```
<View>
        <Name>System.Diagnostics.EventLogEntry</Name>
        <ViewSelectedBy>
            <TypeName>System.Diagnostics.EventLogEntry</TypeName>
        </ViewSelectedBy>

        <ListControl>
            <ListEntries>
                <ListEntry>
                    <ListItems>
                        <ListItem>
                            <PropertyName>Index</PropertyName>
                        </ListItem>
                        <ListItem>
                            <PropertyName>EntryType</PropertyName>
                        </ListItem>
                        <ListItem>
                            <PropertyName>EventID</PropertyName>
                        </ListItem>
                        <ListItem>
                            <PropertyName>Message</PropertyName>
                        </ListItem>
                        <ListItem>
                            <PropertyName>Category</PropertyName>
                        </ListItem>
                        <ListItem>
                            <PropertyName>CategoryNumber</PropertyName>
                        </ListItem>
                        <ListItem>
                            <PropertyName>ReplacementStrings</PropertyName>
                        </ListItem>
                        <ListItem>
                            <PropertyName>Source</PropertyName>
                        </ListItem>
```

```
                        <ListItem>
                                <PropertyName>TimeGenerated</PropertyName>
                        </ListItem>
                        <ListItem>
                                <PropertyName>TimeWritten</PropertyName>
                        </ListItem>
                        <ListItem>
                                <PropertyName>UserName</PropertyName>
                        </ListItem>

                    </ListItems>
                </ListEntry>
            </ListEntries>
        </ListControl>
    </View>
```

This is a pretty simplistic example, but it does serve to illustrate the basics of how and why PowerShell's built-in formatting works. If you scroll to the top of the file, you'll notice that all the <View> tags are contained within a top-level <ViewDefinitions> tag, which is itself contained in the uppermost <Configuration> tag. That's more or less the whole of the formatting file.

---

**Tip**
These files are easier to work with in a dedicated XML editor rather than in Notepad. SAPIEN PrimalScript recognizes and color-codes XML files for easier editing, and the Enterprise edition of PrimalScript includes a Visual XML Editor, which can make XML editing and creation even easier.

---

**By the Way...**
If you just run **Get-EventLog System** without specifying **Format-List**, PowerShell displays the output in a table format. That's because the first view registered for the EventLogEntry type is a table-style format; when we specified a list format, PowerShell had to dig deeper to find a format for EventLogEntry objects that used a ListControl. Fortunately, there was one—otherwise, PowerShell would have constructed a list on its own, possibly using less relevant properties.

## Constructing Your Own Format

A format file thus begins with a <Configuration> tag. Inside that is a <ViewDefinitions> tag, or *node*. Within that, you'll add a <View> node for each object you want to format. Within the <View> node, you'll define an arbitrary <Name> for your view, and you'll build a <ViewSelectedBy> node that tells PowerShell when to use your view. Optionally, the <View> node can also contain a <GroupBy> node, which specifies how PowerShell should group objects. For example, a folder listing is grouped by its parent. Thus far, then, a format file looks something like this:

```
<Configuration>
 <ViewDefinitions>
   <View>
     <Name>MyView</Name>
     <ViewSelectedBy><TypeName></TypeName></ViewSelectedBy>
     <GroupBy></GroupBy>
   </View>
```

```
  </ViewDefinitions>
</Configuration>
```

Actually, there's one meta tag that must appear as the first line in the actual file:

```
<?xml version="1.0" encoding="utf-8" ?>
```

This simply defines the file as XML. For the remainder of this chapter, we'll assume that any format files you're creating already have this line and just focus on the body of the file. Your filename must end in the .ps1xml extension. We recommend you give the file a meaningful name. You'll need to copy the file to any computer where you intend to use the custom formats. Later in the chapter, we'll show you how to load the files into PowerShell.

---

**Tip**
The <Name> of your view allows you to specify it when you use the **Format-Custom** cmdlet. This cmdlet has a **-view** parameter, which accepts the name of the view you want to use to format your output. This allows a view to be selected manually, even if it doesn't match the data type of the objects you're trying to format.

---

Let's cover how that <GroupBy>node works. Typically, you'll populate it with two sub-nodes, <PropertyName> and <Label>:

```
<GroupBy>
 <PropertyName>Myproperty</PropertyName>
 <Label>My Prop</Label>
</GroupBy>
```

Now, when this view is selected, a new header with the label "My Prop"will be generated each time a new value is encountered for Myproperty. Grouping isn't used a lot, though, so let's get back to our basic, in-progress format:

```
<Configuration>
 <ViewDefinitions>
   <View>
     <Name>MyView</Name>
     <ViewSelectedBy><TypeName></TypeName></ViewSelectedBy>
     <GroupBy></GroupBy>
   </View>
 </ViewDefinitions>
</Configuration>
```

From here, you have to decide if you want to make a list, wide, table, or custom view. We'll cover each of these individually, in increasing order of complexity, but we'll start with the above basic template as our starting point for each. For all of our examples, we'll be using the System.Diagnostics.Process class, creating a custom view for Process objects.

## Wide Views

A wide view is probably the easiest to create, primarily because wide views use only a single object property—they're just not that complex. Here's a complete view:

```
<Configuration>
 <ViewDefinitions>
   <View>
     <Name>MyView</Name>
     <ViewSelectedBy><TypeName>System.Diagnostics.Process</TypeName></ViewSelectedBy>
     <WideControl>
        <WideEntries>
           <WideEntry>
              <WideItem>
                 <PropertyName>Name</PropertyName>
              </WideItem>
           </WideEntry>
        </WideEntries>
     </WideControl>
   </View>
 </ViewDefinitions>
</Configuration>
```

Notice that we've filled in the <ViewSelectedBy> section with a .NET Framework type name to which this view will apply. We've added a <WideControl> section, which includes a single <WideEntries> section. Within that, you're permitted one <WideEntry> section, which may contain a single <WideItem> tag. That tag includes the property name you want included in the view—just one property. This may seem like overkill to just display one property, but it's the same basic structure that the other types of views use, so a lot of the excess is just to maintain the structural consistency that XML requires.

You can manually select this view by running:

```
PS C:\> get-process | format-wide -view MyView
```

There's one alternative you can perform with a <WideItem>: Rather than containing a <PropertyName> tag, it can instead contain a <ScriptBlock> tag. For example, suppose we wanted all our process names displayed in lowercase:

```
<WideItem>
    <ScriptBlock>$_.Name.ToUpper()</ScriptBlock>
</WideItem>
```

We've used the special $_ variable, which represents the current object, to access the Name property. Because the Name property is a string, it has a **ToUpper()** method. Thus, our wide view will display all process names in all uppercase characters.

## List Views

List views are only slightly more complicated than wide views, because list views also display properties without a lot of extra formatting. Essentially, a list view is identical to a wide view, except that you can have multiple items—that is, properties or script blocks. Here's an example list view:

```
<Configuration>
 <ViewDefinitions>
   <View>
     <Name>MyView</Name>
     <ViewSelectedBy><TypeName>System.Diagnostics.Process</TypeName></ViewSelectedBy>
     <ListControl>
        <ListEntries>
           <ListEntry>
             <ListItems>
```

```
                <ListItem>
                    <Label>Name</Label>
                    <PropertyName>Name</PropertyName>
                </ListItem>
                <ListItem>
                    <Label>Process ID</Label>
                    <PropertyName>ID</PropertyName>
                </ListItem>
                <ListItem>
                    <Label>CPU Used</Label>
                    <PropertyName>CPU</PropertyName>
                </ListItem>
                </ListItems>
            </ListEntry>
        </ListEntries>
    </ListControl>
  </View>
 </ViewDefinitions>
</Configuration>
```

Also notice that each <ListItem> can have an additional tag: <Label>. The <Label> is the text displayed next to the actual property value. <PropertyName>, as in a wide view, is the property to display. As with a wide view, you can also substitute a <ScriptBlock> for a <PropertyName>; when you do so, you still provide a <Label> that is used to label whatever the script block outputs.

You can manually select this view by running:

```
PS C:\> get-process | format-list -view MyView
```

> **Caution!**
> We're just using these views as examples; generally speaking, you wouldn't include two views with the same name in the same format file. It's actually not a problem to have two views with the same name, provided they're different layouts (e.g., wide and list), because PowerShell can distinguish them by the layout type. However, if you have two views that use the same layout and have the same name, you'll get unexpected results when trying to use that formatting file.

## Table Views

Table views are incrementally more complex than a list view. Like a list view, you can define multiple properties to display (one per column). However, you must define the table's header—the first row, which displays labels for each column—in a separate section. Here's the first part of our example:

```
<Configuration>
 <ViewDefinitions>
   <View>
     <Name>MyView</Name>
     <ViewSelectedBy><TypeName>System.Diagnostics.Process</TypeName></ViewSelectedBy>
     <TableControl>
       <TableHeaders>
        <TableColumnHeader>
          <Label>Name</Label>
          <Width>20</Width>
          <Alignment>Left</Alignment>
        </TableColumnHeader>
```

```
          <TableColumnHeader>
            <Label>Process ID</Label>
            <Width>10</Width>
            <Alignment>Center</Alignment>
          </TableColumnHeader>
          <TableColumnHeader>
            <Label>CPU(s)</Label>
            <Width>4</Width>
            <Alignment>Right</Alignment>
          </TableColumnHeader>
        </TableHeaders>
      </TableControl>
    </View>
  </ViewDefinitions>
</Configuration>
```

As you can see, all we've done here is define the <TableControl> and add the <TableHeaders> section. Within it, we have three <TableColumnHeader> sections, one for each column defined. For each column, we define a text <Label>, the desired <Width> of the column, and the <Alignment> of the column, which may be Left, Center, or Right. You need to keep track of the order in which you define the columns: If you define too many to fit on a user's screen, PowerShell will only display as many columns as it can in the order they're provided in this view. Also, your table *row* entries, which define the data shown in the table's rows, must occur in the same order as the table header, or the output won't make any sense.

We'll continue by adding the table row information:

```
<Configuration>
  <ViewDefinitions>
    <View>
      <Name>MyView</Name>
      <ViewSelectedBy><TypeName>System.Diagnostics.Process</TypeName></ViewSelectedBy>
      <TableControl>
        <TableHeaders>
         <TableColumnHeader>
            <Label>Name</Label>
            <Width>20</Width>
            <Alignment>Left</Alignment>
          </TableColumnHeader>
          <TableColumnHeader>
            <Label>Process ID</Label>
            <Width>10</Width>
            <Alignment>Center</Alignment>
          </TableColumnHeader>
          <TableColumnHeader>
            <Label>CPU(s)</Label>
            <Width>4</Width>
            <Alignment>Right</Alignment>
          </TableColumnHeader>
        </TableHeaders>
        <TableRowEntries>
          <TableRowEntry>
            <TableColumnItems>
             <TableColumnItem>
                <PropertyName>Name</PropertyName>
              </TableColumnItem>
              <TableColumnItem>
                <PropertyName>ID</PropertyName>
              </TableColumnItem>
              <TableColumnItem>
                <PropertyName>CPU</PropertyName>
```

```
        </TableColumnItem>
       </TableColumnItems>
      </TableRowEntry>
     </TableRowEntries>
    </TableControl>
   </View>
  </ViewDefinitions>
</Configuration>
```

We've added the <TableRowEntries> element, which includes a single <TableRowEntry> node. Within that is a single <TableColumnItems> element, containing one <TableColumnItem> for each column defined in the header. The <TableColumnItem> elements contain either a <PropertyName> or a <ScriptBlock> tag, which work exactly as they did in the wide and list views.

........................................................................................................................

**Remember!**
Our example isn't including a <GroupBy> section, but it could—refer to our earlier discussion on the <GroupBy> element for information.

You can manually select this view by running:

```
PS C:\> get-process | format-table -view MyView
```

## Custom Views

Custom views are a completely different beast, and they're much more complicated. They're made more complicated than necessary, really, by the fact that (as of this writing) the PowerShell SDK documentation doesn't address them, and PowerShell doesn't really ship with any examples. We'll do our best to de-mystify them for you here. They start off simply enough:

```
<Configuration>
 <ViewDefinitions>
   <View>
     <Name>MyView</Name>
     <ViewSelectedBy><TypeName>System.Diagnostics.Process</TypeName></ViewSelectedBy>
     <CustomControl>
       <CustomEntries>
       </CustomEntries>
     </CustomControl>
   </View>
 </ViewDefinitions>
</Configuration>
```

This is enough like the pattern of the other three view types that you can probably figure out what comes next: Within the <CustomEntries> section, we'll create <CustomEntry> elements that define our view. Within the <CustomEntry> nodes will be <CustomItem> elements that actually determine what gets displays. You're right: That's what'll happen. It's what goes *inside* those <CustomItem> sections that becomes more complicated.

Here's a simple custom format. Really, this isn't any more complicated than a wide view, because this custom format is simply displaying the name of the Process objects. You'll notice that it takes more XML to get this result: For example, the <CustomItem> has an <ExpressionBinding> sub-element that contains the familiar <PropertyName> tag. As with the other views we've covered, that <PropertyName> could also have been a <Scriptblock> tag.

```
<Configuration>
 <ViewDefinitions>
   <View>
     <Name>MyView</Name>
     <ViewSelectedBy>
        <TypeName>System.Diagnostics.Process</TypeName>
     </ViewSelectedBy>
     <CustomControl>
       <CustomEntries>
        <CustomEntry>
         <CustomItem>
           <ExpressionBinding>
             <PropertyName>Name</PropertyName>
           </ExpressionBinding>
         </CustomItem>
        </CustomEntry>
       </CustomEntries>
     </CustomControl>
   </View>
 </ViewDefinitions>
</Configuration>
```

Here's a slightly more complicated version: We've changed the <CustomItem> to include a <Frame>, with a <LeftIndent> of 4. This will "draw" an invisible "box" around our results, and indent the entire box by four characters. Within the <Frame> is another <CustomItem>, this time with our <Scriptblock> and a <NewLine /> tag. The <NewLine /> tag places a blank space after each object that's output in our view. To save space, we're only including the <CustomControl> portion of the XML—nothing else has changed.

```
  <CustomControl>
    <CustomEntries>
     <CustomEntry>
      <CustomItem>
        <Frame>
          <LeftIndent>4</LeftIndent>
           <CustomItem>
              <ExpressionBinding>
                <Scriptblock>$_.Name.ToUpper()</Scriptblock>
              </ExpressionBinding>
              <NewLine />
           </CustomItem>
        </Frame>
      </CustomItem>
     </CustomEntry>
    </CustomEntries>
   </CustomControl>
```

Here's a further evolution. This time, we've added a <Text> tag to the custom item, creating a "Process:" label. We've also added an <ItemSelectionCondition> to the <ExpressionBinding>. Only processes with a Handles property greater than 50 will be selected to have their name displayed.

```
  <CustomControl>
    <CustomEntries>
     <CustomEntry>
      <CustomItem>
        <Frame>
          <LeftIndent>4</LeftIndent>
           <CustomItem>
              <Text>Process: </Text>
```

```
<ExpressionBinding>
  <ItemSelectionCondition>
    <Scriptblock>$_.Handles -gt 50</Scriptblock>
  </ItemSelectionCondition>
  <Scriptblock>$_.Name.ToUpper()</Scriptblock>
</ExpressionBinding>
             </CustomItem>
           </Frame>
         </CustomItem>
       </CustomEntry>
     </CustomEntries>
   </CustomControl>
```

Here's what a portion of the output looks like:

```
Process: ACPRFMGRSVC
Process: ACSVC
Process: ACTRAY
Process: ACWLICON
Process: AUDIODG
Process: AWAYSCH
Process: BTTRAY
Process: CSRSS
Process: CSRSS
Process: CSSAUTH
Process: DLLHOST
Process: DLLHOST
Process: DWM
Process: EXPLORER
Process: EZEJMNAP
Process: HKCMD
Process:
Process:
```

You'll notice that processes that don't meet the criteria aren't displayed, although the Process: label is still displayed, because that label is defined apart from the <ItemSelectionCondition>. So, the label is displayed, regardless, using this view.

Our next step is to remove the <ItemSelectionCondition>, and to add some additional <Text> elements and a new <ExpressionBinding>. Now, we're displaying each process' ID in parentheses, next to the process name:

```
<CustomControl>
  <CustomEntries>
    <CustomEntry>
      <CustomItem>
        <Frame>
          <LeftIndent>4</LeftIndent>
          <CustomItem>
            <Text>Process: </Text>
            <ExpressionBinding>
              <Scriptblock>$_.Name.ToUpper()</Scriptblock>
            </ExpressionBinding>
            <Text> (ID: </Text>
            <ExpressionBinding>
              <PropertyName>ID</PropertyName>
            </ExpressionBinding>
            <Text>)</Text>
          </CustomItem>
        </Frame>
```

```
        </CustomItem>
      </CustomEntry>
    </CustomEntries>
  </CustomControl>
```

Here's a snippet of the output:

```
Process: ACPRFMGRSVC (ID: 1412)
Process: ACSVC (ID: 2436)
Process: ACTRAY (ID: 1488)
Process: ACWLICON (ID: 2696)
Process: AUDIODG (ID: 1236)
Process: AWAYSCH (ID: 4052)
Process: BTTRAY (ID: 680)
```

Combined with the <NewLine /> tag we used earlier, you can begin to see how fairly complicated formatting is possible. One last iteration:

```
<CustomControl>
  <CustomEntries>
   <CustomEntry>
    <CustomItem>
      <Frame>
        <LeftIndent>4</LeftIndent>
         <CustomItem>
           <Text>Process: </Text>
           <ExpressionBinding>
             <Scriptblock>$_.Name.ToUpper()</Scriptblock>
           </ExpressionBinding>
           <Text> (ID: </Text>
           <ExpressionBinding>
             <PropertyName>ID</PropertyName>
           </ExpressionBinding>
           <Text>)</Text>
         </CustomItem>
      </Frame>
      <Frame>
        <CustomItem>
        <NewLine />
        <ExpressionBinding>
           <Scriptblock>"Handles: " + $_.Handles `
           + " / CPU(s): " + $_.CPU</Scriptblock>
        </ExpressionBinding>
        <NewLine />
        </CustomItem>
      </Frame>
    </CustomItem>
   </CustomEntry>
  </CustomEntries>
 </CustomControl>
```

This time, we've added an all-new <Frame> to contain new information. It starts with a <NewLine />, and then displays a text message including the number of handles and the CPU seconds measurement for the process. It concludes with another <NewLine />. Examine this, and then a sample of its output:

```
Process: ACPRFMGRSVC (ID: 1412)
Handles: 135 / CPU(s): 0.1404009

Process: ACSVC (ID: 2436)
```

```
Handles: 257 / CPU(s): 0.624004

Process: ACTRAY (ID: 1488)
Handles: 85 / CPU(s): 0.1092007

Process: ACWLICON (ID: 2696)
Handles: 82 / CPU(s): 0.1404009
```

Custom views are certainly complex, and, trust us, we've barely scratched the surface of what they can do. However, this should get you started on creating your own custom formats. Why bother? One reason we can think of is to create output that's more suitable for management or auditing reports.

By the way, we generated all of this output after importing our format file via **Update-FormatData** (of course), and then running:

```
PS C:\> get-process | format-custom -view myview
```

Where are custom views practically useful? We've mentioned elsewhere that all of PowerShell's built-in help is displayed and formatted using custom views; anytime you're dealing with especially complex data that needs to be laid out in a particular way—not necessarily a list or a table—then a custom view might make sense. Typically, however, administrators are usually working with several objects—such as processes, services, event logs, and so forth—and any time you've got a collection of objects, a list or a table is usually easier to make and presents the information in a way that's easier to use.

## Importing Your Format

When you're ready with a working format, move the .ps1xml file to its permanent location. Personally, we like keeping these files in our personal documents folder ("My Documents" on Windows XP, or "Documents" on Windows Vista), so that our files "follow" us if we're using a roaming profile. We don't recommend storing your files in PowerShell's installation folder, since there's always a possibility that your files will be overwritten by some future update.

Before you can start using your new views, you have to import them into the shell. You'll first need to decide if you want your new formats to come *before* or *after* PowerShell's built-in formats. Remember, when PowerShell isn't given a specific view by name, it goes looking for one that matches the object type it's working with. The first matching view it comes across is the one it uses, so if your views are loaded first, then they'll become the defaults for your data types. If your views are loaded last, then they'll be available on demand, but they won't become the default views (unless PowerShell defines no other views for the object types you've selected).

- To load your files before PowerShell's, run **Update-FormatData -prependPath** *filepath*.

- To load your files after PowerShell's, run **Update-FormatData -appendPath** *filepath*.

Running **Update-FormatData** *registers* the view or views you've defined in the specified file and makes those views available to PowerShell's Format cmdlets.

**Oops...**

If you made a mistake in your format XML, PowerShell will display any errors when it tries to load the file. After fixing any problems, you'll need to close and re-open PowerShell before you can try to re-load your format file.

Unless you add these cmdlets to your profile, you'll need to run them each time you open a new PowerShell session; PowerShell does not persist this information in any other way. Also, keep in mind that .format.ps1xml files can be digitally signed just like .ps1 files; if your shell's ExecutionPolicy requires a signature for scripts, then you'll need to sign your format files, also.

**Warning**

As you read this chapter, you might be tempted to simply modify the format files that shipped with PowerShell. Don't. These files are digitally signed by Microsoft. If you modify them you will break the signature, and unless you're Microsoft, you won't have any way to resign them. Also, when a new version of the file ships from Microsoft, your changes will be lost.

# Formatting Rules

PowerShell's formatting rules are a bit complicated, so it's worth reviewing them. When PowerShell needs to format objects, it follows these rules and uses the *first rule that matches*. Also note that these decisions are all made by examining only the first object in the pipeline—all objects are formatting, according to the decision driven by the first object.

- If you haven't specified a table, list, wide, or custom format (by using one of the Format cmdlets), then PowerShell will look to see if a view has been registered for the data type of the pipeline object. If at least one view has been registered, PowerShell will use the first one it finds—selecting table, list, wide, or custom, based on whatever the view uses.

- If you used a Format cmdlet to specify a list, table, wide, or custom format, but didn't specify a particular view by name, PowerShell will grab the first registered view for the object's type that matches the layout you specified. If no registered view exists, PowerShell will "fake it" and do the best job it can to construct the appropriately formatted output for you, using the "default" properties defined for the object ("default" properties are defined in PowerShell's Types.ps1xml file).

- If you specified a list, table, wide, or custom format, *and* specified a particular view (by using the -**view** parameter of the Format cmdlet), PowerShell will look for that view. However, it'll only be able to use it if the view uses the same layout—table, wide, custom, or list. If the view you specify doesn't match the layout you specified, you'll receive an error.

- If there is no registered view for the type of object in the pipeline, and you didn't specify any formatting, PowerShell will use a table if the object has fewer than five properties. Otherwise, it'll use a list. PowerShell won't automatically select a wide or custom format under these circumstances. If PowerShell decides to use a list, it will—by default—only display properties that are marked as "default properties" for that object type in PowerShell's Types.ps1xml file. If that object type isn't defined in Types.ps1xml, or if no properties are marked as "defaults," then PowerShell will display *all* of the properties in a list.

# Chapter 39
# The PowerShell Ecosystem: Third-Party Extensions

Perhaps one of the most important aspects of PowerShell is the fact that it has quickly developed a rich and active following of independent users and companies who support and extend it. In other words, PowerShell doesn't exist entirely on its own: It is part of a diverse and growing ecosystem, which includes many companies, individual enthusiasts, and more. Why is a rich ecosystem important? Well, one concern with PowerShell—or any new technology—is whether or not it will become adopted widely enough for people like you to invest time in. Of course, if enough people think that, then it's a catch-22: Nobody invests the time, so nobody feels it's worth investing the time. With PowerShell, however, you don't have to worry about that: *Lots* of people have invested serious time and money already. It goes beyond Microsoft, too, although the support for PowerShell within Microsoft's various product teams is significant and expanding. Outside of Microsoft, many third-party manufacturers and independent programmers are extending PowerShell's functionality by providing sets of cmdlets, tools and utilities, and much more.

In this chapter, we'll examine some of the more complete offerings—that is, commercial and free extensions that are mature and immediately usable. By the time you read this, it's almost certain that all of these will have released new versions, so our goal here isn't to completely document these, but rather to give you an idea of what's out there, and what these various tools and components can do for you in your daily work.

Note that, with the exception of the software manufactured by SAPIEN Technologies, neither of the authors of this book have any affiliation or association with the software we're discussing in this chapter. We're not endorsing or recommending any of it, and no manufacturer paid us any kind of compensation to include this software in the book. We simply wanted to give you a springboard for further research and help you realize what a diverse and flexible tool you've found in PowerShell. Hopefully, by getting a glimpse at what others are enabling PowerShell to do, you'll be able to find the perfect thing to solve whatever unique administrative problems you find yourself faced with.

## PowerGagdets

PowerGadgets, LLC (www.PowerGadgets.com) has made an extremely cool, very useful snap-in for Windows PowerShell. PowerGagdets takes input data—say, performance data from the WMI performance counter classes—and turns that data into charts, gauges, and maps. For example:

```
PS C:\> gwmi win32_perfrawdata_perfos_memory | out-gauge -value availablembytes -floating
```

This uses WMI to query the "Available Memory" performance information from the local computer and display a "free memory" gauge. Of course, since **Gwmi** supports remote connectivity, you could just as easily pull the available memory—or CPU information or anything else—from another computer, as well. The graphical gauges and charts can be free-floating, displayed as desktop icons, or they can be docked in the Windows Vista SideBar. They can also auto-update themselves on an interval you specify, making them an easy way to create customized, task-specific dashboards.

A graphical Wizard allows you to create new gadgets outside of PowerShell, if desired—for example, you can use a database on your network, or a Web service, as the data source for a new gadget. Several gadgets can be combined into a group, which helps to prevent on-screen clutter (trust us, it's easy to get carried away with these things). You can even automatically e-mail an image of a gadget, if desired—that'll show the boss who doesn't believe your servers are hitting 90% CPU capacity!

PowerGadgets Creator lets you author complex gadgets in a graphical environment, and then save them as .PGF files, which you can distribute to other administrators—they simply need the PowerGadgets Client (which is less expensive) installed in order to use these files. For example, you might create a "map" gadget that shows the status (up or down) of your organization's servers, and then distribute that to other technicians on your network for use in their personal "dashboard." Gadgets that retrieve their data from a source other than PowerShell have no dependency on PowerShell; they can be viewed without having PowerShell installed. Gadgets can even be digitally signed, helping you to keep them safe and secure.

## PrimalScript

SAPIEN PrimalScript (www.PrimalScript.com) is a visual development environment geared specifically toward scripting, and with specific support for Windows PowerShell (it was in fact the first commercial tool to support PowerShell). It offers a number of features that help make PowerShell scripting easier:

- Syntax color-coding, making your scripts easier to read and making it easier to catch typos.

- Live syntax checking, which is somewhat like live spell-checking in Microsoft Word.

- Code hinting, including pop-up syntax reminders for PowerShell cmdlets.

- Integrated help, allowing you to place your cursor over PowerShell cmdlets, press F1, and get the cmdlet syntax in a pane right within the editor.

- Code completion, including pop-up menus for PowerShell cmdlets and other language elements.

- The ability to package PowerShell scripts into standalone executable (.Exe) files that run under alternate credentials.

- Source control integration, providing enterprise-level change control and rollback capabilities.

- The ability to run PowerShell scripts right within the editing environment, with script output appearing in a dedicated "output" pane.

- Integrated security, including the ability to modify the local ExecutionPolicy, and to automatically apply a digital signature to PowerShell scripts each time they're saved (making it easier to use the safer AllSigned ExecutionPolicy).

- The ability to undo changes made to a file even after weeks or months of not working with the file—the "undo stream" is saved along with the file itself, not stored in memory.

- Built-in Snippets, which are short, pre-written chunks of commonly-used code that you can drag into your scripts, or add with a hotkey. You can save your own commonly used segments of code as custom Snippets and use them alongside the built-in ones.

The list of features goes on and on—PrimalScript as of last count included well over 200 distinct features; many of these are not necessarily PowerShell-specific, but still contribute to a more efficient scripting experience. A 45-day free trial is available from the product's Web site, and it can be purchased from various software resellers and from www.ScriptingOutpost.com.

## PowerShell Community Extensions

Go to http://www.codeplex.com/powershellcx and you'll find an open-source, community-driven treasure trove of PowerShell extensions: The PowerShell Community Extensions. As this book was being written, v1.1 was the current version, and it sports almost 60 new cmdlets, dozens of functions and filters, a collection of useful scripts, and more. Many of these cmdlets provide access to things that Windows can do, but which PowerShell itself doesn't support: reparse points, name resolution, pinging, symbolic links, ZIP and TAR file creation, terminal sessions, hard links, clipboard management, data conversion, and more. In fact, looking at the list, it's hard to imagine how any hardworking administrator could live without these dozens of useful tools. It even includes a PSDrive provider for Active Directory, allowing to you connect your domain as a "disk drive" and browse it using PowerShell's familiar commands like **Cd** and **Dir**. And, best of all, these extensions are absolutely free.

Let's take a quick look at the Active Directory provider, which many of you will find appealing. When you install the PowerShell Community Extensions, a new PSDrive is created called COMPANY that is "mapped" to the root of your Active Directory domain. All you need to do is change drives and you can navigate your domain as if it were a file system:

```
PS COMPANY:\> dir

    LastWriteTime Type              Name
    ------------- ----              ----
7/28/2006 10:11 PM builtinDomain       Builtin
7/28/2006 10:11 PM container           Computers
7/31/2007 11:28 AM organizationalUnit  Desktops
7/28/2006 10:11 PM organizationalUnit  Domain Controllers
7/24/2007 12:36 PM organizationalUnit  Employees
7/28/2006 10:11 PM container           ForeignSecurityPrincipals
7/28/2006 10:11 PM infrastructureUpdate Infrastructure
7/28/2006 10:11 PM lostAndFound        LostAndFound
7/28/2006 10:11 PM msDS-QuotaContainer NTDS Quotas
7/28/2006 10:11 PM container           Program Data
7/28/2006 10:11 PM container           System
7/28/2006 10:11 PM container           Users

PS COMPANY:\> cd employees
PS COMPANY:\employees> dir

    LastWriteTime Type              Name
```

```
     ------------- ----              ----
7/30/2007 11:10 AM user             Don Jones
7/24/2007 10:11 PM user             Jeff Hicks
7/24/2007 3:44 PM organizationalUnit  QA
7/30/2007 9:33 AM organizationalUnit  Research
7/24/2007 9:52 PM organizationalUnit  Sales


PS COMPANY:\employees>
```

You can create a new organizational unit almost as easily as creating a new folder:

```
PS COMPANY:\employees> new-item Finance -itemtype organizationalunit
```

Creating a new user takes a few steps:

```
PS COMPANY:\employees> $amy=get-adobject -distinguishedname (new-item "Amy Admin" '
>>-itemtype user).distinguishedName
>>
PS COMPANY:\employees> $amy.sAMAccountname="aadmin"
PS COMPANY:\employees> $amy.sn="Admin"
PS COMPANY:\employees> $amy.givenname="Amy"
PS COMPANY:\employees> $amy.displayname="Amy Admin"
PS COMPANY:\employees> $amy.Description="Company help desk admin"
PS COMPANY:\employees> $amy.userprincipalname=aadmin@company.local
PS COMPANY:\employees> $amy.UserAccountControl=544 #enable account
PS COMPANY:\employees> $amy.title="Help Desk Supervisor"
PS COMPANY:\employees> $amy.SetPassword("P@ssw0rd")
PS COMPANY:\employees> $amy.SetInfo()
```

The **Get-ADObject** cmdlet that is part of the community extensions is abstracting the underlying .NET Framework classes in much the same way as using the [ADSI] type adapter. But because it is a cmdlet, it is a little easier to use. In our example, we are using the -distinguishedname property to instruct the cmdlet what object to get. In this case, it is the distinguishedname of a new user object we create using **New-Item**. The expression creates a new user object for Amy Admin and returns a PowerShell object, $amy, that we can work with.

If you pipe $amy to **Get-Member()** you'll see some properties but not all. However, as long as you know the name of the user property, you can set it as we do here. You can also call the **SetPassword()** method, and don't forget to call **Set-Info()** to write your changes to Active Directory. As you can see, this is a lot of work. We recommend you check out the Quest AD cmdlets that we talk about below. You can use them in conjunction with the AD provider.

## SAPIEN Extensions for Windows PowerShell

This is a free snap-in available at www.PrimalScript.com/freetools. This is the one piece of software that we, the authors of this book, are directly associated with, since we actually created these extensions. They're under constant revision and enhancement, so be sure you're periodically checking back for the latest version. Currently, the Extensions provide more than a dozen cmdlets that are useful in logon scripts (checking for local group membership, retrieving the user name and domain name, and so forth), retrieving local management information like available memory, connecting to databases and executing queries, pinging computers, and even speaking aloud (that's right—you can have PowerShell talk to you). We also included a couple of cmdlets that mimic the MsgBox and InputBox functionality from VBScript, in case you're used to working with VBScript and miss those simple graphical prompts.

## SAPIEN's PowerShell Help

PowerShell's built-in help facility provides detailed information not only on cmdlets, but on a number of more general topics. While these are all easily accessible from within the shell using the **Help** function, sometimes you want to be able to read help information while you're piecing together a complex command-line instruction. In those cases, having to run **Help** can be distracting. At www.PrimalScript. com/freetools, you'll find a PowerShell Help utility. This tool extracts all of the help information from PowerShell, and displays it in a graphical window. This allows you to browse the help information *alongside* the console window, so that you can see examples *while* you're piecing together complex instructions.

## CodePlex

CodePlex (www.codeplex.com) is Microsoft's answer to SourceForge: It's an open-source project hosting site that charges projects no fees. We have a project named PowerQuest hosted there (www. codeplex.com/powerquest), which is a text-based adventure game that takes place within the PowerShell console. The PowerShell Community Extensions also live on CodePlex. However, if you type "PowerShell" into CodePlex's search engine, you'll come up with more than a dozen PowerShell-related projects, including:

- Extensions that support Windows Installer
- PowerShell Remoting
- A SharePoint PSDrive provider, allowing SharePoint servers to be connected as "drives" within PowerShell
- An implementation of JungleDisk, which uses Amazon's S3 storage services
- A NewsGator provider

It's worth stopping by CodePlex every now and again to see what's new—there's an active and growing community of programmers extending PowerShell's capabilities every day.

## Quest PowerGUI

Even though PowerShell is a management shell, there are still plenty of administrators who feel more at home with a graphical interface. The PowerGui tool acts as a graphical front end to PowerShell.

Starting PowerGUI

The console organizes likely tasks in a tree pane. When you select an item, you get a graphical output of an underlying PowerShell expression. Here, you can see the where we've retrieved a list of System event logs filtered to return the last 100 errors:

PowerGui UI Mode

When you click the PowerShellCode tab, you can see the actual PowerShell code that is executed:

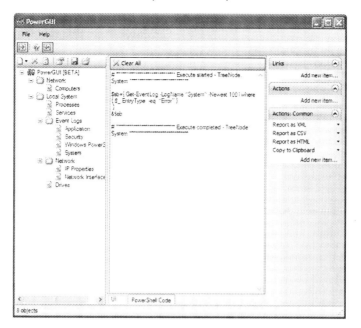

PowerGui PowerShell Code mode

This lets you manage systems with PowerShell in a graphical format yet still learn how to do it from the command line.

The PowerGUI can be extended by including other snap-ins and user-developed extensions. You can use PowerGUI as a front end to Exchange 2007 and System Center 2007. You can download the application and learn more at www.powergui.org.

## Quest Cmdlets for Active Directory Management

Even though the current version of PowerShell has limited functionality related to Active Directory, Quest Software has stepped in and developed a set of free cmdlets you can use to manage Active Directory. These cmdlets are bundled as part of their ActiveRoles Management Shell for Active Directory, which you can download from www.powergui.org.

The list of included cmdlets is deceivingly short and more are added with each new release:

- Add-QADGroupMember
- Add-QADPasswordSettingsObjectAppliesTo
- Connect-QADService
- Convert-QADAttributeValue
- Disconnect-QADService
- Get-QADComputer
- Get-QADGroup
- Get-QADGroupMember
- Get-QADObject
- Get-QADPasswordSettingsObject

- Get-QADPSSnapinSettings

- Get-QADUser

- New-QADGroup

- New-QADObject

- New-QADPasswordSettingsObject

- New-QADUser

- Remove-QADGroupMember

- Remove-QADObject

- Remove-QADPasswordSettingsObjectAppliesTo

- Set-QADObject

- Set-QADPSSnapinSettings

- Set-QADUser

However, don't let the quantity deceive you. These cmdlets let you create and work with Active Directory objects like users, groups, and computers. Creating a new user can be as simple as this:

```
PS C:\> new-qaduser -parentcontainer "OU=Employees,DC=company,DC=local" `
>> -name "Charles Dickens" -samaccount "cdickens" -userpassword "P@ssw0rd" `
>>-userprincipalname "Cdickens@company.local" -displayname "Charles Dickens"
>>

Name              Type           DN
----              ----           --
Charles Dickens   user            CN=Charles Dickens,OU=Employees,DC=company,DC=local


PS C:\>
```

But because these are cmdlets, they can also take advantage of the pipeline. Suppose we have a CSV file of new user accounts to be created:

```
PS C:\> cat newusers.csv
First Name,Last Name,Title,Department,Telephone
Anne,Tern,Sales Intern,Sales,555-1234
Ben,Jay,Finance Intern,Finance,555-1235
Charlie,Robin,Research Lab Asst.,Research,555-1236
David,Cardinal,Research Lab Asst.,Research,555-1237
Ed,Nightingale,QA Technician,QA,555-1238
Fiona,Thrush,Outside Sales Rep,Sales,555-1239
```

We can take the contents of this file and run them through **New-QADUser**:

```
$file='C:\newusers.csv'
PS C:\> Import-Csv $file | %{new-qadUser -parentcontainer `
>> ('OU=' + $_.Department + ',OU=Employees,DC=company,dc=local')`
>> -name ($_.'First Name' +' ' + $_.'Last Name') `
>> -samAccountName (($_.'First Name').Substring(0,1) + $_.'Last name') `
>> -firstname $_.'First Name' -lastname $_.'Last Name' `
>> -title $_.title -department $_.department -company "Company.com" `
>> -phonenumber $_.Telephone -userpassword "P@ssw0rd" `
```

```
>> -userprincipalname (($_.'First Name').Substring(0,1) + $_.'Last name' `
>> + "@company.com") -displayname ($_.'First Name' + ' ' + $_.'Last Name') `
>> -objectattributes @{"userAccountControl"=544} `
>> | set-qaduser -objectattributes @{"pwdlastset"=0}
>> }
>>

Name              Type           DN
----              ----           --
Anne Tern         user           CN=Anne Tern,OU=Sales,OU=Employees,DC=compan
Ben Jay           user           CN=Ben Jay,OU=Finance,OU=Employees,DC=compan
Charlie Robin     user            CN=Charlie Robin,OU=Research,OU=Employees,DC
David Cardinal    user            CN=David Cardinal,OU=Research,OU=Employees,D
Ed Nightingale    user            CN=Ed Nightingale,OU=QA,OU=Employees,DC=comp
Fiona Thrush      user            CN=Fiona Thrush,OU=Sales,OU=Employees,DC=com


PS C:\>
```

In a matter of seconds we've created fully populated user accounts. The output of the **Import-Csv** cmdlet is piped to the **ForEach** cmdlet, which is represented by the % alias. We'll use the values from the different columns in the CSV file to provide property values for the **New-QADUser** cmdlet. Remember that $_ will represent the current user record from the CSV file. The first record has these values:

```
First Name : Anne
Last Name : Tern
Title     : Sales Intern
Department : Sales
Telephone : 555-1234
```

The parent container is built from the department property of the first record. In our test domain, each department has a child OU under the Employees organizational unit. The user's account name is a combination of the First Name and Last Name fields from the CSV file:

```
-name ($_.'First Name' +' ' + $_.'Last Name')
```

Next, we create the sAMAccountname by taking the first character of the first name and concatenating it with the last name:

```
samAccountName (($_.'First Name').Substring(0,1) + $_.'Last name')
```

The user principal name is constructed in much the same way:

```
-userprincipalname (($_.'First Name').Substring(0,1) + $_.'Last name' '
>> + "@company.com")
```

The remaining properties are either hard coded, like "Company", or associated with the corresponding CSV field:

```
>> -title $_.title -department $_.department -company "Company.com" `
```

In order to enable the accounts, we set the "UserAccountControl" property to 544:

```
-objectattributes @{"userAccountControl"=544}
```

After each account is created, we pipe the result to the **Set-QADUser** cmdlet to change the "PwdlastSet" property, which forces the user to change their password at next logon:

```
set-qaduser -objectattributes @{"pwdlastset"=0}
```

This allows us to set the same password for each user but then force them to change it immediately.

The Quest cmdlets also make it easy to modify existing accounts, add users to groups, and much more. Using these cmdlets, which technically are still in beta, in conjunction with the DirectoryServices PSDrive provider from the PowerShell Community Extensions, will make managing Active Directory a snap.

## Full Armor

Full Armor's WorkFlow Studio presents a graphical front end to Windows PowerShell and the WorkFlow Foundation in the .NET Framework 3.0. This tool let's you drag and drop graphical objects that represent PowerShell cmdlets and scripts and link them together in a workflow. As you drag each element, you can modify its parameters and customize the process.

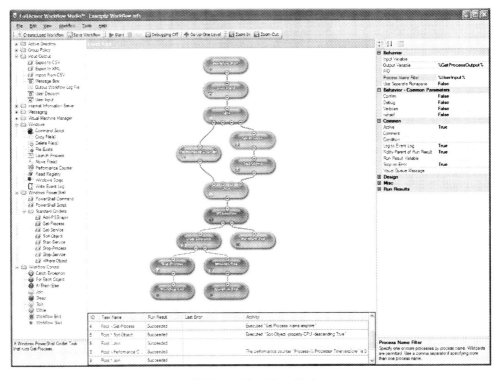

Full Armor WorkFlow Studio

Once you have a workflow process that meets your needs, you can save it and run it at any time, even as a scheduled task. You can learn more about this product from www.fullarmor.com.

## SDM Software

SDM Software focuses on Group Policy management solutions. They have released two free cmdlets for working with Group Policy from within PowerShell. The cmdlets require the Group Policy Management Console to be installed first.

The first cmdlet, **Get-SDMgpo**, will retrieve information about your group policy objects:

```
PS C:\> get-sdmgpo "corp desktop"


DisplayName              : Corp Desktop
Path                     : cn={7F283C5A-2C6B-4F9F-96A2-9959BD3F7EC6},cn=policies,cn=system,DC=com
pany,DC=local
ID                       : {7F283C5A-2C6B-4F9F-96A2-9959BD3F7EC6}
DomainName               : company.local
CreationTime             : 8/8/2007 1:15:02 PM
ModificationTime         : 8/8/2007 1:22:18 PM
UserDSVersionNumber      : 14
ComputerDSVersionNumber  : 1
UserSysvolVersionNumber  : 14
ComputerSysvolVersionNumber : 1
```

You can also use a wildcard character and return information about all group policy objects:

```
PS C:\> get-sdmgpo *
```

Because the cmdlet is using the Group Policy Management Console, you can also do things with your policy objects, such as back them up or generate a report:

```
PS C:\> foreach ($gpo in $gpos) {$gpo.Backup("E:\GPOBackups\","Weekly Backup")}
```

You can create a blank Group Policy Object with **New-SDMgpo**:

```
PS C:\> new-sdmgpo "Sales Users"


DisplayName              : Sales Users
Path                     : cn={E045D7E3-D128-4BBC-9642-7E7344F177A2},cn=policies,cn=system…
ID                       : {E045D7E3-D128-4BBC-9642-7E7344F177A2}
DomainName               : company.local
CreationTime             : 8/8/2007 2:28:54 PM
ModificationTime         : 8/8/2007 2:28:56 PM
UserDSVersionNumber      : 0
ComputerDSVersionNumber  : 0
UserSysvolVersionNumber  : 0
ComputerSysvolVersionNumber : 0
```

You can't specify policy settings but you can take steps such as disabling the policies computer node. In fact, we can put the two cmdlets together:

```
PS C:\> foreach ($gpo in (new-sdmgpo "Finance Users")) {
>> (get-sdmgpo $gpo.displayname).SetComputerEnabled($False)
>> }
>>
```

Here we've created a new Group Policy Object called "Finance Users" using **New-SDMgpo**. Using **ForEach** we iterate the results of the expression and pass the policy's displayname to **Get-SDMgpo** where we invoke the **SetComputerEnabled()** method.

And if that weren't enough, SDM Software has also released a PowerShell based tool called the GPExpert Scripting Toolkit. You can use PowerShell to modify individual GPO settings.

Here we connect to the XP Firewall GPO using the **Get-Sdmgpobject** cmdlet from the GPExpert Scripting Toolkit:

```
PS C:\> $gpo=get-sdmgpobject -gponame "gpo://company.local/xp firewall"'
>> -openbyname $true
>>
PS C:\> $gpo
```

```
GPName                      : gpo://company.local/xp firewall
UserName                    :
Password                    :
AuthEnum                    : None
OpenByName                  : True
CentralStore                :
Containers                  : {Computer Configuration, User Configuration}
GPCComputerVersion          : 8
GPCUserVersion              : 2
GPTComputerVersion          : 8
GPTUserVersion              : 2
Name                        : XP Firewall
Guid                        : CE36149F-6862-4A6C-9BDB-73BA70BF41FD
DisableComputerConfiguration : False
DisableUserConfiguration    : True
Type                        : AD
ADRoot                      : System.DirectoryServices.DirectoryEntry
FSPath                      : \\Alpha-DC.company.local\SYSVOL\company.local\Policies\{CE36149
PolFileManager              : GPOSDK.Providers._Common.PolFileManager
AdmManager                  : GPOSDK.Providers._Common.AdmManager
```

You can also use this tool to manage local group policy settings:

```
$gpo = Get-SDMgpobject -gpoName "gpo://ComputerName/Local/"

$cnt = $gpo.GetObject("Computer Configuration/Administrative Templates/System/Logon");
$settname = "Do not process the run once list"

$stng = $cnt.Settings.ItemByName($settname);

"'Listing properties of the setting" + $settname

$proplist = $stng.GetPropertyNames();
$set_vname = "";
foreach ( $propname in $proplist ) {
   $propname + ' = ' + $stng.Get($propname);

}
```

Let's connect to the domain firewall setting container. This is a single line command:

```
PS C:\> $cnt=$gpo.GetObject("Computer Configuration/Administrative Templates/Network/Network
 Connections/Windows Firewall/Domain Profile")
```

We want to modify one of the Allow ICMP Exception settings:

```
PS C:\> $setting=$cnt.settings.itembyname("Windows Firewall: Allow ICMP exceptions")
```

We can see that the current "Allow redirect" setting is turned off:

```
PS C:\> $setting.Get("Allow redirect")
0
```

So, we'll turn it on and save the change:

```
PS C:\> $setting.Put("Allow redirect",1)
PS C:\> $setting.save()
```

With this tool, you create a GPO and define all of its settings all with a PowerShell script. There is much more to this tool that we think you'll find intriguing. You can download software and read more at http://www.gpoguy.com/powershell.htm.

# /n Software

Even though the .NET Framework is quite extensive when it comes to networking, PowerShell has very few native networking cmdlets. Fortunately, /n Software has released NetCmdlets. This group of cmdlets can be used to work with SNMP, send SMTP mail, run FTP or TFTP sessions, as well as get low-level packet information.

For example, you can use their **Get-Dns** cmdlet to retrieve DNS information about a specified computer:

```
PS C:\> get-dns exch07.company.local A


ADDRESS      : 192.168.10.25
Type        : A
Fields      : {ADDRESS}
Values      : {192.168.10.25}
Domain      : exch07.company.local
TTL         : 1200
RecordSource : Answer
```

Another cmdlet you might find useful is **Get-Packet**, which allows you to capture packets from a particular adapter. It is not as full-featured as a packet capture program like Wireshark, but it does allow you to do something like this:

```
PS C:\> $cap=get-packet -time 60
PS C:\> $cap | where {$_.protocol -eq "TCP"} | format-table
>> Source,SourcePort,Destination,DestinationPort -autosize
>>


Source          SourcePort Destination     DestinationPort
------          ---------- -----------     ---------------
192.168.127.200       3333 72.14.219.104                80
192.168.127.200       3333 72.14.219.104                80
72.14.219.104           80 192.168.127.200             3333
192.168.127.200       3333 72.14.219.104                80
72.14.219.104           80 192.168.127.200             3333
72.14.219.104           80 192.168.127.200             3333
72.14.219.104           80 192.168.127.200             3333
72.14.219.104           80 192.168.127.200             3333
192.168.127.200       3333 72.14.219.104                80
192.168.127.200       3333 72.14.219.104                80
72.14.219.104           80 192.168.127.200             3333
72.14.219.104           80 192.168.127.200             3333
192.168.127.200       3333 72.14.219.104                80
72.14.219.104           80 192.168.127.200             3333
```

Above, we've captured 60 seconds worth of network traffic and then selected the source and destination. The company also is working on a PowerShell remoting solution, which is currently in beta. Read more about these cmdlets and download a trial at http://www.nsoftware.com/powershell/default.aspx.

Chapter 40
# The .NET Framework for Windows Administrators

With all these talk of .NET and PowerShell, it's easy to think that you *need* to know about the Framework in order to use PowerShell effectively. Some of the more ambitious PowerShell users will blog at length about loading up .NET assemblies and doing crazy stuff with them. Well, the news—good or bad, however you want to view it—is that you can be *very* effective in PowerShell *without* touching the .NET Framework directly. Sure, everything in PowerShell is .NET under the hood, but PowerShell's primary purpose is to *adapt* the Framework into something more administrator-friendly. That said, the Framework has a lot of powerful capabilities lurking under the hood, and if you don't mind the complexity, PowerShell *will* let you access all that power. So, that's what this chapter is all about: understanding the framework enough to be able to utilize it from within PowerShell.

## What is the Framework?

The Microsoft .NET Framework is essentially a *huge* collection of prepackaged functionality provided to programmers by Microsoft, to make the programmers' work easier. For example, the .NET Framework knows how to send e-mail, how to resolve computer names to IP addresses, and how to ping a remote computer; if you're writing an application in the Framework, then, you just instruct it to do those things, rather than writing them yourself. By building all this great functionality into the common Framework, Microsoft allows developers to be more productive: All the developers have to do (more or less) is piece together the various pieces of the Framework to accomplish whatever task the developers are trying to accomplish.

For example, if we sat you down with a copy of C++ and asked you to write a program that would stop a Windows service, would you know where to begin? We certainly wouldn't. Because that's such a commonly needed task, however, Microsoft built that functionality into the Framework, in the form of the

System.ServiceProcess.ServiceController class. See, the Framework consists almost entirely of these various *classes,* and they're organized into a fairly consistent naming convention—called a *namespace*—to help make them a bit easier to remember. For example, nearly anything having to do with the Windows system falls under the System namespace, including System.IO for input/output tasks (like writing files), System.XML for working with XML documents, System.Web for working with Web-related stuff, and so forth. A .NET Framework class serves pretty much the same purpose as a WMI class: The class describes how some piece of software functions. Think of a class as a *definition* for something; a definition for a service, for example, specifies that the service have a name, the ability to start, stop, and pause, and so forth. When you're actually talking about a *specific* service, then you're talking about an *instance* of that class. The instance has all the properties and methods that are defined in the class, and those properties and methods allow you to manipulate that instance—stopping it, starting it, reconfiguring it, and so forth.

So, at its heart, the Framework is an enormous collection of classes, which is referred to as a *class library.* And we do mean *enormous*: Visit the documentation at http://msdn2.microsoft.com/en-us/library/ms644560.aspx and you'll see exactly how enormous. But, by organizing classes into the various namespaces, the class library is somewhat easier to browse and learn about.

## PowerShell's Framework Adaptation

Normally, PowerShell doesn't force you to work directly with the Framework's classes. Instead, PowerShell gives you task-oriented cmdlets, which simplify the underlying Framework classes and, in some cases, make them more consistent. For example, some Framework classes use a Length property to indicate their size, while others use Count; PowerShell "adapts" these so that they consistently appear to use the Count property when accessed from within PowerShell.

WMI is a really good example of the hard work PowerShell does to adapt Framework classes into something more administrator-friendly. For example, try running this:

```
PS C:\> gwmi win32_operatingsystem | gm


   TypeName: System.Management.ManagementObject#root\cimv2\Win32_OperatingSystem
```

We've retrieved a WMI instance and piped it to **Get-Member (Gm)**. We see that the TypeName— that is, the Framework class name—is System.Management.ManagementObject. Okay, that means PowerShell asked the Framework to go get this particular WMI instance, and what came back was this object type. Let's look it up in the documentation (it's at http://msdn2.microsoft.com/en-us/library/system.management.managementobject.aspx). If we look at the *members*—that is, the properties, methods, and so forth—of this class, we see that there aren't that many properties and methods. There *certainly* aren't as many properties as PowerShell lists:

```
Name                        MemberType  Definition
----                        ----------  ----------
Reboot                      Method      System.Management.ManagementBas...
SetDateTime                 Method       System.Management.ManagementBas...
Shutdown                    Method      System.Management.ManagementBas...
Win32Shutdown               Method       System.Management.ManagementBas...
Win32ShutdownTracker         Method        System.Management.ManagementBas...
BootDevice                  Property     System.String BootDevice {get;s...
BuildNumber                 Property     System.String BuildNumber {get;...
BuildType                   Property    System.String BuildType {get;set;}
Caption                     Property    System.String Caption {get;set;}
CodeSet                     Property    System.String CodeSet {get;set;}
```

```
CountryCode                                   Property      System.String CountryCode {get;...
CreationClassName                             Property      System.String CreationClassName...
CSCreationClassName                            Property       System.String CSCreationClassNa...
CSDVersion                                    Property      System.String CSDVersion {get;s...
CSName                                        Property     System.String CSName {get;set;}
CurrentTimeZone                               Property      System.Int16 CurrentTimeZone {g...
DataExecutionPrevention_32BitApplications Property      System.Boolean DataExecutionPre...
DataExecutionPrevention_Available            Property       System.Boolean DataExecutionPre...
```

And that's just a partial list! No, the Framework object is much more generic. If we were actually using the Framework directly, we wouldn't have all of these properties; instead, we'd use the ManagementObject class' **Get()** method to retrieve the property we wanted. For example, object. Get("BuildNumber") would get the BuildNumber property. But in PowerShell, we don't have to do that, because PowerShell has *adapted* the object for us. The clue is in the TypeName shown by **Get-Member**:

```
TypeName: System.Management.ManagementObject#root\cimv2\Win32_OperatingSystem
```

PowerShell's tell us that it's adapted this object to directly represent the root\cimv2\Win32_ OperatingSystem WMI class. What PowerShell has done is gone in and retrieved all of the WMI class properties, and constructed a customized object with all the properties that the WMI class has. That way, what we get in PowerShell "looks" like we think a Win32_OperatingSystem WMI class should look like. PowerShell also adapts the WMI class' methods, such as **Reboot()** and **Shutdown()**, so we can call them directly. The Framework would have us call the **InvokeMethod()** method, which is more cumbersome. By and large, then, PowerShell's adaptation makes it easier to work with Framework objects.

# Adaptation Details

Sometimes, however, you need to work *directly* with the *actual* Framework object. Sometimes this is because PowerShell isn't adapting some function or feature that you want to use; often times, it's because—as in the case of WMI—PowerShell's adaptation is actually creating an entirely different object from the one the Framework returned. Therefore, PowerShell provides four different "views" of an object:

- The adapter view, which is called PSADAPTED
- The actual, raw object, which is called PSBASE
- Just the elements that PowerShell has added to the object, called PSEXTENDED
- The adapter object itself, called PSOBJECT

As we covered in the "Working with XML Documents" chapter, PowerShell does a ton of working adapting an XML document to look like an object hierarchy; XML looks nothing like that in the raw Framework world. For example, you can create and view a simple XML document object as follows:

```
PS C:\> $x = [xml]"<root><tag /></root>"
```

To see what PowerShell has done with that, just pipe $x to **Get-Member**. PowerShell will claim you've got a System.Xml.XmlDocument type of object, which is true enough (the **Get-Member** output is lengthy, so we're not including it here—try it for yourself). However, if you look at the various other objects, you'll see something different. For example, try this:

```
PS C:\> $x.psbase
```

```
NodeType            : Document
ParentNode          :
DocumentType        :
Implementation      : System.Xml.XmlImplementation
Name                : #document
LocalName           : #document
DocumentElement     : root
OwnerDocument       :
Schemas             : System.Xml.Schema.XmlSchemaSet
XmlResolver         :
NameTable           : System.Xml.NameTable
PreserveWhitespace  : False
IsReadOnly          : False
InnerXml            : <root><tag /></root>
SchemaInfo          : System.Xml.Schema.XmlSchemaInfo
BaseURI             :
Value               :
ChildNodes          : {root}
PreviousSibling     :
NextSibling         :
Attributes          :
FirstChild          : root
LastChild           : root
HasChildNodes       : True
NamespaceURI        :
Prefix              :
InnerText           :
OuterXml            : <root><tag /></root>
```

Looking at $x.psadapted, however, reveals the *adapted* object, in which the XML's document structure is converted into an object hierarchy:

```
PS C:\> $x.psadapted

root
----
root
```

The adapted object is what you work with normally, so just typing **$x** is the same as typing **$x.psadapted**. The point is that the PSBASE version—the raw object—provides very different properties and methods. So, what are the differences? Well, for example, $x alone won't allow us to access the native XML DocumentElement property:

```
PS C:\> $x.documentelement
PS C:\>
```

PowerShell simply returns nothing, because the *adapted* view of $x doesn't have a DocumentElement. We can access that via the PSBASE, however:

```
PS C:\> $x.psbase.documentelement

tag
---


PS C:\>
```

Thus, PSBASE is a means of accessing the raw, un-adapted Framework class. Most PowerShell objects are adapted to some degree or another; for example, let's look at the various views for a process object obtained using **Get-Process**:

```
PS C:\> $p = get-process
PS C:\> $p.psbase

Length         : 70
LongLength     : 70
Rank           : 1
SyncRoot       : {acrotray, Ati2evxx, Ati2evxx, audiodg...}
IsReadOnly     : False
IsFixedSize    : True
IsSynchronized : False


PS C:\> $p.psextended


                                                                 Count
                                                                 -----
                                                                    70

PS C:\> $p.psobject

Members            : {Count, Length, LongLength, Rank...}
Properties         : {Count, Length, LongLength, Rank...}
Methods            : {Get, Set, Address, get_Length...}
ImmediateBaseObject : {acrotray, Ati2evxx, Ati2evxx, audiodg...}
BaseObject         : {acrotray, Ati2evxx, Ati2evxx, audiodg...}
TypeNames          : {System.Object[], System.Array, System.Object}

PS C:\> $p.psadapted

Length         : 70
LongLength     : 70
Rank           : 1
SyncRoot       : {acrotray, Ati2evxx, Ati2evxx, audiodg...}
IsReadOnly     : False
IsFixedSize    : True
IsSynchronized : False
```

You can see that the extensions—PSEXTENDED—is actually a count, since what **Get-Process** returns is a collection. Normally, $p wouldn't have a **Count** property; the extensions—part of PowerShell's adaptation, in other words—provides this property. The PSBASE shows that the *normal* property name is Length. However, PowerShell adds the **Count** property to maintain consistency with other portions of the Framework, which use **Count** rather than **Length**. In other words, the PowerShell team decided to standardize on Count, and added it to those objects that were already using Length.

**It's a Bypass!**

If PSBASE still isn't making sense to you, then think about it this way: Normally, PowerShell tries to simplify Framework classes for you, and what you see in PowerShell is that "simplified" version. PSBASE allows you to bypass the simplification, when desired, and work directly with the "under the hood" Framework class.

# Using Framework Objects Directly

Of course, you can use PSBASE to work directly with any Framework objects that PowerShell is retrieving for you. But what about *other* Framework objects, ones that PowerShell isn't already adapting and loading for you? PowerShell does have the ability to load Framework assemblies (DLLs) and utilize the classes they contain. Perhaps the best example we have of this is loading up the Framework's speech synthesizer (available in version 3.0 and later of the Framework).

## Loading Assemblies into PowerShell

Framework classes are contained in assemblies, which are stored in files on your hard drive, primarily as DLL files in the %windir%\Microsoft.NET\Framework\\*version*\ folder. We want to work with the System.Speech.Sythesis.SpeechSythesizer class, which is conveniently documented at http://msdn2.microsoft.com/en-us/library/
system.speech.synthesis.speechsynthesizer.aspx; even more conveniently, the documentation tells us right at the top of the page that this is in the System.Speech.dll file. Here's how to load the assembly:

```
PS C:\> [system.reflection.assembly]::LoadWithPartialName("System.Speech")
```

Simple enough. Now the classes within that assembly are available to us.

## Using a Framework Class

When you load up a class for the first time, you're executing a special method of the class called its *constructor*. Sometimes, classes have multiple constructors that accept different input arguments; some classes will have a constructor that doesn't require any arguments at all. According to the SpeechSythesizer documentation, the only available constructor for this class doesn't have any arguments at all. So, creating a new instance of the class is as easy as this:

```
PS C:\> $speech = new-object system.speech.synthesis.speechsynthesizer
```

We put the new instance into a variable, $speech, which will give us access to its properties and methods:

```
PS C:\> $speech.speak("This PowerShell stuff rocks!")
```

Remember, piping $speech to **Get-Member** will reveal its properties and methods; some of these may seem complicated because for objects like this PowerShell isn't doing any adaptation—you're getting the raw object from the Framework.

On our system, the default voice is a female voice. If we wanted to switch to a male voice, we'd—well, we'd look in the online documentation, is what we'd do. The page listing the members of the SpeechSynthesis class is at http://msdn2.microsoft.com/

en-us/library/system.speech.synthesis.speechsynthesizer_members.aspx, and we see a property named Voice. Clicking on that property to learn more, we see that it's a read-only property. That means we can't change it, so it's not what we're looking for. Back to the members page.

There's a method called **SelectVoice()**—that looks promising. The docs say that it takes one argument, which is the name of the voice to select. No clues on what might be valid values here, though, so it's off to our favorite search engine to try to find an example. We punch in **speechsynthesizer selectvoice method** and hope for the best; we're quickly sent to http://www.codeproject.com/useritems/Vista_Speech_Recognition.asp?msg=1977267, which offers a full tutorial on the topic.

> **Why the Runaround?**
> Why are we sharing this exploration process with you? Because this book isn't going to be a complete reference—or even an incomplete reference—to the .NET Framework. Our goal is to show you *how we find this information*, so that you can duplicate our self-education techniques and learn to educate yourself about other useful Framework classes.

It turns out after reading the fairly lengthy tutorial that we could do this faster with the **SelectVoiceByHints()** method, which allows us to pass a gender and age, and lets the Framework figure out what "voice" fits that. There's no clue as to how we specify a gender, so we decide to just guess. We run this in PowerShell:

```
PS C:\> $speech.selectvoicebyhints("male",35)
Cannot convert argument "1", with value: "35", for "SelectVoiceByHints" to type "System.S
peech.Synthesis.VoiceAge": "Cannot convert value "35" to type "System.Speech.Synthesis.Vo
iceAge" due to invalid enumeration values. Specify one of the following enumeration value
s and try again. The possible enumeration values are "NotSet, Child, Teen, Adult, Senior"
."
At line:1 char:27
+ $speech.selectvoicebyhints( <<<< "male",35)
```

Well, it bombed, but it gave us a great clue! Now we try this:

```
PS C:\> $speech.selectvoicebyhints("male","senior")
PS C:\> $speech.speak("How's this, young man?")
```

And it works great. So, you've seen how to actually find the assembly that a class lives in, load that assembly, create a new instance of a class, and then utilize the class—along with an Internet tour of how to find out *how to use a class*.

# Fun (and Useful) Tricks With the .NET Framework

You can do a number of useful things with the Framework. In the next few chapters, for example, we'll show you how to use it to access databases, build your own graphical user interfaces from within PowerShell, utilize Web services, and much more. Right now, however, we offer a few short, incredibly useful techniques.

## Sending E-Mail

Sending e-mail from within PowerShell is easy, thanks to the Framework's built-in System.Net.Mail classes. And there's a bonus: Because these functions live in the base System.dll assembly, you don't need to load any additional assemblies into PowerShell! The starting point is the System.Net.Mail.

MailMessage class, which is a shortcut class used to create quick, ad-hoc e-mail messages. Once you create a new instance of the class, you simply set a few properties (such as the body of the message, who it's going to, and so forth), and you're done. Here's where you start:

```
PS C:\> $mail = new-object system.net.mail.mailmessage
```

Now, we need to create the sending and recipient e-mail addresses. Note that these are actually entirely new classes of the MailAddress type, so we'll create them and assign them to variables:

```
PS C:\> $from = new-object system.net.mail.mailaddress("don@sapien.com")
PS C:\> $to = new-object system.net.mail.mailaddress("jhicks@sapien.com")
```

Next, we'll assign the $from address to the **From** property of the message. Note that the **To** property of the message is actually a collection, because we can add multiple recipients. To add onc, we'll use the collection's **Add()** method, passing in the address we want to add. We can do this as many times as needed to add all the recipients. Finally, we'll set the **Subject** and **Body** properties, which are simple text strings. Note that you *can* add attachments, set Bcc and Cc recipients, and so forth; look up the System. Net.Mail.MailMessage class in Microsoft's MSDN Library (http://msdn.microsoft.com/library) for details.

```
PS C:\> $mail.from = $from
PS C:\> $mail.to.add($to)
PS C:\> $mail.subject = "Test message"
PS C:\> $mail.body = "Hi, Jeffery!"
```

Last, we create one more new object, this time of the System.Net.Mail.SmtpClient class. Creating the class requires us to pass along the name of our SMTP mail server; we then use the SmptClient's **Send()** method, passing in our mail message object, to actually send the message:

```
PS C:\> $client = new-object system.net.mail.smtpclient("mailserver")
PS C:\> $client.send($mail)
```

And that's it. Of course, your mail server's security comes into play, as well: For example, if your SMTP server requires authentication, than this technique won't work as-is. Instead, you'll also have to set the Credentials property of the SmtpClient object. It can also use a custom SMTP port, be forced to use SSL, and so forth; consult its documentation in MSDN Library for details on these options.

## Resolving Names by Using DNS

Here's something fun to do with the System.Net.Dns class. This is an interesting class; if you look in the documentation at http://msdn.microsoft.com/library, this class is listed as *static*, with a comment that says, "The members of a static class are accessed directly without an instance of the class." That means you don't need to create an instance of the class by using **New-Object**; instead, you can use the class directly:

```
PS C:\> [system.net.dns]::gethostaddresses("msn.com")


IPAddressToString : 207.68.172.246
Address           : 4138484943
AddressFamily     : InterNetwork
ScopeId           :
```

```
IsIPv6Multicast   : False
IsIPv6LinkLocal   : False
IsIPv6SiteLocal   : False
```

This example illustrates the value of reading the documentation—without it, you could spend all day trying to run **New-Object System.Net.Dns** and just keep getting error messages. The documentation also reveals the other tasks this class can help accomplish, such as getting a host name by passing its IP address (reverse lookup), getting the DNS host name of the local computer, and so forth.

## Accessing Remote Event Logs

The System.Diagnostics.EventLog class provides access to event logs, including those on remote computers:

```
PS C:\> $log = new-object System.Diagnostics.EventLog Application,Server2
```

The $log variable now represents the Application log of Server2. You can then use the log's **Clear()** method, for example, to clear it:

```
PS C:\> $log.Clear()
```

The log also provides **WriteEntry()** and **WriteEvent()** methods which can be useful, as well as methods like **ModifyOverflowPolicy()**, which can reconfigure the log itself.

## Making a Notification Icon

The Framework has the ability to place a notification icon in the task bar notification area. Using it, you can display balloon tip-style notifications. You start by loading the System.Windows.Forms assembly into the shell:

```
PS C:\> [reflection.assembly]::loadwithpartialname("System.Windows.Forms")
```

Because we need an icon for this, we also need to load the System.Drawing assembly:

```
PS C:\> [reflection.assembly]::loadwithpartialname("System.Drawing")
```

Next, we create a new icon and load a standard Windows .ICO file:

```
PS C:\> $icon = new-object system.drawing.icon("c:\myscriptsicon.ico")
```

Now, we create a new NotifyIcon and set its icon to be the icon we just created. We also set its Visible property to $True so that it displays:

```
PS C:\> $notify = new-object system.windows.forms.notifyicon
PS C:\> $notify.icon = $icon
PS C:\> $notify.visible = $true
```

Now we can display a balloon tip:

```
PS C:\> $notify.showballoontip(10,"Title","Message",[system.windows.forms.tooltipicon]::
warning)
```

The last bit determines the icon shown in the balloon tip; you can select Error, Info, None, or Warning. The first number is the number of seconds that the balloon remains visible.

# Chapter 41
# Reading and Writing Information in Databases

Let's get one thing clear from the outset: This chapter isn't about managing database systems like Microsoft SQL Server or Oracle, and it isn't about designing and creating databases. Right now, none of those database management systems provide PowerShell-specific capabilities for administration—that is, they don't provide cmdlets. Microsoft SQL Server does provide a set of .NET Framework classes called SQL Management Objects (SMO) to accomplish administrative tasks, but using them is more complicated than we can do justice to in a single chapter—it's a book of its own, and it's pretty difficult, compared to how easy it'll be once SQL Server provides a set of cmdlets for administration. Instead, our goal is to help you utilize existing databases—whether those are SQL Server, Microsoft Access, Excel spreadsheets, MySQL tables, or nearly any other type of database you may have—in your PowerShell scripts. We'll do so through the use of a few special .NET Framework classes.

## Connecting to a Database

The first thing you'll need is a database *connection string*. The Framework treats SQL Server and other databases somewhat differently, so we'll start with a non-SQL Server connection. Go to www.ConnectionStrings.com and locate the type of database you want to connect to. We'll use an Access 2007 database; if multiple connection strings are shown, look for one that says "OLE DB" or "OLEDB." For example, the Access 2007 connection string is shown as follows:

```
Provider=Microsoft.ACE.OLEDB.12.0;Data Source=C:\myFolder\myAccess2007file.accdb;Persist Security
Info=False;
```

We, of course, need to modify that somewhat to meet our specific needs, primarily by specifying the correct path to the database file:

```
Provider=Microsoft.ACE.OLEDB.12.0;Data Source=C:\users\don\documents\sample.accdb;Persist Security
Info=False;
```

Finally, we'll paste that into PowerShell, assigning the string to a variable for easier use:

```
PS C:\> $connstr = "Provider=Microsoft.ACE.OLEDB.12.0;Data Source=C:\users\don\documents\s
ample.accdb;Persist Security Info=False;"
```

Next, we need to import the assembly that contains the Framework's database functionality: System. Data:

```
PS C:\> [system.reflection.assembly]::LoadWithPartialName("System.Data")
```

And we'll create a new OleDbConnection object. This is the object you use to connect to non-SQL Server databases (SQL Server uses a SqlConnection object—it has a different name, but you use it exactly as shown here). After creating the new object, we'll set its ConnectionString property to be our connection string, and then we'll open the connection.

```
PS C:\> $conn = new-object system.data.oledb.oledbconnection
PS C:\> $conn.ConnectionString = $connstr
PS C:\> $conn.open()
```

That's it - our connection is open and the database is ready for use.

## Building a Command

Next, we need to tell the database to do something. The instruction language used, no matter what type of database we're actually connected to, is the Structured Query Language, or SQL. This book isn't intended as a learning guide for SQL; suffice to say that SQL has four main operations:

- SELECT, which queries rows from the database
- INSERT, which adds rows to the database
- DELETE, which removes rows from the database
- UPDATE, which changes existing rows in the database

We're going to start with a SELECT query. We begin by putting the query itself into a variable:

```
PS C:\> $query = "SELECT * FROM Test ORDER BY ColumnA"
```

Next, we create a new Command object (specifically, an OleDbCommand; SQL Server uses a SqlCommand that works the same way). We'll set it to use our existing, open Connection, and give it our query text:

```
PS C:\> $cmd = new-object system.data.oledb.oledbcommand
PS C:\> $cmd.Connection = $conn
PS C:\> $cmd.CommandText = $query
```

# Executing the Command and Working with the Results

Because our query is expected to return rows of data, we need to store those rows someplace. We'll use a variable; what comes back from the Command will be a DataReader object, containing the rows our query returned, and that object will be placed into our variable:

```
PS C:\> $reader = $cmd.ExecuteReader()
```

As an aside, if our query *wasn't* expected to return any rows—if it were an INSERT, UPDATE, or DELETE query, for example—we'd use a slightly different method:

```
PS C:\> $cmd.ExecuteNonQuery()
```

Notice that we don't save the results into a variable this time, because there are no results expected back. However, in our example, we do have the $reader variable, which contains our query results. The first thing we need to do is position the DataReader's internal "pointer" to the first row of data:

```
PS C:\> $reader.read()
True
```

The return value of TRUE, which could also have been saved in a variable, tells us that there's at least one row beyond this one when we're ready for it. Right now, we're on the first row of data and ready to access its columns. We have some choices in how we do this: If we know what order the columns are in the database, we can access the columns' values using their ordinal position:

```
PS C:\> $reader.GetValue(0)
Value1
PS C:\> $reader.GetValue(1)
Value2
```

If we only know the columns' names, and not their position, it's a bit trickier:

```
PS C:\> $reader.GetValue( $reader.GetOrdinal("ColumnA") )
Value1
```

Here, we've used the **GetOrdinal()** function to get the ordinal, and passed that to **GetValue()**, which only accepts ordinals. When we're done working with those rows and want to go on to the next one, we execute **Read()** again:

```
PS C:\> $reader.read()
True
PS C:\> $reader.read()
True
PS C:\> $reader.read()
False
```

When **Read()** finally returns FALSE, it means we've moved past the available data. Now, any attempt to access the columns will result in an error. Of course, in a script you'd be more likely to place this into a loop of some kind:

```
While ($reader.read()) {
    $reader.getvalue(0)
}
```

Remember: To change data, there's no "SetValue" method; instead, you issue a *new* query using UPDATE. Keep in mind, however, that so long as a DataReader is open on a connection, that connection can't be used for anything else—so you may have to create a second connection in order to make database changes. In order to free up the connection being used by the DataReader, close the DataReader:

```
PS C:\> $reader.close()
```

You should also close the overall database connection when you're finished using it:

```
PS C:\> $conn.close()
```

## The SQL Server Difference

SQL Server works almost the same way, but has special Framework objects:

- For connections, use System.Data.Sql.SqlConnection
- For commands, use System.Data.Sql.SqlCommand
- Executing a command returns a System.Data.Sql.SqlDataReader

Apart from these differences in object names, the objects work identically to their OleDb counterparts. The only other major difference is that the connection string expected by the SqlConnection object is somewhat different. www.ConnectionStrings.com lists them, under the heading "SQL Native Client." For example:

```
Driver={SQL Native Client};Server=myServerAddress;Database=myDataBase;Uid=myUsername;Pwd=myPasswo
rd;
```

A number of variations exist depending on what kind of security connection SQL Server is configured to use, and so forth; the Connection Strings Web site lists them all and provides examples.

## A Practical Example

Here's a real-world example: We'll populate a database with computer names and write a script that reads those names, retrieves the computers' service pack version numbers, and places those numbers into the database.

### SPInventoryToAccess.ps1

```
# Assumes database is Inventory.accdb
# Assumes table name is SPInventory
# Assumes column names are ComputerName and SPVersion
# and that both columns are text (not numeric) values

function GetSP($computer) {
        $wmi = gwmi win32_operatingsystem -computer $computer
        foreach ($item in $wmi) {
```

```
                    $item.servicepackmajorversion
        }
}

function SetSP($computer,$spack) {
    $connstr = "Provider=Microsoft.ACE.OLEDB.12.0;" + `
      "Data Source=C:\users\user\documents\inventory.accdb" + `
      ";Persist Security Info=False;"

        # Open Connection
        $conn = new-object system.data.oledb.oledbconnection
        $conn.ConnectionString = $connstr
        $conn.open()

        # Create query
    $query = "UPDATE SPInventory SET SPVer = '$spack' " + `
      "WHERE ComputerName = '$computer'"

        # Execute query
        $cmd = New-Object system.Data.OleDb.OleDbCommand
        $cmd.connection = $conn
        $cmd.commandtext = $query
        $cmd.executenonquery()

        $conn.close()

}

[system.reflection.assembly]::LoadWithPartialName("System.Data")

# Connection String
$connstr = "Provider=Microsoft.ACE.OLEDB.12.0;" + `
  "Data Source=C:\users\user\documents\inventory.accdb" + `
  ";Persist Security Info=False;"

# Open Connection
$conn = new-object system.data.oledb.oledbconnection
$conn.ConnectionString = $connstr
$conn.open()

# Create query
$query = "SELECT ComputerName, SPVersion FROM SPInventory"

# Get Records
$cmd = New-Object system.Data.OleDb.OleDbCommand
$cmd.connection = $conn
$cmd.commandtext = $query
$reader = $cmd.executereader()

# Read rows
While ($reader.read()) {
        $computer = $reader.getvalue(0)
        $spack = GetSP $computer
        SetSP $computer $spack
}

# Close everything
$reader.close()
$conn.close()
```

Note that our script makes some assumptions about the location and structure of the database, so we've documented those assumptions in the script's initial comments. We've created separate functions to retrieve the service pack version and to write the service pack to the database; this simply helps to encapsulate those particular tasks. Also notice that the SetSP function creates an all-new connection to the database. Some notes on what we did there:

- By using the same variable names as the main script, this function is creating *new* variables in its own private scope. See our discussion on scope in the chapter "Scripting Overview."

- The function can't use the main script's connection, because that connection is being used by the DataReader. So long as the DataReader is open, that connection is locked to it and can't be used to issue other queries.

- Opening and closing a connection over and over again isn't necessarily resource-efficient, but it keeps the function self-contained. An alternative would have been to open a second connection in the main body of the script, and to pass that connection as a third input argument to SetSP. That way, the function could stay open throughout the script and be re-used by the function. We'd just have to remember to close the second connection before the script finished.

Here's a complete walkthrough of the script, one section at a time. First up is our GetSP function, which simply uses WMI to query a specified computer. It outputs that computer's ServicePackMajorVersion property:

```
function GetSP($computer) {
        $wmi = gwmi win32_operatingsystem -computer $computer
        foreach ($item in $wmi) {
                $item.servicepackmajorversion
        }
}
```

Next is the SetSP function. We begin by defining our connection string:

```
function SetSP($computer,$spack) {
    $connstr = "Provider=Microsoft.ACE.OLEDB.12.0;" + `
     "Data Source=C:\users\user\documents\inventory.accdb" + `
     ";Persist Security Info=False;"
```

Then we open the connection:

```
# Open Connection
        $conn = new-object system.data.oledb.oledbconnection
        $conn.ConnectionString = $connstr
        $conn.open()
```

And we create a new SQL UPDATE query. Notice our use of the input arguments, $spack and $computer, to provide values to the SQL query:

```
# Create query
$query = "UPDATE SPInventory SET SPVer = '$spack' " + `
 "WHERE ComputerName = '$computer'"
```

Finally, we create a new command, execute it, and close the connection:

```
# Execute query
        $cmd = New-Object system.Data.OleDb.OleDbCommand
        $cmd.connection = $conn
        $cmd.commandtext = $query
        $cmd.executenonquery()
```

```
        $conn.close()

}
```

Here's the first line of the script that executes—remember, the functions are just *defined* at this point; we haven't actually called them yet. The first line of the script loads the System.Data assembly:

```
[system.reflection.assembly]::LoadWithPartialName("System.Data")
```

Note that this won't create an error if the assembly is already loaded, so it's safe to execute even if the assembly might have already been loaded by something else. Next we define and open our connection to the database—the one that the main body of the script will use:

```
# Connection String
$connstr = "Provider=Microsoft.ACE.OLEDB.12.0;" + `
 "Data Source=C:\users\user\documents\inventory.accdb" + `
 ";Persist Security Info=False;"
# Open Connection
$conn = new-object system.data.oledb.oledbconnection
$conn.ConnectionString = $connstr
$conn.open()
```

We create a SQL SELECT query:

```
# Create query
$query = "SELECT ComputerName, SPVersion FROM SPInventory"
```

And then we execute that query, saving the resulting DataReader object into $reader:

```
# Get Records
$cmd = New-Object system.Data.OleDb.OleDbCommand
$cmd.connection = $conn
$cmd.commandtext = $query
$reader = $cmd.executereader()
```

We use a loop to move through the returned rows one at a time, retrieving the first column as the computer name. This is passed to GetSP to get the service pack version, and both the computer name and service pack version are passed to SetSP to update the information in the database:

```
# Read rows
While ($reader.read()) {
        $computer = $reader.getvalue(0)
        $spack = GetSP $computer
        SetSP $computer $spack
}
```

Finally, when we're all done, we close everything:

```
# Close everything
$reader.close()
$conn.close()
```

As you can see, working with databases is reasonably straightforward, and they provide a good deal of extra functionality for your scripts.

# Chapter 42
# Working with Windows Forms

Windows Forms, or WinForms, are a segment of the .NET Framework that allows developers to create graphical applications. The idea is that all the common graphical user interface controls—buttons, checkboxes, and so forth—are contained with the Framework itself, so that all you have to do is tell the Framework where to put them, what size to make them, and other details. The Framework actually takes care of drawing them and managing them on the screen. Well, because PowerShell is built on the Framework, it can access all of WinForms, meaning you can use PowerShell to construct graphical user interfaces.

## Caveats, Restrictions, and Can't-Dos

Before we get carried away, however, you should know that building a GUI in PowerShell isn't necessarily easy. For one, there's no Visual Studio-like GUI that lets you drag UI elements around; instead, you'll be manually positioning these elements on a pixel-by-pixel basis. For another, PowerShell can't interact with *all* of the various controls that WinForms supports. That's because PowerShell has some restrictions on the type of events it can easily hook up to—which means now we need to discuss what events actually are.

### Introducing Events

You've already learned that objects, generically speaking, have properties and methods. Properties describe what an object is and does, while methods tell an object to do something. Objects also support *events*, which are things that can happen *to* an object. For example, when you move your mouse around the screen in Windows, little "MouseMove" events are happening to everything you pass your mouse over. Most objects don't react to this particular event; others—like the window minimize and maximize controls in Windows Vista—may react by highlighting themselves or some other action.

When an event occurs, we say that the event is *raised*. You can write code, called an *event handler*, which is executed when the event is raised. Event handlers are what allow you to *do* something when an event happens. For example, when a user clicks a button, the "Click" event is raised, and your "Click" event handler, if you've written one, is executed. This is broadly referred to as *event-driven programming*, since your code only executes in response to events that are raised. This is a different model than the *procedural* programming normally done in PowerShell, where a script simply contains a set of instructions that are followed in sequential order—the script doesn't wait around for things to happen, it just executes one line at a time.

The number of and type of events supported by a given control, such as a button or checkbox, is determined by Microsoft, and these are hard coded into the Framework. So, if a particular control doesn't support a "MouseMove" event, then you won't be able to "detect" that event happening to the control, and you won't be able to write code that responds to that event.

When an event *does* occur to a control, the Framework sends your event handler some input arguments. These arguments allow your event handler to determine, for example, what control the event occurred to. Sometimes, the arguments might also contain *state* information, such as whether a Shift or Ctrl key was held down at the time the event occurs. The exact arguments passed into your delegate differ depending on the control and the event. For example, some simple controls, like buttons, pass a minimal number of arguments for their "Click" event; other, more complex controls might pass additional arguments for a "Click" event. The exact arguments passed by a particular control's event are collectively referred to as the event's *signature*. In a bit, we'll look at how you can access these arguments, but first let's start building a graphical user interface.

## PowerShell and Events

PowerShell allows you to "connect" your code to an event, but *only if* the event uses a particular *signature*. We'll get into this in more detail later in the chapter—it'll make more sense after we've shown you some of this working. The good news is that, as an administrator, you probably only want to create fairly simple graphical user interfaces, and PowerShell won't have any problems with those. So, let's get started.

## But First...You Need to Read the Docs

Throughout this chapter, we're going to be referring to the .NET Framework documentation. You can find it online, for free, at http://msdn.microsoft.com/library. Because browsing through the documentation's table of contents is extremely time-consuming, we're primarily going to be relying on the search function within MSDN Library to look up specific classes by their type name. *We urge you to follow along.* We're not going to be republishing the information in the documentation, since what's online is already free and up-to-date, and if you're going to be working with WinForms, you're going to need to know how to use the documentation—so you might as well start getting used to it now!

# Creating a Form

When you look at a window, or a dialog box, or pretty much anything similar in Windows, you're looking at a *form*. A blank form doesn't contain anything you can interact with directly, except perhaps minimize, maximize, and close buttons in the form's title bar. Rather, a form is a blank canvas on which other controls are placed. In fact, a form is often referred to generically as a *container control*, meaning it is a control that can contain other controls.

To create a new form, we first need to load the Framework assembly that contains the WinForms classes. Then, we'll instantiate a new form, set some of its properties for size, appearance, and position, and then display the form.

```
# load WinForms
[Reflection.Assembly]::LoadWithPartialName("System.Windows.Forms") | Out-Null

# create form
$form = New-Object Windows.Forms.Form
$form.text = "PowerShell Menu"
$form.top = 10
$form.left = 10
$form.height = 250
$form.width = 200
$form.visible = $true
```

Of course, if you run this script, you'll see a window quickly appear and disappear. That's because the $form variable is created within the scope of this script; when the script ends, the scope goes away—and so $form is discarded and the window it represents disappears. Were you to dot-source this script, or simply type it into the command line directly, the window would stay visible. We can also make one minor change to the last line of our script:

```
$form.visible = $true
$form.showdialog()
```

This will remove our explicitly setting the form's Visible property, and instead call the form's **ShowDialog()** method, which makes the window *modal*. In other words, no other code will execute until the window is closed. Use the window's close button (in its title bar) to close it, and PowerShell displays "Cancel," which is the value returned by **ShowDialog()** when a form is closed in this fashion. Here's the form so far:

## Adding Controls

Okay, now we've got a window—what are we going to do with it? We could probably start by adding some controls. We're going to focus on the simpler controls provided by the Framework. Here are their Framework class names, along with the URL of the control's member list (listing its properties, methods, and events):

- Label: System.Windows.Forms.Label
  http://msdn2.microsoft.com/en-us/library/
  system.windows.forms.label_members.aspx

- Button: System.Windows.Forms.Button
  http://msdn2.microsoft.com/en-us/library/
  system.windows.forms.button_members.aspx

- Checkbox: System.Windows.Forms.CheckBox
  http://msdn2.microsoft.com/en-us/library/
  system.windows.forms.checkbox_members.aspx

- Radio button (or option button): System.Windows.Forms.RadioButton
  http://msdn2.microsoft.com/en-us/library/
  system.windows.forms.radiobutton_members.aspx

- Text box: System.Windows.Forms.TextBox
  http://msdn2.microsoft.com/en-us/library/
  system.windows.forms.textbox_members.aspx

- Combo box (drop-down list box): System.Windows.Forms.ComboBox
  http://msdn2.microsoft.com/en-us/library/
  system.windows.forms.combobox_members.aspx

- List box: System.Windows.Forms.ListBox
  http://msdn2.microsoft.com/en-us/library/
  system.windows.forms.listbox_members.aspx

To create a new control, all you need to know is its class name:

```
$button = new-object System.Windows.Forms.Button
```

To customize the control's appearance, simply modify one or more of its properties (which are listed on the members page we referenced above). Note that each control will have a Top and Left property, which are measured from the *top left corner* of the *parent control*. So, a Button with a Top of 10 and a Left of 10 will appear 10 pixels down and to the right within whatever form it is eventually placed in. To actually add the control to the form, use the form's Controls collection, which has an **Add()** method, as shown here:

```
# create button
$button = New-Object Windows.Forms.Button
$button.text = "Close"
$button.height = 20
$button.width = 150
$button.top = 2
$button.left = 25
$form.controls.add($button)
```

Of course, make sure you move any call to the form's **ShowDialog()** method to the *end* of this code!

Right now, were you to run the form, clicking the button wouldn't do anything. That's because we haven't created an event handler yet, nor have we "attached" the event handler to the button's Click event. Here's our form with the button added:

You'll notice that we have some tweaking to do with that button's position, but hopefully you get the idea behind adding a simple control to a form.

## Creating Event Handlers

Event handlers are simply PowerShell script blocks, which execute in response to a given event. For simple events—that is, those using the simple signature we examined earlier—you can use a simple syntax to attach the script block to the desired event. As a general practice, we usually attach all of our event handlers *before* we add the control to the form, so the following is a revised example of our script (to save space, we're omitting the code that build the actual form—we're assuming you still have that in there):

```
# create button
$button = New-Object Windows.Forms.Button
$button.text = "Close"
$button.height = 20
$button.width = 150
$button.top = 2
$button.left = 25

# create event handler for button
$event = {
        $form.close()
}

# attach event handler
$button.Add_Click($event)

# attach controls to form
$form.controls.add($button)

$form.showdialog()
```

The $event variable contains our script block—and notice that *this is not contained within quotation marks!* In the event handler code, we're simply calling the **Close()** method of our form object. We attach our event handler to the Click event of the button by calling the special **Add-Click()** "method." You can refer to any event in this fashion: **Add_** followed by the event name. We then attach the button to the form and show the form as a dialog box.

So, the basic steps of working with WinForms are:

- Create the form and set its properties.

- Create one or more controls and set their properties.

- Create event handlers and attach them to controls.

- Add the controls to the form.

- Display the form.

The tricky part, if there is one, is knowing what control properties and events are useful, and tweaking property settings—like control positions and sizes—to achieve the appearance you're after.

## Useful Control Events and Properties

Again, we're going to focus on a few basic controls, along with the form itself. For each of these, we'll call out specific properties and events that we've found to be the most useful, but keep in mind that these are a very small subset of the controls' total capabilities; you'll need to review the Framework documentation (we gave you URLs earlier) for the complete details. Note that some properties, methods, and events might certainly qualify as "interesting," but are very complex to use with a Visual Studio-like graphical designer (and, even if you *have* Visual Studio, it won't do you any good in PowerShell). For example, creating a set of drop-down menus for a form is pretty complex, and involves several different controls; creating this in PowerShell code is beyond the scope of what we're able to cover here.

Also, *all* controls have a Top, Left, Height, and Width property; we won't be adding those to any of the lists that follow, but you'll need to set them in order to achieve the appearance you're after. All controls also have a Name property, which you can set to create a name for the control; this isn't always terribly useful inside PowerShell, though, where you'll primarily refer to a control by the variable that "contains" the control. However, we'll show you some examples later where the Name property can be useful.

### Forms

A Form represents a window, either one that's resizable, or a fixed-size dialog box. Interesting properties include:

- ControlBox – Either $True or $False; controls whether or not the form has a "control box" in the upper-left corner of its title bar.

- Controls – A collection containing all the controls contained on the form. Use this collection's **Add()** method to add new controls to the form.

- DialogResult – You set this property before closing a form that was displayed using the **ShowDialog()** method; this property determines the "result" returned by **ShowDialog()** – can be one of:

    o [System.Windows.Forms.DialogResult]::Abort

    o [System.Windows.Forms.DialogResult]::Cancel

    o [System.Windows.Forms.DialogResult]::Ignore

    o [System.Windows.Forms.DialogResult]::No

    o [System.Windows.Forms.DialogResult]::None

    o [System.Windows.Forms.DialogResult]::OK

- o [System.Windows.Forms.DialogResult]::Retry

- o [System.Windows.Forms.DialogResult]::Yes

- FormBorderStyle – Controls the border style of the form. Set this to one of the following:

  - o [System.Windows.Forms.FormBorderStyle]::Fixed3D

  - o [System.Windows.Forms.FormBorderStyle]::FixedDialog

  - o [System.Windows.Forms.FormBorderStyle]::FixedSingle

  - o [System.Windows.Forms.FormBorderStyle]::FixedToolWindow

  - o [System.Windows.Forms.FormBorderStyle]::None

  - o [System.Windows.Forms.FormBorderStyle]::Sizable

  - o [System.Windows.Forms.FormBorderStyle]::SizableToolWindow

- MaximizeBox, MinimizeBox – Controls whether or not the form has maximize or minimize buttons; set to $True or $False.

- Text – The text shown in the form's title bar.

- TopMost – Set to $True or $False to control whether this form appears "on top" of all other windows.

Interesting methods include:

- Activate() – Gives the form the *focus*, making it the active window.

- BringToFront() – Brings the form to the front of Windows' *z-order*, making it (at least temporarily) the topmost window, but not necessarily making it the *active* window.

- Close() – Closes the form.

- Hide() – Hides the form.

- ShowDialog() – Shows the form *modally*, meaning the remainder of the application (that is, your script) stops running until the form is closed.

- Show() – shows the form *non-modally*, which means your application (your script) continues running.

Forms also have events that you can create event handlers for:

- Click – Raised when the form is clicked.

- Closing and Closed – Raised when the form is asked to close and when it finally closes.

- Resize – Raised when the form is resized.

## Labels

A label is simply a non-editable text area. You could use this to provide a label for a text box, for example. The only property you'll concern yourself with on a label is its Text property, which controls what the label contains. Labels don't have any frequently-used methods or events.

## Buttons

A Button is a clickable command button, which is placed on a form or within another container. One interesting property is Text, which is the text that appears on the face of a button.

Buttons don't really have any methods that you'll frequently use. The main method you'll worry about is Click. The Click method is raised when the button is clicked.

## Text Boxes

Text boxes provide a place for users to type textual input. Apart from their size and position controls, they have a few useful properties:

- Enabled – Set to $False to disable the text box (grey it out); the default, $True, allows the text box to function normally.

- MaxLength – the maximum number of characters that can be typed into the text box.

- MultiLine – Set this to $True to make the text box a multi-line control with built-in word wrapping.

- PasswordChar – set this to a single character, such as *, to force the text box to only display this character for whatever is typed.

- ReadOnly – set this to $True to allow a text box to display text (e.g., you can change the Text property), but to prohibit editing of that text by the user.

- Text – provides access to the text that has been typed inside the text box. You can set this property to pre-fill the text box, if desired.

We've never found ourselves using any of a text box's methods on a regular basis, although there are a couple of events you'll want to know about:

- Click – Raised when the text box is clicked.

- Enter – Raised when the cursor enters the text box.

- Leave – Raised when the cursor leaves the text box.

- TextChanged – Raised when the text inside the text box changes—even by so much as a single character. You have to be careful with this event; if your event handler changes the text, then *another* TextChanged event will be raised, which could easily create an endless loop.

## Check Boxes

Check boxes are used to indicate "yes/no" choices. The primary properties you'll worry about are:

- Checked – $True or $False depending whether or not the check box is checked

- Text – The text that appears alongside the check box

Check boxes don't really have any frequently used methods, but they do have a useful event:

- CheckChanged – Raised when the check box is checked or unchecked

## Radio Buttons

Radio buttons are used to present a short (usually three or fewer items) series of choices, from which the user selects a single choice. Important properties are:

- Checked – $True or $False depending on whether or not this radio button is selected

- Text – The text that appears alongside the radio button

Only a single radio button in a set can be selected at a single time. All radio buttons included on a form are considered part of a set; if you want to have two sets of radio buttons, then at least one of those sets needs to be enclosed in another container-style control, such as a System.Windows.Forms.GroupBox control. Radio buttons don't have any especially important methods, but they do each have one important event:

- CheckChanged – Raised when the radio button is selected or de-selected. Note that this event will usually raise twice: Once for the radio button that was just selected, and then once for the radio button which was subsequently de-selected.

## List Boxes

List boxes contain a list of text choices, from which the user may select one or more. Because multi-select list boxes are somewhat more complicated, we're mainly only covering a list box that's configured to allow a single item to be selected. Important properties are:

- Items – Retrieves a collection of the items within the list box

- SelectedIndex – The zero-based index number of the currently-selected list item; contains -1 if no item is selected

- SelectedIndices – A collection of zero-based index numbers for selected items (if multiple-item selection is allowed)

- SelectedItem – the currently-selected item

- SelectedItems – a collection of selected items (if multiple-item selection is allowed)

- SelectionMode – the means by which items are selected; can be one of the following:

    o [System.Windows.Forms.SelectionMode]::MultiExtended – multiple items can be selected using Shift, Ctrl, and the arrow keys

    o [System.Windows.Forms.SelectionMode]::MultiSimple – multiple items can be selected by holding down the Ctrl key

    o [System.Windows.Forms.SelectionMode]::None – no items can be selected

    o [System.Windows.Forms.SelectionMode]::One – one item can be selected (this is the default)

- Text – The text of the currently-selected item

There is a useful method you should know about:

- FindString() – Finds the first item in the list that matches the specified string (useful for finding the index number of an item when all you know is the item text)

And, of course, an event or two:

- SelectedIndexChanged – Raised when the selection changes

- TextChanged – Raised when the Text property is changed

The tricky part with a list box is, of course, getting items into it: You have to use the Items collection, which has an **Add()** method:

```
$listbox.items.add("New Item")
```

Each time you add an index, it is added to the *end* of the list. However, the method also outputs the new index number. If you don't simply want that number displayed as script output, either capture it in a variable or pipe it to **Out-Null**:

```
$listbox.items.add("New Item") | Out-Null
```

## Combo Boxes

A combo box can take one of two main forms. A true *combo box* allows you to select items from a drop-down list, and to type your own value, which isn't on the list. A more limited form, the *drop-down list*, only permits you to select an item from the list. Useful properties are:

- DropDownStyle – Determines the style of the combo box, and can be:
    - [System.Windows.Forms.ComboBoxStyle]::DropDown – for a true combo box
    - [System.Windows.Forms.ComboBoxStyle]::DropDownList – for a drop-down list
    - [System.Windows.Forms.ComboBoxStyle]::Simple – for a combo box where the drop-down portion is always visible
    - Items – the items in the list – this works the same as the Items property for a combo box, which we've already discussed
    - SelectedIndex, SelectedItem – both refer to the selected list item, either by index or by the item text
- Text – the text in the combo box

There aren't any major methods to call to your attention, but there are some events:

- SelectedIndexChanged – Raised when the selected list item is changed
- TextChanged – Raised when the text is changed (see our comments about this method in the Text box for some cautions)

Items are added to the drop-down list in the same way that they are added to a regular list box.

# Displaying Forms

You have to use the **ShowDialog()** method so that everything stays on one thread—this means your form will "block" the shell. You get a DialogResult property of the form object populated; code WITHIN the form can set this property to return a result to the shell or calling script or whatever. If you just use **Show()**, then the form spins on a new thread, and PowerShell can't stay "connected" to the form's events—so it's effectively useless.

# A Practical Example

We wanted to build a quick little graphical utility that would allow a technician to quickly retrieve key operating system information from a remote computer. The trick is, we didn't want the technician to have to know the computer names: Instead, we'd read those in from a text file (we're hard coding the filename, since we don't want technicians to have to provide it, but you could prompt for that, if desired), allowing us to give each technician just the computer names they need to work with. So, here's our first go-round—we'll show you the entire script first, and then break down each piece.

## WinForms1.ps1

```powershell
function CheckOS($computer) {
        $wmi = gwmi win32_operatingsystem -computer $computer

        # create output form
        $form = New-Object System.Windows.Forms.Form
    $form.text = "OS Info for $computer"
        $form.top = 10
        $form.left = 10
        $form.height = 200
        $form.width = 250
        $form.formborderstyle = [system.Windows.Forms.FormBorderStyle]::FixedDialog

        # create text box
        $textbox = New-Object system.Windows.Forms.TextBox
        $textbox.top = 2
        $textbox.left = 2
        $textbox.width = 246
        $textbox.height = 196
        $textbox.readonly = $true
        $textbox.multiline = $true
    $textbox.text = "Build: " + $wmi.buildnumber + " / Service Pack: " + `
    $wmi.servicepackmajorversion + " / OS: " + $wmi.caption

        # add control to form
        $form.controls.add($textbox)

        # show form
        $form.showdialog() | Out-Null
}

# load WinForms
[Reflection.Assembly]::LoadWithPartialName("System.Windows.Forms") | Out-Null

# create form
$form = New-Object System.Windows.Forms.Form
$form.text = "Check OS Info"
$form.top = 10
$form.left = 10
$form.height = 280
$form.width = 200
$form.formborderstyle = [system.Windows.Forms.FormBorderStyle]::FixedDialog

# create label
$label = New-Object system.Windows.Forms.Label
$label.text = "Select computer to query:"
$label.top = 2
$label.left = 10
$label.width = 180

# create button
$button = New-Object Windows.Forms.Button
$button.text = "Select"
$button.height = 20
$button.width = 180
$button.top = 230
$button.left = 10

# create event handler for button
$event = {
        $form.dialogresult = [system.Windows.Forms.DialogResult]::OK
        $form.close()
```

```
}

# attach event handler
$button.Add_Click($event)

# create list box
$listbox = New-Object Windows.Forms.ListBox
$listbox.height = 200
$listbox.width = 180
$listbox.top = 20
$listbox.left = 10

# populate list box
$names = gc c:\computers.txt
foreach ($name in $names) {
        $listbox.items.add($name) | out-null
}

# attach controls to form
$form.controls.add($button)
$form.controls.add($listbox)
$form.controls.add($label)

# show form
if ($form.showdialog() -ne "Cancel") {
        if ($listbox.selectedindex -ne -1) {
                CheckOS $listbox.selecteditem
        }
}
```

The first thing our code does is define a function—that's not actually executing until later, though, so we'll skip it. The first *executable* code in our script is loading up the Windows.Forms assembly:

```
# load WinForms
[Reflection.Assembly]::LoadWithPartialName("System.Windows.Forms") | Out-Null
```

Next, we create a new form. We apply several attributes to it, including a dialog box-style border.

```
# create form
$form = New-Object System.Windows.Forms.Form
$form.text = "Check OS Info"
$form.top = 10
$form.left = 10
$form.height = 280
$form.width = 200
$form.formborderstyle = [system.Windows.Forms.FormBorderStyle]::FixedDialog
```

Then we create a label, so that the user has some idea of what this little utility is going to do:

```
# create label
$label = New-Object system.Windows.Forms.Label
$label.text = "Select computer to query:"
$label.top = 2
$label.left = 10
$label.width = 180
```

Next up is a button:

```
# create button
$button = New-Object Windows.Forms.Button
$button.text = "Select"
$button.height = 20
$button.width = 180
$button.top = 230
$button.left = 10
```

And then the button's event handler. Notice that all this is doing is setting a DialogResult for the form and then closing the form:

```
# create event handler for button
$event = {
        $form.dialogresult = [system.Windows.Forms.DialogResult]::OK
        $form.close()
}
```

Now we add the event handler to the button's Click event:

```
# attach event handler
$button.Add_Click($event)
```

Next, we create a list box and populate it by reading computer names from a text file:

```
# create list box
$listbox = New-Object Windows.Forms.ListBox
$listbox.height = 200
$listbox.width = 180
$listbox.top = 20
$listbox.left = 10

# populate list box
$names = gc c:\computers.txt
foreach ($name in $names) {
        $listbox.items.add($name) | out-null
}
```

Now we're ready to add our three controls to the form:

```
# attach controls to form
$form.controls.add($button)
$form.controls.add($listbox)
$form.controls.add($label)
```

And now we show the form. Notice that we're calling the **ShowDialog()** method as part of an If block. We're checking to see if the **ShowDialog()** result is "Cancel" or not; if it isn't, we check to see if an item is selected in the list box. If one is, we'll call the function we defined at the beginning of the script, passing the selected list box item as the function's input argument.

```
# show form
if ($form.showdialog() -ne "Cancel") {
        if ($listbox.selectedindex -ne -1) {
                CheckOS $listbox.selecteditem
        }
}
```

Here's what the form looks like:

The function retrieves information from WMI—specifically, the Win32_OperatingSystem class. It then creates a *new* form, adds a text box, and fills that text box with the information we've selected. Finally, it shows the form as a dialog box.

```
function CheckOS($computer) {
        $wmi = gwmi win32_operatingsystem -computer $computer

        # create output form
        $form = New-Object System.Windows.Forms.Form
    $form.text = "OS Info for $computer"
        $form.top = 10
        $form.left = 10
        $form.height = 200
        $form.width = 250
        $form.formborderstyle = [system.Windows.Forms.FormBorderStyle]::FixedDialog

        # create text box
        $textbox = New-Object system.Windows.Forms.TextBox
        $textbox.top = 2
        $textbox.left = 2
        $textbox.width = 246
        $textbox.height = 196
        $textbox.readonly = $true
        $textbox.multiline = $true
    $textbox.text = "Build: " + $wmi.buildnumber + " / Service Pack: " + `
    $wmi.servicepackmajorversion + " / OS: " + $wmi.caption

        # add control to form
        $form.controls.add($textbox)

        # show form
        $form.showdialog() | Out-Null
}
```

Here's the dialog displayed by the function:

The only thing we don't like about this utility is that it has to be run *each time* you want to query a computer. Instead, we'd like it to re-display the first form, so that another computer can be selected. It should continue doing that until we close the form by clicking its "Close" button (in the title bar).

The way we're choosing to do that is to move the CheckOS function *inside the button's Click handler*. Here's the revised script, where you'll notice the relocated CheckOS function. Also within the Click handler is the call to CheckOS, which checks to make sure a computer name was selected before continuing:

## WinForms2.ps1

```
# load WinForms
[Reflection.Assembly]::LoadWithPartialName("System.Windows.Forms") | Out-Null

# create form
$form = New-Object System.Windows.Forms.Form
$form.text = "Check OS Info"
$form.top = 10
$form.left = 10
$form.height = 280
$form.width = 200
$form.formborderstyle = [system.Windows.Forms.FormBorderStyle]::FixedDialog

# create label
$label = New-Object system.Windows.Forms.Label
$label.text = "Select computer to query:"
$label.top = 2
$label.left = 10
$label.width = 180

# create button
$button = New-Object Windows.Forms.Button
$button.text = "Select"
$button.height = 20
$button.width = 180
$button.top = 230
$button.left = 10

# create event handler for button
$event = {
        function CheckOS($computer) {
                $wmi = gwmi win32_operatingsystem -computer $computer

                # create output form
                $form = New-Object System.Windows.Forms.Form
    $form.text = "OS Info for $computer"
```

```
                $form.top = 10
                $form.left = 10
                $form.height = 200
                $form.width = 250
                $form.formborderstyle = [system.Windows.Forms.FormBorderStyle]::FixedDialog

                # create text box
                $textbox = New-Object system.Windows.Forms.TextBox
                $textbox.top = 2
                $textbox.left = 2
                $textbox.width = 246
                $textbox.height = 196
                $textbox.readonly = $true
                $textbox.multiline = $true
        $textbox.text = "Build: " + $wmi.buildnumber + " / Service Pack: " + `
         $wmi.servicepackmajorversion + " / OS: " + $wmi.caption

                # add control to form
                $form.controls.add($textbox)

                # show form
                $form.showdialog() | Out-Null
        }
        if ($listbox.selectedindex -ne -1) {
                CheckOS $listbox.selecteditem
        }
}

# attach event handler
$button.Add_Click($event)

# create list box
$listbox = New-Object Windows.Forms.ListBox
$listbox.height = 200
$listbox.width = 180
$listbox.top = 20
$listbox.left = 10

# populate list box
$names = gc c:\computers.txt
foreach ($name in $names) {
        $listbox.items.add($name) | out-null
}

# attach controls to form
$form.controls.add($button)
$form.controls.add($listbox)
$form.controls.add($label)

# show form
$form.showdialog() | Out-Null
```

At the end, we've piped the output of **ShowDialog()** to **Out-Null**, because at that point, we don't care what the dialog's result is—the only way the dialog can be closed is to click its "Close" button, which means our script is finished.

## Working with Event Arguments

In our examples thus far, we've ignored the fact that data is passed into each event handler. For the most part, we haven't *needed* any data; we just needed to know that the event occurred. That's probably the case for *most* events, actually, but the Framework does sometimes provide additional information that you can work with inside your event handlers. In an event handler, you have two special variables that you can work with: The variable $this represents the control that the event occurred to. For example, if a button was clicked, $this would *be* that button. This allows you to assign the same event handler to multiple controls' events, since you can always use $this to figure out which control actually received the event, and to work with that control directly.

The $_ variable represents the *event arguments* that were passed into the event. Sometimes, such as with a button's MouseClick event, the arguments are of a specific type—MouseEventArgs, for example. Those types may have particular properties. For example, a MouseEventArgs argument has a Buttons property, which allows you to determine *what mouse button* was used to click the control. Here's an example:

```
Switch ($_.Button) {
  System.Windows.Forms.MouseButtons.Right { "Right button"; Break }
  System.Windows.Forms.MouseButtons.Left { "Left button"; Break }
}
```

A complete discussion of every type of possible event handler signature, and every possible event argument construction, is beyond the scope of this book—that's what the Framework documentation is for, actually. For example, if we search for the System.Widows.Forms.Button class, and then click on its MouseClick event, we see that the *handler* is listed as a MouseEventHandler. Clicking on that handler reveals that it passes in the *sender* argument (which becomes $this in PowerShell), and *e* (which becomes $_ in PowerShell), which is a MouseEventArgs. Clicking on MouseEventArgs displays information about it; scrolling to the bottom provides a link to the MouseEventArgs Members, which displays all the properties and so forth that $_ would contain in PowerShell.

> ............................................................................................................
>
> **Hold on to Your Hat...**
> One reason that PowerShell can work with all these varied event signatures is due to a feature called *contra variance* in the Framework. Essentially, PowerShell can handle any event that passes a *sender* argument (which becomes $this), and a second argument that is either of the type EventArgs, or of a type that *inherits* from EventArgs.
>
> For example, look up the System.Windows.Forms.TreeView control in the Framework documentation, and click on the TreeNodeMouseClick event. That takes you to the documentation for that particular event, where you'll see that it wants a TreeNodeMouseClickEventHandler; click *that*, and you'll see that the second argument is a TreeNodeMouseClickEventArgs (we know, these crazy names *kill* us). Click that second argument and, finally, you'll see that it inherits from MouseEventArgs. Click *that* and you'll see that it inherits from EventArgs. Whew
>
> So, because the second argument in the event is a descendent (albeit second-generation) of EventArgs, PowerShell can "hook" an event handler to that event. Some events, however, may have additional parameters, or may have a second parameter that does *not* inherit from EventArgs. In those cases, PowerShell *might not* be able to "hook" your event handler to the event quite as easily. It *is* possible to create an event handler capable of dealing with a different event signature, but it's outside the scope of what we can cover here. And, if you're sticking with the basic WinForms controls and their common events, you won't need to know how to do that.

Using $_ and $this provide additional flexibility in your event handlers. Keep in mind that the overall design philosophy of event-driven programming, which WinForms uses, is as follows:

- Write enough code to get your interface looking like you want.

- Write event handlers that respond to user actions.

In other words, all of your "juicy" code will be in your event handlers, as shown in our WinForms2.ps1 example. This can make your scripts a bit tough to read—and, frankly, a real pain to debug, sometimes—but it's the way things need to be done to properly leverage WinForms.

Chapter 43
# Working with the Web

One of PowerShell's cooler features is its ability to tap into the .NET Frameworks strong Web connectivity. We were originally going to call this chapter, "Working with Web Services," because "Web Services" is such a buzzword these days—but we realized that "Web Services" means a very specific thing and involves protocols like the Simple Object Access Protocol (SOAP). While that's all well and good, it's also pretty darn complicated, and it's not really all PowerShell can do. PowerShell can pull information from the Web in a lot of different ways, and we wanted to be able to touch on some of the other ways that aren't specifically "Web Services." But first, let's make sure we're on the same page with what happens when we use PowerShell to pull information from a Web server.

## Retrieving Data from the Web

Basically, the entire point of the HTTP protocol that makes the Web work is that a client sends a request for a given Web page to a server, and the server (we hope) responds by sending the text of that Web page back to the client. Now, sometimes servers go through a lot of effort to produce that page. For example, servers running a server-side language like ASP.NET, or PHP, or ASP often have to process a lot of programming instructions, access databases, and so forth in order to dynamically "construct" the page requested by a client. In the end, though, what's transmitted to the client is just pure, simple text.

The type of text transmitted back is important, too. For example, most Web pages use a language called HTML, which you've no doubt seen. When this text is received by a Web browser, it *renders* the HTML, meaning it uses the HTML instructions to create the final page that you're accustomed to seeing. Sometimes, though, a Web server will send something other than HTML. A blog, for example, is in an XML format called RSS. Even a Web service uses HTTP, although the text it sends is in an XML format called SOAP (usually; other formats exist for Web services, too).

When you work with data from the Web in PowerShell, though, you're going to be working with that raw, under-the-hood text transmitted by a Web server. PowerShell doesn't render HTML into a pretty page, and it doesn't format an RSS feed the way Internet Explorer or another Web browser might. Instead, you'll be working directly with the text exactly as it was transmitted by the Web server. Sometimes, you might just save that information to a file, so that it can be opened by a "smarter" application, like Internet Explorer; other times, especially when the text is in an XML format, you might use PowerShell's own capabilities to extract bits of data from what the Web server sent you.

## A Simple Request

The .NET Framework's System.Net.WebRequest class is used to make a Web request to a specific URL. It looks like this:

```
$Request = [System.Net.WebRequest]::Create("http://www.sapien.com")
```

The request doesn't *do* anything; it just sort of sits there on your computer. To transmit it, you ask the Framework to retrieve the response to that request:

```
$response = $request.GetResponse()
```

And that's it: The $response variable will contain your HTTP response. As a simple thing, you can check the response's StatusCode property to see if it's "OK:"

```
$response.StatusCode
```

In fact, these three lines of code can combine to make a pretty useful little utility, which we'll write as a function:

```
Function Ping-WebServer($url) {
 $request = [System.Net.WebRequest]::Create($url)
 $response = $request.GetResponse()
 If ($response.StatusCode -eq "OK") {
 $True
 } else {
 $False
 }
}
```

Pass this function the URL of an intranet (or Internet, for that matter) Web server, and the function will output $True of that server is reachable via HTTP, and if the server responds correctly. This is a nice little utility that you could incorporate into a larger script that checks the status of various resources on your network for you. The trick with it is that we didn't care *what* the response was; we just cared that there *was a response.*

## Working with XML Data from the Web

But what if you *do* want to work with the information that the Web server sent back? In that case, we might opt to work with a more full-featured object: The System.Net.WebClient. For example, Microsoft publishes an RSS feed at http://www.microsoft.com/technet/security/bulletin/secrss.aspx, which lists the latest Microsoft security bulletins. RSS is simply an XML format, and we know from our chapter, "Working with XML Documents" that PowerShell knows how to work with XML. So, we'll use the

WebClient to retrieve that RSS feed, and then use PowerShell's XML capabilities to create some formatted output from the feed's contents.

We have to start by loading the Framework assembly that contains the WebClient class and then we'll ask it to download the entire RSS feed into an XML variable:

```
[System.Reflection.Assembly]::LoadWithPartialName("System.Web") | Out-Null
$webclient = new-object System.Net.WebClient
$url="http://www.microsoft.com/technet/security/bulletin/secrss.aspx"
[xml]$data = $webclient.downloadstring($url)
```

Now we need to examine the data. First, we'll check to make sure we *got* some data, but checking to see if $data is null or not:

```
if ( $data -ne $Null) {
```

Now we'll start creating out output, starting with the RSS channel title and the date it was last updated.

```
Write-Host -backgroundcolor Yellow -foregroundcolor blue `
$data.rss.channel.Title

Write-Host "Last Updated" $data.rss.channel.LastBuildDate `n
```

Next, we'll write the title of the first item. Notice that we're setting a variable, $i, equal to zero, and using it to access the first rss.channel.item element.

```
$i=0
do {
write-Host -foregroundcolor White `
$data.rss.channel.item[$i].Title
```

Depending on the severity of the current item, we'll set its description color to be red, yellow, or green.

```
#color code description based on severity
if ($data.rss.channel.item[$i].Description `
-Like "*Rating:Critical*") {

 $color="Red"

}

elseif ($data.rss.channel.item[$i].Description `
 -Like "*Rating:Important*"){

 $color="Yellow"

} else {

 $color="Green"

}
```

Last, we'll actually write the description, using the color we selected.

```
Write-Host -foregroundcolor $color `
$data.rss.channel.item[$i].Description `n
```

Now we increment $i by one and continue looping until we've reached the end of the RSS items.

```
$i++
} until ($i -gt ($data.rss.channel.item).count)
}
```

Finally, here's what happens if our original $data request was null:

```
else {
 Write-Host -foregroundcolor Red "Could not get " $url
}
```

Here's the entire script, with some additional comments to help you follow the flow:

## Get SecurityRSS.ps1

```
#Get-SecurityRSS.ps1
#Query Microsoft's Basic Security Feed for latest bulletins
#Critical bulletins will be displayed in Red
#Important bulletins will be display in Yellow
#Everything else will be displayed in Green

[void] [System.Reflection.Assembly]::LoadWithPartialName("System.Web")
$webclient = new-object System.Net.WebClient
$url="http://www.microsoft.com/technet/security/bulletin/secrss.aspx"
## Get the web page into a single string
$data =[xml]$webclient.downloadstring($url)

if ( $data -ne $Null) {
 Write-Host -backgroundcolor Yellow -foregroundcolor blue `
 $data.rss.channel.Title
 Write-Host "Last Updated" $data.rss.channel.LastBuildDate `n
 $i=0
 do {
 write-Host -foregroundcolor White `
 $data.rss.channel.item[$i].Title
 #color code description based on severity
 if ($data.rss.channel.item[$i].Description `
 -Like "*Rating:Critical*") {
 $color="Red"
 }
 elseif ($data.rss.channel.item[$i].Description `
 -Like "*Rating:Important*"){
 $color="Yellow"
 }
 else {
 $color="Green"
 }
 Write-Host -foregroundcolor $color `
 $data.rss.channel.item[$i].Description `n
 $i++
 }
 until ($i -gt ($data.rss.channel.item).count)
 }
else {
 Write-Host -foregroundcolor Red "Could not get " $url
```

}

This example showed you how to retrieve a Web page into a string. In our example, we converted that to XML by declaring $data as an [XML] type, but you could use [string] instead if you were retrieving a normal HTML page. Once you've got that HTML page, you can work with the contents however you want to.

## Using a Proxy Server for Web Connections

The examples we've shown thus far assume that you have an unimpeded connection to the Internet—that is, you either don't have a Web proxy server to deal with or the proxy server is capable of working "invisibly." If that's not the case, then you'll need to take a few additional steps. Note that these can be tricky, and you'll probably have to do some experimentation to find the exact combination that works for you. Just be prepared for things to not work properly the first time, since every proxy configuration is different!

In *many* cases, the System.Net.WebClient or System.NetWebRequest class will be able to read and use the proxy settings configured in the Internet Options control panel application. Try ensuring that those settings are properly configured first: Open the Control Panel, double-click Internet Options, select the Connections tab, and then click LAN Settings (this may differ slightly on various versions of Windows). If set to "automatic proxy configuration," Windows relies primarily on the WPAD host identified by your DHCP server.

Alternately, you can create a new System.Net.WebProxy class:

```
PS C:\> $proxy = new-object System.Net.WebProxy
```

Once you've done that, you can set the proxy server address:

```
PS C:\> $proxy.Address = "http://myproxy.mycompany.com"
```

You can specify that Windows pass along your logon credentials to the proxy:

```
PS C:\> $proxy.UseDefaultCredentials = $true
```

It is possible to provide alternate credentials to the proxy server, as well. However, the technique is a bit complicated due to the way the Framework classes are designed. For more information, go to http://msdn.microsoft.com/library, search for "System.Net.WebProxy," and then read the information provided for the Credentials property. You'll need to create a new instance of the ICredentials interface and then use its GetCredentials method. Credentials can be supplied on a per-URI basis, so this is something you really have to think through carefully. Whenever possible, we find that configuring a proxy through the Internet Options Control Panel application is far easier.

Once you've gotten your proxy configured the way you want it, you have to assign it to the WebClient or WebRequest:

```
PS C:\> $webrequest.proxy = $proxy
```

Then you can successfully issue your request, which should now be directed to your proxy server. However, we don't want to understate the complexity of using the WebProxy class in environments with unusual older proxy servers; we've been in some situations where we've simply never been able to get the

WebProxy to connect properly. If you run into difficulty, please drop by the Discussion Forums on www. ScriptingAnswers.com and ask for help; in a book like this we can't deal with every individual situation that may come up, but in the discussion forums, we definitely can.

## Working with "Real" Web Services

PowerShell can natively work with "real" Web services—that is, those which communicate using a Web services protocol like SOAP—but it needs some help from you to do so. The .NET Framework requires a *Web services description language* (WSDL) *proxy* in order to handle communications between the Framework and the remote Web service; unfortunately, PowerShell can't build such a proxy itself. Microsoft Visual Studio comes with a command-line utility called Wsdl.exe, which can build such a proxy, but for the purposes of this book, we're not assuming you have access to a licensed copy of Visual Studio.

In his blog, PowerShell MVP Keith Hill shows how you'd do this, assuming you *did* have access to Visual Studio's Wsdl.exe utility. The full post is at http://keithhill.spaces.live.com/blog/ cns!5A8D2641E0963A97!512.entry, and it looks like this, with the first line using Wsdl.exe to compile a WSDL proxy from a weather-forecasting Web service:

```
PS C:\> wsdl.exe http://www.webservicex.net/WeatherForecast.asmx?WSDL
```

Next, he uses the C# compiler to compile the proxy:

```
PS C:\> csc /t:library WeatherForecast.cs
```

Then he loads the compiled proxy assembly into PowerShell:

```
PS C:\> [Reflection.Assembly]::LoadFrom("$pwd\WeatherForecast.dll")
```

With the assembly loaded, he creates a new instance of the object representing the Web service:

```
PS C:\> $weatherService = new-object WeatherForecast
```

And finally calls the Web service's **GetWeatherByZipCode()** method, storing the results in $forecast:

```
PS C:\> $forecast = $weatherService.GetWeatherByZipCode(80526)
```

Last, he displays the contents of $forecast:

```
PS C:\> $forecast
```

A further discussion—since it requires Visual Studio—is beyond the scope of this book, but we wanted you to see that it's *possible* and give you an idea of where to go if you want more information.

## A Practical Example

This'll be fun: Windows Live Search is capable of returning search results in RSS format, which we learned how to read earlier in this chapter. Combining that with some of the knowledge from the chapter "Creating Custom Objects," we've written a function that will accept a query term, and then return a set of custom objects representing the search results. We added this function to our profile so that Get-SearchResults is always available. Here's the function:

## LiveSearch.ps1

```
Function Get-SearchResults {
    param([string] $searchstring=$(throw "Please specify a search string."))

        $client = New-Object System.Net.WebClient

    [xml]$results = $client.DownloadString("http://search.live.com/results.aspx?q=" + `
    $searchstring + "&format=rss")
        $channel = $results.rss.channel

    foreach ($item in $channel.item) {
        $result = New-Object PSObject
        $result | Add-Member NoteProperty Title -value $item.title
        $result | Add-Member NoteProperty Link -value $item.link
        $result | Add-Member NoteProperty Description -value $item.description
        $result | Add-Member NoteProperty PubDate -value $item.pubdate
        $sb = {
                $ie = New-Object -com internetexplorer.application
                $ie.navigate($this.link)
                $ie.visible = $true
        }
        $result | Add-Member ScriptMethod Open -value $sb
        $result
    }
}
```

This is using the System.Net.WebClient class to retrieve a Live Search results page. Notice that we're passing the RSS format request in the URL itself; this is a feature of Live Search that we're simply capitalizing on. We go through each search result and create a new custom object. That object has properties for the Title, Link, Description, and PubDate, and a ScriptMethod named **Open()**. This ScriptMethod is just a PowerShell script block, which we defined in $sb: It creates a new instance of Internet Explorer, navigates to the page represented by the current search result (accessing the URL via $this.link), and makes the browser visible. Finally, the function outputs the search result.

Here's how to use it:

```
PS C:\> $hits = get-searchresults "PrimalScript"
PS C:\> $hits

Title                   Link                    Description            PubDate
-----                   ----                    -----------            -------
SAPIEN Technologies, Inc. .  http://primalscript.c   SAPIEN Technologies: ... 02 Sep 07 08:4
PrimalScript 2007           http://www.scriptingo... PrimalScript 2007 .. ... 01 Sep 07 17:3
Software                    http://www.scriptingo... Software ... Award-Wi... 01 Sep 07 21:3
SAPIEN Technologies - Make.  http://www.sapien        PrimalScript a script... 01 Sep 07 06:0
SAPIEN Technologies - Make.  http://www.sapien.com... SAPIEN Technologies -... 01 Sep 07 01:1
DevGuru Review - PrimalScript http://www.devguru.co... Award-winning web dev... 31 Aug 07:39:0
pixelconsumption Â" Compil... http://blog.pixelcons... Adobe has made a grea... 07 Sep 07 06:5
Flash tutorials - Coding f... http://www.communitym... Flash, Dreamweaver, F... 07 Sep 07 10:4
Coding for Flash with Prim... http://www.communitym... CMX Learning Guides. ... 07 Sep 07 07:0
SAPIEN Press - scripting b... http://www.sapienpres... Get the Most from Pri... 18 Aug 07 02:1

PS C:\> $hits[0].title
SAPIEN Technologies, Inc. - VBScript Editor, PowerShell Editor, ASP ...
PS C:\> $hits[0].link
http://primalscript.com/
PS C:\> $hits[0].open()
```

As you can see, we're able to access individual search results, such as $hits[0] to access properties like Title and Link, or the method we created—**Open()**—to open the search result in a new Internet Explorer window.

# Chapter 44
# Creating PowerShell Cmdlets and Snap-Ins

This is *definitely* an advanced topic. Before you proceed, you should know that cmdlets can only be written in .NET languages, such as Visual Basic (VB) or C# (pronounced, "C Sharp"). We're not here to teach you those things, and, in fact, we're assuming that if you're reading this chapter, you're already familiar with programming in those languages. Cmdlet development is also *definitely* beyond the scope of "systems programming" or "administrative scripting," which is what the rest of this book is about. However, at the time we're writing this, nobody else has really documented cmdlet development, so we figured we'd give it a shot. Honestly, if you're already pretty familiar with VB or C#, then writing a cmdlet isn't really that difficult.

We also need to point out that this short chapter is obviously not a complete work on cmdlet development. We could (and others have) write a complete *book* about this subject; our goal here is just to give you an overview of what cmdlet development looks like and give you a jumping-off point for further exploration, if you find that this topic interests you.

Much of the sample code in this chapter is taken from SAPIEN Technologies' extensions for PowerShell, a free snap-in you can download from www.primalscript.com/freetools. That isn't an open-source project, so we won't be sharing the source code for all of the cmdlets in that snap-in. However, if you visit www.CodePlex.com, and search for "PowerShell," you'll find a number of other projects that *are* open source, and you can check out their source code. Don wrote a game that runs as PowerShell cmdlets, and you'll find it on CodePlex at www.codeplex.com/powerquest.

## Some Terminology and the Basic Process

Remember that cmdlets live in snap-ins, which are basically .NET DLL files. A snap-in can contain more than one cmdlet, but you have to add the entire snap-in and all its cmdlets to PowerShell at the same time; you can't pick and choose. So, creating a new cmdlet involves first creating a snap-in for the cmdlet to live in; from there, you can start adding cmdlets to the snap-in.

When you're finished programming a snap-in (and its cmdlets), you must *compile* it into a finished DLL. That DLL must exist on any system that needs to use the snap-in and the cmdlets it contains. The DLL must initially be *registered* so that PowerShell can detect its existence, and then it can be added to the shell using the **Add-PSSnapin** cmdlet. If you later recompile a snap-in, you can just drop the new DLL on top of the old one; there's no need to re-register it. But you will need to restart PowerShell.

## Getting Started: You Need an Environment

Don't think for a moment that you're going to get away with using Notepad to create cmdlets. Yes, it's physically possible, but only a madman would try. Instead, you'll need a copy of Visual Studio 2005 or later (or one of the free "Express" editions of Visual Studio, at least). Or, if you happen to have SAPIEN PrimalScript Enterprise Edition, you'll find that it does a bang-up job for cmdlet development as well as PowerShell scripting. Because we *do* happen to have PrimalScript Enterprise, we'll be using it and giving you directions to follow along (you can get a free trial of the software from www.primalscript.com/downloadtrial if you want to follow along).

You're also going to need the System.Management.Automation DLL, and you will not believe how far out of their way Microsoft has gone to make this thing difficult to find. Start by going to www.microsoft.com/download, and in the download search box (not the "all Microsoft.com" search box), type "framework sdk" and click Go. You're looking for the .NET Framework 3.0 SDK for your platform (x86 or x64); Microsoft seems to move this thing constantly and it can be quite infuriating to locate. Worse, when you finally get it, you're going to have to install pretty much all of it in order for the "Reference Assemblies" to be installed. We haven't figured out which little component of the SDK does this, so we typically just install the whole SDK on a virtual machine, grab the Reference Assemblies from the Program Files folder, and copy them over to the computer we're actually working on. Fun, huh? Next time you talk to someone at Microsoft, ask them why the heck they can't ship this one little DLL with PowerShell itself.

......................................................................................................................................................................

**Don't Get Excited**
By the way, don't get excited if you find System.Management.Automation.ni.dll. That won't help you; that's a pre-compiled version that's actually used by PowerShell, but *you* can't use it to make new cmdlets. Sorry.

Once you get this thing onto your system, it should be in \Program Files\Reference Assemblies\Microsoft\WindowsPowerShell\v1.0. There are actually five total DLLs that you'll need:

- Microsoft.PowerShell.Commands.Management.dll

- Microsoft.PowerShell.Commands.Utility.dll

- Microsoft.PowerShell.ConsoleHost.dll

- Microsoft.PowerShell.Security.dll

- System.Management.Automation.dll.

## Creating a New Snap-In

To get started, go to PrimalScript's File menu and select New > Project. Then, select either Visual Basic Projects or C Sharp Projects, depending on which .NET language you plan to work in. In the Templates window, select Windows PowerShell Snapin. Give your snap-in a name (we're using "TestToys"), specify a location for it on your hard disk, and click OK.

When PrimalScript displays the workspace browser (usually on the right of the screen), double-click PSSnapin.vb. This is the file that defines your snap-in. Really, all you need to do is modify the strings returned by the various functions, such as the name, vendor name, description, and so forth. The AssemblyInfo.vb files can be used to set the information that is displayed when someone right-clicks the DLL file in Windows Explorer and selects Properties. This information includes the version number, title, description, copyright information, and so forth.

That's it—you've made a snap-in! Of course, without a cmdlet in there, it won't do much good.

This would be a good time, however, to add a reference to the System.Management.Automation.dll. In PrimalScript, expand the References node in the Workspace browser, and you'll probably see the reference already in there; right-click and remove it. We're going to re-add it, just to make sure it has the correct path for *your* system. Right-click References and select Add Reference; on the .NET tab, click the Browse button and find System.Management.Automation.dll and double-click it. Now you should have the proper reference in your project—why not save it at this time?

# Creating a New Cmdlet

To begin adding a new cmdlet, right-click the project name ("TestToys," in our case), and select Add > Add New Item. From the list of categories, select Windows PowerShell Cmdlet, and then select Windows PowerShell Cmdlet from the Templates window. Create a name for your cmdlet—we're going with PingComputerCmdlet—and click OK. To begin working with your new cmdlet, just double-click its .VB file to open that file in the editor window.

Our goal is to create a cmdlet that accepts one or more String objects, which we expect to either be computer names or IP addresses. We'll define a -**name** parameter to accept this input, but we also want to accept input from the pipeline. We want our cmdlet to attempt to ping each specified address, and, if it's successful, to output that same address. Essentially, we're building a filter: Computer names go in, but only the ones that we could successfully ping will come out. Those successful names can then be piped to some other cmdlet, which attempts to connect to those computers.

### Naming Your Cmdlet

The first thing you need to do is pick a name for your new cmdlet. You'll notice that the cmdlet code starts with something like this:

```
<Cmdlet(VerbsCommon.Get, "PingComputerCmdlet", SupportsShouldProcess:=True)> _
```

That's definitely not correct. Rather than VerbsCommon.Get, we want to specify another verb: Ping. The PowerShell SDK lists the allowable verbs. The documentation starts at http://msdn2.microsoft. com/en-us/library/ms714674.aspx, but we're specifically interested in those verbs, which are at http://msdn2.microsoft.com/en-us/library/ms714428.aspx. We see that the Ping verb is listed as a Diagnostic Verb, meaning it'll be VerbsDiagnostic.Ping. We'll change the noun portion of our cmdlet name to Computer, resulting in the following:

```
<Cmdlet(VerbsDiagnostic.Ping, "Computer", SupportsShouldProcess:=True)> _
```

Because our cmdlet doesn't do anything potentially dangerous, we're not going to support the **-confirm** or **-whatif** parameters. Therefore, we're going to set the SupportsShouldProcess metavariable to FALSE:

```
<Cmdlet(VerbsDiagnostic.Ping, "Computer", SupportsShouldProcess:=False)> _
```

That leaves us with this as our entire cmdlet code:

```
<Cmdlet(VerbsDiagnostic.Ping, "Computer", SupportsShouldProcess:=False)> _
Public Class PingComputerCmdlet
    Inherits Cmdlet

    '<Parameter(Position:=0, Mandatory:=False)> _
    'Public Property Name() As String
    '    Get
    '        Return ""
    '    End Get
    '    Set(ByVal value As String)
    '    End Set
    'End Property

    Protected Overrides Sub ProcessRecord()
        Try
            Throw New NotImplementedException()
        Catch ex As Exception

        End Try
    End Sub

End Class
```

Now we're ready to start creating input parameters for our cmdlet.

## Creating Cmdlet Parameters

The cmdlet template provided in PrimalScript has a block of comments that show how to declare a PowerShell cmdlet parameter. We're just going to uncomment that block and use it as-is. Because our cmdlet can't operate without some input, we're setting our parameter, which we'll leave named "Name," to be Mandatory.

```
<Parameter(Position:=0, Mandatory:=True)> _
```

We're also going to declare a variable, which will hold whatever data is passed in through this parameter.

The variable declaration occurs *outside* the parameter's Property block:

```
Dim Address As string
```

Notice that we've defined this as a single string, not an array. Keep that in mind

That the Get block simply returns the current property value. We're storing the current value in Address, so when the Get block is called, we simply want to return whatever's in Address:

```
Get
    Return Address
End Get
```

Similarly, when new data is passed into the parameter via the Set block, we want to put that data into our Address variable so that we can work with it. Therefore, we'll modify the Set block. The variable "value" is provided for us as the variable that receives incoming data; we'll just transfer that into our Address variable for long-term storage.

```
Set(ByVal value As String)
    Address = value
End Set
```

So, our entire parameter declaration looks like this:

```
Dim Address As String
<Parameter(Position:=0, Mandatory:=True)> _
Public Property Name() As String
    Get
        Return Address
    End Get
    Set(ByVal value As String)
        Address = value
    End Set
End Property
```

Since this is the only parameter we need, we're *almost* done with this part. If we did create additional parameters, they'd all need a unique Property name, and they'd need a unique Position value. The Mandatory value could be modified for each one as appropriate. Typically, parameters aren't any more complicated than this.

## Input Validation in Parameters

You could, if you wanted to, perform some input validation in the Set block to make sure that any incoming data is what you expect. For example, let's say we created a parameter that was accepting date input. To check and make sure we got a date, we could do something like this:

```
<Parameter(Position:=0, Mandatory:=True)> _
Public Property Today() As String
    Get
        Return TodayDate
    End Get
    Set(ByVal value As String)
     If isdate(value) Then
         TodayDate = value
```

```
        Else
            Throw New Exception("Bad input")
        End If
    End Set
End Property
```

Here, we've used an If/Then block to determine if the incoming data is a valid date or not. If it is, we go ahead and put it into our storage variable, TodayDate. Otherwise, we have VB throw an exception, which would be passed up to Windows PowerShell.

## Pipeline Parameters

We did say that we wanted out -**name** parameter to accept input from the pipeline, so we need to modify it slightly by adding an additional attribute to its declaration:

```
Dim Address As string

<Parameter(Position:=0, Mandatory:=True, ValueFromPipeline:=True)> _
Public Property Name() As String
    Get
        Return Address
    End Get
    Set(ByVal value As String)
        Address = value
    End Set
End Property
```

By adding the ValueFromPipeline attribute, we're telling PowerShell that complete input objects can be fed to this parameter from the pipeline. That's an important distinction: We want the *complete* input object, which we're expecting to be a String collection. Another option is to only have the parameter accept a single *property* from the pipeline objects. To do that, you'd specify the ValueFromPipelineByName attribute instead. If we did that, then the input objects would have to have a Name property, which would match the name of our parameter. PowerShell would *just* feed the Name properties of input objects to our parameter.

## Overriding an Input Processing Method

Finally, we have to "override" one of the cmdlet's default input processing methods. All cmdlets are built from a template that's essentially built into PowerShell; whenever PowerShell executes a cmdlet, it automatically executes three distinct phases. Remember, these all happen for *each* cmdlet that is run. They are:

- BeginProcessing – This is called when the cmdlet is initially executed.

- ProcessRecord – This is called once for each input object that is passed to the cmdlet.

- EndProcessing – This is called after all input objects have been sent to the cmdlet for processing.

The template that cmdlets are built on defines three methods that correspond to these "execution phases." The trick is that the template's methods *don't do anything*. So, if we do nothing else with our cmdlet, all three methods will execute without error, but nothing will happen. In order to have our cmdlet do useful work, we have to *override* at least one of these methods, substituting our own code for the template's empty methods.

If your cmdlet doesn't accept pipeline input, then it should override the EndProcessing method. Our cmdlet *does* accept pipeline input, so we must at least override the ProcessRecord method:

```
Protected Overrides Sub ProcessRecord()
    Try
        Throw New NotImplementedException()
    Catch ex As Exception

    End Try
End Sub
```

Here's how this works: If 10 objects are pipelined into our cmdlet, then the cmdlet's **ProcessRecord()** method will be executed *10 times*. Each time, our input parameter **-name** will be set to a new pipeline input object. In that fashion, we'll be processing all 10 input objects, although our cmdlet only has to worry about processing one of them at a time.

The default code PrimalScript gives us simply throws an exception indicating that the ProcessRecord method hasn't yet been implemented. We'll remove that default code and substitute our own.

## Coding the Cmdlet

One of the reasons we like working in VB rather than C# is because VB has a neat object called My, which contains a lot of cool functionality. For example, **My.Computer.Ping()** is a method that pings a computer by name or IP address, and returns a TRUE or FALSE value if the computer was reachable or not. Since we already know that our Address variable will contain the address we want to ping, it's pretty easy to build the functional code of our cmdlet:

```
If My.Computer.Network.Ping(Address) Then

End If
```

Now all we need to do is create some output. That is, if the ping was successful, we want to output the same address we received as input. PowerShell provides a built-in function called **WriteObject()** that will do the trick:

```
If My.Computer.Network.Ping(Address) Then
    WriteObject(Address)
End If
```

That's a pretty straightforward, yet useful, cmdlet.

Your finished .VB file should look something like this:

```
Imports System.Management.Automation

<Cmdlet(VerbsDiagnostic.Ping, "Computer", SupportsShouldProcess:=False)> _
Public Class PingComputerCmdlet
    Inherits Cmdlet

    Dim Address As String

    <Parameter(Position:=0, Mandatory:=True, ValueFromPipeline:=True)> _
    Public Property Name() As String
        Get
            Return Address
        End Get
        Set(ByVal value As String)
            Address=value
        End Set
```

```
    End Property

    Protected Overrides Sub ProcessRecord()
       If My.Computer.Network.Ping(Address) Then
        WriteObject(Address)
       End If

    End Sub

End Class
```

## Compiling the Snap-In

Now we're ready to compile the cmdlet into a DLL. From PrimalScript, this is pretty easy: From the Build menu, select Build Workspace. Note that PrimalScript requires you to have installed the .NET Framework SDK in order for compilation to work; that's because PrimalScript is simply calling on the compilers provided with the Framework SDK. If you installed the Framework SDK in order to obtain PowerShell's reference assemblies, then you should be ready to go.

## Registering the Snap-In

The .NET Framework (just the Framework run-time, not the whole SDK) includes an **InstallUtil.exe** utility that registers assemblies like your new snap-in. To use it, open a new PowerShell window and type this:

```
PS C:\> set-alias installutil $env:windir\Microsoft.NET\Framework\v2.0.50727\installutil
```

Note that this is a reference to the .NET Framework 2.0 folder; this is okay even if you're using v3.0 of the Framework, because v3.0 is really just a set of add-ons to 2.0. PowerShell itself is written and compiled in v2.0.

Next, run this:

```
PS C:\> installutil "path\file.dll"
```

You'll provide the complete path and file to your snap-in DLL. Make sure your snap-in DLL is someplace permanent; once you register it this way, PowerShell will always look for it in that location.

## Adding the Snap-In

Registered snap-ins can be added using the **Add-PSSnapIn** cmdlet. If your cmdlet is named TestToys, just run this:

```
PS C:\> add-pssnapin testtoys
```

That's it—you should be able to run **Get-PSSnapIn** and see your new snap-in. To see the cmdlets included in your snap-in run:

```
PS C:\> get-command -pssnapin testtoys

CommandType     Name              Definition
-----------     ----              ----------
Cmdlet          Ping-Computer     Ping-Computer [-Name] <String> [-Verbose] [-Debu..
```

If you want your snap-in to be available every time you start PowerShell, don't forget to add it in your profile.

## Removing the Snap-In

If for some reason you need or want to remove the snap-in after it has been registered, the easy approach is to use the installutil alias:

```
PS C:\> installutil /u "filepath\testtoys.dll"
```

If that fails, you might need to delete the registry entry under HKLM:\SOFTWARE\Microsoft\ PowerShell\1\PowerShellSnapIns and restart PowerShell.

## Using the New Cmdlet

We're going to read a list of computer names from a text file and pipe them to the **Ping-Computer** cmdlet. The contents of the text file are as follows:

```
DON-LAPTOP
LOCALHOST
DON-PC
SERVER2
```

Of these, only the second and third names are actually reachable on our network. Here's the cmdlet in action:

```
PS C:\> get-content c:\computers.txt | ping-computer
Ping-Computer : An exception occurred during a Ping request.
At line:1 char:44
+ get-content c:\computers.txt | ping-computer <<<<
```

Oops. Well, not everything goes perfect the first time. Unfortunately, there's no super-easy way to debug cmdlets. You basically have to try and analyze what happened, modify the cmdlet, re-compile it (which will require you to shut down PowerShell so that the snap-in DLL can be overwritten), and try again.

## Debugging Cmdlets

After a bit of fussing, we got things working properly:

```
PS C:\> get-content c:\computers.txt | ping-computer
LOCALHOST
DON-PC
```

The problem, it turns out, is that the **My.Computer.Ping()** method will generate an exception if it's unable to resolve a name to an IP address. On our test network, which doesn't use DNS, it wasn't able to resolve the first name to an IP address, so it wasn't able to even try pinging it. We solved the problem by simply adding some VB error trapping to our cmdlet, so that any exceptions wouldn't cause it to quit:

```
Protected Overrides Sub ProcessRecord()
    Try
        If My.Computer.Network.Ping(Address) Then
            WriteObject(Address)
```

```
          End If
      Catch ex As Exception
      End Try
   End Sub
```

This isn't a great practice, programming-wise; we *should* be checking to see what error occurred and handling it, if possible. But we know that about the only thing that can go wrong is for the name-to-IP address resolution to fail, and there's nothing we can do about that if it happens—so we haven't put any "error handling" code in the Catch block.

Here's the revised .VB file:

```
Imports System.Management.Automation

<Cmdlet(VerbsDiagnostic.Ping, "Computer", SupportsShouldProcess:=False)> _
Public Class PingComputerCmdlet
   Inherits Cmdlet

   Dim Address As String

   <Parameter(Position:=0, Mandatory:=True, ValueFromPipeline:=True)> _
   Public Property Name() As String
       Get
           Return Address
       End Get
       Set(ByVal value As String)
           Address=value
       End Set
   End Property

   Protected Overrides Sub ProcessRecord()
       Try
           If My.Computer.Network.Ping(Address) Then
            WriteObject(Address)
           End If
       Catch ex As Exception

       End Try

   End Sub

End Class
```

## Making Help

By default, when someone uses the **Get-Help** cmdlet (or the **Help** function) to ask for help on your cmdlets, PowerShell looks for an XML-formatted help file located in the same folder as your snap-in DLL. This XML format is *complicated*, and it's absolutely not worth your time to cobble one together manually. Fortunately, a member of the Windows PowerShell team took the time to build a graphical tool capable of creating PowerShell-compatible help files. Download it from http://www.wassimfayed.com/
PowerShell/CmdletHelpEditor.zip, run it (be sure to read its documentation), and you're ready to go. Your snap-in has to be pretty much finished before you can begin authoring the Help file; the utility looks at your snap-in and sets up appropriate sections for each cmdlet, each parameter, and so forth.

# It's All in the Framework

While we certainly haven't shown you every possible permutation of cmdlet development, we've definitely given you a kick-start. Hopefully, if you're already experienced in VB or C#, you'll have enough to begin creating your own cmdlets and snap-ins and extending the capabilities of Windows PowerShell.

However, as you've seen here, the actual process of creating a cmdlet or snap-in is pretty straightforward. It's the *functionality* of your cmdlets—the code that makes them do whatever it is you want them to do—that's complex. For that, we can't provide a lot of help: You'll need to dig into Microsoft .NET Framework development much deeper than we can do in this administrator-focused book. We do know that many administrators have some programming experience in their background, and that you may already have some Framework familiarity. For those administrators, diving in and creating cmdlets should be pretty simple now that you've seen how it's done.

# A Practical Example

Although the example we showed you is definitely practical, we want to do something a bit more complicated to wrap up this chapter. Our goal is to redo our **Ping-Computer** cmdlet so that it outputs a custom object type for each computer name provided to it. Each of those objects will expose a number of properties, including the computer name that we attempted to ping, whether or not it was successful, and other statistics. Such a custom object is more flexible because we'll be outputting an object even if a ping fails; this allows a subsequent pipeline cmdlet, such as **Where-Object**, to filter the results for whatever you have in mind at the time.

**This is Rocket Science**

Well, it's not *exactly* rocket science, but this is a much more complicated and .NET Framework-centric example. We won't be explaining all of the underlying Framework concepts in exhaustive detail, so if this is a bit over your head, that's okay; you're not missing anything that's actually important to the day-to-day operation of PowerShell. If you're diving this far into cmdlet authoring, we're assuming that you have a good Framework grounding in the first place.

We'll start by defining a new class named PingResult. In .NET, a class is basically the description of what a given object will look like. In this case, we've simply defined four basic properties. Notice that we declare an "internal" variable, whose names we start with an underscore (that's our convention, not something you *have* to do). These variables hold the actual property values; the four Property routines provide a means of changing and retrieving those values.

Next up is our actual cmdlet class. You'll notice that we've abandoned the special **My** object and switched to using WMI to perform the ping; that's because the WMI Win32_PingStatus class provides more detailed information, rather than just a "success" or "failure" rating. Our cmdlet's ProcessRecord() subroutine is called once for each pipeline object passed into the cmdlet; for each one, it attempts to ping the computer name provided. It constructs a new object of our PingResult type and populates the object's properties from values provided by the Win32_PingStatus class. Each PingResult object is written to the output pipeline.

First up, the PingResult class:

## PingResult.vb

```
Public Class PingResult

'the following is one line
 Private _ComputerName As String, _StatusCode As Integer, _ResponseTime As Integer, _
ProtocolAddress As String

   Public Property ComputerName() As String
       Get
           Return _ComputerName
       End Get
       Set(ByVal value As String)
           _ComputerName = value
       End Set
   End Property

   Public Property StatusCode() As Integer
       Get
           Return _StatusCode
       End Get
       Set(ByVal value As Integer)
           _StatusCode = value
       End Set
   End Property

   Public Property ResponseTime() As Integer
       Get
           Return _ResponseTime
       End Get
       Set(ByVal value As Integer)
           _ResponseTime = value
       End Set
   End Property

   Public Property ProtocolAddress() As String
       Get
           Return _ProtocolAddress
       End Get
       Set(ByVal value As String)
           _ProtocolAddress = value
       End Set
   End Property

End Class
```

To add a class in PrimalScript, right-click on your workspace name, Select Add > Add New Item and pick Class from the Code section. Here's the revised cmdlet file:

## PingComputerCmdlet.vb

```
Imports System.Management.Automation
Imports System.Management

<Cmdlet(VerbsDiagnostic.Ping, "Computer", SupportsShouldProcess:=True)> _
Public Class PingComputerCmd
   Inherits Cmdlet

   '<Parameter(Position:=0, Mandatory:=False)> _
   'Public Property Name() As String
   '    Get
```

```
'        Return ""
'    End Get
'    Set(ByVal value As String)
'    End Set
'End Property

Private _Name As String
<Parameter(Position:=0, Mandatory:=False, ValueFromPipeline:=True, _
 HelpMessage:="The name or IP address to ping")> _
Public Property Name() As String
    Get
        Return _Name
    End Get
    Set(ByVal value As String)
        _Name = value
    End Set
End Property


Protected Overrides Sub ProcessRecord()
    Dim Result As New PingResult

    'define query
    Dim Searcher As New System.Management.ManagementObjectSearcher( _
    "SELECT * FROM Win32_PingStatus WHERE Address = '" & _Name & "'")

    'execute query
    Dim PResults As System.Management.ManagementObjectCollection
    PResults = Searcher.Get()

    'run through results
    Dim PResult As System.Management.ManagementObject
    For Each PResult In PResults
        Result.ComputerName = _Name
        Result.StatusCode = PResult.GetPropertyValue("StatusCode")
        Result.ProtocolAddress = PResult.GetPropertyValue("ProtocolAddress")
        Result.ResponseTime = PResult.GetPropertyValue("ResponseTime")
        WriteObject(Result)
    Next

End Sub

End Class
```

Before you compile this, you'll likely need to set Option Strict to Off.

When you use this new version, you can pipe in the contents of a file, or, as in this example, create a new array of strings and pipe that into the cmdlet:

```
PS C:\> @("localhost","don-pc","mediaserver","testbed") | ping-computer
```

| ComputerName | StatusCode | ResponseTime | ProtocolAddress |
| --- | --- | --- | --- |
| localhost | 0 | 0 | ::1 |
| don-pc | 0 | 0 | fe80::e468:3091:f2... |
| mediaserver | 0 | 0 | 192.168.4.103 |
| testbed | 0 | 0 | |

You'll notice that the ProtocolAddress property contains the actual address that responded—in most cases, those are IPv6 addresses, since those computers are newer versions of Windows (running Windows Vista) that automatically configure themselves to use IPv6.

Also notice the value of outputting objects from the cmdlet, rather than just simple strings. Now, PowerShell's formatting cmdlets can take over and create lists and tables automatically, using the objects' properties. Even **Get-Member** can help, as shown here, by displaying the properties. Notice the TypeName: It consists of our snap-in's name (PrimalToys), and the class name we created in VB:

```
PS C:\> $results = @("localhost","don-pc","mediaserver","testbed") | ping-computer
PS C:\> $results | gm


   TypeName: PrimalToys.PingResult

Name                 MemberType Definition
----                 ---------- ----------
Equals               Method     System.Boolean Equals(Object obj)
GetHashCode          Method     System.Int32 GetHashCode()
GetType              Method     System.Type GetType()
get_ComputerName     Method      System.String get_ComputerName()
get_ProtocolAddress  Method      System.String get_ProtocolAddress()
get_ResponseTime     Method     System.Int32 get_ResponseTime()
get_StatusCode       Method     System.Int32 get_StatusCode()
set_ComputerName     Method     System.Void set_ComputerName(String value)
set_ProtocolAddress  Method      System.Void set_ProtocolAddress(String value)
set_ResponseTime     Method     System.Void set_ResponseTime(Int32 value)
set_StatusCode       Method     System.Void set_StatusCode(Int32 value)
ToString             Method     System.String ToString()
ComputerName         Property   System.String ComputerName {get;set;}
ProtocolAddress      Property   System.String ProtocolAddress {get;set;}
ResponseTime         Property   System.Int32 ResponseTime {get;set;}
StatusCode           Property   System.Int32 StatusCode {get;set;}
```

While we won't pretend that creating cmdlets is *easy*, it is at least straightforward. Any complexity comes entirely from the complexity of the Framework itself, and not from the very small amount of overhead required to actually create a cmdlet or a snap-in.

# Part V

# Reference

## Appendix A
# Automatic Variables in PowerShell

PowerShell defines a number of automatic variables that you can use. Note that some of these are context-dependent, meaning they're only available in certain situations. Also, while the majority of these are defined by PowerShell (meaning they're available under any hosting application), some of these are defined by PowerShell.exe and are only available to scripts running under that host, or under a host that is fully emulating PowerShell.exe.

| Variable | Purpose |
|---|---|
| $$ | The last token of the last line received by the shell |
| $? | $True is the last operation succeeded; otherwise, $False |
| $^ | The first token of the last line received by the shell |
| $_ | The current pipeline object (used in script blocks, filters, the **ForEach-Object** cmdlet, and the **Where-Object** cmdlet) |
| $Args | An array of the parameters passed to a function |
| $DebugPreference | The action to take when information is written to the debug pipeline ("Continue" means to display it; "SilentlyContinue" suppresses it) |
| $Error | A collection of objects for which an error occurred |
| $ErrorActionPreference | The action to take when information is written to the error pipeline ("Continue" means to display it; "SilentlyContinue" suppresses it) |
| $False | Boolean value FALSE |
| $foreach | Refers to the enumerator in a foreach loop |
| $Home | Specifies the user's home directory; same as %homedrive%%homepath% |
| $Input | Contains the collection of pipeline objects sent to a script block |
| $LastExitCode | The exit code of the last external executable that was run |
| $MaximumAliasCount | The maximum number of aliases available |
| $MaximumDriveCount | The maximum number of drives available |
| $MaximumFunctionCount | The maximum number of functions available |
| $MaximumHistoryCount | The maximum number of entries saved in the command history |
| $MaximumVariableCount | The maximum number of variables available |
| $PsHome | The folder where Windows PowerShell is installed |
| $Host | Provides an interface to the hosting application |
| $OFS | Output Field Separator: Use when converting an array to a string; by default, is a space character |
| $ReportErrorShowExceptionClass | When $True, shows the class name of displayed exceptions |
| $ReportErrorShowInnerException | When $True, shows the chain of inner exceptions for displayed exceptions |
| $ReportErrorShowSource | When $True, shows the assembly name of displayed exceptions |
| $ReportErrorShowStackTrace | When $True, shows the stack traces for displayed exceptions |
| $ShouldProcessPreference | Specifies the action to take when a cmdlet is used with -**confirm** |
| $ShouldProcessReturnPreference | Value returned by ShouldPolicy |
| $StackTrace | Contains detailed stack trace information about the last error |
| $True | The Boolean value TRUE |
| $VerbosePreference | The action to take when information is written to the verbose pipeline ("Continue" means to display it; "SilentlyContinue" suppresses it) |
| $WarningPreference | The action to take when information is written to the warning pipeline ("Continue" means to display it; "SilentlyContinue" suppresses it) |

# Appendix B
# Common .NET Framework Data Types

As we discussed throughout this book, PowerShell relies on the underlying .NET Framework types to handle data manipulation. This is a benefit for you, because those underlying Framework types pack in a lot of useful functionality. Our goal in this Appendix is to provide a quick reference to those types' *most useful* methods and properties—not a comprehensive reference, but rather a listing—with examples of those properties and methods that an administrator will get the most use from.

In the reference tables that follow, method names are always followed by (), but property names are not. That's how you can tell the difference between a property and a method.

### [Boolean] [Bool] • System.Boolean
Contains TRUE/FALSE values

| Name | Purpose | Example |
|---|---|---|
| ToString() | Returns a string representation of the object; e.g., the word "TRUE" or "FALSE." | $var.ToString() |

### [Byte] • System.Byte
Contains byte values

| Name | Purpose | Example |
|---|---|---|
| ToString() | Returns a string representation of the byte. | $var.ToString() |

## [Char] • System.Char

Contains individual characters

| Name | Purpose | Example |
|------|---------|---------|
| ToString() | Returns a string representation of the object; e.g., the character itself | $var.ToString() |

## [DateTime] • System.DateTime

Contains date and time values—note that the methods and properties produce output based upon your system's regional settings. For the below example, assume that $d or $t contain a date, time, or date/time value.

| Name | Purpose | Example |
|------|---------|---------|
| Add() | This method requires you to create instances of the Framework's TimeSpan class; instead, use one of the AddX() method below. | |
| AddDays() | Adds the specified number of days | $d = $d.AddDays(2) |
| AddHours() | Adds the specified number of hours | $t = $t.AddHours(24) |
| AddMilliseconds() | Adds the specified number of milliseconds | $t = $t.AddMilliseconds(1000) |
| AddMinutes() | Adds the specified number of minutes | $t = $t.AddMinutes(-30)<br>*Adding a negative number results in subtraction* |
| AddMonths() | Adds the specified number of months | $d = $d.AddMonths(6) |
| AddSeconds() | Adds the specified number of seconds | $t = $t.AddSeconds(60) |
| AddTicks() | Adds the specified number of ticks (a *tick* is a 100-nanosecond unit) | $t = $t.AddTicks(100) |
| AddYears() | Adds the specified number of years | $d = $d.AddYears(100) |
| Date | Extracts the date from the value | $d.Date |
| DateTime | Extracts the date and time from the value | $d.DateTime |
| Day | Extracts the day of the month from the value | $d.Day |
| DayOfWeek | Extracts the day of the week from the value | $d.DayOfWeek |
| DayOfYear | Extracts the day of the year (Julian date) from the value | $d.DayOfYear |
| GetDateTimeFormats() | Returns an array with all possible string representations of the date | $d.GetDateTimeFormats() |
| Hour | Extracts the hour from the value | $d.Hour |

| Name | Purpose | Example |
|------|---------|---------|
| IsDaylightSavingTime() | Returns $True or $False if Daylight Saving Time is active | $d.IsDaylightSavingTime() |
| Kind | Indicates whether the time is based on local time, Coordinated Universal Time (UTC), or neither | $d.Kind |
| Millisecond | Extracts the milliseconds from the value | $d.Millisecond |
| Minute | Extracts the minutes from the value | $d.Minute |
| Month | Extracts the month from the value | $d.Month |
| Second | Extracts the seconds from the value | $d.Second |
| Ticks | Extracts the ticks from the value. A tick is 100 nanoseconds. | $d.Ticks |
| TimeOfDay | Extracts the time of day from the value | $d.TimeOfDay |
| ToBinary() | Returns a 64-bit integer value representing the date | $d.ToBinary() |
| ToFileTime() | Returns a Windows file time | $d.ToFileTime() |
| ToFileTimeUtc() | Returns a Windows file name translated to Coordinated Universal Time (UTC) | $d.ToFileTimeUtc() |
| ToLocalTime() | Converts the time to local time | $d.ToLocalTime() |
| ToLongDateString() | Converts the value to a long date string | $d.ToLongDateString() |
| ToLongTimeString() | Converts the value to a long time string | $d.ToLongTimeString() |
| ToOADate() | Converts the value to an OLE Automation date | $d.ToOADate() |
| ToShortTimeString() | Converts the value to a short time string | $d.ToShortTimeString() |
| ToString() | Returns a generic string representation of the date. | |
| ToUniversalTime() | Converts the value to Coordinated Universal Time (UTC) | $d.ToUniversalTime() |
| Year | Extracts the year from the value | $d.Year |

## [Decimal] • System.Decimal

Contains decimal values

| Name | Purpose | Example |
|------|---------|---------|
| ToString() | Returns a string representation of the decimal | $var.ToString() |

## [Double] • System.Double

Contains double-precision floating-point numeric values

| Name | Purpose | Example |
|---|---|---|
| ToString() | Returns a string representation of the number | $var.ToString() |

## [Float] [Single] • System.Single

Contains single-precision floating-point numeric values

| Name | Purpose | Example |
|---|---|---|
| ToString() | Returns a string representation of the number | $var.ToString() |

## [Hashtable] • System.Collections.Hashtable

Contains associative arrays (also called dictionaries or hashtables)

| Name | Purpose | Example |
|---|---|---|
| Add() | Adds an element with the specified key and value | $ht.Add("Key","Value") |
| Clear() | Clears the hashtable of all elements | $ht.Clear() |
| Contains() | Returns $True if the hashtable contains the specified key | $ht.Contains("MyKey") |
| ContainsKey() | Returns $True if the hashtable contains the specified key | $ht.ContainsKey("MyKey") |
| ContainsValue() | Returns $True if the hashtable contains the specified value | $ht.ContainsValue(5) |
| Count | The number of key/value pairs in the hashtable | $ht.Count |
| IsFixedSize | $True if the hashtable is a fixed size | $ht.IsFixedSize |
| IsReadOnly | $True if the hashtable is read-only | $ht.IsReadOnly |
| Item | Gets or sets the value associated with the specified key | $ht.Item("MyKey") = "MyValue" <br> Write-Host $ht.Item("MyOtherKey") |
| Keys | Gets an array of the hashtable's keys | $a = $ht.Keys |
| Remove() | Removes the element having the specified key | $ht.Remove("MyKey") |
| ToString() | Returns a string representation of the entire hashtable | $ht.ToString() |
| Values | Gets an array of the hashtable's values | $a = $ht.Values |

# [Int] • System.Int32

Contains 32-bit (regular) integer values

| Name | Purpose | Example |
|------|---------|---------|
| ToString() | Returns a string representation of the number | $var.ToString() |

# [Long] • System.Int64

Contains 64-bit (long) integer values

| Name | Purpose | Example |
|------|---------|---------|
| ToString() | Returns a string representation of the number | $var.ToString() |

# [Regex] • System.Text.RegularExpressions.Regex

Contains regular expression strings; below examples assume $r contains a valid regex

| Name | Purpose | Example |
|------|---------|---------|
| GetGroupNames() | Returns an array of capturing group names for the regex | $r.GetGroupNames() |
| GetGroupNumbers() | Returns an array of capturing group numbers that correspond to the group names in an array | $r.GetGroupNumbers() |
| GroupNameFromNumber() | Gets the group name that matches the specified number | $r.GetGroupNameFromNumber(1) |
| GroupNumberFromName() | Gets the group number that matches the specified name | $r.GetGroupNumberFromName(0) |
| **IsMatch()** <br><br> *Returns $True if a single match is found* | Returns $True if the specified string matches the regex | $r.IsMatch("Test") |
| | Start the regex comparison at a specified character position | $r.IsMatch("Test",2) |
| | Returns $True if the specified string matches the specified regex | $r.IsMatch("Test","\w+") |
| **Match()** <br><br> *Returns the first match found* | Returns a match where the specified string matches the regex | $r.Match("Test") |
| | Start the regex comparison at a specified character position | $r.Match("Test",2) |
| | Returns a match where the specified string matches the specified regex | $r.Match("Test","\w+") |

| Name | Purpose | Example |
|------|---------|---------|
| **Matches()**<br><br>*Returns an array of all matches found* | Returns a collection of matches where the specified string matches the regex | $r.Matches("Test") |
| | Start the regex comparison at a specified character position | $r.Matches("Test",2) |
| | Returns a collection of matches where the specified string matches the specified regex | $r.Matches("Test","\w+") |
| Replace() | Within the specified input string, replace all strings that match the regex with the specified replacement string | $r.Replace("Input","Replace") |
| Split() | | |
| ToString() | Returns the regex expression as a string | $r.ToString() |
| Options | Returns the options that the regex uses to operate | $r.Options |
| RightToLeft | Returns $True if the regex searches from right to left | $r.RightToLeft |

## [Scriptblock] • System.Management.Automation.ScriptBlock

Contains strings which are used as script blocks

| Name | Purpose | Example |
|------|---------|---------|
| Invoke() | | |
| InvokeReturnAsIs() | | |
| ToString() | Returns a string representation of the script block | $var.ToString() |
| IsFilter | | |

## [String] • System.String

Contains True/False values. Examples below assume that $s contains "SAPIEN Press"

| Name | Purpose | Example |
|------|---------|---------|
| Chars | Converts the string into an array of [char] objects | $c = $s.Chars |
| EndsWith() | Returns $True if the string ends with the specified character(s) | $s.EndsWith("Press")<br>$True |
| IndexOf() | Returns the character position of the specified string | $s.IndexOf("SAP")<br>0 |

| Name | Purpose | Example |
|------|---------|---------|
| IndexOfAny() | Returns the index of the first occurrence of any character in the specified array | $a = @("A","P") <br> $s.IndexOfAny($a) <br> 1 |
| Insert() | Inserts the specified string at the specified index position | $s = $s.Insert(5,"Insert") <br> $s <br> SAPIEN Insert Press |
| IsNormalized() | Returns $True if the string is in the "C" Unicode normalized form | $s.IsNormalized() |
| LastIndexOf() | Returns the last index position of the specified string | $s.LastIndexOf("s") <br> 11 |
| LastIndexOfAny() | Returns the last index position of any character in the specified array | $a = @("r","e") <br> $s.LastIndexOfAny($a) <br> 9 |
| Length | Returns the length of the string | $s.Length <br> 12 |
| Normalize() | Returns a version of the string which is in the normalized Unicode form "C" | $s = $s.Normalize() |
| PadLeft() | Adds the specified number of spaces to the left of the string | $s.PadLeft(5) |
| PadRight() | Adds the specified number of spaces to the right of the string | $s.PadRight(5) |
| Remove() | Deletes the specified number of characters beginning at the specified position | $s.Remove(0,7) <br> $s <br> Press |
| Split() | Returns an array of strings, using the specified character to split the existing string into individual elements | $t = "One,Two,Three,Four" <br> $t.Split(",") |
| Substring() | Retrieve the specified number of characters starting at the specified position | $s.Substring(2,7) <br> PIEN Pr |
| StartsWith() | Returns $True if the string starts with the specified character(s) | $s.StartsWith("Press") <br> False |
| ToCharArray() | Converts the string into an array of [char] objects | $c = $s.ToCharArray() |
| ToLower() | Returns a lowercase version of the string | $s.ToLower() <br> sapien press |
| ToUpper() | Returns an uppercase version of the string | $s.ToUpper() <br> SAPIEN PRESS |
| Trim() | Removes whitespace from the beginning and end of the string | $s = $s.Trim() |
| TrimEnd() | Removes whitespace from the end of the string | $s = $s.TrimEnd() |
| TrimStart() | Removes whitespace from the beginning of the string | $s = $s.TrimStart() |

We have omitted some of PowerShell's types, such as [XML] and [WMI], because PowerShell provides a better adaptation for these types of objects that you get just working with the Framework type. Refer to the appropriate chapter on these technologies for more information. We've omitted the [ADSI] type adapter here because it's discussed more thoroughly in the chapters dealing with ADSI and directory services.

# Appendix C
# Regular Expression Syntax

PowerShell uses a fairly standard implementation of regular expression syntax; Web sites like www.regegbuddy.com, www.regular-expressions.info, and www.regexlib.com provide tools, tutorials, and examples that can be used in PowerShell without any major adjustments. This Appendix is not intended as a tutorial; rather, it's intended as a quick reference to the major syntax elements supported by PowerShell. Our "Regular Expressions" chapter covers using regular expressions and provides several real-world examples.

| Standard Regular Expressions Format | Logic | Example |
|---|---|---|
| value | Match the exact character specified | "book" -match "oo" (matches "oo") |
| . | Match any single character | "copy" -match "c..y" (matches "copy") |
| [*value*] | Match at least one of the characters in the brackets | "big" -match "b[iou]g" (matches "big") |
| [*range*] | Match at least one of the characters within the range; use – to specify a contiguous range | "deal" -match "d[a-e]l" matches ("deal") |
| [^] | Match any character except those in the brackets | "hand" -match "h[^brt]nd" matches ("hand") |

| Standard Regular Expressions Format | Logic | Example |
|---|---|---|
| ^ | Anchor match to the beginning of the string | "book" -match "^bo" (matches "bo") |
| $ | Anchor match to the end of the string | "book" -match "ok$" (matches "ok") |
| * | Match zero or more instances of the preceding character | "shaggy" -match "g*" (matches "gg") |
| ? | Match zero or one instance of the preceding character | "hairy" -match "r?" (matches "r") |
| \ | Match the character that follows as a literal character (escaped) | "$5.00" -match "\$5" (matches "$5") |
| \w | Match a word – any character except whitespace | "SAPIEN" -match "\w" (matches "S") |
| + | Match one or more instances of the preceding directive or character | "SAPIEN" -match "\w+" (matches "SAPIEN") |
| \W | Match any non-word character (space, tab, etc) | "One Two" -match "\W" (matches the space) |
| \s | Matches any whitespace character | "One Two" -match "\s" (matches the space) |
| \S | Matches non-whitespace character | "abcde" -match "\S+" (matches "abcde") |
| \d | Matches any digit | "abc123" -match "\d" (matches "1") |
| \D | Matches any non-digit | "abc123" -match "\D" (matches "a") |
| {n} | Specify exactly n matches | "abc" -match "\w{2}" (matches "ab") |
| {n,} | Specify at least n matches | "abc" -match "\w{2,} " (matches "abc") |
| {n,m} | Specify at least n matches, but no more than m matches | "abc" -match "\w{2,3}" (matches "abc") |

# Appendix D
# Reading PowerShell's Help

By now you know how easy it is to ask PowerShell for help and how a well-written cmdlet is self-documenting. But deciphering a help screen can be a little confusing to first-time PowerShell users. We want to show you how easy it is to read a help screen.

Here's what you might get when asking for help on the **Get-Service** cmdlet:

```
PS C:\ > help get-service

NAME
    Get-Service

SYNOPSIS
    Gets the services on the local computer.


SYNTAX
    Get-Service [[-name] <string[]>] [-include <string[]>] [-exclude <string[]>]
[<CommonParameters>]

    Get-Service -displayName <string[]> [-include <string[]>] [-exclude <string[]>]
[<CommonParameters>]

    Get-Service [-inputObject <ServiceController[]>] [-include <string[]>] [-exclude
<string[]>] [<CommonParameters>]
```

The Synopsis should be self-explanatory. But what about the Syntax? The first thing to notice is that there are three different ways you can use **Get-Service**. Each version has its own syntax, although with this cmdlet, they are very similar.

Anything you see in square brackets is optional. You don't have to specify it as a parameter. If it is a required item—more on that in a bit—PowerShell will prompt you for a value like this:

```
PS C:\ > get-eventlog

cmdlet get-eventlog at command pipeline position 1
Supply values for the following parameters:
LogName:
```

When you see something like <string[]>, this is informing you of the expected type for that particular parameter. Thus, the displayName parameter is expecting a string value:

```
-displayName <string[]>
```

Some PowerShell parameters are positional. That is, you don't have to specify the parameter name. PowerShell will determine the parameter property based on the position. Ever wonder why you can run an expression like this without having to specify any parameters?

```
PS C:\ > get-service spooler
```

If you look again at the syntax for the first variation, notice that **-name** is in square brackets:

```
Get-Service [[-name] <string[]>]
```

This indicates that the parameter name is not required and is a positional parameter. The **Get-Service** cmdlet only has one such parameter.

If you need a bit more clarification, look at the full help for a cmdlet:

```
PS C:\ > help get-service -full
```

In addition to the summary we've already looked at, you get full information about each parameter. Here's an excerpt for **Get-Service**:

```
PARAMETERS
    -name <string[]>
        Specifies the service names of services to be retrieved. Wildcards are permitted. By
        default, Get-Service gets all of the services on the computer.

        Required?                 false
        Position?                 1
        Default value             *
        Accept pipeline input?      true (ByValue, ByPropertyName)
        Accept wildcard characters? true

    -include <string[]>
        Retrieves only the specified services. The value of this parameter qualifies the Name
        parameter. Enter a name element or pattern, such as "s*". Wildcards are permitted.

        Required?                 false
        Position?                 named
        Default value
        Accept pipeline input?      false
        Accept wildcard characters? True
```

Notice that these parameters are not required, which we already knew because they were enclosed in square brackets.

The Name parameter has a position value of 1, which means the first string after the cmdlet name will be treated as a service name. Again, this confirms what we already knew, because -**name** was shown in square brackets in the help summary. The
-**Include** parameter is not positional:

```
        Position?                   named
```

The help syntax informs you that you must specify the parameter name.

Look at the default value for the -**name** parameter. Help tells you that it is the * wildcard. Finally, you can also see that the parameter can accept pipelined input. Since all the parameter is expecting is a string, you can run an expression like this:

```
PS C:\ > @("spooler","alerter","browser") | get-service

Status  Name             DisplayName
------  ----             -----------
Running Spooler          Print Spooler
Stopped Alerter          Alerter
Running Browser          Computer Browser
```

Each array value is piped to **Get-Service**, which assumes the passed value is the name of a service.

The last piece of important information in PowerShell help is to look at what types of objects the cmdlet can accept as input and what type of objects, if any, the cmdlet produces:

```
INPUT TYPE
   Object


RETURN TYPE
   System.ServiceProcess.ServiceController
```

This snippet from the **Get-Service** help shows that the cmdlet can accept any type of input object and that it returns a ServiceController object. You can confirm that by running an expression like this:

```
PS C:\ > (get-service alerter).Gettype()

IsPublic IsSerial Name                      BaseType
-------- -------- ----                      --------
True     False    ServiceController         System.ComponentModel.Component
```

With a little practice, you'll be able to decipher the mysterious PowerShell help screens, which will make you a more efficient PowerShell user.

# Index

## X–Y–Z

# ADSI Scripting: TFM™

SAPIEN Press

Finally, everything you need to know about ADSI Scripting is contained in one definitive volume. This is the VBScript-oriented, comprehensive reference to ADSI scripting that only SAPIEN Press could produce. Every ADSI object, every class, every property, and every attribute are all located in one place. You'll also find GUI-to-attribute mappings and detailed information on using the WinNT and LDAP ADSI providers. Finally - the complete ADSI scripting reference you've always wanted!

## TABLE OF CONTENTS

Cade A. Fassett

SAPIEN
PRESS

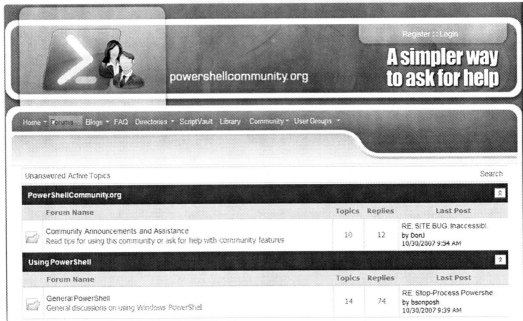

# Need expert training?
# Look no further!

**Expert, Guru-Led PrimalScript, VBScript, and
Windows PowerShell™ training,
designed with your busy schedule in mind:**

SAPIEN provides on-site, customized training for your company or individual needs, and we also offer off-site classes in a city near you.

All sessions are taught by expert SAPIEN scripting gurus Don Jones and Jeffrey Hicks. We also offer training courseware that is designed for delivery by professional trainers and professional training centers.

Whether you are a beginner or an expert user, SAPIEN has the flexible, comprehensive training options you need.

SAPIEN | scripting simplified™

**FOR MORE INFORMATION:**
www.scriptingtraining.com
or call SAPIEN Technologies
866.774.6257

# PrimalScript Resource Kit

The **PrimalScript Enterprise Resource Kit** is perfect for Windows administrators working with VBScript or Windows PowerShell. You'll start with our award-winning, top-of-the-line PrimalScript Enterprise visual script environment, and also receive:

- ScriptingAnswers.com University Class-On-Disc titles: VBScript 101, 201, and 301, as well as Windows PowerShell 101.
- Physical books of three popular SAPIEN Press titles: ADSI Scripting: TFM, Windows PowerShell: TFM and WSH and VBScript Core: TFM.
- A full set of VBScript Snippets and Windows PowerShell Snippets that make scripting faster.
- A printed, bound copy of PrimalScript 2007: TFM, the official manual for PrimalScript 2007.

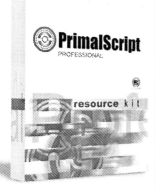

The **PrimalScript Professional Resource Kit** is perfect for Windows administrators working with VBScript. You'll start with our award-winning PrimalScript Professional visual script environment, and also receive:

- ScriptingAnswers.com University Class-On-Disc titles: VBScript 101, 201, and 301.
- Physical books of two popular SAPIEN Press titles: ADSI Scripting: TFM and WSH and VBScript Core: TFM.
- A full set of VBScript Snippets that make scripting faster.
- A printed, bound copy of PrimalScript 2007: TFM, the official manual for PrimalScript 2007.

**PrimalScript Universal** includes nearly everything that SAPIEN has to offer! You'll start with the award-winning PrimalScript Enterprise, our most full-featured visual scripting environment. You'll also receive:

- One license for SAPIEN PrimalScope, our standalone VBScript and JScript debugger.
- The complete ScriptingAnswers.com Electives series of training videos, including VBScript-focused videos that cover IIS 6.0 automation, Exchange Server 2003 administration, Advanced HTML Applications, and Enterprise Best Practices.
- The ScriptingAnswers.com Library, which includes short-subject training videos on VBScript and Windows PowerShell topics, and several full-length training videos covering a number of VBScript-related topics, including ADSI, WMI, HTML Applications, and much more.
- ScriptingAnswers.com University Class-On-Disc titles: VBScript 101, 201, and 301, and Windows PowerShell 101.
- eBooks of our most popular SAPIEN Press titles, including ADSI Scripting: TFM, WSH and VBScript Core: TFM, and Windows PowerShell: TFM.
- A full set of Snippets that make scripting faster, including Snippets for VBScript, KiXtart, HTML Applications, and Windows PowerShell.
- A CD full of additional exclusive tools and resources.

SAPIEN

Class-on-Disc

These self-paced "Class-On-Disc" courses include hands-on exercises, instructor video, narrated demos, extra exercises, self-assessment quizzes, and a variety of other learning elements. Each course is completely immersive, requiring up to several days to properly complete. Everything is included on the disc, and presented in an innovative, Flash-based interactive learning environment.

# VBScript Fundamentals

**VBS101:**

Go from zero to sixty in just eight 30-minute modules. Starting with no prior VBScript experience, you'll learn everything you need to know to start writing your own administrative scripts, including login scripts, basic configuration scripts, and more. This course provides the essential knowledge you need to master intermediate and advanced VBScript topics. Select modules are followed by a self-assessment opportunity, and all samples are attached directly to the presentation for your convenience.

# VBScript Intermediate

**VBS201:**

Extend your VBScript skills to include powerful Windows administrative technologies like Windows Management Instrumentation, Active Directory Services interface, and much more. You'll also learn best practices that help make scripting easier and more effective in both small business and enterprise environments. Assumes that you already understand the VBScript core language (or have completed our VBScript 101 course). Select modules are followed by a self-assessment opportunity, and all samples are attached directly to the presentation for your convenience.

# VBScript Advanced

**VBS301:**

Master advanced scripting topics and take your scripting skills to the next level! Learn to work with databases, e-mail, and other enterprise technologies, and learn the tools and techniques needed to make powerful, self-contained scripting tools quickly and easily. You'll even learn how to apply your scripting skills to create graphical scripts, called HTML Applications (HTAs). Select modules are followed by a self-assessment opportunity, and all samples are attached directly to the presentation for your convenience.

# Windows PowerShell

**101:**

Windows PowerShell 101 Class-On-Disc from the ScriptingAnswers.com University. In it, Don Jones leads you through the process of learning Windows PowerShell through videos conceptual animations, narrated demonstrations, hands-on exercises, self-assessment quizzes, and more. This Complete Class-On-Disc comprises more that 20 total hours of training activities.

SAPIEN

## TO ORDER:
### www.scriptingoutpost.com
### Or Call Customer Service at:
### 866.774.6257

# Windows Server 2008: What's New/What's Changed

Microsoft has released its next server operating system – Windows Server 2008 – and you need to know more about it. But you don't need the basics. You already know Windows 2003. You just need to know what's new and what's changed in Windows Server 2008. Read-Only Domain Controllers, the Group Policy Central Store, Terminal Server RemoteApps, Fine-Grained Password Policies. This quick and entertaining guide, written by Windows insider Greg Shields does just that. Focusing on the new technologies for installing, managing, and securing Windows Server 2008, you'll quickly ramp up your skills. Save yourself some time and money by skipping the basics and using your existing skills to master Microsoft's new server O/S.

Automate server installations * More effectively manage servers through Server Manager * Gain insight with Reliability and Performance Monitor * Implement powerful new Group Policy * Reduce your attack surface with Server Core * Complete better Active Directory backups * Deploy apps using Terminal Services * Secure your servers with the new Windows Firewall.

SAPIEN PRESS

# WSH and VBScript Core: TFM

A complete reference to the VBScript and Windows Script Host language - for the Windows administrator. Far more than a mere syntax reference, **WSH and VBScript CORE: TFM** provides you with detailed administrative script examples for each function, statement, keyword, object, property, method and more. If a function can be used in three different ways, you'll find three different and complete examples. No more guessing about what the docs mean and no more hunting around on the Web trying to find the exact example you need. You'll never again wander through examples meant for developers because this book was written entirely and specifically for Windows administrators! **WSH and VBScript CORE: TFM** is the last VBScript and Windows Script Host reference you'll need, because it's accurate, complete, and designed especially for Windows administrative scripting.

**ORDER YOUR COPY:**
www.scriptingoutpost.com
or call SAPIEN Press
866.774.6257

SAPIEN
PRESS